Modern

Rhetorical

Criticism

The Scott, Foresman/Little, Brown Rhetoric and Society Series
Bruce G. Gronbeck, General Editor

Modern

Rhetorical

Criticism

RODERICK P. HART

The University of Texas at Austin

Scott, Foresman/Little, Brown Higher Education
A Division of Scott, Foresman and Company
Glenview, Illinois   London, England

To Chris and Kate

And the other college students I have known and loved

Acknowledgments for the copyrighted materials not credited on the page
where they appear are listed in the Acknowledgments section beginning on
page 515. This section is to be considered a legal extension of the copyright
page.

Library of Congress Cataloging-in-Publicaton Data

Hart, Roderick P.
    Modern rhetorical criticism / Roderick P. Hart.
    p.   cm/
    Includes bibliographical references.
    ISBN 0-673-18030-1
    1. Rhetoric.   2. Criticism.   3. Persuasion (Rhetoric)
    4. Literature—History and criticism—Theory, etc.   I. Title.
    PN175.H37   1989
    808—dc20   89-27684
                                                                                   CIP

    2 3 4 5 6 - MPC - 94 93 92 91 90

Preface

Rhetoric was studied by ancient Greeks and Romans, medieval courtiers, Renaissance theologians, and by political thinkers in the emerging democracies of the eighteenth century. In each age there was a sense that something powerful happened when a firebrand mounted a public platform, entered a church pulpit, or delivered a scathing editorial. Because this same feeling continues today, there has been a renewed interest in the study of rhetoric. Here is why: Hitler's rise to power, the Iran-Contra hearings, the resurgence of David Duke, televised evangelism, the politicized novel, advocacy journalism, apartheid protest rallies, AIDS awareness campaigns, Weight Watchers International, soap operas, and the Ayatollah Khomeini. All of these characters and events collect in the rhetorical arena. All of them change people's lives. To ignore them is to incur possible political, moral, health, and financial risks.

Modern Rhetorical Criticism is a comprehensive, up-to-date guide to public rhetoric, written for those taking courses in rhetorical criticism and for students of literary criticism interested in the rhetorical approach to ideas. Its goals are threefold: (1) to broaden the reader's conception of persuasion so that its uses in law, politics, religion, and commerce are seen as different in degree—not in kind—from its less obvious uses in literature, science, education, and entertainment; (2) to survey the major critical studies of rhetoric produced in the United States during the past thirty years; and (3) to equip the reader with the critical tools and attitudes needed to see how rhetoric works its magic.

The reader, however, will not find in *Modern Rhetorical Criticism* a complete history of rhetorical thought or a history of rival schools of criticism. Rather, the book emphasizes the more recent U.S. tradition of critical inquiry. Unlike the European tradition, which has been popular among students of literature and has focused largely on stylistic matters, the American tradition (beginning in the early 1900s) has featured public debate and emphasized the spoken word. In an era of electronic mass media that has given public speech a kind of power never before witnessed in human history, such an emphasis seems especially warranted.

Features of the Text

The book begins with two overview chapters, one on the nature of rhetoric and one on the nature of criticism. These introductory discussions present the basic terminology of rhetorical study and examine the reasons criticism is so central to intellectual life. Part Two goes deeper into rhetorical texts themselves by providing the basic tools needed to understand the situations, ideas, arguments, structures, and styles that make up rhetorical exchanges. Finally, Part Three treats more ambitious forms of analysis—those dealing with role, culture, and drama—and also shows why certain recent schools of criticism—feminism, Marxism, and postmodernism—must be understood by anyone hoping to produce intelligent criticism in the latter part of the twentieth century.

Several features make this book unique. For example, in addition to a wide array of critical techniques and summaries of critical studies, the book contains numerous pieces of original criticism. Sometimes, the texts analyzed are masterworks—patriotic oratory, Shakespeare's plays, congressional debates, and Orwell's *Animal Farm*—and sometimes they are more practical—Army recruitment literature, bureaucratic propaganda, radio drama, and junk mail circulars. These sample analyses are intended to demonstrate the way creative criticism can "open up" a text that the persuader has (consciously or unconsciously) wrapped up tightly.

Still other features make *Modern Rhetorical Criticism* distinctive. These include:

- **Critical Probes** Specific, concrete questions that can be asked of a given text are scattered throughout the book. These probes are, essentially, the critic's tools. When used carefully, patiently, and imaginatively, these questions shed light on textual matters often ignored by the average listener or reader.
- **Chapter Headnotes** Each chapter begins with a sample persuasive message that graphically previews the chapter's content. These headnotes range from Richard Nixon's resignation speech to Broadway lyrics, from contemporary funeral prayers to children's textbooks, and from avant-garde poetry to social protest rhetoric.
- **Critical Profiles** These are brief, intriguing summaries of some of the most interesting research studies produced in the area of rhetorical criticism. They are grouped under such headings as Rhetoric and the American West, Rhetoric and Corporate Life, Rhetoric and the Law, and Rhetoric and the Popular Arts. Col-

lectively, they demonstrate how vast rhetoric's influence has become and how many disguises it wears in the contemporary world.

· **Appendixes** Two highly practical appendixes also help the reader. Appendix A directs the critic to library materials suitable for rhetorical analysis. Complete bibliographical citations are included, as are library call numbers. Among the materials listed are patriotic orations, editorial cartoons, political campaign speeches, government propaganda, court transcripts, underground magazines, corporate reports, and television newscripts.

Appendix B helps the aspiring critic do the background reading necessary for producing a complete criticism. Here, readers are advised how to do literature searches (for both popular and scholarly periodicals and books), how to use historical sources to sketch out cultural background, how to access popular reactions to major rhetorical events, how to find relevant audio-visual materials, and how to search computerized data-bases for background ideas.

The very existence of *Modern Rhetorical Criticism* shows how widespread rhetorical inquiry has become during the last thirty years. In colleges and universities, more academic courses are devoted to rhetorical matters every year. When taught in Departments of Speech or Communication, courses on rhetoric bear such titles as Speech Criticism, Contemporary Public Address, Political Communication, Persuasion and Propaganda, Rhetoric and Media, or Historical/Critical Research Methods. In Departments of English, they fall under such headings as Rhetoric and Literature, Text and Language, Stylistics, Rhetoric and Genre, or Advanced Composition and Exposition. Moreover, sociologists, anthropologists, political scientists, historians, and religious scholars have all demonstrated increasing interest in rhetorical issues. But no matter what such courses are called, they tend to tell the same tale: rhetoric has always been studied and used, and always will be. *Modern Rhetorical Criticism* is designed to prepare its reader for that reality.

Acknowledgments

For me, this book has been a long time in coming. The idea for it was germinated when I first began teaching rhetorical criticism in the early 1970s, and the book largely reflects the intellectual routes I have traveled since that time. Professor Carroll Arnold of Pennsylvania

State University started me on that journey. A truer guide than he is surely not imaginable. His influence and the influence of Professor Richard Gregg have been profound, no matter how remote those influences may seem at this late date.

More recently, I have benefited from the advice of many others. Professor Jill McMillan of Wake Forest University encouraged this book from the beginning. Professor Charles Stewart of Purdue University, my former colleague, talked with me about rhetorical criticism for nine happy years. Professor Kathleen Jamieson of the University of Pennsylvania carefully read each word in this manuscript and gave me the benefit of her oh so gentle counsel. I also must acknowledge Professor Edwin Black of the University of Wisconsin, Professor Richard Cherwitz of the University of Texas, Professor Bruce Gronbeck of the University of Iowa, Professors Carol Jablonski and David Payne of the University of South Florida, and Professor Kathleen Turner of Tulane University. Each directed me away from certain pitfalls. I alone am responsible for the other pitfalls into which I may have inadvertently fallen.

I am most grateful to Barbara Muller and Richard Welna of Scott, Foresman/Little, Brown, the former for having stuck with this project during its several incarnations and the latter for having provided assistance so often and so cheerfully. I also appreciate the many graduate students who wrote Critical Profiles for *Modern Rhetorical Criticism*, and I am especially thankful to Roger Cude, Suzanne Daughton, David Fowler, David McLennan, Jim Mackin, Deanna Matthews, John Pauley, Charlotte Richards, Deborah Smith-Howell, and Kerry Strayer for having made the nettlesome aspects of writing this book less nettlesome.

Above all, I am thankful to my family, especially to my mother, who is the best rhetorical critic I know, and to my wife who is, simply, the best.

R.P.H.

Contents

CRITICAL PROFILES

Rhetoric and Political Psychology

Rhetoric and Literature

Rhetoric and Corporate Life

Rhetoric and the American West

Rhetoric and Personal Psychology

Rhetoric and National Strife

Rhetoric and Social Protest

Rhetoric and Modern Science

Rhetoric and the American Presidency

Rhetoric and Women's Identities

Rhetoric and Televised News

Rhetoric and Social Class

Rhetoric and the Law

Rhetoric and the Popular Arts

Rhetoric and Print Journalism

Rhetoric and Policy Formation

Rhetoric and Human Passion

Rhetoric and Education

Rhetoric and Everyday Life

Rhetoric and Image Management

Rhetoric and Mass Entertainment

Rhetoric and Political Religion

Rhetoric and Personal Change

Rhetoric and Cultural Identity

Rhetoric and the American South

Rhetoric and Religious Experience

FIGURES

TABLES

PART ONE

Introduction to Criticism

CHAPTER ONE

The Rhetorical Perspective

❖
❖

Because as they cut it was that special green, they
　　decided
To make a woman of the fresh hay. They wished to
　　lie in green, to wrap Themselves in it, light but not
　　pale, silvered but not grey.
Green and ample, big enough so both of them could
　　shelter together
In any of her crevices, the armpit, the join
Of hip and groin. They—who knew what there was to
　　know, about baling
The modern way with hay so you rolled it up like a
　　carpet,
Rather than those loose stacks—they packed the
　　green body tight
So she wouldn't fray. Each day they moulted her to
　　keep her
Green and soft. Only her hair was allowed to ripen
　　into yellow tousle.

The next weeks whenever they stopped cutting they
　　lay with her.
She was always there, waiting, reliable, their
　　green woman.
She gathered them in, yes she did,
Into the folds of herself, like the mother they
　　hadn't had.
Like the women they had had, only more pliant, more
　　graceful,
Welcoming in a way you never just found.
They not only had the awe of taking her,
But the awe of having made her. They drank beer
Leaning against the pillow of her belly
And one would tell the other, "Like two Adams
　　creating."

And they marveled as they placed
The cans at her ankles, at her neck, at her wrists so she
Glittered gold and silver. They adorned what
   they'd made.
After harrowing they'd come to her, drawing
The fountains of the Plains, the long line
Of irrigating spray and moisten her up.
And lean against her tight, green thighs to watch
   buzzards
Circle black against the pink stain of the sunset.

What time she began to smolder they never knew—
Sometime between night when they'd left her
And evening when they returned. Wet, green hay
Can go a long time smoldering before you notice.
   It has a way
Of catching itself, of asserting that
There is no dominion over it but the air. And it
   flares suddenly
Like a red head losing her temper, and allows its
   long bright hair
To tangle in the air, letting you know again
That what shelters you can turn incendiary in a
   flash.
And then there is only the space of what has been,
An absence in the field, memory in the shape of a
   woman [Macdonald, 1985:75–76].

This is not a book about poems. It is a book about rhetoric. It is also a book about criticism. It is a book that invites careful attention to the messages of daily life. The book encourages us to pick and probe at messages designed to influence human thoughts and actions. Because it is a book about rhetoric, it is about *the art of using language to help people narrow their choices among specifiable, if not specified, policy options.* Not a very sophisticated definition, perhaps, but one that is intuitively attractive. For example, we know, intuitively, that the poem involves a special use of language. But is it language designed to *narrow* the choices of other people? Not in any obvious sense. Our day-to-day experience with obvious forms of rhetoric—advertising, political speeches, televised evangelism—tells us that if poet Cynthia Macdonald is attempting to persuade us of something special, she has chosen a strange tack indeed. Macdonald uses language well—beautifully, in fact. She paints her pictures with dexterity, making us see the plain beauty of the bountiful pasture she describes, making us hear the casual conversations of the laboring brothers, making us feel the alternating softness and hardness of the carefully baled hay, making us smell the acrid smoke of the Hay Lady as she gives up her all. Poet Macdonald also evokes rich feeling states: the sense of almost womb-like comfort provided the tired farm hands by the Hay Lady, the wonder of watching nature's earthen blackness blend into the "pink stain" of her sunsets, the sadness that all humans experience when something close to them—pets, people, bales of hay—expires. Macdonald gives us precisely what a good poet should give us—old thoughts thought anew, old feelings felt anew—but she does not give us rhetoric.

The following speaker, in contrast, provides rhetoric aplenty. He offers "Kudos for Condos":

> Mr. Speaker, two decades ago, a group of men and women took advantage of a new idea in American real estate by completing the first condominium conversion in the United States. Now, as the residents of this building prepare to celebrate its twentieth anniversary, they can look back proudly at having set the standard that all other real estate conversions would do well to emulate.
>
> This historic building is located at 9410 64th Road, in Rego Park, Queens County, New York. Its residents have had true success by allowing tenants a real choice; in fact, one tenant who decided not to buy his apartment lived on under rent-control protection for almost twenty years.
>
> Mr. Speaker, in the story of this modest structure in Rego Park and of the creative people who transformed it, I think we can see a truly American spirit of inventiveness and the can-do-ethic. It is precisely this kind of innovation to meet challenges that has allowed this nation to sustain such a tremendous history of growth.
>
> As always, it was the people involved in this enterprise who made the difference. David Wolfenson was the landlord of the building twenty years ago; it was his initiative that started the entire process. Edward Schiff gave the expert legal advice necessary to complete the project; twenty years later, he still represents both sponsors and tenant groups.
>
> Mr. Speaker, I call now on all of my colleagues in the U.S. House of Representatives to join me in congratulating the men and women of 9410 64th Road on the twentieth anniversary of their successful conversion, and in wishing them the best of luck for the future [Ackerman, 1986:16].

Any person of aesthetic sensibility will be almost embarrassed by the stark contrast between Cynthia Macdonald's mellifluous lines and Representative Gary Ackerman's crass lionizing of his constituents in the halls of Congress. In contrast to Macdonald, who demands nothing but thoughtful relaxation from her readers, Ackerman makes us squirm with his tedious pontificating ("they can look back proudly . . ."), his tiresome clichés ("a truly American spirit of inventiveness . . ."), and his ponderous overstatements ("It is precisely this kind of innovation to meet challenges . . ."). Tedious pontificating, tiresome clichés, ponderous overstatements. This is rhetoric. Or at least some of it. The worst of it, perhaps. But each day, in every profession, people like Gary Ackerman produce rhetoric, much of it trivial, some of it important, all of it purporting to help others sort through their choices.

Modern Rhetorical Criticism invites us to study why the *Congressional Record* is filled with such stuff, why Representative Ackerman's constituents were flattered by his blandishments, and why his colleagues in the House smiled benignly when he read his remarks into the *Record*. Because he operates as something of a classic persuader here, Ackerman tries to "cut off" the many options for response available to his audience. Ackerman's **policy options** are clearly specified ("let's cheer for condos"), whereas Cynthia Macdonald never tells her audience exactly what she expects them to *do* as a result of reading her poem. This lack of specificity is what makes reading verse such a pleasure: It gives us room to wander; it permits a vacation from choosing between this concrete possibility and that concrete probability. Congressman Ackerman, in contrast, is all business.

But must all rhetoric be as pedestrian and self-serving as Gary Ackerman's? Clearly not. Human history has been written by great persons authoring great orations for social betterment. Often, these great statements have seemed more poetic than pragmatic, as satisfying to the heart as they have been to the head. Consider, for example, the remarks that Holocaust survivor and Nobel laureate author Elie Wiesel made when accepting a Medal of Freedom from Ronald Reagan in April of 1985, shortly after Mr. Reagan had unwisely accepted an invitation to speak at a German cemetery where S.S. troops are buried:

Today is April 19, and April 19, 1943, the Warsaw ghetto rose in arms against the onslaught of the Nazis. They were so few and so young and so helpless, and nobody came to their help, and they had to fight what was then the mightiest legion in Europe.

Every underground received help except the Jewish underground, and yet they managed to fight and resist and push back those Nazis and their accomplices for six weeks, and yet the leaders of the Free World, Mr. President, knew everything and did so little of nothing, or at least nothing specifically to save Jewish children from death.

You spoke of Jewish children, Mr. President. One million Jewish children perished. If I spent my entire life reciting their names, I would die before finishing the task.

Mr. President, I've seen children, I have seen children being thrown in the flames—alive! Words, they die on my lips. So I have learned, I have learned, I have learned the fragility of the human condition.

And I am reminded of the great moral essayist, the gentle and force-ful Abe Rosenthal, having visited Auschwitz, once wrote an extraor-dinary reportage about the persecution of Jews, and he called it, "For-give Them Not Father, for They Knew What They Did."

I have learned that the Holocaust was a unique and uniquely Jewish event, albeit with universal implications. Not all victims were Jews. But all Jews were victims.

I have learned the danger of indifference, the crime of indifference. For the opposite of love, I have learned, is not hate, but indifference.

Jews were killed by the enemy but betrayed by the so-called Allies who found political reasons to justify their indifference or passivity.

But I've also learned that suffering confers no privileges. It all depends what one does with it.

And this is why survivors of whom you spoke, Mr. President, have tried to teach their contemporaries how to build the ruins, how to invent hope in a world that offers none, how to proclaim faith to a generation that has seen it shamed and mutilated, and I believe, we believe, that memory is the answer, perhaps the only answer.

[Wiesel, 1985:22]

This is hardly Ackerman-like discourse. A great man, not an average man, is speaking. And he is speaking of great matters, not of expedient matters. Like poet Macdonald, Wiesel conjures up word-pictures that galvanize, draws on our psychic histories, uses language that sears the emotions. But there is an awkwardness to Wiesel's language also. He repeats himself frequently, begins sentences and then begins them again, uses more words than he really needs for clear communication. Wiesel's message could use a good editing: greater specificity, less choppiness, fewer clichés. But to call for such changes would be to miss the point of the rhetorical exchange, for Elie Wiesel had no intention of producing poetry that day. He wanted one thing: to convince Ronald Reagan to cancel his trip to the Nazi graves. Wiesel's eloquence derived from the emotional investment he made in his message, from his per-sonal experiences during the war, and from his clarity and forthright-ness of expression. All of this made for an *artistry* not seen in Repre-sentative Ackerman's speech on condos, but it also made for an *insistence* not apparent in Cynthia Macdonald's poem. In short, Elie Wiesel mustered as much artistry as his insistence would allow.

Modern Rhetorical Criticism will probe these subtleties of human interaction. The book presents practical techniques for uncovering the wishes and schemes often hidden in public discourse. It sketches some major studies of public persuasion and helps the reader learn how important answers can be gotten if the right questions—the most important questions—are asked. It details a number of theoretical per-spectives for "taking apart" the messages we hear each day so that we can better appreciate why, rightly or wrongly, the Gary Ackermans of the world far outnumber the Elie Wiesels and the Cynthia Macdonalds. But before considering these techniques and studies and perspectives, let us consider what rhetoric is and what it is not.

THE ARTS OF RHETORIC

The premises in this chapter are threefold: (1) Rhetoric is a special sort of human activity; (2) it takes a special perspective to understand rhetoric; and (3) by understanding rhetoric, one acquires a special perspective on the world. We can get some sense of the special nature of rhetoric by contrasting the messages above. After reading Macdonald's poem, each of us has a unique set of feelings, remembrances, and expectations. Macdonald develops many images, trips off many associations. She seems to demand nothing in particular from us as readers. Ackerman, in contrast, clearly seeks universal agreement from his listeners about a narrowed set of choices. He is more businesslike in his approach, taking pains to provide common background for his listeners, using language in highly conventional ways, mentioning specific names and dates and places, being obvious when identifying good ("innovation") and evil (the lack of a "real choice" in housing), telling his listeners directly what he wishes them to do next (applaud). There is a purposiveness in Ackerman's remarks that is missing in Macdonald's poem. Ackerman seems less patient than Macdonald; he is almost boorish in his concern that we get his story straight. Macdonald, in contrast, seems more willing to let us find our own story within her story. She wants us to be different after reading her poem, but she seems content to let *us* explore the dimensions of that difference. Both rhetoric and poetry tell a story, but the rhetor (one who uses rhetoric) takes special pains to be sure that the moral of the story is clear to the audience.

But what is the moral of Cynthia Macdonald's story? Is she operating as some sort of naturalist, innocently employing imagery drawn from primitive life forces, hoping only that in reading the poem we will come to appreciate anew the essential connectedness of the human and natural worlds? Or could she be a retrograde sexist, heralding a masculine world of physical dominance in which woman becomes a pliable object to be freely manipulated by men? Or is she an avant-garde feminist, surrealistically describing a world in which Man (the laborers) is deceived into believing that he can "possess" Woman (the Hay Lady), who suddenly, and imperiously, leaves for parts unknown? All of these interpretations are possible, and they are the sorts of things that critics debate. But the important thing to note here is that *the poet herself does not resolve these disputes.* The poet keeps her own counsel, content to provoke such questions in her readers but not to answer them.

Like poetry, rhetoric is an art. Like poetry, rhetoric creates a story out of nothing, using symbols to bring to life feelings we had forgotten we had, plans we had not yet considered adopting. As we see in Ackerman's speech, rhetoric uses common ideas, conventional language, and specific information to change listeners' feelings and behaviors. Rhetoric always tells a story with a purpose; the story is never told for its own sake.

Given our definition of rhetoric, every rhetorical task involves five basic moves: (1) The speaker tries to effect change by using **language** rather than nonsymbolic forces (like guns or torture); (2) the speaker must come to be regarded as a **helper** rather than an exploiter; (3) the speaker must convince the listener that new **choices** be made; (4) the speaker must **narrow** the listener's options for making these choices, even though (5) the speaker may become subtle by not **specifying** the details of the policies advocated.

Thus, the user of rhetoric peddles choices, even though most people naturally resist making choices unless forced to do so. And if forced to do so, people also naturally resist having their search for a solution prematurely constrained by someone else. So persuasion takes work: The speaker must "help" without appearing gauche or paternalistic, and the speaker must establish that the world is not yet fundamentally right (hence requiring new choice-making by the listener), but that it can soon be set right by making the (narrowed) choice the speaker endorses. The average TV commercial tells this tale a thousand times daily, with New Bride being driven to despair (and choice) by the ring-around-the-collar spotted by Handsome Husband. Mature Neighbor quickly arrives on the scene with her bag of groceries *and* a box of the New and Improved Narrowed Choice. Marital bliss is quickly restored, we are led to believe, and choice-making recedes into the background until crabgrass strikes fifteen minutes later. Not all persuasion is this predictable, of course, but all of it involves the art of managing choices.

But if rhetoric is an art, it is an art far different from the arts of poetry and painting. It is an art with these characteristics:

1. *A cooperative art.* Rhetoric is an art that brings speakers and listeners together. It cannot be done in solitude. To speak by oneself in a closet is possible, but it is hardly normal. Rhetoric makes little sense unless it is made for others. After all, the reactions of other people will be its measure: their votes, their purchases, their conversions, their affection. So rhetoric is a reciprocal or transactive art, because it brings two or more people together in an atmosphere of potential change. By sharing communication, both speakers and listeners open themselves up to each other's influence. In that sense, communication is not something that is *done* to others. Rather, it is something that people choose to do to themselves by consenting to communicative contact. By agree-

ing to rhetorical exchange, says Arnold [1972:16], people acknowledge their dependence upon one another. In the world of rhetoric, a speaker succeeds only when he or she can induce listeners to "contribute" their knowledge, feelings, and experiences about the matter in question. The rhetorical critic studies such invitations to cooperate.

2. *A people's art.* Rhetoric is an ordinary art. Its standards of excellence are the standards of ordinary people. Rhetoric is rarely as graceful or as lilting as poetry, because the people for whom it is made are too busy to bother with grace and lilt. Rhetoric works within the constraints of everyday logic, the logic of people who live in condos and like them. The heroes in rhetorical history are people like Louisiana populist Huey Long, who severely mangled the King's English whenever he spoke, but who was loved by his constituents because of it, not in spite of it. Rhetoric is often neither pretty nor fetching, although it can be both. At times it is even heavy-handed, although it tries never to be seen as such. At its best, rhetoric is ordinary language used extraordinarily.

3. *A temporary art.* Normally, rhetoric is rooted in the age of its creation. The people who create rhetoric speak today's language, not yesterday's. Such speakers use time-bound examples, time-bound statistics, time-bound jargon, caring little how it will sound on tomorrow's tomorrow. That is why most of the rhetoric we hear each day sounds more like Gary Ackerman's than Abraham Lincoln's. Or, more precisely, that is why only one or two of Lincoln's speeches continue to be read today. The remainder of his speeches dealt with issues and personalities that no longer concern us. Only on a few occasions did he turn rhetoric into poetry. Like Elie Wiesel, Lincoln knew that most rhetoric was meant to be consumed, not savored.

4. *A limited art.* As Bitzer [1968] reminds us, rhetoric is only deployed when it can make a difference. Rhetoric cannot really move mountains, which is why so few people stand at the bases of mountains to orate. Similarly, Arabs normally cannot move Israelis by speaking to them and that is why, sadly, they often do not try (and vice versa). Neither of these situations is "rhetorical" in Bitzer's sense, because human discourse cannot seem to change them. Rhetoric can do much, but it cannot do everything.

5. *A frustrating art.* There are no laws of rhetoric. There are important rules of thumb, but little else. To be effective in persuasion one must have a delicate touch, an ability to use the right argument and the deft phrase at precisely the right time. When deciding what to say, the rhetor always swims in a sea of uncertainty, because (1) people usually argue only about uncertain matters (for example, Should euthanasia be permitted?) rather than about that which is fixed (for example, the inevitability of death) and (2) people are so complex, so

changeful, and so ornery about so many matters. Thus, when thumping for space program funding, the NASA spokesperson must often leave the best scientific arguments at home, because it is ordinary citizens and their representatives, not scientists, who fund space missions. Rhetoric, then, deals with the probable, the best case that can be made under limited circumstances. It is used to decide the undecided question and to solve the unsolved problem [Bryant, 1972:20–21]. People talk when they can think of nothing else to do but feel that they must do something.

6. *A generative art.* Contemporary writers [Cherwitz and Hikins, 1986] tell us that rhetoric produces most of what passes for everyday knowledge. They claim that rhetoric helps us learn what other people think (for example, whether or not space funding should be increased) and also to learn our *own* minds about things (for example, an old dictum claims that one never really knows something until one can teach it to someone else). By arguing with one another we produce what is called social knowledge, the sort of knowledge that determines much in human affairs. Today in the United States, for example, witches are no longer burned, blacks are no longer limited to plantation employment, and Japanese-Americans are no longer interned. But in other eras, *when other arguments prevailed,* such "truths" were taken for granted and, more important, were used as the basis for social policy. So rhetoric never produces complete truth, only partial truth, truth for these times and for these people. As Johnstone [1969:408] says, "the only way to tell whether what I have is a truth or a falsehood is to contemplate its evocative power," that is, its power to secure the agreement of others. And lest we think that such social knowledge is not really knowledge, we need only reflect upon the comparatively recent history of witches, blacks, and Japanese-Americans.

THE RANGE OF RHETORIC

One way of understanding rhetoric is to consider what it is and what is is not or, better, *how much* of a thing it is and *how much* of another thing it is not. In Figure 1.1, "the rhetorical" is depicted as an area bordering on other domains, but one that is nonetheless special. For example, rhetoric resembles science in that both the scientist and the rhetor want to be taken seriously. The persuader wants listeners to believe that calamity will strike unless the speaker's warnings are heeded. Like the scientist, the persuader marshalls evidence (for example, the testimony of experts, certain statistical trends), uses this evidence to comment upon some real, not imagined, feature of the observable world (for example, "overpopulation will inundate the

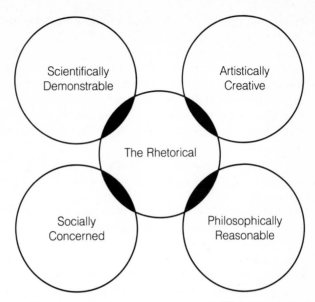

infrastructure of this city''), and then employs this package of arguments to support a policy recommendation (for example, ''We must put
an immediate moratorium on building permits.''). But even though
both the scientist and the persuader seek to make things demonstrably
true, the persuader is willing to treat the perceptions of *ordinary people*
as the acid test of demonstratedness. The scientist, in contrast, normally is expected to meet a more exacting standard of truth (empirical
verifiability, the judgments of experts, experimental replication), while
the persuader's truth is often fifty-one percent truth: the majority judgment of ordinary citizens. For most persuaders on most issues, fifty-
one percent truth is judged sufficient.

As we have mentioned, the persuader, like the poet, is artistically
creative. Both work with symbols to breathe life into ideas. Neither
uses tangible tools (like pick axes) to effect random changes in tangible
phenomena (like rocks). Rather, both the artist and the persuader use
their imaginations to engage their audiences' imaginations. But as we
have noted before, the persuader's creativity is often exercised in
behalf of decidedly short-term gains (for example, assent on the particular issue at hand), and the persuader, because he or she is a ''nar-
rower,'' is unlikely to give listeners the intellectual and emotional freedom normally permitted them by the artist. The imagination of the
persuader is not likely to be as uncontrolled as that of the traditional
artist, because, as we have said, rhetoric is a *social art*. It does little good
for the rhetor to take flights of fancy unless the audience can come
along.

RHETORIC AND POLITICAL PSYCHOLOGY

Critical Profile 1.1   "You See, Doctor Cronkite, I Have This Problem . . ."

Former President Gerald Ford's televised interview with Walter Cronkite during the Republican National Convention in July of 1980 baffled political analysts. Presidential hopeful Ronald Reagan had made the unprecedented move of inviting a former president (Ford) to be his Vice Presidential running mate for the 1980 campaign. Political analysts saw the interview, in which Ford and Cronkite openly discussed the possibility of a "co-presidency," as a significant but inexplicable historical event. How could Ford, a veteran politician, make the mistake of being so publicly open about the personal and political motivations for his (ultimately negative) response to Reagan's offer?

Rebecca Cline, now of the University of Florida, offers an alternative perspective on the event. Rather than viewing Ford's actions as politically disastrous, she focuses on his self-revelations as a form of interpersonal communication. Political analysts, by assuming that Ford's intended audiences were the media and the public, virtually ignored Cronkite's role in the interview. Cline discovered in the interview signs of a therapist-client relationship between the two men, offering an explanation for Gerald Ford's openness. In other words, Ford was not aiming his comments and replies toward the political community, but was instead speaking to Cronkite in an attempt to work things out in his own mind.

In the interview, Cline noted several parallels between Cronkite's behavior and that of a nondirective therapist and between Ford's expressiveness and that of a typical patient. Cline labeled many of Cronkite's behaviors "facilitative," while Ford engaged in what she called "problem-expression." Problems can be "ignored, acknowledged superficially, or dealt with directly." Cline used a seven-point scale created by psychotherapists to measure the degree to which Ford dealt with his problems directly. Throughout the interview, Ford scored well above the midpoint on this scale. When Cronkite asked how Ford would respond to being "drafted" by the party, the former president replied, "It would be tough. . . . I would not go to Washington, Walter, and be a figurehead Vice President. If I go to Washington . . . I have to go there with the . . . belief that I will play a meaningful role. . . . For me to go there and go through the ceremonial aspects, it wouldn't be fair to Betty, it wouldn't be fair to me, it wouldn't be fair to the President, and it wouldn't be right for the country." Cline's use of the therapeutic analogue therefore helps to make sense out of one of the most puzzling field-days of self-disclosure in American political history.

Profiled by: Suzanne M. Daughton
Citation: Cline (1985)

Critical Profile 1.2   A Diabolical Enemy

The President may be Commander in Chief, but only Congress can declare war. This means that a chief executive must first rally Congress behind his crusade. Historically, the favored strategy for doing so has been a systematic "diabolization" of the enemy—the Germans were described as "Huns," the Japanese as "yellow and dastardly," and the British as "jackal[s] who pander to . . . [an] insatiable appetite." Ronald Hatzenbuehler and Robert Ivie, then of Washington State University, argue that in order to rally a nation to war, the inherent conflict between the twin values of peacefulness and protectiveness have to be reconciled. Identifying a scapegoat purges the guilt created by these conflicting ideals, thereby justifying "the breach of peace as it promises to eliminate the source of trouble."

In a study of congressional speeches delivered before war was declared against the British in 1812, the authors found ample evidence of diabolism being used in the still-young United States. During a decade of debate on the "British question," the prowar Republican leadership gradually created an image of a brutal enemy determined to recolonize America. Couched in dramatic, almost theological, language, an otherwise preposterous conclusion—that the British wanted the colonies back—was rendered increasingly reasonable to the nation's citizens.

Republicans talked of being "trampled," "wrested," "bullied," "kicked," and "pounded" by Great Britain. Ominous predictions of lost sovereignty and dignity filled the debate. The few, isolated incidents of British/American tussling were recast into an urgent crisis demanding immediate reprisal. John C. Calhoun reasoned, for example, that "The evil still grows . . . and in each succeeding year swells in extent and pretension beyond the preceding." The citizens of Norristown, Pennsylvania, evidently agreed with the Senator. On May 19, 1812, the town council resolved that the British government was an "object of detestation [to] the civilized world" whose "crimes" and "perfidy" were a threat to the "very existence of this Nation as an Independent Republic." A month later, President Madison demanded a declaration of war on Great Britain.

Diabolism is not unique to American culture, nor is it just an occasional visitor to the nation's shores. Variations of it have been used to castigate Jews and Catholics during the days of the Ku Klux Klan, to intern Japanese-Americans in World War II prison camps, and to threaten Vietnamese fishermen off the U.S. coast in the 1980s. Perhaps the most unsettling thing about this strategy was amply demonstrated in the debates of 1811 and 1812: It can create an enemy *out of nothing* (or out of very little). Such a strategy transforms yesterday's random events into today's incendiary words and, all too often, into tomorrow's protracted battles. Calling people names feels good. But, as Hatzenbuehler and Ivie show, names have consequences.

Profiled by: Patricia Powell
Citation: Hatzenbuehler and Ivie (1983)

Critical Profile 1.3   Lee Harvey Oswald: A Leader Without Followers

---

On November 22, 1963, Lee Harvey Oswald assassinated President John F. Kennedy. For almost three decades since that time, we have heard speculation that Oswald was part of a wide-ranging political conspiracy. None of the conspiracy theories has been fully convincing. But the notion that Oswald acted alone in mad frustration has likewise not seemed sufficient to explain the crime. Assassination is the kind of terrorism we associate with movements. Was Oswald part of a movement? If so, who else was involved?

Leland Griffin of Northwestern University offers a novel answer to those questions in his rhetorical analysis of Oswald's writings. Griffin argues that Oswald did in fact act alone, but that "he saw himself as the leader of a movement, imaginary though it was" and that "impelled by the rhetorical dynamics of that movement, he murdered in its name." The manuscripts that Griffin examined were not intended for publication. Oswald appeared to be writing to himself. But, paradoxically, he also seemed to be addressing an audience (when he used pronouns like "our," "your," and "yours"). Oswald considered himself an expert because he had lived under both American capitalism and Soviet communism. He found both systems to be unsatisfactory. In his writings, he offers an "allturnative" that is directed to imaginary "supporters": "In making such a declaration I must say that in order to make this allturnative effective supporters must prepare now."

Oswald envisioned the creation of a "special party" of "radical futurists." And Oswald had a vision of Utopia for the new party: "The emplacement of a separate, democratic, pure communist society is our goal." He mentions membership, organization, and "distribution of information about this movement to others." At this point, Griffin writes, the movement existed in Oswald's mind, "and he had found his identity as its leader." Toward the end of his writings, Oswald names his Utopian system "The Athenian System" and positions it as a "system opposed to communism, Socialism, and capitalism."

As Kennedy moved toward detente with the Soviet Union, he came to symbolize both opposing systems to Oswald. Oswald's followers—the "auditors in the theater of his mind"—compelled him to act as their leader. When the opportunity presented itself, he shot "not Kennedy alone, but Kennedy/Khrushchev, the combined symbol of the corrupt powers of capitalism/communism that governed the world." Oswald's motive, according to Griffin, was his own imaginary movement, a movement generated by the force of his own internal rhetoric.

Profiled by: Jim Mackin
Citation: Griffin (1984)

The persuader also tries to be philosophically reasonable, to insure that an argument makes the kind of *patterned sense* it must make to be understood by others. The rhetor typically avoids the incomplete mental image, the sudden self-interruption, or the discordant use of language that lends excitement to more purely artistic endeavors. However, the persuader typically uses what works and is less scrupulous in argumentation than the philosopher would recommend. The rhetor uses, in Aristotle's terms, all the means of argument available, not just those recommended in the logic books. As we shall see in Chapter Five, there is a special logic to persuasion, a psycho-logic, and it is to these informal methods of reasoning that the practical speaker most often pays homage. Thus, as Windt [1972] points out, it even sometimes makes "sense" for certain speakers (for example, radical anti-war protesters) to stomp their feet and to act crazed. The logic of persuasion is sometimes a curious logic.

Finally, the persuader is socially concerned, at least in part. The persuader is a public person, seeking to change not just one life but many lives. When abandoning solitude, the persuader promises that many people's lives will be improved in some important way. But the persuader is not a social worker. As McGee [1975] says, persuaders present *their* versions of what "the people" believe, often taking great liberties with public opinion. Thus, the persuader's social concern is limited to his or her private version of the ideal life, a life in which everyone owns a Ford automobile or votes a straight Socialist ticket or gives witness to biblical truths daily. The persuader wants to make a particular kind of change, a public change. Those who dream social dreams need the aid of others.

Because it borders on the domains of the poet, the scientist, the philosopher, and the community worker, the realm of the rhetorical is a powerful realm. The rhetor draws upon each of these worlds and yet steps back from each simultaneously, seeking to become a poet, but a poet of practical consequences; a scientist, but a scientist unencumbered by footnotes. The persuader also becomes an easygoing logician and a social worker with an eye on the bottom line. By blending these roles as skillfully as Ronald Reagan did when serving as president, persuaders become highly influential. For this reason alone, they bear watching. Watching them is the job of the rhetorical critic.

The definition of rhetoric is obviously generous, one designed to encompass a variety of messages. Included within this broad definition would be the television docudrama, the cooing of lovers on a park bench, the scientific treatise, the invocation at the City Council meeting, the reprimand from the boss at work, the presidential address, the college lecture, the adolescent's whining during dinner, the blockbuster movie, the top sergeant's welcome to boot camp, the Burger King commercial, the psychiatrist's counseling session, and much else. All of these situations require the use of language and all of them can result in both obvious and not obvious forms of influence. It is a hallmark of the critical perspective that all messages be examined carefully, especially those that seem to lie outside the realm of rhetoric. Currently, rhetorical critics are launching just such investigations into such seemingly nonrhetorical areas as aesthetics, science, philosophy, and friendship formation in order to witness subtler forms of persuasion.

For the most part, however, this book will treat the more common sorts of rhetorical influence, largely because it is in these areas that scholars have worked longest and most profitably. More often than not, the focus here will be on (1) the *verbal* features of persuasive messages rather than their nonverbal aspects (gesture, iconography, intonation), (2) *public* rather than private interpersonal encounters (we will be more likely to focus on lawyers than on lovers), and (3) *consecutive* rather than interrupted discourse (we shall more often consider the speech and the essay rather than serial conversations). Because the research is most plentiful in these areas, this threefold emphasis will be our tendency, but not our preoccupation. The world of rhetoric is a wide one and we will invite the reader to consider both its depth and its breadth.

Indeed, the most basic job of the rhetorical critic is to be able to discover *when* rhetoric is being used in the first place. Persuaders, after all, do not always own up to their profession. Often, they would like to be mistaken for a scientist or a poet or a philosopher. By keeping a sharp eye peeled for the essential features of rhetoric, however, the critic can discover when rhetoric comes to call. Normally, three features make a message rhetorical: (1) **delineations of the good,** (2) **resonance for a particular audience,** and (3) **clear or clearly implied policy recommendations** ("policy" being conceived here in its broadest sense, including proposals of marriage, requests for repentance, voter solicitations, and much else).

Table 1.1 presents three similar yet different lists of events ranging from the obviously to the less obviously rhetorical. As one moves from right to left, notice how the events change in subtle yet important ways, increasingly lending themselves to more immediate and more powerful rhetorical uses. In the case of the photographs, for example, it is not hard to imagine how the picture of an Appalachian shack could be used in the hands of a community activist seeking federal funding. Such a picture presents a special invitation to the viewer to think *now* about matters of right and wrong. The fact that this is an "American" shack makes Americans especially uncomfortable, because it calls into

Table 1.1   Types of Rhetorical Events

Messages	More Obviously Rhetorical	Uncertain	Less Obviously Rhetorical
Photographs	An Appalachian shack	The White House	A South Sea hut
Telephone call	From Handicapped Workers of America	From a son at college	From a rich friend
Drama	Guerrilla theatre	Off-Broadway drama	Broadway musical
Signs	On a highway billboard	At an hourly parking lot	On a restroom door
Commercials	About hamburgers from Wendy's Restaurants	About drugs from the National Basketball Assn.	About Picasso from the National Endowment for the Arts
Magazines	*Moral Majority Report*	*Harpers*	*Time*
Guided tours	At Budweiser plant	At Lincoln Memorial	At Yellowstone National Park
Humor	Political jokes	Ethnic jokes	Animal jokes
Poetry	Langston Hughes	Wallace Stevens	E. E.Cummings
Trip directions	From Big Al to his car lot	From a new boyfriend to his lake cabin	From Rand McNally to Salt Lake City
Statistics	From Int'l. Assoc. of Oil Producers	From Mobil Oil Corp.	From U.S. Dept. of Energy
Music	Folk songs	Church hymns	Rhythm and blues
Football	Half-time pep talk	TV color commentary	Cheerleaders' cheers
Storytelling	Religious testimonials	Folklore	Fairy tales

question certain aspects of the national dream. Perhaps because of this audience resonance, the policy recommendations seem to jump out of the picture for many Americans ("Let us put a stop to this kind of poverty" or "Why don't those people get a job and live better?").

The picture of the White House is more ambiguous. One can imagine the photograph being used in patriotic ways in the United States ("the seat of our democracy") and quite differently in Iran ("home of the jackal"). It could be used for comedic effect on *Saturday Night Live* ("The Prez's house") or for purely crass boosterism on a multicolored flyer ("Bring your convention to Washington. Hotel rates have never been lower."). The South Sea hut, in contrast, might lend itself to any number of uses. Previous rhetoric in the U.S. culture, at least, seems not to have marked it yet for special use, and hence it makes fewer immediate and specific demands on us as viewers (Should it be used for a travel brochure? In connection with religious missionary work? As a symbol of exploitation in the Third World?). As one moves from right to left in Table 1.1, one gets the feeling that (1) the speaker's exact purposes for persuasion become less ambiguous, (2) perhaps as a result, the emotions of the speaker lie increasingly close to the surface, (3) increasingly specific "policies" are being recommended to the audience or at least broadly hinted at ("Give now," "Commit yourself fully," "Follow the Word"), (4) the question of essential good and evil has become less of a question, and (5) finding an "ideal audience" for the message would become easier, because fewer and fewer people can fill the bill as the rhetoric heats up. In short, as we move from right to left, things become more rhetorical.

This is not to say that we should turn our backs on less obvious rhetoric. Indeed, critics have become increasingly interested in these subtler messages precisely because most people (that is, most potential audience members) are oblivious to the *hints* of good and evil or *implied* policy recommendations buried within them. Thus, for example, critics are now looking at the range of meanings provided by the Vietnam Memorial in Washington, D.C. [Foss, 1986], at stereotypes in popular romance novels [Hubbard, 1985], at the rhetoric of newscasting [Gregg, 1977], and at the politics of public service announcements [Paletz, et al., 1977]. Throughout this book, therefore, we will look for rhetoric in all its haunts and discover tools refined enough to understand even the most subtle of its manifestations.

THE FUNCTIONS OF RHETORIC

We have discussed what rhetoric is and what it is not, where it can be found, and what shapes it takes. It now remains for us to examine what rhetoric *does*, how it functions in human society. Of course, we will be studying the uses of rhetoric throughout this book, but here, briefly, we can examine some of its less frequently noticed uses.

1. *Rhetoric unburdens.* People who make rhetoric do so because they must get something off their chests, because the cause they champion overwhelms their natural reticence. Such people refuse to let history take its slow, evolutionary course and instead try to become part of history themselves. The history they make may be quite local in character (for example, picketing a neighborhood abortion clinic), but rhetorical people typically do not hang back. They sense that the world

---

RHETORIC AND LITERATURE

Critical Profile 1.4   A Good Woman Is Hard to Find

How influential are romance novels? Do they provide readers with simple escape, or do they encourage the adoption of an idealistic world view? Marsha Vanderford Doyle of the University of South Florida used a technique called fantasy theme analysis to examine the romantic rhetoric of Barbara Cartland, the bestselling author in the world. Doyle found several intriguing features of the novels that provide, through repetition, potentially influential lessons for readers about male/female relationships. One of the most significant features Doyle discovered was an answer to the question: How does one react to a society lacking "high standards, noble ideals, and decency"? Cartland provides her millions of faithful readers with visions of "moral fantasy," illustrating the difference in behavior and beliefs of desirable and undesirable women. Cartland believes that her novels, with their formulaic characters and plots, provide "a guide to happiness" for "the young and idealistic."

The undesirable woman is pictured as "assertive, persistent, independent, immoral, and sexual." She will ultimately be rejected by men in favor of the traditional woman. While the heroine in Cartland's novels is "fragile, dependent, submissive, moral, and spiritual," the rejected woman is "associated with physical pleasure and is described as less-than-human: 'Moving lithely as a snake, she drew him down on top of her . . . desire seemed to make her more animal than human.'"

The concept of an ideal can be constructive as well as destructive. Obviously, Cartland's heroine displays the traditional virtuous limitations, which can be incapacitating in the pursuit of a career. However, Doyle notes that the phenomenal success of Cartland's novels shows that they fulfill a need: Romance novels provide stability and validation for traditional behavior and values in a time of changing and confusing sex roles. Readers may account for the imperfections in their lives by calculating their deviations from the ideal. Women who read Cartland's novels may gain from this vision hope as well as a sense of increased control over the events in their lives. Readers may feel that if they could only be more like the heroine, their lives would be more fulfilling. One can only wonder how such readers square the stories they read with the stories that life itself tells daily.

Profiled by: Suzanne M. Daughton
Citation: Doyle (1985)

---

around them is not yet set, and so they approach it aggressively, often convinced that they can make a difference, always convinced that they must try.

On occasion, however, the need to speak produces ambivalence. For example, Charles Manson, who in 1969 engineered a series of horrible crimes in California (known as the Tate-LaBianca murders) and who is currently serving a life sentence in prison, seems especially conflicted about such matters. Manson recently consented to an interview with journalist Keven Kennedy, and his remarks tell us much about his rhetorical mindset:

> *Kennedy:* Do you want to be released from prison?
> *Manson:* Released? I just want to be left alone. You see, I dismissed the world a long time ago. Really I did. I dismissed it. It's gone from my mind. It comes over and says, "You pay me some attention." I say, "No." "Will you accept our God as being *the* God?" I say, "All right. I'll accept anything. Now, can I get on with my business?" [Manson, 1985:28]

At this stage in his life at least, Manson appears to have quit the business of leadership. He seems unwilling to make the sorts of adjustments communication requires. But less than two minutes later in the interview Manson had this to say:

> *Manson:* I just learn to reflect people back at themselves. Because man is not working—why tell anybody? If you start informing people that are misinformed, you'd spend the rest of your life informing people that are misinformed. *I would feel that I had achieved something if we could stop the misinforming of people and inform them properly* [Manson, 1985:29, italics mine].

In this latter statement, Manson captures the rhetorical person's basic instinct: to step out of the shadows of anonymity and make a difference by "informing them properly." Although his years in prison have no doubt quelled his ardor for social contact, Manson's desire to lead lurks just beneath the surface of his consciousness. While he seems to have lost a bit of heart over the years (for which we may all be thankful), even the fifty-year-old Charles Manson harbors the persuasive instinct. In a sense, then, communication is a kind of arrogant imposition on other people. When A tries to persuade B, for example, A affirms (1) that something is wrong in B's world and (2) that A can fix it. Thus, if it is true that the poet is an escapist, it is also true that the rhetor is an infiltrator. Naturally, the arrogance of the rhetorical act is normally well disguised by the practicing persuader, who is, after all, only there to "help" ("You owe it to *yourself* to sign this contract," "The *handicapped* do indeed appreciate your contribution," "Do this for the *Lord's* sake"). Still, a rhetorical engagement is no less intrusive just because its intrusions have been camouflaged.

2. *Rhetoric distracts.* A speaker wants to have all, not just some, of our attention. To get that attention, the speaker must so fill up our

---

Critical Profile 1.5   The Power of the Parable

A man traveling across a field encountered a tiger. He fled, the tiger after him. Coming to a precipice, he caught hold of a wild vine and swung himself down over the edge. The tiger sniffed at him from above. Trembling, the man looked down to where, far below, another tiger was waiting to eat him. Only the vine sustained him.

Two mice, one white and one black, little by little started to gnaw away at the vine. The man saw a luscious strawberry near him. Grasping the vine with one hand he plucked the strawberry with the other. How sweet it tasted!

Why are parables, like this one attributed to the Buddha, so popular? Why are parables found in nearly every culture? To what does the parable owe its rhetorical power? After pondering questions like these, William G. Kirkwood of East Tennessee State University developed the following answer: We do not yet know why and how parables work, but, equally, we cannot become contented with our ignorance of them.

As brief narratives, parables primarily instruct rather than entertain and are popular because they "enliven otherwise remote ideas, call attention to forgotten or unsuspected possibilities, and confront listeners' attitudes and actions." The parable works on two levels—the metaphorical and the exemplary. That is, the parable *as metaphor* provokes insight by revealing "tacitly an 'extraordinary,' transcendent reality within 'ordinary' events and actions." The Great Supper, for example, can be understood "as a metaphor

---

minds that we forget, temporarily at least, the other ideas, people, and policies usually important to us. Naturally, we do not just give away our attention, so it takes rhetoric at its best to sidetrack us. One way of doing so is for the speaker to control the premises of a discussion. As McCombs and Shaw [1972] have demonstrated, the power of the mass media derives not so much from their ability to tell us what to think but from their ability to get us to think about the topics they favor. When choosing to report on industrial lead poisoning, for example, a local TV station simultaneously chooses *not* to cover the crowning of the Apple Queen or the win-loss record of the local Double-A farm club. By "setting the agenda" in this fashion, by controlling the premises pertaining to newsworthiness, the media can influence any conclusions drawn from the premises they have set in place.

So the rhetor constantly requests listeners to think about this topic, not that one; to consider this problem, not those they are currently thinking about; to try out this solution, not that endorsed by the oppos-

---

Critical Profile 1.5   The Power of the Parable (*continued*)

for the kingdom of God itself." The parable *as example*, on the other hand, dramatizes "familiar moral precepts," illustrating behavior to be emulated or avoided.

Kirkwood's claim is that most scholars, particularly those who study New Testament stories, have *overstated* the metaphorical power of the parable and have thereby "failed to appreciate the significance of stories as examples." For Kirkwood, the parable as example does more than relate a moral; it portrays "a particular state of awareness." The Buddha's parable is not merely "a poetic metaphor reflecting humanity's existential condition"; it actually induces the state of awareness suggested as an antidote to the human condition—in the face of adversity, "pluck and enjoy the strawberry."

Unless close attention is paid to the exemplary features of the parable, Kirkwood argues, much of its rhetorical power remains undetected, particularly in the case of parables from more "contemplative and mystical traditions." If Kirkwood is right, scholars still have much to recover—both from the New Testament and from the narratives of other societies. It may be the case that cultures bury their knottiest problems in these intriguing rhetorical forms. Thus, for example, we find in Jesus' parable of the Good Samaritan much of the ethnic and class enmity of ancient Jewish society. In short, to learn about parables may be to learn about the forces that vex people's souls most grievously.

Profiled by: Kerry Riley
Citation: Kirkwood (1985)

---

ing speaker. In this sense, rhetoric operates like a good map. Maps, after all, have a distinctive point of view: They "favor" interstate highways (by coloring them a bright red) over rural roads (often a pale blue); they emphasize urban areas (blotched in yellow) over small towns (a small dot); they adapt their appeals to vacationers (by highlighting Yosemite) rather than to truckers (no diners are listed). Like the rhetor, the road map bristles with integrity, implying by the precision of its drawings that it provides the complete story: all the highway news that's fit to print.

Rhetoric, too, tries to narrow our latitudes of choice without giving us the feeling that we are being thereby hemmed in. Rhetoric tries to control the *definition* we provide for a given activity ("Your church offering isn't a monetary loss; it's a downpayment on heaven") as well as the *criteria* we employ to solve a problem ("Abortion is not a religious issue; it's a legal one"). By also emphasizing one speaker *category* over another (for example, George Bush as commander-in-chief of the

Critical Profile 1.6   Mark Twain: Patron Saint

A glance at today's social and political scene reveals a problem for democracy that even an optimist cannot deny. The problem might be thought of as overspecialization or information overload. How, for example, can the average citizen make decisions regarding such issues as deployment of new missile systems or creation of a new regulatory agency? Frederick Antczak of the University of Virginia summarizes what technology has meant for democracy: "Each issue seems entangled in the next, and of each only one thing is sure: it is probably more complicated than we yet know and politicians will be inclined to admit." Complicating the difficulty of maintaining a democracy, says Antczak, is an excessive concern for public image that manipulates people instead of genuinely informing them.

Antczak believes that there is a way out of our democratic predicament: a return to a form of rhetoric that builds a public of critical decision-makers, people who are unwilling to settle for answers offered by either politicians or journalists. A look to our past reacquaints us with discourse that emphasizes issues over image, and Mark Twain was master of that genre. He provides an example of speech that would remake an uncritical people into a thinking, questioning public. Antczak contends that Twain's sarcasm and irony were the tools of a democratic educator who used his humorous devices to share contradictions with his audience. "What Twain built with one hand, he tore down—sometimes, it seemed, gleefully—with the other." While the tearing down might have been the medicine a democratic society needs, the humor made the medicine easier to swallow. In Twain's words, "Humor makes me reflect . . . Always, when I am thinking, there comes suggestions of what I am, and what we all are, and what we are coming to." Twain's entertaining rhetoric thus constructed a more educated public by presenting them with a model of a person who joyfully criticized bad thinking.

What, then, is the role of the modern critic? Antczak's research suggests that the critic is one who educates the public by questioning popular assumptions, one who reveals truths normally hidden within a crafty piece of discourse. In a sense, Mark Twain might well become the patron saint of contemporary rhetorical criticism. At its best, after all, criticism is more than cold-blooded description and interpretation. It is also an indirect and playful way to make people think about possibilities they usually ignore and to question the conventional wisdom that swirls about them each and every day.

Profiled by: John Theobald-Osborne
Citation: Antczak (1985)

armed forces versus George Bush as the Republican legatee of Richard Nixon), persuaders invite us to focus on this and not that, on here and not there, on now and not then.

3. *Rhetoric enlarges.* In some senses, modern persuaders are like the heralds of old. They move among us singing the siren song of change, asking us to open our worlds a bit and to study a new way of looking at things, to consider a new solution to an old problem (or an old solution to a problem we did not know we had). Rhetoric operates like a kind of intellectual algebra, asking us to equate things we had never before considered equatable. Thus, for example, Adolph Hitler rose to fame (and infamy) by linking German nationalism with increased militarism and Germany's economic woes with Jewish clannishness. Corrupt equations, but, for him, useful ones.

Often, the **associations** encouraged by rhetoric are no less sophisticated, or honorable, than those created by Adolph Hitler. Nevertheless, these linkages are the workhorses of persuasion, devices suitable for asking listeners to expand their horizons. For example, manufacturers of personal computers are now virtually assuring unwary parents that computing skills will translate instantly into educational achievement for their children. It is interesting to note that persuaders rarely ask for major expansion of their listeners' world views. They imply that only a slight modification is in order. Persuasion moves by increments of inches.

Often, persuaders **disassociate** ideas in order to expand the viewpoints of their listeners. For example, Bankamericard changed its name to Visa in the early 1970s so that the more international flavor of the new name would offset the growing anti-Americanism found in Western Europe at the time. Similarly, during the neophyte's first meeting at Alcoholics Anonymous, an attempt is made to break the intimate connection between the person's self-image and the use of stimulants. Naturally, the alcoholic, like all listeners, initially resists such "enlarging" perspectives. It becomes the persuader's task to demonstrate that any such alterations are a natural extension of thoughts and feelings the listener *already* possesses and that any such new notions can be easily accommodated within the listener's *existing* repertoire of ideas. Thus, for example, patently unnatural cosmetic products are sold to American women as devices for enhancing their natural beauty. That is why rhetoric is called an art.

4. *Rhetoric names.* To understand the power of rhetoric we must remember that creatures and noncreatures alike (people, frogs, rocks, bicycles) are born without labels. People are, as best we know, nature's only namers. And they name things with a vengeance: Orville Reddenbacher's Popcorn, Sri Lanka, the Children of God, black holes, the

Utah Jazz, McCarthyism. People take their naming seriously: Newly enfranchised Americans anglicize their names to ward off discrimination; professional women often retain their maiden names to avoid being seen as the captives of their mates; fights sometimes erupt when black youngsters play a name-calling game known as "the Dozens."

No doubt, naming is as important as it is because meaning is such a variable thing. A tornado-ravaged town, after all, is but wind and torment until it is publicly labeled by appropriate people ("The clear will of the Lord" or "an obvious candidate for Federal disaster assistance"). Some executions spawn massive religious movements (for example, the death of Jesus Christ) or excite political passions (for example, the Rosenbergs during the 1950s), while other executions are met with mere curiosity (for example, that of Gary Gillmore, the first person to be executed in recent times). The facts in each of these cases were different, of course, but so too was the rhetorical skill of the executed's namers and the aggressiveness with which they pursued the naming.

The naming function of rhetoric helps listeners become comfortable with new ideas and provides listeners with an acceptable vocabulary for talking about these ideas. Through rhetoric, "white flight schools" are transformed into "independent academies"; "labor-baiting" becomes the "right-to-work"; a "fetus" is seen as an "unborn child"; "suicide" is replaced by "death with dignity"; and a vague assemblage of disconnected thoughts and random social trends is decried as "secular humanism." A major challenge for the rhetorical critic, then, is to study how namers name things and how audiences respond to the names they hear.

5. *Rhetoric empowers.* Those who decry the art of rhetoric often do so because its users embrace many truths, not just one. Traditionally, teachers of rhetoric have encouraged speakers to consider alternative modes of saying things and not to just utter the first thought that comes to mind. This attitude, too, brings censure to the rhetorical arts. Those who embrace absolute standards of right and wrong or totalistic systems of thought have always had problems with rhetoric, because, above all, rhetoric permits and encourages flexibility. Flexibility, in turn, provides options: to address one listener or several; to mention an idea or not to mention it at all; to say something this way and not that way; to tell all one knows or only just a bit; to repeat oneself or to vary one's response. Rhetoric encourages flexibility, because it is based on a kind of symbolic Darwinism: (1) speakers who do not adapt to their surroundings quickly become irrelevant; (2) ideas that become frozen soon die for want of social usefulness.

Such flexibility, in turn, permits continual growth, for the individual as well as for society. Rhetorical theorists contend that there are as many ways of making an idea clear to listeners as there are listeners [Hart and Burks, 1972]. Moreover, because it encourages adaptability, rhetoric permits personal evolution for speakers as well. Nineteen fifties racist George Wallace, 1960s arch-conservative Barry Goldwater, and 1970s radical Tom Hayden all continued to be prominent political spokespersons in the 1980s, not because they changed their beliefs fundamentally, but because they found new *ways* of telling their truths as they matured politically (and rhetorically). And when people's fundamental beliefs *do* change over time, rhetoric can also accommodate such reincarnations: of Pat Boone from a rock 'n roll idol to a religious evangelist, of Gerry Rubin from a social revolutionary to a corporate yuppie, of Dan Quayle from a campus playboy to a stodgy conservative.

Social power, then, often derives from rhetorical strength. Grand ideas, deeply felt beliefs, and unsullied ideologies are sources of power too, but, as Plato has told us, none of these factors can be influential without a delivery system, without rhetoric. Purity of heart, honest intentions, and a spotless record of integrity are assets to a political speaker, but they are hardly enough to sustain a campaign unless they are *shared* with the voters. As Bryant [1972:23] remarks, if they are to be used with confidence "a bridge or an automobile or a clothes-line must not only *be* strong but must *appear* to be."

6. *Rhetoric elongates.* What does rhetoric make longer? Time. Time, that most precious of all substances, can be extended—or, more accurately, seem to be extended—when rhetoric is put to use. Consider the Reverend Martin Luther King, Jr. When he came on the scene in the 1950s, King no doubt knew that civil rights laws would not be enacted just because he mounted the public platform. *But King succeeded in making the future seem to be the present,* because his appeals reached so deeply into people's souls and because his futuristic images were painted so vividly: "I have a dream . . . that one day, right here in Alabama, little black boys and black girls will be able to join hands with little white boys and white girls as sisters and brothers. I have a dream today!" [King, 1964:374]. Naturally, King's speeches did not immediately change the legal and social landscapes. But for his followers, the devastations of the past commanded less of their attention when they listened to him describe a future of genuine possibility. In his presence, listeners lingered in the future and felt better because of it. As Hart [1984a:764] says, rhetoric can become a "way station for the patient."

Most persuaders sell the future, to move listeners to a better place, a better time, a happier circumstance. Whether it is more robust health through Herbalife, a slimmer figure with Lean Cuisine, or fewer taxes with Bob Dole, rhetoric transports us, momentarily at least, across the boundaries of time. Admittedly, this is a kind of surrogate, or false, reality. But genuinely effective rhetoric makes such criticisms of literal falseness seem small-minded. When tempted with visions of untold wealth via Amway or a glorious afterlife via Jesus, many people relax their guards.

It is also true that rhetoric can be used to appropriate the *past.* When doing so, most skilled persuaders use the opportunity to do some historical housecleaning. Thus, as Warner [1976] tells us, most patriotic celebrations in the United States omit from their oratory stories of racial, ethnic, or religious persecution. The Fourth of July speaker steers clear of these unquestionable historical facts, because ceremonial rhetoric has its own, more up-beat, story to tell. Rhetoric tells a *selective* history, taking us back in time for a brief, heavily edited, tour of history. But as the good eulogist knows, not everything about the dearly departed need to be told at the funeral. The eulogist reminds us of the deceased's grandest virtues, his or her most endearing qualities, because only the best of the past can make the present seem less tragic. So, while rhetoric often tells literal lies, most of us would have it no other way.

CONCLUSION

In this chapter, we have covered the essentials of rhetoric. We have seen that rhetoric has special features that are not found in other creative arts like painting and music and poetry. Rhetoric's creations are practical creations, and because they are the creations of real people living in the real world, rhetoric is a controversial thing to study. Many people do not like rhetoric, which is to say they like their own rhetoric best. But human beings have little choice but to use rhetoric if they wish the world to be different than it is. Jonas Salk may have invented a vaccine for polio, but no further vaccines will be discovered at the Salk Institute unless its fund-raising goes well. Neil Armstrong may have set foot on the moon, but he was permitted to do so only because Congressional arms were twisted by the space lobby in the United States. Similarly, those Americans who enjoy riding on an interstate highway system or watching rock videos should thank the structural and acoustic engineers who made such marvels possible, but they should thank, too, the rhetorical engineers whose persuasive appeals found funding sufficient to nurture those inventions when they were being developed.

So rhetoric is with us, for both good and ill. It is with us because most worthwhile ideas come from *groups* of people working in concert. For religions to thrive there must be apostles. For ideas to be understood there must be teachers. For justice to be served there must be lawyers. For space exploration to take place there must be Carl Sagans. To turn our backs on rhetoric would be to turn our backs on sharing ideas and values, which would be to turn our backs on any practical notion of human community. So rhetoric is with us because it must be with us.

But just because rhetoric exists and just because we must use it does not mean that it is easily understood. This book is dedicated to the proposition that rhetoric can and must be understood. The assumption here is that the more lenses available for viewing rhetoric, the greater will be our understanding of human discourse. Thus, each chapter of this book will dissect persuasive messages. In some chapters, we will use wide-angled lenses to examine such broad features as setting, role, and purpose. In other chapters, we will use more refined lenses when viewing argument, form, structure, and language. We will consider what various schools of criticism have to say about persuasion and then look at some of the fascinating things scholars have found about the many forms of rhetoric. But we should do none of that until we have an instrument for doing so. And so we will now examine a microscope suitable for examining rhetorical exchange: the critical perspective.

CHAPTER TWO

The Critical Perspective

❖
❖

I would be most happy if you would attend a Cabinet luncheon next Tuesday the nineteenth. If you want to bring your press secretary and any other member of your staff I'll be glad to have them. If you can arrive at about twelve fifteen I'll have General Smith and the Central Intelligence Agency give you a complete briefing on the foreign situation. Then we will have luncheon with the Cabinet and after that if you like I'll have my entire staff report to you on the situation in the White House and in that way you will be entirely briefed on what takes place. I've made arrangements with the Central Intelligence Agency to furnish you once a week with the world situation as I also have for Governor Stevenson.

Harry S. Truman [1952]

This letter was sent to Dwight D. Eisenhower, who, when he received it (on August 14, 1952), was the Republican candidate for the U.S. presidency. Mr. Truman's letter bears the stamp of his efficient informality: "If you can arrive at about twelve fifteen," "I've made arrangements," "I'll . . . give you a complete briefing." Also in evidence is his vigor of expression and personal openness: "I'll be glad, " "I would be most happy," "if you like I'll have my entire staff . . ." Although Truman's prose is businesslike, its intent is clear: To put the good of the country above political partisanship by giving the Republican candidate the same information he provided Democrat Adlai Stevenson somewhat earlier.

Informal conversation, a light lunch, a cordial briefing. Who could ask for more? Dwight Eisenhower, for one:

Dear Mr. President:
Thank you for your offer to have me briefed by certain agencies of the Government on the foreign situation. On the personal side I am also grateful for your luncheon invitation.

In my current position as standard bearer of the Republican Party and of other Americans who want to bring about a change in the National Government, it is my duty to remain free to analyze publicly the policies and acts of the present administration whenever it appears to me to be proper and in the country's interests.

During the present period the people are deciding our country's leadership for the next four years. The decision rests between the Republican nominee and the candidate you and your Cabinet are supporting and with whom you conferred before sending your message. In such circumstances and in such a period I believe our communications should be only those which are known to all the American people. Consequently I think it would be unwise and result in confusion in the public mind if I were to attend the meeting in the White House to which you have invited me.

As you know, the problems which you suggest for discussion are those with which I have lived for many years. In spite of this I would instantly change this decision in the event there should arise a grave emergency. There is nothing in your message to indicate that this is presently the case.

With respect to the weekly reports from the Central Intelligence Agency that you kindly offered to send me, I will welcome these reports. In line with my view, however, that the American people are entitled to all the facts in the international situation, save only in those cases where security of the United States is involved, I would want it understood that the possession of these reports will in no other way limit my freedom to discuss or analyze foreign programs as my judgment dictates.

Very respectfully,
Dwight D. Eisenhower [1952]

Dwight Eisenhower an ungrateful wretch? Only a critic can tell for sure. This chapter will focus on the attitudes and skills needed to make sense of human discourse. We will see that there is always more to rhetoric than first meets the eye and that even a pleasant invitation for lunch can, in the hands of a wily politician, become something quite different indeed.

But what exactly is Mr. Eisenhower saying here? And why is he so rude? Most likely, he is using the Truman invitation to establish his independence and authority as a presidential candidate and to offset what he sees as Truman's political ploy. Although Eisenhower is careful to observe the amenities ("on the personal side I am also grateful"), he quickly points out that his role as "standard bearer of the Republican party" makes special demands upon him. Eisenhower seems worried that the speech-act of chatting with an opposite-party incumbent might make it seem as if he, the candidate, were a mere child being summoned to the principal's office. So Eisenhower counterattacks by launching arguments about the Democratic party's failures of leadership and about his own vast experience as a world leader ("The problems which you suggest for discussion are those with which I have lived for many years"). Also, by the very form of his letter (much longer than Truman's, less informal, more hortatory), Eisenhower tries to shift the direction of the exchange so that he, not Truman, takes the principled stand.

The astute critic will also note Eisenhower's veiled attack of Truman's motives. Eisenhower implies that Truman is using the letter to cover up his own rank partisanship (Ike's remarks about the Democratic candidate "with whom you conferred before sending [me] your message"). Ike also hints that the luncheon has been designed as a photo opportunity *for Truman*, because there seems to be no real need for the discussion ("I would instantly change this decision in the event there should arise a grave emergency"). Finally, Eisenhower's clever use of language makes Truman seem sneaky and underhanded ("our communications should be only those which are known to all the American people"), while Eisenhower himself emerges as open and honest, a man in charge ("I would want it understood that the possession of these reports will in no way limit my freedom to discuss or analyze foreign programs as my judgment dictates"). Rhetoric can indeed be complicated stuff.

Rhetorical criticism is the business of identifying the complications of rhetoric and explaining them in a comprehensive and efficient manner. This definition implies several things: that rhetorical texts are indeed complicated, that there is an orderly way of describing these complications, and that the best criticism describes them parsimoniously (simply yet completely). So when confronting messages, the critic examines such factors as role, language, arguments, ideas, and form in order to reduce the confusion persuaders intentionally create for audiences—and for critics.

Modern Rhetorical Criticism is, therefore, something of a guidebook to confusion. It invites us to be less spontaneous and simplistic when responding as critics, since persuaders try so hard to make us spontaneous and simplistic when responding as audience members. The book outlines methods for inspecting persuasive messages in order to see what news about people might lie within them. Before considering critical techniques, however, we need to know something of the critical enterprise itself, an enterprise designed to expose the clever rhetoric of clever politicians like Harry Truman and Dwight Eisenhower. This chapter offers just such a perspective on cleverness.

THE PURPOSES OF CRITICISM

In the passage above, Dwight Eisenhower operates as both a persuader and a critic. As a critic, he dissects Harry Truman's message with care, and, as a persuader, he slyly accuses Truman of using the luncheon to salve his own guilty conscience. Eisenhower portrays Truman's politeness as political manipulation and refuses to become part of the President's elaborately staged demonstration of statesmanship. When responding as he did, Ike did what all good critics do: he examined rhetorical texts to account for *all* of their important meanings, not just those the persuader featured.

Naturally, another critic might argue that it was Eisenhower who acted ungraciously when transforming Truman's luncheon invitation into something sordid. In either case, the critic would be doing what all good rhetorical critics do: building an argument about social conditions by observing what people say. Naturally, only a community of informed persons could judge whether Eisenhower was the rhetorical criminal or the rhetorical victim here. This community of critics would listen to the contrasting arguments, examine the evidence offered, and then render its judgment. So that is what rhetorical critics do. But why do they do it? There are several possibilities:

1. *Rhetorical criticism documents social trends.* Rosenfield [1972:133] sees the critic as a special sort of sports analyst, who takes part in the swirl of life but who also has perspective on it. Rosenfield distinguishes between the fan, who enjoys the game of persuasion, and the expert commentator, who both appreciates and comments knowingly upon it. Criticism, therefore, requires special discernment: the ability to stand simultaneously in the midst of and apart from the events experienced. Like the sports commentator, the critic provides an instant replay of the event, pointing out features that the too-involved fan was unable to see because of the immediacy and excitement of the event itself. The critic reviews the scene of the action, calling attention to features of persuasion that the listener saw but did not notice.

The good critic magnifies without distorting, focusing upon rhetorical characteristics that, while seemingly incidental, may nevertheless be important. Thus, for example, Hart [1978] noticed that the pamphlets issued by radical atheists were raggedly produced, containing grammatical faults, typographical errors, and even missing words. The following is an example of such rhetoric:

By hypnotic methods, by imposing fear of God or devil, beliefs contrary to science, common sense are implanted into the subconscious

minds of the children, and then by massive propaganda, which sat-
urates the TV, the press, often schools and libraries, the victims are
brain stuffed into accepting religion, on "faith," which is attempting
to believe things which cannot be proven, and are contrary to common sense, intelligence and reason [Johnson: n.d.].

Although seemingly insignificant, such run-on sentences led Hart to
conclude that a hurried, telegraphic rhetoric is well suited to a group
that has to make an impression on its hard-to-get readers quickly. He
went on to describe the philosophical world view and psychological
mind-set of the atheists, citing in each case the minor but important
features of the garbled style he noticed.

The good critic notices verbal trends, features that are too regularized to be accidental and too suggestive to be unimportant. According
to Farrell [1980], the critic thereby treats messages as symptoms of
some larger social fact. The critic says: "I see a bit of 'X' here and am
willing to bet that there is more 'X' to be found in society at large." So,
for example, Leathers [1973] has shown that radical right persuaders
often use the *nonexistence* of facts as proof of their existence (that is,
"you can't see It because 'they' won't let you, which only proves that
It is there in massive quantities"). Leathers worries about the rhetoric
he describes, fearing that such shoddy reasoning will become attractive
to people who cannot or will not listen carefully to what they hear.
Thus, the critic acts as society's vanguard, spotting in today's rhetoric
the smoke that becomes tomorrow's fires.

As Brockriede [1974] has said, all rhetorical critics are arguers.
Feminists argue that articles in popular magazines demean women.
Physicians argue that beer commercials glorify alcoholism. Social
activists argue that ethnic stereotypes in situation comedies undermine
minorities. In each case, a critic is arguing that *regularized* features of
rhetoric have become dangerous to society. In other circumstances, it
is the absence of regularity that causes alarm: Appeals to national unity
drop off in political campaigns and letters to the editor become self-
centered rather than community-centered. Combining these perceptions, the critic might posit the rise of a new narcissism and then spec-
ulate about its consequences for society at large. In short, the critic's
job is to discover trends and then see where they lead.

2. *Rhetorical criticism provides general understandings via the case-
study method.* By scrutinizing a small number of texts, the critic restricts
the range of available insights. Even if a thousand televangelised sermons were collected for study, the critic would still be examining messages rooted in a peculiar political circumstance, in a specialized
medium, and in a unique cultural backdrop. Even with such a large
sample, the critic would still only have a sample, a mere whisper of

history's religious utterances. Because the critic's focus is tight, the critic's challenge is to tell the largest story possible given the necessarily limited evidence available.

So the critic is a sampler, and samplers must be both modest and cautious. But modesty and caution do not insure unimportance. What the critic gives up in *scope* is offset by the *power* of insight made available. What insures power? Choosing a provocative text for study, asking important questions of that text, and making intriguing extrapolations from it. The critic is indeed a sampler, but what is sampled— human discourse—is hardly trivial, since people imbed in their talk some of their most complicated motivations. It is the critic's job to sort through these imbeddings, finding evidence of the universal in the particular and yet, as Leff [1986] cautions, also respecting the integrity and particularity of each message/event.

The critic, therefore, operates like the anthropologist, who may find in the smallest ritual the most complete depiction of tribal history and culture. The good critic never studies a particular text simply because it exists, but because it promises to tell a story larger than itself. This means that no message is too modest for careful inspection. If ego-defense is a powerful human motivation, both the advertisements on match covers and the character sketches in the modern novel should bear witness to it. If human brutality is on the rise, it might as well be in evidence in the interviewing styles of late-night radio commentators and in the rhetoric of the Ku Klux Klan. If gender animosity is a universal feature of human history, it should be discoverable in the scripts of both soap operas and grand operas.

Like all research activities, criticism requires that one (1) *isolate* a phenomenon for special study (the rhetoric of U.S. space exploration), (2) *describe* special manifestations of that phenomenon (that rhetoric's heavy reliance on metaphors), (3) *classify* features of that phenomenon (its dependence on frontier metaphors versus temporal metaphors), (4) *interpret* the patterns noticed ("the American people are still not capable of thinking in terms of fixed borders"), and (5) *evaluate* the phenomenon ("Will the U.S. become extraterrestrial imperialists?"). These five intellectual skills are central to all forms of disciplined inquiry, but they constrain the critic in particular ways, as we will see throughout this book.

3. *Rhetorical criticism produces meta-knowledge* (that is, explicit understanding of implicit realizations). There are many similarities between literary criticism and rhetorical criticism. Both require acuteness of perception; both demand textual exploration; and both expose human wants and desires as expressed in language. But there is also a major difference: While few of us speak poetry in the day to day, all of us, as Molière reminds us, speak prose. We are, all of us, persuaders of

a sort, even if our rhetorical successes are usually modest. But if we are human, we manipulate symbols in the presence of others. Because this is so, rhetorical criticism is criticism of life itself, of our own participation in the experience of living.

And because this is so, everyone is capable of doing rhetorical criticism without ever reading *Modern Rhetorical Criticism.* By having lived and talked for several decades or more, all of us have done the homework necessary to do criticism. Consider, for example, the following rather ordinary message:

> SPE 390R. *Seminar in Contemporary Rhetorical Criticism.* May be repeated for credit when topics vary. Representative topics include dramatistic criticism, content analysis, and methodologies for movement studies. Prerequisite: Upper-division standing.

What sort of message do we have here? Without question, a course description from a college catalog. But how do we know such a thing? How is it possible for a reader who has never opened the course catalog of the University of Texas at Austin to make such a perception? And why do we have such *confidence* in that perception? Why could we not possibly mistake this message for a chili recipe or a love letter or the lyrics to a rock song or the preamble to the Constitution or a page from Fodor's latest guide to Austria? Wherein lies the "implicit knowledge" necessary to identify this textual fragment? If we know this much about rhetoric, what else do we know that we don't know we know? And how do we know such things?

Last question first. We know such things because we are members of life's audience. We know it because each day, without effort or conscious attention, we are voracious consumers of messages. Each day, from dawn to dusk, we swim in a sea of rhetoric: commercials for underarm deodorants, letters from loved ones, newspaper editorials, political oratory, *People* magazine. Each year, from January to December, we process, discard, and reprocess a virtual blizzard of discourse. Each lifetime, from birth to death, we add to our extraordinary catalog of messages, constantly increasing the complexity and subtlety of our rhetorical knowledge. There is not a course description alive that could escape our detection.

Alas, the knowledge just described, while useful, is normally inert. While most people can identify messages accurately enough, few are able to explain *how we know what we know.* Few people pay attention to the details of their rhetorical experience. Upon reflection, however, upon the doing of criticism, almost everyone can do so. For example, the form of our course description is revealing: no complete sentences, abnormal punctuation patterns, and inconsistent italicizing, all of which suggest a hurried, businesslike tone, a message totally uninterested in wooing its reader. In addition, its reasoning patterns are telegraphic. Concepts like "seminar," "credit," and "prerequisite" are never explained, creating a heavy demand on the reader to supply the ideas necessary to make logical sense of the message. The language is also formidable: excessive use of jargon, polysyllabic words, and opaque phrases (SPE 390R).

Also revealing is what is not found in the text. Nobody runs or jumps or feels here. No doing is being done. This absence of verbs suggests institutionalization, hardly what one would expect from what is essentially a piece of advertising. But this is a special sort of advertising, advertising without adjectives. The topics mentioned are not "new and improved" topics, just topics; the movement studies are not "innovative and exciting," just plain vanilla. And much else is missing. There are no extended examples to help the reader see what the course will be like, no powerful imagery to sustain the student's visions of wonder while standing in the registration line, no personal disclosure by the author to build identification with the reader. It is almost as if this message did not care about its reader or, for that matter, even care about itself. It does nothing to invite or entice or intrigue. It does not unburden itself.

There is one thing that almost all college students know about such course descriptions: They cannot be "trusted." Students know that they are written by groups of people and, therefore, do not bear the marks of the instructor's personality. Students know that such descriptions are processed by a complex bureaucracy that impresses its rigidities onto them. Students know that they must sample the rhetoric of their peers and the rhetoric of the professor who will teach the course before signing up. These latter rhetorics, students reason, will have the color, detail, and humanity central to proper decision making. And so course descriptions dutifully sit in college catalogs: unread, unrespected, unloved. A hard life.

Frequently, then, criticism reminds us of what we already know about the world. It asks us to compare each new message to the data bank of messages already accumulated over a lifetime of reading and listening. Criticism asks us to make our implicit knowledge explicit, since only explicit knowledge can be used in practical ways. So rhetorical criticism is quite ecological: It invites us to become more active in retaining each day's messages so that they can later be recycled for use in understanding new messages.

4. *Rhetorical criticism invites radical confrontation with otherness.* Perhaps this phrasing is a bit melodramatic, but criticism is a wonderful way to get outside of oneself. Naturally, most of us resist leaving our own perfect worlds to enter the strange, dark habitats of others. Our

worlds are orderly, theirs chaotic; ours enlightened, theirs bizarre. But we also have wanderlust, a curiosity about the not-us, which is why vacationing in strange lands is such a prized experience. Rhetorical criticism can also be a kind of vacationing, a way of visiting the not-us by examining what they have to say. As with all vacationing, though, criticism requires preparation—attitudinal preparation. We must remember that all persons have reasons for doing what they do even if their reasons are not our reasons and that we cannot understand others unless we are willing to leave our own tastes, experiences, and prejudices at home. And if we are unable to leave them at home, we should at least store them in a seldom used suitcase when exploring.

This is not a moral injunction (criticize others as you would have them criticize you). It is an intellectual injunction, which says that one cannot *understand* others unless one appreciates how they reason and behave. But this injunction is not easy to follow. Consider, for example, the following streetcorner materials distributed each day in each city of the United States:

- *Jesus and Mary Speak to the World through Veronica Luken*
  (Our Lady of Roses Shrine, Bayside, New York)
- *Active Involvement for a Better America*
  (United States Jaycees)
- *Heard any Good Fag Jokes Lately?*
  (National Gay Task Force)
- *Marijuana in America: The Facts*
  (National Organization for the Reform of Marijuana Laws)
- *How to Strengthen Your Motivation to Succeed*
  (Weight Watchers International)
- *Fight Forced Busing*
  (National Socialist White People's Party)
- *Smoking in Public: Let's Separate Fact from Friction*
  (R.J. Reynolds Tobacco Co.)
- *A Patriot's Prayer*
  (First Church of God-in-Reagan)
- *Dear Recreational Vehicle Owner*
  (The Good Sam Club)

Many people's first response to this smorgasbord of motives and attitudes is: "Only in America!" From the standpoint of criticism, this is actually a healthy response. At least initially, the good critic examines all rhetoric in a spirit of wonder rather than one of censure: What do R.V. owners have to say to one another? How does a tobacco company conceal its self-interest in a public service announcement? Is *The Patriot's Prayer* serious or a spoof? What do Weight Watchers know about motivation that I do not? And who, pray tell, is Veronica Luken?

Questions like these pull us into rhetoric and thereby pull us toward people, people who experience the world in special ways. If done well, criticism forces us outside the comfort and familiarity of how we think and feel. It asks, for example, why racists are racists. What experiences have made them so different? Why are they so afraid of racial integration? What *really* threatens them? Bus riding? Black skin? Inferior education? Perhaps. But could it also be rapid change or technological advancement or social mobility or mass anomie or perhaps just life in general? All of these are possibilities, and only careful, critical inspection of *Fight Forced Busing* could help us sort through them.

Because the rhetorical critic examines messages meant for other people at other times, it is hard to do criticism and remain provincial. Rhetoric brings us face to face with otherness: experiences that differ from ours, anxieties that seem remote, dreams that do not compel us. Thus, when examining texts the critic is almost always an intruder, an uninvited guest. The good critic remembers this and offers explanations of rhetoric as it was constituted, not as he or she would have had :t constituted. The critic operates in this fashion not because it is nicer to do so but because it is smarter.

It is often not easy to be a good guest at someone else's party. Critics are people too, after all, who often feel strongly about the public matters they study. So it is useful to remember certain ground rules when doing criticism, ground rules that foster an enlightened sense of otherness:

1. *All public messages make sense to someone.* Because rhetoric is a people's art, it is sometimes easy to feel superior to it. Despite their noxious appeals, someone must like the collection of athletic misfits who make up the Miller Lite gang on television. Someone must appreciate their swagger and bravado and faintly ironic touch. Someone must be able to love them despite their mangled grammar and soft-core sexism. It is the critic's job to presume such attractiveness and to discover the "operating consensus" [Brummett, 1984b] that makes a particular message atttractive for particular others.

2. *All criticism is autobiography.* This is George Bernard Shaw's famous phrase, and it is as true today as it was at the turn of the century. Try as hard as they might, critics can never be completely objective about rhetoric. Nor should they be. But they should at least be *conscious of their subjectivity*, aware of the biases they bring to the critical task, and willing to explain those biases when sharing their observations with others.

3. *Description before evaluation.* The critical instinct—I like it/I hate it—is a powerful instinct. It will rear up within the critic

each moment of each day. But to make sense out of something that is radically other, the critic must first get the lay of the land. Thus, the ultimate challenge is to explain rhetoric with which we disagree or to find flaws in rhetoric to which we are instinctively attracted. The good critic tries to appropriate the psychology of the *natural* audience before asking: What does this message do for me?

Although these attitudes cannot solve all critical problems, they can be useful for those wishing to understand themselves by understanding others. Rhetorical criticism puts us in direct touch with humanness, because it examines what humans do most artfully—write—and most instinctively—talk. The critic of rhetoric stands in a privileged place.

THE QUALITIES OF CRITICISM

Not all critics are born equal. There is no Declaration of Critical Independence to insure that each critic will be perceptive. Even when examining a rich and suggestive piece of rhetoric, some people fail to appreciate its nuances. The gifted critic, on the other hand, can build a provocative story out of the humblest message. So, for example, Philipsen [1975] sat and listened each day to blue-collar youths in South Chicago, eventually using cues in their everyday talk to build a fascinating tale of what manhood meant in such a community. To be sure, the rhetoric Philipsen examined was quite ordinary, so he had to be especially creative to find the truths hidden in its informality. But perceptiveness and creativity are not completely inherited. They can be nurtured. It is possible to become more perceptive as critics if we (1) adopt a useful set of critical attitudes and (2) ask the right sorts of questions when inspecting rhetoric. Each chapter in this book will suggest some of these questions, but it is our job here to examine the characteristics of the ideal critic.

1. *The good critic is skeptical.* There is no other way to say it: The good critic does not take life at face value. Skeptics treat life on their terms, not on life's terms, and, most assuredly, not on the persuader's terms. The good critic is one who stands back and watches, who will not be drawn into the pyrotechnics of rhetoric until fundamental questions about the speaker's motives have been resolved. Skepticism, however, need not lead to cynicism. The skeptic is one who insists on taking a second look at everything simply because there is always more to a story than first meets the eye. The cynic, on the other hand, is a skeptic gone sour, one who refuses to take even a first look because of past disappointments.

RHETORIC AND CORPORATE LIFE

Critical Profile 2.1   "Big Oil" Goes on the Defensive

Few rhetorical tasks are as demanding as the one faced by major oil companies in the mid-1970s. In the wake of the 1973–1974 "energy crisis," petroleum producers were identified with "windfall profits," "gas shortages," "pollution," and every other imaginable form of greed and irresponsibility. How did the corporate giants deal with the problems of public opinion thereby created? For Mobil Oil, the answer was *Observations,* a series of newspaper advertisements that ran from 1976 to 1980. In a study by Richard Crable and Steven Vibbert of Purdue University, *Observations* was described as a series of "apparently non-controversial messages" that provided the foundations for blatant pro-oil company persuasion. *Observations* was written in a casual manner, sprinkled with quotations, cartoons, and chatty news items of a populist orientation. Their conversational quality made *Observations* a far cry from the aggressive and hard-hitting Op-Ed page editorials typical of corporate rhetoric.

Crable and Vibbert argued that the advertisements subtly attempted to change popular sentiment about Mobil by identifying the company with conservation of resources and the promise of science. The authors explain *Observations* as an appeal to the Promethean myth. Prometheus was a mythic figure who "gave the stolen gift of fire to humans." As a tool that symbolizes energy and control of the natural environment, fire represents a unique step in the civilizing of humanity. Certainly, all energy producers have such characteristics, but there is another dimension to the myth. Prometheus also stood as a symbol of rebellion against superior power. The mythic figure stole the fire from Zeus, who intended to keep it from the possession of mortals. Mobil embodies this myth by speaking out aggressively, alone among major oil companies. By presenting itself as the irreverent maverick among the energy giants, Mobil took on the mythic role of Prometheus to perfection.

Crable and Vibbert conclude that Mobil's *Observations* "are the viewpoints of a self-proclaimed American hero, clad in the surprisingly appropriate garments of ancient myth." Their universal appeal makes them a potentially potent form of advocacy, both directly and as a basis for later persuasion. These seemingly innocent advertisements incorporated a subtle series of identifications, yet they were presented as if they were just another "part of America's Sunday afternoon."

Profiled by: John Theobald-Osborne
Citation: Crable and Vibbert (1983)

Two key presuppositions of the skeptic are that all rhetoric denies itself and that good rhetoric denies itself completely. There are, of course, a few forthright persuaders to be found—the used car dealer, the politician, the streetcorner evangelist—who tacitly admit to their

---

Critical Profile 2.2   Economics as Poetry

Literary economics—the phrase appears to be a contradiction in terms to anyone who has glanced at a recent economics textbook. Such books are replete with equations, mathematical terms, and statistical formulae. But the University of Iowa's Donald McCloskey, who holds degrees in both economics and history, has recently turned to the field of rhetoric to help explain concepts in both disciplines. From his studies, McCloskey concludes that economics is essentially scientific poetry.

McCloskey claims that although economists' "official rules of speaking well, to which they pay homage in methodological ruminations and in teachings to the young, declare them to be Scientists in the modern mode, . . . economists are not experts; they are basically persuaders." For example, when the price of a commodity goes up, consumers buy less of it. Economists call this the "Law of Demand." But empirical tests have found that this law is only true sometimes. So what enables economists to base theory on a law that is empirically weak? And what makes their arguments in this regard convincing? Bewitching language, says McCloskey.

Economists write about "hypothesis testing," "statistically significant coefficients," and "rational dynamic models" to support their arguments. While these phrases may not have the poetic quality of Shakespeare's comparing thee to a summer day, they have similar rhetorical effects on their intended audiences. When he wrote, after all, Shakespeare was obeying current literary fashion by using metaphor to describe his love. Similarly, economists obey conventions by using the metaphor of the scientific method, thereby cloaking their conclusions in the magical aura of scientific thought.

For example, economists use mathematical tests to determine whether or not two things are significantly different from each other. Unfortunately, such tests only determine if the difference is *statistically* significant; they say nothing about the *economic* significance of the results. "The point here . . . is that once a comparison or a regression is finished it must be interpreted," says McCloskey. That is, economists must ultimately *make meaning* out of the numbers they manipulate.

Too often, people taking in economic rhetoric allow scientistic metaphors to cast spells upon them. They come away thinking they have been enlightened when, in fact, they have simply been enchanted. Enchantment, of course, has its virtues. But so, too, does a rigorous skepticism. To paraphrase another poet, Humpty Dumpty, if economics is poetry, the only important question becomes whether the poet or the reader will be its master.

Profiled by: Nancy Roth
Citation: McCloskey (1985)

Critical Profile 2.3   Accommodating Crisis on the Job

Traditionally, critics have studied the rhetoric of radical social movements. But change can be propelled by enduring social institutions as well, says Jill McMillan of Wake Forest University, who has investigated the rhetoric of the modern organization. In her study, McMillan examined newsletters produced between 1965 and 1980 by four very different kinds of institutions— The Presbyterian Church in the United States, Reynolds Metals Company, the Kansas Democratic Party, and the Tennessee Education Association— and focused particularly on how these groups used internal persuasion to maintain their external influence. McMillan picked this particular era because the nineteen sixties and seventies were turbulent and because she wanted to learn how organizations talked about such turbulence.

McMillan found that when facing a crisis, institutions creatively translated "news" into persuasion by enlisting routine vehicles (such as newsletter features) in the battle. When Reynolds faced pressure from environmental interests, for example, the traditional newsletter contest format was used to promote recycling among employees, thereby deflecting charges of societal unconcern. Organizations also reduced the fears of employees by showing members that crises like the Vietnam war and the civil rights movements were either "nothing new" or that they could be handled by a prescriptive, institutional approach. On several occasions, for example, Reynolds tried to normalize crisis by "rehearsing" employees in the newsletters so that they could handle attacks made on aluminum by their customers and friends. "All employees are spokespersons" this rhetoric implied.

Institutions also used a kind of "symbolic expansionism" to solidify employee support. Reynolds, for example, identified itself with the entirety of American private enterprise, thereby implying that what was good for Reynolds was good for America. McMillan notes that the purpose here was "to 'talk as if' and to make members 'feel as if' a new and holistic organization really existed." Organizations in crisis also "flatten the hierarchy" (that is, by making employees feel equal to their bosses). For example, newsletter requests for employee feedback, even if the data are never used, can strengthen links between member and institution, reinforcing what McMillan calls the "illusion of participation." When energy prices rose, Reynolds "asked" employees for cost-cutting suggestions. Rather than changing real power allocations, then, institutions often divert employees' attention by encouraging institutional loyalty. As Reynolds once editorialized, "It's important for government officials and legislators to know what we do, and to trust us."

Institutions are a powerful force in society. They endure because they can recognize and cope with crisis. Organizations that adapt, live. Organizations that adapt well, live well. In short, rhetoric ensures survival of the fittest organizations.

Profiled by: John Llewellyn
Citation: McMillan (1982)

status as persuaders. But even here there is legerdemain. The used-car dealer agrees to take less for the automobile because he "was young once too and remembers his first car." The politician is never the crass solicitor but one biding her time until canonization, when her "dream for the nation becomes a reality for all people." And the evangelist is never motivated by personal ego when buttonholing passersby, but is "compelled from afar to do the work of the Lord." These people do not wish to be seen only as persuaders; they wish to be seen as something more exalted.

Still others deny the rhetorical function entirely. Lessl [1985] tells us that astronomer Carl Sagan wraps himself in the mantle of both poet and priest in order to "teach" his viewers about the value of space exploration. McMillan [1982] tells us that corporate managers weave politically tinged values into their "explanations" of company policy. Adams [1986] tells us that newscasters look to a geographical region's popularity with American tourists before deciding which natural disasters to "report." In each case, these teachers, managers, and reporters-turned-persuaders have sought to have influence without acknowledging their attempts to do so. They have sought to escape critical detection by holding up signs emblazoned with the statement "No persuasion here. Look elsewhere for objects of criticism." The good critic does not look elsewhere. The good critic does not even blink.

As Fisher [1984] and others explain, persuaders often use narratives to throw the critic off the persuasive scent. Storytelling, as Ronald Reagan well understood, signals a time out: "Listen to this story as a story. You need not worry about argumentative propositions being advanced here." Most of us relax in the presence of narratives. Thus a "mere" story, *Uncle Tom's Cabin*, became one of the most potent pieces of civil rights rhetoric the United States has ever known. And thus business executives sell stock options during cocktail parties, those "time out" events that advance rhetoric by denying its possibility. In some senses, then, the nonpersuader is the best persuader and the non-appeal the ultimate appeal.

2. *The good critic is discerning.* One need not be a genius to be discerning. Sherlock Holmes was not brilliant, but he was discerning. He knew when to pay attention (when others were not around), how to pay attention (by looking to the left when others looked to the right), and where to pay attention (by looking in the scullery kitchen rather than in the public parts of the mansion). Holmes's eyes took in no more information than did those of the local constable. But unlike the local constable, Holmes had better categories for sorting and storing the information he collected. Both noticed the brown shoes on the body of the deceased, but Holmes also noticed the absence of scuff marks, because he had a theory of scuff marks. To the constable, shoes were

shoes, but to Holmes the way people scuffed their shoes was a function of the purposiveness of their walk, which was a function of their lifestyle, which in turn was a function of their social habits and, ultimately, their mental habits. And that is why a man wearing unscuffed shoes would never have died a natural death while roaming through the moors. *That* sort of person detests moors.

Like Holmes, the good critic is very hard to distract. Concentration is a precious gift for a critic, since persuaders try so hard to divert their audiences' attention. As a result, the good critic pays attention to textual details that most audiences ignore. Thus, by simply noticing the raw frequency of certain word choices, Hart [1986b] concluded that Ronald Reagan's first inaugural address was more ideological than was normal for a ceremony, a kind of rhetorical hangover from a very ideological campaign. Of course, Ronald Reagan himself did not assume that his choice of individual words would be of much interest to his listeners. He no doubt presumed that his lectern-thumping would be muffled by the colorful metaphors he used and by the pleasant stories he told. That is why, when examining the Reagan speech, it proved useful to look elsewhere.

Most good critics look elsewhere. To understand the routines of social power in the United States, for example, Whittenberger-Keith [1989] inspected neither economic charts nor voting patterns but manners books. To determine the extent of contemporary racism, Rainville and McCormick [1977] looked not at open-housing laws but at the descriptions of black and white athletes provided by sports commentators. In both cases, the critics assumed that: (1) All texts are filled with data, even if some of these data seem irrelevant at first blush; (2) what is *not* present in a message is often more important than what is present; and (3) how an idea is phrased may sometimes be less important than the fact that the idea is mentioned at all. The good critic asks questions of texts that audiences and poor critics rarely ask.

But discernment should not be confused with eccentricity. Few critics ask how often the letter "e" is used in a passage, because nobody has yet generated a *good reason* for doing so. Rather, the good critic has a sense for significance, a sense that matures as more and more discourse is examined. Thus, when Chesebro and Hamsher [1975:321] urge the critic to become more discerning by going "beyond data collection to pattern recognition," they are trying to make the critic more like Sherlock Holmes.

3. *The good critic is imaginative.* Almost anyone can gather facts about a message. But it takes a good critic to know what to do with them. For example, most people have seen the late-night public service announcements urging safe driving. Murray Edelman [1977] has observed them, too. But because he was both skeptical and discerning,

as well as imaginative, Edelman thought harder than most people about this ostensibly innocent rhetoric. Although controversial, his conclusion about the safe-driving advertisements is provocative: Such campaigns place responsibility for highway safety completely *on the driver* and deflect attention from a major source of highway carnage—automobile manufacturers. Not only did Edelman see rhetoric where there appeared to be none, and not only was he able to zero in on just the right features of the texts he analyzed, but he was also able to link his observations to a larger story about how entrenched economic interests use persuasion to maintain positions of privilege.

One need not be a leftist to appreciate how Edelman operated here. The larger story he told—his theory—gave an enriched purpose to his inquiries. He did not investigate public service advertisements because he enjoyed them (who does?) but because when watching them late one night he was struck with a *general idea* about how political pressure operates in the United States. Naturally, this one analysis by Edelman could not establish some grand new law of political influence, but his case study did raise several general questions that he and others could then proceed to answer by collecting more evidence. But it was the imaginative leap from data to theory that made Edelman's observation such an important one.

A message is worth analyzing if it tells a story larger than itself. This means that the good critic always has a rationale for examining a text. These rationales take many forms: (1) the study may be worth doing because the speaker has dealt with a **classic dilemma** (How can a president apologize for backing misguided legislation without losing his authority?); (2) the speaker may have dealt imaginatively with **unresolved tensions** (How can a president appeal to the farmers without losing the urban vote?); (3) the speaker may have addressed **projected problems** (How can a president make the nation comfortable with life in a nuclear world?); (4) the speaker's situation may be a **parallel instance** of a continuing one (How did early presidents change citizens' economic habits?); or (5) the speaker may have been the first to confront some **unique circumstance** (What persuasive tools can a president use during an impeachment trial?).

There are, of course, countless such good reasons for doing rhetorical criticism. Notice that in all of the above instances, however, the critic has addressed issues of universal interest. Concern for the larger story, therefore, should animate each piece of criticism written. This same principle suggests several guidelines for developing a critical rationale:

1. *No message is inherently worthy of study.* Just because a given text fascinates the critic does not mean that study of it will be worthwhile. Often, criticism becomes eccentric and too specialized

because the critic fails to develop a clear reason for doing criticism. This produces scholarship-by-whim. Thus, when picking a text, the critic should be asking: *Why* does this message intrigue me? "Just because" is not a sufficient answer.

2. *The past speaks to us constantly.* Examining the rhetoric of the past, even the rhetoric of the distant past, can be quite useful, because it gives us perspective on the lives we live today. Naturally, as Wichelns [1973:43] reminds us, all rhetoric is "rooted in immediacy" and we must be careful not to distort the past in a headlong rush to find within it contemporary relevance. But people are people. And cultures are cultures. And rhetoric is rhetoric. The past has much to teach us if we but open our ears to its voices.

3. *People who are larger than life may not be lifelike.* "Tabloid scholarship" [Hart, 1986a:293] presumes that persuasion by "great" persons will be especially worthy of study. This is a poor assumption. It is easy to become distracted by high-profile speakers like presidents and popes, people who often say interesting things but who are far removed from the lives most people lead. The good critic remembers that the messages of ordinary people are often highly suggestive, because they better represent how persuasion-in-general functions.

4. *Imitation is not the sincerest form of flattery.* All too often, critics fail to go far enough in their analysis, because they merely "translate" a message rather than explain it. This is especially true for the beginning critic, who is tempted to latch onto an existing critical system and then superimpose it on an innocent piece of rhetoric. The result is criticism that succeeds only in finding new examples of old persuasive strategies.

No set of guidelines will insure brilliant criticism. But the guidelines above will insure that the critic asks *why* criticism is being done in the first place. Skepticism and discernment are central to good criticism, but unless the critic makes an imaginative leap from text to idea, criticism becomes wasted time and wasted paper. Persuasion is too interesting and criticism too productive to be overturned by unasked and unanswered whys.

THE STANDARDS OF CRITICISM

Evaluation seems to leap out of a word like criticism. Most people in daily life are "critics" in this sense when they complain about the local transit system or the tardiness of mail delivery. Normally, however, these everyday evaluations are not reflective. Few people are

---

RHETORIC AND THE AMERICAN WEST

Critical Profile 2.4   Sagging Archetypes:
                         What Happened to the American West?

America loves its Westerns. Tales of the West—whether songs, novels, or films—are staples of the entertainment industry. But Janice Hocker Rushing, now of the University of Arkansas, sees trouble on the range. According to her, Western stories in the 1980s have threatened the myth of the American West by failing to provide ways of resolving the inherent tensions between individualism and community.

The 1950s produced classic Westerns such as *High Noon* and *Shane*. These films depicted a balance between the competing urges of individualism and communalism, creating what Rushing calls "dialectical reaffirmation," a blending of these paradoxical elements that allowed 1950s viewers to draw strength from the synthesis. In contrast, the West of the 1980s, as epitomized by the film *Urban Cowboy* and the television serial *Dallas*, failed to affirm the tension between individual and society. Rather, they wished it away. Professor Rushing labels this practice "dialectical pseudo-synthesis," because these important paradoxes and their contradictory impulses are glossed over. "Rhetorically, this pattern gives the appearance of reaffirming the potency of the Western myth, whereas in reality, it is subversive of the original archetype," Rushing notes.

In the classic Western of the 1950s, the hero came from outside the community and did not become a member of the society even as he was protecting it. He also avoided communal temptations like sex and gambling. After saving the town, the hero remained distant, either by becoming ruggedly diffident or by actually leaving for parts unspecified, thereby validat-

---

willing to visit the offices of the transit company, do a time-and-motion study of its operations, interview its personnel, pore over maps of urban geography, calculate the economies of scale produced by different routings, and then do the massive data synthesis necessary to determine if there is, in fact, sufficient reason to be perturbed by the late bus at the corner of Maple and First. So it is important to distinguish between general complaining and *reflective complaining*, better known as criticism. Equally, it is important to distinguish between gushing compliments and *reflective compliments*, which is also criticism. The judicious critic is, therefore, one who knows when and how to render an evaluation.

Most faulty critical statements result from premature evaluation, from judging the goodness or badness of a rhetorical message before having carefully inspected its pieces and parts, before having collected data sufficient to sustain critical judgment. Another type of faulty eval-

---

RHETORIC AND THE AMERICAN WEST

Critical Profile 2.4   Sagging Archetypes:
What Happened to the American West? (*continued*)

---

ing the society he had saved and yet, at the same time, reinforcing his own sense of self. In the 1980s, however, the Western hero offered very different answers to the paradox of individualism and community. *Urban Cowboy* attempted to resolve this perennial tension by emphasizing appearance over reality. For example, the frontier itself was domesticated; the most expansive setting in the film was a three-acre bar and dance floor. The only "wildlife" depicted was a mechanical bull that patrons rode in an attempt to establish their virility. What has the Western myth come to, Rushing asks, when men try to prove themselves by conquering a machine in animal's clothing? Rushing repeats such plaintive questions in her analysis of *Dallas*, where the corporate greed of J.R. Ewing and his crowd represent to her a total perversion of the frontier hero.

Should we mourn the passing of the Western archetype? Is the hyper-realism of *Urban Cowboy* good for us as a culture? In becoming so cerebral and so ironic, have we pushed things too far? Would the simple moral structure of *Shane* serve us better in the 1990s and beyond? Do we need more heroes? Or has hero-worship been the source of our troubles in the past? Even movies pose important questions, if we are keen enough to notice them.

Profiled by: John Llewellyn
Citation: Rushing (1983)

---

uation occurs when the critic fails to explicate the standards used in the evaluation. We react differently to a critic who says, "My mother is a terrific cook because she only buys food in yellow containers," than we do to one who argues, "My mother is a good cook because she prepares tasty foods low in cholesterol." The first critic seems to be using absurd standards for judgment while the second seems more reasonable; reasonable, that is, in the eyes of other reasonable people. In this connection, Black [1978:7] has made the critic's obligations clear:

> The person who hears a speech and says, "I like it," is not making a critical statement. He is reporting the state of his glands; he is speaking autobiographically. If we happen to like the person or if we are curious about the state of his glands, we may be interested in his report. Certainly his psychoanalyst would be interested in it. But neither the analyst nor we should confuse the statement with criticism.

Critical Profile 2.5   "Go West, Young Disciple"

What could possibly unite and incite the most varied Protestant denominations to come together in a Restoration Movement aimed at establishing *one* church? Nothing less than a "rhetorical vision" of a popular "social drama," argues Carl Wayne Hensley of Bethel College, who based his work on Ernest G. Bormann's theory that persuasion occurs when "several fantasy theme dramas combine to catch up a large number of people in common symbolic reality." Hensley claims that the tremendous revivalism and unity effected by the Disciples of Christ in the nineteenth century can be attributed to the *secular* rhetorical vision they employed, one that presented the contemporary drama of winning the West as the model for winning the world for Christ.

As proponents of postmillennialism, the Disciples of Christ appealed to independent Westerners to "reject abstract creeds and formal ritual" (just as they had rejected the old social order in the East), in order to restore the primitive purity of the church and thereby hasten Christ's return. The primary source of the Disciples' vision was the Bible "with its dramatic unfolding of creation, corruption, conflict, and conquest." For the Disciples, "the scene of the completion of [God's] plan was America, particularly the West." According to the rhetoric, the American church "would move out to conquer the world; the millennium would be ushered in; and the drama would climax in Christ's second coming and the ultimate restoration of paradise." In short, the pioneers of the West were united by these biblical themes and were recast as the pioneers of *reformation*.

A common rhetorical ground for unity was not easily won, however. Time and time again, various denominational creeds and confessions were rejected as insufficient for a basis of union. Finally, the "Bible, the whole Bible, and nothing but the Bible" emerged as the "platform and bond of union" and "sectarian names of human origin such as 'Methodist,' 'Presbyterian,' etc." were abandoned for biblical names such as "Christian" or "Disciple of Christ."

The Restoration Movement stands not only as an important contribution to American culture but also as an example of how a rhetorical vision can attract adherents "by setting forth familiar dramas with a unique emphasis," dramas that offer "auditors participation with unseen but omnipotent forces in controlling the world's destiny." As a religious enactment of the American fascination with its Western frontier, the story of the Disciples of Christ reminds us of the power of dreams and of the persuader's special ability to dream in public.

Profiled by: Kerry Riley
Citation: Hensley (1975)

Critical Profile 2.6 Saving Nature—The Birth of Modern Consciousness

Modern Americans are no longer strangers to the alternative side of "prog-ress," namely, preservationism. National Parks, land use planning, and environmental regulation stand in opposition to nuclear waste sites, sprawl-ing development, and piecemeal destruction of nature. But such *political* respect for nature is a recent development. Only a few generations ago, there was little public consciousness of how nature was being destroyed or how such damage might be prevented. Why do we now care so deeply for nature? What started our concern? And why are we now willing to pay for that concern?

One answer might be found in the person of John Muir, the so-called "father of preservationism" and the primary figure in creating Yosemite National Park in 1890. In a study of this early environmentalist, Christine Oravec of the University of Utah argued that Muir's rhetorical appeals changed basic American attitudes toward nature by unifying "the aesthetic, rational, and ethical response to nature." She describes Muir as a poet-persuader.

Muir's basic approach was to try to tap the imaginations of those who read his accounts of California's Sierra Nevada mountain range and thereby move the federal government to preserve Yosemite from fragmentation and development. Muir's persuasion rested on conveying the urgency of the problem, the destruction of "the most divinely beautiful and sublime [landscape] I have ever beheld." Muir intended that the great park include not only the central valley of Yosemite but also the surrounding watershed, which he described in highly metaphorical, organic terms: "The branching cañons and alleys of the basins of the streams that pour into Yosemite are as closely related to it as are the fingers to the palm of the hand—as the branch, foliage, and flowers of a tree to the trunk."

Oravec contends that Muir's rhetoric reordered public priorities concern-ing nature by introducing the organic purity of the environment as an alter-native to material progress. That is, rather than basing his appeals on the (now familiar) "scientific" arguments for preserving the ecology, Muir used highly poetic descriptions of nature to heighten people's consciousness. By creating a visualization of natural perfection, Muir helped to construct a new "artistic" consciousness based on the experience of untouched nature. His word-paintings continue to motivate to this day, and for nearly a century Muir's vision of the natural has symbolized citizens' opposition to unregu-lated industrial development in the United States and, particularly, in the West.

Profiled by: John Theobald-Osborne
Citation: Oravec (1981)

It is not criticism, because, although it may be stimulated by an object, it is not *about* an object; it is a statement about the speaker's own feelings, and nothing more.

Rhetorical critics have used quite a variety of critical standards to evaluate the rhetoric they have studied. Although we shall not detail these standards here, it is interesting to see the tremendous variety of approaches available to the critic. Clearly, any of these standards can be used intelligently or foolishly. The judicious critic is one who knows which standard is being used and, most important, why. And the exceptionally judicious critic is one who gives fair attention to the many alternative standards by which persuasion may be evaluated, some of which are:

1. *The utilitarian standard:* Given the limitations of the situation, did the message do what it was intended to do? Did people react as the speaker hoped? Compared to other speakers on this topic in situations like this, did this speaker do as well as could be expected?
2. *The artistic standard:* Was the use of language exceptional? Did the message meet the highest standards of beauty and well-formedness? Did it so stimulate the imagination that it brought new ideas to life?
3. *The moral standard:* Did the message advance "the good" and encourage public virtue? Was there sufficient moral instruction by the speaker so that listeners were moved toward worthy, not just convenient, goals? Did it meet acceptable standards of right and wrong?
4. *The scientific standard:* Did the message accurately represent reality? Did the speaker's arguments have a factual base and did conclusions follow directly from the evidence presented? Could the claims in the message be independently verified?
5. *The historical standard:* Was there anything in the message for "the ages"? Is it likely that the ideas presented and the values endorsed will outlast the speaker? Did the speech set processes in motion that resulted in major changes?
6. *The psychological standard:* Did the message purge the emotions of the speaker or the audience? Did the speech present an opportunity to calm important fears and anxieties? Were people so motivated by the speech that social energy and personal commitments were renewed?
7. *The political standard:* Did the message advance the goals of the social groups the critic endorses? Will the "right" sort of people be advantaged by the speech? Will any harm be done to the most deserving people in society because this speech was given?

Two things should be clear about this list of standards. First, it is incomplete—each critic can, and should, freely supplement the list. Whichever standard is chosen, the critic still has the obligation of defending the appropriateness of the choice made. A second important point is that messages that meet one standard may fail miserably in light of another. So, for example, a speech at a Billy Graham Crusade may succeed in increasing donations to the church (the utilitarian standard) and, because its description of the afterlife is so masterful (the artistic standard), the congregation's guilt over their indulgent lifestyles may be removed (the psychological standard). On the other hand, in describing sin the Reverend Graham may have grossly distorted the extent of the national drug problem (the scientific standard) by making it seem as if it were only a problem for minority groups (the political standard), thereby making it unlikely that anyone in the future would have much respect for the remarks he made (the historical standard). Clearly, one must operate thoughtfully when choosing critical standards as well as when deploying them. Rarely do we have trouble deciding whether we like a thing or dislike it. Explaining why we feel this way takes something else. It takes a judicious critic.

CONCLUSION

Criticism can be complicated, but it can also be highly rewarding. To look carefully at what people say and how they say it is to take the human enterprise seriously. People are complex, but they are also fascinating. One of the most fascinating things about them is their rhetorical natures. Communication is an attempt to build community by exchanging symbols. Since the building of community is what most makes people people, listening to what they have to say is to pay them the ultimate compliment. This is true even if we, as critics, sometimes listen more carefully than is normally expected—or desired. And in paying this much attention to what people say, we also pay attention to ourselves, which makes criticism the ultimate self-compliment as well.

Throughout this book, we will consider the best advice available about the doing of rhetorical criticism. Part Two covers the most productive questions that can be asked of any persuasive message. Part Three presents four kinds of analysis that have been particularly useful in critical studies lately. The Appendix offers two practical aids for the critic: (1) how to find texts for critical study and (2) how to access reference materials for illuminating the rhetorical situation under examination. *Because these Appendix materials are especially useful to the beginning critic, the reader should consult them now.*

There is nothing magical about good criticism. Good criticism is the art of developing and then using critical probes, which are nothing more than intelligent and specific questions to be asked of a given text. Dozens of these critical probes are distributed throughout this book. By using them, the critic cannot help but become more discerning. Also, because the subject matter here is rhetoric, this book no doubt will add to the reader's supply of skepticism. And because the work of professional critics will be examined throughout, the reader will be presented with many examples of judiciousness. But the imagination necessary for productive criticism will have to derive from another source, from inside critics themselves. Let us hope that imagination abounds for all who would be critics.

PART TWO

General Forms of Criticism

❖
❖

CHAPTER THREE

Analyzing Situations

❖
❖

[I wish I could sing!] I speak to you as an American Jew.

As Americans we share the profound concern of millions of people about the shame and disgrace of inequality and injustice which make a mockery of the great American idea. As Jews we bring to [this] great demonstration, in which thousands of us proudly participate, a two-fold experience—one of the spirit and one of our history.

In the realm of the spirit, our fathers taught us thousands of years ago that when God created man, he created him as everybody's neighbor. "Neighbor" is not a geographic term; it is a moral concept. It means our collective responsibility for the preservation of man's dignity and integrity.

From our Jewish historic experience of three and a half thousand years we say:

Our ancient history began with slavery and the yearning for freedom.

During the Middle Ages my people lived for a thousand years in the ghettos of Europe.

Our modern history begins with a proclamation of emancipation. It is for these reasons that it is not merely sympathy and compassion for the black people of America that motivates us. It is above all and beyond all such sympathies and emotions a sense of complete identification and solidarity born of our own historic experience.

[Friends], When I was . . . [in] . . . the Jewish community in Berlin under the Hitler regime, I learned many things. The most important thing that I learned in my life, and under those tragic circumstances, is that bigotry and hatred are not the most urgent problem. The most urgent, the most disgraceful, the most shameful, and the most tragic problem is *silence*.

A great people which had created a great civilization had become a nation of silent onlookers. They remained silent in the face of hate, in the face of brutality, and in the face of mass murder.

America must not become a nation of onlookers. America must not remain silent—not merely black America, but all of America. It must speak up and act from the President down to the humblest of us, and not for the sake of the Negro, not for the sake of the black community, but for the sake of the image [the dream], the idea, and the aspiration of America itself.

Our children, yours and mine, in every school across the land, every morning pledge allegiance to the flag of the United States and to the Republic for which it stands, and then they, the children, speak fervently and innocently of this land as the land of "liberty and justice for all."

The time, I believe, has come for us to work together, for it is not enough to hope together—for it is not enough to pray together—to work together, that this children's oath—pronounced every morning from Maine to California, from North and South—that this oath will become a glorious, unshakable reality in a morally renewed and united America.

[Thank you.]

This chapter begins with a question: Who gave this speech? Here are several more: Can we be sure that this was a speech and not an essay? If a speech, when was it given? Where? Under what social and psychological circumstances? What of the audience? Were they wealthy, middle-class, or poor? Were they Jewish, like the speaker, or were they religiously and ethnically diverse? How did they feel about the topic? Sympathetic or hostile? Excited or bored? What about the speaker? Male or female? Educated or uneducated? Of high status or low? Young, middle-aged, or elderly? What was the speaker's occupation?

Such questions may seem bizarre. Few people must deal with mystery messages. Most texts come prepackaged, replete with the information needed to make sense out of them. Most messages are understandable because we confront them in their natural habitats: in a particular place, at a particular time, with other, particular people. Besides, if we ever did happen upon a mystery message, surely there are reference books available to provide any information needed.

This chapter will presume that no such reference books exist. It will also presume that most persuasive messages contain information that normally slips past but still influences the unperceptive observer. We will see here that every message contains "genetic markers" that reveal much about its intellectual, psychological, and social parentage— where it came from, how it matured, and why. We will discover that since each persuasive message is produced in a unique rhetorical situation, thereby constituting a unique speech-act, *the situation itself can make a statement* apart from the statements contained in the words of the message.

In a sense, all criticism is a kind of guessing game, with the critic trying to shed light on the especially shadowy parts of rhetorical messages. By inspecting a message carefully—more carefully than most listeners do, more carefully than speakers would prefer—the critic turns presumed knowledge into tested knowledge. So how do we know that the speech above is, in fact, a speech? The clues are several. For instance, it would be presumptuous for a writer to pen the first sentence in the first paragraph, since these remarks seem part of a *continuing* dialogue with somebody the speaker never identifies. While writers sometimes start in the middle of things, they rarely leave their readers without background clues for long, certainly not forever. But a speaker talking to a live audience could make such a reference if he or she had just shared some sort of musical experience, which seems to be the case here. Also, the language in the message does not seem quite smooth enough for written composition. The sentences are often short—simple, declarative—and they contain few of the embedded clauses common to essay or textbook writing. There is much direct address here ("we share," "our fathers taught us"), a feature often found in personal correspondence. But there is also much *formal* direct address here ("Friends . . . ") that would be off-putting if found, say, in a loved one's postcard from Tahiti. The words in the passage are common ones, so the message could be a popular editorial, but the speaker ends by thanking the audience for their attention, something that writers never do. After all, while a writer can presume that time is being freely provided by readers (who can pick up or put down the printed matter at their leisure), the speaker is always aware that attention is a gift that busy and easily bored listeners give to speakers. And so we have a speech.

A contemporary speech? Possibly, although one gets very little flavor of today's hard-nosed pragmatism and P.A.C.-controlled politics here. There is no talk of funding possibilities, enactable legislation, or factual precedent. Rather, the speech seems to be a *beginning* ("The time . . . has come"). We hear of plans being made, not of victories being savored. Moreover, the speaker attempts to turn his individual listeners into some sort of collective ("our children, yours and mine"), as if he could not presume that they already shared the same priorities.

What else do we have? We have singing, Jews, blacks, collective responsibility, repudiation of silence, pledges of allegiance from North to South, a post-World War II time frame, and, most pregnantly, the Emancipation Proclamation. This is also a short speech, perhaps one of many given that day. Moreover, either the speaker is rudely ignoring local personalities and local conditions or is reaching out to a *national* constituency ("from Maine to California"). All in all, this sounds like the language of the 1960s, an era in which even political rhetoric sounded religious and in which a term like "great demonstration" had an ideological rather than a mercantile meaning. This sounds like the era of the gospel-singing Mahalia Jackson, who preceded our speaker, and of Martin Luther King, Jr., who spoke just after our speaker. The place: Washington, D.C. The scene: the Lincoln Memorial. The audience: some two hundred thousand civil rights marchers. The date: August 28, 1963.

And our speaker? What does the message/situation tell us? A male, no doubt, for few women addressed such large crowds in the United States in 1963. The mere *act* of speaking at a massive demonstration like this was an outward sign of power and the roots of sexism held fast in 1963, even within the then-forming civil rights establishment. The language is full of male forcefulness ("I speak to you as an American Jew"). The gentle paternalism ("'Neighbor' is not a geographic term; it is a moral concept") and historic persona ("During the Middle Ages my people . . . ") clearly suggest the thoughts of an older speaker (or a self-important younger one). Finally, even though the phrase "a rabbi" was removed in the first line of the ninth paragraph, the speaker himself signals his occupation with his scholarly distinctions ("not for the sake of the black community, but for the sake of . . . "), his spiritual exhortations ("a glorious, unshakable reality in a morally renewed and united America"), and his sermonic style ("in the face of hate, in the face of brutality, and in the face of mass murder"). The speaker was Rabbi Joachim Prinz [1963], then national president of the American Jewish Congress and one of several speakers who shared the platform with Dr. King on that historic day in 1963.

So our critical work is done. But was it worth it? Would it not have been easier to simply look up the required information in a handy reference book? Easier, yes. More informative? Decidedly not. In the language of Chapter Two, use of a reference book would not have explained how we knew that we knew important distinctions between contemporary and noncontemporary speech, between male and female speech, between religious and secular speech, between private and public speech, between mature and immature speech, between formal and informal speech, and between speech and nonspeech. In this chapter, we will come to understand that all messages "do" as well as say and that all messages bear the imprints of the social situations that produced them, thereby making rhetoric a *situated art* that can only be understood when text and context are considered simultaneously. In this chapter, we will see that the best reference book of all is that housed in the critic's personal library of rhetorical knowledge.

THE MEANINGS OF SPEECH-ACTS

A basic fact about speaking often goes unnoticed: It is an activity. That is, by addressing another, a speaker both says something *and does something*. Many critics miss this "doing" function in their headlong rush to study words. But as Hart [1987:xxi] has said, "by choosing to utter words to another, a speaker makes at least these decisions—to speak to A and not to B; to speak now and not then or never; to speak here and not there; to speak for this period of time, not longer or shorter. These rhetorical decisions contain 'information' for us as observers if we are wise enough and patient enough to track these decisions." Daily life often teaches these lessons about speech-acts. Sometimes painfully: Despite his gift for storytelling, a guest overstays his welcome at a party; despite her good intentions, a young executive is fired for sharing classified information with a colleague in a public restaurant; despite their affability, a married couple insults their new neighbors by greeting them with a wave instead of an extended conversation. In each of these cases, the messages exchanged were innocent enough, but matters of place, timing, and relationship undid them. Philosopher J.L. Austin [1970] has labeled this "extra" dimension of persuasion its **performative** character. Austin himself was particularly intrigued by situations whose performative features dominated its message features (if said in the right context, "I do" both communicates loving sentiments *and* gets one married.) But as Benjamin [1976] has observed, all rhetorical messages probably have important performative aspects to them, which is why the critic is urged to calculate a message's performative features *before* doing any sort of careful textual analysis.

Even the most basic speech-act can be examined profitably from the performative standpoint. Arnold [1974:38–43] and Hart, et al. [1983:13–14] have isolated a number of "implicit messages" that attend *any* instance of public discourse. They argue that the agreement to share communication in any context means at least these things:

1. *The speaker feels that something is wrong.* This wrong thing may not approach calamity status, but even a friendly greeting is an attempt to ward off the forces of alienation and to increase goodwill in society. Preachers preach and teachers teach because of the sin and ignorance they hope to offset. Politicians speak politics when they envision that their legislative mandate is in trouble. Indeed, politics is inevitably rancorous, because it focuses upon the most persistent of problems: poverty, disease, war, natural disaster. Even a speech at a happy event, such as a toast at a wedding, is designed to wave away nonhappiness for the couple. People talk when they are troubled. During all other moments they are quiet. The first question the critic must ask, therefore, is : What's wrong?

2. *The speaker is not yet desperate.* Rhetorical people are optimists; they believe that talk can change human affairs. By speaking, people signal hope to one another. Total desperation, in contrast, drives peo-

ple away from rhetoric, away from human solutions and toward more "transcendent" remedies such as contemplation or narcotics. So where there is rhetoric there is hope, or so implies the person who takes the trouble to speak. It is for these reasons that nuclear arms limitation talks always make front-page headlines. The mere agreement to talk documents that hope abides.

3. *The speaker is committed.* To something. Not necessarily to the subject matter of the speech. Perhaps just to himself or herself. Perhaps to this particular audience. Perhaps to the proposal being advocated. But speech, especially public speech, implies a dramatic sort of commitment primarily because of the substantial risks attendant to it. Often, these commitments are strongly emotional (for a social activist) and often these commitments to speak cost us time (a campaigning politician), money (a poorly paid campus evangelist), relationship (a lecturer traveling the country without her family), or sleep (a late-night television commentator). In each case, the speaker signals that speaking is worth what it costs.

4. *The audience is open to change.* Listening, too, is a commitment, a tacit acknowledgement that listeners are not set in their ways. To listen to a live speech, after all, is to interrupt what one is doing, to don coat and hat and dodge the raindrops, sometimes to stand in line for tickets, occasionally to be seated in uncomfortable surroundings, often to be confronted with strange thoughts and uncomfortable emotions. Satisfied teenagers have no need for education; satisfied citizens have no need for politics; satisfied people have no need for rhetoric.

McGuire's [1976] study of Catholic Pentecostals nicely demonstrates these implicit messages of listening. McGuire became interested in glossolalia—speaking in tongues—and in what such uncommon speech patterns meant to those who used them. Typically, scholars have been interested in the psychological features of tongue-speakers, but McGuire felt that the *social agreements* among glossolalics and their listeners contained the richest story. By speaking in tongues, McGuire found, such persons signaled (1) that they spoke as God's "medium" and not for themselves as individuals, (2) that because of their "surrendered" status they could use more metaphorical and poetic language than could ordinary worshippers, and (3) that their rapturous experience did not blind them to norms of common social politeness in church. McGuire also found that listening to glossolalia required congregation members to be unusually "active" as auditors. They listened to confirm, not to question, often reading much into the messages they heard. After one glossolalic experience, for example, "one woman testified to having 'laid hands upon' a leaking faucet to 'cure' it; another member's confirmation of a scripture reading involved an inaccurate hearing of a key word in the text; another testimony involved a detailed mathematical calculation of the number who would be saved on the Last Day" [McGuire, 1976:14–15]. In short, McGuire made sense out of the worship services by asking not what was being said but *what was being done.*

Thus, a key question for the rhetorical critic is this: By speaking on this topic to this audience in this setting at this time, what "news" is the speaker making? Sometimes, the "news" lies in the **speaker-topic** relationship, as when a conservative such as Ronald Reagan addressed the growing AIDS crisis in the United States, thereby signaling that this was indeed a crisis. At other times, the news lies in the **speaker-setting** relationship, as when Mr. Reagan spoke at Notre Dame University to commemorate Knute Rockne's football coaching career and Mr. Reagan's previous role in a movie on Rockne's life. Or the story could lie in the **speaker-audience** relationship, as when President Reagan reluctantly, and belatedly, spoke to reporters about the Iran-Contra affair. In each of these situations, both a statement and a meta-statement were made by Mr. Reagan. It is this larger statement that the critic must examine in each instance of persuasion.

It would matter little, for example, what the Pope said about papal infallibility should he ever agree to discuss it. The mere *fact* of his doing so would send an important message. Similarly, when Egypt's Anwar Sadat traveled to the Knesset in Jerusalem to speak in 1977, it made little difference what he said, because his going there said enough. As Branham and Pearce [1985:29] point out, when the Chicago Seven conspirators (a radical group in the 1960s) refused to take part in their own conspiracy trial, they too said a great deal even though they said nothing. And as Brydon [1985:148] observed, the mere agreement of a political incumbent to debate a challenger can send a message of great strength or great weakness to voters, media personnel, and challenger alike. At times, not to speak is to say a good deal.

THE FUNCTIONS OF SPEECH-ACTS

Because the natural tendency of the critic is to be fascinated with words and their meanings, it is not always easy to focus on the "action" of a speech-act. This was less of a problem for Maurice Bloch [1975] and his colleagues, who studied the speaking activities of people in nontechnological societies. Because they were comparative strangers to the tribes they studied, the researchers could shift their attention from the words spoken to the speaking activities *as activities.* In his book, Bloch presents the work of ten different anthropologists who

RHETORIC AND PERSONAL PSYCHOLOGY

Critical Profile 3.1   Corporate Loyalty Equals Economic Disaster

U.S. corporations spend millions of dollars annually producing newsletters, brochures, and glossy magazines for their employees. According to communication scholar George Cheney, now of The University of Colorado, this expensive practice is believed by top management to yield important benefits: hardworking, loyal employees. Using subtle rhetorical techniques, such publications encourage employees to identify with the company, to see themselves as one of "us" rather than one of "them." They strongly imply that if the corporation does well, its employees will bask in its reflected glory. They "present [the corporation's] interests as the interests of the employee member."

These appeals sound innocuous. Based on them, Cheney argues, "the employee self-consciously makes the decision to 'behave organizationally.'" But sometimes the manipulation is so subtle that the employee does not make this decision consciously. "What is desired by large corporations," says Cheney, "is something more: the internal motivation that arises when the two voices speak in unison." Not surprisingly, corporations use in-house publications to encourage employees to unconsciously tie their ideas about self-fulfillment, pride, and personal identity to those of the company.

Such close identification with corporations can have results that are dangerous for individuals and for the institutions that have developed to protect their interests. For example, Cheney asserts that corporate identification has led to the decline of labor unions as a powerful voice protecting the rights of workers. During an economic period that has seen laborers give up previously hard-won benefits and wage increases "for the good of the corporation," this is an alarming outcome. Close identification also leads to a personal paradox: How is it possible for workers to "find themselves" and simultaneously make decisions that place the organization's needs before their own?

Furthermore, employees who are completely taken in by the company line seldom question the way things are done. They have little motivation to innovate. They preserve the status quo. At a time when American industries are lagging seriously behind foreign competitors in many major industries, is it really desirable for corporations to foster "identifying" employees? Such rhetoric may be necessary for efficient business functioning in the short term, but in the long term it may be disastrous for the American economy and for the spirit of independence that built that economy in the first place. To many managers, independence of thought on the part of employees may seem meddlesome, time-consuming. But Cheney's study asks if corporate identification does not, ultimately, cost much more indeed.

Profiled by: Nancy Roth
Citation: Cheney (1983)

Critical Profile 3.2   Heaven on Earth: God *and* Mammon

"I have what I call spiritual indifference, and I practice it. Someone has said, 'When you get enough hell you'll look for heaven.' I've had enough hell."

So responds Frederick J. Eikerenkotter II, better known as Reverend Ike, to critics of his Science of Living Ministry. In contrast to what the evangelists of his day were doing, Rev. Ike discarded the fundamentalist's preoccupation with suffering in 1966 for what William Wiethoff of Indiana University terms "a more marketable approach." Wiethoff found Rev. Ike's rhetorical enterprise to be a unique synthesis of the secular and the sacred. Although the cornerstone of Rev. Ike's Social Gospel is the common philosophy of positive thinking and its monetary rewards, Ike delivers this message "with an evangelistic fervor." Consonant with Wiethoff's definition of a rhetorical enterprise ("organized efforts to reinforce secular satisfactions of individuals' needs through a quasi-religious gospel"), God and mammon have merged in Rev. Ike's plan of salvation. Repentance is not the issue. Thoughts of personal prosperity are the "psychic currency" that purchases heaven on earth.

In addition to a fundamental belief in self, there are three guidelines Ike uses to synthesize "spiritual and material comfort while sanctioning simple, conventional means to the ends:"

1. "All life is mind. All life is psychology. . . . Set your Mind in Motion and your very own God-Given Mind Power will instantly bring you the good you deserve."
2. "The *lack* of money is the root of all evil."
3. You can "learn to earn." (The Science of Living Institute offers degrees to those who master this truth.)

Note that Rev. Ike's rhetoric is not aimed at social change but rather at a modification of self-perceptions. His approach induces a psychological condition of symbiosis between the ministry and the believer, one in which the believer "is encouraged to perceive himself as less discontented, better informed, and more highly motivated." Therefore, heaven on earth is a matter of fervent *reinforcement* of traditional ethics rather than a genuine spiritual change.

The absorption of the frustrated, not adaptation to audience, is the key to Rev. Ike's success. Ike's rhetorical strategy of synthesis rather than invention is attractive to many. He offers "easy" answers. They are easy because they demand so little of listeners yet promise so much. "Easy rhetorics" like Rev. Ike's need to be watched carefully. Many rhetorics argue that virtue is its own reward. For Rev. Ike, reward is its own reward. The real question becomes: Who is being rewarded?

Profiled by: Kerry Riley
Citation: Wiethoff (1977)

Critical Profile 3.3   Guilt and the "Me" Generation

American mythology waxes eloquent about the rugged individualism of its people. In the late nineteen sixties and seventies, the nation's youth so embodied that spirit that they were dubbed the "me" generation. How is it possible, then, that the American people are also known for their social activism—an activity that requires participants to put the good of society before individual achievement? And why did so many social movements sweep the country at the height of the coming of age of the "me" generation?

David Payne of the University of South Florida asserts that these questions can be answered with one word: guilt. He explains that "guilt identifies a pervasive and prototypical way of assigning 'personal responsibility.'" If people can be made to feel individually culpable for a social phenomenon, they can be persuaded to act. The "acceptance of guilt offer[s] therapeutic resolutions" through action, says Payne.

How do people become aware of their guilt? Payne suggests that rhetoric is employed "to assault [their] perception of present circumstances as normal or tolerable and shake [their] complacency about circumstances and the adaptations [they] make to them." Speakers and writers often use vivid, doomsday imagery to demonstrate how bad things have gotten and how individuals have contributed to the catastrophe. Paul Erlich used such imagery in his 1968 book *The Population Bomb*. Writing at a time when Americans were becoming conscious that natural resources were limited, Erlich offered "a grim view of 'mass famine' and overcrowding on a 'moribund globe'" if couples continued to have more than two children. He argued that every citizen of planet Earth participated in "ecosystem destabilization" and

---

fanned out all over the world to study what political speechmaking "did" for the societies they studied.

One of these researchers studied the Merina of Madagascar and found the oratory to be depersonalized, bearing no distinctive stamp of the speaker. Indeed, even the orator's intonation patterns had been fixed by tradition, suggesting that for the Merina the act of speaking was, ipso facto, an act of tribal submission. In another case, among the Tikopia of the Solomon Islands, the chief of the tribe rarely showed up for the speaking activities, thereby insuring that his authority could never be directly questioned by those in attendance. In the speeches of the Kaoleni of Kenya, researchers found few references to heirarchy or leadership, since to mention such matters would have been to call attention to sharp economic cleavages in that society.

The general impression one gets from such traditional oratory is one of *constraint*. Political speaking in such societies seems more a pro-

---

Critical Profile 3.3   Guilt and the "Me" Generation (continued)

was responsible for ultimate planetary apocalypse unless he or she took personal responsibility to limit the number of children born.

From this emotional rhetoric, the "zero population growth" movement was born. In ensuing years, the rate of U.S. population growth declined for the first time since the nation's founding. Rugged American individualists had forgone the personal pleasures of having large, loving families for the certain knowledge that they had done their part to save the world. Intent upon expiating their guilt, the "me" generation took Erlich at his word. They joined social movements in droves, working on issues ranging from gay rights to making the oceans safe for endangered whales. Only then could they feel good about themselves.

Payne's book questions whether or not the "me" generation was aptly named. He also raises fundamental questions about the American character that are not easily answered. How, he asks, could a generation so consumed by consuming be simultaneously attracted to a variety of "Eastern" religious cults? How could a generation that created the "Yuppie" also be concerned with Biafran relief programs? How could the same generation revere both Mick Jagger and Mother Teresa? Payne's answer is that guilt has become a rhetorical constant in the United States and that it creates a kind of emotional standoff between national achievement and national selfishness. Guilt, Payne says, has become one of the U.S.'s greatest natural resources.

Profiled by: Nancy Roth
Citation: Payne (1989)

---

cess of putting on a show than of solving problems in a direct and clinical fashion. Speaking generally about such traditional peoples, Bloch [1975:8] observes that "the orator's words are almost entirely not his own, in the sense that he sees them as handed down from the ancestors. He will have learned all the proverbs, stories and speech forms and his main aim is to repeat them as closely as possible." Bloch [p. 9] goes on to say that listeners in these societies also make clear social statements when they take part in such speaking events: "On these occasions if you have allowed somebody to speak in an oratorical manner you have practically accepted his proposal ... When someone speaks to you in this way there quite simply seems to be no easy way of saying 'no' or commenting on the substance of what is said." In short, Bloch and his colleagues found that such speech-acts were symbolic tokens of basic political structures. For them, speaking *was* political action.

Closer to home, Hart [1987] conducted a comprehensive study of the basic rhetorical decisions made by recent American chief executives. Rather than examine the texts of presidential messages, Hart simply recorded the date, place of delivery, occasion, topic, audience, and political circumstance of each of the presidential speeches delivered between 1945 and 1985. This amounted to a data base of some ten thousand speech events. By looking at the pattern of speech decisions made by the presidents—to whom they talked, about what, when, and where—he hoped to catalog the most primitive, relational functions of presidential discourse. As Hart [1987:61] says, "Even before speaking to an audience, for example, a speaker makes a commitment to the members of that audience by agreeing to address them. To speak to a listener is to choose that listener above all other listeners, to acknowledge that the attitudes of that audience are somehow important." The basic question Hart asked—what does speech do?—focuses on a fundamental set of meta-messages and, therefore, should be asked during any rhetorical inquiry:

1. *Speech situations index power.* Hart observes that the first audience addressed by Ronald Reagan after the assassination attempt upon him consisted exclusively of press correspondents, suggesting how central the media now are to a president's image of strength. Also, even though Mr. Reagan opposed affirmative action, he spoke extensively to women's groups early in his administration, signaling how important such groups had become to liberal and conservative presidents alike.

2. *Speech situations index ego needs.* Hart discovered that Lyndon Johnson gave an unusually large number of speeches in his home state, probably because Texas audiences confirmed for him that he had finally "made it" as a national figure (something he never seemed quite sure of himself). A reverse finding was that Richard Nixon never spoke in the state of Massachusetts while president, perhaps because he suffered from a "Kennedy complex" and felt threatened when speaking in the shadow of Harvard.

3. *Speech situations index social obstacles.* Hart concludes that the presidency is becoming more difficult because chief executives are increasingly delivering preplanned speeches to preselected audiences instead of putting up with the give-and-take of press conferences. Also, presidents sharply increased their regional speaking when Congress was controlled by the opposing party, no doubt because they hoped to build grass roots support for their legislation and to use that support for Congress-bashing.

4. *Speech situations reveal speaker priorities.* Unlike any of the other chief executives, Jimmy Carter continued to speak extensively in the

two months *following* his 1980 defeat for reelection. The reason? He was a dogged individual strongly committed to the policies the electorate had just repudiated. Similarly, Democrat Lyndon Johnson traveled unusually often to *Republican* states in order to enlist support for prosecuting the war in Vietnam and, by crossing party lines, thereby showed how important such policies were to him.

5. *Speech situations reveal audience priorities.* Presidental speaking has now become a full-time business; the American people cannot get enough of their chief executive. Presidents now speak extensively during both election years and nonelection years and during the summer months as well as during all other seasons of the year. For whatever reason, the American people seem to have developed an insatiable appetite for presidential oratory.

6. *Speech situations reveal speaker-audience relationships.* Presidents are now spending more and more of their time speaking to private groups behind the closed doors of convention halls than to ordinary citizens in town squares. No doubt, such changes have been occasioned by alterations in patterns of political fund-raising, a fact also reflected in recently increased speaking activities in the Sun Belt, a part of the country undergoing great surges in population (and infusions of capital). In short, presidents use speech to flatter the people they must flatter.

Our concern in this section has been on *pre*-rhetorical analysis, not on words but on word-using. Because speech is always a situated activity, speakers must structure the right "configuration" of elements—audience, topic, setting—to have maximum impact. Shortly, we shall turn to a more detailed analysis of these elements, but before doing so let us consider the first question to be asked of any rhetorical event: *What act is being performed?* This is a simple question, but answers to it are usually complex. An elementary way of answering this question is to reduce the speech activity to one word, a gerund. Admittedly, such an approach is somewhat simplistic, but that is precisely its value: It reduces the speech-act to its most basic performative feature. Although the critic is free to choose any characterizing term for this purpose, Table 3.1 presents a starter's list, borrowing from the work of Gaines [1979] and supplemented by other suggestions as well.

The key move here is to describe, not to evaluate, the speech-act. Naturally, as with all criticism, the critic must be able to defend the characterizing term chosen for the speaking event in question. No doubt, different critics analyzing the same event would spot different "performances." That is as it should be, since this sort of exercise only provides a first, quite partial, glimpse of the event in question. But there is real utility in attempting this critical procedure, not for the answers

Table 3.1   Available Terms for Characterizing
Speech-Acts

activating	disputing	ordering
amusing	distracting	placating
angering	diverting	praising
announcing	edifying	promising
avoiding	enacting	refuting
calming	encouraging	reminding
challenging	enlightening	reporting
commencing	entertaining	requesting
confusing	escalating	retracting
consecrating	finishing	rousing
continuing	frightening	shocking
deceiving	humiliating	soothing
delaying	inciting	startling
demanding	inspiring	surprising
deterring	insulting	teaching
displaying	intimidating	warning
disposing	leading	

derived but for the questions raised. It seems clear, for example, that our rabbi at the Lincoln Memorial was not attempting to amuse or promise or continue or entertain or surprise. Equally, it appears that he was not trying to confuse or deter or escalate or frighten or startle. But was he commencing something or continuing something? Was he warning or encouraging his television audience? Was he soothing or challenging the tired civil rights workers? Was he inciting or diverting or doing both at the same time? And what was he doing most of most often? Questions like these focus on the most general terrain of a speech-act and help orient any subsequent textual analysis. They also throw light on the overall architecture of the rhetorical act—who said what to whom and why—and thereby raise questions asked all too rarely but almost always profitably.

THE COMPONENTS OF SPEECH-ACTS

This section will consider how a critic can better understand a message by reckoning with its larger social situation. According to Bitzer [1968], a number of situational factors operate to suggest what can and cannot be said by a person in a given instance. Some of these suggestive factors lie within the speaker (knowledge, experience, psychological state), while others are external (the time of day, what others are saying). In either case, a message becomes a public record of how the speaker coped with the suggestions built into the rhetorical situation. Figure 3.1 captures the most basic of such factors. Several features of the model are worth noting:

1. *The model situates the message within an array of social forces.* No piece of discourse can be understood outside its natural habitat. While an ancient poem may delight persons living generations later, that is rarely the case with rhetoric. Old rhetorical messages seem to warn subsequent readers: "You really should have been there." Thus, Arnold [1968] notes that when the parliamentary speeches of William Butler Yeats were anthologized, the editor provided the situational details necessary to make sense out of the speeches. In contrast, collections of Yeats's poems rarely contain such situational markers.

2. *The model describes a system of elements.* Any speech-act is always more than the sum of its parts; to change one element is to change the whole. Anyone who has seen the "same" convention audience underwhelmed by a Michael Dukakis and overwhelmed by a Jesse Jackson knows that changing *one* element of a rhetorical system can produce changes throughout that system.

Figure 3.1
Elements of a Rhetorical Situation

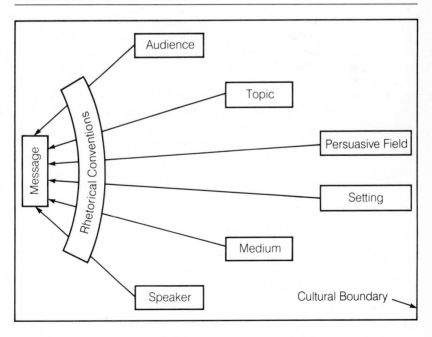

RHETORIC AND NATIONAL STRIFE

Critical Profile 3.4   Words and the Atomic Bomb

Words are often thought of as distinct from real life. Sometimes words correspond to reality (for example, when we tell the truth), and sometimes they contradict it (for example, when we lie). But a study by James Hikins, now of Ohio State University, considered how words can produce a reality of their own, a distinct reality that reduces our options as citizens and directs us toward a particular path of action. In his study, Hikins examined a number of foreign policy statements during World War II. He argues that these speeches, which demanded the "unconditional surrender" of Japan, created a set of conditions that forced President Harry Truman to drop the atomic bomb on two Japanese cities to end the war.

The rhetoric of unconditional surrender began with the entry of the United States into the war the day after the December 7, 1941, bombing of Pearl Harbor. Immediately, newspapers were filled with bitter public statements: "We shall wreak the vengeance of justice on the violators of peace, these assassins who attack without warning. . . . The United States answers Japan's challenge with steel-throated cannon and a sharp sword of retribution." A study of speeches, newspaper editorials, and other public policy statements reveals that this rhetoric of retribution quickly became a philosophy of national unity. A few months after Pearl Harbor, a State Department committee on foreign policy reached the consensus that the only acceptable outcome of the war would be "unconditional surrender." Throughout the war, President Roosevelt and others repeatedly called for "the unconditional surrender of the criminal forces who plunged the world into storm and ruin." Over and over again for the next three-and-a-half years, demands for unconditional surrender were repeated by public figures and supported by U.S. citizens.

According to Hikins, such rhetoric produced an unbending force that rejected—ahead of time—any compromise. When Harry Truman became president upon the untimely death of Franklin Roosevelt, the political forces unleashed by the language of unconditional surrender gave Truman no option but to use the ultimate weapon: the atomic bomb. If cooler heads had prevailed, compromise might have ended the war earlier and made the atomic bombing unnecessary. But rhetoric tends to make heads hot, not cool, and these demands for unconditional surrender gave Truman no room to negotiate. Hikins writes that such demanding rhetoric, once unleashed, may be as irresistible as any military weapon. Surely those who mourn the Japanese of 1945 will attest to that.

Profiled by: John Theobald-Osborne
Citation: Hikins (1983)

3. *All situational elements operate within a unique cultural boundary.* It is often hard to see the effects of culture upon human interaction. Nevertheless, the critic must try to do so, since culture penetrates all message-sending and all message-receiving. The themes found in a *Rocky XXI* film may seem quite universal to the average American moviegoer, but it takes only the slightest cultural sensitivity to be able to trace its sexism and nationalism to a long cultural history of conservative U.S. values.

4. *A message is the visible record of a complex interaction.* The rhetorical critic focuses heavily on message cues, because that is all that is left after a dynamic human encounter has occurred. Often, the message itself contains only the slightest traces of this complexity and so the critic must "put back" such elements to make the message/situation as whole as possible.

5. *The message is the rhetorical critic's touchstone.* Anthropologists may study social settings; sociologists may study audiences; psychologists may study media effects; philosophers may study human thought; and historians may recount the careers of great speakers. But it is the rhetorical critic who uniquely examines the marks *left on messages* by these various forces.

Our model, then, conceives of messages as repositories of information about situational elements. As Branham and Pearce [1985:25] observe, text always implies context and context always implies text, which is why, they argue, the off-color jokes of comedian Lenny Bruce could be shocking in the uptight 1950s and seem almost quaint thirty years later. One way of discovering the context within the text is to inquire into the social "parentage" of a given message. Sometimes, inspecting a message for audience, speaker, topical and other imprintings can lead to confusion, as the critic tries to cope with the wealth of data unearthed. But as Rosenfield [1968] and Booth [1979] indicate, to restrict one's vision artificially is to insure getting a static look at the message. Thus, let us proceed through this configuration of factors and consider the situational analyst's critical probes:

SPEAKER VARIABLES

- **Besides discussing a particular topic in a particular location, is the speaker making some sort of *social statement* by speaking?**
- **Does the audience have firsthand knowledge of the speaker that the speaker can draw upon rhetorically?**
- **Is the speaker "sainted" or "victimized" by stereotypes listeners have of "speakers like this?"**

Critical Profile 3.5   Public Response and the War to End All Wars

After securing a formal Congressional declaration of war against Germany in the spring of 1917, President Woodrow Wilson was faced with the rather immediate problem of how to deal with public opinion. It was one thing to sign a piece of paper declaring war and quite another to motivate people to actually *fight* that war, especially since the American public was deeply divided over the issue of U.S. involvement with the Allies. If they were to make the sacrifices demanded in wartime, Americans had to see the war as both justifiable and honorable. Thus, President Wilson created the Committee on Public Information (CPI), which, claims Thomas A. Hollihan of the University of Southern California, served as an immense public relations organization designed to "assure that Americans would have the will necessary to sustain a prolonged war against a powerful enemy." The CPI was successful beyond Wilson's imaginings.

All the devices of the then-primitive mass media were used to persuade the American public of the virtues of war. Hollihan shows how CPI artfully created vital pseudo-battles to be fought by average American citizens in their average American towns, battles that carefully corresponded to the war taking place on European soil. Even though the strategic utility of such local activities was questionable from a military standpoint, they did serve as a practical *outlet* for patriotic feelings and, hence, for getting people to make a behavioral commitment to the war effort. For example, in order to localize an abstraction like "the enemy," the CPI went on the attack by making "people aware that German spies and saboteurs might be in their midst." One CPI ad warned:

German agents are everywhere, eager to gather scraps of news about our men, our ships, our munitions . . . Do not wait until you catch someone

---

- **Is the speaker able to roam freely when specifying his or her motives for speaking?**
- **Has the speaker subscribed to a particular ideology or doctrine that expands or limits what can be said?**
- **Does the speaker possess any unique assets or liabilities when speaking on this topic?**
- **Is there textual evidence that the speaker considered these factors when framing the message in question?**

Naturally, these are only a very few of the questions relevant to the speaker-message relationship and the influence of the speaker's unique self on message-creation. These questions deal with how social role, personal ideology, and public image constrain, sometimes dictate,

---

Critical Profile 3.5 Public Response and the War to End All Wars
(*continued*)

---

putting a bomb under a factory. Report the man who spreads pessimistic stories, cries for peace or belittles our efforts to win the war . . .

In a similar vein, those who refused to purchase war bonds (which was described as "a litmus test for patriotism"), were subject to "mild forms of terrorism." German-Americans were also attacked: "You are in contact with the enemy *today*, just as truly as if you faced him across No Man's Land. In your hands are two powerful weapons with which to meet him—discretion and vigilance. *Use them.*" At the behest of the CPI, defense councils and security leagues emerged in virtually every American community. The enemy was thereby rendered concrete, no longer a distant evil fighting American troops in distant lands.

During wartime, the verbal excesses of groups like the CPI seem thoroughly defensible, even admirable. But it is important to consider what sorts of rhetorical seeds might have been sown in the United States at that time: cultural defensiveness, mindless nationalism, and ethnic prejudice, to name but three. These moral lapses still bedevil contemporary Americans and one wonders if the CPI helped to nurture them.

Profiled by: Susan Whalen
Citation: Hollihan (1984)

---

what a speaker says. On occasion, for example, a college teacher must struggle mightily to keep a lecture free of personal bias in order to keep students from questioning everything the lecturer has to say (about this, and all other, topics). In such cases, personal ideology wages a ferocious war with social role in the presence of public image. The message produced—the lecture itself—often carries the battle scars. In other instances, the mere fact of speaking can carry the most important message. Philipsen [1986] has observed, for example, that when he engaged a college professor in a heated public exchange, former Chicago mayor Richard Daley's loss of composure signaled that his political power was beginning to wane. Jamieson [1988b] has also observed that the real advantage of modern presidential debating lies not in the political information provided the citizenry but in the debates' abilities

---

Critical Profile 3.6   The Boston *Massacre?*

At nine o'clock in the evening of March 5, 1770, a cold, dark street became the scene of the legendary Boston Massacre. How did a struggle between obscure working-class Bostonians and provoked British soldiers become elevated to a moral drama? Why were the radical patriots so successful in their attempt to make the King Street altercation a conflict between good and evil, between liberty and tyranny? Questions of this sort encouraged Kurt W. Ritter, now of Texas A and M University, to study how the Boston radicals used the confrontation as a potent rhetorical device. Ritter analyzed the incident comprehensively, drawing upon original transcripts of the testimonies from the likes of John Adams and Thomas Hutchinson and focusing on the important issue of moral drama.

One of Ritter's initial observations seized upon the raw power implicit in the very name "Boston Massacre:"

Even strong words such as "killings," or "murders" would not have had the impact . . . of "massacre," which implied massive butchering of unresisting victims. A murder might occur in the passion of the moment but a massacre required a cool, calculated conspiracy.

Ritter reveals several inconsistencies that make the rhetorical ploy of using the term "massacre" particularly significant. First, virtually no one present at the scene could relate precisely what had happened during the clash. One witness testified that "it was difficult to determine which were the Aggressors—the soldiers or the townspeople." Second, the questionable characters

---

to insure that the candidates themselves become informed on the issues of the day! Speakers may create messages, but, often, messages re-create speakers as well.

AUDIENCE VARIABLES

- **Regardless of the practical outcome of the interaction, has the audience made any significant *social statement* by coming to listen?**
- **To what extent is this audience a "rhetorical audience," that is, one that can directly implement the change the speaker is requesting?**
- **Can the speaker capitalize on existing common ties with the audience when speaking to them?**
- **What previous personal or philosophical commitments (for**

Critical Profile 3.6   The Boston *Massacre? (continued)*

of the victims suggest that the soldiers may have been goaded into firing their deadly muskets. In fact, during the December, 1770, trials, the distinguished John Adams, acting as defense attorney for the soldiers, described not five hundred victims, but *five* victims:

> The plain English is, gentlemen, most probably a motley rabble of saucy boys, negroes, and mulattoes, Irish teagues and outlandish jack tarrs. And why we should scruple to call such a set of people a mob, I can't conceive, unless the name is too respectable for them.

Third, copious amounts of rhetorical propaganda were shuttled from one end of the colonies to the other and then on to England and back. Each newspaper account, pamphlet, or moving oration contributed to the reality that became known *not* as the "unhappy transaction" (as the Tories had dubbed it), nor as the "Boston Conflict," nor even as the "Boston Murders." As Ritter says, "The rhetoric became the reality of the Boston Massacre." Indeed, how could anyone resist becoming alarmed when confronted by rhetoric of the following sort: " . . . (it was) a most shocking spectacle; the gutters of the street running with blood, and the snow dyed crimson, with the blood and brains of . . . [their] fellow citizens?" Of such stuff, revolution is made.

Profiled by: Christine Keffeler
Citation: Ritter (1977)

---

example, group memberships) has the audience made that may affect their responses to the speaker?
· **What contrary information or attitudes does the audience have that can inhibit the speaker's success?**
· **What recent experiences has the audience had that may affect their responsiveness?**
· **Is there textual evidence that the speaker considered these factors when framing the message in question?**

Simply agreeing to become part of an audience can constitute a major social statement. In pretechnological societies, for example, Starosta [1979] tells us that the simple willingness to sit and listen to a public speech signaled a people's shift toward formalization of governance. Similarly, Campbell [1983:105] observes that the rhetorical technique known as consciousness-raising (a form of communication in which speaking and listening roles are exchanged frequently) was particularly well-suited to the early women's movement, then made up largely of at-home women who were used to conversational, rather than public, modes of interaction. We do not normally think of listening as a form of commitment, but many professional speakers do, which is why they work so hard to match audience with message. Thus, when Harry Truman rode across the United States in a Pullman car during the 1948 election, giving some four hundred odd speeches in some four hundred odd places, Truman produced a rhetoric-in-search-of-an-audience. He knew that there were people who shared his real-life experiences (as a nonurbanite) but who did not know that his administration was being hamstrung by a Republican-controlled Congress. Truman also knew that most of the really influential newspapers of the day favored his opponent, Thomas Dewey, so the President brought his rhetoric directly to people who were less affected by the opinions of the elite press: rural and small-town voters. In so doing, Truman capitalized on what was "built into" his audiences via their demography.

TOPIC VARIABLES

- Is this topic socially acceptable? Is the fact that it is being discussed a significant *social statement?*
- Is the topic volatile or innocuous? Is public opinion highly polarized on this matter?
- How complex is the topic? Can it be reasonably discussed with this audience in this setting?
- Because of how this topic has been discussed before, must the speaker deal with it in a certain way?
- Does the topic have any special features that make its discussion via this medium advantageous or risky?
- Is there textual evidence that the speaker considered these factors when framing the message in question?

Pity Teddy Kennedy. The senator from Massachusetts can discourse confidently about tax reform, the Trilateral Commission, oil import fees, Third World relief measures, and Star Wars research and development. About such matters he is smooth, often profound. But should some reporter mention the word Chappaquiddick, the good senator turns pale and inarticulate. Introducing such a wild card into a Kennedy speech situation throws his entire rhetorical system out of kilter. This subject matter—no matter what the setting and no matter what the medium or audience—brings up old and terrible memories for Mr. Kennedy, making him perhaps the only person in public life whose presidential aspirations have been undone by a single speech topic. On the other hand, if Kennedy had not quickly offered a dramatic public explanation of the events at Chappaquiddick in 1969 (thereby making a social statement about his forthrightness and leadership abilities), his career might well have been ended by the incident and not just hampered by it.

Each speech topic has a "range of discussability." Some topics (for example, the Golden Gate Bridge) let a speaker roam freely when discussing it, while others tightly rein one in (for example, the Chappaquiddick bridge). It is difficult for many Americans to talk about such indelicate matters as hemorrhoidal treatments or vaginal sprays, products requiring advertisers to be especially inventive rhetorically. The range of discussability for a topic may also be constricted by that topic's complexity. For example, some years ago the Mathematical Association of America opened its annual meeting to the press in order to gain wider public understanding of the important work that mathematicians do. Alas, the experiment failed: Only four of the eighty invited reporters bothered to attend [Kolata, 1975:732]. At other times, linking a speaker (say, a politician) to a topic (say, extramarital sex) within a specialized medium (say, *Playboy* magazine) can create enormous rhetorical difficulties—if you are Jimmy Carter and if the year is 1976 and you are running for the highest office in the land. In short, any one element in the configuration of elements can create topical difficulties. Several operating at the same time can create rhetorical nightmares.

PERSUASIVE FIELD

- **Taken as a whole, can the speech situation be seen as a *counterstatement* to some other set of messages?**
- **Have the speaker's previous remarks to this audience expanded or limited current persuasive possibilities?**
- **What statements have other people made in the past that constrain what can be said now?**
- **What sort of immediate "verbal competition" (for example, heckling) is the speaker being subjected to?**
- **Can any future rhetorical messages be envisioned that require anticipatory strategies now?**
- **Is there textual evidence that the speaker considered these factors when framing the message in question?**

The persuasive field consists of all those other messages impinging upon an audience in a given speech situation. These messages could have been authored by the speaker previously, by other members of the audience, or by persons not present. During a news conference, for example, a president often must cope with rumors that have been circulating for days in the newspapers, with recent Congressional attacks on his administration, or with the complaints of protesters massed outside the White House. All of these forces are added to the mix when the president approaches the microphone for the first question.

At times, the persuasive field will be unusually message-filled as, for example, during the Watergate phase of the Nixon administration. During that time, Mr. Nixon largely abandoned the press conference format for the much less competitive format of weekly radio addresses, refusing to share "his" airtime with his opponents in the press corps. Toward the end of the Nixon administration, reporters like Dan Rather asked unusually sharp questions during these press conferences, thereby restimulating the persuasive field. Moreover, modern presidents are now subjected to "instant analysis" immediately after speaking so that, while speaking, they must anticipate and counteract messages that do not yet exist. For these and other reasons, presidents often begin their press conferences with formal statements, trying to establish a base of rhetorical operations before receiving flak from the press corps. In other words, all messages contain the ghosts of other messages. Thus, Gilberg, et al. [1980] found that today's presidential speech often tracks last week's newspaper, since presidents are now so responsive to the persuasive field energized each day by media reports.

SETTING VARIABLES

- Is any *social statement* being made by the speaker by speaking at this time in this place?
- Is there a special kind of "history" attached to where the speech is being given? Does that place affect what can be said?
- Do any nonverbal events (for example, aspects of sight, sound, feeling, etc.) affect the speaker's game plan?
- Is any event likely to occur in the future that will affect what can be said now by this speaker?
- Is there textual evidence that the speaker considered these factors when framing the message in question?

Over time, some physical locations take on special social (and rhetorical) significance. When announcing his bid for the 1988 presidential campaign, for example, Gary Hart stood atop a magnificent mountain peak in Colorado, thereby declaring himself, both verbally and nonverbally, a man of Western vision. A very different image is presented by the poor acoustics and overcrowding of political convention halls (designed to add excitement to the oratory delivered), while the ornate quietude of a great cathedral permits, and denies, still other rhetorical possibilities. As Edelman [1964:96] says, many physical settings have a contrived character and are "unabashedly built up to emphasize a departure from men's daily routine, a special heroic quality to the proceedings they are to frame." A good example of such contrivances occurs in courtrooms, says Edelman [1964:99], who notes that "The judicial bench and chambers, formal, ornate, permanent and solid, lined with thick tomes, 'prove' the deliberateness, scholarliness, and judiciousness of the acts that take place in them, even though careful study of these acts in a university or newspaper office (different settings) may indicate they were highly arbitrary, prejudiced, or casual."

Aspects of time (the hour of the day) and timing (when an event occurs relative to other events) are also important factors. As Gronbeck [1974:86] says, a persuasive message may fail because the speaker is the wrong person for the moment, because the audience is not yet "primed" to take the appeal seriously, or because the message is otherwise presented too soon or too late. For example, Gerald Ford got a great deal of political mileage out of the bicentennial celebrations held in 1976, which also happened to be the year he was running for reelection. By linking his personal political calendar with the nation's cultural calendar, Ford was able to "preside" over the American people even as he solicited their votes. His opponent in that campaign, Jimmy Carter, was also a student of judicious timing. Timing is also important in the business world, where product-messages are carefully adapted to the entertainment schedule. This is why beer is advertised during football telecasts and why soap is advertised during, well, soap operas.

MEDIA VARIABLES

- Is the speaker making any important *social statement* by delivering his or her message via this medium?
- Does the modality chosen (that is, spoken or written) enhance or detract from the speaker's message?
- Does the size of the audience the medium can reach present or deny any important rhetorical possibilities?
- Are there any important "sponsorship effects" associated with messages presented via this medium?
- Does the medium chosen permit the speaker's personality to become an important force of persuasion?
- Do subaudiences exist because of the medium chosen for the message?
- Is there textual evidence that the speaker considered these factors when framing the message in question?

A medium is what "carries" a message. At the simplest level, for example, we are aware of the very different rhetorical possibilities of speaking versus writing. Normally, marriage is proposed in person—while speaking—rather than by telegram, because speech is personal and intimate, while telegrams are both too cold and too terse for something as complicated as love. On the other hand, "Dear John" is more likely to receive a letter than a phone call from "Love, Sue," because writing helps one focus one's thoughts, craft one's arguments, and, above all, circumvent the emotionalism of the moment. The Dear John letter, of course, is one of the most hated messages yet devised by humankind, because its sender makes such a powerful social statement by choosing a distanced medium for a former intimate. It is highly likely, therefore, that most such letters are destroyed before they are read through. No matter how carefully the words may be phrased, the rhetorical *act* is a fundamentally alienating one.

With the advent of the mass media, persuasion has been changed in dramatic ways. Before, when speakers addressed throngs of listeners in a live setting, the speaker's message could not be dispersed widely, but the speaker could reach out and touch the immediate audience. With radio and television, many more listeners can be solicited simultaneously, but they are now presented with "images" rather than with flesh and blood speakers in close proximity. Scholars are only beginning to sort out these complexities of the mass media.

But some things we already know. For example, the mass media create "sponsorship effects," with listeners now having built-in expectations for *any* televised message. That is, TV viewers have come to expect informality rather than formality, personalized rather than impersonal arguments, visual rather than bland supporting materials, interactive rather than monologic formats, and much else. Also, because so many persons can now be reached at the same time via television, rhetorical messages are becoming increasingly complex, as speakers adjust different parts of the same message to the different subaudiences they face simultaneously. So, for example, Smith [1972] found that Richard Nixon's 1968 acceptance address at the Republican National Convention succeeded because it somehow managed to appeal to both the partisan convention-goers as well as to the less partisan, more easily distracted, viewers at home. More recently, Wander [1984] showed that any presidential foreign policy address must now speak directly to the voters, as well as to their journalistic overhearers, and to friendly and unfriendly members of Congress as well. It gets even more complicated: At the very same time, the president must send signals to the Soviets without missending signals to U.S. allies. No doubt, this overlapping of audiences makes politics sound as strange as it does at times.

RHETORICAL CONVENTIONS

· **Has this configuration of elements ever come together before?**
· **If so, are there rules of interaction that must be followed by the speaker?**
· **If this speech situation is a new one, must any general rhetorical guidelines be honored here?**
· **Does any *one* element (speaker, audience, topic, etc.) have special weight on this occasion?**
· **Is there textual evidence that the speaker considered these factors when framing the message in question?**

Without question, people are efficient. Rather than invent a completely new message for each new social event, they formulate rhetorical guidelines to deal with stock situations. The first moment or two of the ordinary street corner conversation, for example, is highly predictable. We discuss health, the weather, the local ball club, and little else. Although seemingly insignificant at first, such standardized locutions tell a good deal about cultural assumptions. For example, it is noteworthy that even on a comparatively bawdy TV show like *Designing Women*, indiscriminate adultery, personal arrogance, and corporate rapaciousness are—in virtually every single instance—ultimately punished. Admittedly, compared to the television dramas of the 1950s, it now takes longer for the transgressions to be discovered and the transgressors disciplined. But it has long been part of the American code that such behaviors are deserving of censure, and so we have developed formulas for discussing such things. Colonial values are still powerful in the United States and so, were he to return, Puritan preacher Jonathan Edwards might well be able to guest-direct an episode or two of *Designing Women*, so well does he know the story line of American morality.

At times, configurational elements go together so often that rituals of interaction develop. In such instances, speakers become tightly constrained in what they can say, and listeners learn to appreciate the sameness of rhetorical exchange. So, for example, eighty percent of the content of any Roman Catholic mass is predetermined, with worshippers being comforted by the emotional predictability of a powerful ritual. Presidential inaugurals, marriage ceremonies, eulogies, graduation exercises, bar mitzvahs—all of these are heavily constrained by rhetorical conventions, signaling that standard problems (that is, transitional moments) persist and that these problems are so important that public solutions must be found for dealing with them.

Even when full-blown rituals are not present, one can spot conventions at work. There are, for example, strong sanctions against quietly talking to oneself in the corner of a room. Equally, however, raising one's voice in public is often not permitted. One can discuss athletics in mixed company, but not athletic supporters. The term black is now acceptable, but the term negro is not. The careful critic will spot such rhetorical rules and then ask *why* they exist, largely because these verbal habits so often point up a society's special preferences as well as its special vulnerabilities.

CONCLUSION

This chapter has emphasized two things: (1) The very *decision* to speak can be an important kind of social action and (2) the various elements of a rhetorical situation often become *imprinted* upon the message, thereby becoming a valuable source of insight for the critic. Let us conclude our discussion with an example. The case in point is an interesting piece of rhetoric portrayed in the movie *Patton* but based on a real speech given in July of 1944 by General George S. Patton [1946] prior to crossing the English Channel for an assault on the German armies in France. Even a brief excerpt from Patton's speech reveals its distinctive tones:

> Men, this stuff you hear about Americans wanting to stay out of this war is a lot of b___s___! Americans love to fight, traditionally. All real Americans love the sting of battle. When you were kids, you all admired the champion marble player, the fastest runner, the big league ball player, the toughest boxer. The Americans love a winner, and cannot tolerate a loser. . . .That's why Americans have never lost, and will never lose a war. The very thought of losing is hateful to an American. . . .
>
> You are not all going to die. Only two percent of you here would die in a major battle. Death must not be feared. Every man is frightened at first in battle. If he says he isn't he's a goddam liar. Some men are cowards, yes. But they will fight just the same, or get the hell scared out of them watching men who do fight, who are as scared as they. The real hero is the man who fights even though he is scared. . . .
>
> An Army is a team: It lives, sleeps, eats, fights as a team. This individual heroic stuff is a lot of crap. The bilious bastards who wrote that kind of stuff for the *Saturday Evening Post* don't know any more about real battle than they do about f___! . . . We have the finest food, the best equipment, the finest spirit and men in the world. . . . Why, by God, I actually pity those sonsofbitches we are going up against: by God, I do! . . .
>
> The kind of man I want is like the lieutenant in Libya who, with a Luger against his chest, jerked his helmet off, swept the gun aside

with the other hand, and busted hell out of the Boche with his helmet. Then he jumped on the Hun and went out and killed another German. By this time, the lieutenant had a bullet through his chest. Now, that is a MAN for you. . . .

Even a cursory look at Patton's remarks will reveal some of the major *social statements* being made in this situation: a great general taking the time to talk to raw recruits; the soldiers seated together, building esprit de corps prior to an important battle; the candor of Patton dealing directly with such topics as courage, self-image, mortality, and immortality, signaling with this choice of topics that the moment was important to him. The clear sense of counterstatement is also obvious, with Patton using the speech-act to argue that the rumormongers, Tokyo Roses, and *Saturday Evening Posts* were wrong in every detail. By meeting with the men (on their turf) so soon before battle, Patton no doubt sent them an important message of solidarity, as he did by giving a live speech rather than a radio address.

The imprints of the various situational elements are also unmistakable. The speech is Pattonesque: coarse, crude, unyielding, defiant, a clear indication of a **speaker variable** at work. In some senses, Patton's reputation was so much larger than life that he may even have had to overstate his positions in order to meet the men's exalted expectations of him, which may be why the text combines both superpatriotism with a faint sort of anarchism. Evident here too is the everyday talk of the everyday soldier, a hint of the **audience variables** with which Patton had to deal. Patton's images are earthy and his language colorful, because earthiness is the constant companion of the foot soldier and colorfulness his only respite. In some senses, the speech treats the individual **topic variables** in conventional ways, but by *combining* deeply philosophical topics (the purpose of life) with brutishly practical matters (getting fed), Patton gives his listeners an exhilarating rhetorical ride. In some senses, the structure of the speech is conventional (one is reminded of football coaches at half-time), but the language used— imperative rather than declarative sentences, contrast devices rather than comparison devices—is unmistakably Patton's.

A comparison of Patton's speech with the trimmed-down version delivered by George C. Scott in the movie *Patton* shows how **media variables** can change things considerably. In the original speech, for example, Patton spent a good deal of time talking about the importance of the hard training his men had recently experienced, something omitted in the movie speech because the popcorn-eaters had no doubt been otherwise employed in recent weeks. The original speech also spends a great deal of time talking about the reality of death, giving it a kind of authenticity missing in Scott's speech. There is also a great deal of detail in the original speech missing in the movie version (for example, of a soldier near Tunis fixing a telephone wire in the thick of battle). Comments like these possess a real-world integrity demanded by the **setting variables** impinging on a real general speaking only moments before a real war.

Moviemakers have their own rhetorical challenges, however. For example, they deleted Patton's careful instructions to his men not to mention that they had seen him (a security measure), since the average theatre patron would hardly have understood the historical context for these remarks. Also, the movie version is only half the length of the original speech and has none of the internal repetition found in the historical version. These patterns are found because there are very tight **rhetorical conventions** affecting moviemaking, conventions dictated by the fast pace expected in the war film genre. Whereas George Patton had to reach out to real soldiers experiencing real fears, George C. Scott needed only to make a quick and dramatic impression on his listeners so that they would be set up to enjoy the next two hours in the darkened theatre. In a sense, then, neither George Patton nor George Scott owned their speeches. Their audiences did.

For the student of rhetoric, situational analysis must be the first procedure in any critical operation. Getting a broad-based perspective on the speech-act is important, because rhetoric torn away from its context makes no sense or makes distorted sense. Future chapters in this book will delve deeper into the sinews of messages. These anatomical excursions will be important, because in detail lies precision. But the good surgeon reaches for the scalpel only after having done an overall physical workup of the patient. The critic should do likewise by treating rhetorical situations in all of their complexity. To do less would be a kind of critical malpractice.

CHAPTER FOUR

Analyzing Ideas

A pool table; don't you understand? Friend, either you're closing your eyes to a situation you do not wish to acknowledge, or you are not aware of the calibre of disaster indicated by the presence of a pool table in your community.

Well, you got trouble, my friend. Right here, I say, trouble right here in River City. Why, sure, I'm a billiard player; certainly mighty proud to say, I'm always mighty proud to say it. I consider that the hours I spend with a cue in my hand are golden. Help you cultivate horse-sense, and a cool head, and a keen eye. Did you ever take and try to give an iron-clad leave for yourself from a three-rail billiard shot? But just as I say it takes judgment, brains, and maturity to score in a balkline game, I say that any boob can take and shove a ball in a pocket.

And I call that sloth, the first big step on the road to the depths of degradation. I say, first, medicinal wine from a teaspoon—then beer from a bottle. And the next thing you know your son is playing for money in a pinched-back suit, and listenin' to some big out of town jasper hearin' him tell about horse-race gamblin'. Not a wholesome trottin' race. No! But a race where they set down right on the horse. Like to see some stuck up jockey-boy settin' on Dan Patch? Make your blood boil? Well, I should say.

Friends, let me tell you what I mean: You got one, two, three, four, five, six pockets in a table, pockets that mark the difference between a gentleman and a bum, with a capital "B" and that rhymes with "P" and that stands for "POOL."

And all week long your River City youth will be a fritterin' away; I say your young men will be fritterin'. Fritterin' away their noontime, suppertime, choretime, too. Get the ball in the pocket—never mind gettin' dandelions pulled or the screen door patched or the beefsteak pounded; and never mind pumpin' any water 'til your parents are caught with the cistern empty on a Saturday night. And that's trouble!

Yes, you've got lots and lots of trouble. I'm thinking of the kids in the knickerbockers, shirttailed young ones, peekin' in the pool hall window after school. You got trouble, folks, right here in River City. Trouble, with a capital "T" and that rhymes with "P" and that stands for "POOL." [Hill, 1958]

Professor Harold Hill, that consummate salesman-cum-shyster depicted in the delightful play *The Music Man,* is a man filled with ideas. He is filled with old ideas (like loving hard work and avoiding sin) as well as new ideas (music as salvation), and he is filled with the best idea of all: combining these ideas in order to make a profit. When he spoke, Professor Hill showed that he was a fine student of American culture, which is itself a complex amalgam of old and new ideas. In fashioning his sermon/advertisement, Hill focused not so much on the particular ideas the residents of River City, Iowa, favored in the 1930s. Rather, he concentrated on the enduring ideas their forebears had resonated to at the turn of the century and that their great-grandchildren would also appreciate in the 1990s. In doing so, Mr. Hill proved himself a fairly decent intellectual historian of the United States, and he proved, too, that all good speakers must first become good listeners.

And Harold Hill was a fine listener indeed. His constant meandering through the Midwest selling anything he could carry in a (preferably lightweight) display case had taught him much about the plain-speaking, plain-thinking middle-Americans who were his customers. Even before walking on the sidewalks of River City he knew the people he would pass. He knew, for example, that the clean streets and neatly trimmed lawns were maintained by people who respected Western assumptions of rationality and orderliness, ideas having their presuppositions in the Enlightenment and their implications in getting the dandelions pulled. He knew that country folks at the turn of the century in the United States had been raised on a stern diet of Calvinism (no matter what their religious denomination) and on concepts of incremental spirituality ("And I call that sloth, the first big step on the road to the depths of degradation"). For such people, sin was not only progressive but also concrete. Theirs was a Christian world view, not a Platonic one, and so unpounded beefsteak could stand as a sign of perdition just as surely as the death of Jesus Christ had stood as real-world rejection of pagan philosophizing. Theirs was a life of immediacy, of planting and tending and harvesting, of coping with nature. Thus, they distrusted foolishness—"boobs" and the like—favoring instead "horse-sense," since animals were so central to their material survival and since material survival was tied up in complicated ways with moral matters. Because rural life makes land and its care the measure of the individual, and because the greater the expanse of one's land the greater one's personal risk, there was also a self-imposed provincialism to Harold Hill's customers that made them instinctively wary of "out of town jaspers." At the same time, River City residents were heirs to American pluralism. Their resulting friendliness made it possible for them to be seduced by an out-of-towner even as they were being warned of same.

As it turns out, Harold Hill was as much a philosopher as a peddler of slide trombones. For him, persuasion involved understanding the assumptions people make about the world, since human decisions are so often based on people's first premises, their basic assumptions. The study of philosophy is the study of these first premises and *the study of rhetoric is the study of first premises-in-use.* Harold Hill was probably not a self-conscious philosopher. He knew what he knew in the way most practical people know things: by imitation and observation. But unlike most, Hill had a special ability to ground persuasion in people's most basic thoughts. The measure of Hill's artfulness is that his rhetoric did not sound "philosophical" at all. It sounded practical, not abstract; it sounded cozy, not antiseptic; it sounded partisan, not neutered. Miss Marian, River City's resident rhetorical critic (and later Hill's inamorata), quickly saw through his rhetoric. She did what the best critics do: She traced the ideas Hill used to their first assumptions and reasoned that these were probably *not* the assumptions held by the average cosmopolitan professor of musicology. Miss Marian traced Hill's ideas to their roots and found them lying in River City and not in Harold Hill. Smart lady, Miss Marian.

In a sense, Harold Hill made something out of nothing when he contrasted godlessness with euphonic piety. Neither euphony nor piety invited this linkage, but Hill persevered until these wellsprings of belief produced usable ideas. To do so took considerable rhetorical imagination (Would Dan Patch be pleased that he became both savior and shill in River City?). But persuaders have always been opportunistic in these ways, a fact that produces horror, admiration, or bemusement in critics. Miss Marian, a librarian and hence a person sensitive to texts and to the cataloging of ideas, reacted in all three ways from time to time. These will be our options as well, and Miss Marian will be our inspiration as we consider how persuaders use ideas and how critics can catch them doing so.

THE STUDY OF IDEAS

In a way, all rhetorical critics study ideas. And, in a way, each chapter in this book focuses upon the rhetorical uses of ideas. But this chapter will focus on the basics, on how persuasive appeals come to be. Here, we will emphasize the gathering of elementary rhetorical facts, echoing Hopper, et al.'s [1986] belief that the most scientific thing a scientist does lies not in the use of computers or measuring instruments but in the scientist's ability to *describe* a phenomenon in detail and with precision. Careful description is especially important in rhetorical criticism, since rhetoric is such an emotional thing to study. That is, if the rhetoric being studied is powerful, the natural tendency is to applaud or decry it. The descriptive impulse arrests this very natural, but critically dangerous, inclination by asking what is known for sure about the message in question.

Good description requires gathering facts before doing interpretation or evaluation. But description itself can be problematic. For instance, for some observers the essential fact about the statue of a Confederate general in a town square is that that person fought for the Confederacy. To others, the statue symbolizes universal (not Southern) leadership or loyalty. To a leftist, the statue is an abomination because it glorifies war; to a rightist, the statue is an abomination because it is covered with pigeon droppings. A teenager tuned in to a Sony Walkman may find the statue boring because its inscription is too flowery, while the geologist standing next to him may be fascinated by the volcanic traces in the rock quarried for the statue. Thus, if we can be unsure what a thing (like a statue) is or what its most central feature is (its Southernness?, its geological qualities?), then finding the essential nature of anything as dynamic as a rhetorical exchange becomes even more difficult.

Because of the complexity of rhetoric, it makes sense initially to (1) isolate and (2) list a message's main ideas. This chapter will present two techniques for doing so, each of which has these benefits:

1. *Analyzing ideas tells what is present and what is not.* A strange proposition, at first, but an important one. By examining a persuasive text, we confront the speaker's final set of ideas, the speaker's best guess of what could be said in the rhetorical situation at hand. But the ideas *not* chosen can also be informative, even though this presents something of a dilemma for the critic: Whereas the message itself records what was said, what was not said obviously includes everything else potentially sayable. Harold Hill talked of pool tables, but he did not talk of inflation or medieval weaponry or plane geometry or cabbages or kings. The solution to the critic's dilemma is obviously to discover what *important* things Harold Hill did not say. Accordingly, this chapter includes a "universal" list of idea-types for the critic's use. This is not a perfect solution. After all, no list of anything human can ever be exhaustive, and anything that is listlike can become artificial. But the benefits seem to outweigh the liabilities, and so our universal list will be recommended for use.

2. *Analyzing ideas alerts us to rhetorical patterns.* Throughout this book, the critic will be urged to pay special attention to patterns of ideas. Even though exceptions to patterns can be important, the concept of exception makes no sense apart from the concept of pattern. As a result, there is a sense in which all critics are mathematicians,

because, whether they are aware of it or not, they count things when making discriminations. For example, a critic may say, "The speaker's use of language was brilliant." (Translation: "Compared to a group of speakers, this speaker deviated substantially from the mean on a number of language variables.") The point here is not to make the critic sound like some sort of crazed scientist but to dramatize how much the critic depends on perceptions of rhetorical pattern and how often, knowingly or unknowingly, the critic makes statements of proportion: for example, "I was surprised that the speaker ignored the budgetary argument." (Translation: "Given the amount of time most people spend talking about money, spending this much time on aesthetics seems out of the norm.") But even though critics depend on rhetorical patterns, they do not always acknowledge this dependence, nor do they always document their claims about matters of proportion. The critical techniques in this chapter can improve upon that condition.

3. *Analyzing ideas helps to explain rhetorical "tone."* A word like "tone" almost always appears in quotation marks. Tone is the sort of thing that all persons feel but few can describe. Tone is like other phrases that also appear in quotation marks, phrases referring to the "feeling state" or "emotional residue" or "psychic power" of a message. Placing such phrases in quotation marks is not so much to disparage them as it is to admit critical defeat: We know tone when we see it, but few of us can talk about it intelligently. And yet even though the tone of a message can be hard to describe, it is often not hard to identify. For example, when students of criticism were asked to describe the Hill speech as well as the Prinz and Patton speeches discussed in Chapter Three, they did so with ease and with impressive unanimity. When asked to position these speeches on the scales presented in Figure 4.1, their agreement approached 90 percent.

As is often the case with tone, the students could not be shaken in their judgments of these speeches, but they were hard pressed to state *explicitly* how they knew what they knew. However, by stepping back a bit, by taking the time to sketch the flow of ideas, by using standard idea-lists to describe the messages being examined, and by asking the question constantly "What, specifically, is telling me what I know to be the case?", the students became more precise. One ancient, simple technique they used was to translate the texts into their own language via outlining, thereby derhetoricalizing what the speaker had made rhetorical. This chapter will present more ambitious techniques, thereby giving the critic a **technical language** for discussing the hard-to-discuss. Such techniques are no cure-all, but they can advance the scholarly discussion and that is the spirit in which they are offered here.

Figure 4.1
Scales for Describing Rhetorical Tone

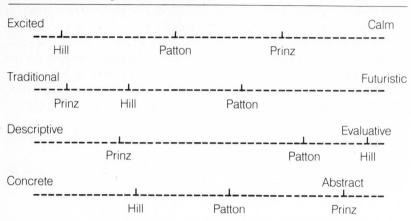

A TOPICAL APPROACH TO IDEAS

Nobody knows precisely where ideas come from—or why some ideas bubble to the surface of public discussion more often than others. And yet our daily experiences require us to establish priorities about ideas. The person described as having a "personality problem," for example, is often just a person with an "idea problem"—that is, one who thinks differently from us. Travel to a foreign country can be difficult for the same reason. The impatient American who drums her fingers on the table of the Roman cafe while waiting for service learns that some ideas (like efficiency) are not revered equally in all cultures. Indeed, the very concept of "culture" is a shorthand designation for groups of people who prefer the same kinds of ideas and who go to the same sorts of places to find new ones.

At times, it may seem as if there are as many ideas in the world as there are people. The proof of this is found each day in the pages of the *National Inquirer,* a journal that specializes in the idiosyncratic ("Boy marries great aunt," "Honors students dismembers algebra teacher"). But there is a *predictable* idiosyncracy to the stories published in the *National Inquirer,* as if the editors rewrote the same stories each week, changing only the names and locations of the aunts and algebra teachers mentioned. Such constancy implies that the millions of individual stories in the world derive from a limited number of "master stories." This chapter assumes that there are sixteen places from which such stories are drawn. This chapter also assumes that knowing about these places increases a critic's sensitivity to rhetorical ideas.

RHETORIC AND SOCIAL PROTEST

Critical Profile 4.1   Name-Calling in Public Places: The Birth of a Nation

The city of Philadelphia is popularly regarded as the center of revolutionary sentiment in the decade prior to the American Revolution. But the Philadelphia of the 1760s was a very different city indeed. Its citizens were prosperous and emotionally attached to "Mother England." Nevertheless, the citizens of Philadelphia became swept into a fever of revolution by the forces of rhetoric in a relatively short period of time. As Stephen Lucas of the University of Wisconsin points out, prerevolutionary Philadelphia was a city marked by its communication structure. That system of communication included several newspapers with Whig sentiments, efficient printing, and easy distribution of pamphlets and broadsides, as well as a tradition honoring vigorous public discussion. All of these factors proved crucial in the development of a spirit of questioning, or protest, and, later, of revolution in the City of Brotherly Rhetoric.

To effect such changes in Philadelphia required protesters to engage the city's "large and aggressive middle-class," "the most important audience for Philadelphia protesters." Using all of the available communication channels, the leaders of the revolution brought Philadelphia into the protest by first identifying an enemy and then objectifying and vilifying it. By making the enemy personal, the leaders of the rebellion were able to attract the leading citizens of Philadelphia where they might otherwise have failed. As rhetorical strategies, objectification and vilification are, according to Lucas, "ways of identifying adversaries, affixing blame, and enlarging the distance between the enemy and the protesters." The strategies both personalized and distanced the opposition. For instance, a description of the British General George Gage as "a common highwayman . . . who perpetuates a robbery upon the property and liberty of a whole province" depicts a particular villain, both naming and portraying him in the darkest terms possible. Objectification also creates a plural enemy from vilified individuals. "The rhetoric of protest in Philadelphia was replete with denunciations of vague but 'powerful legislative usurpers,' 'a lordly faction at home,'" and so on. By envisioning such a larger-than-life enemy, Philadelphians were able to see the "struggle with England [as one] between good and evil."

The success of revolutionary rhetoric in Philadelphia points up an often overlooked issue: No rhetoric can be successful without an efficient delivery system. Lucas makes this clear by showing the relationship between rhetoric and the mass media systems present in Philadelphia. For those who think that the mass media only began to influence politics during the Vietnam era, they need to think back anew on the country's founding days. Even then, mass sentiment was a function of mass messages mass-ively consumed.

Profiled by: Donald Nobles
Citation: Lucas (1976)

Critical Profile 4.2   In Rhetoric, Winning Isn't Everything

Social movements do not always succeed. As a matter of fact, the social movement that attains all of its objectives is a historical rarity. But James Andrews of Indiana University warns that we should not assume that a failed social movement had no rhetorical effect. Every social movement arises in a context and, somehow, the rhetoric of that movement will alter its context—often in not obvious ways. To illustrate his point, Andrews examined the Chartist movement, a social movement that failed in Victorian England but that nevertheless left its historical mark.

The Chartists were radical democrats attempting to reform the aristocratic English Parliament in the 1830s. The Chartists drew their name from the "People's Charter," which called for universal male suffrage, the ballot, elimination of property qualifications for members of Parliament, payment of members of Parliament, and other provisions that were intended to increase the power of the unpropertied working class. Although these demands may seem mild to us, in Dickens's England the Chartist program was considered radical.

The movement failed to reform the government. The ruling classes responded with a counter-rhetoric that defended property and the traditional aristocratic institutions. The House of Commons defeated a proposal to consider the Charter by a vote of 235 to 46. The Chartists themselves suffered from internal dissension over the question of their right to use force to achieve their ends. By the 1850s, "the Chartists decisively lost their hold on the main body of the working class."

But this failed movement had affected its larger social scene. Other reforms of the period that benefited the lower classes, such as the repeal of the Corn Laws, the shortening of the work day, and the reform of the Poor Law, "were secured under the pressure of the torchlight meetings, the riots, insurrectionary plots and strikes of Chartism." In addition, the Chartists "left a rhetorical legacy." Later labor movements in England had as resources "a memory of strategies which failed," "a stock of arguments to be exploited in other ways," and above all "the example of working-class leadership." For better or worse, the political and rhetorical scene in England was permanently altered by the Chartist movement. Even though it failed to meet its short-term goals, the movement opened up a new area of public dialogue and stands as eloquent testimony that even losers affect history.

Profiled by: Jim Mackin
Citation: Andrews (1973)

Ever since persuasion has been studied, scholars have been interested in the common themes of public discourse. The ancient Greeks thought of these traditional themes (they called them *topoi*) as the ideas underlying all ideas; similarly, the ancient Romans conceived of a limited set of commonplaces capable of "housing" all conceivable argu-

---

Critical Profile 4.3   Hard Questions, Easy Answers

Is it ever justifiable to violate a moral code to accomplish a pragmatic good? For example, if abortion is murder, should a woman who conceives after being raped have the right to abort the fetus? For many people this question promises a painful journey into ethical relativism. For others, the answer is, categorically, no: ". . . even the first small step away from principle is a complete change of direction after which all other steps are but inevitable downward progressions." We have here a rhetoric of ascent toward (and descent from) moral innocence, a powerful theme underlying anti-abortion rhetoric. Randall A. Lake of the University of Southern California used the parallel vocabularies of theology ("words about God"), deontology ("words about moral obligation"), and logology ("words about words") to illuminate the characteristic ascent-descent pattern of anti-abortion rhetoric.

Anti-abortion rhetoric argues in quasi-syllogistic form: "Thou shalt not kill innocent beings. A fetus is an innocent being. Therefore abortion (which kills a fetus) is murder and hence always wrong." This argument, based on abstract rules of conduct rather than a concern for what is possible, is stated in deontological form. In deontological ethics, priority is placed on avoiding evil rather than on doing good, and moral behavior is enacted simply by obeying preordained rules. Thus, good *intentions* do not mitigate rule violations. When deontology is combined with theology, the source of rules is identified as God, whose inflexible code shall be obeyed regardless of practical consequence. Logology, Kenneth Burke's term for the study of relationships among terms within a vocabulary, parallels deontology in its emphasis on the hortatory negative ("thou shalt not") and its descriptions of Order (pious obedience) and Disorder (impious dissent). According to Lake, anti-abortion rhetoric utilizes a theological/deontological vocabulary and is thus particularly well-suited to analysis through logology.

In anti-abortion rhetoric, the fetus is a "perfect" child, innocent and, because not yet born, unfallen. The circumstances of conception are thus irrelevant. Because abortion is total victimization of a perfect victim, it is emblematic of the depths to which humanity has plunged in its willful disobedience of the Order of God's creation. Anti-abortion activists feel that social repudiation of abortion would be a reversal of this direction. It would replace the despair engendered by humanity's descent into degradation with the hope of ascendent adherence to moral law. In joyous reaffirmation of God's Order, anti-abortion activists battle that behavior which "shortcircuits Redemption, imposing Disorder upon the world in perpetuity." Traditionally, the American people have never been attracted for long to a rhetoric so sure of its premises. Still, one wonders if they will ultimately make an exception for a rhetoric that deals so centrally with the essence of life itself.

Profiled by: Elizabeth Macom
Citation: Lake (1984)

ments. Two thousand years ago, to be trained in persuasion was to be trained in how to fashion public arguments from these ideas-behind-all-ideas. More recently, Wilson and Arnold [1974] identified a useful list of **universal topics** from which most ideas derive. Their claim is that some variation on these topical themes can be found in any public or private message. Say Wilson and Arnold [p. 76]:

> For a good many centuries scholars argued that people talk on a fairly limited number of themes, that they vary the treatments of basic ideas but not the basic ideas themselves. You need not hear or read many speeches or essays to see that these thinkers were right. We all discuss the same general types of ideas over and over. This is not a sign of laziness, it is the natural result of the kinds of things people feel they need talk to each other about. We all discuss and argue chiefly about human affairs, and the ways you can think about human affairs are limited within any culture. The result is that we can actually predict in advance many of the categories of thought any talker will use. . . .

Throughout history, topical systems like Wilson and Arnold's have been used as autosuggestive or cueing devices to help students invent ideas for speaking or writing. Rather than being asked to "just think" about a given subject matter, for example, students have been given a list of topics to help stimulate their imaginations. Research by Nelson [1970] found that such devices significantly increased the number and effectiveness of ideas students generated when preparing rhetorical messages. But systematic use of these universal topics in criticism has not been as common, even though such a system can be helpful to the critic for these reasons: (1) It is a reasonably *complete* way of categorizing persuasive arguments; (2) it is a simple and efficient method of *reducing* a message to its essential rhetorical character; (3) because it is a fixed system, it can help reveal *patterns* of argument that might not have been noticed otherwise; and (4) it allows the critic to make *proportional* statements about the themes of a given message.

Listed below are the sixteen universal topics Wilson and Arnold have isolated in their studies. Next to each are examples (from Hart, et al. [1983:452–453]) of how the topic might be developed in a hypothetical argument by a hypothetical Surgeon General discussing the not-so-hypothetical problem of hearing disorders:

1. Existence or nonexistence of things ("Over 50 percent of the elderly have hearing disorders; workers in a noisy environment are especially prone to hearing problems.").
2. Degree or quantity of things ("Hearing problems can range from mild ringing in the ears to total deafness and even death.").

3. Spatial attributes, including adjacency, distribution, place ("There is an intimate connection between brain and ear; the ear covers only a small area of the body but magnifies sound incredibly.").

4. Temporal attributes, including hour, day, year, era ("One can lose hearing overnight; many middle-ear infections occur between 4 and 7 years of age.").

5. Motion or activity ("Fast movement can cause dizziness because of inner-ear problems; rapidly moving sound waves can cause temporary loss of hearing.").

6. Form, either physical shape or abstract categories ("Some hearing losses result from inner ear versus outer ear problems.").

7. Substance, physical or abstract; the fundamental nature of a thing, often signaled by definitions ("The roots of hearing loss sometimes lie in basic, psychological trauma.").

8. Capacity to change, including predictability ("The inner ear can improve itself; surgery can correct middle-ear damage.").

9. Potency, power, or energy, including capacity to further or hinder something ("Hearing problems can make us unable to discriminate any sort of speech.").

10. Desirability, in terms of rewards or punishments ("Audiological difficulties hinder social interactions and can adversely affect employment opportunities.").

11. Feasibility, workability, or practicability ("Auditory training can be established for those with residual hearing problems; lip reading training is also possible in some cases.").

12. Causality, the relationship of causes to effects, effect to effects, adequacy of causes, etc. ("Abnormal growths in the ear cause problems; high fever and infection can also cause damage.").

13. Correlation, coexistence or coordination of things, forces ("Hearing difficulties can be related to viral diseases.").

14. Genus-species relationships ("Hearing specialists are an important part of the larger medical community.").

15. Similarity or dissimilarity ("There is sometimes a distinction between the hearing problems of older people and those that affect children.").

16. Possibility or impossibility ("The inner ear cannot be corrected by surgery, but hearing aids can provide some measure of relief.").

When using this list of universal topics for criticism, students have found these guidelines to be helpful: (1) Work with two or three other critics, designating each member of the team a "specialist" on four or five of the universal topics; (2) proceed through the message on a statement-by-statement basis, with relevant members of the critical team making "bids" for "ownership" of individual statements; (3) assign each statement to no more than two of the categories listed; if uncertainties develop (and they will) delay resolving them until the entire message has been inspected; (4) if disagreement persists after thorough discussion of problematic statements, assign the statement to multiple categories on a proportional basis. Classroom exercises using these techniques have shown that these categories can be learned fairly quickly and that after only a few group experiences students can master the system and then use it in their own critical projects. The goal here is surely *not* to develop scientific precision but simply to provide a rough "topical translation" of the message being inspected.

While this approach seems to make sense theoretically, the worth of any critical system lies in its utility. Accordingly, Table 4.1 presents the topical sketches that student critics developed of the Prinz and Patton speeches presented in Chapter Two and the Hill speech presented earlier in this chapter. When doing their work, the students asked (1) which topics were used? (2) which were not? and (3) why?

Clearly, the three passages present very different profiles. But before discussing the differences, the similarities should be noted, the most dramatic of which is that all three speakers used correlation quite often. Given the different speech situations they faced, what could such a finding mean? Most likely, it suggests that each speaker felt the need to be something of a bridge-builder, perhaps because each was in some sense an outsider. Harold Hill's case is an obvious one. He spends much of his time linking pool halls and sin in the first part of

Table 4.1   Comparative Use of Universal Topics

Universal Topics	Rabbi Prinz	Harold Hill	George Patton
Existence	2	14	5
Degree	9	7	6
Spatial	6	9	3
Time	10	11	2
Motion	5	11	5
Form	0	0	2
Substance	18	0	13
Capacity to change	5	2	4
Potency	8	7	6
Desirability	7	28	7
Feasibility	0	1	9
Causality	4	7	13
Correlation	9	8	13
Genus-species	5	0	0
Similarity-dissimilarity	8	1	4
Possibility-impossibility	4	1	9

his speech and, later, linking musical instruments with virtue. It is probably the obviousness of these strained linkages that makes us smile as we easily uncover Hill's deviousness. *We* can see that Hill is "using" these good Iowans by appropriating their values and anxieties for his mercantile purposes. But it is also true that Hill's status as a geographical outsider left him with little choice other than to be a builder of bridges. Sloth and degradation, frittering and corruption, medicinal wine and riotous living—disingenuous correlations for a seller of band instruments, but not unlike those still used weekly at many a religious crusade.

Rabbi Prinz was not so much a geographical outsider as he was a cultural outsider, and so he too offered equations: of Jewish and black ghettos, of Jewish and Christian morality, of Old World and New World dreams. His correlations are more uplifting than Hill's, but in some ways they are remarkably similar. Both took the "high road" morally, Prinz because he was a cleric, Hill because he was a conniver. And George Patton's exalted status made him an outsider of sorts as well, one presumably removed from the life of the everyday soldier. As a general among generals, Patton had to demonstrate clear relationships between the war he was fighting and the war he expected his men to fight. His equations were graphic in their simplicity: the Army life and the sporting life; dehumanization and German militarization; American virtue and all virtue.

To a lesser extent, all three speakers made use of potency, motion, degree, and desirability. They did so because each in his own way was a highly energized persuader with a message to share and a grand new world to describe. Harold Hill's world included a powerful army of young people striding splendidly down Main Street, virtuous and energetic young people marching toward the good (and carrying his band instruments). General Patton, too, paints a vibrant picture—of strong, active soldiers doing strong, active things, overcoming a vicious and morally bankrupt enemy. Although he is less histrionic than either Hill or Patton, Rabbi Prinz takes pains to link degree ("the most urgent, the most disgraceful, the most shameful, and the most tragic problem") with potency ("a glorious, unshakable reality in a morally united America") in order to pound home his themes of justice and equality for all.

All three speakers were activists and their rhetoric reflects that fact. But none was a college lecturer and hence none spent time detailing abstract, structural relationships (form or genus-species relationships). Also, because each speaker meant to begin dialogue on the matters they treated rather than to nail down practical policies, they generally avoided discussion of such sticky issues as how change would be implemented, at what price, with what difficulties, and how soon. Other speakers on other occasions would tackle these detailed issues, they seemed to reason.

In this sense, Harold Hill was the classic salesperson: long on promises and short on application. Notice that he develops a 28:1 ratio of desirability to feasibility, not at all unlike the sales pitch for the power mower delivered weekly in the Sears Garden Shop. In the rousing conclusion to his speech, for example, Hill links the soon-to-be River City Boys Band to Maine, Plymouth Rock, and the Golden Rule, but he never mentions the price of a piccolo. Hill also spends considerably more time on the topic of existence than the other speakers, perhaps because he had a problem: He had no problem. That is, there was no good, compelling reason for the quiet folks in River City, Iowa, to have their collective ears assaulted by the screeches of adolescent music-making (and to pay good money for the privilege of doing so). Harold Hill knew this, and he also knew that the motivating "problem" had to be a major one. So he used what he had—a pool hall—and he willed that shameful instance into a universal sin. His speech is thus really two speeches, with existence dominating the first and desirability the second.

Rabbi Prinz made the bravest attempt of all three speakers at capacity to change ("America must speak up and act from the President down to the humblest of us"), but his attempt is still modest, perhaps because his primary rhetorical purpose was to set up the magnificent oration of Martin Luther King, Jr., immediately following, an address that would amply discuss such themes. It is also noteworthy that the rabbi completely eschewed feasibility, perhaps because to raise such matters would take more time than he was allotted, perhaps because a discussion of pragmatics would have been inappropriate in a ceremonial setting, or perhaps because the civil rights movement was then in its infancy and nobody knew exactly *how* human justice could be achieved. Given such limitations, the rabbi was wise to stick with substance. He spent most of his time defining key concepts like dignity, the American idea, neighborliness, silence, hatred, and morality. Such a scholarly (Talmudic?) approach cost the rabbi Harold Hill's energy and George Patton's assuredness, but it no doubt helped him play the part he was intended to play at the March on Washington.

A somewhat different tone emerges in the Patton speech. Patton used some amount of feasibility and possibility, no doubt because a desirable but unfeasible or impossible speech would hardly have been motivating to men about to enter battle. More subtly, however, he also stressed causality, explicitly telling his men which actions would produce which effects ("Every man in the mess hall, even the one who heats the water to keep us from getting diarrhea, has a job to do"). A causally driven speech like Patton's is indeed heartening. It is clean, clear, linear, pragmatic, and thoroughly Western in its philosophical orientation. Such a speech raises no question (for example, cowardice, defeat) that it does not also answer. Patton begins his speech with causal patterns (hard work produces athletic success) and he ends it in the same way (bravery under fire insures immortality in the eyes of one's grandson).

Equally interesting is Patton's use of substance. It is this topic that distinguishes Patton's remarks from persuasion heralding surefire success or a money-back guarantee. The substance of which Patton speaks is bravery and patriotism. Placed alone in a speech, such matters could have produced empty abstractions. And, indeed, there is a real sermonic quality to Patton's statement, with only Rabbi Prinz (at 18 percent) surpassing him on substance. The thing that makes Patton's speech so interesting is that he manages to run both theoretical *and* practical themes against one another, with the former whetting listeners' appetites and the latter insuring them sustenance. The result is a great amount of rhetorical energy, perhaps explaining why students were so ambivalent when describing the tone of Patton's speech (see Figure 4.1).

As mentioned earlier, the statements in a verbal text indicate where a speaker *ended* thought about the subject at hand. But that is only part of the story. It is also important to know where a speaker *began* looking for thoughts. Topical analysis lets the critic look "beneath" words to find the essential places from which those words emanated. Because it focuses on such basic matters, topical analysis is particularly useful for examining public controversies, arenas in which people often talk past one another precisely because they have *begun* their arguments in different places. Imagine, for example, how rancorous discussion could become between a speaker who operated from feasibility ("let's do it this way because it will work") and another who operated from substance ("let's do it this way because people must be protected from their baser natures"). According to Einhorn [1981], that is precisely the situation in which John Madison and Patrick Henry found themselves during the Virginia ratification debates, with Madison arguing on the basis of practicality and Henry arguing philosophically. Wiethoff [1981] found contrary premises also operating during the Roman Catholic Church's debate over the use of vernacular during church services, while Medhurst [1985] implies that the public argument between conservatives and the rest of society often hinges on different rhetorical treatments of desirability and feasibility.

Several studies have used ideational analysis to explain the success or failure of individual speakers or movements. Solomon [1983], for example, implies that the STOP ERA movement could not get past the universal topic of dissimilarity. Because it had based virtually all of its rhetoric on the supposed differences between men and women, the movement could not engage in meaningful dialogue with feminists who operated from similarity. More important, the movement could not secure the cooperation of nonideologues, people concerned with more practical matters like desirability, feasibility, possibility, etc. As Zyskind [1968] has shown, desirability and feasibility are the hardiest rhetorical topics in American cultural history. Any movement that cannot deploy such arguments must probably resign itself to marginal status.

An interesting study by Kaufer [1980] showed how some speakers habitually operate from the same topical premises no matter what the rhetorical situation. Kaufer studied Clarence Darrow's famed defense of Loeb and Leopold during their trial in the early 1920s (they were accused of having wantonly killed a fourteen-year-old). According to Kaufer, Darrow was remarkably consistent in his use of causality, arguing that mercy should be shown to Loeb and Leopold because their cultural and psychological upbringing (the cause) left them no choice but to commit the crime they did (the effect). In a sense, Darrow asked for a guilty verdict against society and mercy for the defendants (who were both wealthy and well educated). Kaufer notes that Darrow's persistent use of causality even in such a preposterous situation revealed the depths of Darrow's commitment to what is now known as behaviorism, a philosophy that still undergirds much political and judicial decision making in the United States today.

The topical approach is only one of many ways of examining ideas. Also, such a general approach only begins the process of criticism. But being somewhat systematic when first approaching a text has its uses. After all, one of the most perplexing things about doing criticism is knowing where to start. The suggestion made here is that critics should start their criticism where persuaders start their persuasion.

A JUDGMENTAL APPROACH TO IDEAS

The topical approach for describing ideas tends to be speaker-oriented. A second approach is Arnold's [1974], which focuses on the judgments *audiences* are asked to make by a speaker. Arnold's approach is based on these assumptions: (1) When speakers speak, they assume that audiences will make judgments about their remarks; (2) a verbal text is a record of the kinds of judgments audiences are being asked to make; (3) a text records only the *potential*, not the actual, judgments audiences make; (4) because rhetorical occasions are often standardized, there are a limited number of *classic* judgmental requests.

RHETORIC AND MODERN SCIENCE

Critical Profile 4.4   Science and Scientism: The "Spocking" of America?

The study of rhetoric is the study of contingent issues. How should the national debt be handled? Should affirmative action programs be eliminated? How should the AIDS epidemic be dealt with? These and other questions are debated in Congress, in the White House, and in the national media. Such questions are never analytically "solved" as in mathematics, but are, rather, collectively "settled." Lately, however, Thomas Lessl of the University of Georgia has identified a change in the nation's problem-solving style—the rise of scientism. "Science out of context is scientism," says Lessl, "a faith in the supremacy of scientific methods, the belief that scientific methods are applicable to the solution of all questions or that all questions are scientific questions."

Lessl's conclusions are drawn from his study of the rhetoric of public scientists who have spoken on behalf of the American space program. His study concludes that "the public scientist subtly, but definitely, recreates the world in the image of science." These interpretations have led to a change in the ideological character of the American public. Now, says Lessl, when public problems are examined as scientific problems, the moral questions that have always been central to rhetoric are made to seem irrelevant. He points out that America's response to increased teenage sexual activity, for example, has been to treat it "as a technical problem to be resolved through training in the various methods of birth prevention." Because of the scientism surrounding them, politicians and educators are reluctant to propose ethical or moral instruction even as an adjunct to "technical information."

Scientism not only ignores key elements of public decision-making but also distorts the true process of science and invites false confidence in what technology can produce. Lessl cites the arms race as an instance where "Instead of each side seeking disarmament which would be the appropriate response to the acknowledged immorality and futility of nuclear arsenals, the superpowers seek a new kind of futility, some new technology [like 'Star Wars'] that will undermine the nuclear threat."

In selling science, space advocates often sound like entrepreneurs, featuring scientific "spinoffs" in their rhetoric rather than scientific exploration itself. This makes strategic sense, since it takes money as well as brains to make a rocket ship. Lessl notes that science and capitalism, though apparently different, share a love of accumulation, "something less pejoratively called 'progress.'" And so we find a paradox here: Although scientistic rhetoric is unscientific, it is eminently useful in public debate. Thus, for economic as well as rhetorical reasons, even Pure Science has come to depend on the charms of its bastard cousin–New Age Scientism.

Profiled by: John Llewellyn
Citation: Lessl (1985)

Critical Profile 4.5   Nuclear Energy: Amateurs Need Not Apply

An early advocate described it as "a healthy horse" and added that there was no need to change the horse but rather to change the track from "a steeplechase to a well prepared fast, flat oval." A day at the races? No, a more weighty issue, one which has been a matter of contention since it burst into public consciousness with the use of the first atomic weapon in 1945. Nuclear power—a fundamentally uncontrollable force or a farm animal to be "hitched up" and put to work? This question, so central to the debate over the use of nuclear power as an energy source, has plagued the American people for over forty years and may well be the most important question of the millennium.

Michael Vickery of Texas A & M University examined the rhetoric of pro-nuclear advocates to determine how they argued for the acceptance of nuclear power. He discovered two primary arguments in such rhetoric, one of which claimed that the use of nuclear power to generate electricity was absolutely essential to sustain "the comforts and luxuries that go with the progressive society we have created." The second theme, called forth by nuclear "accidents," was that nuclear power could be mastered. The Three Mile Island incident in 1979 was labeled "instructive" by these nuclear advocates who employed a circular logic: From the accident, scientists had learned enough to correct any further flaws. The accident at Chernobyl in 1983 hardly daunted them either; it merely proved that *American* safety measures were sound.

These arguments fall under the larger rhetorical strategy Jacques Ellul has called *technique*. The rhetoric of technique presumes the existence of "experts" who measure progress and declare it good for a technologically naive public. These same experts profess the *inherent* ability to extricate the country from any problems created by an intrusive natural world or by the nuclear industry's inevitable technical mistakes. Although the rhetoric of technique is initially encouraging to people, Vickery argues, it is ultimately impenetrable, "a rhetoric which subjugates all questions . . . to the mechanistic imperative to use things." In an increasingly technological world, the inability of average citizens to question the goodness of public policy matters renders them politically and socially helpless, incapable of moral argument, able only to endorse technical solutions to technical problems. This death of moral argument, notes Vickery, is exemplified in a statement issued by the Boy Scouts of America in support of the use of nuclear power. The statement concluded that "in the United States we have laws to protect people from being exposed to radiation." The trends Vickery found in pronuclear rhetoric clearly disturb him. He warns that if we become trapped in a technical system whereby law becomes the handmaiden of science and where industry serves as the patron of education, moral argument will be reduced to a faint, irrelevant curiosity from yesterday's yesterday.

Profiled by: Kerry L. Strayer
Citation: Vickery (1988)

Critical Profile 4.6   The Rhetoric of Controlled Panic

"And that's the way it was," Walter Cronkite used to intone at the end of each night's newscast, and millions of Americans switched off their television sets, confident that they were adequately informed about the news of the day. But observers have noted that something changed in 1979 when an accident occurred at the Three Mile Island nuclear power plant in Pennsylvania: For five days, millions of Americans went to bed wondering if they were going to wake up the next morning.

In "a world where the public is forced to endure an unsteady relationship with technology and the environment," where even the experts do not know the answers and where mass panic could cause thousands of deaths—how do newscasters and scientists decide what and how to tell the public about a technological disaster? After reviewing reports of the TMI accident, Thomas Farrell and G. Thomas Goodnight of Northwestern University concluded that current media practices are inadequate. "Whatever or whoever was to blame [at TMI], the net result was failed communication."

But if the scientific establishment and the nightly news cannot be trusted to get the story straight, who can? After all, most people like to think that even though they may not understand the complicated issues facing them, *someone* does and that someone is acting decisively. Generally speaking, the American people do not know how to handle ambiguity. Interestingly, say the authors, neither do the mass media.

If there was a hero during the TMI crisis, it might well have been Pennsylvania Governor Richard Thornburgh, who spoke and acted decisively even though he knew less about the situation than did the conflicting experts. Few Americans doubted his decision to evacuate the area near the disaster. Thornburgh was willing to take a clear position in the face of an ambiguous, potentially fatal, situation and, equally important, he knew how to make his position seem authoritative. But Farrell and Goodnight's research raises several vexing questions for those who did not follow Thornburgh's lead. Given the complexity and potential dangers of today's technologies, can Americans afford to be ignorant of conflicting scientific opinion on a given issue? If they choose ignorance, might they now be betting their lives on their decisions as never before? If, on the other hand, people become fully informed, might the "enlightened panic" that results create an even more dangerous condition than that created by collective ignorance? Can experts and politicians, on the other hand, be taught how to communicate effectively about modern technologies? Can a society create a rhetoric that has never before existed, a rhetoric that helps people understand life in a technological world? And if such a rhetoric is developed, will it make people dangerously susceptible to authority figures? Nuclear technologies are new. Nuclear rhetorics are even newer. At Three Mile Island, both proved to be frighteningly fragile.

Profiled by: Nancy Roth
Citation: Farrell and Goodnight (1981)

In building his system, Arnold catalogued these standard rhetorical occasions and concluded that four arguments predominate in the social world: What is empirically true? What is morally correct? What makes us happy? How should we proceed? Arnold reasoned further that most rhetorical statements reflect one or more of these "stock" issues" and thus that all statements radiate from one of four classic judgmental requests. Modified a bit they are:

1. *Factual:* Statements that ask listeners to consult the world around them when judging the speaker's remarks. Such consultations can be focused on the past ("John Adams was the second U.S. president"), the present ("Nobody beats the prices at Acme"), or the future ("Let's meet for dinner in Boston next Tuesday"). Because these statements occur in rhetorical texts, they often do not meet a scientist's rigorous standards of factuality. Rather, they are treated as commonsense facts. Thus, even a controversial statement like "The United States is second to Japan in technological know-how" is treated as a factual request, because the listener is being encouraged to consult real-world conditions when judging the speaker's assertion.

2. *Optative:* Statements that ask listeners to consult their own general wishes and preferences or those of their social grouping when judging the speaker's remarks. Unlike factual statements, optative requests have a clearly evaluative flavor. The values undergirding them include taste ("New Yorkers are too pushy for me"), efficiency ("Georgians take too long to get things done"), beauty ("Ohioans let themselves get too heavy"), or practicality ("Californians are completely unrealistic"). The obviousness of these evaluations often differs sharply ("She seems nice" versus "What a great person!"), but Arnold's system does not require making subtle distinctions about such matters.

3. *Adjudicative:* Statements that ask listeners to consult some sort of formally proclaimed code of behavior when judging the speaker's remarks. Adjudicatives are judgmental neighbors to optatives, since both are evaluative. But when a speaker makes adjudicative requests, the speaker asks that formal, institutional (often written) standards be consulted mentally before passing judgment. Such codes are normally more specific and rigid than the more general optative standards. The specifications they make can include law ("The accused has committed a heinous crime, your Honor"), religion ("The Bible fully endorses tithing, my children"), etiquette ("One should never kiss on the first date"), or political ideology ("The true spirit of communism denounces this practice, comrades").

Over time, subgroups of people often transform general, optative standards into adjudicative ones so that some sort of dogma results. For example, the "Miss America Code" replaces for beauty contestants what normally serves as general standards of propriety for the rest of us. The "IBM Doctrine" replaces general notions of efficiency for Big Blue's new employees. The "scientific procedure" is ingrained in young chemists, replacing their earlier standards of ordinary carefulness. To become indoctrinated is to learn to use such codes when making decisions. Knowing such things, and knowing that code-based judgments are often more reliable than more general wishes and preferences, persuaders are strongly attracted to adjudicative statements.

4. *Promissory:* Statements that ask listeners to consult their hopes and dreams when judging the remarks of the speaker. Promissory statements (or, as Arnold calls them, predictive of desirability statements) explicitly or implicitly detail the positive consequences of adopting a new attitude or standard of behavior. Rhetorical messages often differ dramatically in how clearly they explicate the good that will result from speaker/listener agreement. In some persuasion, for example, the promises are bold and unmistakable but fairly sketchy ("10.8% home loans at Bank of America. They've never been lower"), while other forms of persuasion (for example, a brochure for a resort hotel) detail the wonders that await the tourist. The promises in yet other rhetoric are all too clear: "Miller Lite: less filling, tastes great." In still other cases (for example, perfume advertising), factuals and optatives fill the verbal text, while pictures (for example, a wind-swept beach in Bermuda) are used to hint at promises. Normally, then, "hard-sell" and "soft-sell" can be measured by calculating the (1) frequency, (2) explicitness, and (3) detail of the *verbal* promises made.

A helpful way of employing the judgmental approach is to catalog the individual statements making up a text, using the definitions and examples above as a guide. The experience of critics who have used this system suggests that in addition to the four "pure" types of judgments, most rhetorical messages will contain a good number of mixed statements. Often, it is the critic's ability to account for these mixed perceptions that makes Arnold's system especially useful. That is, while a statement like "I joined Nate's Health Spa" clearly makes a factual request, a statement from a commercial like "I joined Nate's Health Spa and lost 75 pounds in only one month" operates very differently. In the second (factual/promissory) statement, the speaker clearly implies "And you can too!" even though this statement never appears in the text itself. Intuitively, we "know" that the second statement differs markedly from the first, but it is initially hard to say exactly how the two statements differ. Arnold's system gives us a technical language for talking about such subtle, but undeniably important, differences in rhetorical texture.

Table 4.2 presents the eight most common types of judgmental requests along with brief commentary on their likely uses in persua-

Table 4.2   Some Common Types of Judgmental Requests

Judgment Type	Example	Use
1. Factual	"You can't get to Boise by airplane."	A workhorse strategy in persuasion. Used to establish substantiveness.
2. Optative	"It's not worth the paper it's written on."	Used to establish the desirability or undesirability of a claim.
3. Adjudicative	"Anyone who would say that is not a real American."	A "high-profile" strategy often used when the audience subscribes to a clear-cut code of right and wrong.
4. Promissory	"With Smith in our camp, we can't help but win the election."	A very obvious "pitch" in which a speaker delineates the forthcoming benefits of a proposal.
5. Factual/optative	"Mr. Jones told me that your work has been unsatisfactory lately."	Usually appears as (formal or informal) testimony. Used to substantiate evaluations offered.
6. Factual/adjudicative	"If you pursue this course of action, the Church will roundly condemn you."	A strategy that borrows the credibility of another code or institution in order to heighten the acceptability or unacceptability of a policy.
7. Optative/promissory	"Anyone as sweet as you will go places in this world."	Often used in "hard-sell" persuasion. Shows that the evaluation given means something (that is, it has observable consequences).
8. Factual/promissory	"Fred's high I.Q. will make him a great deal of money later in life."	A narrative approach that hopes that the listener will make a subtle transference to his or her life. Hints that if good things happened in Case A, they will also happen in Case B.

sion. While the individual critic may find even other judgmental combinations (especially as the often peculiar rhetorics of subgroups are examined), this list should be sufficient for most purposes. As with the topical system, the critic might proceed through a message statement by statement, noting which judgmental clusters develop, where in the message they are found, and which judgments are conspicuously absent or underrepresented. Especially when first trying out this system, it is useful to work in teams with other critics. However, the ideal methodology is for the critic to make these judgmental discriminations alone and only *later* compare notes with others. In that way, the perceptiveness of the individual analyst is buttressed by the breadth of group vision.

Students of criticism using the judgmental system have made several interesting points about the three speeches mentioned earlier. For example, they noted that the "military code" produced a number of adjudicative requests from Patton (for example, "this individuality stuff is a bunch of crap"), but that he warmed up his audience first by making a number of culturally sanctioned, optative requests (for example, "Americans traditionally love to fight"). Students who compared the real Patton speech to the movie version found 50 percent fewer factual requests in the latter, indicating that real soldiers need hard data, but that movie audiences are primarily interested in "color" (that is, in Patton's undeniably evaluative language).

Uses of promissory judgments differed radically from speech to speech, with virtually all of the latter half of the Patton speech being promissory, but virtually none of the statements in the Prinz speech being of this sort. Indeed, roughly 90 percent of Prinz's speech contained nothing but factuals and adjudicatives. Apparently, the rabbi saw his job as one of (factually) establishing the similarity between Jewish and black experience and then adjudicatively aligning the goals of the civil rights movement with appropriate religious and Constitutional mandates. The result is a somber tone (no optatives) as well as a sober tone (no promissories), both of which contrast sharply with Harold Hill's message. The first third of Hill's speech (the portion presented here earlier) is a salad of optative judgments based on simple pleasure ("the hours I spent with a cue in my hand are golden") or modes of relaxation ("Not a wholesome trottin' race. No!"). Warming to his subject, Hill piles in an equal assortment of adjudicative judgments in the second third of his speech ("We've . . . got to figure out a way to keep the young ones moral after school") and closes this segment with a stark adjudicative admonition: "That game with fifteen numbered balls is the Devil's tool." The final third of Hill's speech (the famous "Seventy-Six Trombones") is heavily promissory, as Hill marches his now-duped, soon-to-be customers all around the town square. The irony of the speech, of course, lies in the riotous *mixing* of optatives and adjudicatives as well as in Hill's presumptuous use of sacred codes for the selling of band instruments.

Having made these observations, however, can we say that the judgmental system is truly helpful? Does it promise more than critical jargon? There seem to be at least six major advantages to this approach:

1. *The system highlights speaker-audience relationships.* One of the first studies to use this system [Douglass and Arnold, 1970] found it to

be much less sterile than other critical procedures, because it forces the critic to pay attention to *social* realities and not just to the verbal eccentricities of a given message. By conceiving of a speaker as one who constantly makes requests of listeners, the critic is reminded again and again how cooperative communication must be if it is to succeed. Hart [1970] found, for example, that true believers (for example, American Communists or John Birch Society members) began and ended their messages with adjudicative arguments, sandwiching between them whatever facts of the day they were discussing. Because this pattern was so consistent, Hart concluded that all such speeches were designed to celebrate the truths these speakers and audiences shared. In contrast, speakers facing unfamiliar audiences made almost half of their requests on optative bases, since they could only depend upon audiences' general wishes and preferences. Intriguingly, speakers facing hostile listeners made twice as many promissory requests as most speakers, ostensibly because they were trying to "buy off" the hostility with hints of things to come.

2. *The system exposes patterns of rhetoric.* In Chapter Six, we will discuss generic studies of rhetoric, studies focusing on how certain messages can be grouped together in distinctive classes. Most of us are aware of these classes. Using such information, we sort each day's mail: personal letters, bills, charitable solicitations, and a large assortment of junk mail. But what rhetorical markers help us do the sorting? How, exactly, does a letter from Uncle Joshua differ from a letter from Uncle Sam? Most likely, Uncle Joshua loads his letter with factuals and optatives ("had a lovely day at the lake last week with your cousin Ben"), whereas Uncle Sam tends more toward the adjudicative ("the penalty for not replying to this notice within 30 days is . . ."). The coupon sent to us by Aunt Jemima, in contrast, is filled with promissories ("ten cents off on your next purchase," "best tasting syrup you've ever put on a pancake"). Often, clever persuaders try to transport the tone of one rhetorical class (for example, a revival meeting) to another situation (for example, a pitch for band instruments) so as to disguise their persuasive intentions. Using the judgmental system, the critic can become sensitive to the tonal features of these different rhetorical classes.

3. *The system identifies influential situational factors.* Most people know that the mass media have changed how persuasion operates, but what do those changes look like? What adaptations must a reporter make, for example, when relating a story to a television audience rather than writing it for the local paper? (More detailed factuals in the latter?) What is the essential rhetorical difference between a legal drama on television and an actual trial in the county courthouse? (Fewer dull adjudicatives in the former?) How will members of Congress change

their styles now that C-Span carries their spoken remarks live to almost every home in the United States? (More lively optatives?) Now that even out-of-the-way speeches by a presidential barnstormer can be videotaped and replayed for a national audience, how will campaign speeches change? (Less obvious promissories?) Because the judgmental system is so sensitive to changes in rhetorical tone, the system holds real promise for monitoring situational influences.

4. *The system increases sensitivity to ideology.* A real advantage of the Arnold system is that it distinguishes between optatives and adjudicatives, that is, between informal and institutionalized beliefs. As Hart [1971] and Clark [1977] found, religious and secular discourse often differ sharply, with the former depending on adjudicatives and the latter having to settle for optatives. Along a different line, Jablonski [1979a] discovered that even though many sociological changes swept through the Roman Catholic Church in the 1960s, the judgmental patterns in its rhetoric did not change, suggesting that *rhetorical* conservatism may inhibit philosophical radicalism. Campbell [1975] made a parallel discovery. He found that in order to escape theological censure for his new theory of evolution, Charles Darwin dramatically abandoned the scientific code (factuals + adjudicatives) at crucial points in his writing, often going off on highly personalized, moralistic, and sometimes even frankly nationalistic tangents in order to disguise the rather startling implications of his new theory. A reverse situation presented itself in a Jehovah's Witness's tract entitled "Are They Harmless Observances?" [1974] wherein the author attempted to prove (adjudicatively) that celebrations of Valentine's Day, May Day, and Mother's Day must be decried, because the Bible enjoins its readers to "quit touching the unclean thing." By comparing the use of formal and informal evaluations, then, the critic can often make uncommon discoveries about public discourse.

5. *The system helps explain rhetorical momentum.* Some messages seem to trudge along slowly, making their cases with deadly precision, while others fly by, dazzling the eye with rhetorical fireworks. Often, this latter effect is generated by linking one promissory statement after another, as we see in the following rather breathless piece of advertising:

> Ski. Mix. Meet. Vail is tall and tan and single and every night's like Friday. It's a swift track down an alpine bowl in tandem with that Austrian accent who rode up in the gondola with you. And helped with your bindings and gave you goose bumps.
> Vail is wineskins at noon at a romantic level called timberline. It's gaslight, fondue, and accordions. Discovery in a boutique. Youth. And experience that ages well. There's even a trail called Swingsville. . . .
> [Vail Resort, n.d.]

This excerpt might serve as a baseline against which all messages could be judged for momentum! Most texts do not contain such energy. From the studies done thus far, promissory statements comprise about 10 percent of the average public speech; normally, such statements are found in conclusions. The proportion in advertising is probably much higher; the ad from which the passage above was extracted approached 80 percent promissory statements. Often, the proportion of promissory statements in a message will be a good indicator of rhetorical subtlety, so the critic should be especially attentive to both the number and placement of these judgments. Developing sensitivity to rhetorical momentum can be the best ally of the critic interested in consumer protection.

6. *The system can be used to index cultural change.* Because the judgmental system is simple and yet suitably comprehensive, it helps detect alterations in rhetorical fashion. As we shall see in Chapter Ten, changing cultural values are often reflected in popular rhetoric. The judgmental critic can sometimes detect these changes ahead of time. For example, in 1987, McDonald's ran a national advertisement extolling its virtues. Standard enough. But the virtues it described were not its traditional ones (cheap and tasty food served quickly), nor did the advertisement contain the usual visual claptrap (smiling faces; colorful logos; lots of red, white, and blue). Rather, the advertisement was densely written and visually simple. Its arguments were particularly interesting:

- "At McDonald's, we serve you beef that's leaner than the kind of ground beef most people buy in the supermarket . . ."
- "No fillers. No additives. 100% pure American beef . . ."
- "Grade A milk in our milk shakes, sundaes and cones . . ."
- "Buns from top-quality enriched American wheat—baked locally."
- "We believe you can't turn out the best meals unless you have good nutritious food to start with. So that's where we start." [McDonald's, 1987]

The ad went on to make reference to the U.S. Department of Agriculture, dietary guidelines, the basic food groups, saturated fat and cholesterol, balanced meals, and it ended by offering free information from its "Nutrition Information Center." Heady stuff for a fast-food operation.

With the exception of its sign-off ("It's a good time for the great taste"), the ad contained very few optative statements. Virtually all of the evaluations it offered (and there were some forty rather long statements in the message) emerged from the "dietary code" now being promulgated by physicians, nutritionists, health clubs, and school nurses. Naturally, the ad—because it was an ad—was heavily promissory as well. But the really impressive piece of cultural news lay in *what* it promised (adjudicative allegiance), indicating the great popularity of the new nutritional consensus in the United States. When a fry-'em-up operation like McDonald's feels the need to bow at the altar of the U.S. Department of Agriculture, cultural change must surely be in the wind.

CONCLUSION

In this chapter, we have explored two major ways of examining ideational content. Clearly, the topical and judgmental approaches are only two among many. But both are good places for a critic to start. Both systems take some getting used to, but they give the critic a fairly precise way of talking about an art—rhetoric—that is so often imprecise. Both systems urge the critic to "violate" the natural structure of a message by reducing it to its most basic ideational units. In so doing, the critic runs the risk of somewhat distorting the rhetorical experience listeners themselves underwent. But this seems to be a risk worth running, especially if it helps the critic discuss the listening experience in ways that listeners themselves might find strange, but which they could not disavow.

Persuaders, of course, do not encourage such dismantling of their arguments. That is why the critic must attempt it. In many ways, the simple act of recategorizing a speaker's ideas is a fundamentally revolutionary act, for it means that *the critic's system*, not the speaker's system, will guide the critic's perceptions. In this sense, rhetorical criticism is a game of cat-and-mouse played by critic and speaker. The topical and judgmental systems of analysis give the critic an extra advantage in this continually fascinating game.

CHAPTER FIVE

Analyzing Argument

My fellow Americans: I come before you tonight as a candidate for the vice-presidency and as a man whose honesty and integrity has been questioned. Now, the usual political thing to do when charges are made against you is either ignore them or to deny them without giving details. I believe we have had enough of that in the United States, particularly with the present administration in Washington, D.C. To me the office of the vice-presidency is a great office, and I feel that the people have got to have confidence in the integrity of the men who run for that office and who might attain them. I have a theory, too, that the best and only answer to a smear or to an honest misunderstanding of the facts is to tell the truth. And that is why I am here tonight. I want to tell you my side of the case.

I am sure that you have read the charge, and you have heard it, that I, Senator Nixon, took $18,000 from a group of my supporters. Now, was that wrong? And let me say that it was wrong . . . I am saying it, incidentally, that it was wrong, not just illegal, because it isn't a question of whether it was legal or illegal: that isn't enough. The question is, was it morally wrong? . . . I say that it was morally wrong—if any of that $18,000 went to Senator Nixon, for my personal use, I say that it was morally wrong if it was secretly given and secretly handled. And I say that it was morally wrong if any of the contributors got special favors for the contributions they made.

And now, to answer those questions, let me say this: Not one cent of the $18,000 or any other money of that type ever went to me for my personal use. Every penny of it was used to pay for political expenses that I did not think should be charged to the taxpayers of the United States.

It was not a secret fund. As a matter of fact, when I was on "Meet the Press"—some of you may have seen it, last Sunday—Peter Edson came up to me, after the program, and he said, "Dick, what about this fund we hear about?" And I said, "Well, there is no secret about it. Go out and see Dana Smith, who was the administrator of the fund," and I gave him his address. And I said, "You will find that the purpose of the fund simply was to defray political expenses that I did not feel should be charged to the government."

And, third, let me point out, and I want to make this particularly clear, that no contributor to this fund, no contributor to any of my campaigns, has ever received any consideration that he would not have received as an ordinary constituent. I just don't believe in that, and I can say that never, while I have been in the Senate of the United States, as far as the people that contributed to this fund are concerned, have I made a telephone call for them to an agency, nor have I gone down to an agency in their behalf. And the records will show that, the records which are in the hands of the administration.

Well, then, some of you will say, and rightly, "Well, what did you use the fund for, Senator? Why did you have to have it?" Let me tell you in just a word how a Senate office operates. First of all . . .

* * * * *

Now, let me say this: I know that this is not the last of the smears. In spite of my explanation tonight, other smears will be made. Others have been made in the past. And the purpose of the smears, I know, is this, to silence me, to make me let up. Well, they just don't know who they are dealing with. I'm going to tell you this: I remember, in the dark days of the Hiss trial, some of the same columnists, some of the same radio commentators who are attacking me now and misrepresenting my position, were violently opposing me at the time I was after Alger Hiss. But I continued to fight, because I knew I was right, and I can say to this great television and radio audience that I have no apologies to the American people for my part in putting Alger Hiss where he is today. And as far as this is concerned, I intend to continue to fight.

Why do I feel so deeply? Why do I feel that in spite of the smears, the misunderstanding, the necessity for a man to come up here and bare his soul, as I have—why is it necessary for me to continue this fight? And I want to tell you why. Because, you see, I love my country. And I think my country is in danger. And I think the only man that can save America at this time is the man that's running for President, on my ticket, Dwight Eisenhower . . .

And now, finally, I know that you wonder whether or not I am going to stay on the Republican ticket or resign. Let me say this: I don't believe that I ought to quit, because I am not a quitter. And, incidentally, Pat is not a quitter. After all, her name was Patricia Ryan and she was born on St. Patrick's Day, and you know the Irish never quit.

But the decision, my friends, is not mine, I would do nothing that would harm the possibilities of Dwight Eisenhower to become President of the United States. And for that reason I am submitting to the Republican National Committee tonight through this television broadcast the decision which is theirs to make. Let them decide whether my position on the ticket will help or hurt. And I am going to ask you to help them decide. Wire and write the Republican

National Committee whether you think I should stay on or whether I should get off. And whatever their decision is, I will abide by it.

But just let me say this last word. Regardless of what happens, I am going to continue this fight. I am going to campaign up and down America until we drive the crooks and the Communists and those that defend them out of Washington, and remember, folks, Eisenhower is a great man, and a vote for Eisenhower is a vote for what is good for America. [Nixon, 1952]

This is the introduction and conclusion to what may well be the most famous speech in American political history. Given in September, 1952, by Richard M. Nixon, the vice presidential candidate on the Republican ticket headed by Dwight Eisenhower, the speech was remarkable in several ways. For one thing, it was unprecedented: Never before had an American politician used the then-young mass media to combine personal appeals with political appeals. Never before had an American politician given an itemized accounting of every penny he owned, as Richard Nixon does in the body of this speech. Never before had an American politician used the visual power of television to conduct a public conversation, with the candidate himself moving freely across a homey set and his wife sitting demurely across from him on a couch. Never before had an American politician directly asked U.S. voters to contact party leaders on his behalf, many of whom were then urging Nixon to resign from the ticket. And never before was an American politician exonerated so speedily—less than twenty-four hours after delivering his address. In the speech, Nixon used his parents and their home mortgage, his wife and her Irish ancestry, his children and their dog, Checkers, but he did so so disarmingly that his speech became a rhetorical classic and Mr. Nixon himself something of a political classic.

There are many interesting features of Nixon's "Checkers Speech." Mr. Nixon saw rhetorical opportunities with television that nobody had seen before. A master strategist, Nixon understood that the best defense (he had been accused of using secret monies illegally) was a good offense and that a TV appearance at the eleventh hour would take his detractors completely by surprise. (It did.) Mr. Nixon succeeds because he denies his rhetorical essence, framing his speech as a response to an attack on an honest man who only incidentally happens to be a politician. In the language of Chapter Three, Mr. Nixon's speech-act was itself fascinating. The message stood as bravery incarnate: an embattled man unfairly attacked by left-leaning ideologues, a man who had been compelled "to come up here and bare his soul." Indeed, Nixon intersperses themes of anti-Communism throughout his speech, making frequent allusions to Alger Hiss, a person who became the object of Nixon's scorn for his alleged Communist leanings. The conclusion to Nixon's speech even goes so far as to link the standard bearer of the Democratic Party, Adlai Stevenson, to Communist infiltration ("any man who called the Alger Hiss case a red herring isn't fit to be President of the United States"). Such appeals encouraged the audience to view the speech as action rather than reaction, as statesmanship rather than electioneering. These framing strategies were critical to Nixon's success: If his audience had remembered his timid introduction rather than his fire-breathing conclusion, he never would have regained the momentum the fund scandal cost him. His speech-act provided just such momentum.

In the language of Chapter Four, the Checkers Speech is a salad of ideas, with Nixon combining all four judgmental types: a factual listing of his credits and debits; optative appeals to middle-American values (he says at one point that his wife is without a mink but has "a respectable Republican cloth coat"); adjudicative flag-waving when he rides forth to slay the Communist dragon; and even a good deal of promissory campaigning ("remember, folks, Eisenhower is a great man, and a vote for Eisenhower is a vote for what is good for America"). There is a remarkable boldness to Nixon's speech, a weaving together of seemingly disparate themes (humility and patriotism, money and morality, family values and warfare, domestic can-do and international communism). Only Mr. Nixon's emotional intensity tied the pieces together and prevented people from viewing his remarks as political parody.

In this chapter, we will examine argument—the linking of ideas in support of identifiable propositions. We will track how speakers move their listeners from one assertion to the next and, ultimately, to some overriding assertion. In analyzing argument and reasoning, we must rethink what we know about them, for the logic of persuasion is a *human logic* in which reasoners are able to build bridges between ideas that professional logicians would find flimsy. Because the logic of persuasion is also an *informal logic*, the critic must be reminded that listeners' reasoning standards are looser than those used by scientists in the laboratory or by judges in court. It is a logic based as much on feeling as on thinking. More accurately, it is a logic that presumes that all feelers think and that all thinkers feel. Thus, Richard Nixon's emotional speech "made sense" to a great many of his listeners even though it was filled with pandering and irrelevancies. Here, we will try to discover what sort of sense Mr. Nixon made and for whom he made it.

It is important to view "sense" as something that is indeed *made.* In persuasion, sense is negotiated by people who use their beliefs, hopes, fears, and experiences to guide them. When listening, listeners never start from scratch. They hear each message in the context of everything they have heard previously. Clever speakers like Richard Nixon understand this and build "reasoning aids" to their messages. In this chapter, we will use three different tools to examine how people like Mr. Nixon reason, and we will see that each model tells us something different about the Nixon speech. But perhaps the most important thing that can be learned about reasoning is taught by Mr. Nixon himself. When he asks the rhetorical questions, "Why can't we have prosperity built on peace, rather than prosperity built on war? Why can't we have prosperity and an honest government in Washington, D.C. at the same time?", he responds with classic rhetorical reasoning: "*Believe me*, we can." In persuasion, reasoning and credibility are never separated for audiences. Critics may wish it otherwise, but it is never otherwise. It is this fact that will begin our discussion of argument.

THE LOGIC OF PERSUASION

Many people become frustrated by what passes for logic in the practical world. Ronald Reagan, a popular unionist during young adulthood, becomes a reactionary during his senior years. Jane Fonda, a radical critic of the Vietnam war during the 1960s, becomes a health guru fifteen years later. Gordon Liddy, a Watergate-convicted felon in the 1970s, becomes one of the most popular campus lecturers in the 1980s (because of his expertise on crime!). This makes sense? Has the public gone mad? Is nothing constant? Are people without memory? Has logic lost its logic? Questions like these can be maddening, but the rhetorical critic cannot indulge them. To understand persuasion is to understand a new kind of logic.

Traditional logic—the logic of the scientist, the judge, and the philosopher—has always stood as Grade A, approved logic, as well it should. Traditional logic, or technical logic, posits certain rigid rules of reasoning (syllogistic forms), emphasizes certain modes of fact-gathering (the scientific method), promotes certain modes of inference (arguing from legal precedent), and preaches the gospel of exhaustive research and rigorous testing of propositions. These intellectual tendencies are said to best distinguish humankind from lower animals and to undergird the most important human discoveries. When the space shuttle disaster occurred in the late 1980s, for example, evidence indicated that scientists had reasoned poorly when designing the crucial O-rings for the rocket boosters. The post-disaster hearings conducted by the military and Congressional bodies often were models of traditional logic, as computer printouts, weather charts, and laboratory reports were examined in microscopic detail.

But the public hearings were often something else as well. With the astronauts blaming the scientists and the scientists blaming the military and the military blaming the manufacturers and the manufacturers blaming the politicians and the politicians blaming the gods, the hearings were a field day for name-calling, flag-waving, excuse-making, question-begging, back-stabbing, rank-pulling, grandstanding, obfuscating, and every other brand of argument known to civilization. But the astronauts and the scientists and the military and the manufacturers and the politicians could not be blamed entirely for reasoning in these ways, for they all shared one damnable trait: They were human. As humans, they were imperfect logicians. As humans, they had fears, anxieties, memory lapses, biases, and worries about job security that clouded their thinking. As humans, they could reason like machines only so long before reaching for more shameless rhetorical materials. And those charged with deciding the truth in the case—the American people—had to fight through their own prejudices to make sense of a senseless tragedy.

So the logic of persuasion is neither tidy nor pretty. What passes for sense-making in everyday rhetoric stretches the boundaries of traditional logic. In persuasion, the guidebooks of technical or scientific reasoning must be set aside and a new standard employed:

> In general communication, "reasonable" and "logical" occur as terms *people* use when they want to report that something "hangs together" for *them*, seems adequately developed for *their* purposes, seems free of inconsistencies insofar as *they* have noticed. It seems to me we *must* admit that in rhetoric and drama at least, "reasonable" is in the final analysis what the consumer is willing to call "reasonable" [Arnold, 1971:22].

Admittedly, the critic can overlook this advice by using the dictates of traditional logic to censure informal arguers. But the critic who wishes to understand *how* people reason will try to understand the sort of logic that makes these assumptions:

1. *In persuasion, everything is rational to the behaver at the time of behavior.* This means that people always have "good reasons" for doing what they do. Even though these reasons will often not meet the critic's personal standards of goodness, this proposition suggests that any message that becomes popular will have a powerful logic to it. The consumer who responds to an advertisement featuring a scantily clad model standing next to a new Chrysler should perhaps be censured for sexism, not to mention stupidity. But the critic's job is to discover why this message works: What unspoken needs does it meet for consumers?

What fantasies does it trip off? What values does it herald? Rhetorical criticism is the study of *other people's* sense-making; it is the critic's job to re-present such sense-making faithfully. To do less would be to miss an important part of the human story.

2. *The logic of persuasion is always credibility-driven.* Persuasion comes to us embodied: Most people cannot separate the substance of a message from its author. This is especially true in spoken persuasion where the speaker's attitudes, voice, and personal appearance interact constantly with what the speaker says. While the examples of reasoning found in formal logic books are often unattributed (for example, *Who* was it exactly who first claimed, "All men are mortal. Socrates is a man. Therefore . . ."?), examples in rhetoric books almost always have a name attached. Thus, genetic studies by a neo-Nazi have no chance of being taken seriously by the scientific community, no matter what their inherent scientific worth. In persuasion, inherency lies *within people*, not within ideas. This is why small children are constantly in danger of accepting rides from strangers, since they have long been taught that adults are authoritative and well-intentioned. Speakers with high credibility are thus allowed to ramble, to become patently unclear, or to present distressing evidence and yet retain their appeal. Under such conditions, listeners themselves seem somehow willing to fill in the logical gaps. Thus, as Foss [1983] reports, the birth control controversy in the Catholic Church hinged more on people's feeling about the *authority* of the Church than on either natural law or respect for tradition. In persuasion, speaker and message are always wed, as are reasoning and attitudes.

3. *The logic of persuasion is always saliency-driven.* Saliency is the other great law of persuasion. It states: The listener will virtually always find the *important* and the *immediate* to be most reasonable. In a technical logic designed to test universal facts and establish enduring truths, this proposition would make no sense at all. But in the world of people, logic is a sometime thing. Needs and experience, not abstract truths, guide human decision making. It is one thing to discuss the clinical utility of euthanasia and quite anther to remove the life support system from *one's own mother*. During such moments, medical charts and sociological abstractions become dry as dust as the immediacy and importance of such a decision overwhelms one. On a less momentous front, the old advice not to shop for groceries while hungry is good advice, since the law of saliency decrees that people never decide in the abstract even when they think they do.

4. *The logic of persuasion is audience-dependent.* The logic of persuasion is "weak" rather than "strong" logic. Its standards of reasonability vary sharply from audience to audience and from situation to situation. This is what makes criticism such a fascinating enterprise: It

opens up for inspection an endless variety of reasonings. The rhetoric of skin color, for example, will sound different at a conference of dermatologists than it will at the annual meetings of the National Collegiate Athletic Association, and different still at a gathering of the Ku Klux Klan. As Black [1970] points out, each message contains within it the speaker's conception of the ideal listener (something Black calls the "second persona") as well as the speaker's expectations of how that listener will reason. In other words, a message becomes a record of what the speaker hoped the listener would "add" to the logical stew. Thus, when he found an excessive number of cancer metaphors in the rhetoric of the radical right, Black concluded that these speakers expected their listeners to feel (1) on the brink of ruin, (2) deceived from within, but (3) also willing to fight to the death. As Carleton [1975:87] says, the critic must be ready to account for such "local logics," since universal rules of reasoning rarely shed light on the given case. The good critic finds logic wherever rhetoric is found.

5. *The logic of persuasion is a logic of association.* While technical logic focuses on causality, rhetoric is guided by the weaker dictates of association. In a court of law, for example, even though an indictment establishes no necessary (causal) link between a crime and its perpetrator, juries are often swayed by the very fact of indictment ("Innocent people don't wear handcuffs in court, do they?"). Similarly, a smear campaign in politics often is fueled by associations. Although it makes no causal sense to launch a federal investigation merely because of one's work history or ethnicity, it can make associative sense to do so. So when a Congressional committee looked into his former business dealings, one-time U.S. Labor Secretary Raymond Donovan charged that former building contractors (like himself) always seem worthy of federal investigation, that former building contractors from New Jersey seem automatically indictable, and that former New Jersey building contractors who also happen to be Italian seem automatically guilty.

Because determining true causality is so rare in human affairs, ordinary arguments rarely prove things with scientific certainty. Rather, they trade on the logically weaker, but psycho-logically attractive standards of plausibility and rationalization. So, Duffy [1984] reports that when televangelists lashed out at "secular humanists," they included under that umbrella widely divergent people and viewpoints, few of which shared common roots. Nevertheless, as Duffy points out, there is great efficiency in such an appeal (that is, it gives one the chance of killing many birds with one stone), despite its weakness as formal argument (Do birds of a feather really flock together? On all occasions?).

6. *The logic of persuasion is often a logic of emotion.* The old Western dichotomy between the heart and the head makes little sense in the

world of rhetoric. Most students of persuasion [for example, Delia, 1970] agree that to contrast people's "logical" versus "emotional" tendencies is to separate human features that should not be separated in analysis, since they cannot be separated in fact. When they react to anything—persuasion included—people react with all of themselves. Thus, to describe some rhetorical appeals as logical in nature (for example, monetary arguments) and others as emotional (for example, patriotic arguments) is to deal artificially with a complex process of thinking/feeling. During each moment of each day, people think/feel. Speakers think/feel when they speak and listeners think/feel when they listen. The plain fact of the matter is that some people get quite emotional about money, while others feel most patriotic when talking about nuclear throw weights. When studying persuasion, therefore, the critic must be primarily concerned with the **emotional authenticity** of a speaker (Is the speaker really experiencing the emotion he or she seems to be experiencing?), with the **emotional integrity** of a performance (Does the speaker's background give him or her the "right" to be this emotional on this matter?), or the **emotional register** of an argument (Is the speaker's state of arousal too high or too low for the matter being discussed?). And it must be remembered that questions of this sort are questions about *reasoning*, about how packages of emotions and ideas serve as arguments in the ordinary world.

Given the six features above, the logic of persuasion may seem a completely dishonorable logic: Advertisers convince us that we need clothing we do not need; lawyers encourage clients to cry on the witness stand to win jurors' sympathies; preachers claim they will die if church donations don't increase by 200 percent. In persuasion, these claims stand as argument. Shame on persuasion.

In light of these features, the critic has two choices: (1) to honor traditional logic by ignoring persuasion completely or (2) to study how and why such appeals work and then to warn others about the logic of everyday rhetoric. This second option seems most sensible. After all, the first is defeatist, not to mention faintly elitist. But the second option encourages closer study of people, a fundamentally humane act indeed.

EVIDENCE AND REASONING

The success of a persuasive argument is often determined not by notions of formal validity but by questions of *sufficiency:* Is there enough here to go on? Will more support be required? Is the case over-

RHETORIC AND THE AMERICAN PRESIDENCY

Critical Profile 5.1   "Mr. President, Sir, Your Policy Is Stupid"

How does one criticize the President of the United States before thousands of Americans without appearing churlish? And should one worry about being churlish? These dilemmas, facing each journalist during a presidential news conference, are described by C. Jack Orr, now of West Chester State University in Pennsylvania, as a "counterpoised situation" in which two great institutions come into contact.

In his study, Orr details the rule book for such encounters. For example, the press must operate within the constraints of their roles as "participants, adversaries and allies of officials . . . and good citizens who must exercise appropriate restraint." A journalist can (and is expected to) challenge the president but must also signal proper deference to the President's position. Explicit criticism by a reporter is normally eschewed, for example, and Orr interprets this walking-on-eggs approach as politically, and culturally, functional. He argues that direct criticism by reporters could ultimately restrict the powers of the President. Also, explicitly stated criticism would place the reporter in a more judgmental position than is considered institutionally appropriate by the American people and, therefore, could lead to press censorship.

In his analysis of news conferences, Orr found reporters using three key strategies to maintain institutional balance. Typically, the reporter began the confrontation by addressing the head of state as "Mr. President" or "Sir." Then, the criticism leveled against the President was attributed to some external source, not to the reporter himself or herself. Finally, the President was asked for an *open-ended* response to the challenge. Orr presents a number of examples to illustrate the rhetorical dexterity required in such settings: "Mr. President, . . . I was in Richmond shortly after your reelection, at a public meeting, and a state senator, who was a Negro, got up and asked me, when is Mr. Nixon going to stop kicking the blacks around? And I thought you might like to respond to that." In this example, attributing criticism of Richard Nixon's civil rights policy to someone else enabled the reporter to appear respectful of the *institution* of the presidency while at the same time commenting on a serious charge against the *individual* currently in office. As many reporters discovered when meeting face to face with the feisty Richard Nixon, maintaining this delicate balance between person and office was often difficult.

In short, Orr found presidential news conferences to be generally polite. But is such civility a genuine blessing? Might it foster timidity on the part of reporters and, hence, insure political ignorance for the rest of us? In short: What price politeness? And who, ultimately, pays that price?

Profiled by: Patricia Powell
Citation: Orr (1980)

Critical Profile 5.2   Winning the Debate and Losing the Argument

Political scientists and historians often assume that "objective reality" shapes world events. In this view, nations, parties, and people are motivated by hard-nosed economic and political forces. However, J. Michael Hogan, now of Indiana University, argues that such "real" events are often themselves shaped by the arguments used to debate an issue. To show this, Hogan analyzed the debate over the 1979 treaty President Jimmy Carter negotiated vis-à-vis the Panama Canal. To some, Hogan notes, Carter "gave away" the canal; to others he was a "courageous" president who did what was right. The important thing, in Hogan's view, however, is that the public debate on the Panama Canal was not "so much a contest between truth and falsehood as a competition for persuasiveness."

For most of the twentieth century, Hogan argues, Theodore Roosevelt's internationalist vision of the canal "remained so emotionally compelling, so inextricably linked to national pride," that few politicians risked criticizing America's role in Panama. This rhetorical heritage was very much Carter's foe in the 1979 debate and, as Hogan shows, Carter was not successful in changing most Americans' views on the canal. Hogan describes the pro-treaty arguments as "intellectually untenable and emotionally unappealing," "incomplete," and an affront to "common sense." The anti-treaty arguments, on the other hand, appealed to the image of "American greatness" and promised a return to the "good old days."

Why, then, was the 1979 treaty ratified? Polls at the time indicated that the public would be more favorable toward the treaty if American defense interests were protected. Indeed, Hogan says, the Senate debate continually returned to military issues and while the Senate rejected strongly worded amendments, it did pass weaker "leadership amendments" addressing defense concerns. Most senators, according to Hogan, then voted for ratification, believing that the leadership amendments satisfied public opinion.

As Hogan notes, however, this was an imaginary shift in public opinion. The polls the senators based their decision on "failed to distinguish between the leadership amendments and stronger guarantees of defense rights rejected by the Senate." Thus, the treaty was ratified because the pollsters initially (presumably, unintentionally) misrepresented public opinion. Hogan reasons that this misreading had major political consequences and that while the pro-treaty forces won ratification they may have lost the argument and contributed to the subsequent ousting of Carter and many pro-treaty senators. "Observers from Jimmy Carter to Richard Viguerie," Hogan notes, "agree that the debate was a key factor in the conservative renaissance of the late 1970s."

Profiled by: David R. Harvey
Citation: Hogan (1986)

Critical Profile 5.3   Modern Picnics at Modern Hangings

The Watergate and, more recently, the Iran-Contra hearings demonstrated the fascination people have for political corruption. For weeks, many Americans stayed glued to their TV sets to follow the testimony of the day. Besides entertainment, is there a positive role for such political corruption in a democracy? Bruce E. Gronbeck of the University of Iowa argues that there is indeed. To show this he examines cases ranging from Aeschines' charges against Demosthenes to Richard Nixon's fall from the presidency. Defining political corruption as acts where "private gain is made at public expense," and demonstrating how these acts are turned into "value affirming occasions" by a society, Gronbeck argues that the public outcry "has a salutary effect upon a country," because it reaffirms the principles and power of the State. One of the more interesting aspects of this reaffirmation is what Gronbeck calls "the complete and final purgation of the offender." One of the examples he uses to demonstrate this process is the Watergate affair during Richard Nixon's administration. The break-in at the Democratic National Headquarters in 1972, Gronbeck argues, was merely "a third rate robbery" until "invested with institutional and cultural meanings." This "investment" happened in stages. Nixon, at first, tried to focus public attention on the "facts" and denied any significance to the event. But as Nixon's antagonists persisted in uncovering more information, the "wheels of judicial bureaucracy" continued to escalate the significance of the break-in until, finally, the House Judiciary Hearings *ceremonialized* the event. Rhetorically, Gronbeck argues, such public spectacles convert "everyday crimes" into "constitutional outrages" and change a public figure's image from "savior" to "subverter."

But because this is a ritualized ceremony, Gronbeck also argues that it must be done correctly. The process "takes rhetors skilled with symbols and imbued with patience." If the accusers are not convincing in their confrontation with the corrupted figure, they themselves may end up losing. If, for example, Nixon's accusers were seen as motivated by their own political concerns, the public may well have turned their dissatisfaction on the accusers themselves or have merely laughed at the entire spectacle (as many people did later in the Iran-Contra affair). If convincing, however, the ceremony "allays social fears" and shows that the principles of a society can eliminate corruption. "Thus it is," Gronbeck says, "that a country such as this one literally *celebrates* corruption and its public purgation."

Profiled by: David R. Harvey
Citation: Gronbeck (1978)

stated? As Perelman [1979:117–118] claims, ". . . [popular] arguments are never correct or incorrect; they are either strong or weak, relevant or irrelevant." A good approach for the critic, then, is to examine the weight of the arguments offered in a given message. By contrasting heavily documented propositions to those mentioned in passing, the critic can detect the speaker's areas of confidence and also the rhetorical trouble spots. Naturally, the evidence used in public arguments rarely meets rigorous standards of empirical testing. Although Richard Nixon presented a great many financial facts in his Checkers speech, they were hardly the sort of facts that would stand up in a court of law. Rather, his presenting them gave listeners the sense that Mr. Nixon was a man of probity, that he took the charges against him seriously, that he had emotional and intellectual resources in the heat of battle, that he was in command of his life. On many occasions for many listeners, some evidence is enough evidence.

When inspecting arguments, the critic asks questions like these:

1. Generally speaking, does the message make heavy use of supporting material or is it flatly assertive?
2. Does the speaker use a large number of sketchy arguments or build a tighter case with few propositions but more evidence?
3. Which arguments have ample supporting materials, which are given short shrift, and why?
4. What *kinds* of evidence does the speaker use and do they change from point to point in the message?

Table 5.1 (based in part on Hart, et al., 1983) presents some standard kinds of rhetorical evidence. Also included are a variety of critical probes to see how a given message functioned and how its author perceived the rhetorical circumstances. Because evidence forms the foundation and supporting walls of discourse, the critic who uses these critical probes becomes something of a building inspector, prowling around in the basement and walking amidst the scaffolding to see if the rhetorical architecture is as good as it should be and, if not, why nobody noticed.

Table 5.2 presents a rough estimation of how frequently various clarification devices were used in the Nixon speech and in some of the speeches examined previously. A quick inspection shows that each speech presents a different picture, with some messages resembling others on some dimensions but none being duplicates. This makes sense, since one of the speeches was purely fictional (Harold Hill), while another was quite real (Patton). One was religious with a political tone (Prinz), while another was political yet confessional (Nixon). It is little wonder, then, that the evidentiary profiles are distinctive.

Table 5.1 Analyzing Clarification Devices

Type	Functions	Example*	Critical Probes
Serial examples	Adds totality to a speaker's remarks by presenting, in scattered fashion, numerous instances of the same phenomenon.	"Parents can act as our reference groups, as can friends, political groups, religious organizations, social fraternities, and so on."	How frequently are groups of examples found in the message? Is there any overall logic to the types of illustrations chosen? Which arguments are devoid of examples? Why?
Extended example	Adds vivacity to a speaker's remarks by presenting a detailed picture of a single event or concept.	"Let's consider what happened to John Jones, a college undergraduate who has had trouble 'sorting out' his reference groups. John started school like most people, and soon . . ."	How many different extended examples are used? How much detail is provided within them? Are "story qualities" clearly apparent in the examples? Are the examples real or hypothetical? Is the narrative interrupted at any point? Why?
Quantification	Adds a feeling of substantiveness to a speaker's remarks by means of concrete enumerations.	"Some experts estimate that 70 percent of our decisions are affected by our reference groups, and that one out of every three people experiences tensions in relation to reference group choice."	How often are dates, sums, and quantities provided in the message? When are they used? What sorts of arguments do they support? Which arguments that could be quantified are not quantified? Why?
Isolated comparisons	Adds realism to a speaker's remarks by drawing analogically upon a listener's past experiences.	"Reference groups are like spouses— you can't live without them, but sometimes it's darn hard to live with them!"	What sorts of "equations" are set up by the speaker? Do the two elements of an equation "naturally" go together or is the equation novel? In offering the comparisons offered, what assumptions about the audience does the speaker seem to be making? Are the assumptions justified?
Extended comparison	Adds psychological reference points to a speaker's remarks by successively structuring his or her perceptions along familiar lines.	"A reference group is similar to a mother—it nurtures our feelings when we are hurt; it disciplines us for violating its norms; it helps us mature by . . ."	Are extended comparisons extensively or infrequently used? What sorts of arguments are developed with this device? Is the "known" half of the comparison well adapted to the audience so that they can appreciate the "unknown" half?

*(Example: A sociology lecture on the topic of "reference groups")

Table 5.1   Analyzing Clarification Devices (*continued*)

Type	Functions	Example	Critical Probes
Testimony	Adds to the inclusiveness of a speaker's remarks by quoting appreciatively from known or respected sources or depreciatively from sources of ill-regard.	"Sociologist Carolyn Sherif has said that none of us can really escape the influence of the groups we identify with—our reference groups."	What sorts of persons/ sources does the speaker depend upon? How often is this dependency manifested? Is there an obvious logic to the persons/sources chosen for support? How careful is the speaker's documentation of the sources quoted? What types of persons/sources are never quoted?
Definition	Adds to the specificity of a speaker's remarks by depicting opposed elements.	"Let's consider what is not meant by a reference group. It is not just any group we belong to, nor is it always identifiable. Rather it is . . ."	Is any major attempt made here to define important concepts? Which terms/ ideas are defined fully? Which key terms/ideas are presented without definition? At what point in the message are definitions offered?
Contrast	Adds a dramatic quality to a speaker's remarks by depicting opposed elements.	"Those who identify with many groups have very different attitudes from those who are more individualistic."	What sort of "reverse equations" are presented by the speaker? Are both elements of the contrasts drawn from listeners' experiences? Is dependence on contrasts heavy, moderate, or light? Do contrasts overshadow comparisons and is it significant that they do?

Table 5.2   Comparative Use of Clarification Devices

Clarification Services	Rabbi Prinz (%)*	Harold Hill (%)	George Patton (%)	Richard Nixon (%)
Serial examples	0	11	18	14
Extended examples	14	50	30	31
Quantification	0	11	2	10
Isolated comparisons	17	15	14	12
Extended comparisons	37	0	0	7
Testimony	8	0	4	14
Definition	6	7	17	5
Contrast	17	6	16	17

* Proportion of message using the devices listed

These clarification devices can be thought of as reasoning aids, as argumentative promises to listeners: "If you don't like my comparative argument, here's one with contrast." "If these serial examples make an idea clear for you, this extended example will make it even clearer." "If you're having trouble moving from Proposition A to Proposition B, listen to how a respected source made that same intellectual movement." Some speakers choose poorly when selecting evidence: The wrong device may be chosen for the wrong argument; the right device may be chosen but then developed poorly; an argument needing support may be overlooked while a self-evident argument receives unneeded attention. Making the right choices about such matters is what rhetorical excellence is all about.

The evidentiary choices made by our four speakers seem sensible. General Patton saw his job as one of giving his men a clear sense of purpose. His heavy use of definition shows that. In his speech, he explains the real-life meanings of teamwork and patriotism and does little else. Since his time before battle was short, Patton chose a streamlined argument, hoping that his men would at least take away a fresh understanding of these two concepts. Patton also uses a good deal of contrast, distinguishing the fighting ability and moral superiority of the American troops from their German counterparts. Fairly heavy use of contrast creates "division"—sharp distinctions, opposed viewpoints, observable differences—the kind of black-and-white thinking that keeps confusion to a minimum during battle. All in all, then, a good day's work for Patton or, more precisely, a good five-minutes' work.

Harold Hill's speech could not be more different. He defines very little, makes no extended comparisons, offers no testimony. Such devices would have slowed his speech to a crawl. The producers of *The Music Man* wanted something snappy and hence wrote only a patina of support into Hill's script. They have Hill trying primarily to generate shock and concern in his listeners and, then, a grand enthusiasm for band instruments. Hill bases most of his speech on the extended example of the pool table, figuring that this speech would be but the first in an extended campaign to separate the good folks of River City from their currency. Like Patton, Hill sought simplicity. But unlike Patton, Hill hoped to build intensity of motivation, motivation that might have been dissipated if spread over a wide range of arguments in behalf of tuba-playing. Hill's extended example thus became what professional debaters call a need case, a kind of problem-stating that ultimately invites a "plan," which Harold Hill just happened to have handy in his display case.

Rabbi Prinz's speech resembled Hill's, in part, because he too needed a streamlined performance. Rather than use examples, however, the rabbi made dramatic use of the extended comparison, showing how the experiences of Jews in Nazi Germany paralleled those witnessed daily by blacks in the United States. This heavy use of comparison springs directly from the very speech-act in which Prinz participated: His physical presence at the March on Washington said, "We Jews stand with you blacks on this matter." So the social action of the *event* neatly parallels the rhetorical action of the *text*. Comparisons, however, have their rhetorical costs. They tend to be listlike and, when used in great profusion, better suited to lectures or scientific reports than to half-time speeches or advertising copy. Moreover, unlike examples (which the rabbi almost never uses), comparisons can put audiences to sleep. But given the rabbi's role—that of rhetorical helpmate to Dr. King—he apparently felt it was enough to take his stand on the right side of the issue, make a simple, unembellished statement, and then quit the scene. He did so movingly.

Compared to the other speakers, Richard Nixon's heavy use of testimony is significant. No doubt because he was an object of suspicion at the time, Mr. Nixon quotes Republicans, Democrats, reporters, several imaginary citizens, and a real one. At one point in the speech, he even quotes from accountants and lawyers:

> I am proud to report to you tonight that this audit and this legal opinion is being forwarded to General Eisenhower, and I would like to read to you the opinion that was prepared by Gibson, Dunn and Crutcher [a law firm in Los Angeles], based on all the pertinent laws and statutes, together with the audit report prepared by the certified public accountants:
>
> "It is our conclusion that Senator Nixon did not obtain any financial gain from the collection and disbursement of the funds by Dana Smith [a Nixon aide]; that Senator Nixon did not violate any federal or state law by reason of the operation of the fund; and that neither the portion of the fund paid by Dana Smith directly to third persons, nor the portion paid to Senator Nixon, to reimburse him for office expenses, constituted income in a sense which was either reportable or taxable as income under income tax laws."

No politician wants to be placed in a position of having to use testimony extensively. Quoting others puts them on stage rather than oneself, a despised prospect for any elected official. Also, using direct quotations signals rhetorical trouble, as if the speaker had neither the wisdom nor the authority to carry the day. Quotations also often slow down an oral message for listeners who, unlike readers, cannot skim the text. But Mr. Nixon's back was against the wall; he had no choice but to find credibility where he could find it.

The Checkers Speech is interesting because it is two speeches rolled into one: a speech of moral exoneration and a political stump speech. Because he had so many different jobs to do in his speech,

Nixon found himself using all the evidentiary devices available. Fully a tenth of his speech presented quantitative evidence of his innocence. Almost half of his speech relates examples (of his early life, of his wife's devotion, of Communist evil). A fifth of his speech uses comparisons. Here, he compares his early life to the lives of all young marrieds; his service record with the service records of all heroes; his children with all of America's children; his view of the world with Abraham Lincoln's view (they both loved common people, said Mr. Nixon). This persistent string of comparisons helps to give the Checkers Speech a heavily sentimental tone as Nixon searches under every emotional rock to show what a regular fellow he is. Some forty years later, such devices seem overly obvious, almost a caricature. But Richard Nixon had a way of offering such comparisons without batting an eye, as if they were the most natural comparisons in the world.

Roughly another fifth of Nixon's speech uses contrasts, a Nixon favorite. Perhaps because he always saw himself as the odd man out in society or perhaps because he had such a dialectical cast of mind (the kind that finds fundamental opposition rather than fundamental synchrony in the world), Nixon reveled in contrasts. In his 1952 speech, he distinguished himself from Democrats (who put their wives on the political payroll), from other lawyers (who were richer than he), and from other politicians (who could be bought). He also contrasted his wife with other wives, his party with the opposition party, his political gifts with other political gifts (all he got was Checkers). The sharpness of Nixon's contrasts increases as he draws to the end of his speech and lambastes the Democrats. Always the ex-debater, always the person who never quite fit in, Richard Nixon's gift for contrast lay not in elegance but in the sharpness of the distinctions he drew and in the emotional intensity with which he drew them.

Although it is a humble type of analysis, examining argumentative support reveals how speakers work their minds rhetorically. Often, these patterns of evidence reveal the focus of an argument in especially telling ways. For example, Dicks [1981] discovered that the kind of evidence found in legal advocacy best predicted the issues upon which a jury trial would hinge. In a related study, Ritter [1985] tracked the patterns of evidence used in the first Alger Hiss trial in 1949 (Hiss was a State Department official accused of being a communist) that ended in a deadlocked jury, and compared them to those used during the retrial one year later (which succeeded in convicting Hiss of perjury). According to Ritter, the rhetorical approaches used by the prosecution in the two trials differed sharply. The first trial featured a "courtroom drama" (that is, a parade of larger-than-life personalities and much showmanship), while the second featured a "crime drama" (that is, one which focused on past activities and on forty-seven different pieces of typewritten evidence). Not only did the reasoning patterns differ sharply, says Ritter, but so too did the resulting rhetorical tones of both the prosecution and the defense. A third legal study [Bennett, 1979] discovered that the kind of evidence used in court will be useful only if it reinforces the overall "story" being told by prosecution and defense, a matter to which we will turn in greater depth shortly.

A fairly clear connection has been established between the kind of ideological position a speaker takes and the kind of evidence that speaker uses. Hart [1970], and later Clark [1977], found that doctrinal speakers, persons closely tied to some book of truth, used twice as much testimony as speakers who depended upon an audience's general wishes and preferences. The rhetorical value of testimony has also been established by Smith [1977], who found that "politically paranoid" speakers (persons well out of the societal mainstream) documented their remarks heavily, either because of ideological constraint or because they hoped to imitate "scholarly" discourse, thereby increasing their believability. Yet another study of documentation by Stewart [1965] compared the biblical citations in sermons delivered immediately after the Lincoln and Kennedy assassinations. Stewart found a 30 percent drop in the number of Old Testament quotations over the years, which he ascribes to changes in world view brought about in American theology during the intervening century. Whereas the Lincoln eulogists ascribed the tragedy to God's mysterious ways (hence the biblical quotations), the Kennedy preachers attributed his assassination to human enmity.

Sometimes, the kind of definition used in discourse can be important. For example, Zarefsky, et al. [1984] argue that it was Ronald Reagan's undefined use of such key phrases as "an economic safety net" and "the truly needy" that gave him needed rhetorical room in domestic politics. By using such terms but by refusing to define them, Mr. Reagan was able to appear concerned about the economic plight of the poor without abandoning his conservative principles. Naturally, examining evidence patterns of this sort cannot tell us everything that needs to be known about persuasion. But these patterns can often point up what is *at issue* in discourse. Reasoning is more than the marshalling of evidence, but it is no less than that as well, and so it should be studied with some care.

NARRATIVE AND REASONING

At first, narrative and reasoning seem antithetical. "Poets tell stories" is our initial response, "scientists reason." But a growing number of scholars feel that there is a logic to storytelling, a logic the rhetorical critic must understand. According to such thinkers [for example, Fisher, 1987], much public policy is determined by the stories persuaders tell.

Sometimes, these stories are complex, springing from deep cultural roots; often, stories told today are but updated versions of centuries-old tales. Because they are practical people, persuaders do not tell these stories with the novelist's richness of detail or sense of abandon. Persuaders normally tell only snippets of stories, an anecdote here, an abbreviated fable there, always moving listeners forward to some propositional conclusion. But narratives do advance persuasion because: (1) They disarm listeners by enchanting them, (2) they awaken within listeners dormant experiences and feelings, and (3) they expose, subtly, some sort of propositional argument. Recent scholars have shown that people reason differently in the presence of narrative. Its native features suggest why.

1. *Narrative occurs in a natural time-line.* There are beginnings, middles, and endings to narrative. Once we start on a narrative, we feel compelled to follow it through to its conclusion. All stories, even bad stories, inspire the need to see how they turn out. Narratives always tempt us with closure.

2. *Narrative includes characterization.* People are interested in people. Narratives are the stories of what people do. Often, narratives introduce interesting people, sometimes grand people, to an audience. When we read or hear such narratives, our natural sense of identification makes us want to find out more about the lives of the people described.

3. *Narrative presents detail.* A good story, such as a fine novel, transports us to another time or place by offering fine-grained treatments. When the narrator describes the clothes people wear or the customs they follow or the dialect they speak, we come to know that time and place as if it were our own. Details captivate.

4. *Narrative is primitive.* No culture exists without narrative. Most cultures celebrate their sacred narratives on a regular basis (for example, a Fourth of July celebration) and indoctrinate their young by means of narrative (for example, fairy tales). Narrative appeals to the child in us, because, unlike life, it contains a complete story with certain consequences.

5. *Narrative doesn't argue . . . obviously.* If a narrator tries to make a point too forcefully, we feel cheated. Good narrative holds open the illusion that we—as listeners and readers—help to determine its meaning. Narrative is depropositionalized argument, argument with a hidden bottom line. Narrators charm audiences because they only promise a story well told.

These propositions apply to all narratives, but rhetorical narratives have special features, special obligations, in addition. For example, because rhetorical narrative is *narrative*, opponents find it hard to attack ("it's only a story, after all"). But because rhetorical narrative is also *rhetorical*, because it is storytelling-with-a-purpose, it must also abide by certain rules of purposiveness. Thus, rhetorical narratives are (1) normally brief, (2) often repetitive, (3) sketchy in characterization, (4) frequently interrupted, and (5) rarely exotic. In the middle of his Checkers Speech, for example, Richard Nixon launched into just such a narrative. He did not produce great poetry at that time, but he did produce passably good rhetoric, especially for the white, Protestant, middle-income voter that he especially wanted to reach:

> I was born in 1913. Our family was one of modest circumstances, and most of my early life was spent in a store, out in East Whittier. It was a grocery store, one of those family enterprises. The only reason we were able to make it go was because my Mother and Dad had five boys, and we all worked in the store. I worked my way through college and, to a great extent, through law school. And then, in 1940, probably the best thing that ever happened to me happened. I married Pat, who is sitting over here.
>
> We had a rather difficult time, after we were married, like so many of the young couples who might be listening to us. I practiced law. She continued to teach school.
>
> Then, in 1942, I went into the service. Let me say that my service record was not a particularly unusual one. I went to the South Pacific. I guess I'm entitled to a couple of battle stars. I got a couple of letters of commendation. But I was just there when the bombs were falling. And then I returned. I returned to the United States, and in 1946, I ran for Congress. When we came out of the war, Pat and I—Pat during the war had worked as a stenographer, and in a bank, and as an economist for a government agency—and when we came out, the total of our savings, from both my law practice, her teaching, and all the time that I was in the war, the total for that entire period was just a little less than $10,000. Every cent of that, incidentally, was in government bonds. Well, that's where we start, when I go into politics.
>
> Now, whatever I earned since I went into politics—well, here it is. I jotted it down. Let me read the notes. First of all, I have had my salary as a congressman and as a senator. Second, I have received a total in this past six years of $1600 from estates which were in my law firm at the time that I severed my connection with it. And, incidentally, as I said before, I have not engaged in any legal practice, and have not accepted any fees from business that came into the firm after I went into politics. I have made an average of approximately $1500 a year, from nonpolitical speaking engagements and lectures. And then, fortunately, we have inherited a little money. Pat sold her interest in her father's estate for $3000, and I inherited $1500 from my grandfather. We lived rather modestly.
>
> For four years we lived in an apartment in Parkfairfax, Alexandria, Virginia. The rent was $80 a month. And we saved for the time that we could buy a house. Now, that was what we took in.

What did we do with this money? What do we have today to show for it? This will surprise you, because it is so little, I suppose, as standards generally go of people in public life. First of all, we've got a house in Washington, which cost $41,000 and on which we owe $20,000. We have a house in Whittier, California, which cost $13,000, and on which we owe $3,000. My folks are living there at the present time. I have just $4,000 in life insurance, plus my GI policy, which I have never been able to convert, and which will run out in two years. I have no life insurance whatever on Pat. I have no life insurance on our two youngsters, Patricia and Julie. I own a 1950 Oldsmobile car. We have our furniture. We have no stocks and bonds of any type. We have no interest of any kind, direct or indirect, in any business. Now, that is what we have. What do we owe?

Well, in addition to the mortgage, the $20,000 mortgage on the house in Washington, a $10,000 one on the house in Whittier, I owe $4500 to Riggs Bank, in Washington, D.C., with interest at 4 percent. I owe $3500 to my parents, and the interest on that loan, which I pay regularly because it is a part of the savings they made through the years they were working so hard—I pay regularly 4 percent interest. And then I have a $500 loan, which I have on my life insurance.

Well, that's about it. That's what we have. And that's what we owe. It isn't very much. But Pat and I have the satisfaction that every dime that we have got is honestly ours.

I should say this, that Pat doesn't have a mink coat. But she does have a respectable Republican cloth coat, and I always tell her that she would look good in anything.

One other thing I probably should tell you, because if I don't they will probably be saying this about me, too. We did keep something, a gift, after the election. A man down in Texas heard Pat on the radio mention the fact that our two youngsters would like to have a dog, and, believe it or not, the day before we left on this campaign trip we got a message from Union Station in Baltimore, saying they had a package for us. We went down to get it. You know what it was?

It was a little cocker spaniel dog, in a crate that he had sent all the way from Texas, black and white, spotted, and our little girl, Tricia, the six-year-old, named it Checkers. And, you know, the kids, like all kids, loved the dog, and I just want to say this, right now, that regardless of what they say about it, we are going to keep it.

There are many attractive aspects to Mr. Nixon's narrative. Nixon displays himself as a **reluctant narrator,** reminding us that "this is unprecedented in the history of American politics," giving us the sense that the story is being pried out of him and is, therefore, especially worthy of attention. It is also an **uncontrived narrative.** That is, Nixon discounts his own heroism ("I was just there when the bombs were falling") and interrupts himself several times ("incidentally, as I have said before, I have not engaged in any legal practice . . ."), establishing that the story has not been prepared, that it is pouring out of his soul, not out of his head. The **familiar characters** contained in the story are also comforting: a hard-working young man, a selfless wife, sacrificing parents, dog-loving children. Characters like these can be found nightly in almost any television drama and they serve to humanize the protagonist as only storytelling can.

According to Mader [1973], a narrative must also have **rhetorical presence,** a vividness of detail that brings to life the ideas advanced. Mr. Nixon achieves this by nicely weaving into his narrative specific places (the South Pacific, Alexandria, Whittier), sums and dates ("we've got a house in Washington, which cost $41,000 and on which we owe $20,000"), buildings (the Riggs Bank, Union Station), and, most important, people (Pat, Tricia, and Julie). He also uses some amount of **dramatic variety,** weaving the serious (his wartime experiences) with the whimsical (the beloved Checkers), as well as displaying a nice touch for **dramatic understatement** by suddenly introducing facts that have no obvious argumentative burden (for example, he could not convert his GI policy; his folks are living in a home he owns; he has a 1950 Oldsmobile). Finally, Mr. Nixon is careful to establish **narrative authenticity** by never commenting explicitly on the principle guiding his narrative or the generalization he hopes listeners will draw from his story. Rather, he presents the story as just a story, asking only that the audience permit him to tell his humble tale. In 1952, this tale left many a moist cheek.

Scholars who have investigated the rhetorical uses of narratives seem both fascinated and alarmed by what they find. Bennett and Edelman [1985], for example, observe that the narrator's role is an extraordinarily powerful one, a role whose innocence inhibits listeners from thinking about the arguments embedded in the tales being told them. These authors note that political elites (which includes both office-holders and journalists) often tell simpler stories than is warranted by the facts and often mislead audiences in their rush to tell the simplest and most comforting story possible. Bennett and Edelman warn that life itself is rarely as simple as storybook life and rarely permits pat solutions to life's problems. Rhetorical narratives can become addictive for listeners, they warn, and they observe that stories like Mr. Nixon's leave out a thousand facts for each one they include. For a number of reasons, then, it is useful for the critic to examine narratives carefully. The following critical probes seem especially suited to doing so:

1. *Does the narrative spring from a master narrative?* Hillbruner [1960] notes that many contemporary narratives have their roots in older narratives and that the critic who is sensitive to such antecedents can discover the new implications of these old stories. He found, for

example, that the ancient Greek notion of a great chain of being, wherein all life-forms occupied a different rung on some mystical ladder with God at the top, was still being used by U.S. segregationists twenty centuries later to justify their treatment of blacks (blacks supposedly being a rung down from whites on the great chain). Similarly, Bass [1985] found that Lyndon Johnson used an ancient rescue/salvation narrative to justify the nation's involvement in the Dominican Republic in 1965. In yet another study, Conrad [1983] found evidence of romantic narratives in the rhetoric of the Moral Majority, rhetors who fancied themselves as modern knights of the round table obliged to care for society's most defenseless members (the "unborn" child).

2. *What propositional content is the narrative designed to reveal?* Although narratives do not argue explicitly, they do indeed argue. Their style of argument is devastatingly natural, because it uses a realistic time line to tell who did what when. But behind any narrative lie primitive rhetorical decisions for the speaker: Which facts to stress and which to ignore? Which characters to mention, which to amplify? When to start the story, when to stop it? By making each of these decisions and dozens more like them, the persuader/narrator is also deciding which *ideas* to amplify and which to thrust into the background. Perry [1983], for example, notes that one of the most popular narratives in Nazi Germany conceived of the Jew-as-parasite, an organism that had infiltrated German society and later undermined it. Perry argues that the power of such a story lies in its "figurative logic," in the way it encouraged audiences to think of Jews as "evil, unnatural, and destructive" [p. 234] and hence not worthy of concern. By "bracketing" the Jews in this way, by removing their human status, the parasite story licensed new conclusions about their cultural and political status as well. To accept such a metaphor, says Perry, was to accept a whole new way of thinking as well.

3. *What propositional content is the narrative designed to mask?* This probe encourages the critic to inquire into the underlying purpose of the narrative at hand. When telling a story, after all, the persuader operates preemptively by *not* doing something else. Instead of telling his tale, for example, Richard Nixon could have straightforwardly detailed (1) whose idea it was to have an expense fund, (2) how many dollars were given to how many persons for what purposes, and (3) when the last expenditure was made and why. Dealing directly with these matters would have been uncomfortable for Mr. Nixon. So he told a story.

Kirkwood [1983] comments on the mood-changing power of narrative (it comforts us; it relaxes us) and observes how fiction or a shocking tale suspends "ordinary rationality" and places it in the service of escapist visions. He notes that the humble parable, for example, is really a very powerful form of argument, because it (1) shifts the discussion from actual fact to imagined or re-created fact, (2) subsumes the discussion of principle to the discussion of narrative detail, and (3) reduces the listener to childlike (that is, story-loving) status. Because the narrator takes on a "mantle of spiritual parenthood" [p. 72], says Kirkwood, narrative is not a small matter. When narrative is on stage, then, the critic is wise to look off stage.

Some critics would have us add a fourth, less descriptive, question about narrative: *How effectively and how faithfully does the narrative deal with its subject matter?* This, of course, is the evaluation question and it is important to ask, because storytelling seems so innocent. Fisher [1987] argues that any narrative will have varying amounts of both **narrative probability** (good story qualities: followability, completeness, believability) and **narrative fidelity** (reliability and truthfulness) and that the critic should inspect narrative closely for both features. General guidelines for effective rhetoric can help the critic judge narrative probability, but, as Warnick [1987] notes, we do not yet have clear standards for measuring either truthfulness or reliability. As for reliability—the extent to which the narrative matches the reality it purports to describe—individual critics will have to use their own good judgment by determining (1) what was knowable in a given case, (2) what was knowable by the speaker in particular, and (3) how faithfully the resulting narrative captures what was known.

Ultimately, of course, there can be no final determination on such matters, for accuracy and goodness often exist in the eye of the beholder. But it seems clear that narrative must be inspected carefully. Alone, narrative can be diverting. When combined with rhetoric and introduced into discussions of public policy, however, its diversions must be studied for a basic reason: Rhetorical stories have entailments, they imply consequences. Narrative demands vigilance, because the reasoning it encourages is often as facile as the stories themselves are compelling.

TOULMIN AND REASONING

A useful method for understanding reasoning is based on the work of Stephen Toulmin [1958], who outlined a new way of thinking about informal human argument. Toulmin's approach was a reaction to the models of formal logic then popular in philosophical circles. He felt that such models were too static to deal with something as dynamic as human thought and so he proposed a system better adapted to the actual logics used by actual people. Toulmin did not prescribe how

RHETORIC AND WOMEN'S IDENTITIES

Critical Profile 5.4   Power and Money: Marks of a Woman's Success?

Browsing through the multitude of popular advice books on career women's success, contemporary readers may conclude that "if you've seen one, you've seen them all." Not so, say Barbara Bate and Lois Self of Northern Illinois University. Behind the apparent similarity of such books lie differing, sometimes dichotomous, views of success. From their analysis of seventeen books, Bate and Self found that authors not only prescribe several ways to attain success but that these prescriptions "imply their own world view and its strategic approach to achieving success." How authors conceive of success holds important implications for career women, they argue.

Bate and Self identify three different orientations toward success held by the authors. External markers reflect a view that measures success in terms of money, power, or advancement. Books such as *Beating Men at Their Own Game* and *Wising Up* promote the idea that success is worth any personal investment. Yet, these same books neglect to acknowledge that human costs are incurred or that "external determinants may not be fully satisfactory." In contrast, other authors believe that success is evidenced by internal markers such as self-awareness and personal integration. *Having it All* and *Paths to Power* operate from the premise that "self-knowledge is essential for individual women's happiness." (Success is being able to balance one's personal and professional life.) A third world view defines success ambiguously. *The Effective Woman Manager* assumes that success naturally follows from working for a prosperous organization. Scheele's *Skills for Success* claims that success can be partly measured by external criteria. But at the same time, Scheele underscores the "personal and social dimensions unique to individuals." No explicit criteria for success are offered and readers are left wondering which is the more important pursuit—external or internal markers.

Bate and Self believe that the different philosophies underlying the rhetoric of career women's success books are no trivial matter. They argue that such philosophical differences are significant because what contemporary women "choose as their own definition of success will guide their career choices," as well as the *actions* they take to achieve success. With that sound advice, career women may want to keep in mind the old proverb that "you can't judge a book by its cover."

Profiled by: Yvonne Becerra
Citation: Bate and Self (1983)

people ought to reason; instead, he tried to describe how they actually behaved. Toulmin's approach was quickly seized upon by rhetorical theorists [Ehninger and Brockriede, 1963], and later critics [for example, Arnold, 1974] used the system to analyze actual texts. Another application was that of Hart [1973], who inspected some

Critical Profile 5.5   Finding the Real Bottom Line

Sometimes rhetoric is at its most effective when it seems to have no clear purpose or strategy. A case in point: the startlingly philosophical, almost poetic, tone and uncharacteristically tragic perspective of Elizabeth Cady Stanton's 1892 farewell address as retiring president of the National American Woman Suffrage Association. Titled "The Solitude of Self," the speech was so favorably accepted that when it was read before the U.S. House Committee of the Judiciary, the committee ordered 10,000 reprints. Karlyn Kohrs Campbell, now at the University of Minnesota, notes that despite its success the speech "violates nearly all the traditional canons" of rhetoric: In addition to providing no introduction, conclusion, or apparent logical structure, "it makes no arguments; it provides no evidence." The speech is unlike Stanton's nearly forty-year repertoire of careful argumentation; indeed, it is unique among the rhetoric of the nineteenth century American women's movement. And yet it was, and is, a masterpiece. Why?

Campbell argues that the unusual form of the speech supports its unusual subject—the tragic but empowering idea that each person, man or woman, is "unique, responsible, and alone." The speech is thus a philosophical rather than a practical justification for feminism which subsumed the issues of the day—legal equality, the vote, etc.—within a discussion of the underlying principles of feminism, the same individualistic principles, Stanton asserted, on which the nation was founded. According to Stanton, each person is responsible for his or her own life; it cannot be otherwise: "Who, I ask you, can take, dare take on himself, the rights, the duties, the responsibilities of another human soul . . . ? The talk of sheltering woman from the fierce storms of life is the sheerest mockery, for they beat on her from every point of the compass, just as they do on man, and with more fatal results, for he has been trained to protect himself, to resist and to conquer."

According to Campbell, Stanton turned poetry into rhetoric by discussing the hard-to-discuss. By focusing on the tragic but noble isolation of the individual, Stanton strengthened her audience's commitment to the American notion that rights inhere in people rather than being granted to them by governments, a belief central to advancing the practical goals of the suffrage movement. The effectiveness of Stanton's nonrhetorical yet rhetorical strategy argues for an expanded view of political speechmaking. At times, it appears, a uniquely gifted speaker can cut through the banalities of everyday politics and reach people where they really live—inside their own souls and minds and hearts.

Profiled by: Elizabeth Macom
Citation: Campbell (1980)

Critical Profile 5.6 "Stop Taking Our Privileges"

Does the traditional role of women in American society contradict such basic American values as self-reliance, achievement, and independence? Are American women culturally "handicapped," as the National Organization for Women has asserted? According to Phyllis Schlafly, organizer of STOP ERA, these charges are "the fraud of the century." In contrast to "sharp tongued, high-pitched whining complaints by unmarried women" (her characterization of supporters of the Equal Rights Amendment), Schlafly claims that "[o]f all the classes of people who ever lived, the American woman is the most privileged. . . . The truth is that American women never had it so good. Why should we lower ourselves to 'equal rights' when we already have the status of 'special privilege'?" Martha Solomon, now of the University of Maryland, examined the ideology, ultimate terms, and rhetorical implications of STOP ERA, concluding that its popular success can be ascribed to Schlafly's ability to reconcile women's traditional roles with honored American values. Solomon notes that discourse is most persuasive when it harmonizes attractively with audience members' self-images. Schlafly appeals to her chosen audience by exalting women's traditional roles through a rhetoric of reaffirmation and privilege, concretized in the image of the "Positive Woman." According to Schlafly, the Positive Woman channels her normal American desires into the preservation of her current privileged status; she "has a near-infinite opportunity to control her own destiny, to reach new heights of achievement, and to motivate and influence others. Her potential is limited only by the artificial barriers erected by a negative view of herself or by the stultifying myths of the women's liberation movement."

But while openly celebrating traditional American values, Solomon argues, STOP ERA rhetoric covertly sponsors a less well-accepted ideology of manipulation and fatalism. STOP ERA is less concerned with American concepts of social justice than with the maintenance of privilege, says Solomon. Women are urged to accept the beneficial inequality of American society and to act to preserve it. Schlafly advises that the Positive Woman uses flattery and devotion to bind her husband to her, giving him "the appreciation and the admiration his manhood craves," so that men will continue "to pay premiums on their life insurance policies to provide for her comfort when she is a widow." Rhetorically constructing the situation as a struggle to prevent the ERA's negativistic attempt to strip American women of honored status, Schlafly's goal is capsulized in her group's acronym: "Stop Taking Our Privileges with the Extra Responsibilities Amendment."

Profiled by: Elizabeth Macom
Citation: Solomon (1978)

fifty-four different messages using a modified version of Toulmin's approach. It is this modified version that will be considered here.

Toulmin's system reduces arguments to a kind of outline so as to establish their overall logical movement. By collapsing a text to its skeletal structure, the critic becomes less encumbered by the great amounts of diversionary or supporting material normally contained in a message. Used in this rough fashion, the Toulmin system is more robust than it is precise, but it does provide an economical way of talking about large quantities of discourse. At the simplest level, the critic using the Toulmin system "translates" a message into Toulminian terminology. At a more ambitious level, the system allows the critic to (1) make patterned sense out of discourse by focusing on its most essential logical movements; (2) use the Toulmin layout of a message as a general starting point for more fine-grained analyses; and (3) employ a standard system so that many different kinds of discourse can be compared on the same basis.

As modified by Hart [1973], the Toulmin system asks the critic to isolate in a given message three key features:

1. **Major claims** (a) are the broadest, most encompassing, statements made by the speaker, (b) lie at a level of abstraction higher than all other statements the speaker makes, (c) represent what the speaker hopes will become the "residual message" in listeners' minds (that is, the main thoughts remembered when the details of a message have been forgotten), and (d) are frequently repeated or restated in the message.

2. **Major data** lie at a level of abstraction immediately beneath that of the major claim. Major data are the supporting structures of discourse, statements answering the listener's questions: What makes you say that? What do you have to go on? Major data themselves subsume what might be thought of as subdata: facts, illustrations, bits of evidence, and other clarifying devices used to ground the speaker's assertions.

3. **Warrants** are the keys to the Toulminian approach. They make the "movement" from major data to major claim possible. Toulmin [1958:98] described warrants as "general, hypothetical statements which can act as bridges and authorize the sort of step to which our particular argument commits us." So, for example, if a speaker makes the assertion that "Ransom money should never be paid to free U.S. hostages seized abroad" (major claim) because "you can't deal with terrorists" (major data), the "missing" part of the argument is something of the sort: "Only terrorists would seize an airplane" (warrant).

Ehninger and Brockriede [1963] describe three types of warrants commonly found in public argument: (1) **substantive warrants**—ideas based on what is thought to be actual fact (such as the terrorists-are-irresponsible notion used above); (2) **motivational warrants**—ideas suggesting that some desirable end must be achieved or that some desirable condition is being endangered (for example, the argument "We must pay the ranson money" [m.c.] because "the people will crucify us in the upcoming elections if we don't" [m.d.] somehow depends for its reasonability on the notion that "getting re-elected is a good thing" [w]; (3) **authoritative warrants**—ideas based on the credibility of the speaker or on the source of testimony offered by the speaker (for example, to warrant the argument "We can't pay the ransom" [m.c.] because "I've told the people in the past I wouldn't do so" [m.d.], a speaker would be depending on some such notion as "inconsistent people are crucified in politics" or "this ransom issue isn't worth my political scalp" [w].

In laying out a given message, the critic follows some fairly simple steps: (1) Isolate the major claims being offered by the speaker, keying particularly on repeated or reparaphrased statements; (2) isolate the major data presented, many of which (but not all of which) will be found contiguous to the major claims made; (3) without consulting the message directly, isolate the range of warrants that could reasonably authorize such data-claim movements; (4) categorize these potential warrants, using the tripartite system described above; and (5) determine which of these warrants were *explicitly supplied* by the speaker and which were left unspoken.

Step 5 is especially crucial in criticism. Most, if not all, discourse depends heavily on the cooperation of listeners to complete the reasoning circuit begun by the speaker. A street corner shout to "get out of the street [m.c.], a bus is coming [m.d.]" hardly needs to be attended by the warrant "buses can make mincemeat out of you." Our reactions to such a cry of warning are instinctual: We quickly help the argument along by supplying from our knowledge (of physics) and our biases (self-preservation) the missing pieces and parts needed to make sense out of the warner's "argument." Thus, most persuaders rarely say everything that could be said, trusting that if the correct data are chosen for the correct claim the audience will allow the argumentative movement, if not propel it. From such a perspective, the persuader becomes a solicitor, one who uses language to entice listeners to participate silently in an argumentative exchange. The Toulmin system encourages us to search for such "missing" elements, since examining the *unstated* in discourse provides the most subtle understanding of speaker-audience relationships.

To understand the value of the Toulmin system, let us consider a simple example, a letter to the editor in a small-town, midwestern newspaper that is neither subtle nor argumentatively complex:

> On the Democratic ticket you see Ben Anderson's name. He is a good Christian man. He is an honest man, and you can trust him.
>
> Let us all go to the polls and vote for Mr. Anderson. I've known him for a long time.
>
> We need good men in our offices and more like him.
>
> Let's you and I go and vote for Mr. Anderson.

Figure 5.1 lays out the letter's argument. Several things are striking: (1) Four of the claims are simply asserted. No data are supplied to establish their validity. This gives the message its choppy, telegraphic feeling; (2) the central argument—that Anderson should be elected—is supported by four different pieces of data, none of which has subdata. This gives the message its confident and businesslike tone; (3) none of the data-claim movements is explicity warranted. The

Figure 5.1
Toulmin Layout of Letter to the Editor

Major claims	Warrants	Major Data
	A = authoritative M = motivational S = substantive 0 = suppressed ** = supplied	† = subdata provided 0 = subdata omitted
1. Anderson is a democrat.	(None)	(None)
2. He's running for office.	(None)	(None)
3. Let's vote for him.	3-1. Christians make good officials. (M/0)	He's a Christian. (0)
	3-2. Honesty is important in government. (M/0)	He's honest. (0)
	3-3. Trust is important in government. (M/0)	You can trust him. (0)
	3-4. You can rely on my judgment. (A/0)	I've known him for a long time. (0)
4. We need good men.	(None)	(None)
5. Let's vote for Anderson.	(None)	(None)

tone; (3) none of the data-claim movements is explicity warranted. The three needed motivational warrants (that Christianity, honesty, and trustworthiness are desirable) are omitted as is the one authoritative warrant (that the letter-writer is credible). These missing warrants give the message its homey, emotional touches. Neighbors speaking over the back fence do not need to supply warrants, and people who are sounding off often do not supply them either. As a result, this message is "presumptuous." The argument demands a good deal from the newspaper reader because of its sketchiness, a feature somewhat required by the enforced brevity of these letters, but also expected from anybody letting off steam. These distinctive, often charming, qualities make letters to the editor the most popular feature in almost any local newspaper.

The Toulmin approach can also describe more complex discourse—like that of Richard Nixon—and so Figure 5.2 presents a Toulmin layout of the Checkers Speech. One of the real advantages of the Toulmin system is that by outlining a message skeletally, it emphasizes a message's value appeals and deemphasizes its beguiling use of language. A Toulmin sketch tells us, for example, that Nixon took a two-pronged approach in his speech. Not only did he defend himself against the charges but he also used the occasion to launch a blistering attack on the Democratic party. Data-claim movements 1–5 present the defense, data-claim movements 7–14 the offense. Data-claim movement 6 is particularly interesting. It forms a kind of transition between the two speeches, with Nixon arguing that the Chairman of the Democratic National Committee had affirmed "that if a man couldn't afford to be in the United States Senate, he shouldn't run for the Senate." Nixon reasons that such a notion runs contrary to Republican philosophy and quotes Abraham Lincoln to that effect. After offering the Lincoln quotation ("God must have loved the common people, he made so many of them"), Nixon is off on his political rounds, slashing away in campaigner's style at the evils of the day.

A major difference between Nixon's two speeches is how tight his arguments in d-c movements 1–5 are and how distended his arguments become later. Early on, Nixon densely packs his arguments: Most major claims are attended by two or three different pieces of data, with d-c movement 5 being the densest of all (ten identifiable pieces of major data). This is a lawyerly Nixon, one who makes his case by trying to overwhelm his listener, offering them a variety of data but (as in d-c movement 5) never letting them forget the major claim—that he is innocent.

In the remainder of the speech, however, Nixon wanders. He shifts his focus quickly (Democrats, communists, Eisenhower, quitting),

Figure 5.2
Toulmin Layout of Nixon's Checkers Speech

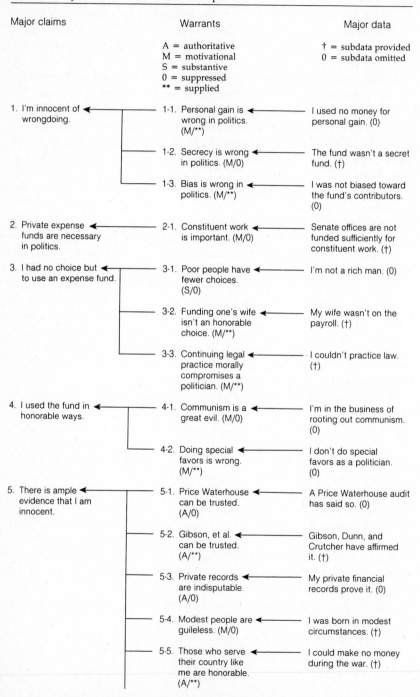

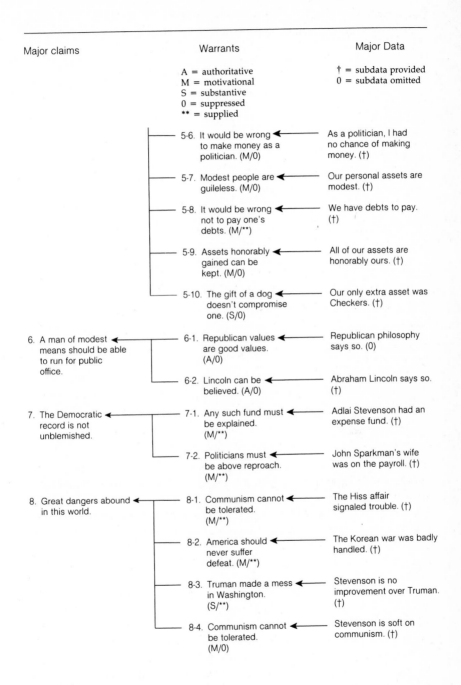

Major claims	Warrants	Major Data
	A = authoritative M = motivational S = substantive 0 = suppressed ** = supplied	† = subdata provided 0 = subdata omitted

5-6. It would be wrong to make money as a politician. (M/0) ◄— As a politician, I had no chance of making money. (†)

5-7. Modest people are guileless. (M/0) ◄— Our personal assets are modest. (†)

5-8. It would be wrong not to pay one's debts. (M/**) ◄— We have debts to pay. (†)

5-9. Assets honorably gained can be kept. (M/0) ◄— All of our assets are honorably ours. (†)

5-10. The gift of a dog doesn't compromise one. (S/0) ◄— Our only extra asset was Checkers. (†)

6. A man of modest means should be able to run for public office. ◄—

6-1. Republican values are good values. (A/0) ◄— Republican philosophy says so. (0)

6-2. Lincoln can be believed. (A/0) ◄— Abraham Lincoln says so. (†)

7. The Democratic record is not unblemished. ◄—

7-1. Any such fund must be explained. (M/**) ◄— Adlai Stevenson had an expense fund. (†)

7-2. Politicians must be above reproach. (M/**) ◄— John Sparkman's wife was on the payroll. (†)

8. Great dangers abound in this world. ◄—

8-1. Communism cannot be tolerated. (M/**) ◄— The Hiss affair signaled trouble. (†)

8-2. America should never suffer defeat. (M/**) ◄— The Korean war was badly handled. (†)

8-3. Truman made a mess in Washington. (S/**) ◄— Stevenson is no improvement over Truman. (†)

8-4. Communism cannot be tolerated. (M/0) ◄— Stevenson is soft on communism. (†)

Figure 5.2
Toulmin Layout of Nixon's Checkers Speech (*continued*)

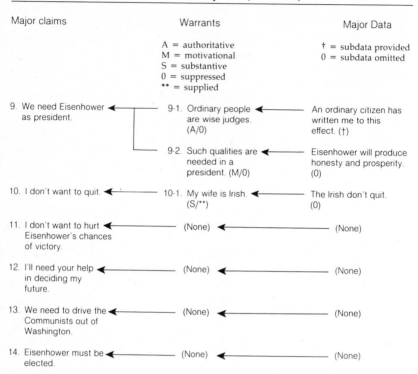

Major claims	Warrants	Major Data
	A = authoritative M = motivational S = substantive 0 = suppressed ** = supplied	† = subdata provided 0 = subdata omitted
9. We need Eisenhower as president.	9-1. Ordinary people are wise judges. (A/0)	An ordinary citizen has written me to this effect. (†)
	9-2. Such qualities are needed in a president. (M/0)	Eisenhower will produce honesty and prosperity. (0)
10. I don't want to quit.	10-1. My wife is Irish. (S/**)	The Irish don't quit. (0)
11. I don't want to hurt Eisenhower's chances of victory.	(None)	(None)
12. I'll need your help in deciding my future.	(None)	(None)
13. We need to drive the Communists out of Washington.	(None)	(None)
14. Eisenhower must be elected.	(None)	(None)

developing no argument in real depth. In his "second" speech, he almost never offers subdata (facts, testimony, etc.), which is probably why the first five of his fourteen d-c movements account for almost *two-thirds* of his speech text. Indeed, his last four major claims are simply asserted; not even major data are offered. The conclusion of his speech (presented as part of the headnote to this chapter) shows the effect of such an argumentative approach: intense political emotion.

Perhaps the most interesting thing about Mr. Nixon's remarks is how explicit he warrants his d-c movements. This single feature probably explains why the "Checkers Speech" has been the object of so many political barbs by journalists over the years. Journalists appreciate subtlety and Mr. Nixon was anything but subtle. Apparently, he felt that he could not take the chance that the members of his audience would voluntarily warrant his arguments, so he did so himself. When stated, warrants often sound aphoristic as well as sermonic, as if they had come from *Poor Richard's Almanac*. Here are some snippets from Mr. Nixon's litany of warrants:

- "I have a theory, too, that the best and only answer to a smear or to an honest misunderstanding of the facts is to tell the truth."
- "I say that it was morally wrong if [money] was secretly given and secretly handled."
- "The taxpayers should not be required to finance items which are not official business, but which are primarily political business."
- "Gibson, Dunn and Crutcher, lawyers in Los Angeles, [is] the biggest law firm, and incidentally, one of the best."
- "I pay [my parents back] regularly because it is part of the savings they have made through the years they were working so hard."
- "A man that's to be President of the United States, a man that is to be vice-president of the United States, must have the confidence of all the people."
- "A war which costs us 117,000 American casualties isn't good enough for America."
- "The Irish never quit."

Although Mr. Nixon's listeners already knew that political thievery, war casualties, and deadbeat sons were undesirable, Nixon reminds them again anyway. Such obviousness made the journalists of his day groan and today's audiences smile when they watch the speech replayed. But Mr. Nixon's target audience in 1952 responded enthusiastically, inundating the Republican National Committee with thousands upon thousands of telegrams immediately after the speech. Mr. Nixon's warrants may have been overly sentimental, but their clarity won him the day.

Research using the Toulmin system has proved its critical usefulness. Hart [1970], for example, probed speaker/audience relationships when contrasting "doctrinal" and "hostile" rhetoric. Whereas speakers in the former situations (who spoke to accepting listeners) rarely provided explicit warrants, the latter offered an average of two such statements per d-c movement and also showed an unusual fondness for authoritative warrants, ostensibly because they felt that their disagreeing audiences would not cooperate with them argumentatively. A study by Clark [1977] found that religious sermonizing was distinguished by a compactness not found in the secular rhetoric he also studied. The preachers used only a small number of d-c movements, telling a narrow, but well embellished, tale. Secular speakers, in contrast, felt the need to cover more issues, perhaps because they required as many *different* bases of support as they could get with their unindoctrinated listeners.

The Toulmin system also helps explain tone. For example, the boldness of the Patton speech mentioned earlier probably resulted from his rapid transition from major data to major data, all of which are placed in the service of one major claim ("We will be victorious") but none of which is developed via subdata. In contrast, the frivolous tone of Harold Hill's speech results from his dependence upon sacred warrants (the wages of sin, the importance of industry, communal obligations, etc.) for profane purposes (the selling of band instruments). The presumptuous tone of The Student's Lament (that end-of-the-semester whine resulting in the major claim, "I simply must have an 'A' in this course") is often signaled by the highly questionable warrants needed to legitimize the movement from data to claim: *The Puritan Ethic* ("I've worked really hard in here"), *Ego Unbounded* ("I've really liked your course"), *In Loco Parentis* ("I'll flunk out of school unless you help me out"), or *Capitalism Incorporated* ("A lesser grade will hurt me on the job market"). Because these values are so deeply ingrained in U.S. culture, students using them are bewildered (not to mention irritated) when instructors call attention to these warranting structures. The professor who responds to such a request with the faintly European assertion, "Only excellence, not character, is rewarded in here," comes across as a cultural alien.

The critic using the Toulmin approach is equipped, finally, with a system that may explain why a given message failed to persuade. Like other critical tools, the Toulmin approach provides the critic with a technical language for describing rhetorical trends that cannot easily be described in lay language. So, for example, a message may be said to fail because its major claims are too disparate (the speaker rambles), because claims are offered without data (a speaker rants), because major data are offered but not linked to the claims they are intended to reinforce (the speaker becomes anecdotal), because there are no culturally available warrants for the data chosen (the speaker seems irrelevant), or because the speaker explicates warrants too insistently (the speaker becomes pontifical). Thus, the Toulmin system seems the best method developed thus far for explaining that curious brand of thinking/feeling known as human reasoning.

CONCLUSION

For many years, the study of reasoning was solely the province of the philosopher. Later, the children of philosophers, psychologists, began to explore the workings of the human mind. Whereas the philosopher treated ideas in their pure forms (their most abstract forms), the psychologist investigated what people felt when thinking about ideas. More recently, the rhetorical critic set out to discover how persuasive messages mediate human reasoning. The critic interested in practical argument does not become as abstract as the philosopher nor as individualistic as the psychologist. Instead, the critic searches for evidence of *social reasoning* by looking "through" messages to the human beings cooperatively producing them. The study of public argument is, therefore, the study of how minds meet.

This chapter has championed a psycho-logical model of argument, taking the position that reasoning is more than ciphering. As a result, the critic has been urged to inspect all arguments through the eyes of the human beings who are attempting to reason collectively. This model abandons the thinking/feeling dualism so often found in Western culture and the elitism found in technical or idealist models. It urges the critic to study the rules of *ordinary* reasoning, even if those rules spring from the humble advice found in everyday proverbs [Goodwin and Wenzel, 1979]. It urges the critic to study the rhetoric of "peculiar" people, because learning about strangers so often translates into genuine self-knowledge [Hill, 1973]. It urges the critic to study the "intuitive validity" a message has for listeners, even if the listeners' standards for validity are not the critic's [Brummett, 1984b]. Finally, it reminds the critic that reasoning is something that people do in their own marvelously complicated ways. May that ever be the case.

CHAPTER SIX

Analyzing Form and Structure

LEAR: Attend the lords of France and Burgundy, Gloucester.
GLOUCESTER: I shall, my liege. [Exeunt Gloucester and Edmund.]
LEAR: Meantime we shall express our darker purpose.
   Give me the map there. Know that we have divided
   In three our kingdom: and 'tis our fast intent
   To shake all cares and business from our age;
   Conferring them on younger strengths, while we
   Unburthen'd crawl toward death. Our son of Cornwall,
   And you, our no less loving son of Albany,
   We have this hour a constant will to publish
   Our daughters' several dowers, that future strife
   May be prevented now. The princes, France and Burgundy,
   Great rivals in our youngest daughter's love,
   Long in our court have made their amorous sojourn,
   And here are to be answer'd. Tell me, my daughters,
   Since now we will divest us, both of rule,
   Interest of territory, cares of state, Which of
   you shall we say doth love us most?
   That we our largest bounty may extend
   Where nature doth merit challenge. Goneril,
   Our eldest-born, speak first.
GONERIL: Sir, I love you more than words can wield the matter;
   Dearer than eye-sight, space, and liberty;
   Beyond what can be valued, rich or rare;
   No less than life, with grace, health, beauty, honour;
   As much as child e'er loved, or father found;
   A love that makes breath poor, and speech unable;
   Beyond all manner of so much I love you.
CORDELIA: [Aside] What shall Cordelia do? Love, and be silent.
LEAR: Of all these bounds, even from this line to this,
   With shadowy forests and with champains rich'd,
   With plenteous rivers and wide-skirted meads,
   We make thee lady: to thine and Albany's issue

> Be this perpetual. What says our second daughter,
> Our dearest Regan, wife to Cornwall? Speak.

REGAN: Sir, I am made
> Of the self-same metal that my sister is,
> And prize me at her worth. In my true heart
> I find she names my very deed of love;
> Only she comes too short: that I profess
> Myself as enemy to all other joys,
> Which the most precious square of sense possesses;
> And find I am alone felicitate
> In your dear highness' love.

CORDELIA: [Aside] Then poor Cordelia! And yet not so;
> since, I am sure, my love's
> More richer than my tongue.

LEAR: To thee and thine hereditary ever
> Remain this ample third of our fair kingdom;
> No less in space, validity, and pleasure,
> Than that conferr'd on Goneril. Now, our joy,
> Although the last, not least; to whose young love
> The vines of France and milk of Burgundy
> Strive to be interess'd; what can you say to draw
> A third more opulent than your sisters? Speak.

CORDELIA: Nothing, my lord.

LEAR: Nothing.

CORDELIA: Nothing.

LEAR: Nothing will come of nothing: speak again.

CORDELIA: Unhappy that I am, I cannot heave
> My heart into my mouth: I love your majesty
> According to my bond; nor more nor less.

LEAR: How, how, Cordelia! mend your speech a little,
> Lest it may mar your fortunes.

CORDELIA: Good my lord,
> You have begot me, bred me, loved me:
> I Return those duties back as are right fit,
> Obey you, love you, and most honour you.
> Why have my sisters husbands, if they say
> They love you all? Haply, when I shall wed,
> That lord whose hand must take my plight shall carry
> Half my love with him, half my care and duty:
> Sure, I shall never marry like my sisters,
> To love my father all.

LEAR: But goest thy heart with this?

CORDELIA: Ay, good my lord.

LEAR: So young, and so untender?

CORDELIA: So young, my lord, and true.

LEAR: Let it be so; thy truth, then, be thy dower . . .
> [Shakespeare, 1603:983–984]

Thy truth, then, be thy dower. Not a happy epitaph for a would-be heiress. And not a very rhetorical epitaph either. Young Cordelia, faithful daughter of her aging and self-indulgent father, need only have uttered sweet nothings to inherit a kingdom. Cordelia's sisters, Goneril and Regan, surely had no trouble meeting Lear's challenge. They understood the speech-act implicitly: Tell him you love him and make him forget that he forced you to say such things. When in human history have such riches hung upon the mere saying of a speech?

And Lear was hardly choosy here. Were he our contemporary, the lyrics to any Top Forty love ballad would have sufficed. So what's wrong, Cordelia? Why not "mend your speech" for a moment or two? Why let your audience confuse your integrity with a lack of tenderness on your part? Why get philosophical when the situation so clearly invites you to be mercenary?

Cordelia's defense of her actions is hardly compelling. She pleads lack of rhetorical competence: a love "richer than her tongue." She stands on personal principle: an unwillingness to "heave her heart into her mouth." But Cordelia's outrage seems even more basic: She resents using a standard rhetorical form to show unstandard love of a parent. She resents being trooped across Lear's stage, the third in a line of singing princesses, forced to mimic speech that is neither exalted nor subtle. Cordelia was not unloving, nor was she unwilling to discuss her love. Rather, she felt that love has its own timetable and that it is diminished when employed unfeelingly and by command. Above all, Cordelia resents the formulas of love: formulas repeated daily to her father by courtiers, formulas her sisters have turned into rites of devotion. In rejecting these formulas, Cordelia became less rhetor than critic. Sadly, critics almost never please kings.

This chapter discusses forms and formulas. It is concerned with three things. First is **structure**—the apportionment and sequencing of message elements. Structural decisions revolve about which ideas should be given what amount of attention and how ideas should be arranged for maximum impact. For example, an important structural feature of Cordelia's speech is the balance struck between discussions of her love for her father and the love she someday expects to have for a husband. This equivalence made little sense: Lear was clearly not interested in sharing the rhetorical spotlight, especially not with a non-existent son-in-law. Cordelia's sisters, on the other hand, were highly conventional. Their rhetoric placed Lear on stage by himself, dominating all with his several fascinations. They did not confuse their father, covering less ground in their speeches but with greater impact. Cordelia's rhetorical ambition, in contrast, prompted only scorn.

This chapter's second concern is **form**—the patterns of meaning listeners generate when they take in a message. Form refers to the "shape" of meaning, how ideas are linked together by listeners. Some ideas (for example, inflationary spirals) sit in a listener's mind alone and unloved, associated only with abstruse economic principles, boring political editorials, and a vague sense of unpleasantness. Other ideas (say, a circus) generate a host of pleasant associations: hot dogs, clowns, elephants, calliopes, popcorn, colorful tents, earthy smells, fancy costumes, and memories of innocence. Thinking of a circus fills up the mind in ways that inflationary spirals cannot. If it has been a long time since our last circus, the booming welcome of the ringmaster will immediately help to "fill out" the mental form of the circus, making us properly anticipatory as circus-goers.

Implicitly knowing such things, Goneril tells Lear that her love surpasses those things her father already prizes ("eye-sight, space, and liberty"). Her speech asks Lear to think of life's most precious qualities ("grace, health, beauty, honour") and then to round out this mental picture by adding her love to the concoction. Cordelia, in contrast, runs competition with herself, asking her father to ponder her affection in the company of such unpleasant things as contracts ("I return those duties back as are right fit") and jealousy ("that lord whose hand must take my plight"). Law, envy, and love—hardly a comfortable mixture of ideas for a defensive old man.

Finally, this chapter treats **genre**—a class of messages sharing important structural and content features that creates special expectations in listeners. Genre exists because speakers are imitative, borrowing from yesterday when deciding what to say today. A genre—the religious invocation at a sporting event, the political commercial on television, the gold-watch speech at a retirement dinner—develops because people's life experiences are so similar: They are born, they grow up, they fall in love, and they die. They always have, and they always have needed to speak of these experiences, resulting in pink and blue birth announcements, bar mitzvah speeches, marriage proposals under the stars, and moving funeral orations. Each of these messages echoes its forebears, at least in part.

Naturally, history can be tyranny. Utilizing the formulas of speech requires a Faustian bargain: guaranteed social acceptability in exchange for independence of thought. Lear's daughter Regan opted for this deal, drawing upon a rich tradition of courtly love ("I profess myself an enemy to all other joys"), thereby anticipating her father's anticipations. Cordelia, in contrast, intentionally violated the generic rules. She combined biology ("you begot me") with sociology ([you] "bred me") and delivered herself of a dispassionate, intellectually balanced college lecture. Good genre. Wrong audience.

This chapter probes how message structure interacts with expected patterns of meaning (form) to produce persuasion. Structure and form are a complex business, but examining rule-following and rule-violating is almost always profitable. This chapter's thesis is that by knowing who follows rhetorical rules and who does not, the critic can learn much about the whys and wherefores of these rules. Perhaps this is why Shakespeare opened his great tragedy with the generic struggle presented above. Perhaps he sensed that an important moral lesson could be taught by depicting who used rhetoric and who was used by it. With Shakespeare as our first teacher, then, let us become better students of structure and form.

FORM AND STRUCTURE IN RHETORIC

The key distinction between structure and form is this: Structure is something that speakers do and form is something that listeners do. Structure is identifiable in texts, form emerges in listeners' minds. Figure 6.1 provides a clear, albeit elementary, example of this distinction. If asked the question, "Which picture has the *clearest* meaning?," most people would pick Figure A. If then asked, "Which picture has *special* meaning?," they would give the same answer. Figure A symbolizes the United States of America. Versions of it have been planted on the moon, on the hills of Iwo Jima, on Kuwaiti oil tankers in the Persian Gulf, on Olympic team jackets, on the lapels of conservative bankers, and on the coffins of heroes in Arlington National Cemetery. Figure A has also been worn on the backsides of student protesters in the 1960s, burned in the streets of Teheran in the 1970s, and displayed during Fourth of July automobile sales in the 1980s. Figure A inspires many, infuriates others. It is drenched in meaning.

But Figures B, C, and D show that Figure A's content is not exceptional. It is merely a special arrangement of iconic characters: stars, bars, and backgrounds. Its meaning, the *form* it takes in the perceiver's mind, is heavily dependent upon its basic *structural* elements. Even a slight rearrangement of these elements (Figure B) changes the evocative power of the symbol completely. A more ambitious rearrangement (Figure C) removes virtually all of its "Americanicity." While Figure C possesses a certain raciness not present in Old Glory, it is still unlikely to draw a salute.

Figure D seems so distorted as to be sacrilegious. It takes perceptual gymnastics to see that its content is identical to that of Figure A. Upon viewing it, schoolchildren would wonder and patriots would quake, both assuming that there is only one "right" way to assemble such elements. They would resist *any* arbitrary arrangement of these features, sensing that even the slightest variation on the "true" optical theme would rob it of its formal meaning. When it comes to Figure A, Americans become visual fundamentalists.

Figure 6.1
Relationships Between Content and Structure

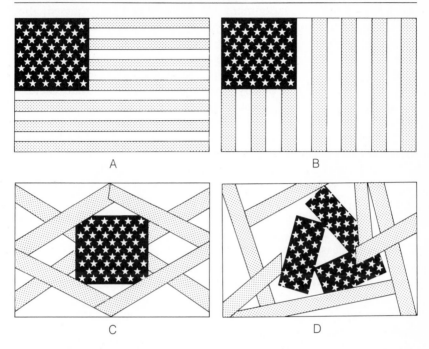

A

B

C

D

Figure 6.1 teaches an important lesson: Structure and content cannot be separated easily. As we moved from Figure A to Figure D, the contents of the messages became increasingly radical. *Only* Figure A is acceptable if conventional meanings are to be shared. Figure D meant nothing to us. We were incapable of forming its elements into something sensible, never mind into something important, never mind into something motivating. As Heath [1979] argues, certain message structures arouse particularized expectations within perceivers, who are often unwilling to change those expectations—or forms—once they have been aroused (for example, once stars and bars have been presented in the same visual field). Thus, formulating rhetoric involves selecting and arranging message elements and predicting how listeners will react to these elements additively. As Arnold [1974:137]notes, listeners *will* generate forms in their heads constantly. The speaker uses structural devices to guide this process of forming.

The centrality of structure to content is best seen in the absence of structure (as in Figure D) or in its misapplication. For example, if a preacher somehow forgot to ask the bride and groom to exchange vows during a wedding, the event would not be "formed" as a proper ceremony by those in the church pews. Upon first noticing the omission, the wedding guests might well treat the experience as a novelty, as a preacher's ritualistic experiment. As the ceremony progressed, they would try to re-form this newly evolving reality into traditional meanings ("perhaps the vows will be exchanged just before the recessional"). As Gregg [1978] notes, form is constantly emerging across time for listeners as they try out new interpretations of new data. Ideally, the speaker helps out by structuring messages so that listeners' formings become whole, consistent, clear, meaningful, and comforting. Should the speaker shirk such responsibilities, listeners will take over the task themselves: "Poor Pastor Johnson has become addle-brained" or "maybe John and Sue are putting us all on."

Critics have often treated structure formalistically by applying a set of prescriptive laws to message organization. Research by Douglass and Arnold [1970], however, shows that few real-life messages fit these standard patterns. A more promising line of inquiry, they suggest, is to treat structure as a psychological, not as a linguistic, process, and to examine a message not as a set of self-contained statements but as a *stimulus to reasoning* for listeners. They warn critics that while structure can be found in messages, the more important element, form, is found in listeners' reactions to these structures. So, for example, Douglass and Arnold urge critics to search for the kinds of "organizational help" a speaker provides and for the inferences listeners are likely to draw as a result. By asking which ideas were emphasized and which were not, which came first and which last, which were interrupted and which were not, a critic begins to learn what listeners "did" with the rhetorical materials they were asked to process. Thus, a speaker who tells a long-winded story without a point or who relates facts in reverse chronological order is likely to frustrate listeners' forming instincts. Ideally, then, a critic looks through message to listener, through structure to form, to find rhetorical effect.

A useful way of examining message structure is to ask a set of questions about how rhetorical materials have been arranged in a given case. These probes deal with **message design** (the use of standard structural devices), **message emphasis** (the comparative treatment of individual ideas), **message density** (the depth of coverage of individual ideas), and **message pacing** (the distribution of ideas through time). In each case, the critic is urged to look for the effects message patterns have within listeners. The first of these questions has to do with message design:

Does the speaker use an (1) identifiable and (2) consistent type of traditional message structure?

Is this approach used throughout or only from time to time?

Here, the critic inspects a text's overall architecture to see if it conforms to any of the classic patterns of message structure. Table 6.1 presents those patterns, although it must be emphasized that only rarely will textbook examples of these patterns be found in real-life persuasion (since speakers often take shortcuts). Also, merely identifying these patterns is of little use unless they can also shed light on the overall rhetorical situation being studied. Since message structure relates so closely to how people think, it can tell much about a speaker's mental habits or an audience's operating hierarchy of beliefs. These structural cues are suggestive, because people often do not think about *how* they will present ideas but only about what they will say. Thus, asking why a speaker's first argument came first and not last forces the critic to explain what nonarbitrary logic the speaker used when making the always arbitrary decisions of firstness and lastness. And the fact that these decisions never *seem* arbitrary to a speaker adds to their capacity to shed light on unstated intellectual and cultural premises.

Some of our earlier messages show the importance of message design. Harold Hill, for example, used causal sequence to prove that all versions of local sin could be attributed to the goings-on in the pool hall. After making this case, Hill returned to the high school gymnasium and presented a second speech ("Seventy-Six Trombones"), which functioned as the conclusion to his overarching problem-solution strategy. Perhaps the most interesting thing about Hill's structure is its purity. His speeches emerge in the play as set pieces, unadulterated examples of classic rhetorical design. The unerring way in which they unfold seems to be the playwright's tip that Hill is up to no good. These structures are so pure, so self-propelling, that the theatre audience becomes enthralled with Hill-the-strategist and, at the same time, begins to feel slightly superior to him. This sense of superiority is important, since if Hill's manipulativeness cannot readily be seen by the audience, they will be unable to appreciate his eventual reconstruction. Thus, Hill uses the sin-then-salvation motif to perfection, which, in turn, stands as evidence of his imperfection.

Things are more disorderly in real life. George Patton, for example, rambled when speaking, moving from discussion of a winning spirit to the availability of superior equipment, to the psychology of combat, to the need for toughness, and finally to the immortality of bravery. Such a topical structure is not without its advantages. Rambling gives the audience the sense that they are being let in on the speaker's unconscious; it allows Patton to become human, even though he almost never refers to himself in the speech. Similarly, his transitions are no more elaborate than the word "now." These brief punctuations signal to the audience that something else has just occurred to Patton and that he might as well get that off his chest too. This sort of lazy structure

Table 6.1 Common Structural Techniques in Persuasion

Structural Type	Rhetorical Function	Example (State Legislative Debate)	Main Advantages	Main Disadvantages	Critical Probe
Chronological sequence	Places time relationships in the foreground so that narrative becomes clear	"In the 1970s, we tried a sales tax and that proved inadequate. We moved to sin taxes in the '80s. The '90s require something new: a tax on professional services."	Builds suspense as the past unfolds into the present (or future)	Propositions the speaker is advocating can become subordinated to the telling of the "story"	What appears to be the speaker's rationale for discussing the particular points-in-time chosen for discussion?
Spatial sequence	Shows relationships between parts and parts or between parts and wholes	"The opportunities in this state are enormous. The lake area has tourist development. The tri-city area is luring high-tech industry. And the plateau region has the new Space Command Center."	Makes ideas "visual" for listeners	Too much detail may cloud the ideas being advanced	What devices did the speaker use to demonstrate the "adjacency" of the elements described?
Ascending/ Descending sequence	Ideas are arranged according to their relative importance, familiarity, or complexity	"I agree with Senator Davenport that cable regulation must be at least considered this session. And I agree with Senator Foley that the open-meeting law is important. But we can't even think about those things	Gives a sense of precision by emphasizing the relationship of one concept to another	Once begun, the sequence must be completed, with all necessary stages being discussed	What specific strategic advantage is the speaker hoping for by emphasizing climaxes or anticlimaxes?

Causal sequence	Links observable effects to underlying factors allegedly responsible for those effects	"until we agree on funding basic state services." "Ladies and gentlemen of the legislature, I ask you to reflect on industrial development in this state. What's responsible for our growth in that area? I'll tell you what: a superior educational system. Let's never forget that."	Western listeners particularly appreciate causal structures	Listeners have been taught to distrust *simple* cause-effect linkages	What steps did the speaker take to guard the *credibility* of the causal attributions made?
Problem-Solution sequence	Appropriate courses of action are endorsed on the basis of their capacity to remedy problems	"You and I both know that we need a revenue bill that's at least three things: timely, fair, and adequate. That's what my plan is about."	Builds on the common psychological need within people to overcome difficulties	If listeners are unconvinced of the seriousness of the problem, boredom results	Did the speaker spend the most time emphasizing problems or were solutions primarily stressed?
Withheld-Proposal sequence	Favorable materials are piled up and the speaker's solution mentioned only briefly at the end	"Let's reflect for a moment on what the park system has done for this state. It's the best run system in the nation and it adds four hundred million dollars a year in tourist revenue to our budget each year. Let's keep all of that in mind when we discuss funding for the parks this year."	An ostensibly "innocent" approach and therefore especially useful for a hostile audience	Highly dependent for effectiveness on the speaker's knowledge of what the audience currently knows and feels	Does the speaker make the *transition* from general to "preferred" materials gracefully and non-manipulatively?

Table 6.1 Common Structural Techniques in Persuasion (*continued*)

Structural Type	Rhetorical Function	Example (State Legislative Debate)	Main Advantages	Main Disadvantages	Critical Probe
Open-Proposal sequence	Direct, deductive presentation of a proposal followed by support for that proposal	"You people have already heard the conservative approach to doing things. Tonight I'm going to give you another perspective: We need to raise taxes immediately. Here's why."	A simple and clear sequence which appears "fourthright" as a result	Can be boring for listeners if they feel that they have "heard it all before"	How does the speaker compensate for the lack of suspense such an approach entails?
Reflective sequence	A variation on the problem-solution sequence in which the speaker professes no particular preferences for a solution	"Quite frankly, I'm not sure how to proceed at this point in the debate. State revenues have never been lower and welfare needs have never been higher. The problems are obvious. But what are the solutions?"	Sets up an "exploratory" mood by involving listeners directly in problem-solving	Can be seen as manipulative if the speaker suddenly opts for a particular solution	Does the speaker maintain a sense of *mutual* problem-solving by actively considering all possible alternatives?
Elimination sequence	A solution-oriented approach in which all but one remedy is successively eliminated by the speaker	"So we've looked at five different options this morning and found each of them wanting. What choice	Highly useful when the audience readily acknowledges	Can be seen as manipulative if the speaker seems to be using a strawman argument	What does the speaker do to guard against listeners' *impatience* with

	Characteristic	Example	Rationale	Limitation	Evaluative question
		do we have other than to adopt the Harris plan forthwith?"	the relevance and importance of the problem		such a lockstep structure?
Motivational sequence	Speaker follows a fixed pattern of attention, need, satisfaction, visualization, and action	"Ten thousand. That's the number of state-funded abortions performed last year. Without more money, pretty soon only rich women will be able to afford abortions and the welfare rolls will swell. We simply must pass H.B. 21 and we must do it *today*."	Parallels what is thought to be a universally attractive and psychologically "whole" sequence of thought	A fairly vague series of steps that are not always easily distinguished from one another	How much time does the speaker spend on each "stage" of the sequence and were such allocations of time justified?
Topical sequence	Breaks a subject matter into several equivalent sub-parts and then treats them in somewhat arbitrary order	"This has been a really productive legislative session. We've solved the budget crisis; we've tackled deregulation; and we've begun the Industrial Development Commission. I congratulate each and every one of you on a job well done."	Perhaps the simplest method available of organizing a message	Speakers are often seduced into giving equivalent treatment to subtopics that do not merit equivalent treatment	Is there a strategically sound *ordering* to the sub-topics selected for treatment by the speaker?

(after Arnold, 1974)

also signals the novelty of Patton's situation: a hastily called speech delivered by a busy general who just happened to be in the area and who had no time to prepare a formal message.

This was hardly Rabbi Prinz's case; his brief remarks were well scripted and carefully choreographed to fit into the overall scene of the March on Washington. Prinz generally followed a chronological pattern (yesterday's Jewish ghettos, today's black ghettos, tomorrow's ghettoless America), although he is not compulsive about it. Ceremonial situations normally demand a conventional structure, which is perhaps why so many have cursed so mightily when watching the Academy Awards show each year. (Gushing non sequiturs are occasionally charming but more often irritating.) Prinz's use of the past in service of the future was, therefore, sensible given his role (as a teacher) and his status (as an elder). Anything more experimental on his part would perhaps have seemed out of character.

Richard Nixon was hardly ceremonial. He was an arguer. Portions of his Checkers Speech establish how carefully he linked evidence with conclusions. He used the elimination sequence to show why his only choice was to use a campaign fund, causality to point up the Communist threat to the nation, and the withheld-proposal technique as well ("I leave the decision up to you. Write and call now"). But the open-proposal approach can also be found in his speech ("I'm innocent and here's the evidence") as can chronology (his life and times).

Nixon's speech was, therefore, a complex speech: Its early structure differs from its later structure and its substructures contain substructures. This complexity points up the complexity of Richard Nixon himself, a man never reducible to an easy gloss. It also shows the complexity of his political circumstances: How exactly does one combine a jury summation with a solicitation for votes? And it reveals the complexity of reaching a TV audience, some of whom love you, some of whom hate you, and many of whom would rather be watching something else. It is little wonder, then, that Mr. Nixon's speech was as complex in design as it was obvious in content.

A general inspection of a message's design features is useful for the overall questions it raises. More specific questions can also be asked, some of which have to deal with message emphasis:

**How rigidly does the speaker adhere to the *topic-proper?*
Does the speaker roam widely from subject matter to subject matter or is the message highly constricted in content? Why?**

Are a great many arguments presented in scattergun fashion or are just a few arguments *developed* (but developed in depth)?

Are the interconnections of evidence and arguments made clear via previews, transitions, and internal and concluding summaries? Why?

Does an idea's *context* give it special importance or attractiveness?

Do the statements made just before or just after an idea make it less likely or more likely that that idea will be received well (understood and accepted)?

The first two sets of questions urge the critic to examine how tightly, or formally, the speaker developed his or her case. Such inquiries help the critic examine the crucial matter of rhetorical tone. We know, for example, that an attractive element of informal conversations is that they proceed at their own pace, with each new topic having only a marginal relationship to the foregoing topic. At times, we are attracted to structureless dialogue, which is perhaps why "talk radio" is so attractive to so many people. At other times—in a legal contract, newspaper editorial, performance appraisal—only clear, and clearly coordinated, arguments are tolerated. Douglass and Arnold [1970] warn the critic not to take a purist's approach to message structure, since much real-life discourse does not slavishly utilize standard organizational patterns. Jamieson [1988a] extends this argument by documenting the growing disuse of formal argument during political exchanges on the mass media. She claims that the structural rules of everyday conversation (be interesting, be relevant, be anecdotal) best match the structural patterns of televised speechmaking. Jamieson further claims that because of television, traditionally "masculine" speech patterns (patterns emphasizing classic structures) are giving way to the traditionally "feminine" qualities of personalization, ornamentation, and causal organization.

Ronald Reagan, a person who constantly substituted narrative structures for propositional structures, frequently proved Jamieson's point. An interesting example occurred in Mr. Reagan's summation during his third debate with Walter Mondale in 1984. After arguing that the meaning of the election lay in the future and that economic growth was important, Mr. Reagan suddenly made the following observations:

> Several years ago, I was given an assignment to write a letter. It was to go into a time capsule and would be read in a hundred years, when that time capsule was opened. I remember driving down the California coast one day. My mind was full of what I was going to put into that letter about the problems and the issues that confront us in our time and what we did about them.

> But I couldn't completely neglect the beauty around me: the Pacific out there on one side of the highway, shining in the sunlight, the mountains of the coast range rising on the other side. And I found myself wondering what it would be like for someone . . . wondering if someone, a hundred years from now, would be driving down that highway, and if they would see the same thing.
>
> With that thought, I realized what a job I had with that letter. I would be writing a letter to people who know everything there is to know about us. We would know nothing about them. . . . [Reagan, 1984:1609]

It is hard to know what Mr. Reagan had on his mind here. The story has nothing to do with the economy (his immediately preceding statement) or with the remarks that followed (nuclear weapons, preserving freedom, and George Bush), topics which were themselves disconnected. The argument of his story is unclear and even its narrative plot line is off kilter. Mr. Reagan appears to be free-associating, moving his mouth while his brain searches for a conclusion to the debate. There are no previews, transitions, or internal summaries; his speech is a digression within a digression. But Mr. Reagan's supporters hardly seemed bothered by his closing remarks. For them, his informality had a mythical warmth, the stamp of a person willing to share even his moments of reverie with his audience. His remarks had "conversational structure," signaling his trust in them as listeners, which is why they were charmed by it.

Reagan's critics, in contrast, used this example to describe a mind unable to structure thought, to connect evidence with conclusions, or to process information consecutively. His critics argued that digressive speech signals a digressive mind and that the *context* within which his remarks were found—during a national debate on foreign policy—was especially damning. How could such an undisciplined mind be trusted, they asked, to cope with the complexity of a nuclear age? In a sense, both Reagan's admirerers and his critics were making the point made earlier: structure argues. They differed as to what Mr. Reagan's structure said (A man who retained his humanity even when discussing nuclear war? A man out of touch with the dangers of his times?), but in both cases they showed the effects produced when an argument appears in one context rather than another.

In a similar fashion, LeRoi Jones's play *The Baptism*, which treated themes of Roman Catholicism and homosexuality simultaneously, raised a furor twenty years ago even though the author made no causal links between religion and gay life-styles in the script. Similarly, Gary Hart's fate was sealed in 1987 when stories of his presidential candidacy began appearing in the tabloids rather than in the journals of opinion. In other words, special rhetorical effects can be produced merely by the *common placement* of two ideas. When *Harper's* magazine [1984] presented (with absolutely no commentary) a boxed list of yearly expenditures for the Solidarity workers movement in Poland ($74,568) and one month's expenditure for Johnny Carson's third wife ($21,625), it used a simple structural device to make an eloquent statement about bourgeois priorities. In this case, as in the cases above, context said what content alone did not.

> **Which points are *emphasized* and which given short shrift by the speaker?**
>
> **Does the speaker cover the waterfront of ideas or home in on just a few?**
>
> **Do these decisions expose the persuasive obstacles being faced?**
>
> **How much time is spent on the introduction of *novel* information?**
>
> **How much time is spent recasting the familiar?**
>
> **Does this known/unknown ratio reveal anything important about the rhetorical situation?**

These two groups of questions relate to message density, the extent to which individual ideas are allowed to predominate in a given text. As mentioned in Chapter One, rhetoric is often an attempt to spotlight certain ideas or to push other ideas backstage. For example, when a young couple begins house-hunting, they become locked in an ideational struggle with the realtor (whether they know it or not). The realtor's job is to highlight the built-in curio cabinet, the mauve carpeting, and the easy-care lawn and at the same time to deflect attention from the price of the home, the windowless family room, or the cracks in the Sheetrock. Naturally, the realtor will continually justify this rhetorical coverage during the home tour, so wary consumers must not only know their price but their topic as well. As long as the purchasing decision hinges on mauve versus persimmon carpeting, the realtor is equally advantaged. Thus an important rhetorical principle suggests itself: Whoever controls the shape of the discussion controls its consequence as well.

In confrontational situations, topical emphasis becomes especially important as the disputants try to elbow aside their rivals' topics. This is true in court, where the lawyer for the defense uses the grounds of direct relevance to keep the toxicologist from testifying. It is also true in political affairs, as, for example, during the Watergate era of the Nixon administration. One fabled press conference, that of August 22, 1973, was especially interesting. Until this point, Mr. Nixon had been avoiding press conferences for over five months, but he ultimately had to face the press. But he did not come unarmed. After being badgered with one Watergate question after another, Nixon made a bold attempt to shift the direction of the discussion:

> *Question:* Mr. President.
> *The President:* Just a moment. We have had thirty minutes of this press conference. I have yet to have, for example, one question on the business of the people, which shows how consumed we are with this [Watergate]. I am not criticizing the members of the press, because you are very interested in this issue, but let me tell you, years from now people are going to perhaps be interested in what happened in terms of the efforts of the United States to build a structure of peace in the world. They are perhaps going to be interested in the efforts of this Administration to have a kind of prosperity that we have not had since 1955—that is, prosperity without war and without inflation—because throughout the Kennedy and throughout the Johnson years, whatever prosperity we had was at the cost of either inflation or war or both. I don't say that critically of them. I am simply saying we have got to do better than that [Nixon, 1973a:719].

Mr. Nixon's ploy did not entirely change the direction of that day's discussion, but it did reinforce those who felt that he was being hounded out of office by the press. Particularly interesting was how Mr. Nixon justified his attempt to change the subject: He reached for transcendent goals, painting himself as a statesman and the press as small-minded. Throughout his career, Richard Nixon was a hard charger. He never let anyone else set his rhetorical agenda.

What is newsworthy about the *sequence* of arguments?

Do first-saids and last-saids reveal anything important about the speaker's rhetorical circumstances?

What would have happened if the arguments had been reversed?

Does the speaker alternate the *mood* of the message?

Is narration or verbal intensity or itemized lists or rhetorical questions dominant in certain portions of the message and absent in others, thereby creating peaks and valleys of rhetorical pressure on the audience?

Does the *beginning* of the message anchor later ideas and arguments?

Does the speaker begin as if listeners already possessed common feelings on the subject or does the speaker try to disabuse listeners of currently held values and beliefs?

When, if at all, are unusually *controversial* or *complex* ideas introduced in the message? Early, middle, late, or not at all? What sort of material precedes or follows such potentially troublesome segments?

Message pacing is another important structural matter. It is concerned with *when* in time ideas are presented. Because listeners (unlike readers) cannot "turn back the pages" when they miss something, order effects are especially important in oral persuasion. For many years, researchers tried to determine which sequence of arguments was most influential. By using the same arguments in each case but by varying the ordering of appeals from test audience to test audience, these researchers determined that familiar ideas should be placed before unfamiliar ideas, that an attention/stress/solution pattern is especially effective, that first ideas and last ideas are remembered better than those in the middle, that a withheld-proposal sequence may backfire with hostile listeners [Karlins and Abelson, 1978]. But such studies are limited in generalizability and rarely help the critic understand the nuances of a particular message. Typically, it is more useful to examine a given sequence of arguments, tracing how that speaker approached that unique set of rhetorical problems.

An example of the importance of message pacing was the U.S. Army's [1972] "Eleven Point Checklist for Job Hunters." The checklist began with this statement: "If you are a young man about to graduate from high school, you certainly want the best possible job you can find. To help you in accomplishing this task, we have prepared a checklist for your use. We sincerely wish you the best of luck." Having thus offered its services as a guidance counselor, the Army proceeds through its checklist as follows: (1) Pay; (2) Vacations; (3) Education; (4) Allowances; (5) Leisure time; (6) Medical care; (7) Marketing [that is, shopping]; (8) Retirement; (9) Travel; (10) Bonuses; (11) Training. Each point on the checklist had specific advice for the job hunter (for example, "Travel—Your employer should agree to relocate you at your request anywhere in the U.S. or Free World at his expense. If married, this includes your family.") At the bottom of the page the audience was invited to use the checklist when weighing other job offers and then was left with the preferred suggestion: "Better yet, don't waste your time, see your Army Representative today."

Several items are of structural interest here. For one thing, no item on the checklist asked the job hunter to consider the *kind of work* he or she would be doing. Apparently, soldiers' day-to-day activities were not attractive enough to merit even a twelfth position on the hierarchy. And the checklist is indeed a hierarchy, with four of the first five relating to either money or time off. While education is placed in third position, no details are given. In contrast, the benefits associated with most other items are amply provided: 30 days PAID vacation, a $10,000 bonus to stay more than three years. Given the age of the target audience, the authors were wise to drop retirement to the bottom of the list with training. Two other items at the bottom, travel and bonuses, are essentially restatements of vacations and pay at the top of the list and are thus filler material. Also, at no point in the sequence is the reader more than one item away from a monetary argument. The organizational pattern is thus carefully adapted to the Army's perpetual target audience: America's underprivileged. Financial opportunity reaches out from beginning to end in this message.

While the Army example is elementary, it shows how mood must be carefully modulated in persuasion. One person who deftly monitors mood is the Reverend Jesse Jackson. He masterfully mixes highs and lows by use of cleverly timed stories and extended contrasts. Jackson will pack one part of a speech with rapidly delivered facts and then languish for awhile, toying with a heavily embellished metaphor. At other points he will suddenly substitute ribaldry for seriousness or philosophizing for case-making. Rhetorically, Jesse Jackson is a whirling dervish of moods, constantly accelerating, decelerating, and then accelerating again. It is Jackson's *packaging* of powerful rhetorical elements that makes his supporters ecstatic and his detractors nervous. The former sense that there is a wholeness to his appeals, a simultaneous accommodation of virtually all their mental states. The latter sense that the emotional complexity of his speech can become a tinderbox for social unrest. The history of rhetoric could support either case.

A number of critics have examined the effects of pacing. Hart [1973] noted, for example, that highly ideological speakers often load up their speeches with anxiety after anxiety, not releasing the pressure until the ends of their speeches. In contrast, speakers addressing uncommitted audiences rarely discussed problems for so long. Himmelein [1974] monitored how several different messages oscillated through time and found that periods of activity alternated with periods of inactivity (as measured by uses of active verbs), that self-references and abstractions were more common in the beginnings of speeches than at the ends, and that absolute language and evaluation statements predominated in the conclusions of speeches.

Another approach was Davis's [1978], who found that the most distinctive feature of the televised documentary lay in its *ratio* between visual and verbal materials. Davis found this ratio to hold across subject matter and network, arguing that it is this ratio that gives documentary both its credibility ("If you don't accept my words, here is the visual evidence") and its tediousness ("Why talk so much? Let me just look at the pictures"). Yet another study by Blankenship [1986] examined TV's juxtaposing of Ronald Reagan's sedate first inaugural with the simultaneous, chaotic release of American hostages from Iran. Blankenship argues that this tug-of-war between such incompatible images deprived American viewers of the emotionally "whole" feelings inaugurals are designed to generate.

All of the studies mentioned here have tried to understand how listeners form meanings and how speakers' structural choices guide them when doing so. The critic's job is to talk with precision about such structural regularities (or irregularities) and then monitor them in actual texts. And this is to do more than document the obvious. While many people may sense that introductions differ from conclusions, that polarized speakers differ from neutral speakers, or that TV documentaries are distinctive, precise *explanations* of such "known" realities have been rare. Thus, there is much work to be done by the structural critic. Such studies can help us learn how we know what we know and how we know it *when* we know it.

FORM AND STRUCTURE: A CASE STUDY

In 1938, Orson Welles shocked many in the United States when he presented a radio broadcast of H.G. Wells's *War of the Worlds*. Most radio listeners were caught unaware by the broadcast and believed the tale of the Martian invasion completely. In some parts of the country, people fled into the streets in panic. Police switchboards were lit up for hours on end with excited callers describing imminent doom. Even some newspaper reporters were tricked into believing the fantastic story of how Martians subdued earthlings and bred a new super race until the extraterrestrials themselves were undone by the common cold.

Thirty years later, on Halloween night in 1968, WKBW radio in Buffalo, New York, broadcast an updated version of the Wells classic [WKBW, 1968]. Even though station personnel preceded their show with twenty-one days' worth of announcements, alerted all local media and city officials, and issued press releases liberally, some amount of panic again occurred, this time in western New York. The local telephone company, for example, logged four thousand calls directly attributable to the broadcast.

WKBW's updated version utilized the many media routines that had been developed since the original Welles broadcast, many of which were structural in nature. Aspects of structural pacing, emphasis, density, and design caught listeners off guard. Also, because the performers' voices were already well known to the Buffalo audience, listeners had form-related expectations when hearing these voices. The

RHETORIC AND TELEVISED NEWS

Critical Profile 6.1   The Documentary: Facts for Self-Reflection

Americans yearn to get the facts. In the last century, items ranging from Upton Sinclair's *The Jungle* to the current popular television program *20/20* are evidence that the public feeds on factual data. What intrigues Thomas Benson is how the public interprets and makes everyday use of such facts. Benson, who teaches at The Pennsylvania State University, believes Frederick Wiseman's documentary film *Primate* "helps to understand how meanings are made by audiences," and how facts become symbols by which audiences comprehend their world.

It turns out that Wiseman's method of filmmaking makes constant use of the rhetorical device of comparison. "Every image in the film invites us to make comparisons," says Benson, the film's title itself suggesting a comparison between men and apes. In a birth scene, for example, women in nursing gowns mother infant apes with toys, baby bottles, and a rocking chair—a scene where "the researchers themselves invite the comparison." Wiseman uses the birth scene to reinforce a comparison of baby apes with human babies, thereby having the "rhetorical effect of causing us to establish a sentimental identification with the apes." But that feeling of identification is ultimately reversed for viewers as a small monkey is shown screaming as it is taken from its cage by a man with protective gloves. The man, a research scientist, pins the monkey's arms behind its back and clamps its neck. Later scenes depict the gruesome vivisection of apes by scientists.

Wiseman's comparative approach invites viewers to draw their own conclusions about the relationship of animals to humans. Research techniques such as vivisection are cruel to animals, but the research that eventuates is often beneficial to humankind. At the same time, viewers who become sentimentally attached to the apes are disturbed by the inhumane research methods used on the animals. Thus, Wiseman's approach rhetorically forces viewers to deal with the ethical question: How can one accept the use of inhumane research practices without accepting the ethical argument that apes are not like humans? Comparison, explains Benson, "both justifies and condemns the research" and thereby heightens rhetorical tension considerably, forcing us to consider "paradoxes of our institutions and ourselves." As Benson says, we begin to "realize that the shame and rage we direct at the primate researchers is directed at them as representatives of ourselves. It is not that we cannot forgive them, we cannot forgive ourselves."

Profiled by: Yvonne Becerra
Citation: Benson (1985)

Critical Profile 6.2   Electronic Detective Stories

Since the nineteenth century, Americans have sat on the edges of their seats intrigued by detective stories. Even the most clever villains were no match for Sherlock Holmes, Auguste Dupin, or Sam Spade. These sleuths' superior intelligence and cool demeanor allowed them to gather facts, unravel mysteries, and produce a sense of morality and order in society. Somehow, all was right with the world when the Great American Detective was on his beat.

A modern version of the classic detective story appears weekly in the popular news show *60 Minutes,* according to Richard Campbell of the University of Michigan. One reason for the popularity of *60 Minutes,* says Campbell, is its use of detective-style narration. Often while wearing trench coats, reporters like Mike Wallace, Harry Reasoner, and Morley Safer stand at the scene of the crime; they "carry no weapon but rely on rational analysis and their ability to outwit characters." As they confront the villains of the week, these intrepid reporters assume risks, but fearlessly solve the crime, mediating familiar human tensions between "safety and danger," "individuals and institutions," and "honesty and deception."

60 Minutes, says Campbell, stresses the reporter's role as a mediator of conflict. Reporters appear in medium camera shots, totally in control of the space around them. In contrast, villains and unsuspecting victims appear in tight close-ups. Even the slightest movement of the head makes the subject appear as if he or she were "trying to escape scrutiny." Like the classic detective, the *60 Minutes* reporter is portrayed as having superior control, detachment, and intelligence, a person with the metaphoric status of a "heroic detective who champions Middle American individualism and integrity in the face of heartless bureaucracy." Reporters are portrayed as "loners," free from the constraints of the camera, producers, and editors, which, collectively, enhance their "narrative position" as mediators and "affirmers of individualism."

Like classic detective stories, says Campbell, the popularity of *60 Minutes* lies in its use of narrative tensions that, when resolved, simplify and transform experience. *60 Minutes* taps into our desire for "truth, honesty, and intrigue," and provides a middle ground where audiences may discover who they are. Naturally, all of this is quite formulaic, rhetorically, and one wonders what vision of "truth" is being served in *60 Minutes*'s mad dash to produce first-rate theatre. Detective stories, after all, rarely challenge us intellectually. "Whodunit?" is an eternally interesting question, but, one might ask, is it always an important question?

Profiled by: Michael G. Lacy
Citation: Campbell (1987)

Critical Profile 6.3   A Stately Chaos, a Calming Tension

Rhetorical critics have often been interested in how figures of speech and thought affect persuasion. Little attention, however, has been focused on the oxymoron, a figure which puts together contradictory terms ("a happy accident" or "a pained smile") in order to achieve dramatic effect. Jane Blankenship of the University of Massachusetts examined the coverage by ABC of the first Reagan inaugural on January 20, 1981, and the simultaneous release that day of American hostages held in Iran. Blankenship claims that the entire coverage of the day's events gave ABC's viewers "a miscellany of contrasting information, interpretations, and modes of presentation." Among her examples of oxymorons, Blankenship makes a strong case that the visual and the verbal were frequently at odds, thereby creating an uncomfortable dramatic tension for viewers.

Blankenship claims that "'Real life' and 'manufactured' mini-dramas were juxtaposed" in ABC's inaugural coverage. For example, the presidential inauguration was characterized by orderliness and planning, the hostage release by disorder and confusion. The events of the inauguration were carefully orchestrated and timed, while news of the hostage release was sketchy and sporadic throughout the day. In addition, the television cameras pictured one event while news personnel spoke of the other; frequently, the two processes occurred at the same time. For example, while ABC cameras provided a close-up of inaugural dignitaries, reporters provided Associated Press reports that the hostages had left Teheran.

Since ABC did not, or could not, set the scene for viewers and since it had no overarching metaphor for the two stories of the day, it presented the audience with the conflicting dialectical tensions of the oxymoron. The result for the audience was that it had to make a choice, mirroring ABC's, among phenomena. The juxtaposition of important and diverse, yet related, stories forced the audience to develop a framework for itself. Used to having the media "package" things neatly for them, the ABC audience that day had to package things for themselves based upon their own experiences with figures and tropes. Because of the "oddness" of having to use the oxymoron, the ABC audience saw "heightened, compressed *contrasts*," rather than a unified and complete pictorial and verbal account of the day's events. In other words, viewers had to do something that television audiences rarely have to do: they had to think.

Profiled by: Donald Nobles
Citation: Blankenship (1986)

---

performers took advantage of these expectations by initially conforming to radio routines and then gradually causing the ground to shift beneath their listeners' feet. Old structures (music, weather, and sports) were replaced by interim structures (fast-breaking news events) and then by radically new structures (the invasion story itself). The bril-

Table 6.2   Rhetorical Progression of WKBW's "War of the Worlds"

Feature	Phase 1	Phase 2	Phase 3	Phase 4	Phase 5
Station I.D.	6.0	4.0	1.0	0.0	2.8
Commercials	14.5	5.8	3.2	0.0	0.0
Music	44.5	22.0	0.0	0.0	0.0
Studio reporting	3.5	13.3	9.8	27.6	27.2
Studio interviewing	0.0	27.0	47.0	22.4	25.6
Eyewitness reporting	0.0	6.0	39.0	50.0	44.4
Disc jockey patter	21.0	4.8	0.0	0.0	0.0
Disc jockey reporting	10.5	17.5	0.0	0.0	0.0

*Each phase approximately 18 minutes
(% Distribution of rhetorical features)

liance of the show lay in its seamlessness: Listeners did not notice these gradual shifts in continuity. Because the WKBW program teaches so many interesting lessons about structure and form, we will examine its features at length.

Because it lasted for some ninety minutes, the show can be divided for analysis into twenty-three separate time periods (each of which lasted for roughly four minutes) and their rhetorical features can then be examined in detail. Thematically, the show appears to be composed of five major phases (roughly 18 minutes each) and so our analysis will proceed phase by phase. Table 6.2 presents some general quantitative information about the broadcast.

Phase One: Normalcy?   The first twenty minutes of the show proceeded with the usual interspersing of music, commercials, and disc jockey patter. The attempt here was to decrease the vigilance of the audience by employing familiar structural patterns and to give listeners the feeling that full attention need *not* be paid to the goings on. Presuming (1) that a relaxed listener is a persuadable listener and (2) that suggestion works best during moments of inattention, the disc jockey even did some subtle prefiguring (at the end of Period 1) just after playing a record:

> *Disc jockey*: Everybody do it! Santana! WKBW with the eleventh biggest hit this week on the Keep Me Company series. Jackson Armstrong on a Sunday night, Halloween Night, rocking along, baby. And did you hear that remark Joe Dounty made about the explosions on Mars and all the debris out in space and everything and all the big explosions there earlier tonight? I'll tell you, I wouldn't go out to space for nothing. Why not? Well, suppose you were to go to the moon or someplace like that and were supposed to land, right, land with some kind of a vehicle and get out. Yeah, well suppose you open the door to get out and somebody got in. Not me, man.

During the second period, Armstrong (the disc jockey) continues on his merry way, interrupting his chatter at one point with a message from NASA that its space-watch facilities expected communications difficulties that evening. Again trying to desensitize the listener, Armstrong trivializes this report by saying that it dealt with "sun spots and things like that." He then inquires, "Can you hear me down there in South Carolina? As long as you can hear KB, what difference does it make about communications?" The D.J. keeps up his bantering until (at the end of Period 3) he interrupts himself with the statement, "We have an important news development and here's Joe Dounty with the information." The report states that authorities in the town of Grand Island (across the river from Buffalo) have reported a series of explosions and fires and that motorists had been asked to stay clear of the area.

Despite the news report, however, Period 4 proceeds as usual. The show *returns* to the music/commercial/chatter routine, thereby convincing listeners that they need not "undo" their standard mental associations. By thus reestablishing listeners' form-related expectations, the producers of the show hoped to make credible the deviations-from-pattern that would soon appear. Phase One, however, dulled listeners' senses with heavy doses of normality. While foreshadowing has taken place, the warning signs were subtle and hence seen as irrelevant by listeners.

Phase Two: Raising Questions. Interruptions are important because they are points of structural intersection, moments when one rhetorical routine overlaps with another. Interruptions signal that listeners' expectations may not be borne out by forthcoming events and hence they heighten attentiveness. Some formats (for example, deejay patter) are presumably more interruptable than others (for example, a song or a commercial) and so the interruption we find in Period 5 is of special interest:

> *Disc jockey:* All right, all right excuse me a minute here folks. I know normally we don't come in on the top of a record or things like that when it's not over but, ah, Joe Dounty has a special interrupt story on this thing that's happening in Grand Island. So let's go to the newsroom and Joe Dounty.

At about twenty-two minutes into the show, we have the first real break in format after having had four songs presented in close succession without interruption. As Table 6.2 shows, the disc jockey's role shifts slightly in this phase, with Armstrong fielding duties as a substitute (that is, low-key) newsperson and generally engaging in less disc jockey palavering. His language also changes subtly in Periods 5 and 6, when he uses such phrases as "special interrupt story" and later opines "Hmm, apparently this thing is a little more serious than anybody suspected initially." Period 5 is also the occasion of the first *location shift*, with the rhetorical action passing from the entertainment booth to the newsroom. Psychologically, the listener is also being asked to shift his or her position (from lightness to seriousness), as the Grand Island story begins to take shape.

And that story is indeed becoming more interesting, although sharp details are not yet available. Slowly, the facts dribble out, structurally demanding that listeners use their imaginations and also stay tuned:

> *Studio reporter 1:* All available firefighting equipment has been called to Grand Island and much of the apparatus has already arrived there. The cause of the alarm is a reportedly large meteor that has struck in the vicinity of Grand Island Boulevard. Several persons have been injured and some are believed dead, although we have no confirmed number on those people reportedly killed in the crash and explosion. Details are still rather sketchy. We expect to hear from KB newsmen who are already on their way to the scene.

Immediately after this report, the disc jockey replies, "Thank you very much, Joe. I guess while we're waiting for further information on this whole thing, I can get into some more music at KB, huh, right?" This is an important statement. It does several things: (1) It foreshadows that Armstrong's role as disc jockey is changing from one of dominance to one of irrelevance; (2) it acknowledges that the musical format is becoming background rather than foreground; and (3) it warns that listeners' expectations for the evening may no longer be justified.

Those expectations continue to be questioned. The third song in a row is interrupted; a format shift from the studio to the field occurs; casualties in Grand Island are first mentioned; the station's program director (Jeff Kay) takes over the reportage; the effortless verbal ping-pong of the radio personalities breaks down as *unanticipated events* disrupt continuity:

> *Disc jockey:* Thank you, Don. KB News is going to keep you informed of the developments as they come up tonight here on the . . .
> *Program director:* Jack, Jack, we're going to take this story because of the importance of it, we are going to take it live . . .
> *Disc jockey:* Oh . . .
> *Program director:* . . . from the newsroom . . .
> *Disc jockey:* Oh, okay, well . . .

Program director: . . . on the spot. And we'll take it into there as soon as we can pick up the equipment and get it hot.

Disc jockey: Oh, all right. That's Jeff Kay, our program director, folks, and he's just informed me that we're going to cover this Grand Island news story live and direct from Grand Island. So I guess what we'll have to do is just go on to the news department. So, with further developments, this is WKBW, Buffalo, New York, to our news department.

This disjointedness helps loosen listeners' emotional moorings and urges them to re-form the available information. Their expectations about normality are rocked further at the end of Period 8 as things become even "busier" structurally: Mobile reporters begin to send in reports; a deputy sheriff is interviewed; military personnel are called to the scene of the Grand Island explosions. The attempt here is to keep listeners moving intellectually so that they cannot retreat to conventional explanations of how the world is. Moreover, the interviewers' questions change in character: They are now used to *predict the news,* not just to help report it. The questions themselves begin to have answers built into them. The interview with the deputy sheriff is a case in point:

Studio reporter 2: Can you give us an estimate on the number of deaths or injuries?

Deputy: No, there's no count at this point. We don't know. But there are several lives lost.

Studio reporter 2: Are you in communication with all parts of the island yet, and with your units in the field?

Deputy: Most of our communication lines are down here.

Studio reporter 2: How about electrical and gas failures? Have you had any reports on that?

Deputy: There's been about three electrical failures that we know about.

Studio reporter 2: Any looting, things like that?

Deputy: I can't tell you that at this moment. I really don't know.

Phase Three: The Edge of Crisis.   At forty minutes into the program, the action is fast and furious. It now seems that a tragedy of major proportions has struck Grand Island. But no larger explanation, no theory of events, has yet been offered. Phases One and Two have decentered the listener; the job of Phase Three is conversion. As is often the case, the conversion starts with a seemingly innocent question asked of a Niagara University astronomer:

Studio reporter 2: Dr. Moore, can you tell if that was an extraterrestrial body that landed on Grand Island?

Naturally, the good professor denies this outlandish possibility, but the seed has now been planted.

Another decentering technique also involves a structural shift. Up to this point, the listener has been addressed directly. In Period 9, the listener suddenly becomes an overhearer. The reporters begin to talk to one another as if they were not being observed; by the end of the program, the listener is almost completely "forgotten" rhetorically. This window-on-the-world technique is seductive indeed:

> *Remote reporter 1:* Jim, this is not Hank, it's Don. I am presently on the East River Road. Could you give me your present location, please?
>
> *Remote reporter 2:* I'm on the Moses Expressway and I'm headed south just beyond the Falls now.
>
> *Remote reporter 1:* I'm having a lot of trouble here with traffic. I can't seem to make any headway at all on Grand Island. We're on the East River Road. Do you have any taping equipment with you, Jim?
>
> *Remote reporter 2:* Yes, I've got the Sony tape recorder in the back here.
>
> *Remote reporter 1:* Okay, good. As soon as you get on the scene, try and get us a report back with Dr. Moore and also some police officers. I'm attempting to pick my way through this traffic. I should be there in not too long. It's really congested down here.

This sort of technical byplay dominates Periods 9 and 10, although the hand is not overplayed. Occasionally, the anchor person suddenly takes charge, like a weaving boxer attempting to right himself after a series of roundhouses:

> *Studio reporter 2:* This is Henry Brock in the WKBW newsroom. This just off the wire: United Press says it has unconfirmed reports that Governor Rockefeller is preparing to mobilize the National Guard in light of the developments on Grand Island. New York Telephone Company has requested that only emergency telephone calls be made by private individuals. The lines are beginning to be swamped with calls and police and fire official switchboards have been overburdened with calls. Fire officials in the city of Buffalo are concerned at this time. The fires that have broken out on the island have bled off a great deal of equipment. And extra units in the city have been called in. Commissioner Falsetta of the Buffalo Police Department has requested that all off-duty policemen report to the precincts.

This passage also reveals a shift in message emphasis, as we see in Table 6.2 and Figure 6.2. Structurally, Figure 6.2 shows that conversational turn-taking has now increased dramatically, with the action being especially hectic in Phase Three. Phase Three is also the credibility phase, with named authorities (both institutions and individuals)

Figure 6.2
Rhetorical Changes During WKBW's "War of the Worlds"

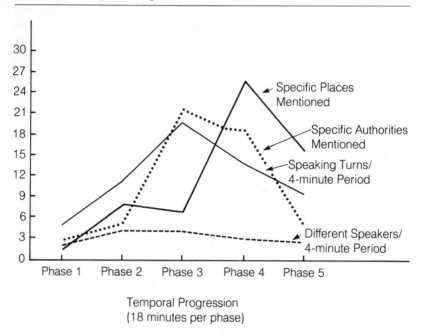

Temporal Progression
(18 minutes per phase)

being mentioned frequently. Moreover, destroyed houses, injured persons, raging fires, and a certain giant crater are described by a bevy of overlapping voices, some of which are not even identified for the listener. These rapid structural shifts create conceptual static as the listener searches out the meaning of the growing crisis. The reporters often add to the confusion by feigning incapacity, thereby calling into question any and all traditional explanations of events:

Remote reporter 1: Yes, Henry, it's not, it's not a meteor, Henry. I'm standing on the edge of the crater right now. And I can look down into it and there are clouds of white, hot steam rising from the face of what looks like some sort of a metallic, cylindrical object. It's a very large object that's, that's lying in the bottom of the crater. So far, there has been no one around that I have been able to talk to, to find out what it might be. It's, it's, it's hot, intense heat around this crater at the present moment. And I just . . . I just don't . . . don't . . . I can't describe it very well. I can't describe it all that well. Perhaps you can hear the sound that's coming from the crater. It's a pulsating sound. It's a high-pitched sound. I don't know exactly what it is at all. I don't know. I haven't got any idea.

Table 6.2 shows that in Phase Three studio interviewing dominates even eyewitness reporting, no doubt signaling that *leading questions* were constantly being asked of reporters on the scene (for example, *Studio reporter 2:* "What was it? It sounds like space debris. Was it space debris?"). Table 6.2 also shows that by now virtually all structural signals of normality (music, commercials, station I.D.) have been extinguished. At the very end of Phase Three, the first graphic detail of the Martian landing is presented. If listeners are not hooked at this point, they cannot be hooked.

> *Remote reporter 2:* My God, Don, there's something crawling out of the top of this thing. Something or someone. I can see two discs of some sort. They're eyes. They appear to be eyes. It might as well be a thief, for all I know. Something's wriggling out of this capsule. Wait a minute, wait a minute. Tentacles, that's what they are. I can see them now. The police lights are on them. This thing is large. The body glistens, like it's soaking wet. That face. I can hardly look at it, Don. I can hardly look at it. The eyes are black. The mouth is C-shaped and it's dripping saliva. It's finding it very difficult to move, but it's now beginning to move. It's weighed down by something. I can't say what it is. This thing is rising up. I've got to get out of here. The crowd's moving back. I'm moving back. I'm getting out of here.

Phase Four: The Beginning of the End.   The passage just quoted foreshadows the shift in language that comes to dominate Phase Four. The eyewitness reporters now become hyperbolic and seem to lose control of the action (*Remote reporter 2:* " . . . he and the professor are now approaching the, this monster. Good God Almighty Abraham, there was some sort of red beam. They've burst into flames—the professor, the lieutenant . . ."). This apparent loss of control licenses listeners to jettison conventional explanations and to accept the "Martian" interpretation of events. But, again, the show's producers do not attempt too much too soon. Period 14, for example, is *narrated* by studio personnel, thereby departing radically from the wildness of the preceding field reports. Once again, these rapid shifts in format are designed to keep rhetorical momentum flowing against the listener. Persuasion often thrives when uncertainty abounds.

Phase Four also signals a shift in message density. As Figure 6.2 reports, the names of specific places are increasingly mentioned, thereby enlarging the scope of the apparent invasion. The listener is made to feel a smaller and smaller part of a larger and larger scene:

> *Program director:* Stand by one moment please. I have a report here somewhere. Landings have been reported in Toronto, Oshawa, Erie,

Pittsburgh, the Finger Lakes region, Bradford, and the Dunkirk area of Western New York. And now I understand in the Batavia area. Scientists are speculating, at this moment, that they are indeed allied with the phenomenon that occurred on Mars. And I have just been handed another message. A report from Grand Island says that National Guard, regular Army, U.S. Air Force, police, and sheriff's deputies numbering in the vicinity of about a thousand men have almost been totally destroyed by a single fighting machine from what is believed to be the planet Mars. There are approximately twenty survivors, the rest remain trampled by the huge metal feet of this Martian fighting machine or cindered by the heat ray. And at last report we understand that the charred body of Jim Fagan is also . . . was discovered. Another report is that further explosions are now being witnessed by the Jodrell Bank Observatory in England on the planet Mars. We understand that Jamestown, Lewistown, Lockport, all of the towns surrounding the Niagara County area and Erie County around Grand Island are all being evacuated at this moment.

Rather than run the risk of letting the listener become distanced from the scene of the action, however, Phase Four ends with a *local* disaster: Thousands of persons are swept into a raging river when fleeing Grand Island. Ostensibly, these quick structural shifts from there to here and from here to there cut off the listener's routes of attitudinal escape.

Phase Five: Humanizing Evil.   Phase Five begins with the following battle report:

> *Remote reporter 1:* . . . There's a total of three machines here. They're coming into the refinery. The artillery is now turned around from its perimeter. They're firing. We apprently got, we got one! We got one! It's down! It's down! It's down! We got it, it's down! Artillery blasted it. They just shot it down. The other two have joined it. And now they are emitting something, they're emitting some sort of a smoke screen it looks like from here. It's . . . it's . . . they're not very far away from me. It's thick, black smoke. It's about as tall as a man. It's starting to encompass the entire area. The smoke is coming from . . . from these things. And the artillery, the weapons, they're continuing to fire into the center, into where these three machines are located. The smoke cloud is now coming toward me, Harry. It's . . . it's . . . My God, there's a man, there's a man falling. It's not smoke. It's gas. [cough, cough]

This is the first "live" death heard on the show and it removes the listener's remaining props. One by one, the familiar radio personalities lose their lives until the program director reports "we have one more unit left in the field." In Phase Five, the rhetorical action shifts away from the mass destruction depicted earlier. Now, cameo stories are presented in rapid succession: the U.P.I. man in Dunkirk who sends his last message; the sole remaining remote reporter who asks the program director to phone his wife; the program director himself, who cannot find a match to light his last cigarette. These finely etched portraits are interspersed with talk of fleeing "refugees" and with the destruction of familiar landmarks: the Ashland Oil Refinery, Bethlehem Steel Company, Delaware Park, City Hall. All of these descriptions serve to localize the rhetoric and to place the invasion on a human scale. The show closes with the program director answering the telephone:

> *Program director:* KB News. You want to talk to who? [Laughing. Hangs up.] They wanted to talk to Herb Weinstein. He's . . . he's dead. Is anybody else in this building? What am I going to do? I'm the only one left. I wonder if anybody is listening. I wonder if anybody has got a radio that's operating. The transistor. Yeah, the transistor. I can take the mike. We'll go outside. That's what I'll do. I'll go outside. Get this thing unhooked from the stand. Weinstein's dead. They're all dead. What the hell am I going to do? I'll go outside. . . .

This analysis of the "War of the Worlds" has not told all that needs to be known about form and structure. But it does reveal some of the organizing strategies available to persuaders. Naturally, our analysis could easily have focused on why these strategies *failed* to convince most people that the Martians had landed. What told them the story was a phony? No doubt, they got their answers by asking structural questions: Are these same rhetorical patterns in place on rival radio stations? Is the tale unfolding too quickly? Can an air war really be fought in three minutes? Are TV's visual structures in sync with radio's verbal structures? Thus, whether convinced or not convinced, listeners consulted what they knew, or thought they knew, about discourse structures when determining what really happened on Grand Island twenty years ago.

GENRE AND FORM

As defined earlier, a genre is a class of messages having important structural and content similarities, which, as a class, create special expectations in listeners. Inaugural addresses, then, constitute a genre, because they share textual features and are delivered in similar circumstances every four years. Thus, when he first spoke as president, George Bush did not sound exactly like John Kennedy or Abraham Lin-

RHETORIC AND SOCIAL CLASS

Critical Profile 6.4   Politicians: Are They What They Eat?

What was the political significance of Ronald Reagan's appetite for jelly beans? Did this trait make him more suited or less suited for the presidency? What does it mean to label a group "quiche-eating liberals"? Barry Brummett of the University of Wisconsin-Milwaukee has explored, of all things, the curious role of foods in shaping political images and his findings are not at all as trivial as the topic might suggest.

Synecdoche is the rhetorical device that represents a whole object by referring to one of its parts. Brummett explains his particular interest: "Gastronomic reference . . . uses only part of what one eats to represent all of what one eats and thus, by extension, to represent the person who eats." Food, Brummett suggests, offers a clue to the social class loyalties of a candidate or group. American politics does not normally permit such matters to become the focus of public attention, largely because class-related tensions are so volatile and because they lie so close to the surface of a still-immigrant nation. Nevertheless, says Brummett, the successful political candidate is often the one who stays close to middle-class norms—whether in values or food—and who can find a rhetoric sensitive enough to signal such membership without appearing to have done so.

In the 1980 campaign, for example, independent candidate John B. Anderson and his followers mounted a broad-scale effort for public support. Media treatments of Anderson, however, used his taste in food to suggest an elitist political philosophy. Anderson was described as "split-level suburban; his palate runs to J&B on the rocks and a slab of prime ribs, though he will accept such rigors of the road as a fried bologna sandwich." Without saying anything about Anderson's policies, this description spoke volumes about his values. In contrast, Senator Edward Kennedy, more wealthy and more patrician than Anderson, was described as having a taste for the middle-class staples of ice cream and daiquiris. Kennedy's describers also noted his penchant for occasional overindulgence in these foods—making him seem even more middle-class.

Brummett indicates that these "innocent" characterizations show that rhetoric can be a powerful tool for directing attention in subtle ways. The story rhetoric tells is not necessarily untrue, but its story is always a carefully edited one: A candidate's handlers suggest parallels to a popular former president; opponents question a candidate's name, age, or hair style; journalists make a fragment of the politician represent his or her entire self. In a real sense, then, voters must be on the alert to listen for the "whole" politician and not just for his or her "parts" as popularly described. The ultimate significance of the food issue is not what the candidate really eats but, rather, what the public is willing to swallow.

Profiled by: John Llewellyn
Citation: Brummett (1981b)

Critical Profile 6.5   "I Hear You, Reverend!"

How many of us go to church on Sunday morning expecting to "talk back" to the preacher with an "Amen" and to enjoy a spiritual jam session among musicians who "get a thang goin'"? For those of us who do, it is perhaps because the "residue of an African heritage persists undiminished and intact in the call-response pattern of black communication," say Jack L. Daniel and Geneva Smitherman of the University of Pittsburgh.

The authors describe the traditional black church as the "holy-rolling, bench-walking, spirit-getting, tongue-speaking, vision-receiving, intuitive-directing, amen-saying, sing-song preaching, holy-dancing and God-sending church." Communication here means spontaneity, interaction, and interdependence: all legacies of the African heritage, all necessary for creating a sense of unity among the parishioners. This form of communication depends upon the call-response pattern and follows a hierarchical progression, another African legacy. The church hierarchy begins with God, who, respectively, is followed by the Minister, the Mother of the Church, the Elders, the Deacons, the Trustees, the Saved Adults, and downward . . . to the Sinners. God inspires the minister, who, in turn, inspires the congregation. Call-response is set in motion, starting with God, who *calls* the preacher to *respond* by becoming His servant.

Following a "warming up" period in which the spirit of the Lord is invoked, the preacher announces his or her beginning call: "My theme for today is Waiting on the Lord." Typical congregational responses include: "Take your time," and "Preach, Reb," and "Come on up, now." As the preacher becomes more emotional, the call becomes stronger; likewise, the response heightens. "Yessuh!" and "Watch yo-self now!" complement non-verbal responses such as "nodding of heads, clapping of hands, stomping feet, jumping up and down, jerking the body, holy dancing and 'shouting.'" As this interactive process begins to work, the preacher is increasingly moved by the congregation's response and the spirit "takes over." People speak in tongues; folks pass out from exhaustion; the church is filled with song. The call-response has achieved community.

The call-response pattern, then, is vital to the traditional black church and to obtaining a sense of community among its parishioners. The message behind this message could not be clearer: *Because all persons talk, all persons are important.* Is it any wonder that this religious formula still survives? And is it any wonder that it remains a rhetorical refuge for a people with no other refuge?

Profiled by: Christine Keffeler
Citation: Daniel and Smitherman (1976)

Critical Profile 6.6   The Original Untouchables

He dared not refer to his food grain as rice but must call it "dirty gruel." His children he must call "monkeys" or "calves," and if he got a piece of silver he had to call it copper. When referring to parts of his own body . . . he spoke of his "old eye," "old ear," "old hand."

Was this plucked from the pages of a child's fairy tale? Part of an evil spell? A Charles Dickens story? None of the above. Rather, it is the kind of talk described by Penn State's Robert Oliver in his book *Communication and Culture in Ancient India and China*, in which he captures the rhetorical reality of the Untouchables, the lowest caste of the Hindu religion.

"Caste as Rhetoric in Being" is one of Oliver's most riveting chapters. In it, he explores the ancient Indian caste, whose origins are "lost in prehistory," as an extraordinarily powerful form of rhetoric. The caste literally dictated *all* cultural patterns, which, in turn, petrified all forms of social interaction. The Untouchables, like members of all castes in India, complacently accepted their respective stations in life. "Why?" the Westerner may ask. The answer: Karma, the Hindu principle of causality, which decrees that the joys and woes of one's present life hinge upon the goodness or sins of one's past life. Thus, the higher castes in Hindu society were *not* seen to be responsible for the subjugation of the Untouchables. Rather, their lowly status was determined for them at birth.

Restrictions placed upon the Untouchables were myriad and extreme. For instance, they typically were required to walk around, rather than through, a village; they could not drink the water from the village well; their animals could not graze on shared pasture land. Additionally, the "rhetoric

---

coln, but he did not sound completely unlike them either. Mr. Bush spoke in a 1989 sort of way because he spoke to 1989 sorts of people. But 1989 Americans were still Americans; while they were curious about new possibilities, they were also attracted to old realities. So, when writing his inaugural address, George Bush had help—the help of the ages—whether he wanted it or not. Because he was part of an historical process, he labored under generic constraints.

Generic study is the study of such constraints. It describes patterns of discourse and explains their recurrence. It asks questions like these: Why does this text seem more rule-governed than another? Why are certain rules operating here rather than other rules? What happens if these rules are violated? Why do people care about rules at all? The generic critic intentionally looks for structural and content similarities and then tries to explain them. The generic critic is something like the naturalist who traces the regularities, and interesting irregularities,

---

Critical Profile 6.6   The Original Untouchables (*continued*)

---

of being" began at birth with Untouchable names being given them such as "the lame one," "the one-eyed," "the poor cripple," thereby constraining all future conversations along caste lines. One of Oliver's most colorful, albeit saddest, examples of restrictions being placed against intercaste communication involved the Unseeables, a group of Untouchables so named because the "mere sight of one of them would pollute other people." Says Oliver:

> They were allowed to move about only at night, and then must drag a palm branch behind them—partly so that the rustling would warn others of their approach and partly to erase their footprints. . . .

In fact, the communication of such unfortunates was limited to arranging planned murders and to collecting payment for their labors. The rhetoric of being an Untouchable was clearly the rhetoric of being a pariah.

For Hindus who are born into the Untouchable caste today, life remains much the same as it did thousands of years ago—they are prisoners of inviolable *communicative* prejudice, perhaps the most denigrating form of prejudice that exists. After all, to take away one's livelihood is one thing; to take away one's sense of belonging is quite another. But worst of all is to take away the natural possibilities of speech. With speech, after all, there is always hope.

Profiled by: Christine Keffeler
Citation: Oliver (1971)

---

found in the natural world. But tucking all of life's speeches into their own generic beds is hardly worthwhile if it results in nothing more than taxonomical fascination [Hart, 1986a]. Rather, it is *the story behind the taxonomies,* the general ideas about the natural condition, that intrigue both the entomologist and the generic critic. Thus, when doing criticism, the generic critic operates on the following assumptions:

1. *Generic patterns necessarily develop.* Black [1978a:133–134] argues that there are a limited number of situations in which a speaker can be found and a limited number of ways of responding to these standard situations. As a result, says Black, messages form identifiable clusters over time. So, for example, when he invented the first inaugural address, George Washington could not know that subsequent inaugurals would resemble his. But he might have guessed such a

thing, because the thoughts and feelings of a culture will be similar from age to age. Whoever addresses such people—in any era—must reckon with such constancy.

2. *Generic patterns reveal societal truths.* The generic critic examines message patterns in order to comment on the universal as manifested in the particular. The generic critic looks for basic truths about people by examining the sometimes modest, often indistinct, trends that develop when they talk to one another. Thus, the "odd case," the text that breaks the pattern, will be of particular interest, because it highlights the *rationale* behind the generic formula exposed. If a new president fails to mention God in an inaugural address (something that has never been done), the resulting furor would call attention to the persistence of the special bond between religion and government in the United States.

3. *Knowledge of generic forces is largely implicit.* People can distinguish between a sincere and an insincere apology, because they somehow understand the pure form known as "apology." Thus, when the generic patterns in the "War of the Worlds" began to shift from "entertainment" to "news," many listeners became instinctively alarmed even though unaware of the rhetorical cues stimulating that alarm. Speakers are no different. When a crisis is on the horizon, disc jockeys automatically become less frivolous, somehow sensing that a generic boundary has just been erected. The implicitness of such rules is important, because the not-noticed throws light on people's *first premises*, beliefs so fundamental that they are not called to conscious attention. Disc jockeys are serious during Martian invasions, because the concept of community must be honored—in thought as well as in speech.

4. *Generic patterns stabilize social life.* Genres are conservative. They keep things in place. To speak in established ways by following the rules is to tip one's hat to the forces that be. Thus, the two-year-old expresses displeasure by wailing and the adolescent by sulking, but the teenager slowly learns to disagree without being disagreeable. Parents take delight in such maturity, in the child's growing ability to express emotion in generically sanctioned ways. Should that teenager someday become a U.S. Representative, he or she would learn how to express contempt even more elegantly: "The honorable gentleman from Missouri must surely be mistaken." Formulas like this develop because society has decreed that talking is superior to fighting. So, even though generic formulas sometimes seem silly, careful inspection finds them perpetuating important, agreed-upon truths.

5. *Generic perceptions affect subsequent perceptions.* Hirsch [1967] has argued that all critics are generic critics whether they know it or not. That is, when approaching a text, critics bring preconceptions of

generic types and compare that text to the data bank of texts they have studied previously. Because there is no "semantic autonomy of texts" [p. 74], says Hirsch, a critic's initial, categorizing judgment will color all subsequent judgments of that message. A statement like "John, I'd like to talk to you" immediately starts the categorical search: Is this going to be a reprimand? Until that generic question is satisfactorily answered, John is unlikely to rest easy.

As Rosenfield [1968] has observed, any message will look different alongside another message. The teacher's scathing remarks on a student's term paper seem horrific until other papers are examined to find "that's the norm with old Ellis." Viewed in isolation (perhaps an impossibility), a message may seem distinctive. But a careful dissection often shows that it has borrowed some features from Category A and others from Category B. Finding such generic tracings in no way detracts from the brilliance of a given text. Nor does it detract from its individuality, which properly lies in the creativity of its borrowing, in the uniqueness of the rhetorical assemblage.

An interesting example of Rosenfield's observation occurred upon the death of Lyndon Johnson. Columnist Nicholas von Hoffman [1973:B1] penned a statement about the late president, a portion of which went like this:

> Ah, Lyndon, you're not cold yet and they're calling you great. That's what happens when one politician dies: The rest of them call him great, but, Lyndon, you deserve better than patriotic hagiography. You were better than the eulogistic junk they're saying at the memorial services.
>
> Lyndon, you got your teeth into us and we got our teeth into you. Those five years of you in the White House were a barroom brawl, and, just four years ago almost to the day, when we staggered out of the saloon, dusty and bloody, we didn't hate you anymore. We understood better how you got us into Vietnam than how Nixon got us out and we liked you more, you cussed, cussing bullheaded, impossible, roaring, wild coot.
>
> You had your credibility gaps and your silent sullennesses, but we read you. Oh, man, Lyndon, did we know you! You were the best and the worst of ourselves, the personification of our rational deliriums. You were always so completely, so absolutely you. Kennedy had Pablo Casals to play for him, Nixon's got Pat Boone to pray for him, but you, Lyndon, you had Country Joe and the Fish singing songs soaked in four-letter words at you. . . .

Upon first reading von Hoffman's column, most will notice its irreverence. A more careful analysis shows that, despite its color, the editorial is also a fairly standard eulogy. Naturally, von Hoffman operates on the fringes of that genre, but he is still well within its bounds. Eulogies place one person on stage exclusively. Von Hoffman does that. Eulogies isolate the distinctive features of the deceased. Von Hoffman clearly does that. Eulogies make the dearly departed seem more dear by reframing his deficiencies and less departed by recalling his personality. Von Hoffman does both. And eulogies tell a selective history and project a diminished future because of the dead person's passing. Von Hoffman does those things as well. Naturally, this is not a pure eulogy. Had he been asked to speak at the graveside service in the presence of Lady Bird, von Hoffman would have been more restrained. Equally, however, von Hoffman shows us that the eulogy and the editorial are not incommensurate genres and that his column cannot be appreciated without understanding both of its generic parents.

Rhetorical studies show that genres perform a number of important functions. For one thing, genres are *preservative;* they keep established social patterns viable. Von Hoffman, for example, did not have total license when he wrote, since Lyndon Johnson was a president (and hence part of an institution) and because Johnson was dead (and hence defenseless). Similarly, Jamieson [1973] has shown that the papal encyclical's regal phrasing, doctrinal allusions, and use of the Latin language help to slow the introduction of radical ideas into church governance. Asante and Atwater [1986] also advance this conserving theme by arguing that some genres (lecturing, sermonizing, formal criticism) require the speaker to "stand above" the audience and hence preserve existing hierarchies of power. As they say [p. 171], "the rhetorical condition is established as soon as the form is chosen." Lucas [1986] indicates that Washington's first inaugural took the form it did because it borrowed liberally from British monarchial history and Protestant religious heritage. Consequently, America's first president spoke like a priestly colonial king. This rhetorical complexity perfectly reflects the political complexity built into the American form of government, and it also shows how the new always carries tracings of the old.

Other studies of the inaugural address show that generic alterations often proceed slowly. Finkelstein [1981] found that inaugural texts have become shorter over time, more figurative in language, and less linguistically complex. Finkelstein attributes these changes to the increases in size and diversity of the American audience and to the difficulty of finding nonpolarizing words for a diverse populace. Hart [1986b] examined Ronald Reagan's first inaugural and discovered that even an ideological president must tone down the language of change. While Mr. Reagan's first speech as president was more partisan than the average inaugural, he used a number of linguistic devices (impersonality, abstractness, and a simple vocabulary) to conform to the traditional, centrist mandate of his new office. If generic constraints can hem in even Ronald Reagan, they can be powerful indeed.

Another important feature is that genres suggest verbal *possibilities*. Because he had heard many eulogies before writing his, Nick von Hoffman did not have to start from scratch. His generic knowledge let him benefit from established patterns that had worked well previously. Analogously, Snow [1985] found that Martin Luther King, Jr.'s "Letter from a Birmingham Jail" used an epistle to turn the tables on clergymen who had decried his civil disobedience. By directly addressing a letter to his fellow preachers (in the manner of the biblical Paul), King turned a political matter into a religious matter, thereby making it hard for his opponents to use political quibbles to stall racial integration. A different study is that of Cherwitz and Zagacki [1986], who noted a rise in "consummatory" discourse, discourse designed to "give form to public anger" [p. 321], about international affairs without starting a nuclear holocaust. They note that when American hostages are captured or when American soldiers are attacked in the Middle East, an American president can either fight or not fight. Consummatory rhetoric provides a third alternative: fighting with words. That is, the president can sharply denounce the incidents and place America's enemies on warning, thereby establishing "a therapeutic 'buffer' between the desire for revenge and the necessity of rational deliberation [p. 321]."

Other studies also show the practical advantages of generic knowledge. Windt [1972] notes that the radical Yippies of the 1960s harkened back to the speech patterns of the ancient Greek Cynics in order to be heard. Knowing that the electronic media feed on novelty, the Yippies became bizarre, destroying sacred symbols and using obscenity, since "the more people you alienate, the more people you reach [p. 12]." By substituting an odd genre for normal public dialogue, the Yippies reshuffled the political deck of cards. Jamieson and Campbell [1982] show that the **generic hybrid,** a message borrowed from two or more generic traditions, also alters standard social arrangements. They observe, for example, that eulogists sometimes issue a call for political action in memory of the deceased, thereby adding a policy-related bottom line to the ordinary funeral oration. Similarly, Jablonski [1979b] notes the creativity of **generic transference,** the substitution of one *kind* of message for another. She cites the example of Richard Nixon, who, rather than hold a standard press conference to announce his replacement for the just-disgraced Spiro Agnew (Nixon's first vice president), actually conducted a formal ceremony in the East Room of the White House. Apparently reasoning that people behave better during ceremonies than during press conferences, Nixon pulled the generic rug from beneath his detractors. Jablonski [p. 171] describes his rhetorical wisdom thus:

> . . . the East Room provided a vivid counterpoint to Nixon's earlier Watergate speeches delivered from the Oval Office. The East Room,

which typically accommodates formal state affairs, was filled on this occasion with a formally attired audience of Washington dignitaries. As television cameras panned the elaborate chandeliers of the East Room, viewers at home could hear the invited guests chatting amiably, their laughter rising occasionally above the soft music played by the Marine Corps Band. Then, like bridesmaids, the majority and minority leaders of the Congress, the Cabinet, and Nixon's family filed in, processional-style. After a heightened pause, trumpets sounded the familiar "Ruffles and Flourishes" and the President and Mrs. Nixon were announced.

In a grand setting like this, it was easy indeed for listeners to forget that Mr. Nixon's first vice president was under indictment and that the president himself was currently being charged with high crimes and misdemeanors.

A third function of genres is that they facilitate *listening*. As Burke [1931] notes, recurring forms create "appetites" in audiences by promising, and then meeting, rhetorical expectations. People can miss several days of a soap opera, because its predictability (who slept with whom, when, and where) lets them catch up easily. But just as genres can help audiences, its misapplication can be a problem. Jamieson [1973] notes that when the existential tragedy/farce *Waiting for Godot* first played in Miami

> the audience rioted because they expected to see a Broadway comedy! This is why speakers often provide generic clues for proper listening: "I come before you tonight with a heavy heart. . . ."

Some genres have become especially useful. One of these, the jeremiad, is a religiously tinged oration calling people back to their solemn duties under God. Johannesen [1985] reports that the jeremiad has been popular in the United States since colonial times because it gives an ultimate rationale for less than ultimate political activities. The jeremiad describes sin, threatens punishment, demands repentance, and promises heavenly reward. Using it, John Kennedy embarrassed Americans into attempting a moon race, Lyndon Johnson intimidated them into fighting the Vietnam War, and Ronald Reagan shamed them into tax reform. Ritter [1980] reports that the jeremiad has been equally attractive to both Republicans and Democrats, suggesting the centrality of the "chosen people" theme to the American mindset.

Research on genre recommends this approach to the critic for a variety of additional reasons:

1. *Generic study exposes cultural tastes.* Gronbeck [1978b] notes that the continued popularity of political debate in the United States

reflects the essential contentiousness of the American people and their unwillingness to submit to a single, consistent ideology.

2. *Generic study explains rhetorical power.* Jamieson [1975a] argues that one cannot understand why some rhetoric (for example, the papal encyclical) has the influence it has unless one also understands its "chromosomal imprints," the rhetorical features it retains from its historical roots (in this case, the speeches of Roman emperors).

3. *Generic study indexes social change.* Downey [1982] observes that physical alterations in the world (for example, the existence of nuclear weapons) have necessarily changed how the genre of political saber rattling is conducted (it now has to be done with a more deft political touch).

4. *Generic study reveals psychological style.* Vartabedian [1985] argues that some speakers are "generically blind," excessively committed to one style of speech. He notes, for instance, that Richard Nixon tried to justify himself rather than his policies in Vietnam largely because self-justification had served him so well earlier in his career (for example, the Checkers Speech).

5. *Generic study uncovers latent trends.* Brummett [1984c] has tracked the increasing use of apocalyptic rhetoric (talk of imminent doom and gloom) and warns that its use may cause people to despair of peaceful solutions to the world's problems and make them increasingly susceptible to defeatist rhetoric: "Things are so bad that we might as well try anything."

6. *Generic study provides evaluative standards.* Jamieson [1975b] observes that by knowing the generic rules for a particular kind of speech the critic can better judge its instances. She notes, for example, that satire is essentially generically based criticism, an explicit commentary on lock-step rhetorical formulas (for example, *Saturday Night Live's* imitations of conventional family life).

When doing generic research, the critic uses critical probes to explain textually distinctive trends. Among the most useful of these questions are the following:

1. Do verbal *patterns* give unity to the ideas, values, language, or methods of organization employed in the text?
2. Have these patterns been observed so often that they have become *standard*?
3. Do these patterns dominate the message? That is, how *idiosyncratic* is the speaker?
4. What *generic label* best fits this text? Is the message characterized merely by topic (a sermon), situation (a televised sermon),

or can it be described with more conceptually ambitious labels (a religious diatribe)?

5. How *tight* are the generic constraints and what accounts for their rigidity or looseness?

6. If the rhetorical situation is partly *traditional* (a western movie), does it also have novel rhetorical features (a Chinese cowboy in the lead)?

7. If the rhetorical situation is comparatively *unprecedented* (a televised advertisement for condoms), is any generic borrowing being done (a scientist's testimonial for the product)?

8. Does the speaker provide generic *clues* to help listeners ("I'm your psychiatrist, not your mate. We can be candid but not lovers"). Is the specter of prevous rhetorical events invoked ("Speak to me as if I were an old friend")?

9. Does the speaker offset generic *interference* by distinguishing this message from its ancestors ("Dear Friend, this is *not* just another piece of junk mail. . . .")?

10. Given the generic constraints in place, was the speaker *successful* (on strategic, psychological, moral, or other, grounds)?

While generic study can be highly useful, it can also be misapplied or used excessively. There is no particular merit in classifying discourse for its own sake. Its value lies, rather, in its utility: Does it identify a rhetorical trend that might have been missed? Does it explain why a given speaker failed or succeeded? Does it highlight an interesting rhetorical problem that might have been missed? In other words, the most creative generic research asks and answers important questions.

CONCLUSION

As King Lear painfully discovered, he had raised a radical for a daughter. She refused to honor the rhetorical conventions established for receiving a piece of his kingdom. Cordelia was not offended by the content of the speech Lear wanted her to give. The woman did love her father. But she could not separate the what of Lear's love from the how of her own. She knew that for love to be love it had to be her kind of love, that it had to meet her generic expectations. She, not Lear, had to find the time and the place of love as well as its language. She understood that to use the formulas of love would be to lose love. She knew that love by generic proxy was a cheat.

Cordelia's message is thus the message of this chapter: structure and content are siblings; form is a cousin. They cannot be treated separately without fundamentally destroying the natural complexity of human communication. If content gives speech its substance, structure gives it its variety. People become wedded to their ways of doing things (a cup of coffee with the morning paper, another while opening the mail). They come to believe that these patterns make them distinctive as individuals and, in a grander sense, make life worth living. People also feel special about their ways of saying things. At some level, they may sense that everything worth saying has already been said at least once. But they sense that it has not yet been said *in their way* and that feeling, too, gives life meaning. Because they are social creatures, people will imitate one another. That is where genres come in. Because they are individuals, people will give speech its color by exploring its variations. That is where rhetoric comes in. And because they are complex, they will sometimes say more than they realize they are saying. That is where critics come in.

CHAPTER SEVEN

Analyzing Style: Syntax and Imagery

[T]he scene amidst which we stand does not permit us to confine our thoughts or our sympathies to those fearless spirits who hazarded or lost their lives on this consecrated spot. We have the happiness to rejoice here in the presence of a most worthy representation of the survivors of the whole Revolutionary army.

Veterans! You are the remnant of many a well-fought field. You bring with you the marks of honor from Trenton and Monmouth, from Yorktown, Camden, Bennington, and Saratoga. Veterans of half a century! When in your youthful days you put everything at hazard in your country's cause, good as that cause was, and sanguine as youth is, still your fondest hopes did not stretch onward to an hour like this! At a period to which you could not reasonably have expected to arrive, at a moment of national prosperity such as you could never have foreseen, you are now met here to enjoy the fellowship of old soldiers, and to receive the overflowings of a universal gratitude.

But your agitated countenances and your heaving breasts inform me that even this is not an unmixed joy. I perceive that a tumult of contending feelings rushes upon you. The images of the dead, as well as the persons of the living, present themselves to you. The scene overwhelms you, and I turn from it. May the Father of all mercies smile upon your declining years, and bless them! And when you shall here have exchanged your embraces, when you shall once more have pressed the hands which have been so often extended to give succor in adversity, or grasped in the exultation of victory, then look abroad upon this lovely land which your young valor defended, and mark the happiness with which it is filled: yea, look abroad upon the whole earth, and see what a name you have contributed to give to your country, and what a praise you have added to freedom, and then rejoice in the sympathy and gratitude which beam upon your last days from the improved condition of mankind! [Webster, 1825]

* * * * *

Throw [these enclosures] away within 24 hours. The sexual abuse of children is so ugly, so unbelievable, so Satanic that no one wants to think about it.

But someone's *got to rescue kids from incest, beatings, and rape.* *"Momma, Momma, make him stop hurting me!!" they cry.*

That someone's you . . . and me . . . we are the ONLY ones who can stop the incest, beatings, and rape.

An eight-month-old baby rushed to the hospital with gonorrhea of the throat! How does an eight-month-old baby get gonorrhea of the throat? You can figure it out. A booklet, "How to Have Sex with Kids" telling a man (1) how to penetrate the vagina of a four-year-old, (2) how to keep it hush-hush so that she does not tell her parents, and (3) that "hey . . . you're doing the kid a favor by deflowering her."

Please send a check for 1,000 dollars or 1500, or 2,000 or 200 or 100 or 50 . . . whatever.

You want to sacrifice hard and tough for this one. Sell a car, land, borrow (I did), or go to your savings account. I challenge YOU to be the one to send the $10,000 or $5,000 check.

An Ivy-League philosopher, I abandoned university teaching to work at this full time.

And I'm not alone. You're with me. We—*you and me*—stop the sexual abuse of kids.

Read the enclosed. Cry. Rage. Tell others. And rescue.

I'll send to anyone (including you) a free copy of my tape, "How to STOP the Sexual Abuse of Children." Send me names. The other side of the tape is "How to Protect You and Your Family from Attack." *Please help me to send this tape out to thousands and thousands of people* . . . [Gallagher, 1984]

These passages were authored by different persons. No surprise. In different time periods. Again no surprise. To different audiences. Obvious as well. Their genres are also different: The first passage bears the marks of the commemorative oration and the latter that of junk mail. The texts are so different that even placing them next to one another is an ironic exercise. Indeed, an admirer of the first author (Daniel Webster) might be offended by even a remote comparison between Webster's intellect and that of the second author, one W. Neil Gallagher of Tupelo, Mississippi, whose greatest distinction seems his access to mimeograph equipment and stamps. So the passages are predictably different. Any fool could tell that. But it takes a special kind of fool, a stylistic critic, to tell why.

This chapter focuses on **style,** the sum total of language habits distinguishing one message from another. Here, we will examine language microscopically, noting which words a speaker chooses and how they collectively produce special effects. We will investigate tone and nuance, features that audiences sense but cannot describe. We will discover why some words provoke more intense reactions than their synonyms, why language sometimes hides rather than reveals meaning, and why the imagery of poetry and the imagery of rhetoric sound alike yet different. Mostly, we will try to become precise about imprecise things: Why does one word sound stronger than another? Why does some rhetoric seem sacred and other rhetoric profane? How does language contribute to passion? To majesty? To mystery? To boredom? What makes a lawyer's language tedious when written in contracts but gripping when presented to a jury? How must the language of advertising change when Cadillacs are being sold rather than Yugos? Why do physicians' words insulate them from public scrutiny and why is this almost never the case with politicians?

But the most basic thing we will do in this chapter is look closely at language. Most people do not. Most people pay attention to the big picture in persuasion: ideas, arguments, examples, pictures, stories. So by looking carefully at language, the critic has a natural advantage over the casual listener. Most contemporary Americans, for example, could quickly tell that Daniel Webster's Bunker Hill oration was alien to their era and culture. "But why?" the stylistic critic asks. To ask such a basic question is all too rare, but to ask it is to begin to find its answer.

For example, Black [1978a], a preeminent stylistic critic, explains that Webster's sentimental style is now unfashionable, because people no longer respect absolute values and are unwilling to surrender to great persons espousing great ideas. But for the right people, says Black, Webster's style permits an emotional "recreation under sanctioned auspices" [p. 78], a way of being shielded from unpleasant realities. To describe war veterans as the "remnant of a well-fought field" is to indulge language and thereby to indulge oneself. This is the language of melodrama, language that elevates ordinary soldiers to "fearless spirits," that turns a battlefield into a "consecrated spot," and that transforms helpfulness into "succor in adversity." This is grand language and hence distasteful to modern Americans. A statement like "We have the happiness to rejoice here in the presence of a most worthy representation . . ." cries out for the journalist's editorial pen. Raised on a diet of glib advertising phrases, modern Americans would be asleep by the time Webster got past the dependent clauses in the sixth sentence: "At a period to which you could not reasonably have expected to arrive, at a moment of national prosperity such as you could never have foreseen . . ."

Perhaps because they read few books and watch much television, modern Americans hate language that calls attention to itself: "May the Father of all mercies smile upon your declining years." Modern Americans also like verbs rather than adjectives, action rather than embellishment. In their scientific detachment, they are suspicious of "heaving" breasts, "contending" feelings, or "agitated" countenances and embarrassed by excessive emotionality: "The scene overwhelms you, and I turn from it." While modern Americans still remember their dead and recognize their military heroes, they are more businesslike about it. Modern Americans might feel an ideological kinship with Daniel Webster, but, stylistically, he alienates them.

Neil Gallagher's style alienates many of them too, but for different reasons. Unlike Webster, Gallagher has plenty of verbs: "read," "cry," "tell," "rescue." Unlike Webster, Gallagher's adjectives are short, pungent: "ugly," "Satanic," "hard and tough." Unlike Webster, Gallagher does not shield his readers from reality. He pours fact upon fact ("incest, beatings, rape"), trying to impress his audience with quantitative rather than qualitative experience: "hundreds and hundreds of . . . workshops," "thousands and thousands of people." Because he is writing rather than speaking, Gallagher tries hard to address his listeners personally, seeking in one brief message both to commence and consummate a relationship: "Sell a car, land, borrow—I did—or go to your savings account." While Webster's promises to his audience are philosophical, Gallagher's are concrete: "I'll send to anyone . . . a free copy of my tape." While Webster invites his listeners to reach up to him, Gallagher reaches down to his.

Despite his verbal energy, Gallagher misses the mark. His words demand too much too soon ("throw this away within 24 hours"), and his emotionality seems excessive for a person we hardly know. While his streamlined sentence structure is simpler than Webster's, Gallagher piles too many disjointed thoughts into too little space and hence they become a tumult: four-year-olds, money, gonorrhea, the Ivy League, land sales, free tapes. While his language is informal ("kids," "hush, hush," "Momma"), its staccato pace is inelegant and emotionally abrupt. Gallagher's too-rapid treatment of the victims he claims to care for (one brief paragraph) and the speed with which he repairs to his own bottom line ("send the $10,000 or $5,000 check") make him seem a hit-and-run artist. At times, Gallagher's gracelessness makes us yearn for Webster.

To say that a nineteenth-century commemorative speech differs from a mass mailing on child abuse is hardly profound. But even our brief examination of them has exposed two different worlds; it is these worlds of meaning that the stylistic critic tries to understand. In making their language choices, Webster and Gallagher revealed—wittingly and unwittingly—a bit about themselves and their audiences. According to Ohmann [1959:19], style reflects a writer's mode of experience, how that author tries to "impose order on the world." Webster wanted to make the world slow down in order to better savor the past; Gallagher sought a faster rotation in order to better salvage the future.

All persuaders, many unconsciously, develop a style. They do so, according to Gibson [1966:24], partly as "a matter of sheer individual will, a desire for a particular kind of self-definition." If Daniel Webster and Neil Gallagher were somehow placed in the midst of a modern cocktail party, they could be found because of their styles: Webster would hold court, Gallagher would buttonhole. But there is more to style than personality. Style is also imposed upon speakers by time (the nineteenth century versus the twentieth century), by occasion (known versus unknown audiences), and by genre (eulogies, mass mailings, cocktail party chatter). As Klaus [1969:61] notes, style is important because it often "does not originate within the man; it exists apart from him, as an inheritance, a legacy, that shapes his conceptual ends as surely as he does."

Although it is intellectually promising, studying style is often a humble business. Noting that Daniel Webster habitually used the passive voice while Neil Gallagher used the active voice may seem trivial. But it is less trivial to say that Daniel Webster's world was one in which audiences felt dominated by great ideas (freedom), great myths (heroism), great beliefs (Christianity), great events (Yorktown), and great people (himself). This entire system of beliefs, this world view, may have resulted in Webster's use of the passive, since, as Milic [1971:87] says: ". . . even some of the greatest [writers] knew very little about what they were doing when they wrote." Gallagher's breathy use of the active voice may, in contrast, have signaled the onrushing events of his times and a confusing world in which children must become warriors to protect themselves. Gallagher's language may reflect a whole way of seeing the world, a take-charge way. When choosing their verbs, then, Webster and Gallagher may have been reaffirming the times in which they lived. Equally, they may have been doing nothing more than choosing verbs.

The good critic knows that to emphasize a single stylistic feature in a text is to risk getting a hasty impression of that text. Thus, in Chapters Seven and Eight, we will urge the critic to use as many tools as possible when studying language. Approaching the same message from numerous perspectives builds in safeguards against foolishness. To appreciate the subtlety of language, one must get beyond impressionism by cataloging and counting, by gathering different kinds of linguistic data, by sorting them out in complex ways, and then by thinking some more. Language is wonderful. It charms and delights. All of us love it. But like any lover, it must not be taken for granted. The good stylistic critic never does.

EXAMINING SYNTAX

Despite centuries of interest in it, rhetorical style remains elusive. Turner [1973] notes that some would do away with the concept completely, treating it like the physicist's ether, a seemingly important but impossible-to-find phenomenon. But few have followed this lead, primarily because daily life documents the importance of style. How, for example, would historians have treated the first moon landing if Neil Armstrong had not said the pefect thing: "That's one small step for man, one giant leap for mankind"? Neil Armstrong was no stylist, but his statement does have a pleasing parallelism and a dash of imagery. The remarks of other ordinary stylists are also remembered. We remember the World War II general who, when asked to surrender, replied to the enemy in an exceedingly economical way: "Nuts." We remember the head coach of the Washington Bullets who, when asked if his team had a chance to win, drew on his Italian heritage and replied: "It's never really over 'til the fat lady sings." We remember the embattled Interior Secretary who, when asked to defend his hiring practices, responded with the statement: "We have every kind of mix you can have. I have a black, I have a woman, two Jews and a cripple." And we remember the baseball slugger who, when asked what his role on the team was, replied "I'm the straw that stirs the drink." the drink."

In their ordinary ways, all of these speakers were stylists. While few scientists speak in balanced couplets, ambassadors often do and, in July of 1969, Neil Armstrong was an entire planet's ambassador. Similarly, in his one-word statement, Anthony McAuliffe captured the no-nonsense, tough-it-out style of his fellow soldiers and hence inspired them. Dick Motta's comparison between basketball and opera was so bizarre that it quickly put a smile on the nation's face. In contrast, James Watt turned the nation's head as well as its stomach with his tasteless aside, and it eventually cost him his job. Reggie Jackson's metaphor was rather high-style for a baseball player and it also had the pungency fans had come to expect from Mister October.

When the individual words of such memorable phrases are viewed in isolation, they are often not impressive. As Blankenship [1968:53] notes, 195 of the 265 words spoken in Abraham Lincoln's Gettysburg Address were of one-syllable, indicating that style emerges from *word patterns*. That is, words that seem weak on their own gain strength when they come together. The genius of style is, therefore, the genius of architecture, not of brick-making, a fact made plain in 1863: ". . . that government of the people, by the people, for the people, shall not perish from the earth." Pascal's famous comment on style is as apt today as it was in the seventeenth century: "Words differently arranged have a different meaning, and meanings differently arranged have different effects." Beardsley [1969:14] proves this point when noting that even a slight rearrangement of Thomas Paine's words by Madison Avenue would obliterate its impact: "Soulwise, these are trying times."

In short, stylistic excellence often lies in **syntax,** the way in which words are arranged. The truth of this proposition can be seen by looking at the components of style. Although the diagramming of sentences has lost favor recently, it can still be useful. Arnold [1974], for example, urges the critic to separate the grammar of a message into what can be called its (1) **primary** and (2) **secondary** structures. Primary structure often consists of an initial noun phrase, a verb phrase, and a final noun phrase (containing either a prepositional phrase or what was formerly called the direct object). All other words found in a given sentence can be assigned to the secondary structure, including predicate modifiers, dependent clauses, and adverbial phrases. By segmenting a message in this way, its natural linguistic intricacy is disrupted. But this can be an excusable intrusion if it helps the critic better appreciate the basics of style.

Nothing is more basic than a chain letter. Rhetorically, it is completely predictable: It promises that individual good fortune results from a conspiracy of letter-writing. All participate, all win. Although nominally illegal in most states, chain letters will not die. Often, the impulse behind them is financial, a pyramid scheme based on people's willingness to become pests to their friends. The rhetoric of such letters mixes threats for breaking the chain with rewards for maintaining it. "Everyone an entrepreneur" goes the appeal, and the letters clog the mail.

Given the rhetorical circumstances of chain letters—an unknown author, a questionable product, and an uncertain recipient—one might expect basic rhetoric from them. Figure 7.1 justifies those expectations. The letter examined [Kiss, 1985] could hardly be simpler, with 13 of the 34 sentences consisting of *nothing but* primary structures (the figure's boldface elements). The remaining sentences are only slightly less pure: Almost none begin with a dependent clause; only a few sentences are compound; there are virtually no embedded constructions. This is Dick-and-Jane language. An avalanche of simple sentences cascades on the reader, as if the slightest violation of primary structure would ruin persuasion. Nouns and verbs predominate, transitions are omitted, and even paragraph breaks are eschewed in the original typescript. The basic conceptual appeal of the letter is only slightly more subtle than its grammar: "Keep the letter going or you, too, might die like Helen Fairchild."

Fifty-nine percent of the words in the chain letter are contained in its primary structure. In contrast, Figure 7.2 presents a letter from General John Pershing [1919], whose primary structure accommodates only 23 percent of his remarks. *All* thirteen of his sentences are burdened by secondary structures. His primary segments are weighted down in front by dependent clauses and in the rear by a compound structure or a series of prepositional phrases. Also, adverbs frequently peek between Pershing's verb phrases, further slowing down the message. It is as if the General could not leap into a sentence without first

Figure 7.1
Grammatical Structure of the Chain Letter

(1) **This paper→has been sent→to you**
                                        for good luck.

(2) **The original copy→is→in New England.**

(3) **It→has been→around the world**
                                        nine times.

(4) **The luck→has   been sent→to you.**
                now

(5) **You→will receive→good luck→within four days**
                                        of receiving this letter, provided
                                        you, in turn, send it back out.

(6) **This→is→no joke.**

(7) **You→will receive→it→by mail.**

(8) **Send→copies→to people.**

(9) **Do not send→money,**
                        it has no price.

(10) **Do not keep→this letter.**

(11) **It→must leave→your hands→within ninety-six hours.**

(12) **An R.A.F. officer→received→$70,000.**

(13) **Joe Elliot→received→$40,000**
                                and lost it because
                                he broke the chain.

(14)   **Gene Welch→lost→his wife→after receiving this letter.**
        While in the Phillipines

(15) **He→failed to circulate→the letter.**

(16)   **he→received→$7,755.**
        However, before his death

(17)   **send→copies→of the letter**
        Please   and see what happens in four days.

(18) **The chain→comes→from Venezuela**
                                and was written by Saul Anthony
                                deCroof, a missionary from South
                                America.

(19)   **you→must make→20 copies**
        Since the copy must   and send them to your
        make a tour of the world,   friends and
                                           acquaintances.

(20)   **you→will get→a surprise.**
        After a few days

(21) **This→is→true**
                        even if you are not superstitious.

(22) **Do note→the following.**

(23) **Constantina Dias→received→the chain→in 1983.**

                                                    (*continued*)

Figure 7.1 Grammatical Structure of the Chain Letter (*continued*)

(24) **He→asked→his secretary→to make twenty copies**
                                          and send them out.

(25)   **he→won→a lottery→of two million dollars.**
   A few days later

(26) **Eric Deddit,**   **→received→the letter**
       an office employee,   and forgot it had to leave
                                               his hands within ninety-six
                                               hours.

(27) **He→lost→his job.**

(28)   **he→mailed out→the twenty copies.**
   Later, after finding
   the letter again,

(29)   **he→got→a better job.**
   A few days later

(30) **Helen Fairchild→received→the letter**
                              and, not believing,
                              threw the letter away.

(31)   **she→died.**
   Nine days later

(32)   **send→no money.**
   Remember,

(33)   **don't ignore→this.**
   Please

(34) **It→works.**

doing calisthenics. Statements 7 and 8 are particularly noteworthy, as Pershing gets a long running start, only to step across two short primary segments. Balanced constructions ("whether keeping lonely vigil in the trenches, or . . ."), unneeded adjectives ("monotonous drudgery," "overwhelming victory"), and double nouns ("with mind and body," "its efficiency and its valor") abound in the message. Indeed, the chain letter managed to pack thirty-four sentences into less space than it took Pershing to lumber through his thirteen sentences (there are 316 total words in the former and 357 words in the latter). Where the author of the chain letter envisioned an impatient reader, Pershing seemed to anticipate the opposite.

Pershing's expectations were sensible. His letter was distributed on February 28, 1919, to all doughboys returning from World War I. This was a time for reflection, since, for the first time in a long time, General Pershing's men had time. So the General paused and thought of grand things—valor, achievement, dedication, sacrifice, and mortality—sensing that the significance of his ideas justified the grand style. The ideas he treated were timeless, ideas that would help fill the unhurried, reflective moment as his men aged. The chain letter, in contrast, blows away with the first wind or when the next piece of junk mail is opened. Its very style invites, even demands, such treatment. But the Pershing letter issues a different invitation, which may explain why it was found, lovingly preserved, in the attic of a World War I veteran sixty-five years later.

By uncovering the grammatical structure of these two messages, we discover what Lanham [1983] calls the **periodic** (or paratactic) style and the **running** (or hypotactic) style. Each style has a special rhetorical purpose and each responds to a different human psychology. Lanham urges the critic to make an early determination of these features, since they so often reveal the author's voice. The periodic style, exemplified by Pershing, and the running style, exemplified by the chain letter, make different commentaries about the texts that embody them. Lanham urges the critic to listen for this inner, fainter voice to truly understand the subtlety of rhetoric.

The running style is a "verb" style, not a "noun" style. It is also the most natural style because it is simplest. In a running style, the author tells who did what to whom, when, where, and how. Such a style lends itself to narrative development, to "coping with the world. The coping is all small-scale, minute-to-minute tactics, not seasonal grand strategy; the reader is on patrol with the writer, sharing immediate dangers and present perplexities. Things happen as they want to, not as we would have them." The chain letter uses this laundry-list type of development, as fact pours atop fact, event atop event, emotion atop emotion, until the author finally screeches to a halt. Neil Gallagher's diatribe on child abuse is similar. In neither case is the reader given time to reflect. *Immediate* responses are the order of the day and clean primary structures ensure that that order will be carried out.

Lanham points up another feature of the running style when offering Julius Caesar's "I came; I saw; I conquered" as its prototype. Lanham notes that this style typically suppresses information by not ordering phenomena, thereby placing responsibilities on the audience's shoulders. When Caesar placed coming, seeing, and conquering on the same syntactic level, says Lanham [p. 33], he left it up to the reader to determine their relative priority: "If Caesar had written instead 'Since it was I who arrived, and I who saw how the land lay, the victory followed as a matter of course,' he would have said outright what the tight-lipped 'came-saw-conquered' formula only invites us to say about him." Similarly, because the chain letter has so few orienting devices (for example, dependent clauses), the reader is not invited to distinguish between the plight of Joe Elliot (who lost $40,000) and

Figure 7.2
Grammatical Structure of the Pershing Letter

(1) Now that your service with the American Expeditionary Forces is about to terminate,

I→cannot let   you   go→without a personal word.

(2) At the call to arms,   the patriotic young manhood   of America eagerly   →responded   and became the formidable army whose decisive victories testify to its efficiency and its valor.

(3) With the support of the nation firmly united to defend the cause of liberty,   our army→has executed→the will→of the people   with resolute purpose.

(4) Our democracy→has been tested   and the forces of autocracy have been defeated.

(5) To the glory of the citizen-soldier,   our troops→have   faithfully   fulfilled→their trust   and in a succession of brilliant offensives have overcome the menace to our civilization.

(6) As an individual,   your part   in the world war   →has been→an important one→in the sum total   of our achievements.

(7) Whether keeping lonely vigil in the trenches, or gallantly storming the enemy's stronghold; whether enduring monotonous   each→has   bravely and efficiently   played→his part.

drudgery at the rear, or sustaining the fighting line at the front,

(8) By willing sacrifice of personal rights; by cheerful endurance of hardship and privation; by vigor, strength and indomitable will, made effective by thorough organization and cordial cooperation,

you→inspired→the war-torn Allies→with new life
and turned the tide of threatened defeat into overwhelming victory.

(9) With a consecrated devotion to duty and a will to conquer,

you→have served**→your country.**
loyally

(10) By your exemplary conduct

a standard→has been established and maintained
never before attained by any army.

(11) With mind and body as clean and strong as the decisive blows you delivered against the foe,

you→are soon **to return→to the pursuits**
of peace.

(12) In leaving the scenes of your victories, may

I→ask
that you carry home your high ideals and continue to live as you have served—an honor to the principles for which you have fought and to the fallen comrades you leave behind.

(13) It is with pride in our success that

I→extend→to you
my sincere thanks for your splendid service to the army and to the nation.

Gene Welch (who won $7,755 but who also lost his wife). Such facts merely shoot forth, propelled by the noun-verb-noun-verb syntax its excited author has chosen.

The periodic style, Daniel Webster's and John Pershing's style, operates quite differently. If the running style is loose, the periodic style is tight: reasoned, intricate, connected. Here, secondary structures constantly tell the audience what they should do with the primary structures. Lanham [p. 77] notes that the periodic style, "with its internal parentheses, balanced phrasing, and climactic resolution, stops time to let a reader take in the complete pattern." The periodic style does more of the audience's work—categorizing, weighing, proportioning, qualifying—or, as Lanham [p. 54] puts it: "[The periodic style] is like the vast formal garden of a Baroque palace, all balanced squares and parallel paths. The land is rearranged in ways that the visual cortex can easily sort out. The [r]unning style, on the other hand, is like the informal garden, which shapes nature without seeming to. Nature is not dominated and reformed but simply helped on the way it wanted to go anyway."

Periodic speakers trade (1) authority for interest and (2) spontaneous responses for delayed, but more emotionally complex, responses. Webster and Pershing willingly made such trades. Use of a more telegraphic style at such sacred moments would have seemed to them a cultural mockery. If human sacrifice did not warrant a complex style, nothing did, they may have reasoned. On the other hand, because their purposes were so practical, Neil Gallagher and the author of the chain letter also chose the right style. Given the enormity of the child abuse problem, Gallagher's simple, direct language stood as a stylistic signal that a solution was possible, if not imminent. Like other direct mailers, Gallagher did not know his audience; he thus became plain in order to offset the cruelest of fates—being ignored.

Running and periodic motifs deal solely with the structural features of language. *How* these structures are used by individuals is a very different matter. That is, not all running styles need be tacky and not all periodic styles produce poetry (they can as easily result in obfuscation). Dwight Eisenhower was an interesting example in this context. As a writer, Ike had a nice, sprightly, running style, and his memoirs are a pleasure to read as a result. But as a speaker, he often lost his compass amidst secondary structures. This was true even during simple ceremonial occasions as, for example, when he welcomed children to an Easter egg roll at the White House.

This point is dramatized in Table 7.1 by contrasting what Eisenhower [1958:65] said (hypotactically) with what he might have said (paratactically). Clearly, Ike used twice the words he needed and, unlike Webster or Pershing, got no mileage from the extra verbiage.

Table 7.1   Eisenhower's Actual Versus Potential Style

Delivered Version	Potential Version
It is a privilege to welcome you once more to the annual egg-rolling contest on the White House grounds.	Welcome to our annual egg-rolling contest.
I surely hope that the weather cooperates with you properly and that you do not have the discomfort of a shower.	Let's hope it doesn't rain.
Moreover, I just learned this morning that many of the schoolchildren had to go to school on this Easter Monday . . .	I've just learned that some children had to go to school today . . .
and so to them I extend my sympathies for missing the fun of the day . . .	and I'm sorry they're going to miss the fun . . .
that I hope the rest of you will have.	that the rest of you will have.
Mrs. Eisenhower joins me in saying Happy Easter to all of you. Goodbye.	Mrs. Eisenhower joins me in saying Happy Easter to all of you. Goodbye.

His prepositional phrases are unncessary, since his audience already knew they were standing "on the White House grounds" and joined together "on this Easter Monday." The dependent clauses in the second and third statements add neither information nor grace to his remarks, and his bloated syntax ("and so to them I extend my sympathies for . . .") robs the message of elegance. Thus, it is not enough to determine a text's basic stylistic structure. The critic must also reckon with the *effects* achieved, or lost, by them as well.

Gibson [1966] offers a useful way of getting at these stylistic effects. He would describe Eisenhower as a **stuffy** talker because of the length of his clauses, his avoidance of simple words, and his use of the passive voice. In his system, Gibson argues that the combination of more than a dozen language variables creates distinctive styles like Eisenhower's. In addition to the stuffy style, Gibson posits a **tough** style (monosyllabic words, many "to be" verbs, few adjectives) and a **sweet** style (a you-orientation, a good number of contractions, use of the active voice). Gibson has worked out the exact stylistic ingredients for each style and his recipe is presented in Table 7.2.

The Gibson system is useful not because it is precise (it is only a rough guide) but because it helps explain rhetorical voice. "Voice" is a difficult thing to describe, but it is hardly a difficult thing to hear. For example, General Pershing's measured voice is different from Daniel Webster's grand voice, and both differ substantially from the frenetic voice of Neil Gallagher. Gibson's system helps us discuss such felt-but-

Table 7.2   Criteria for Measuring Style

Variables	Tough	Sweet	Stuffy
1. Monosyllables	>70%	61–70%	<60%
2. Words of 3 syllables or more	<10%	10–19%	>20%
3. 1st & 2nd person pronouns	One "I" or "we"/ 100 words	Two "you" per 100 words	No 1st or 2nd person pronouns
4. Subjects (neuters versus people)	1/2 or more people	1/2 or more people	2/3 or more neuters
5. Finite verbs	>10%	>10%	<10%
6. To be forms as finite verbs	>1/3 of verbs	<1/4	<1/4
7. Passive verbs	<1/20 verbs	None	>1 in 5
8. True adjectives	<10%	>10%	>8%
9. Adjectives modified	<1 per 100 words	>1/100	<1/100
10. Noun adjuncts	<2%	>2%	>4%
11. Average length of clauses	<10 words	<10 words	>10 words
12. Clauses (percent of total words)	<25%	<33%	>40%
13. "Embedded" words	<1/2 S/V combinations	<half	>twice
14. Uses of "the"	8% or more	under 6%	6–7%
15. Contractions and fragments	>1 per 100 words	>2/100	None
16. Parentheses & other punctuation	None	>2 per 100 words	None

(From Gibson, 1966)

not-explained phenomena. The example Gibson [pp. 29–30] gives of the tough style is especially vivid and shows the usefulness of his humble counting and contrasting:

> In the late summer of that year we lived in a house in a village that looked across the river and the plain to the mountains. In the bed of the river there were pebbles and boulders, dry and white in the sun, and the water was clear and swiftly moving and blue in the channels. Troops went by the house and down the road and the dust they raised powdered the leaves of the trees. The trunks of the trees too were

dusty and the leaves fell early that year and we saw the troops marching along the road and the dust rising and leaves, stirred by the
breeze, falling and the soldiers marching and afterward the road bare
and white except for the leaves.

The plain was rich with crops; there were many orchards of fruit
trees and beyond the plains the mountains were brown and bare.
There was fighting in the mountains and at night we could see the
flashes from the artillery. In the dark it was like summer lightning,
but the nights were cool and there was not the feeling of a storm
coming.

These are the words of Ernest Hemingway, a tough-talker if there
ever was one. Gibson describes the tough-talker as an experienced,
close-lipped, first-hand reporter who knows what he knows and who
is unafraid to share it. The tough-talker is self-absorbed, sure of his
footing: Hemingway sees things from *his* house, reports *his* sightings
of the artillery flashes. Gibson says there is a flatness to the speaker's
voice here, a self-limiting but unquestionable sense of authority. "You
would not call this man genial," says Gibson [p. 31], since "[h]e
behaves rather as if he had known us, the reader, a long time and
therefore doesn't have to pay us very much attention." Instead, the
"voice" concentrates on facts, describing things as they are, not as they
seem to be. The phrases are short, the sentences compound rather than
complex, and adjectives and adverbs are kept under control by nouns
and predicates. This is the spare language of a clear-headed speaker.

A second style is what Gibson calls sweet talk. It could hardly be
more different from stuffy talk, as the language of advertising so often
shows:

Have you ever tried **Kathy's Kitchen Products** before? You'd be
amazed at how quick and easy they are—and how incredibly tasty as
well. Wait 'til you smell the scrumptious smells of **Kathy's** *new* frozen
dinners, made as always with only the finest of **Kathy's** ingredients.

Tomorrow, help yourself to **Kathy's** new Taco Delight. Loads of
lettuce and cheese, extra helpings of perfectly seasoned beef, the
crispiest taco shells you can buy, and all the hot sauce you'll ever
need. Even a little guacamole on the side. Everything you need for a
stay-at-home fiesta. Olé!

This voice is unquestionably more social: You and your life experiences, your tastes, and your kitchen routines are emphasized. Gibson
notes that sweet talk is filled with clichés ("the finest ingredients,"
"everything you need"), no doubt because clichés are the language of
us all. There is also a more informal (running) style here, because the
speaker seeks action, not rumination, from the audience. Unstated, but

very much present, is the speaker's assumption that he or she has the *right* to counsel the audience. The "voice" knows that you need something quick, something easy, something tasty, even though this voice has never met you before. This claim of unearned familiarity is the hallmark of the sweet style, says Gibson, as is the lavish use of adjectives. The sweet talker is a solicitor par excellence.

Gibson calls the third of his styles stuffy because it removes the tough talker's sense of self and the sweet talker's sense of other. In their place hovers a disembodied assemblage of words. Gibson [p. 93] uses a government report on smoking as his paradigmatic example of the stuffy style:

> Cigarette smoking is causally related to lung cancer in men; the magnitude of the effect of cigarette smoking far outweighs all other factors. The data for women, though less extensive, point in the same direction.
>
> The risk of developing lung cancer increases with duration of smoking and the number of cigarettes smoked per day, and is diminished by discontinuing smoking.
>
> The risk of developing cancer of the lung for the combined group of pipe smokers, cigar smokers, and pipe and cigar smokers is greater than for nonsmokers, but much less than for cigarette smokers.
>
> The data are insufficient to warrant a conclusion for each group individually.

This is the language of the corporation, of the bureaucrat so fearful of personal exposure or, more charitably, so diligent about not misstating the truth, that he or she hides behind qualifications: "the data for women, though less extensive . . ." Stuffy talk removes passion from discourse, substituting for it a sense of detachment in which all variables (in this case, gender and smoking habits) cancel each other out. Gibson [p. 107] notes that the stuffy talker is in some sense scared: "If this is an age of anxiety, one way we react to our anxiety is to withdraw into omniscient and multisyllabic detachment where nobody can get us." The passive voice also helps to confuse ownership of the speaker's ideas. Thus, "smoking" and not "smokers" become the culprit of the report and "the data," not the researcher, become responsible for the bad news about lighting up.

Gibson's system is limited but nevertheless useful. It roughs out the stylistic terrain fairly efficiently and gives the critic a *base point* against which to compare individual messages. Naturally, there is more to style than syntax. The statistics of grammar cannot alone explain why the Webster address seems somehow dated or why the chain letter seems somewhat slippery. It takes other, richer forms of analysis to see why some discourse registers high notes and why other discourse sounds so flat. It takes more than a woodwind to make a melody. It also takes the human genius to play the oboe properly. It is to such aesthetic matters that we will now turn.

EXAMINING IMAGERY

Both the rhetorical critic and the literary critic study imagery. But unlike poetic imagery, the imagery found in rhetoric is often pedestrian. If poetic images invite tarrying, rhetorical images invite movement. Passion, not nuance, are their hallmark:

> This is God's blazing message to America in this hour—and it is without question its very last chance.
> This is the time to energize these spiritual weapons for the salvation of our land. It must be done immediately, fervently, with faith, and with tears!
> If this is done by the Christian people with all of their heart immediately, and with perseverance, this land shall not only be saved, but there shall also explode from this united prayer-power the most astounding revival in all history.
> MORE POWERFUL THAN
TEN THOUSAND HYDROGEN BOMBS
> We have declared spiritual war on God's enemies and our enemies. NOW LET'S WAGE IT! [Boone, et al., 1970:30]

This passage is from a pamphlet entitled *The Solution to Crisis—America*, authored by teen-idol-turned-evangelist Pat Boone and two colleagues. The booklet is a 1970s forerunner of the far right religio-political rhetoric still in evidence today. Its imagery is neither subtle nor novel. It combines temporal metaphors ("this hour," "this is the time"), thermal metaphors ("blazing message"), and kinetic metaphors ("energize," "explode," "prayer power") to produce a sense of urgency. Also included are metaphors of conflict ("hydrogen bomb," "spiritual war," "God's enemies") that add an oppositional force against which the rhetoric can struggle. The physical metaphors ("with tears," "revival," "with all of their heart") humanize the conflict and, by relating it to bodily processes, make the struggle lifelike.

Bombs falling, hearts palpitating, fires blazing—a good deal of action for a short passage. Should a literalist ask how bodily fluids ("tears") could serve as weapons, or how cerebral processes ("prayer power") could rival atomic chain reactions ("ten thousand hydrogen bombs"), the passage would reduce to silliness. But for Pat Boone's readers, the pamphlet makes sense despite its non-sense. For them, its cacophony of images produces an integrated, emotional whole. Many

---

RHETORIC AND THE LAW

Critical Profile 7.1   Convicted in Print, Acquitted in Court

---

To a journalist, Phil Koerner's story was simple. On July 10, 1981, at approximately 11:00 A.M., he got up from his desk and fired a semi-automatic pistol at his boss, Terry Pettus, until the gun chamber was empty. He then promptly turned himself in to the police and confessed to the murder. The *Topeka Capital-Journal*, the local newspaper, anticipated a guilty verdict. All the facts in the case were obvious—a crime had been committed and its perpetrator had confessed. Imagine the community's surprise, then, when the jury acquitted Koerner of all wrongdoing. How could Koerner be innocent when the "facts" were so obvious?

Celeste Condit, now of the University of Georgia, and A. Ann Selzer discovered that if the court of law had followed the same principles of "objectivity" followed by journalists, Koerner would have been convicted. Condit and Selzer argue that because of the discursive restraints generated by the objectivity standard, important arguments used in defense of Koerner were excluded from local newspaper coverage and that, therefore, the readership was unnaturally biased against Koerner. Because journalists are taught to report the facts—the act (what was done), the scene (where it happened), and the agent (who did it)—they "do not need to account for motives and intentions in order to present an objective account of human events. . . ." It is not surprising, then, that coverage of the Koerner trial was limited to who, what, where, and when, nor is it surprising that it also excluded why.

Condit and Selzer found that the defense attorney argued in court solely on the basis of purpose and character: Why did Koerner pull the trigger? What was Mr. Koerner like as a person? The attorney cast Terry Pettus as an evil individual who had tormented Koerner unmercifully. Koerner, a pious fellow, had no choice but to kill Pettus, said his lawyer in court. Presented with these *"subjective facts"* (described by character witnesses), the jury ultimately decided that the death of Pettus was justified and they exonerated what objectively seemed to be a cold-blooded murderer.

Condit and Selzer argue that motive and character are too often given short shrift in newspaper reportage, thereby producing a slanted public understanding of which laws should be made and, thereafter, of how those laws should be applied. But the law, say Condit and Selzer, is a human business. In its rush to present timely, simple, and uncomplicated news, journalism all too often neglects both the subtle and the complicated in human affairs. Such an orientation can unnaturally obscure a defendant's right to a fair trial, the authors warn. By giving short shrift to *human motive*, modern journalism might even foster a prosecutorial mindset in which only actions count and in which jurors become unwilling to do what only human beings can do—judge and interpret.

Profiled by: Patricia Powell
Citation: Condit and Selzer (1985)

Critical Profile 7.2   Narrative Order in the Court

Why did an openly sympathetic jury finally convict heiress and kidnap victim Patty Hearst of armed robbery? Why did a supposedly open-and-shut murder, kidnapping, and conspiracy case against black power activist Angela Davis end in acquittal? How is it that juries comprised of ordinary people without legal training are able to make decisions at all in complicated legal matters? According to W. Lance Bennett and Martha S. Feldman of the University of Washington, formal rules of courtroom procedure permit competing claims of innocence and guilt, but do not show jurors how to interpret those claims. Instead, people bring "a commonsense framework of social judgment" with them to court based on their love of a good (meaning plausible) story.

During a trial, jurors match the information they hear about a crime with "satisfying narratives" they have heard previously (from books, at their parent's knee, or even on television). Angela Davis's attorney, for example, presented a compelling narrative defense to the jury, while Patty Hearst's lawyer searched in vain for a realistic way of telling Hearst's admittedly bizarre story: a millionairess-turned-gangster. So powerful is this need-for-story that some of Hearst's jurors actually expressed public regret that they had not heard a more convincing (narrative) refutation of the prosecution's case.

What does a jury think of as a good story? One factor is a clearly recognizable central action that "incorporates" the chain of secondary events making up the narrative. In addition, a good story is flexible enough to explain away competing narratives without straining belief. In Patty Hearst's bank robbery trial, for example, her attorneys highlighted her *kidnapping* as the narrative's central event. Fearing for her life, they argued, Hearst was forced to participate in the bank robbery, a secondary event (a minor plot?) for which she should not be held legally responsible. In isolation, this interpretation seems plausible. However, the prosecution introduced evidence that this story could not consistently accommodate: During her "captivity," Hearst had taken turns at sentry duty, jogged by herself in public, and had waited alone in a getaway car while her erstwhile abductors robbed a store. This evidence cast doubt on the defense's narrative while meshing well with the prosecution's story of the *bank robbery* as the central action.

Because juries never know what really happened during a crime, they must depend on re-creations of that action, re-creations that depend heavily on the narrative skills of both storytellers and story hearers. Because articulate people tell narratives best, Bennett and Feldman warn that trial-by-story does not necessarily produce a disinterested judicial system. A well-told story may make legal judgments possible. It does not necessarily make them right. That is the other side of the legal story.

Profiled by: Elizabeth Macom
Citation: Bennett and Feldman (1981)

Critical Profile 7.3   Was Blank a Blank?

In early 1968, Joseph William Blank, a graduate student in public administration at the State University of New York at Albany, legally changed his German-derived surname to "White." His reason? To "avoid the opprobrious remarks sometimes associated with a literal translation" of his name. On the morning of September 23, 1970, White—now on medical leave from his position with the New York State Department of Labor—came into work carrying a Christmas-gift-wrapped package containing a semi-automatic hunting rifle. In the next twelve minutes, bypassing a number of his fellow employees, White stalked and killed four young women with whom he had worked. He then placed the rifle barrel in his mouth and fired. Police found in his pocket a cryptic "note of intent" ending "sic transit gloria munde" [sic] or "thus passes away the glory of the world."

A common theme in the newspaper coverage of this multiple murder and suicide was the inability of mourners and officials alike to comprehend Blank/White's motives. Jeanne Y. Fisher, based at the State University of New York at Albany, saw in this otherwise inexplicable event an opportunity to test the application of rhetorical criticism to the analysis of nonoratorical events. Fisher notes that as an enactment of "attitude," purposeful violence is to a greater or lesser degree symbolic. Thus, she claims, Kenneth Burke's theory of human motivation, which bases action in guilt and purification, inherently contains potential for the discovery of rhetorical meaning in violent action.

According to Burke, humans are goaded by feelings of guilt to attempt rebirth through purification. Purification can be obtained symbolically through reidentification, victimage, and/or mortification. Over the years, Fisher argues, Blank's "personality and behavior seem to have become symbolic of the literal meaning of the Anglicized pronunciation of his name." By changing his name, Blank/White sought both to purge himself of the shame of one name and to embody the purity ("whiteness") of the other. But Burke notes that some individuals are not satisfied with partial sacrifice: "total curative victims" may be required. Fisher asserts that Blank/White's final act was the logical result of the failure of his name change to achieve a satisfying symbolic rebirth. Thus, enacting a need that was "apparently of such magnitude that only a high-powered rifle could express it," Blank/White effected "total victimage" (murder) as well as "total mortification" (suicide) in the fulfillment of his lifelong attempt to prove that "Blank is not a blank."

Profiled by: Elizabeth Macom
Citation: Fisher (1974)

of them would be willing to share their quite literal money with Mr. Boone's movement because of the factually untrue truths embedded in his imagery. Throughout history, people have marched off to literal wars because of the metaphoric battles they have already fought—and won.

Not all rhetoric is this rich with imagery. Thus, two important questions for the critic are these:

To what extent does a message employ nonliteral language? What specific purposes does such language serve?

Most people cannot speak without imagery, because imagery increases the range of things that can be said and, more fundamentally, the range of things that can be thought. That is, despite his oppositional images, Pat Boone was hardly ready to kiss his daughter goodbye and march off to trench warfare. If Debbie had questioned his use of language, he probably would have told her that the sacrifices he was willing to make for his cause *felt like* the sacrifices made by the foot soldier during battle. Such martial thinking perhaps freed Boone to take on challenges he would have been unwilling to take on if he had thought of his duties in less exalted terms. Even though he was, literally, only writing a cheap pamphlet for mass distribution and even though he was, literally, intending to go home and not to war after putting his printing press to bed, his wartime imagery made his job seem all the more grand that day. Pat Boone really meant what he unreally said.

When he wrote to thank Mr. Boone for having sent him a copy of his remarks, President Richard Nixon used language that was as literal as Boone's was figurative. Even though the President seemed to appreciate Boone's bequest, his rhetorical style suggested something else entirely:

THE WHITE HOUSE
WASHINGTON

Dear Pat:

I want you to know how much I appreciate your thoughtfulness in letting me have a copy of your recording, "The Solution to Crisis—America," which you gave to Secretary Romney for me at the Religious Heritage Dinner on June 18. It was especially kind of you to remember me with this meaningful and timely message, and you may be sure I am pleased to have this evidence of faith and patriotism brought to my attention.

With my best wishes,

Sincerely,
Richard Nixon [1970b]

This is how presidents talk. Carefully, and with restraint. There are no wild flights of fancy, no embroidered stories, no riotous mixing of images here. Nixon's language is spare, precise, businesslike. While his salutation is suitably informal, the remainder of the message is distanced: Nixon appreciates Boone's "thoughtfulness," not Boone himself; the recording was given to Romney, not to Nixon personally; Nixon is pleased to see such "evidence of faith," but he is not going to *do* anything about it. Boone's gift is described as "meaningful and timely," a phrase that could describe either the Holy Bible or *Newsweek* magazine. The passive voice ("I am pleased to have this . . . brought to my attention") places the rhetorical action in Boone's arena, not in Nixon's. Thus, while Nixon's reply is cordial on the ideational level, on the stylistic level it repudiates Boone's entire message.

By exercising stylistic restraint, Nixon says, in effect, I have heard you, but I am not listening to you. Because the use of imagery often signals a speaker's heightened state of sentiment, an attempt by Nixon to match Boone's style ("You really socked it to 'em in that one, Pat"), would have joined them *emotionally* as well as argumentatively. Thus, by sending a formal, literalistic letter, Nixon's speech-act became his only (muted) statement, a signal that he was unwilling to travel down the slippery slope of partisan politics.

The word "imagery" derives from the same root as "imagination," a transcendence of the normal. Thus, a speaker's relative use of imagery maps that speaker's comfort with life-as-given. Clearly, Pat Boone is ready for a trip somewhere, while Richard Nixon is committed to staying where he is: in the middle of the political road. Of course, establishment politicians often use imagery when they speak. But they rarely do so with the sense of wild abandon displayed by Pat Boone. Also, their imagery typically throws light on specific pieces of policy ("a chicken in every pot," "a New Deal," "the war on poverty") and their pragmatism makes them abandon failed imagery quickly (for example, George Bush's "thousand points of light" from the campaign of 1988). Politicians are afraid of the world-yet-to-be; social activists embrace it willingly, since it, and it alone, fully substantiates their values: a moral "majority," a world safe for "unborn" babies, a "rainbow" coalition. Thus, to track the use of imagery is to track the length of a speaker's wish list.

One standard category of imagery, the metaphor, has been the object of much scholarly inquiry. Metaphor has been variously defined, but here it will be treated as a master form of depiction [Osborn, 1986] that equates one thing with another: For example, builders of earthen dams in Kenya are likened in discipline to destroyers of dams along the Rhine in World War II and hence dubbed a Peace Corps. Lakoff and Johnson [1980] have written perceptively about metaphor and feel that everyday talkers would become mute without it. They also argue that: (1) *Metaphor results from thought* (for example, if one's beliefs are unpopular, one will feel besieged and hence reflect such feelings when one speaks—Pat Boone's fate) and (2) *metaphor stimulates thought* (for example, if one lives on a diet of warlike rhetoric, one begins to look only for martial solutions to life's problems—the fate of many contemporary Iranians). In their book, Lakoff and Johnson describe a number of functions served by metaphor:

1. *Metaphors selectively highlight ideas.* If an idea is important to a person or a culture, it will find its way to imagery. Lakoff and Johnson observe that martial imagery like "I demolished his argument" or "his claims were indefensible" [p. 4] is used because some cultures treat communication as a contestable, rather than a sharable, activity. Communication can be talked about in other ways, of course, such as argument-as-journey: "We've covered a lot of ground" or "you're off in the wrong direction." Thus, the critic tracks the facts of metaphorical usage, looking for the meanings behind the meanings.

2. *Metaphors are often generative.* They help people see things in a new light. For example, if a client thinks of love as madness ("it just happens; you can't control it"), a marriage counselor might introduce the new metaphor of love-as-labor ("a marriage is something you really have to work at"), thereby calling attention to relational possibilities the madness metaphor had hidden. In a sense, to use metaphor is to admit a kind of defeat, to acknowledge that literal language cannot always exploit complex ideas and feelings. Imagery often helps to approximate what literal language cannot even estimate.

3. *Metaphors often mask ideas and values.* As metaphors become routinely used in a given language community, their implied meanings become less and less noticeable. Knowing this, the perceptive critic traces these "forgotten" meanings carefully. Lakoff and Johnson [pp. 236–237] observe that when corporate leaders treat labor as a business "resource" (for example, by placing it on a par with cheap oil), they become blind to the exploitation of workers such a metaphor encourages. As Lakoff and Johnson say [p. 237], "The blind acceptance of [this] metaphor can hide degrading realities, whether meaningless blue-collar and white-collar industrial jobs in 'advanced' societies or virtual slavery around the world."

4. *Metaphors have entailments.* Metaphors mean certain things but also imply other things. A metaphor may bespeak one's personality (a person who believes that "time is money"), one's intellectual world view (love as a journey: "our relationship isn't going anywhere"), or one's cultural assumptions (up and down: "I'm on top of the situation" versus "he's low man on the totem pole."). Entailments are the policy

implications of metaphor. If one believes that argument-is-war ("she shot down my case"), one may make certain *offensive* assumptions when speaking: (1) that people are naturally competitive, (2) that truth is less important than strategy, and (3) that short-term triumph is most important. In contrast, one who sees argument-as-a-container ("his case won't hold water") may argue *protectively*, focusing on the issue's substance rather than its personal dynamics. While people are usually unaware of their preferred images, their preferred images often expose their premises for action.

Given the rhetorical functions of metaphor, how can they best be studied? Most critics look for what Lakoff and Johnson call metaphor's **systematicity.** That is, they urge the critic to look for patterns of metaphorical usage, since, while "complete consistency across metaphors is rare; coherence, on the other hand, is typical" [p. 96]. By proceeding carefully through a message, the critic can often find an underlying thematic unity to the metaphors chosen. Thus, an important critical probe becomes the following:

What *families of metaphors* reside in the text?
Are they internally consistent?
What is their cumulative effect?

A helpful system for examining metaphor is Osborn's [1976], who inspected a large number of public messages from ancient Greece to the present and grouped the metaphors he found into eleven metaphorical families. Osborn says that these patterns "endure in power and popularity despite time and cultural change" [p. 16] because of the almost primordial pictures they paint. While Osborn's categories are hardly exhaustive, they are a good critical starting place, since they touch on basic human experiences. Modified slightly, his categories include:

1. **Water and the sea** ("the ship of state," "I'm going down for the third time")
2. **Light and darkness** ("he's a bright fellow," "I'm in the dark on this issue")
3. **The human body** ("she's my right arm," "just turn the other cheek")
4. **War** ("a battle for the mind," "our team was blitzed yesterday")
5. **Structures** ("that argument won't hold up," "we're operating in different frameworks")

6. **Animals** ("he's a bit too foxy for me," "they really wolfed down that dessert")
7. **The family** ("necessity is the mother of invention," "defeat is always an orphan")
8. **Above and below** ("let's go over the top in this campaign," "she's really in the depths of depression")
9. **Forward and backward** ("let's get this country moving again," "we're falling behind our quota for the month")
10. **Natural phenomena** ("that was a peak experience for me," "I'm between a rock and a hard place")
11. **Sexuality** ("those policies will rape this nation," "that is a genuinely seminal idea")

The good critic will branch out beyond Osborn's general categories, since so much rhetoric is specific to a culture or a subculture. A more narrowly Western supplement to his list, for example, might include **mechanistic** metaphors ("I'm already wired in on this deal"), **monetary** images ("I'm going for broke in my relationship with Jane"), **athletic** metaphors ("I'll knock this exam out of the park"), and others. But using Osborn's list is a good first step because it identifies the speaker's general mental habits and the audience's perceived motivational bases.

Although it is somewhat barbarous to dissect Dr. Martin Luther King, Jr.'s lyrical style, it does give us the intellectual distance needed to see how a powerful rhetoric works its magic. Even the most casual analysis of his famous "I Have a Dream" speech shows that he used metaphor compellingly:

And as we walk, we must make the pledge that we shall always march ahead. We cannot turn back. There are those who are asking the devotees of civil rights, "When will you be satisfied?" We can never be satisfied as long as the Negro is the victim of the unspeakable horrors of police brutality.

We can never be satisfied as long as our bodies, heavy with the fatigue of travel, cannot gain lodging in the motels of the highways and the hotels of the cities. We cannot be satisfied as long as the Negro's mobility is from a smaller ghetto to a larger one.

We can never be satisfied as long as our children are stripped of their selfhood and robbed of their dignity by signs stating "for whites only." We cannot be satisfied as long as a Negro in Mississippi cannot vote and a Negro in New York believes he has nothing for which to vote. No, we are not satisfied, and we will not be satisfied until justice rolls down like waters and righteousness like a mighty stream.

I am not unmindful that some of you have come here out of excessive trials and tribulation. Some of you have come fresh from narrow jail cells. Some of you have come from areas where your quest for freedom left you battered by the storms of persecution and staggered by the winds of police brutality. You have been the veterans of creative suffering. Continue to work with the faith that unearned suffering is redemptive.

Go back to Mississippi; go back to Alabama; go back to South Carolina; go back to Georgia; go back to Louisiana; go back to the slums and ghettos of the Northern cities, knowing that somehow this situation can, and will be changed. Let us not wallow in the valley of despair.

So I say to you, my friends, that even though we must face the difficulties of today and tomorrow, I still have a dream. It is a dream deeply rooted in the American dream that one day this nation will rise up and live out the true meaning of its creed—we hold these truths to be self evident, that all men are created equal.

I have a dream that one day on the red hills of Georgia, sons of former slaves and sons of former slave-owners will be able to sit down together at the table of brotherhood.

I have a dream that one day, even the state of Mississippi, a state sweltering with the heat of injustice, sweltering with the heat of oppression, will be transformed into an oasis of freedom and justice.

I have a dream my four little children will one day live in a nation where they will not be judged by the color of their skin but by the content of their character. I have a dream today!

I have a dream that one day, down in Alabama, with its vicious racists, with its governor having his lips dripping with the words of interposition and nullification, that one day, right there in Alabama, little black boys and black girls will be able to join hands with little white boys and white girls as sisters and brothers. I have a dream today!

I have a dream that one day every valley shall be exalted, every hill and mountain shall be made low, the rough places shall be made plane, and the crooked places shall be made straight and the glory of the Lord will be revealed and all flesh shall see it together [King, 1964:373–374].

King's artistry derives more from human sensitivity than from stylistic trickery. His naturalistic imagery carries a kind of primitive power: "storms of persecution," "winds of brutality," "valleys of despair," "sweltering injustice," "an oasis of freedom." Bodily processes ("all flesh shall see it") and basic social units ("sisters and brothers") also emphasize how emotionally and politically *fundamental* his argument for freedom was. Some of King's metaphors are almost offensive in their roughness: blacks "wallowing," lips "dripping," people "stripped." Perhaps King reasoned that more urbane language would have made him seem effete in the eyes of the underprivileged and a potential object of manipulation in the eyes of the overprivileged. Hence, he proposed no banquets of grandeur but just a "table of brotherhood," no stairways to the stars but just "rough places made plane," no captains of destiny but just "veterans of creative suffering."

King also established a sense of *forward movement* for his people by transmuting the literal march on Washington into a symbolic march in which people "come here out of excessive trials and tribulations." He launched them on a "quest for freedom," forbidding their "turning back," commanding that they "march ahead," "facing" the difficulties of tomorrow, and moving with the swiftness of a "mighty stream." Forward motion was coupled with *ascendent movement* so that King's people could "rise up" to climb mountains "made low" by their efforts. Metaphorically, the only thing that King left standing was justice itself, which was to "roll down" on his people like a cascade.

Virtually all of King's metaphors can be accommodated by the Osborn schema. This fact establishes how "primitive" King's speech was and why, as a result, it had such political and psychological power. The black members of his audience were, after all, historically *landed* people who worked the nation's farms, cooked the nation's meals, built the nation's buildings, and fought more than their share of the nation's wars. King concentrated on these basic images, because the people he loved were so often relegated to basic pleasures. His metaphors of wind and sea and fire remind us of how central the natural world is to human experience and why, since the beginning of time, people have turned their eyes skyward, looking for explanations.

King broke this naturalistic pattern only once, but it was a significant departure. Fairly early in his speech, he produced a small yet captivating cluster of **monetary** metaphors that are curiously juxtaposed to his organic images. This section of his speech is not elegant: Blacks have been issued a "bad check" from the nation, a check returned with "insufficient funds" stamped upon it. The "vaults" of opportunity have been closed to blacks and an important "promissory note" has been "defaulted" upon by the nation. Just as quickly as King introduces this line he abandons it, returning immediately to traditional imagery.

But King's monetary images made his speech genuinely American. Virtually everything else he said could have been said anywhere anytime. But in mimicking the language of capitalism, King staked a claim to the land on which he stood and also made an ironic commentary on his age. By allotting his audience one economic metaphor for every seven naturalistic images, King approximated the comparative economic ratio between the blacks and whites of his day. In other words, only one-seventh of King's speech was fully "American," perhaps because King's people had not at that point been enfranchised in the most traditionally American way: economically. In a sense, then, Dr. King spoke in August of 1963 as something of a stranger in a strange land.

As the King speech makes clear, imagery can propel rhetoric like nothing else can. It becomes a kaleidoscope for the mind's eye, allowing audiences to see ideas that otherwise would be inert and lifeless. Table 7.3 goes beyond metaphor to present a more complete catalogue of images. It can be used by the critic to answer such questions as the following:

How experimental is the text being examined (as measured by the *types* of stylistic devices used)?

What factors explain such liberal/conservative uses of language?

Mohrmann [1970] has warned that stylistic analysis can all too often become a mere exercise, cataloging for the sake of cataloging. To learn that a speaker used three rhetorical questions and eleven hyperboles hardly advances knowledge. All speakers use imagery and do so all the time. The really important questions about style relate to the pattern of devices used and what the speaker gains or loses by such stylizing. The examples in Table 7.3 adequately establish what these forms of imagery are like. There is little need to do criticism solely to find new examples of same. Instead, the good critic concentrates on the *intellectual operations* signaled by the use of these stylistic tokens.

For example, Campbell [1972] studied the speaking of former Vice President Spiro Agnew and noted his heavy use of antithesis. Rather than leave the matter there, however, Campbell went on to explain how Agnew's style revealed his Manichean world view, an us-versus-them mind-set that constantly divided the world into two and only two categories. This black-and-white thinking, warned Campbell, pointed up Agnew's inability to cope with the grayness of political compromise (a dangerous characteristic for an American politician, says Campbell.) In a similar vein, Kaufer [1981] urges the critic to monitor persistent use of irony, because it points up the existence of a **shared code** between speaker and listener. He asserts that irony always has evaluation built into it and that a statement like "Nice weather, huh?" made by (drenched) Person A to (drenched) Person B is an attempt to reestablish that A and B still agree on standards for evaluating weather. Irony is thus an in-joke often used by in-crowds when the pressure is off. It tends to fall flat when used in other contexts (for example, among strangers at a funeral).

In a similar vein, Lakoff and Johnson [1980:39] have examined metonomy and note that it serves as a kind of argumentative spotlight, calling attention to one feature rather than many features. They note, for example, that a metonomic statement like "Reagan invaded Grenada" is a rhetorically powerful way of isolating who was responsible for a given set of actions and, consequently, who would be singled out for praise or blame. Metonomy can, therefore, help to determine the **intellectual focus** of a message.

But what if a text contains little imagery or "dead" imagery? Even here the critic can learn something. Arendt [1963] notes, for example, that the remarks of Adolph Eichmann, the notorious Nazi leader, typically contained only clichés, unoriginal figures of speech (for example, "a bolt from the blue") that stand out because of their banality. Arendt argues that a mind so incapable of stylistic inventiveness was also a mind ideally suited to the dulling themes of Nazi orthodoxy. Arendt found traces of the rhetoric to which Eichmann had become addicted in Eichmann's own rhetoric.

Some of the most interesting criticism has focused on metaphor. Daughton [1988], for example, tracked Lyndon Johnson's metaphors from his early years as a congressman to his final days in the Oval Office and found an increasing complexity in Johnson's metaphors as he matured. While LBJ used familiar images as a young politician (for example, "we have shortchanged our youth"), his presidential metaphors became more ambitious (for example, "education is the guardian and steward of democracy"). Daughton chalks up this effect to the increasing complexity and institutionalization of the political jobs Johnson took upon himself during his latter years in office.

Another study is Jamieson's [1980] novel comparison of Pope Paul VI and former California Governor Jerry Brown. What could such different speakers have in common? Very little. That is precisely what Jamieson found, but her point was more subtle. She discovered that the Pope often used metaphors to increase his authority, a tendency built into the hierarchy he oversaw. For example, Paul used bodily metaphors because bodies have only *one* head; he used dark-light metaphors and placed the light on *his* position; he used familial images because traditional families are headed by a *male* parent. Jerry Brown, in contrast, used powerlessness metaphors. He depicted himself as a Sisyphus pushing boulders up a hill, or as an incidental member of a Greek chorus, or as a little Dutch boy holding his finger in a political dike. These sharp metaphorical differences explain the contrasting **world views** of the Pope and the Governor: One, a dominant, perhaps domineering, religious leader and the other a practical, perhaps pessimistic, politician. Metaphorical patterns like these, says Jamieson, carry the undertones of rhetoric, and it is to these undertones that listeners often respond unconsciously.

Metaphor is also a good device for embodying changing **cultural trends.** Osborn [1977:359, 362–363] notes, for example, that certain

Table 7.3   Some Common Stylistic Devices*

Device	Definition	Function	Example
Anaphora	Exactly repeating a word or phrase at the beginnings of successive clauses	Highlights the speaker's mental grasp of a concept by displaying the *completeness* (and hence determination) of his or her thinking	"We shall not flag or fail. We shall go on to the end. We shall fight in France . . ." (Winston Churchill)
Antithesis	Juxtaposing contrasting ideas in balanced phrases	An "argumentative" piece of imagery that *sharpens* differences significantly	"Naked came I out of my mother's womb, and naked shall I return thither." (Job, I, 21)
Hyperbole	An extravagant statement used as a figure of speech	A conscious distortion used to *describe* something that would otherwise be beyond description	"Publishing a volume of verse is like dropping a rose-petal down the Grand Canyon and waiting for an echo." (Don Marquis)
Metonomy	Using the name of one thing as the name for something else to which it has a logical relationship	Creates a new association among ideas or exploits an old association in order to add *freshness* to thought	"Agonies are one of my changes of garments . . . I am the mashed fireman with breastbone broken." (Walt Whitman)
Oxymoron	A phrase that seems to have an internal contradiction	A contrastive device designed to, first, confuse and, then, *intrigue* listeners	"That building is a little bit big and pretty ugly." (James Thurber)

Synecdoche	Identifying something by naming a part of it or identifying a part by naming the whole thing	A kind of rhetorical shorthand that provides a more *interesting* view of commonly understood objects or ideas	"Wherever wood [a ship] can swim, there I am sure to find this flag of England [the British fleet]." (Napoleon)
Irony	A statement whose "real" meaning is (recognizably) opposite of what is literally said	In-group humor used to *certify* that speaker and listener share the same evaluative code (accomplished by either overstatement or understatement)	"Your well-known integrity has cleared you of all blame, your modesty has saved you, your past life has been your salvation." (Cicero, when attacking Clodius)
Rhetorical question	Declarative statements taking a (falsely) interrogative form	Generates a sense of *commonality* between speaker and listener via imagined dialogue	"Are you better off now than you were four years ago?" (Ronald Reagan [Franklin Roosevelt])
Parallelism	Groupings of similarly phrased ideas presented in rapid succession	*Quickens* the rhetorical pace and therefore generates psychological momentum in listeners	"We shall pay any price, bear any burden, meet any hardship, support any friend, oppose any foe in order to assure the survival and success of liberty." (John Kennedy)

*Based in part on Espy (1983), Arnold (1974), Kaufer (1981).

metaphors died off in popularity over time as people domesticated the sea. Thus, whereas Edmund Burke in the eighteenth century could describe a rival as being "on a wide sea, without chart or compass . . . whirled about, the sport of every gust," such metaphors were eventually replaced by space imagery (for example, Adlai Stevenson's "We travel together, passengers on a little space ship, dependent on its vulnerable reserves of air and soil . . ."). These alterations, says Osborn, signal more than changing rhetorical fashion. To switch from one metaphorical system to another is also to switch from one style of thinking to another. After all, a nation that finds imminent danger lapping at the edge of its own continent may well operate with greater military caution than one brazen enough to see itself as the master of the stars and beyond.

Imagery can change in the short run as well. Hughey, et al. [1987] studied alterations in the AIDS metaphors found in popular news stories, keying particularly on when AIDS was used as the tenor, or subject, of the metaphor ("AIDS is the holocaust revisited") and when AIDS was the vehicle, or object, of the metaphor ("She treats me like I've got AIDS"). Hughey and his associates note that as the AIDS story saturated American culture, there was a dramatic increase in AIDS-as-vehicle metaphors. In an astonishingly short period of time, AIDS moved from the thing clarified to the thing so well understood that it explained yet other concepts. In other words, metaphor can become something of a cultural timepiece for the enterprising critic.

Imagery is important. It is important because it tells us what motivates people, what mystifies them, what frightens them. Animals, oceans, mountains, birth—these things mystify. Money, inventions, voyages, salvation—these things motivate. War, whirlwinds, torture, disease—these things frighten. Rhetoric uses them all, for good and for ill. Edelman [1964] urges us to take metaphor seriously, because it is so sensitive to social changes. Thus, he warns, while a phrase like "an American presence in the Middle East" sounds exceedingly friendly, the sort of visit one cousin might pay another, this is imagery that masks policy and should, therefore, be treated with deadly seriousness by the discerning rhetorical critic.

CONCLUSION

Analyzing style is a complex business. For whatever reason, language will not reveal its mysteries to the casual observer. Stylistic analysis takes patience: noting metaphorical clusters, being sensitive to a

RHETORIC AND THE POPULAR ARTS

Critical Profile 7.4   Portrait of the Artist as a Persuader

Can there be such a thing as a rhetorical painting? Must art exist only for art's sake or can it serve other purposes? After studying a quartet of paintings by Norman Rockwell, Lester Olson, now of the University of Pittsburgh, found that paintings do indeed have distinctly persuasive features. The paintings in question were Rockwell's depictions of "The Four Freedoms." These paintings became part of a campaign in support of the war effort during World War II and Olson offers them as examples of the persuasive power of icon (pictorial images) in political campaigns.

Rockwell's "visual rhetoric" employed the persuasive technique known as identification. In his "Freedom of Speech" poster, Rockwell shows a blue-collar worker speaking at a town meeting to people of varied backgrounds. "Freedom of Worship" depicts people of different faiths behaving as if they were praying together. "Despite the divergent backgrounds and views represented in the painting," Olson writes, "Rockwell presents a view of religious unity rather than religious squabbling, by depicting them in a monochromatic gold light and by portraying them in a similar act."

"Freedom from Want" and "Freedom from Fear" celebrate family values. "Freedom from Want" shows a family gathering at Thanksgiving, complete with turkey and trimmings. The painting thus "fuses family, country, and God into a celebration" of our civil religion. In "Freedom from Fear," the mother tucks the children into bed while the father, holding his newspaper and eyeglasses, looks on. As a stark antithesis to this peaceful scene, headlines in the father's newspaper report of bombings and the slaughter of women and children.

These four paintings constitute a form of epideictic rhetoric—Aristotle's category for discourse that either praises or blames based on virtues defined by the community. Rockwell's epideictic icons praise an idealized group of Americans who symbolized community values. At the same time, hovering in the background, as in the newspaper headlines, was the antithesis—the unspoken enemy who deserves blame for rejecting these values.

With verbal rhetoric, the Roosevelt administration completed the antithesis for citizens unable to complete it themselves—Germany and Japan were the enemy deserving blame. The administration employed these images uniting God, democracy, and family for political action in support of the war effort. Thus, Roosevelt and Rockwell essentially worked in tandem, with Roosevelt turning political matters into moral ones and with Rockwell's pictures showing that "a people's aesthetic sensibilities can be manipulated for pragmatic ends." In times of calamity, apparently, some artists enlist in the war effort by strapping on their palettes.

Profiled by: Jim Mackin
Citation: Olson (1983)

Critical Profile 7.5   Humor Beyond the Pale

Humorists and their audiences often team up to make fun of accepted values. Parody works in part because audiences willingly permit the subversion of established tastes. But what happens when a joke goes too far? How does parody make the transition from good humor to bad taste? And what sorts of constraints do audiences place on humorists? Such questions led Barry Morris of the University of Illinois to study the parody of Joe Bob Briggs, the fictional "drive-in film critic of Rockwall, Texas." Morris notes that humor's mistakes teach more than do its successes. What was Joe Bob's mistake? According to Morris, Joe Bob violated the communal interests of his audience.

Joe Bob Briggs, the pen name of *Dallas Times Herald* columnist John Bloom, was "a self-effacing redneck movie critic" who denounced "Communists, wimps, and just about any ethnic group." His syndicated reviews attracted an avid readership as they parodied movie critics, the cinema, and society in general. As Morris writes, "try as he might, Joe Bob could not go too far." Suddenly, he did. Little did Joe Bob foresee his quick demise, brought on by a parody of "We Are the World," a gently moving, almost spiritual, tune sung by popular entertainers, who, arm-in-arm, raised money to combat world hunger in the mid-1980s.

On April 12, 1985, Joe Bob unveiled a new creation, "We Are the Weird," which included the refrain:

We are the weird, we are the starvin'
We are the scum of the filthy Earth so let's start scarfin'

---

special use of anaphora, remembering who employs the passive voice and who does not. Often, making such discriminations is a tedious business, yielding a handful of message facts but no obvious explanations. Even for non-Catholics, the special friend of the stylistic critic is St. Jude, patron saint of the hopeless.

Naturally, this is hyperbole. Stylistic criticism can be done and it can be done well. The critic begins as all worthwhile projects are begun: slowly, patiently, sensibly. The critic notices an isolated phrase structure here, a strange colloquialism there, and sets to wondering what it all means. These thoughts percolate awhile as adjectives are counted and found to be more plentiful than expected. Then, the critic notices an odd set of repetitions, repetitions missed when the passage was first read. Later, the critic discovers that a rather old-fashioned sort

Critical Profile 7.5   Humor Beyond the Pale (*continued*)

> *There's a goat head bakin' we're callin' it their food*
> *If the Meskins can eat it, they can eat it too.*

Reaction to the column was immediate. Black groups protested, as did many newspapers and their readers. Bloom resigned, and the column was, for a while, discontinued.

Morris notes that parody depends for its success on the formation of "in-groups" and "out-groups." Those who are in on the joke participate closely with the author in subversive humor. Close participation allows audiences to place "phantom constraints" on humorists. But an important ingredient, Morris maintains, is that audiences must be able to integrate membership in a group parody into the other affiliations in their lives. Yet Joe Bob's parody made this difficult: "Many active Joe Bob supporters," Morris writes, "must have been ill at ease considering the possible costs of having to defend We Are the Weird to friends and coworkers." The in-groups, having supported Joe Bob, felt abandoned to social martyrdom. The controversy over a mistaken lampooning of famine relief efforts rapidly escalated into broader social issues of minority hiring and the image of the city of Dallas. Editors and citizens at large found themselves "on the wrong side of important civic issues." Bloom, the author of the column, resigned from the *Times Herald*, a symbolic sacrifice to good humor. Neither he nor Joe Bob Briggs had been aware of the phantom constraints placed upon them by their readers. Their symbolic death is an object lesson to critics and humorists alike.

Profiled by: John H. Bosma
Citation: Morris (1987)

of maternal imagery both begins and ends the message. These isolated observations tumble about in the critic's head as the passage is read again and again.

In some cases, the critic will suddenly shout "Eureka," but more often a vague sense of the rhetor's strategy will gradually, fitfully, develop. At about this time, the critic might become aware that the text is interestingly different from another text just studied, and so the message begins to take on new meaning as it is viewed comparatively. Lanham [1983:155] likens stylistic analysis to pulling first one thread and then another until a pattern begins to unravel for the critic. This thread-pulling eventually helps the critic recognize the speaker's distinctive voice. It is at this special moment of familiarity that the critic's task takes on steam.

Critical Profile 7.6   America Enters World War II and the Beat Goes On

When America found itself at war in 1941, it had just completed two decades in which jazz and dance music had reached enormous popularity in almost every social class. When the war came, one might have expected popular music to lend itself to the war effort, to change its jazzy and sentimental beat to rhythms that would spark fervent patriotism. But G. P. Mohrmann and Eugene F. Scott of the University of California at Davis found that Americans resisted virtually all attempts to "militarize" their music. Instead, they wanted "music to be what it had been, a medium of amusement and entertainment." Consequently, say Mohrmann and Scott, "the advent of war produced no metamorphosis in the popular song." Why the advent of war failed to change musical tastes is what led Mohrmann and Scott to examine war song lyrics.

The authors found that songs published from late 1941 to 1945 clustered into three main themes: "the war in general, the home front, and the armed forces." According to Mohrmann and Scott, "The Flame of Freedom" and "United We Stand," were the most militant, yet, they had "little impact." Song titles like "We'll Nip the Nipponese" did little to get Americans to take the war seriously. The bombing of Pearl Harbor inspired the lyrics: "Praise the Lord and pass the ammunition, and we'll all stay free; Praise the Lord and swing into position," but the public preference for jazzy musical tempos made the lyrics seem more appropriate to "half time" tunes played at college football games. Particularly unattractive was the militaristic spirit that the music industry attempted to create.

Mohrmann and Scott conclude that even during the war, Americans demanded novelty and sentimentality in their popular songs, since escape and diversion were primary needs for them. Prior to World War II, America had already won one major conflict and was still recovering from the effects of the Great Depression. With the conviction that World War II would be another victory, Americans turned to their inner need for reassurance and diversion, feelings reflected in the lyrics: "You gotta accenchuate the positive, Eliminate the negative, Latch on to the affirmative and don't mess with Mr. Inbetween." Thus, patriotism and militarism were themes not only incompatible with the national mood but with the genre of popular music as well. It seems that even during chaos, the beat goes on.

Profiled by: Yvonne Becerra
Citation: Mohrmann and Scott (1976)

Perhaps this makes it seem that stylistic criticism is somewhat mystical. It is. Somewhat. And it will remain somewhat mystical until people become less complicated and until language exposes its several mysteries to one and all. Such a day may arrive, but it is not here yet. And so the critic goes to work.

CHAPTER EIGHT

Analyzing Style: Word Choice

❖
❖

Give rest, O Christ, to thy servant(s) with thy saints, where sorrow and pain are no more, neither sighing, but life everlasting.

Thou only art immortal, the creator and maker of mankind; and we are mortal, formed of the earth, and unto each shall we return. For so thou didst ordain when thou createdst me, saying, "Dust thou art, and unto dust shalt thou return." All we do down to the dust; yet even at the grave we make our song: Alleluia, alleluia, alleluia.

Into thy hand, O merciful Savior, we commend thy servant [Name.] Acknowledge, we humbly beseech thee, a sheep of thine own fold, a lamb of thine own flock, a sinner of thine own redeeming. Receive him/her into the arms of thy mercy, into the blessed rest of everlasting peace, and into the glorious company of the saints in light. . . .

Christ is risen from the dead, trampling down death by death, and giving life to those in the tomb.

The Sun of Righteousness is gloriously risen, giving light to those who sat in darkness and in the shadow of death.

The Lord will guide our feet into the way of peace, having taken away the world.

Christ will open the kingdom of heaven to all who believe in his Name, saying, Come, O blessed of my Father; inherit the kingdom prepared for you.

Into paradise may the angels lead thee; and at thy coming may the martyrs receive thee, and bring thee into the holy city Jerusalem. [Prayer, 1979:484–485]

These are the familiar words spoken at the traditional Christian funeral. They were taken from *The Book of Common Prayer*, an Episcopalian document, but any modern Christian—Baptist, Methodist, Lutheran, probably even Mormon or Roman Catholic—could recognize and approve of them. Even though the edition cited here was dated 1979 with a first printing in 1789, few changes have been made over the years, making its style old yet ageless. While colloquial Americans do not offer formal salutations ("Come here, O Fred") or use antiquated tenses ("didst ordain," "createdst"), they can understand what is being said here. Also, while they now "request" rather than "beseech," "sing" a song rather than "make" one, and refer to each other as "you" instead of "thee," they can still appreciate the prayer. Its imagery is either naturalistic ("formed of the earth," "Sun of Righteousness") or corporeal ("arms of thy mercy", "guide our feet") and hence reaches across the generations. The prayer's themes—human sinfulness, the divinity of Jesus, salvation for all believers—are so well wrought and so familiar that even their archaic language cannot sap them of vitality.

No doubt, *The Book of Common Prayer* could be rewritten to take advantage of modern language habits. Some denominations have done so. But for many believers, these words will do just fine, even if they are very old words. For modern believers, this prayer's language is precious, in part because it is old and in part because it has brought comfort over the years to so many loved ones standing at so many gravesides. Words like these can be counted upon. Their never-changingness connects modern Christians to the first Christians and thence to unborn Christians. "This is *our* language," says the Christian, "it marks us as special. People who cannot love our language probably cannot love our beliefs."

This chapter focuses on **lexicon,** words that have special rhetorical power and that are unique to a group or individual. Lexicons are important to study because they set people apart. For example, even if one had never read the above prayer and was presented with a disconnected list of its constituent words, one could learn something. Even in isolation, words like "martyrs," "humbly," "sheep," "dust," and "guide" warn a prospective group member that *submission* to something or someone is expected in the text. On the other hand, words like "redeem," "mercy," "risen," "glorious," and "kingdom" imply that personal *improvement* can be expected in return for submission. Finally, words uncommon to everyday speech like "paradise," "alleluia," "immortal," "righteousness," and "Jerusalem" add a dimension of *mystery* to the message. In effect, the very lexicon of Christianity tells its story: Repentance for sin will be rewarded eternally by God in paradise.

Lexicons make for efficiency. By using preferred words, a speaker can establish the right to address an audience. But what happens when a speaker does not have access to such a lexicon? What kinds of *ideas* are possible when certain kinds of words are unavailable? This was the situation confronting Mr. F. J. Gould [n.d.:26–28] some years ago when writing *Funeral Services Without Theology* for atheists. Knowing that atheists' loved ones also need to hear comforting words, Gould offered sample messages for the nonbeliever's funeral service. This was one of his remembrances:

We assemble in this place to say a kind and solemn farewell to the remains of _____.

We come as mourners. But the act of mourning is no strange event in human life. Not only do we grieve at the passing of friends. We may often have occasion to grieve over lost opportunities, or lost wealth, or lost health. And whenever a loss brings sorrow, it is our part not simply to mourn, but also to turn the affliction to some wise purpose in our life's experience. In death, therefore, we seek to find a meaning that shall bring consolation, and enable us to draw a hidden joy from the depth of sorrow. And this joy we discover in the thought that the living and the dead make up one vast family. Memory and love unite us to the departed in sacred ties. A household may be divided among various chambers, and the members, though parted by walls, may yet dwell in real union and sympathy. And so, also, we who live in the light of the sun and stars are yet comrades of the dead, bearing their image in our thought, their names on our lips, or their influences in our very blood and ideas and habits. . . .

Life is but the latest note in a music that began with the birth of humanity itself. The music is a song of households knit in the bonds of mutual love; of cities and states built up by courage and self-devotion; of benefits bestowed by wit and labor for the aid of the weak and helpless; of knowledge won from nature; of precious thoughts and teachings imparted by the sages. How immense and how deep is our debt to the past! How much of thankfulness we owe to the goodness, the intelligence, and the energy of men and women who are now dead, and who toiled in faith and patience for the children of their day, and for us remoter children whom they were never to look upon! How few of these forefathers and foremothers can we know as we knew the dead to whom we here offer our parting words! Yet we derive from them our health, our stores of sustenance, our learning, our all. It is one of our profoundest joys to know that we are united to this great past. "To live with the dead is one of the most precious privileges of humanity. . . ."

Each one of us can help in the glorious task of rendering some service to the family which numbers more members dead than living. Each can offer an impulse of pity, of mercy, of justice. Each can add a useful thought, a cheerful and sensible word, a happy song, an effort to express something beautiful. Each can contribute a little bravery, a little wisdom, a little aim accomplished. And, by reason of that little tribute to the general wealth, we may enroll ourselves among the influences that will pass from age to age in fruitfulness and blessing. . . .

Clearly, Gould has been creative here. Denied use of the religious lexicon, he canvasses human sentiments ("joy," "grief," "courage"), human challenges ("opportunity," "affliction," "labor"), and human virtues ("bravery," "intelligence," "goodness"). These are fine words, but they are hardly special in the way that "Dust thou are and unto dust shalt thou return" is special. The metaphors Gould uses are adequate (a "family" of humankind, living in the "light" of the stars, parted at times by "walls" of separation but ultimately heartened by "stores" of sustenance), but they do not have real rhetorical punch. Also, while the Episcopalian memorial is spare and direct, the atheists' remarks are too self-consciously embellished. Each purpose is a "wise" purpose, each joy "hidden," each family "vast." Sometimes it takes double adjectives to make the point ("how immense and deep is our debt"), and the use of the superlative degree ("profoundest joys," "most precious privileges") makes the passage sound almost like advertising copy. Where one noun would have sufficed, the author uses two ("precious thoughts and teachings") or even three ("the goodness, the intelligence, the energy . . . ").

In short, Gould was not short. He overfills his thoughts with words. It is as if he were constantly afraid of offending some constituency and so he includes them all ("forefathers and foremothers," "cities and states," "the living and the dead"). Deprived of Biblical images of hellfire and damnation, denied the stories of saints and sinners, robbed of textured depictions of an afterlife, Gould resigned himself to abstractions. He asked his audience to enroll itself "among the influences that will pass from age to age" without specifying what such influences actually *do.* He says that in death "we seek to find a meaning that shall bring consolation," but the consolation he offers—turning the affliction "to some wise purpose"—is as gray and lifeless as death itself. Gould's abstractions are so intellectualized that at one point he even speaks of the *"impulse"* of pity, not the felt emotion itself.

In a Judeo-Christian culture, it is hard to be an atheist. It is even harder to talk like one. This is not to say that Mr. Gould has done poorly. After all, he was writing a generic eulogy, a fill-in-the-blanks address for no one in particular and hence was almost necessarily driven to the heights of abstraction. The *Book of Common Prayer* is equally generic, and yet its words seem timely as well as timeless. At least in part, this effect is produced by a lexicon whose history authorizes and whose familiarity comforts. As Chapter Seven demonstrated, effective style emerges from words well arranged, both functionally and creatively. But effective style also depends on the *types* of words a speaker chooses. That is the topic of this chapter.

EXAMINING GROUP LEXICONS

Like people, words have histories. That is why even synonyms come to mean (and feel) different. Blankenship [1968:59] makes this point when commenting on variations like "I am thrifty; you are stingy; he's a miser" or "I agree; you must admit; he's forced to confess." Rhetoric requires the speaker to wander through these lexical thickets when deciding what to say. In 1972, for example, vice presidential candidate Thomas Eagleton was dropped from the Democratic ticket when the phrase "mental illness" began to dog him on the campaign trail (he had spent some time in therapy years earlier). In 1968, Governor Nelson Rockefeller's "divorced" status undid his presidential candidacy in many Americans' eyes. More recently, Adlai Stevenson III of Illinois could not shake the sobriquet of "wimp" when campaigning. Did words alone ruin these political careers? Probably not. But words did become wrapped around the candidates like some sort of hideous leech, sapping the life from their electioneering efforts. Their campaigns turned into an endless exchange of words about words (for example, What *really* constitutes mental illness?), rather than into a discussion of policy matters.

Words like "mental illness," "divorce," and "wimp" are part of a disapproved lexicon. Other words tell a happier story: "patriotic," "integrity," "family," and so forth. With political advertising now becoming a blizzard of short, pictorial messages, such words fill the televised air, often disconnected from genuine argument. It is as if the words themselves had magical power, as if by intoning words like "strong defense," "human rights," and "high technology" a candidate could be assured of political worthiness. Similarly, attacking one's opponent with such words as "Soviet aggression," "inflationary spiral," "nuclear waste," or "welfare state" makes it seem as if *the saying* of these words alone ended discussion. Modern politics has, therefore, become a semantic game. The campaign trail is the game board and lexicon, not policy, is how we keep score.

Words that have special evocative power for a society have been dubbed **ultimate terms** by Weaver [1953]. Phrases like "true Americanism," "equal justice for all," and "scientific advancement" are, according to Weaver, modern God terms that make us mentally genuflect when hearing them. Weaver notes that much public oratory is little more than a clever interspersing of such words at appropriate times, which often turns genuine communication into mere word-saying. Weaver also noted that devil terms, terms like "racism," "drugs," "illiteracy," and "deficit spending," give us a clear picture of malevolence and are, therefore, also rhetorically useful.

Weaver urged critics to track uses of such language to get an early reading on emerging societal values. In the 1950s, for example, Senator Joe McCarthy could have called his detractors misfits, scoundrels, or ingrates, but instead he called them Communists and therein lay the story of his decade. In the 1980s, Ronald Reagan could have labeled his pet armaments intercontinental ballistic missiles, but instead he called them peacekeepers and that told volumes about Mr. Reagan's international vision. As Graber [1976:291] notes, using such words allows speakers to suspend the rules of reasoning and to shift the agenda for discussion, especially if its users are specially licensed keepers of the nation's sacred terminology (as Messrs. Reagan and McCarthy were). Weaver himself was deeply disturbed by the potential for unscrupulous use of ultimate terms. Even a brief listing of their rhetorical capacities shows why:

1. *Ultimate terms are abstract.* They normally refer to ideas (like democracy) rather than to objects (like hot dogs). They normally refer to the deceased (George Washington) rather than the living (Teddy Kennedy). Because they are abstract, their meanings can be twisted: "Buy Magic Cola, an all-American drink." They can also be made to encompass more than they were intended to encompass: "A good Christian should vote conservatively." And they can be used in situations for which they were never intended (for example, when "right to work" became a synonym for union-bashing).

2. *Ultimate terms are efficient.* Although it only has three letters, a word like "pig" can trigger powerful emotions. Thus, when the police were called pigs in the 1960s by radical activists, this devil term evoked images of "filthy" individuals doing the bidding of corrupt politicians, of the police's unabated "appetite" for power, and of the monstrous "breeding" practices of the police, who, in the eyes of the Left, always appeared on the scene in excessive numbers.

3. *Ultimate terms are hierarchial.* That is why they are called ultimate. They lie at the top of society's pantheon of values and subsume all lesser terms. For this reason, they are used to pull rank, to make an opponent's case seem small and expedient. The teenager who argues that going to the lake with friends sounds like more fun than staying at home for the evening barbecue can quickly be disadvantaged. The parent who responds, "You don't want to spoil *the family's* plans, do you?" knows full well where "fun" and "family" rank on the value hierarchy.

4. *Ultimate terms are preemptory.* They let a speaker carve out rhetorical territory and then seal it off from others. By calling his bomb a Peacekeeper, for example, Ronald Reagan challenged his opponents mightily: "All *real* Americans are in favor of peace," implied the President. Similarly, Joe McCarthy threatened his opponents with the rhetorical question: "Only the Communists want me to fail. You're not one of *them*, are you?" In persuasion, whoever scrambles to the high ground first can set the parameters for the debate and, often, its necessary conclusion as well.

5. *Ultimate terms have unstable meanings.* This is a particularly important, and dangerous, feature. Being abstract, ultimate terms can change in meaning from age to age and from topic to topic but its *form* never does. That is, "freedom" is spelled the same way today as it was in 1776, but it no longer just means an absence of British troops on New England shores. For that matter, in an age of Russian glasnost, Chinese capitalism, and Cuban baseball, "Communism" no longer just means Stalinist purges. But persuaders try to make us forget this distinction between form and content. They operate as if a word is a word is a word and that a term's final meaning is determined at its christening. Thus, when the "economic freedom" built into a Republican platform is contrasted to the "collectivist tyranny" of the Democrats, the campaigner is inviting the triangulation of colonial Boston in the 1770s, Stalinist Russia in the 1930s, and contemporary conditions. Even though times, meanings, and policies change, language often does not change.

It is easy to think of ultimate terms as mere semantics, as an idle game with no consequence. Nothing could be more dangerous. The lives lost and careers destroyed by Joe McCarthy's rampage remind us how deadly a game labeling can be. But if language is a game, Weaver would observe, the critic must become its referee. After all, God terms like truth, justice, peace, freedom, and love really *are* worth defending from their corrupters. Racism, sexism, poverty, oppression, and ignorance really *are* worth attacking, as long as the attack is a genuine one and not an act of misdirection. A sacred lexicon remains sacred only as long as it is revered in practice, and so the critic must help determine who has the ultimate right to use ultimate terms.

A second approach to lexicon is to analyze **code words,** specialized terms that designate uncommon phenomena or that designate common phenomena in uncommon ways and that are unique to a subgroup. Typically, the more precise a word is, the more remote it becomes (for example, "ribonucleic acid"). This remoteness makes for efficiency. The surgeon who asks a nurse for a trephine, for example, gets what is needed and gets it quickly. To have asked for "that saw-type thing over there" might have produced the same result but more likely would have produced an array of cutting instruments. Such inefficiency can be costly in surgery: A word lost can mean time lost and time lost can mean a patient lost. For similar reasons, code words are used by scientists (they speak of an "angle of trajectory" instead of its tilt), by bureaucrats ("vehicular traffic" rather than cars and trucks), by lawyers ("indemnify" for protect), by athletes ("reddogging," "sky hook," "double-up"), and by other specialists ("downloading," "psychotic disorder," "G-clef," "occlusion"). As tastes become more refined, as people become more segregated, as ideas become more technical, code words become more common.

Code words have an unsavory reputation because they are inherently discriminatory: They set their users apart from the larger society. As a result, many people react to code words defensively, as if such terms constituted a silent rhetorical conspiracy against them. Sometimes, code words are just that, but equally often they result from normal socialization. We use linguistic shortcuts because grunting "torque!" is easier than orating, "Seeing as how I am lying on my back fixing the transmission linkage and hence cannot extricate myself to reach that curious, wrenchlike implement at your feet, would you be so kind as to . . . "

The code words used by others keep us out of the picture and hence we resent them. *Their* code words are arcane, obtuse, an affront to civility. *Our* code words are "the language of our fathers" or our "distinctive linguistic heritage." Our code words are our semantic birthright while theirs become legalese, scientism, or bureaucratic gobbledygook. Especially when it comes to nursery rhymes, their code words make us twitter: "A triumvirate of murine rodents totally devoid of ophthalmic acuity was observed in a state of rapid locomotion in pursuit of an agriculturalist's uxorial adjunct. Said adjunct then performed a triple caudectomy utilizing an acutely honed bladed instrument generally used for subdivision of edible tissue" [Youngquist, 1983:153].

Code words are standard rhetorical tools that perform a number of functions, among which are the following:

1. *Code words insulate.* Code words are a way of hiding in public, of sending messages to select persons without risk of interruption or interference from the unselected. Hayes [1976] documents this in a study of "gayspeak" in which he describes two distinct cultures within the gay community, one that uses code words openly (including such terms as "nelly number," "S/M," and "Chippendale queen") and another that uses ordinary language in jargonized ways ("liberal-minded," "artistic," "tendencies"). This latter group, says Hayes, is seeking to maximize its rhetorical range and to guard against the social isolation the former group reluctantly accepts.

2. *Code words unify.* Turner [1973] makes the point that slang (informal code words) is a token that can be shared with new members of a group to make them feel included. By using slang, the neophyte participates in the group rhetorically but not financially, organizationally, or behaviorally. As Turner says [p. 189], "Slang may even have its usefulness among children as a protection, so that they can begin to

learn social behavior without staking too much of themselves at once." He also notes that the very act of learning code words is an important ritual for new members: "The student of geometry is never to *draw* anything; he may *describe* circles, *construct* a triangle, *produce* its sides and *drop* a perpendicular, so that geometry is in part the learning of new collocations of words special to the subject" [p. 172].

3. *Code words neutralize.* Code words often drain emotion from social or political events. In the language of Chapter Seven, code words are frequently found in the periodic (or noun-filled) style that hides the essential action that verb-styles reveal. Thus, code words help us deal with unpleasantness, a point made some years ago by George Orwell [1956:363]:

> Things like the continuance of British rule in India, the Russian purges and deportations, the dropping of the atomic bombs in Japan, can indeed be defended but only by arguments which are too brutal for most people to face and which do not square with the professed aims of political parties. Thus . . . [d]efenseless villages are bombarded from the air, the inhabitants driven out into the countryside, the cattle machine-gunned, the huts set on fire with incendiary bullets; this is called *pacification*. Millions of peasants are robbed of their farms and sent trudging along the roads with no more than they can carry; this is called *transfer of population* or *rectification of frontiers*. People are imprisoned for years without trial, or shot in the back of the neck or sent to die of scurvy in Arctic lumber camps; this is called *elimination of undesirable elements*.

4. *Code words sanctify.* Code words make bad things neutral (a "cardiac event" seems less threatening than a "heart attack"), neutral things good (explaining one's religion becomes "witnessing"), and good things magnificent (cutting off-tackle becomes a "Heisman move"). Himelstein [1983] observes that code words can desensitize voters by making political issues seem technical issues. In analyzing racism, for example, Himelstein asked [p. 156], "How does one avoid blatant offense to black voters and at the same time communicate faithfulness to the racist canons of the recent past?" The answer? Code words. Words like "ward politics," "sectionalism," and "neighborhood representation" filled the campaign rhetoric Himelstein studied, silently giving voters directions without appearing to have done so: "The politicians had winked, and the voters had understood" [p. 165].

5. *Code words stabilize.* Edelman [1971] observes that code words keep people in positions of power. For example, those who have not learned the language of the bureaucracy or who cannot use it with authority are denied its riches. That is why there is so little semantic creativity in politics, an arena whose numbing technicalities make

ideas technical and audiences numb. It is this numbing, this state of nonfeeling, that makes the voter ripe for political exploitation. For a political figure to avoid code words, warns Edelman [p. 73], and "to speak and write in fresh or unconventional terms while jargon swirls all about one in an organization [would be] to state definitively that one is not buying the accepted values and not docilely conforming to authority." Few politicians run such risks, says Edelman.

When examining code words, the critic does what critics always do—asks questions: Why are code words used here and not there? Why this lexicon and not another? What attitudes and values are the code words walling in? Which are they walling out? Whom do they protect? Whom do they disenfranchise? There are many questions for the critic to ask because there are so many code words. So the critic studies them, sorting out in each instance what is being said and what is not. All too often, code words make ideas do the bidding of language. It is the critic's job to reverse that process.

When studying either ultimate terms or code words, the critic essentially asks: Out of the thousands of words available for choosing, and out of the millions of combinations that could result from them, why were these words chosen? The answers to such questions are often not immediately apparent. It takes a persistent critic to ask them. A fine model of such persistence is Stelzner's [1966] analysis of Franklin D. Roosevelt's "War Message" of December 8, 1941 (the day after Pearl Harbor). Table 8.1 presents an abbreviation of Stelzner's study, but even in its brevity we see a good critic at work. Stelzner's is a kind of **synonymic analysis,** an attempt to compare the lexicon actually used by Roosevelt to slight variations on that lexicon. Naturally, Stelzner's analysis is often quite speculative. He could not read Roosevelt's mind. But by asking the lexical critic's key questions—why these words? why not others?—Stelzner gives a fine tutorial in criticism.

EXAMINING INDIVIDUAL LEXICONS

Thus far, we have focused on the sacred or secret words of groups. But the language choices of individuals are also worthy of study. Indeed, a person's "style" is often judged to be a special way of wearing clothes or shooting a basketball or saying hello. We tune into David Letterman each night, not knowing exactly what he will say but confident that it will be familiar because his style is so distinctive. Style, the sum total of the variations a speaker makes on standard linguistic schemes, is a basic force in everyday interaction. But how much of this sum total must a critic assess? Which of its variations are really important? This section will try to answer these questions.

An interesting example of the importance of individual style occurred in the case of publishing magnate William Randolph Hearst's granddaughter, Patricia, who was captured by the radical Symbionese Liberation Army in 1974 and then became a gun-toting bank robber by the name of Tania. During her trial, Ms. Hearst's lawyers produced a university examination she had written and compared it to a taped message she sent her father two months after her capture. Were Tania and Patty the same person? Did Hearst freely author the statement to her father or was she, as she claimed in court, forced to read SLA propaganda into a tape recorder? Is the person who wrote the cool scholarly exposition the same woman who authored the cant-filled diatribe her father received? Can people change their styles so radically and so quickly? Are the differences in the two messages a function of different audiences (a professor versus her father) or of changing modalities (oral versus written communication) rather than of changing ideology? Or did the passages reflect a genuine philosophical conversion on Hearst's part and, as SLA member Emily Harris said in court, did the SLA actually try to *tone down* Hearst's rhetoric?

Patty Hearst's trial hinged on what Bailey [1979] has termed forensic linguistics. In Hearst's case, neither the jury nor the appeal judge was convinced of her innocence and expert testimony on the contrasting rhetorical styles was not permitted in open court. A subsequent study by Bailey, however, argues persuasively that Hearst underwent only a *partial* conversion and that while she may have authored some semiradical statements she did not author the most damning of them. By examining Hearst's lexical style (use of nouns, proportion of monosyllables, ratio of auxiliary to main verbs, mean sentence length, and so forth) and comparing them to the passages in dispute, Bailey called into question both Hearst's culpability and her gullibility.

Naturally, this sort of lexical analysis is a conjectural business. The evidence available to Bailey was insufficient to establish Hearst's innocence conclusively. But the questions he asked are important: How unique is an individual's lexicon and how can it be reliably determined? To begin to answer these questions, at least two things are required: (1) a sizeable sample of a speaker's style, a sample that represents diverse rhetorical conditions and (2) a sample of others' word choices (so that language norms can be used for comparison). As Enkvist [1971] says, the study of style is, therefore, the study of deviance from known linguistic patterns.

This sort of comparative logic has guided a number of studies. Knapp, et al. [1974] compared the spontaneous (truthful) remarks of

Table 8.1 Stylistic Analysis of Roosevelt's War Message

Roosevelt's Wording	Alternative Wording	Explanation for Roosevelt's Original Phrasing
Yesterday, December 7, 1941, a date which will live in infamy, the United States of America was suddenly and deliberately attacked by naval forces of the Empire of Japan.	(1) Eliminate: the word "yesterday." (2) Eliminate: "December 7, 1941." (3) Eliminate: mention of infamy. (4) Substitute: "Japan attacked us" for "America was . . ."	(1) "Yesterday" is a stark word that ruptures any sense of leisure on the part of the audience. (2) Exact date serves to make the attack "historical" in the minds of listeners. (3) "Infamy" introduces the strong, denunciatory tone necessary for wartime motivation; also places the future on "our" side. (4) Passive voice makes Japan the aggressor and implicitly sanctions whatever countermeasures are needed.
The United States was at peace with that nation and, at the solicitation of Japan, was still in conversation with its government and its Emperor looking toward the maintenance of peace in the Pacific.	(1) Substitute: "country" for "nation" and "request" for "solicitation." (2) Why "its" Government and "its" Emperor?	(1) A formal tone is best suited to a nation about to go to war. (2) This language further distances and dehumanizes a soon-to-be adversary.
Indeed, one hour after Japanese air squadrons had commenced bombing in the American island of Oahu, the Japanese ambassador to the United States and his colleague delivered to our Secretary of State a formal reply to a recent American message. And while this reply stated that it seemed useless to continue the existing diplomatic negotiations, it contained no threat or hint of war or of armed attack.	(1) Substitute: "Yet" or "however" for "indeed." (2) Substitute: "air force" for "air squadrons." (3) Eliminate: details of previous diplomatic encounters.	(1) "Indeed" is more abrupt and emphatic and personalizes matters by reflecting Roosevelt's anger. (2) "Air squadrons" is a sharper, more definable image of fast, tight-knit formations and thus better for showing Japanese perfidy. (3) Dramatizing duplicity amidst diplomacy plays off Oriental stereotypes of excessive formality; also shows enemy incapable of living up to its *own* cultural code.

244

It will be recorded that the distance of Hawaii from Japan makes it obvious that the attack was deliberately planned many days or even weeks ago. During the intervening time the Japanese Government has deliberately sought to deceive the United States by false statements and expressions of hope for continued peace.

(1) Eliminate: "It will be recorded."

(2) Rephrase: verb forms into active voice.

(1) Bureaucratic phrasing makes the United States the rational, historically conscious party in the dispute.
(2) Passive voice continues to establish American moral and legal innocence (that is, it makes it the aggrieved party).

The attack yesterday on the Hawaiian Islands has caused severe damage to American naval and military forces. I regret to tell you that very many American lives have been lost. In addition, American ships have been reported torpedoed on the high seas between San Francisco and Honolulu.

(1) Substitute: "Yesterday's attack" for "the attack yesterday."

(2) Eliminate: "I regret."

(3) Substitute: "inform" for "tell."

(1) Latter construction makes the barbarousness of the *act* itself more prominent than chronology.
(2) This first self-reference is connected, appropriately, with loss of human life (as opposed to more distant, "military" matters).
(3) "Tell" is more informal, more personal than other alternatives.

Yesterday the Japanese Government also launched an attack against Malaya. Last night Japanese forces attacked Hong Kong. Last night Japanese forces attacked Guam. Last night Japanese forces attacked the Philippine Islands. Last night the Japanese attacked Wake Island. And this morning the Japanese attacked Midway Island.

(1) Why the sharp transition from the domestic scene?

(2) Substitute: "began," "commenced" for "launched."

(3) Eliminate: list of specific places.

(4) Substitute: "Yesterday" for "Last night."

(5) Substitute: Passive voice for active voice (as before).

(1) Insures that anger against the enemy, not fear of domestic attack, motivates the American people.
(2) "Launched" contrasts sharply with the civilized negotiations the Japanese were supposedly conducting.
(3) Mention of British possessions links U.S. with an ally and makes American people feel less alone.
(4) "Last night" has two syllables rather than three. Spoken in rapid succession, the phrase quickens the emotions.
(5) Switch to active voice heightens the enormity of the Japanese attack and readies Americans for a world war.

Table 8.1   Stylistic Analysis of Roosevelt's War Message (*continued*)

Roosevelt's Wording	Alternative Wording	Explanation for Roosevelt's Original Phrasing
Japan has, therefore, undertaken a surprise offensive extending throughout the Pacific area. The facts of yesterday and today speak for themselves. The people of the United States have already formed their opinions and well understand the implications to the very life and safety of our nation.	(1) Substitute: "In my opinion" for "the facts speak for themselves." (2) Rephrase: "the people of the United States have . . ."	(1) Moves the discussion beyond political partisanship; makes the correct war policy "scientifically" assured. (2) Use of the past tense and the third person makes Roosevelt seem like a *conduit* of policy rather than an initiator of it.
As Commander-in-Chief of the Army and Navy I have directed that all measures be taken for our defense. But always will our whole nation remember the character of the onslaught against us.	(1) Why the shift to the first person and the active voice?	(1) The facts having been assembled, Roosevelt can now exert a position of principled leadership without seeming untoward.
No matter how long it may take to overcome this premeditated invasion, the American people in their righteous might will win through to absolute victory. I believe that I interpret the will of the Congress and of the people when I assert that we will not only defend ourselves to the uttermost but will make it very certain that this form of treachery shall never again endanger us.	(1) Rephrase: "righteous might." (2) Eliminate: Conflict between tentative phrasing ("I believe," "I interpret") and assured language ("this form of treachery").	(1) This phrase and others like it give the speech a "sermonic" quality that morally justifies America's decision to enter the war. (2) Cautious phrasing certifies the President's due consideration for the balance of powers while strong phrasing reassures the people and warns the enemy.
Hostilities exist. There is no blinking at the fact that our people, our territory and our interests are in great danger.	(1) Eliminate: downbeat phrasing.	(1) Roosevelt needed to prepare the people for a protracted struggle. Also, this statement is "sandwiched" between positive, unyielding statements that serve to mitigate its negative effects.

| With confidence in our armed forces, with the unbounding determination of our people, we will gain the inevitable triumph—so help us God. | (1) Substitute: "We have confidence in our armed forces; our people have unbounding determination, etc."

 (2) Eliminate: overstatements ("unbounding determination," "inevitable triumph," "so help us God"). | (1) Roosevelt's phrasing is oathlike and thereby heightens his sense of commitment as well as his sense of authority.

 (2) This "theological" vocabulary, previewed earlier, is standard political fare in America during times of stress. |
| I ask that the Congress declare that since the unprovoked and dastardly attack by Japan on Sunday, December 7, 1941, a state of war has existed between the United States and the Japanese Empire. | (1) Substitute: "cowardly" for "dastardly."

 (2) Rephrase: Make tenses coordinate ("I ask . . . has existed"). | (1) "Dastardly" is close to "bastardly" and thus permits public catharsis through surrogate profanity.

 (2) Formal language shows that the United States observes the diplomatic amenities even during war and even when its enemy does not. |

(Based on Stelzner, 1966)

RHETORIC AND PRINT JOURNALISM

Critical Profile 8.1   Newsmagazines Heat Up the Cold War

Dateline Moscow—After the death of Soviet premier Leonid Brezhnev, American newsmagazines reported that thousands of Muscovites waited in a "mile-long line" in "cold, wet streets" to view his body. The faces of the "curious citizens" "showed no grief" as they "shuffled" past the coffin. Brezhnev, "the consummate apparatchik," "inspired neither love nor hate." His death had "little impact on the rhythm of Moscow life." "Only a few portraits and bouquets of flowers turned up in shop windows."

The cold war images clustered here are common to American newsmagazines. Soviets are pictured as a less-than-human people living in a bleak and barren landscape. Even though the party leader had died, implied the magazines, grief and love would be wasted in the automated revolution known as Soviet society.

Although American newsmagazines purportedly present "in-depth analyses" of world events, according to one research report these newsmagazines use reportorial techniques more suited to fiction. The Soviet leader's funeral is not merely reported. Instead, says Farrell Corcoran of Northern Illinois University, the reader is exposed to a "selective web of images of the Soviet Union rich in depersonalizing and decivilizing connotations." Corcoran argues that reportage about the Soviet Union functions to reconfirm American myths about who the Soviets really are and allows the American reader to reconcile two competing values—pacifism and justifiable war. As a peace-loving people, Americans cannot make overtly aggressive attacks on other peace-loving peoples. However, Americans can justify aggression toward an enemy that is neither human nor peace-loving. Corcoran finds such justification provided weekly in the imagery of foreign reportage.

Throughout thirty years of coverage of major Soviet funerals, Corcoran found three dominant images: (1) The Russians are a faceless people living in a "remote and inhuman landscape"; (2) the Soviet leader is a man "obsessively power hungry"; and finally, (3) the Soviet premiers are "uncivilized." The average American reader probably does not notice these ideological images when reading news articles, says Corcoran, who argues that the ubiquity of such ideological content makes the rhetorical force of these very subtle images all the more powerful. Consequently, the cold war ideology favoring aggression toward the Soviets is routinely and consistently justified without an overt appeal being made. Thus, as Corcoran notes, these depersonalizing images of the Soviets "create a mythic picture of an enemy that is, and has always been, coercive, irrational, brutal, visceral, [a] cunning savage." In short, American foreign policy may well be played out these days in the seemingly innocent pages of *Time* magazine.

Profiled by: Patricia Powell
Citation: Corcoran (1983)

Critical Profile 8.2 The Man Is the Style

Martin Medhurst and Michael DeSousa of the University of California set out to find a way to describe the rhetoric of political cartoons. How do political cartoonists exaggerate candidates' characteristics to the point that these "styles" (of appearance, speaking, or thinking) come to be identified with the person? How do these artists, these "editors in charge of graphic opinion," help to construct an "ongoing political reality" for their readers? Medhurst and DeSousa collected and analyzed 749 editorial cartoons having to do with the 1980 presidential campaign. They argued that the political cartoonist's job is similar to that of a speaker in the use of traditional rhetorical elements (argumentation, arrangement, style, delivery, and so forth) but differs in the specific techniques involved.

Like public speakers, cartoonists often use time-bound campaign events as resources for their rhetorical invention. For example, in one drawing by cartoonist Paul Conrad, an elephant is depicted walking away from the viewer. The wrinkles on the elephant's backside trace out the unmistakable face of Ronald Reagan. The caption reads "The End of an ERA." A future reader may not be familiar with the debate over the Equal Rights Amendment and might therefore miss the pun Conrad uses here. Some symbols, however, will probably remain understandable to future readers (for example, the depiction of the GOP as an elephant).

Unlike the public speaker, who can develop an idea over the course of several minutes, political cartoonists hope to communicate their message in a single glance. One of their most prized tools, therefore, is the principal of contrast. In the Conrad drawing, the use of contrasts of line and form invite the reader to see Reagan in a particular way. Reagan's face and the shadow of the elephant contrast light with dark, visual planes (vertical and horizontal), and visual directions (the elephant appears to be walking forward but Reagan is looking backward).

The authors note that most cartoons seem to function simultaneously as commentary, explanation, and revelation. They point out that the placement of the picture within the frame causes the elephant's feet to emerge from Reagan's mouth, a commentary on Reagan's propensity for misstatement. Simultaneously, the cartoon explains the Republican party's stand on the Equal Rights Amendment. Finally, the cartoon's subtle visual elements are highly revelatory: "Line is used to fashion the leathery hide of the elephant which doubles as the facial wrinkles of an aging candidate. Not only does Reagan look to the past, he is a relic of it."

It is a cliché to say that a picture is worth a thousand words. But Medhurst and DeSousa show us that sometimes a thousand words may not be enough to account for the many, powerful messages scratched out from the pen of a master political cartoonist.

Profiled by: Suzanne M. Daughton
Citation: Medhurst & DeSousa (1981)

Critical Profile 8.3   The Candidate's New Clothes

Political campaigns have discovered that they can "get their propaganda into newspaper columns by dressing it up in interesting clothes," and they take advantage of this discovery by the careful crafting of press releases. Jan Vermeer of Nebraska Wesleyan University claims that "campaign press releases are an efficient and reasonably effective way for candidates to communicate with large segments of the electorate." Like other campaign materials, Vermeer argues, news releases "are strangely evanescent; no sooner are they produced and used for their intended purpose than they disappear or become buried in mountains of records mixed with refuse." During their relatively short lifespans, however, the use of press releases has proven to be a valuable campaign technique.

Authors of press releases exploit the public's belief that what it reads in the press is the product of independent and impartial reporting. In fact, says Vermeer, the opposite is often the case. Vermeer found that even though editors and reporters contend heatedly that they find little value in campaign press releases, the material in those releases frequently finds its way into published news stories, often unchanged. Even the releases that are changed by the press have considerable value to the campaigns that produced them. In one example, two candidates for the same office sent out 363 releases; of these, 253 were actually used by the press. But more important than the high percentage of use (69.7%) was the fact that each release generated on average almost four stories, thus attesting to the old adage: out of one, many.

The gatekeeping function of the press is nowhere more noticeable than in its use of candidate press releases. "Candidates use press releases as one means of influencing the images voters have of them," but the ultimate decision of what materials to use lies in the press's reaction to those releases. Candidates tend to stress a relatively small number of attributes, repeating these in releases throughout the duration of the campaign. With this kind of repetition, sometimes including negative attributes of the opposition, press releases serve to "set the agenda" for the press, which, in turn, sets the agenda for the public.

Vermeer notes two essential reasons why so many campaign press releases find their way wholly or largely unchanged into daily newspapers. First, the editors and reporters find press releases an easy source to mine. Second, press releases "fill in" the daily need to put stories in all that empty space. Vermeer's study shows us, once again, how crucial it is for modern citizens to become more critical consumers of the information they receive, a job they dare not leave to the guardians of the press.

Profiled by: Donald Nobles
Citation: Vermeer (1982)

people to lies they told at the behest of experimenters. Individuals' styles changed dramatically from condition to condition: fewer words spoken when lying, fewer self-disclosures, more caution in their remarks, more repetition of words, and fewer factual citations. It was as if the "liars" were trying to step away from themselves, as if their natural lexicons would not cooperate with the lies being told. Another study by Osgood and Walker [1959] compared real suicide notes to those fabricated in the laboratory. They found that the real statements had a leaner, more efficient style and more verbal energy. They did not supplicate by using adjectives or large words; they did not make preachy, philosophical statements; and, interestingly, they used more positive language than those in the comparison group, presumably because suicide makes one contemplate about *both* good and evil.

Another study by Sinclair [1985] looked for a "successful" style among preachers whose congregations were growing and an "unsuccessful" style among those losing church members. After gathering statistical data on church growth, weekly attendance, and financial support by the laity, Sinclair examined the language choices of a large sample of preachers. His findings: The growing churches heard sermons that were more pesonal, more narrational, more assured, and more detailed than parishioners in the declining churches, while the less successful preachers used more passive constructions, less interesting language, and a less businesslike, more folksy, style. A more general study by Carbone [1975] compared speakers rated highly credible to those rated unimpressive by a group of dispassionate judges. She found that highly credible speakers used more human interest language, a richer vocabulary, a more concrete style, and less cumbersome sentence structures than those rated low in believability.

In each of these studies, scholars examined what Sedelow and Sedelow [1966:1] call the distributional properties of language use, word patterns varying in some systematic way from speaker to speaker or from condition to condition. Research of this sort has a quantitative bent. It assumes that any claim about stylistic distinctiveness is ultimately a mathematical claim: Feature A does or does not appear in this text; Feature B appears more often or less often than Feature C; Feature D appears less frequently than the norm. Turner [1973:25] makes these same points when he says:

> If there are choices in language, there are probabilities . . . Even such basic concepts as a "rare word" or a "common word" are statistical concepts . . . To take a simple illustration, if I am about to spell an English word, the probability that I will use a particular letter to begin it, say *n* or *g*, can be roughly measured with a ruler and a good dictio-

nary; if I choose *n* to begin with, the probability that the next letter will be *g* becomes zero; if I reach the stage *notwithstandin-*, the probability that the next letter will be *g* becomes certainty.

The stylistic critic need not trade in good sense for a ruler (or a computer). Counting things takes one only so far. But counting the right things at the right times under the right circumstances produces insight. The rest of this chapter will show why.

Figure 8.1 presents a speech John Kennedy [1961b] gave to the Democratic National Committee the day after his inauguration. The speech is not remarkable: It is a back-slapping piece of political celebration. It is brief, convivial, and spontaneous. It includes teasing and bantering. But it is not John Kennedy. Not really. Although the speech conforms to popular stereotypes of the Kennedy style, this speech was not a normal one for him. Most of his speaking was drier, less personal, and more restrained. Table 8.2 shows how we know this to be true.

The information in Table 8.2 comes from analyzing Kennedy's text with a computer. The program guiding the computer (DICTION) was developed by Hart [1985] and tells the machine which words to look for in a passage. The computer breaks a message into its individual words and then searches for word patterns, thereby determining the speaker's basic lexicon. The program does so by employing dictionaries, lists of words the critic specifies ahead of time. If the computer were prompted with a dictionary called Animals, it might look for dog, cat, sheep, and so on. After finding all such usages, the computer would

Table 8.2   Stylistic Features of the Kennedy Speech

Verbal Category	1/21/61 Speech	Kennedy Average	Other Presidents' Averages
Activity (aggressive, planned)	192.0	204.0	200.5
Realism (concrete, specific)	241.0	198.0	91.0
Certainty (assured, totalistic)	196.0	190.0	185.3
Optimism (inspired, praising)	238.0	213.0	220.0
Complexity (large words)	4.70	4.58	5.20
Variety (different words)	.410	.493	.488
Self-reference (I, me, etc.)	18.00	4.68	8.57
Familiarity (everyday words)	135.0	102.0	102.1
Human interest (references to people)	32.0	26.0	27.8
Embellishment (colorizing words)	.042	.070	.066
Symbolism (God terms)	6.00	2.21	5.45

(From Hart, 1984d:19)

print out how many times these words were employed versus those found in other texts previously searched with the Animal dictionary.

DICTION does not have a category called Animals, but it does employ such word lists as **activity** (including words like "achieve," "change," "plunge") **realism** ("city," "buildings," "farmer"), **certainty** ("everyone," "shall," "entire"), **optimism** ("pleased," "generous," "exciting"), **self-reference** ("I," "me," "myself"), and **human interest** ("boy," "friend," "you"). The program searches for God terms (here called **symbolism:** "America," "democracy," "peace") and also calculates how **embellished** a passage is by comparing its proportion of adjectives and adverbs to its number of nouns and verbs. Finally, the program studies the richness of the speaker's vocabulary (a high **variety** score means the text is not repetitive), its use of everyday words (that is, **familiarity**), and how complicated it is (a high **complexity** score means the speaker used large words frequently). Guided by such search tools, the computer proceeds through a message word by word, remembering which terms of which type were used when. Figure 8.1 simulates how the computer did its "looking" when examining the Kennedy speech.

The real value of such a tool is its efficiency. Although computers are dull-witted when compared to a sensitive critic, a program like DICTION has these advantages: (1) It examines every text in exactly the same way; (2) it ignores all words except those it has been instructed to "look" for; (3) it performs its tasks with lightning speed; (4) it never gets tired; (5) it never forgets what it has "learned" about any message; (6) it can track many kinds of words simultaneously (that is, it can tell which portion of a text is highly certain and which is *both* optimistic and certain).

Another advantage is that a computer cannot be seduced by the rhetoric it examines. Because it rather stupidly looks only for what it has been asked to look for, it is never sidetracked by interesting imagery or a humorous aside or a tear-stained narrative. It looks only for words. But afterward, it can report on verbal *patterns* that the imagery-noting critic was too busy to spot when inspecting the same message. DICTION, therefore, operates like the Secret Service personnel who watch the crowd while the crowd (and the president) watch the tennis match. At the end of the day, when the president relaxes with them, recounting the excitement of the contest, the Secret Service folks cannot comment on the overhead smash that won the fifth set. But they can tell the president how the crowd's mood changed when John McEnroe threw his racket in the air. Reporting on crowd behavior can also be a type of tennis criticism.

A computer will never supplant the critic's wisdom, but its comparative information calls attention to features the critic may have

Figure 8.1
Kennedy's Speech as Analyzed by the *DICTION* Program

I WANT to express my appreciation to all of you for your kind welcome, and also to take this occasion to express my great appreciation—and I think the appreciation of us all—to Senator Jackson who assumed the chairmanship of the Democratic Party at the Convention, who was greatly responsible for our success in November and has been an invaluable aid during the transition. Whatever has been done that is useful in the party in the last 5 or 6 months he has played a great part in it. And I feel that the party has served a most useful national purpose—and while Senator Jackson is obligated to serve the people of Washington in the Senate, I know that we can continue to count on him in the days to come for counsel and advice and support. So I hope we will all stand and give a good cheer to Scoop Jackson.

Scoop atuomatically loses his share of the $4-million debt—we are not going to let him in on it. John Bailey has become the proprietor, along with Mac, of this enterprise. I think we are particularly fortunate to have John Bailey. I heard Governor Lawrence in his seconding speech say the trouble with everything is that they don't know enough of what is going on here in Washington; they ought to get out in the field. I agree with him completely. We have got a man from the field who knows what's wrong here in Washington, and I am delighted that John Bailey is going to take over this job. He is more popular today than he will be any time again in his life. I will feel that he is doing a good job when you all say, "Well, Kennedy is all right, but Bailey is the one who is really making the mistakes." That's the way it was in Connecticut. Ribicoff was never wrong, it was always Bailey's fault. So that is what he is going to go down here.

Up beat introduction results from Kennedy's Optimism score of 238, which was one of the highest in the sample.

Heavy use of prepositional phrases and passive voice constructions decrease Kennedy's Activity score.

JFK's Realism score of 241 is exceptionally high and derives from a combination of personal, temporal, concrete, and spatial references.

Semantically, humor is often the product of overly assured language devoid of qualification, all of which results in a high Certainty score.

But/I/am/delighted/that/he/is/going/to/do/it./It/is/a/sacrifice/for/him./But/I/think/we/are/getting/the/services/of/someone/who/works/in/the/party/year/in/and/year/out,/understands/what/the/party/can/do,/understands/what/the/role/of/the/Chairman/is—and/I/must/say/that/I/am/delighted/to/see/him/assuming/the/position/vacated/by/Senator/Jackson.

Lastly, I want to thank all of you for being with us at the inaugural. The party is not an end in itself—it is a means to an end. And you are the people who, in victory and defeat, have maintained the Democratic Party, maintained its traditions and will continue to do so in the future. I hope the relationship between all of us can continue to be as cordial as possible. I believe in strong political organizations in our country. The Republican Party is strong and vigorous today after the election of 1960. I think we are, also. And when we do that, I think we serve great national purposes.

The party is the means by which programs can be put into action—the means by which people of talent can come to the service of the country. And in this great free society of ours, both of our parties—the Republican and the Democratic Parties—serve the interests of the people. And I am hopeful that the Democratic Party will continue to do so in the days to come. It will be in the interest of us all, and I can assure you that I will cooperate in every way possible to make sure that we do serve the public interest. You have done so well in the past We couldn't possibly have won without you help. I look forward to working with you in the future, and I want you to know that here in Washington, we may not know always what is going on as well as you do, but at least we are trying.

Thank you.

missed. Table 8.2 shows this. At first, these findings seem odd, since the popular press continually ran newsclips of the John Kennedy displayed in the D.N.C. speech. The Kennedy in that speech was witty, almost frisky, the same Kennedy who regaled reporters during press conferences. But DICTION shows that this was a *rare* John Kennedy. While this speech did display his characteristically simple style (see complexity and familiarity), in other ways it was singular. He was more concrete here than normal (see realism) and more disclosive (see self-reference); he used many more God terms (see symbolism) and was substantially more upbeat (see optimism). No matter what this speech implies, then, Mr. Kennedy's *general* style was quite dry and institutional. While a conventional critic might have discovered this same thing eventually, DICTION did so more quickly.

An important limitation of programs like DICTION is that it examines words out of context. By not distinguishing between "The boy hit the ball" and "The ball boy was hit" but only noting that the word "ball" appears in both statements, DICTION violates context. But context is not all there is to rhetoric. For example, the fact that the word "ball" appears in both passages signals a common concern with game-related matters (as opposed to religion-related or fashion-related or ostrich-related matters). The traditional critic might well miss these themes. But these themes may have *additive* effects on audiences who hear game-centered reference after game-centered reference, thereby contributing to their perceptions of rhetorical tone. So, when sweeping across a text quickly and "destroying" its linguistic unity, DICTION may simulate what listeners themselves do when processing messages.

The DICTION analysis of the Kennedy speech largely squares with our intuitions. Even a casual reading of the text reveals its personal, pragmatic tones. Then why use a computer? Because computers capture these tones quickly, reliably, and, most important, comparatively. Consider, for example, Table 8.3, which compares the Kennedy text to others examined previously. Few persons would confuse the Kennedy message with Martin Luther King's "I Have a Dream" speech. DICTION is also not confused. It finds an assuredness in the King speech missing in Kennedy's (see certainty), perhaps showing that social movements permit more exhortation than do political celebrations. This difference is striking, since, *for Kennedy*, this was one of his most assured speeches. But as a practical politician, he could not paint with King's broad brush, nor could he be as precise. On the other hand, Mr. Kennedy could be more upbeat than King (see optimism) and do what politicians do best: flatter ("give a good cheer to Scoop Jackson") and promise ("I can assure you that I will cooperate in every way . . .").

All of this is in sharp contrast to Rabbi Prinz's speech, which DICTION profiles as lecturish: heavy use of unfamiliar words, little

Table 8.3   Comparative Use of Rhetorical Style*

Verbal Category	Martin Luther King	Rabbi Prinz	John F. Kennedy	Franklin D. Roosevelt
Activity (aggressive, planned)	low	low	medium	high
Realism (concrete, specific)	high	medium	very high	low
Certainty (assured, totalistic)	high	medium	medium	low
Optimism (inspired, praising)	very low	medium	high	medium
Complexity (large words)	medium	low	medium	very low
Variety (different words)	low	low	low	low
Self-reference (I, me, my, etc.)	medium	medium	high	low
Familiarity (everyday words)	medium	low	very high	very low
Human interest (references to people)	medium	low	medium	medium
Embellishment (colorizing words)	medium	high	medium	medium

*In comparison to a total sample of 861 public messages.

human interest, and heavy embellishment (adjectives usually slow down a message). The activity found in Rabbi Prinz's speech is also the lowest of the four, documenting the philosophical tone of his remarks. It is little wonder, then, that DICTION finds almost no similarity between the Prinz and Kennedy texts.

The main advantage of DICTION is that it remembers the features of nine hundred other messages when analyzing a text. By doing so, DICTION does what listeners also do (without knowing it): It uses old texts to interpret new ones. When they listened to President Roosevelt on December 8, 1941, for example, most Americans knew they were hearing something extraordinary, in part because the president had just asked Congress to declare war, but also because of the new tone in his remarks. DICTION also senses this when featuring the activity in Roosevelt's remarks ("Last night Japanese forces attacked Hong Kong. Last night Japanese forces attacked . . ."). While FDR's language is not hard to understand (see complexity and variety), he does draw on the special vocabulary of war ("hostilities," "air squadrons," "torpedoed") and of international geography ("Honolulu," "Guam," "Midway Island"), thereby scoring low on familiarity. No doubt, the *divergence* between his simple words and his strange words told listeners that something unprecedented was afoot and that listening to Roosevelt at that moment would be like nothing they had experienced before.

Another interesting aspect of the Roosevelt message is its mid-range score on optimism. At first, this seems an anomaly, since Roosevelt was delivering a war message. But DICTION prompts us to think anew about the President's rhetorical task. He had to discuss the war, and words like "infamy," "deceive," "invasion," and "danger" show that he did. But for each negative statement he made, he also included a positive one, thereby creating dialectical tension. Early on, for example, he contrasts the "treachery" of the Japanese ambassadors with the peace-seeking United States. Later, after detailing the evil done the night before, Roosevelt talks of "inevitable triumph," "unbounding determination," and "absolute victory." Naturally, Roosevelt wanted the American people to deal realistically with the new challenges he described, but he also knew that they could not hope to do so unless they had hope to do so. DICTION shows that he provided it.

DICTION also records low certainty and realism scores for Roosevelt, which seems strange, since the President needed to inspire the nation and help it deal concretely with the Japanese threat. But his certainty score is curiously low, resulting from heavy use of the passive voice: "Japan has . . . undertaken," "The attack yesterday . . . has caused," "American ships have been reported . . ." Roosevelt watched his words carefully, perhaps because he did not know precisely what was then happening in other parts of the world, what military response the United States could make (or how soon), or what domestic problems he would face in the immediate future. His low realism score also signaled tentativeness. Roosevelt spoke of "implications to the very life and safety of our nation" without spelling out these implications. He promised that "always will our whole nation remember the character of the onslaught against us" but did not detail specifics. In short, he seems to have used the speech to buy time, to provide emotional reinforcement, and to preserve his military options. Hence, he opted for strategic ambiguity.

Computerized language programs are valuable not because they provide numerical answers but because they suggest new critical questions. This is the approach Hart [1984d] took when examining the speaking of Presidents Truman through Reagan via DICTION. Although his book tells a good deal about the presidents' styles, it more usefully reveals the factors having major impact on a speaker's lexicon. These factors are presented here as a series of useful critical probes:

1. *Does the speaker's social upbringing affect style?* Of all the presidents, Harry Truman used the greatest amount of certainty. His plain-spoken, Midwestern assuredness charmed his friends and irritated his enemies. But neither reaction changed him. Today, in contrast, politicians fear accountability. In such an era, Harry Truman's voice is

missed: "Business was never so productive, vital and energetic as it is today. All this talk about weakening private enterprise is sheer political bunk" [Truman, 1959:497].

2. *Does the speaker's employment history affect style?* Dwight Eisenhower's rise to power in the army resulted more from his bureaucratic skills than from his brilliance as a military tactician. These bureaucratic experiences resulted in a wordy (high in variety) and abstract (low in realism) style. Ike was less a public speaker than a script-reader, one whose mouth was too filled with words, as he once showed when talking about public service with college students: "In government, one must obviously have no special end to serve, but citizens should not, invariably, be required to divest themselves of investments accumulated over a lifetime in order to qualify for public service" [Eisenhower, 1960:464].

3. *Does the speaker's political vision affect style?* John Kennedy scored the lowest of all eight presidents on optimism. At first this seems surprising, since Kennedy motivated a generation of young people to enter politics to do good. Apparently, however, politics for Kennedy was a matter of *righting wrongs*, a sense we get when listening to him on civil rights: "Are we to say to the world—and much more importantly to each other—that this is the land of the free, except for the Negroes; that we have no second class citizens, except for Negroes; that we have no class or caste system, no ghettos, no master race, except with respect to Negroes" [Kennedy, 1963b:547]?

4. *Does the speech setting affect the speaker's style?* Lyndon Johnson could never adapt to television. Out on the stump, he could shake hands with the folks and palaver until dark. But on television he tied himself to his text, causing his self-reference and human interest scores to drop off and his words to become complex and cautious. But in a face-to-face setting, LBJ could be moving indeed: "I'm not 65 yet, but I have known many people in my lifetime who were 65. Some have been mighty close to me. I have seen their eyes when they wondered whether they would be welcome in their old age in their sister-in-law's home, or whether their brother-in-law would be happy when they are all there using the one bath. I have seen them worry about how they were going to pay the doctors or the medical services. I have seen them grateful for the considerations that the preacher and the women of the church had extended to them in times of illness" [Johnson, 1966:777–778].

5. *Does the speaker's strategic mind-set affect style?* Richard Nixon was a rhetorical classic, constantly adjusting his words to whatever situation he faced. Above all, he was controlled; some would call it conniving. Table 8.4 shows how unerring his adaptations were. Confronted with the Watergate disclosures, Nixon watched each word he

Table 8.4   Richard Nixon's Use of Certainty

Certainty Level	Topic	Date of Speech
210.7	Vietnam	5/14/69
189.7	Vietnam	11/3/69
204.5	Vietnam	4/30/70
184.1	Vietnam	4/7/71
202.4	Vietnam	1/25/72
174.7	Watergate	4/30/73
176.7	Watergate	8/15/73
145.4	Watergate	4/29/74

(From Hart, 1984d:145)

spoke, gauging what he said and gauging his omissions and indirections as well. When speaking from a position of strength (for example, during the Vietnam war), however, Nixon pounded his fist on the national podium. The effect of these two styles is sharply different, suggesting that there were at least two Richard Nixons, if not more.

6. *Does the speaker's social power affect the style?* DICTION found that Gerald Ford's use of self-reference was the highest of all the presidents. This makes sense. Having entered office without a political vision or a mandate from the voters, Ford sold the only product he was sure of: himself. While this trust-me-please style rarely sounded presidential, it had its human attractions: "I see no reason why the Congress and the President cannot work together. That doesn't mean that all 535 Members of the House and Senate will agree with me. But I can assure you that what I have said on more than one occasion . . . that I will work with the Congress, and I know many, if not all, in the Congress will work with me" [Ford, 1975:389].

7. *Does the speaker's cognitive habits affect the style?* Jimmy Carter saw himself as a problem-solver, not as a politician. Thus, even though he worked hard at his rhetoric, it never worked well for him, largely because of his high complexity scores (they were twice as high as any other president). This professorial lexicon impressed "businesspersons who heard Carter refer knowingly to 'pension fund regulations,' 'small business initiatives,' 'energy pricing policy,' and 'upward spiral,' 'synthetic alternatives,' and 'windfall profits tax'" but no doubt bored educators who once heard him describe a "'greatly magnified opportunity for the enhancement of better relationships' and who later were promised 'an encapsulation of what they can do in political motivation' when they returned home'" [Hart, 1984d:162–163].

8. *Does the speaker's communicative history affect style?* Compared to his predecessors, Ronald Reagan had exceptionally low embellishment ratings. Deprived of adjectives and adverbs, what does one have? Nouns and verbs. With only nouns and verbs, what can one do? Tell

stories. A sportscaster in his youth, an actor in adulthood, and a pitch-man for General Electric later on, Ronald Reagan was always a story-teller. Thus, even with defense budgets, Reagan could humanize ideas via narrative: "I received a letter from a young lad who's a sailor on one of our submarines. He said he was writing . . . on behalf of his 180 shipmates. And he said he just wanted us to know how good it felt to be an American. And he said, 'We may not have the biggest Navy in the world, but we've got the best'" [Reagan, 1981:1258].

Computer programs like DICTION are hardly omniscient. They cannot think; they can only count. They cannot deal with the majesty of style, just its plumbing. They cannot give final answers, just pose initial questions. Ultimately, it takes an intelligent critic to decide what the printouts say about lexicon. But as we have seen in both this chapter and the preceding one, style is so subtle that even an army of critics could not solve its mysteries entirely. If the computer can free the critic from the more mundane work of sorting and counting words, it seems a useful adjunct to criticism. Given the complexity of style, the critic can always find better things to do than to sort and count.

CONCLUSION

Knowing about ultimate terms, code words, and individual lexicons is important in studying style, but the critic's best tool is developing a sensitivity to word choice. It is this sort of sensitivity that Wallman [1981] demonstrated in her study of blue-collar British politics. She traced the ways in which the word "race" was used by a counter-establishment figure named Enoch Powell. Wallman noted that Powell's discussions of "race" entered into the everyday conversations of British voters, even though the term was *not* used by them to designate skin color. Rather, they used Powell's rhetoric to explain virtually every problem besetting them. Worries associated with immigration, unemployment, economic scarcity, urban violence, state monopolies, Communists, and student demonstrators were all laid at the door of "the race issue." Powell's rhetoric was influential, Wallman observes, because it gave ordinary people a language with which to talk about their difficulties, even though many of its users had never heard of Enoch Powell.

Wallman's study demonstrates the essential message of this chapter: Words are important. This is true even though speakers often choose their words without thinking about them. Lexical study is interesting because words never exist alone textually. They lie nestled in the company of other words, each of which produces its own special

RHETORIC AND POLICY FORMATION

Critical Profile 8.4   Eloquence in Search of an Audience

With Ronald Reagan no longer residing at 1600 Pennsylvania Avenue, the 1990s look to be a lean season for political eloquence. This situation is not without precedent. News commentators paused during 1976 to mourn the apparent demise of public speaking, calling the entire campaign banal and describing the stilted Ford/Carter debates as "an unnatural act between two consenting candidates." Why does the American public have the feeling of being "nibbled to death by ducks, not addressed by titans" in the current age? What is responsible for the decline of eloquence in contemporary public discourse? And what are the consequences of this decline? Barnet Baskerville of the University of Washington addressed these questions in his historical survey of two centuries of American public address, situating current oratorical mediocrity in a cyclical history of rises and declines in American eloquence.

According to Baskerville, eloquence is the essence of persuasion, "the power to move men and women through speech." Driven by "a fusion of thought and feeling, usually arising out of a great moment," eloquence is said to emerge most often in public discourse when called forth by times of grave public crisis. The early 1960s were one such time, calling forth Martin Luther King, Jr., to speak for the civil rights movement. The American Revolution was another time of eloquence. The real revolution, John Adams once stated, was the "radical change in the principles, opinions, sentiments, and affections of the people," a revolution which had ended, he claimed, before the fighting had begun.

From these high-water marks there has been considerable variation in the quality of American public speech over the years. In times of perceived peace and plenty, public discourse has often suffered, consisting of little more than ritual declarations of America's greatness. Yet the history of American public address also shows that vital, policy-oriented public discussion typically returns in times of social turmoil, its passion and eloquence moving people to thought and action.

Public discourse both reflects and influences the public enthusiasms and preoccupations of its era, Baskerville argues, and the public generally gets the level of public argument it wants: "Nixon's no dope," ran the caption of a *New Yorker* cartoon; "if the people really wanted moral leadership, he'd give them moral leadership." According to Baskerville, the current decline of eloquence in American public speech is understandable in the context of historical precedents and is not necessarily permanent. Eloquence will re-emerge when the people demand it. The real question is: What's stopping them?

Profiled by: Elizabeth Macom
Citation: Baskerville (1979)

Critical Profile 8.5   Joe McCarthy and the Verifiably Incredible

---

The period known as "McCarthyism" in the United States has been called, by many, a national nightmare. The avowed Communist-hunter of the 1950s, Senator Joe McCarthy of Wisconsin, still figures as an enigma in American political history. Although thirty years have passed since McCarthy's death, the rhetorical residue of McCarthy's message still troubles political analysts. Nobody has yet found completely satisfactory answers to the questions: Why did McCarthy speak? Why did people listen? In rethinking these events, communication scholar James Darsey of Ohio State University suggests that a key to the puzzle of McCarthy may reside in his use of evidence. That is, McCarthy was a kind of rhetorical "tease," using facts and figures in such a way that he kept the American people constantly wavering between belief and doubt. Creating and sustaining this tension was not easy, however, and so two other elements were needed: the delicate touch of a master tragedian and the special sort of scenery available only in the chambers of the United States Senate.

In post-World War II America, Darsey notes, citizens' basic civic values and commitments were up for grabs. Reeling from a protracted conflagration and lacking the psychological resources needed to make moral sense out of their worlds, many Americans welcomed the unvarnished certainties of McCarthy's politics. In McCarthy's addresses, for example, this certainty took the form of "the objective, the verifiable, the political equivalent of scientific facts." In making his case, McCarthy constantly interjected such phrases as: "Here are photostats of official letterheads . . .", "I have complete unchallengeable documentation . . .", "I have before me an affidavit . . .", "I have before me another document . . .", "The file shows . . .", "I have in my hand . . .", "I hold in my hand official documentation . . .", "Mr. President, I have a file which I desire to insert in the *Record* today, containing photostats . . ."

The presumed, objective certainty of such evidence provided a vital "intellectual" balance to the emotionally spectacular substance of Senator McCarthy's claims. To McCarthy, foreign policy was an "amazing failure . . .", the "picture of treason which I carried in my briefcase to the Caucus room would shock the nation. . . ." When made public, said the senator, one government document would reveal "the astounding position of the Secretary of State," while another would prove to be "incredibly unbelievable" when revealed. McCarthy's basic appeal, therefore, lay in his ability to link the rhetoric of the courtroom to the rhetoric of the laboratory and thence to the rhetoric of the theatre. His documentation appealed to his listeners' highly organized, fact-respecting "left brains," his emotional outpourings to their more spontaneous, affective "right brains." Thereby combining the sobriety of a barrister with the delicate touch of an accomplished actor, Joe McCarthy was a political—and rhetorical—force to be reckoned with.

Profiled by: Susan Whalen
Citation: Darsey (1985)

Critical Profile 8.6   LBJ's War on Poverty: Declared but Never Fought

When a nation goes to war, citizens are often inspired to patriotism, sacrifice, and unified action against a common enemy. On the other hand, during war someone always loses—badly. There is rarely a "partial" victory. According to David Zarefsky of Northwestern University, President Lyndon Johnson's 1964 declaration of "unconditional war on poverty" initially motivated people by stimulating their imaginations. In the end, however, his metaphorical war proved unwinnable.

Of the many factors Zarefsky notes that shaped the Johnson war on poverty in the United States, perhaps the most important was the matter of definition. Zarefsky suggests that the same rhetorical choices that contributed to the early success of Johnson's poverty program (that is, its militaristic "drama") may have influenced the program's dramatic decline. By declaring poverty to be a vicious enemy, the Johnson administration created a sense of urgency about a problem that had not previously concerned most Americans. This sense of passion allowed the Economic Opportunity Act to become law in record time while opponents of the bill looked on helplessly. After all, who could be against a war on poverty?

Once the bill became law, however, it became apparent that the "military" objective had only been defined in vague terms. Thinking of a war is one thing. Fighting one is quite another. Poverty warriors broadened the (originally limited) scope of the program to match the glamorous image of unconditional war. One Senate witness argued: "We don't fight wars on a demonstration basis, suggesting to the opponent that a target area be selected, control groups be established, make a basic decision on which branch of the service is going to be responsible for the war, and then attempt to coordinate the attack by putting 10 federal generals in charge of 86 programs."

Zarefsky shows that while this definitional ambiguity initially had helped to enlist support for LBJ's programs, allowing individuals to see in the war on poverty what they wanted to see, in the actual administration of the program such ambiguity proved fatal, because it allowed the various interest groups to define the war on poverty in their own ways. When the program did not live up to the unrealistically high expectations Johnson's rhetoric had generated, the various factions became dissatisfied and concluded that the war on poverty was lost, thereby insuring, perhaps, that it was lost indeed.

Profiled by: Suzanne M. Daughton
Citation: Zarefsky (1986)

effect and each of which contributes to the overall impact of the message. These streams of words come tumbling rapidly, forcefully, sometimes chaotically, at listeners. At their most powerful, these words become a torrent, sweeping the audience into a sea of persuasion. The critic stops all of this. By examining word choice carefully, often minutely, the critic becomes a spoilsport, refusing to be carried off by an unexamined rhetoric. This is upsetting to persuaders, who prefer that listeners appreciate, rather than study, their words. That is why critics study them.

PART THREE

Specialized Forms of Criticism

CHAPTER NINE

Role Analysis

Good evening. I have just resigned the Presidency, to which I was elected by one of the largest margins in the nation's history. I shall not indulge in the ritualistic hypocrisy of suggesting that my resignation is voluntary. It is not. It has been forced. The force in this instance is as real as if the White House were at this moment under siege by cadres of revolutionary troops with machine guns determined to overthrow our constitutionally chosen government. In this instance, the overthrow has been accomplished by words rather than arms, but the methods and result are identical. The unrelenting battering to which I have been subjected has brought the elected Administration to a standstill. Daily headlines and media reports are as uniformly inflammatory as propaganda designed to incite mob violence. The Congress automatically rejects virtually every proposal of mine because of its authorship, without regard to its merit. Defiance and disloyalty are rampant within the executive. The web now threatens to encompass the secretary of state. I am left with no choice in submitting this resignation. . . .

* * * * * * *

Fellow Americans, I stand before you tonight with a heavy heart. It is evident that my countrymen have lost all faith and confidence in me and my Administration. There is but one thing I now can do for my country, and that is to resign my office—which I herewith do. It is further evident that the responsibility for my failure and disgrace is exclusively my own. I can and will blame no one else. I sought to enlarge the powers of the Presidency beyond anything contemplated by the Constitution and thereby gravely disturbed the balance of the political order. I used the trust and authority reposed in me by the American people to gain special favors for myself and my friends and to inflict penalties on my enemies. I repeatedly deceived Congress and the people. I created an atmosphere in the White House that led unscrupulous associates to commit crimes on my behalf, and when they were threatened with discovery, I did my best to limit the investigation and to cover up their criminality. In short, I sought to remove the American presidency from the constitutional system of continuous accountability and to transform my high office into an elective dictatorship, accountable only once every four years. I abused my power and betrayed my trust. Let my fate stand forever in the memory of Americans as an example to any future President tempted to place himself above the Constitution and the law. . . .

* * * * * * * *

Good evening, ladies and gentlemen, this is your chief executive, Richard ask-me-no-questions-I'll-tell-you-no-lies Nixon, or, as Tricia and Julie call me these days, "Clearasil"—that's 'cause you can see right through the cover-up.

But I wanna tell you, it's really fascinating to live here in Washington. It's the only city where a man can spend one week on the cover of *Time* and the next week doing it.

Why, so many of my advisers are under indictment we're thinking of changing the national motto from "E Pluribus Unum" to "Nolo Contendere." Yessir, you can't say I ran an Administration without convictions. Why, I tried to hold a Cabinet meeting the other day and I was told I had to wait for visiting hours. Whew! . . .

But seriously, folks, I see by the old handwriting on the wall that my time is almost up and I wanna tell you, you're gonna be in good hands with Jerry Ford. You all know Jerry Ford: he's so dumb, when they asked him what to do about the foreign aid bill, he said, "Pay it!" I don't want to say that Jerry is slow, but he thinks executive privilege means a key to the washroom.

Well, before I leave, I just wanna say, to each and every one of you, you've been a great country. . . .

* * * * * * * *

In all the decisions I have made in my public life, I have always tried to do what was best for the Nation. Throughout the long and difficult period of Watergate, I have felt it was my duty to persevere, to make every possible effort to complete the term of office to which you elected me.

In the past few days, however, it has become evident to me that I no longer have a strong enough political base in the Congress to justify continuing that effort. As long as there was such a base, I felt strongly that it was necessary to see the constitutional process through to its conclusion, that to do otherwise would be unfaithful to the spirit of that deliberately difficult process and a dangerously destabilizing precedent for the future.

I would have preferred to carry through to the finish, whatever the personal agony it would have involved, and my family unanimously urged me to do so. But the interests of the Nation must always come before any personal considerations. . . .

* * * * * * * *

I remember my old man. I think that they would have called him sort of a little man, a common man. He didn't consider himself that way. You know what he was? He was a streetcar motorman first, and then he was a farmer, and then he had a lemon ranch. It was the poorest lemon ranch in California, I can assure you. He sold it before they found oil on it. And then he was a grocer. But he was a great man, because he did his job, and every job counts up to the hilt, regardless of what happens.

Nobody will ever write a book, probably, about my mother. Well, I guess all of you would say this about your mother—my mother was a saint. And I think of her, two boys dying of tuberculosis, nursing four others in order that she could take care of my older brother for three years in Arizona, and seeing each of them die, and when they died, it was like one of her own.

Yes, she will have no books written about her. But she was a saint. . . .

Somewhere above is the genuine resignation statement of Richard Nixon, the thirty-seventh president of the United States, who voluntarily relinquished the nation's highest office because some of his more zealous supporters were caught breaking into the Democratic Party offices. Subsequently, the Attorney General of the United States and other highly placed presidential aides tried to cover up the burglary. Eventually, dozens were imprisoned for their crimes, Mr. Nixon resigned from office, and he was subsequently pardoned by his successor, Gerald Ford. But which of the above passages is Mr. Nixon's genuine resignation speech? And how do we know?

The first passage is a possibility, since its language has the formal yet brisk tones of the practiced political speaker. But the passage's hortatory qualities make it seem vaguely unsuitable for the president of a democracy. Its nouns rumble across the text like verbal howitzers being placed in position for battle: "force," "siege," "cadres," "overthrow," "battering." Its adjectives ("revolutionary," "unrelenting," "inflammatory") are more strident than one would expect from a president skilled in political negotiation. Phrases like "ritualistic hypocrisy" and "mob violence" are the language of the firebrand: too hot for a centrist, too self-indulgent for an elected official, too polarizing for a diplomat who opened talks with the People's Republic of China. The language here seems more like that of a radical rightist, one who might have been associated with Senator Joe McCarthy in the 1950s and who still had a chip on his superpatriot's shoulder.

And a rightist it is. The author is Roy Cohn [1974:48], former chief counsel to Senator McCarthy's committee and a notorious anti-Communist. Mr. Cohn had been asked by *New York* magazine to write a resignation speech for Nixon. In doing so, he made the speech more Cohnish than Nixonian. Its distinctive voice is absent in the fourth excerpt, that authored by Nixon [1974a:627] himself. Although a proud man, Mr. Nixon avoided stridency in his speech, in part because he feared legal recriminations and in part because the language of the presidency is a careful language. Roy Cohn, in contrast, felt obligated only to the truth (he wasn't losing *his* job, after all), and so he could vent his spleen. Because he had an audience to worry about, Richard Nixon was cautious ("I have always tried," "I would have preferred") where Cohn was assured; Nixon was abstract ("interests of the Nation," "constitutional process") where Cohn was concrete; Nixon's arguments were functional ("I no longer have a strong enough political base") rather than ideological. As a free agent, Mr. Cohn could shout his message to the rooftops, but presidents are never free agents, constrained as they are by a Constitution and by countless political forces. So, even when resigning a job they dearly love, presidents speak in a muffled voice.

The difference between Cohn and Nixon is one of **rhetorical role,** a regularized set of verbal strategies resulting in a distinctive personal image. The concept of role suggests that, in part at least, many people are the captives of their jobs. Accordingly, the *New York* editors commissioned Roy Cohn because they knew he would play his role as rightist flawlessly. They knew he would submit to **role constraints,** the communicative rules a job imposes on a speaker. Thus, even before the editors of *New York* received the Cohn submission, they knew what it would say. They also knew that the author of the second passage, Arthur Schlesinger [1974:49], would balance Cohn by unfurling the banner of the Left. Mr. Schlesinger's liberal credentials were impeccable: He was a professor, an Easterner, a writer, a former assistant to John Kennedy, and a leader of Americans for Democratic Action. The editors knew that leftist rhetoric is often filled with irony ("I stand before you tonight with a heavy heart"), moral denunciation ("I can and will blame no one else"), overstatement ("my countrymen have lost all faith and confidence in me"), and catch phrases ("unscrupulous associates," "elective dictatorship"). They knew that, even when ghostwriting, Schlesinger would respond to *his* role constraints, not Nixon's. Thus, the editors did not want genuine speeches at all. They wanted a series of role-determined texts that would be predictably different. They knew they could count, oppositely, on both Cohn and Schlesinger.

They also knew they could count on the author of the third passage, Jeff Greenfield [1974:51], although, in his case, they had to count with their eyes closed. As a general political commentator, Greenfield was the wild card in *New York*'s deck, a person unencumbered by ideology or federal office or personal ties with the Nixon family. If he had a role, it was the role of irreverent journalist, a role he plays by latching onto the highly distinctive style of comedian Bob Hope and then eschewing serious politics. Greenfield's passage shows the power of **rhetorical persona,** the complex of verbal features that makes one person sound different from another. Some people, like Bob Hope, have an especially distinctive persona. His famous phrases ("But I wanna tell you") and his standard transitional devices ("and how about that . . .") make him a rhetorical classic, the model for many newer stand-up comics. Greenfield borrows Hope's persona intact and superimposes it upon the Nixon situation, thereby doing both role-switching (a comedian for a president) and generic transference (a monologue for a formal address). Humor is often the child of such rhetorical intermingling.

Because politics is a tinder keg, however, a real president often submerges self to role and speaks conventionally, thereby muting persona. While some situations like press conferences permit more of the person to show through, even there the role (of the president) and the persona (of the speaker) are tied together. Because this is so, the fifth passage delivered by Richard Nixon [1974b:631] to his staff the day after he resigned, is revolutionary. Here we find Nixon the man, shorn of role, groping his way through a set of painful memories as he says farewell to his closest friends and coworkers. The contrasts in persona between passages 4 and 5 are stark, as if two different people had authored them. In a sense, they did, with the politically sensitive, legally aware Richard Nixon authoring the former and a mawkishly sentimental Richard Nixon extemporizing the latter. This latter persona was one that few had seen previously.

This chapter treats the impact of social obligations on discourse, on how roles create rhetorical limitations and possibilities. Jeff Greenfield's role of wry commentator, after all, had both assets (people read what you write) and liabilities (they need not take you seriously). Similarly, a distinctive persona like Bob Hope's or John Wayne's provides instant recognition but also puts one in a straitjacket, which was John Wayne's fate in the 1960s when he temporarily, and unsuccessfully, traded the role of popular actor for that of political commentator by defending the Vietnam war. In addition, we will see here that rhetorical occasions often produce role conflict, as when Mr. Nixon's legal difficulties forced him to become Richard-the-Meek rather than Richard-the-Lionhearted when resigning. In short, this chapter shows how rhetoric is shaped not just by intellectual and linguistic elements but also by *social* demands. To describe people as role-players is not to diminish them but simply to acknowledge that they live in communities.

THE EMERGENCE OF ROLE

If role does not come at birth, it arrives soon after. "Infant" becomes "son" or "daughter" and learns to gurgle or smile on cue. "Infant" also becomes "brother" or "sister" and, despairingly, learns to share. Learning to become a "niece" or a "nephew" is trickier, because aunts and uncles are around infrequently. But these roles, too, are learned and after them "student," "shortstop," "grocery sacker," "best friend," "lover," "lawyer," "homeowner." Each stage of life brings its role, each role a clientele, each clientele a rhetoric.

Rhetorical personae come from many sources. Often, one's **personal rhetorical history** produces a distinctive way of saying things. Being brought up in a particular locale (for example, the Midwest), learning a particular style of speech (for example, folksiness), identifying with a particular group of people (for example, blue-collar workers), having distinctive learning experiences (for example, by becoming an actor), and marrying a particular kind of woman (for example, an actress) can produce an unrepentant liberal like the young Ronald Reagan. But **ideological influences** can also shape the social self. Becoming financially successful, golfing with conservative Republicans, speaking in behalf of the General Electric Corporation, and taking a second, more conservative, wife can produce a sharply transitional Ronald Reagan. And rhetorical role can also be the product of **institutional affiliations.** When making the transition from Hollywood to Sacramento and then to Washington, D.C., Mr. Reagan increasingly spoke in behalf of entrenched social entities (the State of California, the Republican Party, the executive branch of government), entities with longstanding political and rhetorical preferences. Increasingly, his voice became theirs and theirs his.

Mr. Reagan's story shows that the critic has to be careful when doing any sort of speaker-centered analysis, since public people are so tightly role-constrained. This explains the importance of the final vowel in the term persona. Person and persona are not the same. The former is hidden within layers of selfhood, while the latter is presented for public inspection. The American people knew the persona of Ronald Reagan ("the Democratic Party left me, I didn't leave it"), but perhaps only Nancy knew his person. Since a public message is made for a unique audience in a unique situation, it will necessarily bear certain imprints. Thus, the good critic never presumes that a text faithfully reflects the unique mind and personality of its author.

The importance of this notion cannot be overestimated. Too often, critics become amateur psychoanalysts, searching for a speaker's psyche within the metaphors he or she uses. This is a hazardous and unproductive game. Psychologizing about speakers by looking at their public statements is normally both inaccurate and inconclusive. Hart [1986a:286] calls this "personality fixation" and recommends instead that the critic describe a speaker's persona, the person-type the audience is being *invited* to see. Thus, a research question like "What good or evil lurks inside the Ronald Reagan who uttered these remarks?" equates person with persona and hence is unanswerable. But a question of the sort "What sort of person were audiences invited to notice when hearing Ronald Reagan speak?" is answerable, because the critic has Mr. Reagan's explicit and implicit self-descriptions as guideposts. Keeping this biographical fallacy in mind, we can consider several critical probes useful for describing a speaker's persona:

What reasons for speaking are offered by the speaker?

To study claimed motivations is to study the speaker's self-portrait and, hence, the speaker's understanding of audience values. Earlier in this book, for example, we heard Harold Hill proclaim it his solemn duty to stave off the corruption of River City, Iowa. Why a duty and not a whim? What is it about duty-boundedness that sells in Iowa? In his speech, Rabbi Prinz said that he spoke not as a Jew and not as an American, but as an American Jew. Why the double motivation? Would one have sufficed? In his speech, George Patton made no mention of his reasons for speaking. What did his audience make of that? In his resignation speech, Richard Nixon said that he was resigning not for himself but for the American people, that he was doing *them* a favor and that were it his choice (which, of course, it was), he would have stayed the course. Why did he say such complicated things?

As Kenneth Burke [1962] says, motive is never not at issue in rhetoric and that all such situations prompt the question: What is this person trying to do to me? As Arnold [1968] says, motive is especially crucial in oral persuasion. There, the speaker's physical presence and nonverbal behavior (for example, shifty eyes, perspiration) provide personalized information unavailable to the reader. This complicated package of cues brings the humanity of the speaker into the picture more directly, both for good and ill. Naturally, the clever rhetor will try to deemphasize this question of motive, often by providing flattering self-characterizations early in a message. In so doing, he or she also provides an understanding of what it takes to do business with this sort of audience in this sort of culture.

How sharply delineated is the persona of the message?

According to Harrell, et al. [1975], persona gives authority to a text that would otherwise lack it. Earlier, for example, we saw that four of the five "Nixon" personae were clearly etched for the audience. The ideologues—Cohn and Schlesinger—left little doubt as to their feelings. They knew what they knew and made insistent demands on their readers. The Bob Hope persona in Jeff Greenfield's passage was also clear and consistent, as it would be in any successful parody. Mr. Nixon's farewell to his staff, on the other hand, contained a host of characters. It included the rather pitiable momma's boy in the passage quoted, but it also included lucid political reflections, gracious compliments to the Nixon staff, a commentary on Teddy Roosevelt, and a final, meandering dissertation on aging. The personae change rapidly and radically in the text, with Mr. Nixon redefining himself constantly for his audience.

This distinct-but-inconsistent persona contrasts sharply with his indistinct-but-consistent self of the evening before, which was impersonal, abstract, and faintly legalistic, a low-profile image for a high-profile event. Hillbruner [1974] suggests that a critic distinguish in such speeches between the **signature** of the message (verbal tics unique to the speaker) and its use of **archetypes** (cultural stories and traditional languages used by all speakers). In these terms, Nixon's resignation speech was all archetype and no signature. The opposite condition is found in the following variation on a notice that once appeared in a personal column:

> Intelligent guy (38–55) wanted by beautiful woman to love, honor, and obey. Want to leave the hustle and bustle of a superficially glamorous career to raise a family. I'm 35, but can pass for 28. I'm attractive (many say gorgeous, some say cute), sincere, passionate. I like power and settle for nothing less than excellence. I'm also caring, loyal, faithful, monogamous, artistic, spiritual, physically fit, health oriented but indulgent, traditional (I've never written to a personal column before!). Sweet, caring, sexy, bright, demonstrative. Enjoy opera, elegant restaurants, hayrides on starlit nights, goofy affection, Chinese food, satin sheets, bubble baths, Bach, shopping malls, and playing Monopoly by the fire on winter nights. Write on company letterhead to Box 223, *The Times.*

This passage is a benchmark for clarity of persona! Upon reading it, the reader can quickly decide whether or not to pursue the possibility. The self described here is a unity of diversity, all of it well buoyed by perhaps the healthiest ego in human history. Strine and Pacanowsky [1985] describe texts of this sort as having **prominent authorial status,** whereby the author becomes central to the rhetorical action. In sharp contrast is the rhetoric of science, which derives its authority from a distanced, pedantic style containing no self-references or personal reflections. In rhetoric with such **diminished authorial status,** the speaker's faithful adherence to role-constraints, not the speaker's personal flair, provides its suasive force. Critics are now studying the question of which style is least dangerous, the egomaniacal (but ultimately honest) rhetoric seen above or the cool, self-effacing (but remote control) rhetoric of the scientist or bureaucrat. Personal passion or aloof control? The difference is not unimportant.

Does role, not situation, dominate the speaker's message?

This question encourages the critic to track a speaker from situation to situation to find regularities. And it takes a *critic* to do so, since most people pay little attention to their social habits. Even the simple act of raising one's hand in class, for example, marks a learner's deference to the instructor and a willingness to be guided by the norms of politeness. If hand-raising is a product of role constraints, then so too are the infinitely more complex patterns of daily discourse. Hart [1984b] studied these role-related demands by searching for the "natively presidential" features of political language. He tracked the use of ten verbal factors (described in Chapter Eight), comparing Presidents Truman through Reagan to a group of nonpresidents that included preachers, corporation executives, social activists, and candidates for political office. Table 9.1 presents samples from the texts studied.

Table 9.1   Presidential and Nonpresidential Speech Contrasted

Presidential	Nonpresidential
"I have tried to base my decisions and my thinking and my actions on what I think is really best for this country. I believe that is what my country expects me to do" [Johnson, 1966b:659].	"The Democratic Party does not believe that we can hold back and go forward at the same time. We do not believe that we can get ahead by standing still. We do not believe that we can be strong abroad and weak at home" [Johnson, 1960:4].
"We have the chance today to do more than ever before in our history to make life better in America, to ensure better education, better health, better housing, better transportation, a cleaner environment, to restore respect for law, to make our communities more livable, and to ensure the God-given right of every American to full and equal opportunity" [Nixon, 1973b:14].	"There are some threats to our existence which are fundamentally environmental . . . The urbanization problem is so severe over the world today . . . Here is a single example from outside the United States of how we can make very silly mistakes . . . These are the people who are looting and polluting the world" [Erlich, 1972:118–119].
"Now as we strive to bring about that [peaceful] wisdom, there is, in this moment of sober satisfaction, one thought that must discipline our emotions and steady our resolution. It is this: we have won an armistice on a single battleground, not peace in the world" [Eisenhower, 1953:642].	"Mark these words well. This is what the Communists really mean by 'peaceful coexistence.' They do not mean 'peace.' 'Peaceful coexistence' is simply the Communist strategy for world conquest" [Goldwater, 1964:37].

Generally speaking, three features seemed linked to presidential role: (1) **humanity** (presidents used the greatest number of self-references, were most optimistic, and, compared to business executives at least, were more people-centered), (2) **practicality** (presidents used highly concrete language and chose a much simpler style than their counterparts), and (3) **caution** (presidents used less assured language than those running for office and much less than the preachers studied). Not only did these factors distinguish the presidents from the nonpresidents but Lyndon Johnson and Richard Nixon also changed their speaking in these ways when moving from the vice presidency to the presidency.

These findings suggest that the president's *job itself* has rhetorical requirements built into it, dictating that the president humanize highly technical problems and put a happy face on them as well. The president's job also demands language that the layperson can identify with and an avoidance of geopolitical abstractions. Finally, the president must choose words carefully: A Dwight Eisenhower must avoid the formulas of radical politics used by a Barry Goldwater [see Table 9.1]; a Richard Nixon cannot be as pessimistic as environmentalist Paul Erlich; and a President Johnson must personalize issues that a Senator Johnson might have made more general. For several reasons, then, presidents follow a rulebook when they speak, clearly showing how role can dominate person on occasion.

THE MANAGEMENT OF ROLE

Among the most primitive resources in persuasion are the qualities of mind, behavioral habits, and factors of personal appearance that attract people to one another. But like a talented but raw young boxer, one's person must be "managed" if it is to have social effect. Generosity of spirit and a twinkle in the eye cannot advance a speaker's goals if they are not noticed by others. And so rhetoric requires the speaker to make choices in self-presentation and criticism requires the critic to track these choices. Two sets of critical probes are useful for doing so:

What is the speaker's theory of discourse?
How are listeners' and speakers' roles defined in this model?

Everyone has a theory of discourse, whether they know it or not. Mary Poppins's classic refrain, "a spoonful of sugar makes the medicine go down," affirmed that common premises can win over hostile audiences. Similarly, when Harold Hill's fellow salesmen in *The Music*

RHETORIC AND HUMAN PASSION

Critical Profile 9.1   Hitler's Propagandist or Pornographer?

The girl begged for mercy . . . The Jew observed his victim with a sadistic lust. Then he whipped the blossoming white body of the girl . . . until she was silent . . . Then he released the girl, who was covered with a thousand streams of blood, and carried his victim to the bed where he raped her like an animal . . . As the girl left the dwelling of the Jew Schloss that evening, he knew that the girl was now under his devilish power, and was lost eternally to the German race.

Such was the reportage that distinguished Julius Streicher's *Der Stürmer* as "the most infamous newspaper in history." Calvin College's Randall L. Bytwerk, who has chronicled Streicher's career as the most vulgar (and one of the most valuable) of Hitler's administrators, claims that his rhetorical strategies enabled him to spread anti-Semitism more effectively than any other Nazi propagandist. Although he was not directly responsible for atrocities in concentration camps, Streicher, with his "fierce and filthy rag," was "the man who persuaded a nation to hate Jews" and thereby prepared the way for genocide.

Like many propagandists, Streicher had but one argument: Isolated instances of Jewish depravity were evidence of a plot to ruin the purity of the German race, "part in turn of the larger plot to rule the world." For twenty-two years *Der Stürmer* published innumerable variations on this theme. In profane cartoons, photographs, and articles—all no more than embellished shreds of hearsay—Streicher relentlessly accused Jews of the most heinous crimes.

The hallmark of Streicher's allegations was sexual violence. So explicit, in fact, were his accounts of the "racial defilement" of German women that the "citizens of the Third Reich jokingly called him the *Reichspornograph*," or "the national pornographer." Sex was not only an obsession in his rhetoric but also the center of his private life. In 1935, as a direct result of the public hatred aroused by Streicher's portrayal of Jewish sex crimes, Hitler instituted the Nuremberg Laws, which forbade sexual relations between Jews and gentiles.

Although Streicher was executed as a war criminal, his rhetoric, which added a new, sexual dimension to anti-Semitism, has survived. Even today, organizations exist that glorify him as an "educator, writer, and politician" and that reprint issues of *Der Stürmer* in his memory.

Profiled by: Kerry Riley
Citation: Bytwerk (1983)

Critical Profile 9.2   Fire and Brimstone, Anyone?

Why are people attracted to doomsday rhetoric and how does such rhetoric function? These are two of the questions that Ronald Reid of the University of Massachusetts answers in his examination of prophetic writing. He notes that while prophetic writing is popular in fundamentalist religions, it is often ignored by "establishment" scholars, who seem to be particularly uninterested in what he calls apocalypticism—depictions of a horror-filled future in which evil people perish (both actually and spiritually) but in which good people reach their eternal reward. Reid examined the rhetoric of apocalypticism and traced its development through biblical texts and church history. His examination led him to ask why apocalypticism has flourished during some periods of history but not during all.

Reid shows that even though it has been present in some form during all eras, apocalypticism has been "Accepted widely only during periods when substantial numbers of people were dissatisfied deeply with their present and faced with an uncertain future." Reid notes that Daniel, for example, was written during a period when the Jews were rebelling against the tyranny of their Greek rulers. Similarly, Revelation comes from a time when Christians were being persecuted and forced to worship the Roman state. Apocalypticism works in these periods, Reid notes, because the apocalyptic vision "explains the distressing present" and reassures people about the future. In other words, it shows true believers that there is a meaning for the "dark days" and offers a reward, a "utopia par excellence," for their suffering and discomfort.

Despite its recent scholarly neglect, Reid shows that apocalypticism is a potentially powerful rhetorical force in modern culture. Since prophecy has flourished mainly during periods when "people were unhappy with their present and uncertain about their future," Reid notes, "such a situation is not unknown today." Economic worries, cultural diversity, and the threat of nuclear war have created a climate conducive to the rhetoric of prophecy. Reid notes that if the pressures on modern life continue to increase "many who laugh at prophecy today will find it appealing tomorrow." Is it any wonder, then, that one of the best selling books *in 1987* was titled *The Great Depression of 1990*?

Profiled by: David R. Harvey
Citation: Reid (1983)

Man claimed that "you've got to know the territory" they isolated audience analysis as the key to persuasion. And when Eddie Murphy approached the desk clerk in *Beverly Hills Cop* demanding a hotel room he had not reserved, he proved the utility of intimidation. As Johnson [1975] notes, these **implicit communication theories** are just that:

Critical Profile 9.3   Power Talk: Tactics for Hanging On

Groups come and go with the tides of social and political power. But these groups rarely go quietly. In this study, Andrew King, now of Louisiana State University, examines several rhetorical techniques used by established classes, parties, races, and religions throughout history to maintain their power or to rationalize and minimize their declining fortunes. Among these power-maintenance techniques, "Crying Anarchy!" is one of the most powerful options. As King observes, "Most people have a stake in the existing order and when one's substance is being threatened there is an immediate loss of objectivity. To cry anarchy is to do more than brand the activities of the challengers as merely criminal and sinister. As destroyers of society they strike at everyone."

Earlier in American history, Federalists sought to check the rising popularity of Jeffersonian notions of freedom by claiming, "The more free the citizens, the more profligate will be their demagogues." In a similar fashion, modern opponents of equal employment opportunities for women have asserted that women must recognize their own nature or be "forever condemned to argue against their own juices." Those who fought recent Labour government reforms aimed at opening up the elite educational system in Great Britain held that the behavior of the newly admitted students "closely resembles the Chinese Red Guards inasmuch as they have the same objects in mind for destruction: old ideas, old culture, old customs and old habits."

Just as Crying Anarchy helps groups hold on to power, stories of Rebirth and Revenge help them deal with their declining fortunes. The Dakota Indians used a religion founded on a ghost dance to draw on the powers of their ancestors in hopes of vanquishing the white man. In a sharply different context, when confronted with the nineteenth century's emerging commercial order, some uppercrust New Englanders sought to reclaim their power by turning (or returning) to the idyllic Utopianism of Brook Farm. In effect, when people find themselves slipping into irrelevance, they strike out with everything they have, including all of these forms of "emotional logic."

Essentially, King's techniques for power maintenance are conversion devices that help the group in power interpret the contemporary "facts" to their advantage. Through ridicule, for example, those in power attempt to convert challengers into clowns. With the tactic of Crying Anarchy, a challenge to party or policy is rhetorically magnified until it becomes a struggle for the future of the culture. Groups in power have many resources—often including money and guns. As King points out, these groups also have powerful forms of rhetoric to sustain themselves emotionally and to re-secure their positions of influence politically.

Profiled by: John Llewellyn
Citation: King (1976)

implicit. Mary Poppins and Eddie Murphy could not discuss their rhetorical theories with precision, for life had taught them such lessons in its taken-for-granted way. More important, however, Poppins and Murphy *used* these unspoken assumptions when talking, thereby providing the critic with an important, and accessible, object of scrutiny.

Seven such theories seem particularly useful to the critic. For example, Johnson [1975] studied the rhetoric of cabalists, persons who huddled together for fear of worldwide conspiracies. These persuaders operated on a **magical** theory of communication, warning that the forces of totalitarianism were using silent propaganda to undermine people's wills and they colorfully described how their "mindless" neighbors succumbed to these clandestine conspiracies. A related model is more **mechanical** in nature. In it, listeners are warned that society is being worn down by "implements of propaganda" that "overwhelm" the stalwart but "inept" citizen. Within such rhetoric, Benson [1968] found metaphors of poison used to explain why people succumbed to error (they were "helpless" to resist it). With the magical theory, then, the speaker becomes a master wizard who uncovers the vile deceptions of the day. With the mechanical theory, the speaker becomes a kindly but worried physician of the mind who provides the ideological antidote needed for listeners' attitudinal health.

Lake [1983] discusses a third, **experiential,** theory of persuasion. Here, language is seen as an obstacle to truth. Strains of such thought are found in the rhetoric of the American Indian Movement, which argued that the world of words is the white person's world and, therefore, corrupt. These rhetors argue that whites' treaties and conferences have subverted Native Americans and, as a result, that only natural and supernatural forces can be trusted. The persona here is defiant and emotional, a rhetoric suited to insiders. In contrast is the theory of many engineers whose **rationalistic** theory of economic progress often drives their marketing colleagues crazy in modern corporations. When left to their own devices, these engineers create hopelessly detailed manuals for their customers and, when making product announcements at trade shows, rarely mention their personal experiences with the product. The rhetoric their theory produces is, as a result, bland, spare, and remote.

Another popular theory of communication is **parental.** Here, the persona of the speaker is clear and unmistakable, a dominating presence. The image is one of a kindly shepherd leading a flock, helping even the weakest among his charges traverse the difficult course. The speaker operating on this model becomes all-knowing and yet patient, a sage but nonpartisan helpmate to the listener. Leaders of religious and social movements often opt for this image, especially after their movements have reached maturity. Crable [1977] found that Dwight Eisenhower projected this persona and argues that it was the key to Eisenhower's leadership skills during the postwar years.

Speakers operating on the **antagonistic** model of persuasion see the audience as an enemy to be assaulted; submission, not cooperation, becomes the end of rhetoric. The college debater, the rapid-fire salesperson, the Nader-trained consumer advocate, and the fact-spewing trial attorney often project this persona when "attacking the fortress of public opinion." Hart's [1978] study of modern atheists shows this theory in action, with the atheists producing pamphlet after pamphlet, most of which were badly written, poorly documented, and terribly edited but which, as a result, had tremendous rhetorical energy ("We *can* turn the tide!"). The idea here is to produce *enough* persuasion so that religion is washed away in a sea of rhetoric. The logic of this approach also holds that atheistic ideas, even when unadorned, are so powerful that the merest contact with them will produce conversion.

A final, **formulaic,** theory is especially popular today. This model holds that listeners will succeed if they use certain recipes for personal profit. The shelves of bookstores now bend under the weight of these recipes: *Ten Easy Ways to Lose Weight, Dr. Sam's Guide to Instant Health, How to Beat the Stock Market.* The persona here is supremely confident: The formula works for all customers under all circumstances. As a result, people "dress for success," "get it with est," and "feel better with Herbalife." According to Payne [1989], this rhetoric sharply increased during the 1960s, when scores of capitalistic gurus appeared on the American scene. As with other implicit theories, these persuaders endorse a policy ("Reach nirvana, follow The Way") but also peddle a philosophy of listening ("Record this list of tips; don't question them") and a philosophy of life ("Anything worthwhile comes easily").

Most people are unaware of their assumptions about discourse and might well deny these assumptions if brought to their attention. Still, the good critic realizes that to speak is to reveal attitudes—about oneself and one's ideas, but also about one's listeners and what is best for them. The good critic is always on the lookout for such attitudes.

How consistently does the speaker opt for a particular role? What does this show about the rhetorical situation?

Consider the following message:

People today often ask if I mind whether they smoke. No, I don't mind. Because I like the smell of cigarette smoke. I like the way it triumphantly, insouciantly glides through the air.

I like the look and feel of cigarettes. They're streamlined and look like they're weight conscious. There were times when they felt smooth and sexy between my fingers.

One day, I decided to quit smoking. No reason. I just felt like it. At times, I dearly missed that cylinder of tobacco fashionably wardrobed in white.

Just like a modern woman, who fears she's become too dependent on her man, I was curious to find out whether I was liberated enough to live apart from my carton and my lighter. I've been unattached, so to speak, since then. One day, I'll probably renew the relationship. For now, I'm a loner.

On the other hand, my husband will never end his affair with cigarettes. He's devoted to them as deeply and sincerely as he's committed to me. I don't mind. I'm an understanding wife. I know how it is to want something, to find pleasure in it, to be grateful that it delivers on its promises.

I find the odor of cigarette smoke no less appealing than the aroma of perfume. It reminds me that my husband is nearby. The scent teases his clothing and our bed linens. Confidentially, I think it's a turn-on.

Smokers and nonsmokers think I'm strange because I don't object to entering an office where people are permitted to smoke. To me, the smoke creates an atmosphere of industriousness, of assertiveness, and sometimes of a macho presence.

When I stopped smoking, my friends were uncomfortable. "Will it bother you if I smoke in front of you?" they solicitously inquired. I laughed.

"It would bother me if you didn't," I told them. I know what it's like to enjoy smoking yet to feel obligated to deny yourself the pleasure because you're amidst nonsmokers.

When I'm in the passenger seat of our car, I don't order my husband, "Open a window!" When I'm driving, and a friend who smokes is seated alongside me, I immediately put her at ease by pulling open the dashboard ashtray and saying, "Feel free. It doesn't bother me." In those close surroundings, I anticipate the wafts of smoke that will drift my way. Ahhh, yes.

Perhaps I'm merely a temporary ex-smoker. Nevertheless, I continue to be amazed and amused that I offend other ex-smokers when I lean toward smokers, inhale deeply, and say with a broad smile, "Could you blow it in my face" [Sandler, 1987]?

Here is a text to make a contrarian's heart glad. It was published in *Philip Morris Magazine*, perhaps the only available forum for such a set of remarks. Viewed from a strictly argumentative standpoint, the essay says very little. As an "industry" response to the antismoking lobby, it does not comment on health-related matters or on nonsmokers' rights. Although it counters some arguments (for example, that stale smoke smells awful or that secondary inhaling in small spaces is offensive), it does not genuinely debate the issues. Rather, the real news here is the author's **role appropriation.** She presents herself as a *nonsmoker* and hence can adopt a rhetorical posture otherwise unavailable to her. As a "nonsmoker," she can advance the arguments of fair-mindedness, reasonability, and being-a-good-sport without opening herself up to the full savaging of the antismokers.

The author's persona is carefully managed here. She combines modern puritan ("smoke creates an atmosphere of industriousness") with new feminist ("I was curious to find out whether I was liberated enough . . .") and femme fatale ("The scent teases his clothing and our bed linens") but also the little woman ("I'm an understanding wife"). But perhaps the most interesting feature is that this message was published in 1987, when the tobacco industry suffered a sharp drop in profits because of national opposition to smoking. So this text is a case study in rhetorical desperation, a casting off of the traditional role of industry debater for the hydra-headed persona described above. The rhetoric is so obvious that it probably made even the Philip Morris editors blanch when they published it. But the bottom line is the bottom line and desperate people say desperate things. This passage, therefore, establishes an important proposition: role signals circumstance.

Critics have investigated a variety of roles to learn about circumstances. For example, Ware and Linkugel [1973] found that the role adopted above, that of **apologist,** featured four ways of rebuffing attack: outright denial ("I'm not guilty"), bolstering ("We've got better things to be concerned about"), differentiation ("Here's a new way of thinking about it"), and transcendence ("There's a larger principle at stake here"). Along similar lines, Scott [1987] observed that when Senator Edward Kennedy tried to explain the tragic Chappaquiddick affair (in which a young woman drowned), he directed his remarks to the people of Massachusetts (even though the address was televised nationally), thereby claiming the role privileges of a native son. Another study of the apologist by King [1976] detailed the strategies of leaders on the brink of losing their influence. King's study presents a catalog of signals (use of ridicule, crying anarchy, claims of betrayal, and so forth) useful for predicting when power is beginning to shift.

Another rhetorical character is the **agent** who speaks in behalf of some institution. At first, this role seems attractive, since it gives the speaker legitimate authority. But what power gives, power can also deny. As Hart [1971] found, spokespersons for groups like the Mormon Church and the American Communist Party often had to sacrifice their individuality by rarely using personal anecdotes and by quoting heavily from agreed-upon dogma. In a related study, Jablonski [1980] found that when Catholics resisted the reforms of Vatican II in the 1970s,

American bishops increased their use of doctrinal materials, thereby cloaking themselves in the mantle of the Church. Kessler [1981] documents the usefulness of agentry in politics. Surrogates like family members and local officials are often used to try out ideas in a national campaign without the candidate having to take responsibility for those ideas. The downside, of course, is that such agents can misinterpret the party line, thereby creating more trouble than they are worth.

While agents filter their words through revealed truth, the **partisan** strikes out in new directions, speaking the truth powerfully and passionately. For these reasons, partisans prosper during times of turmoil, using their charisma to galvanize public opinion by goading entrenched forces of power. Gregg [1971] notes that such rhetoric is often autosuggestive: Its strong, negative tone better serves to reinforce in-group feelings than to make new converts. Similarly, Woodward [1979] notes that British prime ministers are typically less populist and less conciliatory than American presidents, since British politicians are so tightly tied to their party's apron strings. Even when declaring war, says Ivie [1974], American presidents avoid polarizing language, justifying their decisions on idealistic rather than partisan grounds. The U.S.'s cultural diversity and political complexity, it seems, necessarily removes the color and intensity from institutional discourse.

The role of **hero** is not easy to play, although many try to play it. Ronald Reagan played it better than most. According to Fisher [1982], Reagan's rhetoric combined two key heroic features: a *romantic* quality and a commitment to *action*. One thing a hero does is rescue fair maidens, which Reagan did by reclaiming America's lost loves: the work ethic, moral sobriety, and fiscal responsibility. In a drug-filled, immoral welfare state, Mr. Reagan implied, only a new vision (consisting of many old visions) would do. According to Hankins [1983], however, some heroes are more *ascetic* than Reagan, coming from outside society to reform it internally. Heisey and Trebing [1986] argue that it was Ayatollah Khomeini's unique ability to combine romance, action, and asceticism that let him unseat the staid Shah of Iran. Thus, while it was Ronald Reagan who spoke the following words, he captured the rhetoric of many other heroes when doing so: "So, with the creative energy at our command let us begin an era of national renewal. Let us renew our determination, our courage and our strength. And let us renew our faith and hope. We have every right to dream heroic dreams" [Reagan, 1981a:377].

Whether one attempts to become apologist, agent, partisan, or hero, however, one must bring to that role **emotional integrity** so that its pieces and parts fit together and **dramatic consistency** so that one does not try to become a partisan one day and an agent the next. Role-enactment can fail for many reasons: (1) The role may be played poorly, (2) it may be unsuitable for the times, or (3) different roles may become intertwined. Dan Quayle faced all of these problems during the 1988 campaign when trying to overcome his image as a campus playboy, to cope with his rival's political and intellectual seniority, and to speak for the New Right without forsaking blue-collar support. It is not surprising, therefore, that the 1988 campaign found Mr. Quayle to be strangely quiet. Tracking the maneuverings of people like Dan Quayle can tell the critic much about the theatre of everyday life and about the players who walk its stage.

THE ASSESSMENT OF ROLE

This final section presents two practical ways of analyzing speaker-based rhetorical patterns. Neither approach is especially sophisticated, but together they can round out the critic's analysis of persuasive role. Once again, we will begin our discussion with critical probes:

Does the speaker make *overt* use of credibility devices?
Do these uses vary across time and circumstance?

In September, 1960, John F. Kennedy had a credibility problem: Although his campaign for the presidency was moving apace, he could not shake the charge that his Roman Catholicism would curtail his political independence as chief executive. Because he was heir to several generations of antipapist sentiment in the United States, Kennedy tried to defuse the issue by speaking to the Greater Houston Ministerial Association and thereby making the Catholic issue a nonissue. Kennedy's speech was a remarkable success. Some say it won him the presidency. The speech not only charmed the Texas ministers but also moved the religious issue to the back burner throughout the United States (either by convincing or by cowering his critics).

The speech itself was perhaps less remarkable than the speech-act. Kennedy's willingness to face his detractors in a volatile situation impressed people, even though his message had few rhetorical flourishes. Kennedy began by thanking the ministers for the invitation to speak, commented on several international and domestic problems, and then framed the central issue succinctly: "It is apparently necessary for me to state once again—not what kind of church I believe in, for that should be important only to me, but what kind of America I believe in" [Kennedy, 1960:427]. Kennedy then spoke with unusual

RHETORIC AND EDUCATION

Critical Profile 9.4   When Compromise Means Failure

In 1974, a group of concerned citizens in Kanawha County, West Virginia, tried to prevent the county from purchasing and using "offensive" books in the county's elementary schools. They felt that these books would "undermine the ethical character and social values" of their community and announced "we do not intend to go to Hell, even if the majority of the people vote to do so." Despite the intensity of their protest, however, eventually all of the criticized books were purchased and used. Barbara Warnick, now of the University of Washington, suggests that this failure was an inevitable outcome of "the rhetoric of conservative resistance." Such rhetoric, she says, is designed to "block reform-oriented change" which threatens a conservative group's community values. Using the moralistic rhetoric of the Kanawha book protest as a case study, Warnick shows that one of the most characteristic features of conservative resistance rhetoric is its refusal to compromise.

In this case study, for example, resisters consistently used "unequivocal terms" and pointed to "irreconcilable differences." One leader announced: "There will be no neutral ground. The only way to be neutral is not to have read the books." The moralistic tone of such rhetoric, Warnick argues, alienates audiences, polarizes the issue, and makes compromise impossible. As one conservative resister put it, "He that is not for me is against me." Such a position leads to only two possible outcomes: "complete victory or total defeat."

In practice, Warnick points out, the latter is normally the outcome, since winning genuine acceptance for values in social and political affairs is normally accomplished through compromise and persuasion. Indeed, says Warnick, conservative resisters often fail because their rhetoric blinds *them* to political consequences, making them unable to see the larger political picture. Warnick points out that a narrow rhetoric makes its users susceptible to manipulation by their opponents, who turn the refusal to compromise into a politically disabling tactic. Rather than confront the resisters, she notes, opponents learn to ostensibly give in to the demands of the protesters by merely delaying change. In the Kanawha County protest, for example, the school board agreed to withdraw the most disputed books, "only to return them to the classrooms once the controversy had subsided." In short, rhetoric is sometimes not so much an art of gaining publicity as one of *removing* an issue from public attention.

Profiled by: David R. Harvey
Citation: Warnick (1977)

Critical Profile 9.5   Better Alive Than Read

The ideas and views a lecturer holds on a given topic are not the cards that draw a crowd to his or her performance. In fact, the "text" of a lecture could be as readily conveyed through print or through less formal kinds of talk. The same holds true for the qualifications and personal experiences of the speaker, which could easily be ascertained by reading a bio. Why, then, do people attend lectures? Aside from the university student intent on satisfying a course requirement, why not stay at home and read a good book instead?

The late sociologist Erving Goffman of the University of Pennsylvania claimed that the key to a lecture's success rests on a sort of rhetorical contract subscribed to by the lecturer and audience. The effective lecturer, said Goffman, is one who has "written his reading text in the spoken register; he has tied himself in advance to his upcoming audience with a typewriter ribbon." That is, the effective lecturer generates what Goffman terms "fresh talk"—conversational tokens that convey the impression of immediate responsiveness to an audience. For example, the lecturer might formulate an introduction that acknowledges the special traits of the audience (its gender, its ethnicity, its professional obligations). Alternatively, the lecturer might introduce ironies and sarcasms, irrelevancies and fiendish in-jokes the audience can presumably understand and appreciate. A lecturer can also fib with a wink, milk the audience for a laugh, and engage in asides that otherwise *celebrate the relationship* between speaker and audience.

In doing such things, the lecturer "is conferring himself on those who are participants" in the occasion. That is, the audience senses that it is getting an *exclusive* glimpse into the Self of the lecturer. Because of these special possibilities of spontaneous speech, a social relationship can be forged that could not have been forged had the audience merely read a written transcript of the speaker's remarks. In these ways, the lecturer functions as a "broker" of his or her own text. Fresh talk serves as the rhetorical scaffolding from which the ideas of a speech are hung and it constitutes the real payoff for attending a "live" event.

Thus, the lecturer who thinks that his audience will be satisfied with intellectual bedazzlement, who thinks that fresh talk is unnecessary (given the substance of his or her address), will leave an audience feeling disappointed. As Goffman notes, the audience may even feel that "listening to text transmission is the price they have to pay for listening to the transmitter." In other words, lecturers live and breathe when they lecture. Audiences come to hear new ideas but also to watch this living and breathing. In a sense, then, the simple format of a lecture attests to the essential sociability of the human creature. A pleasant conclusion, it would seem.

Profiled by: Susan Whalen
Citation: Goffman (1981)

Critical Profile 9.6   History As Persuasion

What are the chances that a scholar presenting a paper at an academic convention would have a major impact on America's vision of itself? Slim. But Ronald Carpenter of the University of Florida insists that Frederick Jackson Turner's address, "The Significance of the Frontier in American History," given to a meeting of the American Historical Association in Chicago in 1893, had far-reaching effects on American thought and, ultimately, on national policy itself. Carpenter attributes those effects to the persuasive rhetorical style employed by Turner.

As an undergraduate, Turner had won all of the major oratorical contests at the University of Wisconsin and he brought these skills to bear on his famous lecture. In it, the frontier became the dramatic center of American history—"the meeting point between savagery and civilization." The pioneer was portrayed as an heroic figure of "coarseness and strength combined with acuteness and inquisitiveness" who possessed "that buoyancy and exuberance which comes with freedom."

In large part because of his rhetorical skills, Turner's thesis percolated through American society. Turner had long-term influence not just on the writing of history but also "upon our country's national psychology," says Carpenter. Emulation of the pioneer and continuation of the frontier spirit became a stock argument in almost all American policy debates—from space exploration to gene splicing and from Korea to Vietnam to Central America. The John Wayne image of the frontiersman remains a major feature of U.S. national mythology to this day. That mythology is even projected into the future in popular science fiction epics like *Star Trek* in which an American captain leads his international crew into "space—the final frontier." As Carpenter shows, Frederick Jackson Turner "was indeed instrumental in the development of America's rhetorical vision of itself as a nation and as a people."

Yet, one wonders, why were the American people so ready to adopt the mythic vision Turner offered? Perhaps it was because the immigrant Europeans among them lacked a national mythology rooted *in the land*. Most nations, after all, trace their lineage through family and tribe to the soil on which their ancestors lived. But only the American Indians could establish such ties to a land Europeans called the "New" World. Thus, Turner's frontier myth may have served the function of legitimizing the white settlers' relationship to land that was theirs by taking, not by natural inheritance. The American frontier was thus a frontier only for white Americans. For other Americans, it was a place called home.

Profiled by: Jim Mackin
Citation: Carpenter (1983)

directness about the issues: Would he become a political captive of the pope? Would he encourage mindless bloc voting? Would other religious groups suffer at his hands? No, no, no, he replied.

The second half of the speech was more positive, with Kennedy discussing freedom of speech, the history of religious tolerance, and the sacrifices that had been made for both freedoms: "Side by side with Bowie and Crockett [at the Alamo] died Fuentes and McCafferty and Bailey and Bedillio and Carey—but no one knows whether they were Catholics or not. For there was no religious test there" [p. 428]. In the final portion of his statement, Kennedy made a series of highly specific predictions for his intended administration: No aid to parochial schools, no religious litmus tests on abortion, censorship, or gambling, no untoward alliances with Catholic countries. He concluded his speech with a warning: "If this election is decided on the basis that 40,000,000 Americans lost their chance of being President on the day they were baptized, then it is the whole nation that will be the loser . . . in the eyes of history, and in the eyes of our own people" [pp. 429–430].

When speaking, Kennedy used a number of credibility strategies, six of which are presented in Table 9.2 (a seventh dimension, dynamism, is largely a nonverbal factor signaled by bodily action and vocal activity). While all rhetorical situations involve these dimensions, speaker's *words* perform only some of the work of image-making. That is, credibility is also determined by such factors as human prejudices, the rhetor's sponsor, media effects, the time of day, audience confusion, and so forth. Moreover, credibility bestowed one day is sometimes withdrawn the next, often for reasons having little to do with what the speaker says (for example, the many innocent evangelists who suffered financially because of the Jim and Tammy Bakker scandal in the late 1980s). In short, the devices listed in Table 9.2 are available for control by the speaker but this is not to say that they alone "produce" credibility.

Table 9.3 presents the credibility strategies used by John Kennedy and some of the other speakers discussed earlier. The chart has been produced by using the "Methods of Demonstration" listed in Table 9.2 and searching for sample instances of them in the five messages studied. Nothing like scientific precision is being claimed here, but the results are interesting. Kennedy, for example, tried a bit of everything. He used competence ("the hungry people I saw in West Virginia"), good will ("Today, I may be the victim [of religious prejudice]—but tomorrow it may be you"), idealism ("this is the kind of America I fought for in the South Pacific"), similarity ("I am wholly opposed to the state being used by any religious group"), and even power ("judge me on the basis of my fourteen years in the congress") and trustwor-

Table 9.2   Verbal Dimensions of Credibility

Credibility Dimension	Perceived Capacity	Methods of Demonstration	Example (United Fund Campaign)
Power	Speaker can provide significant rewards and punishments (either actual or psychological) for audience.	(1) Indications of previous victories the speaker has won in behalf of the topic.	"I've had the honor of directing the last three successful campaigns and . . ."
		(2) Suggestions of how listener can share influence already possessed by the speaker.	"I'd now like to pass out the gold pins to the ten-year volunteers."
		(3) Subtle reminders of status differences between speaker and listener.	"Just last week the mayor said to me, 'John, . . .'"
Competence	Speaker has knowledge and experience the audience does not have.	(1) Association with recognized experts.	"Studies of malnutrition by the federal government show conclusively that . . ."
		(2) Unique, personal familiarity with the topic is demonstrated.	"Having worked with the Meals on Wheels Program, I . . ."
		(3) Mastery of relevant technical vocabulary.	"The hospital's new Epidemiology Lab is now complete, thanks to the last campaign."
Trustworthiness	Speaker can be relied upon beyond this one moment in time.	(1) Present and past behaviors are consistent.	"The United Fund stands on its record: low overhead, maximum help to the community."

	(2) Verbal and nonverbal behaviors are consistent.	"A full two-percent of annual salary. That's what I give. Here's my canceled check."
	(3) Explicitly address alternative viewponts.	"Yes, the Harris scandal did set us back. But there are no more skeletons in the closet."
Good will	Speaker has the best interests of the audience in mind. (1) Benefits of speaker's proposal are dramatized.	"People get sick. Those of you who aren't people needn't bother giving to the Fund."
	(2) Reasons for speaker's concern for audience are specified.	"My family's been in town for three generations. *That's* why I kill myself for the Fund."
Idealism	Speaker possesses qualities to which the audience aspires. (1) Socially acceptable eccentricities are revealed.	"Yes, a 'Uni Fnd' license plate is strange. So call me strange. Publicity is publicity."
	(2) Speaker's risks in behalf of the proposal are specified.	"I put in thirty hours a week for the Fund in addition to my regular job. How about you making ten phone calls for us?"
Similarity	Speaker is seen as resembling the audience in important ways. (1) Association with valued beliefs.	"We've got to remember that folks should care for folks. And that's doubly true for folks who have no folks to care for them."
	(2) Disassociation from unattractive beliefs.	"Communism and the United Funds are both collective actions. That's where the similarity ends."

(After Hart, et al., 1983)

Table 9.3   Comparative Uses of Credibility Strategies

Credibility Strategies	Rabbi Prinz	Harold Hill	George Patton	John Kennedy	Richard Nixon
Power	0	9	19	5	1
Competence	44	61	4	22	19
Trustworthiness	0	0	32	8	9
Good will	18	5	26	26	29
Idealism	2	2	9	27	14
Similarity	36	23	18	12	30

(Percent usage in text)

thiness (he cites his previously "declared stands against an ambassador to the Vatican"). Kennedy's speech is quite experimental, since there were no guidelines for handling such an unprecedented situation.

George Patton's situation was obviously more comfortable than Kennedy's so he used trustworthiness heavily. In a sense, Patton's address was a counterstatement to the anxieties his men were experiencing on the eve of battle. He used his longstanding relationship with the military to become part of his men's internal dialogue and to become identified with the emotional life of the foot soldier. Patton also used his speech to empower the troops, explaining that they were braver and stronger than any who preceded them. While Patton used good will and similarity to also show concern for the G.I.s' daily lives, he spent virtually no time on competence, no doubt because he already had a legendary reputation. To have dwelt on his previous exploits at this time would surely have been untoward.

Rabbi Prinz and Harold Hill operated in a remarkably similar manner, a finding that would no doubt be disconcerting to the good rabbi. But their behavior makes sense: Given the time constraints, neither could count on extended interaction with their hearers and, given their status as unknowns, neither could base their case on personal biography. Power, idealism, and trustworthiness were thus eliminated as rhetorical options. So Harold Hill went with what he had—his imagination—and used competence to demonstrate his authority about the wages of sin. He alluded to corruptions found in the pool hall (with its "three-rail billiard shots"), at the racetrack ("some stuck-up jockey-boy settin' on Dan Patch"), and on life's sidewalks ("libertine men and scarlet women"). Rabbi Prinz also used competence but did so far differently: He simply told his own story of persecution. This "I've been there" approach is universally compelling and was especially appropriate for a person trying to build bridges in the early civil rights movement.

Similarity also builds bridges. Prinz offers an almost perfect equation between his life in Nazi Germany and his audience's experiences with racial discrimination in the United States. Hill responds in kind, disassociating himself from middle-American evil (not getting the screen door patched) and associating himself with cherished values and traditions: "Remember the Maine, Plymouth Rock, and the Golden Rule!" As we have seen earlier, Hill's speech is largely a sermonette. The correspondence between its credibility structure and that of a legitimate clergyman like Prinz further attests to Hill's talents at generic transference.

Nobody used similarity with more bathos than Richard Nixon. His hardworking parents, his adorable children, and his wife's cloth coat all came to his aid in 1952. So much similarity produces a syrupy mixture, which may explain why, later in life, Nixon viewed the Checkers Speech as his most humiliating experience in public life. A more expectable strategy was the good will he emphasized during his long-winded paean to his boss: "And remember, folks, Eisenhower is a great man, and a vote for Eisenhower is a vote for what is good for America." Although Nixon also used idealism when reminding listeners of his anti-Communism, he did not do so extensively. Instead, he dwelt on competence by detailing his personal finances. It is this portion of his address that is best remembered, perhaps because it contrasts so sharply with the similarity and good will normally expected in a campaign speech. That Mr. Nixon worked so hard to combine such different appeals surely attests to his moxie, if not his subtlety.

One value of canvassing such strategies is that it shows which aspects of image were *overtly* dealt with by the speaker and which aspects listeners may have supplied on their own. For example, Richard Nixon could have spoken about trustworthiness directly, but since this was the very issue being questioned publicly, he chose a less frontal approach. Documenting his personal consistency over the years or explicating his opponent's charges more completely would have called undue attention to his weakest suit. So he concentrated his efforts elsewhere, hoping that the aspects of credibility he did cover would make the question of his trustworthiness moot, prompting listeners to ask, "How could such a nice young man have done something like that?" That is precisely the response many listeners made to his remarks.

How often does one find self-references in the text?
Why are they there?

I-statements are important because they are not particularly common and because they index a person's feelings and ambitions in especially prominent ways. Some speakers refer to themselves constantly while others never do. What accounts for such patterns? Personality? Social norms? Situation? Do certain rhetorical tasks (being a late-night host on television) encourage self-references while others (being a dip-lomat) discourage them? Why does speaking normally contain twenty times the number of self-references found in writing? Why do presidential campaigners significantly increase their I-statements once elected and why have recent chief executives increased this rate dramatically? [See Hart, 1984b.] Of such questions we have plenty. Answers are less available.

A critic should look with special care at I-statements, since they make special claims on listeners' attention. Even in casual chatter this is true. When a speaker suddenly starts to tell a personal anecdote, listeners' ears perk up as they sense a shift in the discussion. Naturally, their expectations can be quickly dashed if the story turns into a boring monologue. But, temporarily at least, they are open to influence, because identifying with one another is such a basic human instinct.

A useful critical procedure is to extract from a text any phrase or clause containing an "I" and then to lay out these statements one after another (paraphrased, if necessary). Even this simple procedure gives the critic a fresh perspective on the message, as context is torn away and the self is made more prominent. Table 9.4 shows the results of this procedure for an address given by Ronald Reagan on March 4, 1987. This speech was Mr. Reagan's first response to the Tower Commission's report on the Iran-Contra affair. While not charging Mr. Reagan with high crimes or misdemeanors, the Commission did find that the President had been lax in managing those responsible for the arms-for-hostages deal. Because the Commission was a distinguished one (chaired by a Republican) and because its report received ample media attention, Mr. Reagan had little choice but to face the music.

This much-awaited speech cast Reagan in an unaccustomed role—that of apologist—and began a long period of frustration for him as well. To his credit, Reagan accepted a good deal of blame for what went wrong, although he chalked up some of the problem to incomplete reports, faulty memory, irresponsible aides, and general miscommunication. All in all, it was a speech Ronald Reagan did not enjoy giving.

One way of capturing the tenor of his remarks is to categorize his I-statements by means of a crude, but straightforward system consisting of four elements: (1) **emotional/moral action:** the speaker's reports of feelings experienced, moral lessons learned, and hopes and desires for the future. In the Reagan speech, statements 6, 14, 21, 37, and 58 are examples of this type of I-statement; (2) **narrative action:** references to allegedly factual events, sometimes occurring in the distant past, that led up to the speech (exemplified in the Reagan address by statements 1, 5, 16, 27, 35, and 39); (3) **behavioral action:** specific *policy* behaviors the speaker has engaged in immediately prior to the

Table 9.4   I-Statements in Ronald Reagans's Speech of 3/4/87

(01) I have spoken before (from the Oval Office)
(02) I want to talk (to you)
(03) I have been silent (about Iran-Contra revelations)
(04) I guess you're thinking (I'm hiding)
(05) I haven't spoken before (because of sketchy details)
(06) I felt it was improper (to react precipitously)
(07) I have paid a price (for silence)
(08) I have had to wait (for the whole story)
(09) I appointed (Abshire)
(10) I appointed (the review board)
(11) I am often accused (of optimism)
(12) I have had to hunt (for good news)
(13) I will discuss criticisms
(14) I was relieved (by the Tower Commission report)
(15) I want to thank (the panel)
(16) I have studied the report
(17) I accept the Board's findings
(18) I want to share my thoughts (about the findings)
(19) I am taking action (to implement the findings)
(20) I take responsibility (for my actions)
(21) I am angry (about aides)
(22) I am accountable (for their actions)
(23) I am disappointed
(24) I must answer (to the people)
(25) I find secrets distasteful
(26) I told the American people (there'd be no arms trade)
(27) I didn't trade arms for hostages
(28) I undertook (Iran initiatives)
(29) I let my concern for hostages (spill over)
(30) I asked questions (about the hostages)
(31) I didn't ask about the plan (to swap arms for hostages)
(32) I promise we'll try to free the hostages
(33) I must caution (Americans in Iran)
(34) I am confident (the truth will come out)
(35) I told the Tower board (I didn't know about diversions)
(36) I didn't know (about diversion of funds)
(37) I cannot escape (responsibility)
(38) I identify (problems before acting)
(39) I have found (delegating to be effective)
(40) I have begun (to correct problems)
(41) I met (with professional staff)
(42) I defined values (that should guide them)
(43) I want values to guide policy
(44) I told them (integrity was essential)
(45) I want a justifiable policy
(46) I wanted (an "obedient") policy
(47) I told them (freelancing was over)
(48) I can tell you (the NSC staff is good)
(49) I approved (an arms shipment)
(50) I did approve (an arms shipment)
(51) I can't say when (approval was given)
(52) I have been studying (the report)
(53) I want people to know (the ordeal has not been in vain)
(54) I endorse (the Board's recommendations)
(55) I am going beyond recommendations
(56) I am taking action in three areas

Table 9.4   I-Statements in Ronald Reagans's Speech of 3/4/87 *(continued)*

(57) I brought in (a new team)
(58) I am hopeful (that experience will prove valuable)
(59) I am honored (by Baker's acceptance)
(60) I nominated Webster
(61) I will appoint Tower
(62) I am considering other changes (in personnel)
(63) I will move "furniture" as necessary
(64) I see fit (to make staff changes)
(65) I have ordered NSC (to review operations)
(66) I have directed NSC (to comply with correct values)
(67) I expect to have an honorable covert policy
(68) I have issued directives (about covert operations)
(69) I have asked Bush (to reconvene task force)
(70) I am adopting (Tower report's model)
(71) I am directing Carlucci (to improve staff operations)
(72) I have created a post (of legal advisor)
(73) I am determined (to make new policy work)
(74) I will report to Congress (about new policies)
(75) I have taken steps (to implement Board's recommendations)
(76) I have gotten (the message)
(77) I have heard (the message)
(78) I have a great deal to accomplish (in the future)
(79) I want to accomplish much (in the future)
(80) I intend to accomplish much (in the future)

(Paraphrased)

speech event itself (statements 10, 44, 56, 65, 71); (4) **performative action:** a more complex category consisting of references to the speaker's intentions for the speech (statements 13, 18, 24,) or to commitments and certifications being made by the fact of the speech itself (statements 54, 63, 70, 77).

This system highlights the **locus of action** in a text. That is, it describes whether the speaker is being acted upon by events (when the message is high on narratives) or whether the speaker is taking charge (when it is high on behavioral action). The speech Edward Kennedy gave subsequent to the Chappaquiddick tragedy, for example, was almost completely filled with narrative action as the Senator described himself as having been carried away by a rush of events he could not remember. This critical system can also track internal versus external action (Is the speaker a "feeler" or a "doer"?) by scrutinizing the number and types of emotional/moral statements. Finally, the system identifies whether or not the speaker is personally willing to become part of the bottom line for policy initiatives (the number and force of performative statements).

Although Ronald Reagan used all four types of I-statements in his speech on the Iran-Contra affair, the first half of his message was dominated by emotional/moral and narrative action and the latter half by performative and behavioral action. That is, Mr. Reagan commenced his remarks by backpedaling, recounting how the tide of events swept him up: "As angry as I may be about activities undertaken without my knowledge, I am still accountable for those activities" [Reagan, 1987:12]. The locus of *observable* action in the early part of the speech is, therefore, external to Mr. Reagan, while the *emotional* action lies inside, establishing the President as a sensitive, compassionate person ("I let my personal concern for the hostages spill over . . .") who felt deeply about the events of the day but who was not responsible for them.

Reagan corrects this latter error in the second part of his address. There, he takes charge of events by "adopting," "endorsing," "telling," "nominating," "issuing," "creating," and "ordering." Like a phoenix rising from the ashes, Reagan ends his remarks by promising that there will be action, that he is once again in charge, and that his audience need no longer worry. But while the emphasis changes dramatically during the speech, Mr. Reagan never completely abandons the emotional/moral note on which he began. For Ronald Reagan, this was unquestionably the most difficult speech of his life and so he concluded by redocumenting his personal seriousness: "You know, by the time you reach my age, you've made plenty of mistakes if you've lived your life properly. So you learn. You put things in perspective. You pull your energies together. You change. You go forward" [p. 12].

It can also be useful to compare one speaker's I-statements to those of another. Table 9.5 does so by contrasting the Reagan speech to two other apologia: John Kennedy's address to the Houston ministers and Richard Nixon's Checkers Speech. Clearly, all three speakers used a good many I-statements, since each confronted highly personalized obstacles. John Kennedy used the fewest, perhaps because he had very little narrative to describe (unlike Richard Nixon) and no real policy to effect (unlike Ronald Reagan). Instead, he was thrown back on his own moral makeup ("I believe in an America where the separation of church and state is absolute") and whatever promises he could make that would sound believable ("I do not concede any conflict [between church and state] to be remotely possible"). Other than his personal beliefs, John Kennedy had nothing to offer. If the audience did not get to know *him* in the speech, all would be for nought.

Richard Nixon's situation was far different and so his locus of activity differed as well. By doubling John Kennedy's use of narratives, Mr. Nixon tried to establish that he was not an "actor"—that is, that his expense fund had a life of its own and that he was not responsible for the benefits that accrued for him. Mr. Nixon's basic argument was that he had been acted upon by events (even Checkers was sent to him

Table 9.5   Comparative Use of I-Statements

Item	Kennedy (Ministers)	Nixon (Checkers)	Reagan (Iran-Contra)
General information			
No. of Words in speech	1722	4606	2135
No. of I-statements	45	189	80
Words/I-statement ratio	38.3	24.4	26.7
Types I-statements (%)			
Emotional/moral	35.6	30.7	26.3
Narrative	17.8	36.0	22.5
Performative	44.4	24.9	27.5
Behavioral	2.2	8.5	23.8
No. of I-statements/Phase of speech			
Initial 20%	8	28	15
Second 20%	6	33	18
Third 20%	6	42	19
Fourth 20%	9	45	14
Last 20%	16	41	14

without his knowledge) and he followed this line of thought throughout. But his speech is also rather pitiful (some say pitiable), because of its emotional/moral tone, with Mr. Nixon declaring himself in favor of paying his bills, honoring middle-American values, and being proud of his country. To the extent that Richard Nixon could bare his soul, he did so in this address.

In contrast to the Kennedy and Nixon speeches, there is an almost perfect symmetry to Ronald Reagan's I-statements, perhaps reflecting the complexity of his rhetorical challenge. Unlike John Kennedy, Mr. Reagan could not simply claim that his heart was pure (by using emotional/moral statements). A *sitting* president, after all, is expected to be active in ways that a presidential candidate is not, particularly if his personal staff has behaved badly. Thus, policy actions (behaviorals) had to be specified for his audience and there had to be enough of them to make it seem that action of some magnitude had been taken. In point of fact, Mr. Reagan's policy actions amounted to comparatively little: firing some people, hiring some people, and doing a great deal of tongue-lashing. But he ticked off his list quickly, giving listeners the sense that something important was being done.

When his I-statements are examined collectively, then, Mr. Reagan covered the waterfront. His action was both internal and external, theoretical as well as practical. Moreover, his I-statements were spread *throughout* his speech. This, too, is important. It told listeners that Reagan was aware of their concerns and that he had no intention of hiding from his audience. The speech marches along smartly, and personally.

I-statements are only a part of rhetoric and comparatively little is known about them at present. But when examined in the manner suggested here, they can shed light on the motivational dynamics of discourse. Speakers who use a great many self-references hint strongly that a special persona is being created in the texts they produce. They may also hint something of importance about the persons behind the personae, although that is far less certain. Speakers who never refer to themselves also make an important personal statement by not making one, a condition that should be particularly inviting to the imaginative critic. Naturally, tracking such humble uses of language is a speculative business, but if it moves the critical enterprise forward even slightly, it is a worthwhile business.

CONCLUSION

Within one seven-year period, two very different events occurred in the state of Texas. In 1976, President Gerald Ford gave a speech at the Waco Suspension Bridge. His speech was not a magnificent one, but suspension bridges rarely bring forth eloquence. Mr. Ford did his best with the situation presented to him, declaring the bridge "a tribute to your forefathers, their vision, their foresight to have something like this over this great river, the Brazos River" [1976b:1335]. Having made this observation, Mr. Ford could apparently think of nothing else to say and so he thanked the people in attendance and sat down.

Six years later, rock star Ozzie Osbourne urinated on a plaque at the Alamo. Clearly, an ungracious act. Mr. Osbourne's poverty of spirit was explained to him by virtually everyone over the age of nineteen in the city of San Antonio and explained in especially great detail by one irate city judge. What Gerald Ford had given to the Lone Star State, Ozzie Osbourne had taken away.

In this chapter, we have examined the roles speakers play—how those roles come to be, how they are managed, how they can be studied. Although they may not like it, most people play roles. Roles, after all, facilitate social traffic. They help us think of things to say. It is probably true, for example, that even a kindly person like Gerald Ford would have willingly passed up the chance to give his oration at the bridge. But being a trooper he carried on, appropriating a ceremonial role that he might have used previously at the opening of a new restaurant in Idaho or with the fishing fleet in Massachusetts. His persona was friendly, engaging, and respectful and he carried it off without a hitch. His audience in Waco probably knew that he was playing a role but they hardly minded. After all, it was *their* bridge built by *their* ancestors that *their* president had come to commemorate. Mr. Ford's role, in effect, was owned by his audience as well.

As mentioned earlier, it is *motive* that listeners are keen to discover in almost any rhetorical situation. Speakers use roles to help listeners assign them proper motives. This was, among other things, Ozzie Osbourne's problem at the Alamo. Had he been some unfortunate derelict who in a state of inebriation had relieved himself, Osbourne might well have escaped San Antonians' wrath. But Osbourne had motive going for him, or against him. The irreverent persona he had so carefully nurtured over the years via his bizarre stage antics, his antisocial lyrics, and his satanic costuming made it rhetorically impossible for him to claim uncontrollable bladder problems. Osbourne had long since established a *purposive* image and no amount of explaining could make it seem otherwise. That which he had worked so hard to create over the years—persona—and that which he paid his staff thousands of dollars a year to manage for him—role—was the same thing that made him a cause célèbre on that fated evening in Texas. Like Frank Sinatra before him, Ozzie Osbourne did it his way.

CHAPTER TEN

Cultural Analysis

The United States dollar took another pounding on German, French and British exchanges this morning hitting the lowest point ever known in West Germany. It has declined there by 41% since 1971 and this Canadian thinks it's time to speak up for the Americans as the most generous and possibly the least appreciated people in all the earth.

As long as 60 years ago when I first started to read newspapers, I read of floods on the Yellow river and the Yangtze. Who rushed in with men and money to help? The Americans did. They have helped control floods on the Nile, Amazon, the Ganges and the Niger. Today the rich bottom land of the Mississippi is under water and no foreign land has sent a dollar to help. Germany, Japan and to a lesser extent Britain and Italy were lifted out of the debris of war by the Americans who poured in billions of dollars and forgave other billions in debts. None of these countries is today paying even the interest on its remaining debts to the United States. *When the franc was in danger of collapsing in 1956, it was the Americans who propped it up,* and their reward was to be swindled on the streets of Paris. I was there. I saw it.

When distant cities are hit by earthquakes, it is the United States who hurries in to help. Managua, Nicaragua is one of the most recent examples. So far this spring, 59 American communities have been flattened by tornadoes. Nobody has helped.

The Marshall Plan, the Truman Policy all pumped billions upon billions of dollars into discouraged countries. Now newspapers in those countries are writing about the decadent, warmongering Americans. I'd like to see just one of those countries that is gloating over the erosion of the United States dollar build its own airplane. Come on, let's hear it. Does any other country in the world have a plane to equal the Boeing Jumbo Jet, the Lockheed Tri-Star or the Douglas 10? If so, why don't they fly them? Why do all international lines except Russia fly American planes? *Why does no other land on earth even consider putting a man or woman on the moon?*

You talk about Japanese technocracy and you get radios. You talk about German technocracy and you get automobiles. You talk about American technocracy and you will find men on the moon—not once, but several times and safely home again . . .

I can name you 5,000 times when the Americans raced to the help of other people in trouble. Can you name me even one time when someone else raced to the Americans in trouble? I don't think there was outside help even during the San Francisco earthquake. Our neighbors have faced it alone and I'm one Canadian who's damned tired of hearing them kicked around. They will come out of this thing with their flag high and when they do they are entitled to thumb their nose at the lands that are gloating over their present troubles [Sinclair, 1973].

These are the 1973 observations of Gordon Sinclair, a radio personality for station CRFB in Toronto, Canada. When he made these remarks, the United States faced inflation at home and an unfavorable dollar abroad. Unemployment was high and America's superiority in manufactured goods and natural resources was being questioned. The Vietnam war had cost the U.S. considerable prestige in the eyes of Europeans and the Watergate affair was beginning to unravel the Nixon administration. 1973 was not a happy time for the United States and so Gordon Sinclair spoke up for his neighbors during a daily radio commentary.

Sinclair's impact was immediate and dramatic. The full text of his remarks was reprinted in full in many American newspapers and commented upon in virtually all. U.S. radio stations reran his commentary for days on end; television stations conducted endless interviews with him; Sinclair received 50,000 letters of appreciation from U.S. citizens; and Westbound Records eventually distributed a recording of the Sinclair apologia. What accounts for this reaction? What made Sinclair's pedestrian philosophizing so attractive to so many Americans?

Above all, they liked his speech-act, a fearless, assaultive, unexpected, last-minute rescue of an increasingly embattled nation. They also liked his style. It was simple, hard-hitting, unembellished, concrete, and concise, five adjectives often used to describe the American people themselves. They also liked the Sinclair persona, an independent, blue-collar tough guy: John Wayne, Rocky Balboa, and Ross Perot rolled into one.

But the most important feature of Sinclair's statement was his evidence. He did not praise the United States for its educational system, the goodness of its people, its artistic and cultural achievements, or its democratic form of government. Rather, he burrowed into the fundaments of the culture for his central argument: Entrepreneurship makes the U.S. a great nation. It was American money, not American missionaries, he mentioned in connection with Africa. It was American technology, not American diplomacy, he mentioned in connection with the Soviet Union. It was American engineering, not American science, he mentioned in connection with the space program. Sinclair's homage was based not in ethics or social theory but in war reparations, airline safety, moon walks, dam building, and earthquake relief.

Sinclair complimented the American people just as they compliment themselves: for what they have *done*. When listening to Sinclair, Americans remembered seventeenth-century Puritans carving out communities on the windswept Atlantic coast, eighteenth-century farmers venturing into the wilderness, plowing the land with hand-fashioned tools, and nineteenth-century miners and ranchers settling the American West. Because these experiences required them to "face it alone," they, like Sinclair, get "damn tired" of being "kicked around." Yet their supreme confidence ultimately sustains them, allowing them to hold "their flag high" and "thumb their noses" at their detractors. And because the U.S. still has a kind of national chip on its shoulder, Americans are especially delighted when someone like Gordon Sinclair, a citizen in a faintly Eurocentric culture, defends them in the very language they would have selected themselves.

This chapter holds that rhetoric never escapes the influence of culture. While Henry Higgins may have changed some of Eliza Doolittle's speech patterns in *My Fair Lady*, he never changed the engine that drove her language: her feelings, values, and cultural experiences. In the play, Eliza became less a Cockney speaker, but she always remained, in part, a Cockney thinker. This did not make her less of an individual, but it did make her an individual *somewhere*. It is Eliza's somewhere that the cultural critic studies.

Because so much past research has focused on American culture, that culture will be our special focus here. But everyone, everywhere, imbeds culture into their language. Three of these imbeddings are especially important in criticism:

1. Values: deep-seated beliefs about right and wrong that express a person's basic life orientation;
2. Myths: Master stories describing exceptional people doing exceptional things that serve as moral guides to proper action;
3. Fantasy themes: abbreviated myths whose story lines hint at an idealized (not necessarily ideal) set of conditions.

While these elements will be separated for ease of discussion here, they almost always work together. For example, the values Gordon Sinclair champions—charity, technology, freedom of speech—are drawn from the very sinews of the American value system. In that sense, Mr. Sinclair said nothing new when he spoke, but he did say something old in a wonderfully new way. Similarly, he used a number of ancient myths. As a practical art, rhetoric rarely develops these myths as explicitly as do literature, theatre, or film. Instead it uses mythic abbreviations as, for example, when Sinclair drew upon exploration myths (the moon landing), the Good Samaritan myth (floods on the Yellow River), and the savior myth (the Marshall Plan).

But full mythic development takes time and in the world of practical persuasion time is a luxury. So fantasy themes, a kind of mythic shorthand, become its workhorse. Fantasy themes are *fantasies* because they point to an idealized world and *themes* because they are popular, repeated understandings of what such a world is, was, or will be like. So, for example, Gordon Sinclair imagines Europe without American aircraft, Africa without American relief assistance, Paris without American capital, Israel without U.S. materiel. These are the tales Americans tell each other constantly, especially when they are disgruntled or feel unappreciated. In repeating them, Gordon Sinclair became an American for a day.

After peeling away culture from a text, there is often no text left. Our cultural assumptions and treasured stories are so deeply ingrained that we become mute without them. One cannot, for example, appreciate the masculine, hyperactive tone of Saturday morning cartoon shows unless one understands that they were produced in a nation led, historically, by hyperactive males. Fortunately, even the most sophisticated persuaders carry their culture absentmindedly. That is a real boon to the rhetorical critic, who tries to look through message to culture and hence to the roots of persuasion itself.

VALUES: THE BEGINNINGS OF CULTURE

What tells us that a person is a good citizen? The *Webelos Scout Book* says there are "a few signs":

- He obeys the law. If he thinks a law is wrong, he tries to have it changed. He does this by telling people who are elected to make laws.
- He respects the rights of others. He does not try to get special privileges for himself.
- He tries to be fair and honest with everyone.
- He tries to make his country or town a better place.

- If in school, he "does his best" to learn all he can about his country.
- If grown up, he learns all that he can about his government. Then he votes on election day [Webelos, 1979:71].

Litanies like this tell children about their culture, about who they are and are not. The very speech-act of hawking values like honesty and participatory democracy says something important about Americans. It says that values can be *taught*, like mathematics, iambic pentameter, or metal fabricating. Americans, like other Westerners, are linear thinkers and, hence, linear teachers. They become impatient with the elliptical modes of instruction found in the Orient, or with the patriarchal lectures of kinship cultures, or with the experiential teachings of hunting and fishing societies. Americans believe that even value-based instruction can be systematized and delivered efficiently. Their radical notion of universal public education was based on this very premise, so it makes sense to them to teach values to children just as they teach them to drive a car.

Americans are impatient with metaphysics. They believe that a question like "What is a good citizen?" can be answered clearly and behaviorally. They believe that the *act* of voting on election day is important, no matter what brand of madness may lie in the voter's head. They believe that any town can be made "a better place" by human effort. The skyscrapers, hydroelectric dams, and interstate highways they have built stand as their evidence for such claims. Unlike Islamic fundamentalists, they believe that governance is a cognitive matter, not an emotional one, and that learning "all he can about his country" will serve a citizen best. Americans were brought up on change and stimulated by it as well. They believe that if a person "thinks a law is wrong," that law can be altered just as easily as one's name, one's spouse, or one's brand of deodorant. No matter what the evangelical Christians among them argue, Americans are "evolutionists" of the first order.

So the *Webelos Scout Book* tells a simple yet complex story. Like all effective rhetoric, it wears its values on its sleeve and dares the critic to find them. Cultural analysis is, therefore, a subtle business, for it focuses on the *presuppositions* imbedded in discourse, on its *nonargued* premises, on its *taken-for-granted* assumptions. The cultural critic looks at a message once, and then twice, and then once again, because values are sometimes so deep-seated that they seem nonexistent, so integrally a part of the text that they seem irrelevant to it.

This was the experience of Lewis [1972], who did a careful analysis of some three hundred letters of recommendation written for applicants to graduate school (in sociology) and for faculty positions (in chemistry) at such institutions as Cal Tech, Chicago, Berkeley, Harvard, Minnesota, among others. Here are some of the statements he sampled:

1. He is a very serious and determined student of sociology. In most assignments he goes beyond the call of duty [by producing] more than is expected [p. 22].
2. Although she is rather short, she compensates by drive and perseverance and usually attains her goal [p. 22].
3. He is the oldest son in a family wherein the mother is widowed and has contributed substantially to his own education through outside work [p. 22].
4. He has a good sense of humor which is often masked by his usually serious manner [p. 26].
5. There is no question about the fact that he was one of the best liked of our students. He is mature and reserved, yet very friendly and cooperative [p. 25].

Lewis titled his study "On the Genesis of Gray-Flanneled Puritans," but he could just as easily have titled it "The *Webelos Scout Book* Revisited." We see in these endorsements of modern scientists very little that is modern and even less that is scientific. What we do find are American values writ large: effort, stability, overcoming great odds, teamwork, likability. The ghosts of Horace Greeley and Horatio Alger beckon here and there is something of Beaver Cleaver as well. Lewis was distressed by what he found. He warns that replacing traditional scholarly qualities with "the social ethic" and judging professionals' "whole beings" rather than their work could populate universities with personable but incompetent faculty members.

Lewis may be right, but his letter writers used the only language they knew, the language of their culture. Values, it appears, seep inevitably into a society's rhetoric. White [1949] discovered, for example, that Adolph Hitler denied *no* democratic values when speaking to the German people, even though his political actions embraced none of those values. Culture, it appears, preshaped Hitler's remarks, preventing many people from reading between his lines. A similar effect was noted by Prothro [1956], who found that the rhetoric of Franklin Roosevelt's New Deal gained such cultural significance that even a decade after his death it could be found in the speechmaking of Dwight Eisenhower, a person who differed substantially from Roosevelt on many political issues. And Jewett [1973] reports that the Puritan image of America-as-Redeemer-Nation protracted the Vietnam war for many years so that the nation's self-righteous, millennial rhetoric would have its teeth preserved. To retreat from the war, says Jewett, would have been "fiercely resisted and bitterly resented by Americans," because it would have threatened their "mythic base of moral superiority" [p. 222].

Although it is risky to present a list of values for some two hundred and twenty million people, Table 10.1 attempts just that. The list is based on work done over thirty years ago by Minnick [1957] (and by Spranger before him), but it does not differ substantially from the observations of Alexis de Tocqueville, who traveled among the American people in the 1830s. The key test of such a list is whether or not it seems "familiar" to members of the culture. Admittedly, there are things to argue about here: Is economic success alone valued in the United States? Are family values as strong today as they were earlier? Is government still "naturally inefficient"? While some of these values may have waxed and waned over the years, they should still be holding fast if they are, in fact, *basic* life orientations.

When Minnick updated this list of values in the 1950s, he could not have predicted that Americans of the 1980s and 1990s would be purchasing Japanese automobiles, listening in rapt attention to Oliver North's testimony, or coping with waves of Cuban refugees in Miami. But knowing that Americans value efficiency, that they like male ambition, and that they respect minority rights, Minnick might well have guessed at such contemporary events. Thus, because Minnick's schema seems to have long-term appropriateness, it can be used as a checklist for discovering the value emphases in a particular text.

For example, Gordon Sinclair's radio broadcast was, in many senses, a prose version of Minnick's list. Although Sinclair does not touch upon aesthetic values, he otherwise touches many bases, commending the American people for their scientific achievements, their generosity of spirit, their hard work and perseverance, and their sense of justice. Similarly, Lewis's [1972] letters of recommendation seem to have been generated by using Minnick's list as a kind of artificial intelligence system: II.6 + IV.4 + VI.3 = a letter of recommendation. This seems particularly true when examining the unfavorable letters Lewis studied:

1. He is an individual capable of working long hours at his chemistry, with the aid and encouragement of his splendid wife. . . . But I believe he has dissipated a good deal of his energy in nonscientific endeavors—including two unsuccessful and disruptive marriages and a substanial business venture [p. 28].
2. She was something of a "wheeler-dealer" in student politics, and as a result may not have been too well-liked by some of her peers [p. 24].
3. The only objectionable feature that I have noted is that this last semester he has raised a beard. I thought his appearance with-

Table 10.1   A Catalog of American Values

I. Theoretic Values of Contemporary Americans

1. Americans respect the scientific method and things labeled scientific.
2. They express a desire to be reasonable, to get the facts and make rational choices.
3. They prefer, in meeting problems, to use traditional approaches to problems, or means that have been tried previously. Americans don't like innovations, but, perversely, they think change generally means progress.
4. They prefer quantitative rather than qualitative means of evaluation. Size (bigness) and numbers are the most frequent measuring sticks.
5. They respect common sense.
6. They think learning should be "practical," and that higher education tends to make a man visionary.
7. They think everyone should have a college education.

II. Economic Values of Contemporary Americans

1. Americans measure success chiefly by economic means. Wealth is prized and Americans think everyone should aspire and have the opportunity to get rich.
2. They think success is the product of hard work and perseverance.
3. They respect efficiency.
4. They think one should be thrifty and save money in order to get ahead.
5. Competition is to them the most important aspect of American economic life.
6. Business can run its own affairs best, they believe, but some government regulation is required.
7. They distrust economic royalists and big business in general.

III. Aesthetic Values of Contemporary Americans

1. Americans prefer the useful arts—landscaping, auto designing, interior decorating, dress designing, etc.
2. They feel that pure aesthetics (theatre, concerts, painting, sculpture) is more feminine than masculine and tend to relegate the encouragement of them to women.
3. They prefer physical activites—sports, hunting, fishing, and the like—to art, music, literature.
4. They respect neatness and cleanliness.
5. They admire grace and coordination, especially in sports and physical contests.
6. They admire beauty in women, good grooming and neat appearance in both sexes.
7. They think many artists and writers are queer or immoral.
8. They tend to emphasize the material rather than the aesthetic value of art objects.

IV. Social Values of Contemporary Americans

1. Americans think that people should be honest, sincere, kind, generous, friendly, and straightforward.
2. They think a man should be a good mixer, able to get along well with other people.
3. They respect a good sport; they think a man should know how to play the game, to meet success or failure.
4. They admire fairness and justice.
5. They believe a man should be aggressive and ambitious, should want to get ahead, and be willing to work hard at it.
6. They admire "a regular guy" (one who does not try to stand off from his group because of intellectual, financial, or other superiority).
7. They like people who are dependable and steady, not mercurial.
8. They like a good family man. They think a man should marry, love his wife, have children, love them, educate them, and sacrifice for his family. He should not spoil his children, but he should be indulgent with his wife. He should love his parents. He should own his own home if possible.
9. They think people should conform to the social expectations for the roles they occupy.

Table 10.1 *(continued)*

V. Political Values of Contemporary Americans

1. Americans prize loyalty to community, state, and nation. They think the American way of doing things is better than foreign ways.
2. They think American democracy is the best of all possible governments.
3. They prize the individual above the state. They think government exists for the benefit of the individual.
4. The Constitution to the American is a sacred document, the guardian of his liberties.
5. Communism is believed to be the greatest existing menace to America.
6. Americans believe the two-party system is best and should be preserved.
7. They think government ownership in general is undesirable.
8. They believe government is naturally inefficient.
9. They think a certain amount of corruption is inevitable in government.
10. They think equality of opportunity should be extended to minority groups (with notable minority dissent).

VI. Religious Values of Contemporary Americans

1. Americans believe Christianity is the best of all possible religions, but that one should be tolerant of other religions.
2. They think good works are more important than one's religious beliefs.
3. They believe one should belong to and support a church.
4. God, to most Americans, is real and is acknowledged to be the creator of the universe.
5. They think religion and politics should not be mixed; ministers should stay out of politics, politicians out of religious matters.
6. Americans are charitable. They feel sympathy for the poor and the unfortunate and are ready to offer material help.
7. They tend to judge people and events moralistically.

(From Minnick, 1968:218–220)

> out the beard was very nice. I do not know how permanent the
> beard is. Otherwise I am sure you would be well pleased with
> him in this position [p. 26].

Comments like these clearly created rhetorical problems for the three job-seekers. No longer could student 1 present himself as "steady and dependable" (in Minnick's terms), nor could student 2 characterize herself as a "good mixer." Student 3 has a special problem, since, because of his beard, he will be judged deficient in "good grooming" at best or "queer and immoral" at worst. Perhaps the most interesting feature of such value-based remarks is *how automatically* and *how confidently* the letter writers offered them, as if the warrants legitimizing them were beyond question. For many recipients of these letters, they probably were.

This same confidence is found in the rhetoric of Norman Vincent Peale, a cleric who for fifty years offered advice through his radio talks, television appearances, books, newsletters, handouts, prayer cards, and pamphlets. Peale was as much a minister to the nation's psyche as to the nation's soul and his rhetoric was pure Americana. One of his pamphlets, "Help Yourself with God's Help," lists ten steps for problem-solving. These are the first four:

1. **Seeds:** The way to start out in solving a problem is to entertain a solid belief that for every problem there is a solution. Indeed, every problem contains the seeds of its own solution. You can find the answer to your problem if you look deeply into the problem itself.
2. **Calm:** A basic premise for solving a problem is to remain emotionally calm. Uptightness can block off the flow of thought power. And therefore it is important to reduce the stress and tension elements, for the mind can only operate efficiently when the emotions are under control.
3. **Assemble:** In dealing with a problem a proper procedure is to assemble all of the facts connected with it. Then deal with those facts impartially, impersonally, and judicially. Take a scientific attitude toward the elements of the problem.
4. **Paper:** Lay out all of the component parts of the problem on paper, so that you can see them in orderly coherence. Such a procedure will help to clarify your thinking by bringing the various factors of a problem into systematic order. Being able to see clearly, you will be better able to think clearly [Peale, 1977:10].

Peale's approach is interesting on a number of fronts. For one thing, he provides an enumerated list, thereby displaying the preferred Western logical form. Also, the steps he lists are behavioral, things to do. It is interesting, for example, that he urges putting things on paper *before* seeking intuition (which he lists as step 8) or tapping one's creativity (step 10). The fact-gathering he endorses (step 3) is well aligned with the preferred "scientific" approach to problem-solving found in Minnick's list, as is the "calmness" Peale urges in step 2. All of these features are subsidiary to step 1, however, which is the most American feature of all: confidence that every problem can be solved. It is Peale's faith in hope that made him one of the nation's most popular ministers, the mold out of which recent "Happy Face Preachers" have been cast.

A culture's values are often best seen in contrast. Unlike the brooding of German literature, for example, American literature is expansive, not darkly reflective. Unlike the tartness of British humor, American comedy is lighthearted, not bitter. Unlike the cacophony of Italian politics, American politics is measured, not insurrectional. There is nothing inevitable or invariable about such trends, but they are trends, and anyone who stands against them takes on a special rhetorical burden in the United States.

In July, 1979, Jimmy Carter [1979] shouldered this burden when he made a nationwide address to describe a "crisis of confidence" and to correct a "national malaise." He spoke after having spent ten days secreted away at Camp David with business and labor leaders, teachers, members of the clergy, mayors, and other private citizens. The results of his deliberations were presented in prime time and included the following statements:

- I want to talk to you right now about a fundamental threat to American democracy [p. 1236].
- [We have] a crisis of confidence. It is a crisis that strikes at the very heart and soul and spirit of our national will [p. 1237].
- Our people are losing . . . faith, not only in government itself but in the ability of citizens to serve as the ultimate rulers and shapers of our democracy [p. 1237].
- Too many of us now tend to worship self-indulgence and consumption. Human identity is no longer defined by what one does but by what one owns [p. 1237].
- There is a growing disrespect for government and for churches and for schools, the news media, and other institutions [p. 1237].
- The gap between our citizens and our Government has never been so wide [p. 1238.]

In some ways, Jimmy Carter's speech was brave and in some ways it was foolish. When fashioning it, Mr. Carter obviously consulted neither Minnick's list of values nor Peale's recipes for happiness. It was as if the President wished to call the entire American value system into question: its economic basis for success, its sense of self-destiny, its political traditions. To say the least, his address was a resounding flop. The speech came to symbolize not what was wrong with America but what was wrong with Jimmy Carter: too philosophical for a practical people, too introspective for an outward-looking nation, too melancholy for a country of idealists. Ronald Reagan came along just in time to change all of that and *his* rhetoric was the reciprocal of Carter's. Reagan could recite Minnick's list of values by heart. Throughout his administration, Mr. Reagan often did.

Part of Jimmy Carter's speech was quite orthodox, however. While its first half was ruminative, its second half dealt with U.S. energy supplies. In the second half, Mr. Carter presented a summary of conservation policies, an inventory of alternative fuels, and a program for inaugurating the nation's first solar bank. In discussing these matters, Carter was precise and efficient, a style that differed sharply from his earlier philosophizing. How can two such different tones be merged in the same text? How can a speaker move from a discussion of essence to a discussion of shale oil?

Several scholars feel that American rhetoric is distinguished by its blend of **transcendental** and **pragmatic** themes. Kristol [1972] says that the transcendental themes come from the "prophetic-utopian" strains of colonial religion and the pragmatic themes from the rugged mercantilism also motivating the nation's early settlers. Arnold [1977] observes that almost every major debate in American history has borne witness to this struggle between doing the will of the Lord and doing business. The statement Brinton [1938:34] makes about all revolutions—"grievances, however close they are to the pocketbook, must be made respectable, must touch the soul"—has been especially true in the United States, a nation that seems to need a holy purpose for doing almost anything. Jimmy Carter appeared to realize this when he fashioned his energy sermon. While his particular recipe did not work on that occasion, the ingredients he chose were American staples.

The transcendental strain gives discourse an elevated tone. On inauguration day, for example, Americans have been told that they are the guarantors of a "free world," inventors of a "new deal," explorers of a "new frontier." These rich abstractions were, in each case, attended by the levying of new taxes, a bitter shot of pragmatism. But the transcendental chaser helped people swallow it. It helps them swallow a good deal more as well. For example, Solomon's [1983] study of TV evangelist Robert Schuller finds him at the center of the American mainstream with his "get rich/get God" formula. Solomon notes that Schuller has been unusually effective in blending transcendental and pragmatic themes and quotes from him as follows:

> Why should a person strive for success? Isn't that a pretty selfish objective? No, for when we succeed, whether it's in school, marriage, business, or social services—we inspire others to try to win, too . . . *We have a stewardship to attempt to succeed for the glory of God and for the inspiration of others!* Success is not a selfish objective, for there is no way you can succeed unless you find a need and fill it, find a hurt and heal it, find a problem and solve it! . . . Success is *being the person God wants you to be* [p. 179].

The blessing Schuller bestows on American pragmatism is not unique. Clergymen in the United States prominently "preached up" the Revolutionary War [Kerr, 1962], the Civil War [Stewart, 1969], and World War I [Abrams, 1933] and did so less prominently during more recent conflagrations.

In much American rhetoric, then, the critic will find both transcendental and pragmatic forces at work. Smith [1980] even found them when investigating the lyrics to some 2300 country music ballads, many of which depicted a struggle between the transcendental values of life in the South (close family ties, natural beauty, strong religious values) and the pragmatic wisdom of migrating to the North (often depicted as cold but efficient, a source of jobs but also a source of sin). This same struggle was noticed by Frentz and Farrell [1975] in their analysis of *The Exorcist*, a movie that portrays a classic conflict between transcendence (in the person of Father Karras, the exorcist) and scientific pragmatism (or positivism) in the person of the psychiatric community. The authors argue that the popularity of the film in the 1970s signaled America's need to turn away from the pragmatic tragedies of air pollution, presidential assassinations, Vietnam, the rise of pornography, Watergate, and so forth.

While other cultures also blend pragmatic and transcendental themes, the U.S. has had a special need to *balance* them, often doing so during religious and secular rituals. But why? One reason is that Americans are almost completely heterogeneous. Deprived of common ethnic roots, a universal religion, or a monarchial tradition, Americans have long been susceptible to discussions of transcendental purpose. But it is also because they *lack* these common ties that they almost always return to pragmatism. After all, a diverse citizenry can more easily reach agreement about oil import fees, sewer systems, and income taxes than they can about abstract truths. In short, monitoring these twin value-clusters is the special task of the rhetorical critic, especially if he or she is interested in cultural continuity and change in the United States.

MYTHS: THE SUBSTANCE OF CULTURE

Earlier, myths were defined as master stories describing exceptional people doing exceptional things that serve as moral guides to proper action. All cultures have myths and all cultures have myths of all sorts. Included among them are **cosmological** myths: why we are here, where we came from, what our ancestors were like. Myths like these are heard at an early age from parents (why Great Uncle Ezra moved off the farm), in schoolbooks (how the Declaration of Independence came to be), at church (what Moses found in the burning bush), and in popular films (the legend of Davy Crockett). **Societal** myths, on the other hand, teach one the proper way to live: Tales of George Washington's aversion to childhood lies and Abraham Lincoln's trek through the snow to school become more heavily drenched in meaning each time they are told. They also often become more erroneous, but the literal truth of a myth is rarely its measure. Rather, that myth is best that has evocative potential, the capacity to carry the truth of an event, not its factuality.

RHETORIC AND EVERYDAY LIFE

Critical Profile 10.1   Are Women Better Off Drunk?

In the past fifty years, major strides have been made in treating alcoholism. It is currently seen as a disease that cannot be cured but that can be arrested if the alcoholic does not drink and becomes a member of Alcoholics Anonymous. But Thelma McCormack of York University argues that even this enlightened disease model may have little to offer women.

McCormack reviewed the imagery of drunk and sober women in books, movies, and plays and found that women are portrayed as lacking "confidence in themselves as independent, reflexive, self-directive persons." If *sober* women are seen as being "less able than men to make rational responsible decisions," what incentive do alcoholic woman have to forgo the bottles that have become their chief source of comfort? Why should they face life sober? Drunk or sober, the women depicted in these texts are presented as "dependent on men who are carrying out the important business of the world." Those women who do not have men to depend on drink because they are lonely and unhappy. The message is clear: "Although she enjoys her career, it is no substitute for the more fulfilling life of her [married] classmate."

Married women are not safe either, says McCormack. If they are alcoholics, they are portrayed as bad mothers who leave their children with long-lasting scars. Alternately, liquor is seen as unlocking their sensuality, and this normally repressed desire erupts into impulsive, irresponsible behavior. As the sober wives of alcoholic husbands, women are seen as manipulative, shrewish, and demanding. If they try to help their husbands, they are considered too amateurish. In such cases, male professionals must be called in for assistance.

By devaluing women both drunk and sober, popular culture offers women no choices. "There are no pay-offs to being drunk and none to being sober," argues McCormack. What can be done in books, movies, and plays to extricate women from this dilemma? Is it possible to develop and promulgate role models of effective women? Is it possible to portray warm, loving, and supportive relationships among women and between women and men? If such characterizations are created, will this help women choose sobriety as a life-style?

Changing the way women are portrayed in popular culture will not necessarily change how women see themselves or how they are treated in society, although it may help women to see that—freed from the bonds of alcoholism—they have *choices* about how they can live their lives. If rhetoric can be enlisted in this cause, it will do what rhetoric has always done best: it will expand people's options by stimulating their imaginations.

Profiled by: Nancy Roth
Citation: McCormack (1986)

Critical Profile 10.2   Television Viewing and Reckless Driving—Twins?

The answer might be "yes" according to a study by Michigan State University professors Bradley Greenberg and Charles Atkin. Their research suggests that a viewer watching just one hour per day of prime-time television fiction for one year would have witnessed "more than 2700 irregular driving acts, more than 250 acts in which people are endangered, and about 30 deaths and 50 injuries due to auto accidents." How many times in that year would the viewer observe drivers using seat belts? A mere 15. Of course, the average American watches more than one hour per day of such television programming, so the average numbers are much higher.

Do the thousands of incidents of irregular driving affect what happens when television viewers take to the roads? The authors point out that portrayals of reckless driving on television are not definitive proof that television causes dangerous driving. However, exposure to such programming "may encourage behavioral modeling on the part of viewers. They may imitate certain novel acts or feel fewer inhibitions regarding their own driving."

Among the conclusions of the study are that television viewers, particularly those who watch action programs, are more likely:

- to consider irregular driving, such as quick braking and rapid acceleration, as "normal" behavior.
- to regard seat belts as unnecessary.
- to ignore the serious consequences that dangerous driving poses for people or property.
- to believe that dangerous driving is acceptable in rural and hilly environments.

Greenberg and Atkin's study also suggests some important questions about how communication might be affecting us. If television and other media serve as a model for driving, how else might they be influencing our political, religious, or sexual behavior? Or, to put the question another way, is the entertainment industry selling harmless recreation or something much more serious indeed? A world view? A philosophy of life? An attitude toward death? A theory of social responsibility? A hierarchy of values? A guide to proper behavior? We are not used to looking for such grand things in television shows. But Greenberg and Atkin's study hints that they might be hiding there nonetheless.

Profiled by: John Theobald-Osborne
Citation: Greenberg and Atkin (1983)

Critical Profile 10.3   Family Ties: 1920–1977

Have magazine advertisements showing family intimacy increased, decreased, or stayed the same from 1920 to 1977? Did images of Mom and Dad become more or less intimate during the Me Decade of the 1970s when independence and self-enhancement reigned supreme? Bruce W. Brown of Wilkes College sought to answer such questions. His longitudinal analysis explored five general-interest magazines such as *Life, Time,* and *Saturday Evening Post* over a fifty-five year period. An enlightening study emerges, a study of how the American mass media have treated intimate family relationships and what it means that they have done so.

Brown's exploration was carefully constructed. First, he began with the premise that advertisements do not *shape* cultural values but instead *reflect* them. Furthermore, Brown asserts, general-interest magazine advertisements offer a broader view of family life than do comparable advertisements in specialty magazines such as *Better Homes and Gardens* or *Popular Mechanics.* In order to determine family intimacy, Brown chose a widely used measure: physical closeness. For example, a mother-daughter duo classified by Brown as "intimate" was pictured in close proximity to one another in the ad or were actually touching; likewise, a brother-sister team labeled by Brown as "non-intimate" would be, say, five feet apart.

Among Brown's findings, several stand out:

- Husbands and wives were portrayed as increasingly intimate in magazine advertisements published between 1920 and 1977.

Identity myths explain what makes a cultural grouping special. For example, the United State's distinctiveness as a melting pot is reinforced by winsome tales of immigrants who have struggled and succeeded ("Mr. Cosamino began with a pushcart and now owns the Lower East Side"). In a similar vein, stories of the United States as a "peacekeeper" nation distinguish it from its political rivals (the Soviets' commitment to "world conquest") or its economic rivals (the "fanatical" Japanese). Finally, **eschatological** myths tell people where they are going, what lies in store for them in the short run ("a balanced budget," "full employment") and in the long run (a "heavenly reward," the "transmigration of souls").

All rhetoric depends on myth. An announcement of a dramatic rebound on Wall Street is especially heartening if one has heard of the Great Depression. Sermons of hellfire and damnation are especially frightening if the worshipper believes in fundamentalist mythologies. News stories of American hostages are especially enraging if the captors are Libyans rather than Australians. Normally, a rhetor will not retell these mythic tales in full, but instead use some device (a quick

---

Critical Profile 10.3 Family Ties: 1920–1977 (*Continued*)

- An interesting exception to the above finding occurred between 1940 and 1955. Brown speculates that the cause for this may have been twofold: Many husbands were away from home during the war years and the baby boom may have shifted emphasis from husband-wife relationships to parent-child relationships.
- Father-daughter intimacy rose and fell cyclically during ten- and fifteen-year periods. Brown says that this may reflect the "cultural taboo against fathers becoming too close to their daughters; this is particularly plausible because the measurement of intimacy . . . is based on physical distance."
- Brother-sister relationships were portrayed as slightly more intimate than sister-sister or brother-brother relationships, particularly after 1936. Brown argues that the increasingly popular value of having two children, one of each sex, may explain this finding.

Why do the mass media present increasingly intimate portrayals of family relationships to the American public? Perhaps because there is growing awareness of the need to sustain strong family bonds during an era marked by war, drugs, divorce, latch-key children, and anomie. Perhaps, also, commercial advertising is becoming the nation's family counselor. If that is true, should that hearten us or frighten us?

Profiled by: Christine Keffeler
Citation: Brown (1982)

---

allusion, a metaphor) to recall the tale for the audience. But why use myth at all? There are several reasons:

1. *Myths provide a heightened sense of authority.* Speakers expect their audiences to take myths seriously. McDonald [1969:144] claims that "without myths there is no authority and without authority there is no politics," thereby suggesting that no government can succeed unless it can link its preferred policies to its historical truths. Merelman [1966] puts a finer point on the matter. He notes that myths of "the national interest," for example, cut the costs of raising an army. Glory-drenched tales of old victories both legitimize the government in charge and motivate its citizens to fight on, which is why Merelman argues that "in such a situation one could measure the legitimacy of a government by the proportion of enlistees to draftees, all other things being equal" [pp. 552–553].

2. *Myths provide a heightened sense of continuity.* As one event merges into another over time, its meaning becomes hard to discern. Myth, therefore, becomes the great explainer, grabbing up huge

chunks of time and thousands of individual events to make patterned sense of the world. Thus, the radical who argues that a series of apparently isolated crimes is part of some clandestine conspiracy uses myth to fill in the blanks life has created. Myth, in short, gives meaning to the present by making it seem continuous with the past. Woodward [1983] claims that Ronald Reagan demonstrated this principle when using Franklin Roosevelt's populist myths to depict himself as Roosevelt's political reincarnation. Speakers like Reagan can do so, Balthrop [1984] argues, because mythic time is more elastic than historical time and because audiences are not hypercorrect about mythic names and dates.

3. *Myths provide a heightened sense of coherence.* Just as myth reaches across time, it reaches across ideas in order to fashion whole, consistent ideologies. Bosmajian [1974] says that this was the rhetorical genius of Adolph Hitler, who used British nationalism, Marxist imagery, Roman Catholic pageantry, and Freemason eschatology to fashion Nazi whole cloth. Pocock [1971] says that such a rhetoric contains "ancestral ghosts" that bring together diverse parts of an audience's emotional life. King [1985] notes that this is how myth served Gerald Ford when pardoning Richard Nixon. When claiming that the deposed president had "suffered enough" already, Ford used a "tragic frame" for his story, essentially arguing that *how* Mr. Nixon suffered, whether he went to jail or merely had a troubled vacation, was quite beside the point. King also notes that most listeners grudgingly accepted Ford's explanation, because it allowed them as well to close the pages of the Nixon chapter.

4. *Myths provide a heightened sense of community.* The best myths are shared myths. Communities become communities when they admire the same heroes, revere the same moments in history, emulate the same great deeds. Studies of colonial America show that even a diverse and unsettled citizenry can use myth to fashion community. For example, Merritt [1966] studied the newspapers of that era and found that revolutionary fever increased as journalistic references to "the American colonies" (as opposed to "the British colonies") increased. Likewise, Condit [1985] notes that speeches commemorating the Boston Massacre were quite bland at first and only later became incendiary (with vivid descriptions of the murders), thereby providing a useful myth for talk of a growing revolution. As McGee [1975] says, almost all references to "the people" are based more in myth than in history, since few groups possess the unity and passion ascribed to them by their leaders. But this does not, of course, stop their leaders from treating them as if they were one in spirit.

5. *Myths provide a heightened sense of choice.* Myths dramatize alternatives by dialectically featuring good and evil. The struggles myth portrays heighten the importance of the issues at stake and clar-

ify the alternatives. At times, the struggle is between the haves and the have nots, as Williams [1974] observed in an inner-city church where parishioners described *themselves* as "outcasts," "the despised few," and "poor folks." At other times, the struggle is between rationality and irrationality, as Ivie [1980] found when studying myths of savagery in prowar rhetoric. In yet other cases, the struggle is between the actual and the possible as Gerlach and Hine [1968] observed when finding a "positive fatalism" in the rhetoric of religious movements. After all, say Gerlach and Hine, the advances of a group must be acknowledged, but they cannot be overstated lest the movement become overconfident. In effective rhetoric, therefore, evil cannot become impotent.

6. *Myths provide a heightened sense of agreement.* Because myths are abstract, they can be viewed by different persons at different times and still generate roughly the same understanding. The abstractness of a myth like "One Nation Under God," Hart [1977] has argued, has kept church-state tensions at a minimum in the United States for over two hundred years. By sanctioning religious invocations at political banquets, nondescript prayers before sessions of Congress, and other forms of civic piety, the American people have become convinced that their religious similarities outnumber their religious differences. This rhetoric of God and country has kept two thousand different religious denominations from marching in the streets and from clashing in the halls of Congress as well. While there have been exceptions to this civil-religious "contract," the American people have generally used myth, not law, to handle their church-state relations.

Myth and rhetoric have a symbiotic relationship. Myth gives rhetoric something to say and rhetoric gives myth impact in everyday affairs. The poets, artists, or folklorists who also trade in myth can use "language at full stretch" [Rutherford, 1977:52]. But rhetorical myths are more subdued, because they serve propositional purposes. They are also more abbreviated, since matters of "policy" always receive top billing in practical persuasion. Rhetoric, in short, honors myth by employing it.

But how is myth best studied? The work of Claude Lévi-Strauss is perhaps the richest approach available. Lévi-Strauss, the father of **structuralism,** was an anthropologist by training who became fascinated by the folk stories told in the cultures he studied. A broad and imaginative thinker, Lévi-Strauss's work has been seized upon by historians, linguists, literary scholars and, less often, by rhetorical critics. In one of his first essays on the structuralist approach, Lévi-Strauss [1955:431–440] provided six guidelines (here paraphrased) for the critic of myth:

1. The critic should track the **source** of the myth (where it came from, in what forms it existed previously) to understand its emotional power.
2. The effectiveness of a given myth lies not in its individual narrative elements but in how such elements are **combined.**
3. The critic should discover the **harmony** of emotions, images, ideas a given myth provides.
4. The critic should calculate how a given myth treats standard chronology (historical time) versus **synchronic time** (the narrative progression as construed by the storyteller).
5. Narrative elements that are temporal neighbors, that share the same **context,** will lead the critic to the myth's basic "argument."
6. The critic should pay special attention to the **oppositional** forces in a given myth to discover its motivational base.

Lévi-Strauss's suggestions get the critic started, but, as Warnick [1979:258] argues, they must be adapted in the study of rhetoric, because rhetoric always deploys myth in a particular situation. Also, as Harari [1979] notes, Lévi-Strauss's anthropological approach is so broad-based that it often ignores the specific subject matter the myth is intended to vivify. In addition, Said [1979] observes that each time a myth is used it creates new variations of itself that are sometimes more interesting than any consistencies the critic might observe. Finally, McGuire [1977] reminds the critic that rhetorical myths always serve practical ends and, therefore, take a subsidiary place compared to the speaker's propositions. In short, the rhetorical critic of myth asks: Why did *this* speaker at *this* time with *this* audience allude to *this* particular tale?

With these modifications in mind, let us examine one use of myth, a speech given by Major, the aging pig in George Orwell's *Animal Farm.* In his book, Orwell describes a society populated by animals who, like people, must struggle daily with grandeur and pettiness. Early in Orwell's book, Major gives a speech that could serve as the prototype for any revolutionary address. This is Major's speech:

[1] Comrades, you have heard already about the strange dream that I had last night. But I will come to the dream later. I have something else to say first. I do not think, comrades, that I shall be with you for many months longer, and before I die, I feel it my duty to pass on to you such widom as I have acquired. I have had a long life, I have much time for the nature of life on this earth as well as any animal now living. It is about this that I wish to speak to you.

[2] Now, comrades, what is the nature of this life of ours? Let us face it: our lives are miserable, laborious, and short. We are born, we

are given just so much food as will keep the breath in our bodies, and those of us who are capable of it are forced to work to the last atom of our strength; and the very instant that our usefulness has come to an end we are slaughtered with hideous cruelty. No animal in England knows the meaning of happiness or leisure after he is a year old. No animal in England is free. The life of an animal is misery and slavery: that is the plain truth.

[3] But is this simply part of the order of nature? Is it because this land of ours is so poor that it cannot afford a decent life to those who dwell upon it. No, comrades, a thousand times no! The soil of England is fertile, its climate is good, it is capable of affording food in abundance to an enormously greater number of animals than now inhabit it. This single farm of ours would support a dozen horses, twenty cows, hundreds of sheep—and all of them living in a comfort and dignity that are now almost beyond our imagining. Why then do we continue in this miserable condition? Because nearly the whole of the produce of our labour is stolen from us by human beings. There, comrades, is the answer to all our problems. It is summed up in a single word—Man. Man is the only real enemy we have. Remove Man from the scene, and the root cause of hunger and overwork is abolished forever.

[4] Man is the only creature that consumes without producing. He does not give milk, he does not lay eggs, he is too weak to pull the plough, he cannot run fast enough to catch rabbits. Yet he is lord of all animals. He sets them to work, he gives back to them the bare minimum that will prevent them from starving, and the rest he keeps for himself. Our labour tills the soil, our dung fertilises it, and yet there is not one of us that owns more than his bare skin. You cows that I see before me, how many thousand of gallons of milk have you given during this last year? And what has happened to that milk which should have been breeding up sturdy calves? Every drop of it has gone down the throat of our enemies. And you hens, how many eggs have you laid in this last year, and how many of those eggs ever hatched into chickens? The rest of you have all gone to market to bring in money for Jones and his men. And you, Clover, where are those four foals you bore, who should have been the support and pleasure of your old age? Each was sold at a year old—you will never see one of them again. In return for your four confinements and all your labour in the fields, what have you ever had except your bare rations and a stall?

[5] And even the miserable lives we lead are not allowed to reach their natural span. For myself I do not grumble, for I am one of the lucky ones. I am twelve years old and have had over four hundred children. Such is the natural life of a pig. But no animal escapes the cruel knife in the end. You young porkers who are sitting in front of me, every one of you will scream your lives out at the block within a year. To that horror we all must come—cows, pigs, hens, sheep, everyone. Even the horses and the dogs have no better fate. You,

Boxer, the very day that those great muscles of yours lose their power, Jones will sell you to the knacker, who will cut your throat and boil you down for the foxhounds. As for the dogs, when they grow old and toothless, Jones ties a brick round their necks and drowns them in the nearest pond.

[6] Is it not crystal clear, then, comrades, that all the evils of this life of ours spring from the tyranny of human beings? Only get rid of Man, and the produce of our labour would be our own. Almost over-night we could become rich and free. What then must we do? Why, work night and day, body and soul, for the overthrow of the human race! That is my message to you, comrades: Rebellion! I do not know when that Rebellion will come, it might be in a week or in a hundred years, but I know, as surely as I see this straw beneath my feet, that sooner or later justice will be done. Fix your eyes on that, comrades, throughout the short remainder of your lives! And above all, pass on this message of mine to those who come after you, so that future gen-erations shall carry on the struggle until it is victorious.

[7] And remember, comrades, your resolution must never falter. No argument must lead you astray. Never listen when they tell you that Man and the animals have a common interest, that the prosperity of the one is the prosperity of the others. It is all lies. Man serves the interests of no creature except himself. And among us animals let there be perfect unity, perfect comradeship in the struggle. All men are enemies. All animals are comrades . . .

[8] I have little more to say. I merely repeat, remember always your duty of enmity towards Man and all his ways. Whatever goes upon two legs is an enemy. Whatever goes upon four legs, or has wings, is a friend. And remember also that in fighting against Man, we must not come to resemble him. Even when you have conquered him do not adopt his vices. No animals must ever live in a house, or sleep in a bed, or wear clothes, or drink alcohol, or smoke tobacco, or touch money, or engage in trade. All the habits of Man are evil. And, above all, no animal must ever tyrannise over his own kind. Weak or strong, clever or simple, we are all brothers. No animal must ever kill any other animal. All animals are equal.

[9] And now, comrades, I will tell you about my dream of last night. I cannot describe that dream to you. It was a dream of the earth as it will be when Man has vanished. But it reminded me of something that I have long forgotten. Many years ago, when I was a little pig, my mother and the other sows used to sing an old song of which they knew only the tune and the first three words. I had known that tune in my infancy, but it had long since passed out of my mind. Last night, however, it came back to me in my dream. And what is more, the words of the song also came back—words, I am certain, which were sung by the animals of long ago and have been lost to memory for generations. I will sing you that song now, comrades, I am old and my voice is hoarse, but when I have taught you the tune, you can sing it better for yourselves. It is called "Beasts of England":

[10] Beasts of England, beasts of Ireland,
    Beasts of every land and clime,
    Hearken to my joyful tidings
    Of the golden future time.
Soon or late the day is coming,
    Tyrant Man shall be o'erthrown,
    And the fruitful fields of England
    Shall be trod by beasts alone.
Rings shall vanish from our noses,
    And the harness from our back,
    Bit and spur shall rust forever,
    Cruel whips no more shall crack.
Riches more than mind can picture,
    Wheat and barley, oats and hay,
    Clover, beans, and mangel-wurzels
    Shall be ours upon that day.
Bright will shine the fields of England,
    Purer shall its waters be,
    Sweeter yet shall blow its breezes
    On that day that sets us free.
For that day we all must labour,
    Though we die before it break;
    Cows and horses, geese and turkeys,
    All must toil for freedom's sake.
Beasts of England, beasts of Ireland,
    Beasts of every land and clime,
    Hearken well and spread my tidings
    Of the golden future time [Orwell,
      1946:17–23].

Overall, Major's speech is a myth of rebirth. In paragraph 1, he mentions his advancing years, but in the conclusion he returns to a story from his infancy, thereby providing a mythic frame of death and rebirth. His propositional content is analogous: Animals have been horribly exploited in the past, but a new day is dawning. Paragraphs 2–5 amplify the death motif as Major details his comrades' daily horrors, but paragraphs 6–8 proceed differently as Major describes the mythic labor pains attendant to any birth, even the birth of a movement. Like an instructor in a natural childbirth class, Major comforts, coaxes, and inspires his charges during this painful parturition. The final two paragraphs detail the glories of this birth and it is not incidental that Major mentions his own mother's love in paragraph 9.

Within this overall frame, three major substructures can be detected. Table 10.2 sketches one of them, the speech's **dialectical tensions.** Paragraph 1 is comparatively peaceful, with Major reflecting on his dream of the night before. Here, he also foreshadows mythic transcen-

Table 10.2   Myth and Dialectic in Major's Speech

Paragraph	Negative Mythic Elements	Positive Mythic Elements
1	None	Wisdom, nostalgia
2	Unspecific exploitation	Personal freedom
3	Human exploitation	Fruitfulness
4	Human exploitation	Productivity
5	Human exploitation	Longevity
6	Human exploitation	Deliverance
7	Human exploitation	Equality
8	Human exploitation	Personal integrity
9	None	Wisdom, nostalgia
10	Human exploitation	Freedom, productivity, fruitfulness, brotherhood

dence by mentioning his personal hopes for posterity. But this tranquility is sharply arrested in paragraph 2 as Major introduces the first of seven major clashes. He begins on the most general note—freedom—and quickly introduces the theme of exploitation (without immediately revealing its precise source). But by paragraph 3 Major has warmed to his subject: human depravity. Thereafter, he maintains mythic continuity by contrasting human exploitation to the things his listeners most treasure: raw survival in paragraph 3, the evils of capital in paragraph 4, death itself in paragraph 5.

In paragraph 6, the mood shifts substantially as higher needs are introduced: self-achievement, companionship, a sense of honor. In each case, humankind is made the foil, with Major contrasting each animal virtue to a human vice. Finally, in paragraph 9, dialectic fades into synthesis as good subsumes evil. The speech ends on the dream motif with which it began, but this time the dream is amplified majestically.

Structuralists also emphasize the importance of **time** in myth, the second substructure to be analyzed (see Figure 10.1). Unlike historical time, mythic time does not move moment by moment but often rearranges chronology radically in order to place audiences in the proper "emotional time." Major, the patriarch of the community, began his speech in the distant past. He quickly moved forward in time, but, interestingly, returned to the distant past at the end of his speech, thereby sandwiching all that had transpired in between with his omniscience.

Temporally, paragraph 2 is complex, since it foreshadows the entire speech. Here, Major becomes a person of perspective who moves easily across time, thereby establishing that his topic is grounded in the reality of the past, linked to the saliency of the present, but also relevant to the uncertainty of the future. He then juxtaposes the immediate

Figure 10.1
Myth and Time in Major's Speech

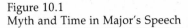

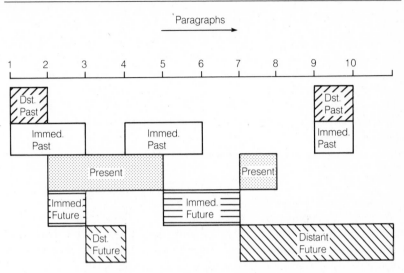

past and the present in paragraphs 2–6. This gives emotional force to the speech, since his data springs directly from his listeners' dreadful lives (he even mentions some of them by name, as if to heighten their sense of personal crisis). The use of the immediate future is especially unsettling, with Major arguing that current desperations cannot compare to tomorrow's hardships. It is this *structural co-occurrence* of present and future—the inevitability of suffering—that makes for such powerful mythic effects.

When Major says in paragraph 3, "Remove Man from the scene, and the root cause of hunger and overwork is abolished forever," he briefly reveals the light at the end of a tunnel he is about to make much darker indeed. He hints at this theme again in paragraph 6 ("Only get rid of Man, and . . . Almost overnight we could become rich and free"), drops it in paragraph 7, develops it in the two penultimate paragraphs, and finally lets it blend into the transcendent future in his concluding paragraph. Moving in and out of the distant future in this way—in effect, teasing his audience—creates mythic tension and sets up the full-bodied myth with which he concludes.

A final, topical pass over Major's speech can be made (see Figure 10.2). **Naturalistic myths** introduce his speech, and properly so, since he is addressing animals. In these passages, images of bodily processes (sleeping, breathing, eating) interact with images of nature (growing, fertilizing). These themes are extended in paragraphs 4 and 5, where

Figure 10.2
Myth and Topic in Major's Speech

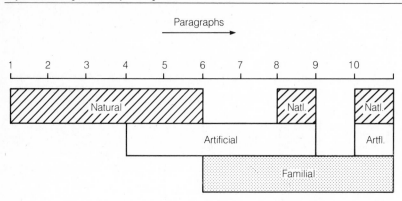

images of fertility (laying eggs, bearing foals) are linked to organic images (excreting, hatching) and aging images (declining musculature, toothlessness). But dialectical tension is also established as Major contrasts these natural wonders to **mythic man's** overconsumption of food, materialistic standard of values, and arbitrary shortening of animal life. Major also contrasts the naturalness of eggs, milk, and dung to human contrivances: knives, blocs, knackers, bricks.

Humanity is also the mythic foil in paragraphs 6–8 as tyranny and selfishness are linked to depraved human habits: sleeping in beds, wearing clothes, drinking alcohol. But a third mythic grouping—**the family**—now changes the speech from one of outrage to one of solidarity. The family myth is developed *across species* ("whoever goes upon four legs, or has wings, is a friend") as well as *across time* ("pass on this message of mine to those who come after you"). Kinship terms (brothers, mother, family) now become more dominant and family rules are laid down. These include political admonishments (references to the "common interest"), sociological enjoinders (human habits should not be imitated), and moral advice (there is to be no killing of other animals). In paragraph 9, this new family is linked, magically, to an ancient family of animals and in paragraph 10 a grand eschatological myth describes a "golden future time" for all.

Although three separate passes over Major's speech have been attempted here, this text, like all texts, is a *coalescence* of mythic structures. These coalescences give to rhetoric its insidious power, since audiences typically cannot unravel what they hear while hearing it. Major, after all, was asking his listeners to deal with his dialectical, temporal, and topical structures *simultaneously*. It is this simultaneity that gives rhetoric its richness and, as Lévi-Strauss has demonstrated, it is the delicate interweaving of these themes that complicates the study of myth. But given the good that myth does in the hands of saviors, and given the evil it does in the hands of tyrants, the patient study of myth is an enterprise that cannot be abandoned.

FANTASY THEMES: THE GRASSROOTS OF CULTURE

This section will take some license with Ernest Bormann's notion of fantasy themes in order to make the construct immediately useful to the critic. As mentioned earlier, fantasy themes are mythic shorthand, story lines describing an idealized (but not necessarily ideal) past, present, or future. If myths are the prized tales of humankind in general, fantasy themes are the local variations of those tales. If myths are vague, fantasy themes are specific. If myths are enduring, fantasy themes are comparatively short-lived. If myths are universally suited to public discussion, fantasy themes change from topic to topic. If myths are cross-cultural, fantasy themes are culture-specific. If myths are studied by historians, fantasy themes are reported by journalists.

An example. A popular master myth is that of America as a New Israel, the conviction that God created the United States for a special purpose: to deliver the world's peoples from a state of darkness. This myth holds that God gave his Chosen People great bounties, but, in recompense, expected the American message (which was really His message) to be spread far and wide. At first, the presumptuousness of this tale seems appalling, especially when it is described in this blunt manner. That is how fantasy themes help. They round out the bluntness by using attractive vignettes to disguise the myth's presumptions. In this way, fantasy themes become the everyday language of myth.

The early Puritans brocaded the New Israel myth and it soon sank deep roots in the American psyche. One of the fantasy themes it spawned held that the United States had to keep itself strong militarily to protect all of God's children. Another set of fantasy themes preached that outer space had to be colonized so that God's word could be taken into the wilderness. Westward expansion in the early 1800s was launched with such fantasy themes, as was Woodrow Wilson's League of Nations, Harry Truman's Marshall Plan, John Kennedy's Peace Corps, Lyndon Johnson's Vietnam war, and Ronald Reagan's Nicaraguan policy. New Israel fantasy themes were used to launch the public education movement in the United States, broaden participation in the Olympic Games, and support a host of charities: The Red Cross, UNESCO, and CARE. Social movements of both the right and left have

RHETORIC AND IMAGE MANAGEMENT

Critical Profile 10.4   Hitler's Story, a Nation's Destiny

Can a book, like a beautiful face, launch a thousand ships? Can a biography lead to a dynasty? Is publishing a prerequisite to revolution? Michael McGuire, now of California State University, argues that because Adolph Hitler's *Mein Kampf* is a rhetorical manifestation of the entire German world view, it galvanized a nation like nothing else could have even though it failed to establish Hitler's intellectual authority. Though it is flawed as literature and as accurate biography, it is a strong rhetorical statement nonetheless.

McGuire points out that *Mein Kampf* is a powerful narrative despite its distortion and omission of facts and despite its neglect of the usual linear chronology. Rather, it is important because it is a grid onto which various mythic "story lines" can be placed and interrelated. For example, in the opening two sentences of *Mein Kampf*, McGuire says, Hitler establishes the importance of a mythic past to the present and the future when he writes, "Today I consider it my good fortune that Fate designated my birthplace to be exactly Braunau on the *Inn*. For this small town lies on the border of those two German states whose reunion seems, at least to us of the younger generation, a life-mission to pursue by every means." Here, says McGuire, a vague history of the German states is associated with the present wish of young Germans to reunite Germany and Austria, thereby turning a factual past into a mythic tomorrow.

In *Mein Kampf*, Hitler's own past is left vague: "One must note Hitler nowhere gives the date of his birth," observes McGuire. This omission associates Hitler's personal past with the former days of German glory. In addition, Hitler relies upon various German myths—strength through suffering, for example—to establish that Fate is important still. Here, Fate represents the personification of nature and is used to demonstrate that his own birth was no accident. Rather, readers are led to conclude, Dame Fate caused Hitler's birth, thereby resurrecting the glory of the German past and insuring leadership for the future.

The implications of McGuire's analysis are quite clear: Hitler presented himself in grand mythic terms to the German people, a nation scarred by political and economic turmoil and facing a bleak future. The mythic Hitler of *Mein Kampf* offered the promise of a brighter future to a nation that had forgotten how to remember as well as how to dream.

Profiled by: Donald Nobles
Citation: McGuire (1977)

Critical Profile 10.5   Nixon, Heroism, and the Silent Majority

---

Only a hero has the character to achieve the divine object of a quest. When President Richard Nixon spoke to the American public about the Vietnam war on November 3, 1969, he presented himself as just such a hero. A "just and lasting peace" was his quest; the "silent majority" of Americans were "the Helpers who with their knowledge and/or magical powers assist the Hero and but for whom he would never succeed." The quest myth is a cross-cultural form that frames political affairs in terms of subjective experience. Hermann G. Stelzner of the University of Massachusetts used W. H. Auden's description of the heroic quest to coax new meaning out of Nixon's much-studied speech.

Stelzner describes two types of quest hero: the clearly superior hero, whose arete (excellence) is evident to all, and the hero of concealed arete, who is called forth only after his apparent betters fail. The "superior" political hero is a visionary: Expressing affairs of state in apocalyptic terms, he proceeds directly toward his target, exhibiting the arrogance of his obvious superiority. Unfortunately, this type of hero is susceptible to a "tragic fall." In contrast, according to Stelzner, the concealed hero is "plodding and pedestrian. He enlists help because unlike his betters he is humble enough to take advice and kind enough to give assistance to people who, like himself, appear to be nobody in particular."

In his speech, Nixon casts John F. Kennedy and Woodrow Wilson as "superior" heroes; he implicitly calls himself the hero of concealed arete. Kennedy, Nixon says, thrilled the imaginations of the young and the idealistic (read impractical), and died a tragic death. Wilson spoke apocalyptically of "the war to end wars," a "dream" which was "shattered on the hard reality of great power politics." Nixon, in contrast, promises no glorious future: "I do not tell you that the war in Vietnam is the war to end wars." Whereas Kennedy's helpers were young, reckless, noisy idealists (who were, in 1969, busy organizing anti-war protests), Nixon constructs his essential support as that "silent majority" of Americans who understood his disciplined, cautious, and pragmatic approach.

Because Nixon's speech was crafted for rhetorical rather than literary purposes, Stelzner cautions that the quest myth form is useful here more for illumination than for evaluation of the Nixon speech. By downplaying his own heroic qualities, by emphasizing the limited magnitude of his quest, and by noting the curious reticence of his helpers, Nixon presented a tale unconvincing as myth but potentially effective as rhetoric.

Profiled by: Elizabeth Macom
Citation: Stelzner (1971)

Critical Profile 10.6   Et Tu, Ike?

Although few presidents will admit in their memoirs that they have engaged in the "act that dares not speak its name"—political advertising—most Americans get their information about presidential candidates from just such ads. Kathleen Hall Jamieson of the University of Pennsylvania argues that "presidential campaigns can be viewed productively through the lens provided by their . . . advertising." In *Packaging the Presidency*, she examines numerous presidential elections and provides insight into the strategies, successes, and blunders of each party, president, and would-be president.

But what one element must a political campaign have above all else? Thematic consistency, says Jamieson. Richard Nixon's first bid for the presidency in 1960 is the example that proves the point. Nixon's strongest claim to the White House in that election was "experience." Having been Vice President under Dwight Eisenhower for the previous eight years, Nixon implied in his ads that he had assisted the President with suggestions, if not actual decision-making. Nixon's Democratic opponent, the young Senator, John F. Kennedy, could take credit for a great deal but could not claim to have served as a presidential understudy.

The strategy made sense. Dwight Eisenhower was still "the most highly regarded public figure in America" and an unequivocal endorsement by him could have helped Nixon's chances tremendously. However, at the end of a long press conference when a reporter virtually asked Ike for his endorsement of Nixon, "for reasons that remain unclear, Eisenhower instead knifed Nixon between the ribs." Of course, the Democrats had a field day with this sequence and included it in their ads:

> *Reporter:* "I just wondered if you could give us an example of a major idea of his [Nixon] that you adopted in that role as the decider and final . . . ah . . ."

> *Eisenhower:* "If you give me a week I might think of one. I don't remember." (Laughter) The announcer concluded, "President Eisenhower could not remember but the voters will remember. For real leadership in the '60's, help elect Senator John F. Kennedy president."

The lack of thematic consistency may well have cost Nixon the election, argues Jamieson. The one person who could have certified the truth of Nixon's claim to experience had instead denied it. Becoming a Caesar is not easy. Advertising helps. But not if one has a friend named Brutus. Or Eisenhower.

Profiled by: Suzanne M. Daughton
Citation: Jamieson (1984)

used such themes, with Teddy Kennedy marching off in the mid-1980s to explain civil rights to South Africans and televangelist Pat Robertson urging greater U.S. involvement in Central America at the same time.

According to Bormann [1972], fantasy themes are needed to *dramatize ideas*, since audiences often lack the imagination to do so themselves. A study by Kidd [1975] illustrates. Kidd was interested in how popular magazines (published between 1951 and 1975) represented the social world to its female readers. She found two major "visions" of the world projected there, one of which stressed that women were fundamentally different from men, that women should avoid conflict at all costs, and that women should follow clear guidelines when establishing relationships. Some of Kidd's examples illustrate this traditional vision:

- In New York City the "career woman" can be seen in fullest bloom and it is not irrelevant that New York City also has the greatest concentration of psychiatrists [p. 33].
- There is no such thing as a worthless conversation provided you know what to listen for. The attentive listener . . . listens for what people unconsciously reveal about themselves while they're talking. Thus [she] can derive meaning from a conversation even though the other person may be talking nonsense [p. 34].
- A man can feel kinship with the gods if his wife can make him believe he can cause a flowering within her. If she doesn't feel it she must bend every effort to pretend [pp. 34–35].

A second, newer vision found by Kidd had a more fluid conception of life, embraced fewer social strictures, and envisioned a greater range of acceptable roles for women. The following excerpts represent that vision:

- Specialists who study family life now agree that it is pointless to compare real marriages with some imagined ideal. The model marriage is a myth . . . We must begin with a basic fact. Not all marriages are alike and they cannot be measured by the same standards [p. 35].
- The idea of permance is an absurd illusion. Change is the most permanent thing you can say about the whole universe [p. 35].
- Unpleasant feelings, petty resentments and frustrations do not go away simply because one refuses to let them show. Rather, they can build up a deadly store of bitterness [p. 36].

Kidd found that most of the stories she read consisted of little more than "case studies" of happy and unhappy women. These stories appeared quite lifelike, thereby adding drama to the author's ideas but also reinforcing either the traditional or newer fantasy themes lying within them.

By finding so many different instances of these visions, Kidd showed that fantasy themes are indeed fantasy *themes*—they are persistent. Bormann [1972] argues that these fantasies "chain out" in society because of their rhetorical power and that, eventually, people repeat these story lines to one another in everyday conversation. Thus, because of fantasy themes in the 1950s, "everybody knew" that Communists had infiltrated the U.S. State Department. In the 1960s, "everybody knew" that racial harmony was imminent. In the 1970s, "everybody knew" that the Grateful Dead subverted American youth. And in the 1980s, "everybody knew" that entrepreneurship would make one rich.

To establish what "everybody knows," critics often consult mass media reports. This approach was used by Cragan and Shields [1977] when studying political campaigns, by Haskins [1981] when studying the rhetoric of civil rights, and by Bormann [1982] when studying international affairs. In each case, the critics established that a particular fantasy echoed through society so often that it reflected shared mythic understandings.

Fantasy theme analysis is particularly useful for understanding subcultures. By keying on Disciples of Christ's fantasy themes, for example, Hensley [1975] discovered how outcasts are able to sustain themselves. Their story line: All "disciples" are reviled at first but ultimate victory is assured them. In a similar vein, Ilkka [1977] traced the rhetoric of the American Communist Party and found that it coped with its minority status by dramatizing the exploits of Communist leaders, thereby replacing argument with hero worship. Gold's [1981] interesting subcultural study investigated local political campaigns in rural Cajun country. He quickly discovered that this brand of Louisiana politics was intolerant of outsiders. As a result, Cajun politicians constantly used familial themes in their rhetoric even if they had to stretch a bit when doing so, as did one Lurlin Lafleur:

> In the past few weeks I have been observing that everyone likes to vote for their kin. . . . Well I've been figuring who would be my kinsmen and I discovered that it's everyone who talks French. *I'm a Cajun, you know. Everyone who talks French—we are all like cousins.* Because you speak French and I speak French, that makes us first cousins. And if you talk English, then *I am the cousin of those who talk English as well*, because I speak English. And if you talk English and French, well

then we are double-cousins, you understand. So don't forget that, my friends, when you vote. Vote for your "Tit coozan," Lurlin Lafleur [pp. 154–155].

Examples like this make it seem that fantasy themes are trivial. But that is quite wrong. A fascinating example of the utility of fantasy themes was reported by Weisman [1980], who studied the activities of prisoners in concentration camps during World War II. Weisman argues that fantasy themes kept many of these prisoners sane. By reciting sacred religious tracts for one another, by engaging in "public dreaming" (for example, by describing the elaborate meals they would prepare upon their release), and by recording their visions of the future in their diaries (a punishable activity itself), some of the prisoners were able to distract themselves from the horrors surrounding them.

A less dramatic testament to fantasy themes is provided by Elpenor [1986], who describes the rhetoric of Alcoholics Anonymous. A recovering alcoholic himself, Elpenor reports that he initially regarded such standard story lines as Count Your Blessings, One Day at a Time, Easy Does It, Live and Let Live, and First Things First as tedious and banal. Eventually, however, he came to realize that such themes give "integrity, coherence, simplicity" to the alcoholic. As part of a "tribal culture which gets passed on by means of stories and maxims," the AA member eventually finds wisdom in these themes because they "are nothing more than condensed stories waiting to be brought to life by his own experience" [p. 47].

Given their importance, how are fantasy themes best studied? Bormann and his students have developed a number of elaborate methods for testing their popularity and power, but let us take an approach better suited to the beginning critic. Table 10.3 presents eight critical queries for this purpose, queries that probe the presuppositions of rhetoric. These questions ask the critic to isolate the story lines most often used in a body of discourse and to ask what lessons they teach: about people's capacities, about right and wrong, about human purpose. Following Bormann's lead, it is not sufficient to answer these questions for a single text. The good critic tracks them *across discourse situations,* since only then can genuine thematizing be established.

A brief example will show how such questions can be used critically. The following passage is excerpted from an oft-circulated flyer entitled "Ideals of a Klansman" by Robert Shelton [n.d.], one-time leader of the Ku Klux Klan. Although the excerpt is brief, it contains many of the Klan's traditional fantasy themes (and its odd punctuation style):

We believe in the upholding of the Constitution of these United States.

Table 10.3   Critical Probes for Fantasy Theme Analysis

1. Given the speaker's story lines, what are people like?
    Are they dependable? Fundamentally deceived? Are people essentially alone? Evil or duplicitous at root? Do they care for one another?
2. Given the speaker's story lines, what are the possibilities of group action?
    Is group effort morally superior to individual effort? Practically superior? Are groups doomed to disharmony? Does group action bring out the best in us? The worst?
3. Given the speaker's story lines, upon what can people most depend?
    Their mental agility? Physical skills? Spiritual resources? Hard work? Other people? Nothing at all?
4. Given the speaker's story lines, what is humankind's fundamental purpose on earth?
    To help others? To self-actualize? To change the world? To fulfill historical mandates? To right wrongs?
5. Given the speaker's story lines, what are the fundamental measures of right and wrong?
    Personal ethics? Some religious code? Social obligations and agreements? Political utility? Legal duty?
6. Given the speaker's story lines, how can success best be measured?
    By assessing quantitative gain? By enhancing self-knowledge? By fulfilling group destiny? By being faithful to certain abstract principles? By defeating an enemy?
7. Given the speaker's story lines, what sort of information is most dependable?
    Book learning? Empirical observation? Personal experience? Folk wisdom? Secret revelation?
8. Given the speaker's story lines, why do things happen as they do?
    Because of some hidden design? Because of individual or group effort? Because of random chance? Because of some extrahuman force?

By upholding the Constitution, is meant the whole Constitution, anyone who violates one clause of the Constitution, would as quickly break every other one if it serves his purpose to do so . . .

We believe in a free press, uncontrolled by political or religious sects.

The press should be free to spread news without coloring it to suit any person or sect: But such is not the case, scarcely a newspaper anywhere dares to publish the truth: the whole truth and nothing but the truth. The press is largely controlled by the Roman Catholic priesthood and Judaism, and as a result the great masses of people are fed on propaganda instead of true facts. When an article is read in either a newspaper or magazine, one does not know but that there is a sinister motive back of it. And a paper that publishes nothing but the truth can hardly exist.

We believe in law and order: In other words, the Klan believes in keeping the laws and enforcing the laws. Many accusations have been brought against the Klan as lawbreakers. These accusations against the order are purely newspaper propaganda. So far we have not heard of a single instance where the Klan, by an official act, has violated any law.

We believe in white supremacy.

> The Klan believes that America is a white man's country, and should be governed by white men. Yet the Klan is not anti-Negro, it is the Negro's friend. The Klan is eternally opposed to the mixing of the white and the colored races. Our creed: Let the white man remain white, the black man black, the yellow man yellow, the brown man brown, and the red man red. God drew the color line, and the man should so let it remain, read Acts 17:26 if you please.
>
> We believe in the protection of our pure womanhood, the home, the church, our public school system, our Constitution, and our American way of life.
>
> This is a stand for the purity of the home, for morality, for the protection of our mothers, our sisters, our wives, our daughters, against the whiteslaver, the home-wrecker, the libertine. And to live up to this principle a Klansman must keep himself pure and above reproach. He must treat other women as he would have those of his own household treated.

This passage finds the world divided into two groups. One, a small one, sees things clearly. Another, much larger, group is composed of those too lazy to see the truth and those who have been duped by the forces of evil (for example, the press). Life, as described by the Klan, is a dog-eat-dog existence. Laws are broken with impunity; immigration threatens to pollute the gene pool; churches deceive their flocks. Only the Klan stands for righteousness; even the courts cannot be trusted. Men are strong, but they are sheep; women are innocent, and they are weak. Such conditions give the Klan a reason for being.

In a world where all is disorder, even a small band of patriots can turn back the forces massing against them. Because the enemy is in *moral* disarray, group action is indeed possible, but only if Klan philosophy is adhered to faithfully by all concerned. That is why there is so much repetition in even this short passage. The redundancy energizes the prose ("the truth, the whole truth and nothing but the truth") and also documents the coherence of Klan philosophy. A small, powerful, easily repeated truth best sustains a crusade.

So the Klan places its faith in doctrine and shows no confidence in great persons leading the group to victory. Given the number of people who have already accepted the "insanity" of civil rights, the Klan also has no hope for human discernment or for change via natural evolution. The Klan's world is fixed: The NAACP is in league with the Communists; foreign ideas are inherently bankrupt; Klansmen are "pure and above reproach." "England for Englishmen, France for Frenchmen, Italy for Italians, and America for Americans," says Shelton elsewhere in the pamphlet. Because so much in the world is set in the eyes of the Klan, the only possibility for change is *complete* eradication of evil, *total* removal of blacks and Jews, and *unqualified* acceptance of the

Constitution ("anyone who violates one clause of the Constitution would . . ."). Given the genetic deficiency of the offending groups, only total revolution will do. Similarly, given the inherent bias of the media, the courts, and the established churches, their pronouncements must be disregarded in toto as well.

The Klan does not find its purpose in life through self-actualizing, through helping others, or through changing public policy in piece-meal fashion. While they do seem motivated by an historical mandate, the source of that mandate is unclear: The advancement of Christian-ity? Strict constructionism? Returning to the chivalric code? Despite this vagueness, the Klan is able to find right and wrong in religion ("an infidel is a person who rejects Jesus Christ") in law ("we have not heard of a single instance where the Klan . . . has violated the law"), and in morality ("this is a stand for the purity of the home"). Given the magnitude of the Klan's goals, success cannot be had quickly. Rewriting an entire nation's laws, disbanding the media, eliminating three-fourths of the world's religions, and removing all foreigners from the U.S. is a tall order. Only the tireless need apply.

The Klansman is an empiricist. He rejects abstractions and believes what his eyes tell him: the pigmentation of skin, the length of a nose, the existence of "true facts" (as opposed to "propaganda"). His sensory organs tell all: "God drew the color line and man should so let it remain." The world he projects is, therefore, a tidy world with people and ideas housed in nativist categories. Books (and, one suspects, edu-cation in general) merely confuse things because they mangle categor-ical distinctions (for example, by conceiving of a black patriot or a white libertine). By keeping his eyes on what he "knows for sure," the Klansman will not underestimate his enemies.

Klan rhetoric has a tired quality to it. Its fantasy themes are now formless and shopworn: rapacious blacks, crooked lawyers, liberated women, power-mongering Catholics, usurious Jews. The pamphlets issued from its national headquarters do not differ from year to year or from decade to decade. It is as if Klan persuaders had long since found their major claims and were now interested only in collecting copycat data. This repetition makes for a lazy rhetoric, a rhetoric that can be heard in any age but which seems peculiar to no age. This may be why the Klan has been consistently relegated to marginal status in the United States, a rhetorical fate for which we may all be grateful.

CONCLUSION

This chapter has treated the rhetoric of new age Klansmen, tele-vision evangelists, writers of recommendation letters, American presi-dents, magazine authors, Boys Scouts, aging pigs, and a U.S.-loving

Canadian. All embraced values. Each depended on myth. All traded in fantasy themes. Each went about rhetorical business in a different way, because each had a special message to share. Each had a vision of what an ideal world would be like and each tried to share that vision with others. Some, like the Boy Scouts, succeeded because their goals were traditional, while others, like Robert Schuller, succeeded because they demanded so little from their listeners. Some, like the Klansmen, failed because the picture they painted was so small, while others, like Jimmy Carter, failed because he did not know which picture he wished to paint. Still others, like Gordon Sinclair, succeeded because he had a message for a moment. But he eventually receded into the background because that was his only message and because there are so many moments.

Each of these persuaders was unique, but each shared something as well: a culture. But having said that, what has one said? After all, each had a different rhetorical goal and each had a distinctive style. But each also had tremendous rhetorical confidence, the sense that his or her message would win the day. Jimmy Carter typified this attitude. Like the Boy Scouts, the Klan, and the advice columnists, Jimmy Carter really believed that his remarks would chip away at the edifice of public opinion. He knew that the odds against him were large, but that did not daunt him. In the same speech he took on political apathy, human selfishness, historical insensitivity, failed resolve, and national greed. Despite these challenges, Mr. Carter, like the authors of the *Webelos Scout Book*, felt sure that he could talk people into behaving better than they had been behaving.

Mr. Carter's instincts sprang directly from the American evangelical tradition in politics. The very act of speaking as he did when he did was a cultural affirmation. Moreover, like the writers of the recommendation letters, Jimmy Carter could not help but fold into his speech half of the American value system: concern for others, self-discipline, response to a challenge, among others. Unfortunately, it was the other half of the American value system—personal independence, self-assuredness, a refusal to acknowledge inadequacy—that undid him. So when he spoke, Mr. Carter was surrounded by his culture. So are all persuaders. But *why* one half of the American value system prevailed that day and why the other half did not is a thorny question. It takes a cultural critic to answer it.

CHAPTER ELEVEN

Dramatistic Analysis

(With David Payne)

Remember when you knew most of your neighbors and their children? Wasn't it a comfort to know if your child was playing a couple of blocks away and had a bump, bruise, or skinned elbow that one of your friends would take care of the immediate problem and let you know, because you'd show the same concern? This is how small neighborhoods used to be. This is how Wimbledon Country is [Wimbledon Country, 1988:3]!

* * * * *

Legend Oaks is a carefully planned neighborhood of nearly 300 thickly-wooded acres in the very heart of Southwest Austin. Here, Mother Nature, preserved and even enhanced by new plantings, lives in harmony with a new standard of neighborhood amenities. Right now, children laugh and swing on our playscape, tennis balls bounce across our lighted court, and the surface of our pool is broken by a swimmer's rhythmic strokes [Legend Oaks, 1988:F12].

* * * * *

When you purchase a home site in Weston Lakes you can enjoy the prestigious Weston Lakes Country Club and build your dream home when you're ready. The country club features one of the finest 18-hole championship golf courses in Texas, adult and family swimming pools, tennis courts, croquet lawn and fine dining. Situated among huge century old pecan and oak trees and shimmering natural lakes, Weston Lakes offers a distinctive and private life style. The lakes act as a clearwater moat surrounding the property and enhance the privacy and security of the development. They are also stocked with catfish and trophy-size bass [Weston Lakes, 1988:5].

* * * * *

The homes in Ember Oaks Estates are built on lush, wooded homesites and are surrounded by gently rolling hills, giving the entire area a peaceful country atmosphere . . . Ember Oaks offers a secluded atmosphere, yet it is close to Southlake, the new IBM complex, Las Colinas, the Mid Cities and Dallas/Fort Worth International Airport [Fox and Jacobs, 1988:J5].

* * * * *

Our company sells houses. Nothing more. If you need to live near the third busiest airport in the United States so that you can travel four days out of five for Big Blue, you're going to hear a lot of planes. Now, we'll be happy to plant a few begonias next to your house so you can be reminded of Mayberry R.F.D., but you'll still be living within twenty miles of three million people. We've been in business for twenty-five years, so see us if you want a house built. As for illusions, you'll have to shop elsewhere. For a hundred and twenty thousand bucks we can't give you prestige—you'll have to earn that by becoming president of your company, playing ball for the Dallas Mavericks, running for Congress, or writing a best seller. Our company can't relieve your guilt feelings about your latchkey kids and we sure as hell can't stop the air pollution you and your neighbors will generate on I-30 each morning. When we build houses, we supply the two-by-fours, the duct tape, the corner molding, the electrical circuits, and the paneling. You supply the baloney.

In the last of these ads, something has gone awry. Or maybe something has gone wry. The first four ads, drawn from the Homes sections of various Texas newspapers, represent their genre nicely. Filled with overly rich images, these ads turn brick-and-wallboard boxes into much grander places by focusing on what their products symbolize rather than what they are. The last ad, however, misses the game plan entirely. Its depressing frankness fails to do an essential job of rhetoric: blend an audience's lived life with its psychic life.

Critic Kenneth Burke says that it takes mystery, adventure, community, and magic to make a human creature. He says that to thwart people's imaginations (as in the fifth ad) is to deny people the resources they need to cope with rootlessness and anomie. He says that the need for drama is not just an affectation that some people have but a basic need that *all* people have, as basic as the needs for food, sex, and shelter. Burke would probably say that the need for drama is so profound that the fifth advertisement could only have been written by a textbook author for ironic purposes. And he would be right.

This chapter details the critical approach of Kenneth Burke, a critic who has explored the complex relationships among aesthetics, politics, language, and social organization. Burke's ideas have influenced countless students of rhetoric and literature as well as sociologists, political scientists, historians, linguists, and philosophers. Burke urges the doing of criticism not because rhetoric is powerful, even though it surely is, and not because criticism is interesting, which goes without saying. Rather, says Burke, tracking the "rhetorical motive" is central to understanding what human beings are at root (symbol-users, he feels), what they strive to do (rise above themselves, he argues), and what they have the potential to do (rise up together, he hopes).

Especially in his younger days, Burke viewed criticism as social activism. One of his most famous essays [1973:191–232], "The Rhetoric of Hitler's Battle," is a trenchant analysis of the persuasion in Adolph Hitler's *Mein Kampf.* Today, of course, academic discussion of Hitler's techniques has been something of a cliché, but it was Burke who traced the trajectory of Hitler's rhetoric in the early 1930s. Unlike his contemporaries, who viewed Hitler as just another politician, Burke treated the Führer as a medicine man who had concocted an elixir for the ailing German spirit.

In 1939, few commentators anticipated the systematic annihilation of the Jew, but Burke saw that potential in the scenarios Hitler sketched in *Mein Kampf.* Burke reasoned that any person who saw himself striding—alone—across a grand political stage could dispatch unthinkingly the lesser characters in his self-made play, much as Shakespeare's kings dismissed their fools with nary a thought. Accordingly, Burke feared Hitler's rhetoric more than he feared Hitler's politics. Burke knew that political systems come and go as a nation's economy, sociology, and demography evolve. But a galvanizing drama can be repeated endlessly, Burke warned, because people's deepest fears and anxieties never change. As a result, Burke became a kind of political Freudian and Hitler became his first, and most disturbed, patient.

Burke wrote his initial book, *Counter-Statement,* in 1931 to "counter" the view that art and literature were merely ornamental. Rather, he said, all of the verbal arts, including literature, drama, speech, pedagogy, and reportage, affect both social knowledge and political decision making. While exploring this thesis, Burke put over six million words in print in fourteen books and in hundreds of essays, lectures, poems, stories, and even a modest novel. Throughout his work, Burke refused to treat life-*as*-drama. Rather, he felt that life-*is*-drama, that people's actions are themselves symbolic statements. In this view, rhetoric employs primitive dramatic forms that make people see more than their eyes alone allow them to see.

Such forms abound in the passages above. In the first ad, the reader is asked to **identify** with a simpler, safer time and place. For many people (urban dwellers, newly arrived immigrants, single-parent families), such a place never in fact existed. But these neighborhoods exist throughout American literature, not to mention in episodes of *The Waltons,* so people can come to view this idealized neighborhood as their neighborhood. Burke would also call attention to how the second passage uses **language clusters** to build its images of innocence. Thick woods, Mother Nature, new plantings, children, water, natural rhythms—these are primal terms, Burke might observe, terms that recall for us the stuff of dreams. Judging by its advertising, Legend Oaks is aptly named.

Burke feels that the principle of **hierarchy** is especially helpful in explaining rhetorical force. The third passage provides evidence of hierarchy with its talk of "prestigious" country clubs, "fine" dining, and "distinctive" life-styles. "Moving up" when buying a home would be more than just a metaphor for Burke, since one's house has psychic as well as material properties and is intimately tied to one's sense of relative worth. When bass are described as "trophy-size," Burke might note, somebody, somewhere, is feeling inadequate. Also, while this passage celebrates old hierarchies with its talk of "century old" pecans, secure "moats," and "croquet lawns," it implies that even the newly arrived can scale the summits if they have the price.

While issues of hierarchy pose the central questions of drama, **transcendence** provides the answers. When considering the fourth passage, for example, Burke might note how "secluded closeness" splits the difference between the inconveniences of rural living and the hectic pace of city life. "Secluded closeness" does not actually make living in the Metroplex easy as much as it transcends such problems by offering a construct around which all persons—country bumpkin as well as city slicker—can rally. Even if it takes an hour on the interstate to get home each day, a "lush homesite" in a "country atmosphere," not a tract home in a subdivision, awaits. This image adds dramatic action to the surburbanite's commute and calls attention to what people are: actors living out their lives speaking scripts to one another.

The dramatistic critic reads these scripts, although there can be danger in doing so. Too often, critics use Burke's ideas merely to label textual elements rather than explain their symbolic power. To avoid this trap, Burke's system will be discussed selectively so that the principles of dramatism, not its terminology, become our focus. But discussing Burke selectively also has its disadvantages, since Burke's mind has ranged so far over so many subjects. Burke's writings show him to be a topical critic, a narrative critic, a structural critic, and a rather scientific student of syntax and lexicon. He has commented on role, imagery, and speech-acts, and his treatment of myth has been consummate. He was also an early devotee of Marxist thought and linguistic skepticism (topics to be treated in Chapter Twelve). Burke, in short, follows his own advice to use all there is to use when doing criticism.

THE PRINCIPLES OF DRAMATISM

Almost as soon as drama existed in Western culture, criticism existed. Among the first critics were the *theoria*, a troupe commissioned to travel about in ancient Greece gathering local information about society. Often, they would comment upon local rituals and festivals, activities designed from the start to call attention to what is noble and what is base in people and their motives. By adopting the dramatistic model for criticism, Burke seized on features of drama that had long been recognized but inadequately developed as a critical paradigm.

Burke presented his theory of dramatism before the advent of television. With so few people going to the legitimate theatre these days, does a dramatistic model still make sense? Indubitably. Current estimates are that the average American child will watch 30,000 television stories by the time of maturity. High drama this is not, but television is often good low drama. Each day, TV reintroduces the child to the very heart of dramatic action: why people do what they do, a phenomenon Burke calls **motive.** Cartoons teach that exasperation leads to irrationality (as with Sylvester and Tweetie); situation comedies teach that callousness can be profitable, if censurable (as with Alex in *Family Ties*); adventure stories teach that evil must be punished at all costs (as in *Miami Vice*). All such dramas throw light on human motives, inviting viewers to examine—and judge—how people behave.

Equally important, television employs age-old dramatic conventions. Because of television, political conventions turn into prime-time extravaganzas; electronic preaching adopts the form of modern morality plays; and George Steinbrenner's Yankees become as intriguing off the field as on. Through television, even the most pedestrian American has been made drama-literate. But when Burke introduced his notion of dramatism in 1939, people were less sophisticated about the mass media (recall that 1939 was the year in which Orson Welles's radio hoax, "The War of the Worlds," capitalized on its audience's ignorance of dramatic forms). Today, in contrast, most of us have a second sense about drama. Burke's critical system depends upon this second sense by making six key assumptions:

1. *The range of rhetoric is wide.* Wherever he looked, Burke found rhetoric. In the language of Chapter One, Burke rarely analyzed obviously rhetorical messages (commercial salesmanship, political solicitation, religious pamphleteering). Instead, he teased out the unspecified policies hidden in implicit rhetoric: poems, plays, polite conversation, signs, maxims, histories, scientific treatises, folklore. As Brown [1969:22] points out, "Burke does not try to write of history as a historian, logic as a logician, politics as a political scientist, language as a

linguist, poetry as a literary critic, and religion as a theologian. He takes them all in his rhetorical stride . . . treating them all as forms of rhetoric themselves."

One of Burke's most famous studies was an analysis of Antony's address to the mob in Shakespeare's *Julius Caesar*. Instead of detailing how Antony cleverly bested Brutus & Co. in the speech ("So are they all, all honorable men"), Burke focused on how *Shakespeare* adapted the play to his Elizabethan audience. Why, for example, did Shakespeare's audience wind up respecting Caesar and not Brutus or Cassius? After all, Caesar was deaf in one ear, suffered from falling sickness, "cried out like a sick girl" on occasion, and was timid and superstitious in addition. Who could identify with such an undistinguished person? Burke asked. And yet is it not crucial that we do so? Burke asked further. He solved his puzzle thus:

> For such reasons as these you are willing to put a knife through the ribs of Caesar.
>
> Still, you are sorry for Caesar. We cannot profitably build a play around the horror of a murder if you do not care whether the murdered man lives or dies. So we had to do something for Caesar—and you would be ashamed if you stopped to consider what we did. I believe we made Caesar appealing by proxy. That is: I, Antony, am a loyal follower of Caesar; you love me for a good fellow, since I am expansive, hearty, much as you would be after not too heavy a meal; and as one given to pleasure, I am not likely to lie awake at night plotting you injury. If such a man loves Caesar, his love lifts up Caesar in your eyes. . . .
>
> [Although I, Antony, was a reveler before Caesar's death], in expanding to my expanded role, I must break the former mold somewhat. Let *savants* explain the change by saying that carefree Antony was made a soberer man, and a bitter one, by the death of Caesar. But it is an obvious fact that if an important cog in the plot vanishes in the very middle of our drama, something has to take its place. In deputizing for Caesar, I found it impossible to remain completely Antony. Let *savants* explain my altered psychology as they will—*I* know it was a playwright's necessity [Burke, 1964:66,67].

Like all good rhetorical critics, Burke focuses here on the speaker-audience relationship, looking through the text to readers' needs and expectations. Because he thereby focused on the "strategic business" of literature, Burke is *persona non grata* for orthodox critics interested in a text's inherent merit. But such inherency does not exist for Burke. He believes that truth is a human thing and, therefore, a negotiated thing, that any attempt to share unaltered reality with an audience is doomed to failure: "Even if any given terminology is a *reflection* of reality, by its very nature as a terminology it must be a *selection* of reality; and to this extent it must function also as a *deflection* of reality" [Burke, 1966:45].

Sharing ideas with others, Burke felt, was always an act of misdirection, a condition required by the complexity of language. Even the simple image of the shepherd, Burke observed, remains innocent only if an audience half thinks about the shepherd's duties. A fuller consideration of that job reveals ominous portents: "If the shepherd is guarding the sheep so that they may be raised for market, though his role (considered in itself as guardian of the sheep) concerns only their good, he is implicitly identified with their slaughter. A total stress upon the autonomy of his pastoral specialization here functions *rhetorically* as a mode of expression whereby we are encouraged to overlook the full implications of his office" [Burke, 1966:301–302].

Like most rhetorical thinkers, Burke calls attention to the artificial hidden within the natural. He also highlights the contrivances of life in order to expose the motives of life's contrivers. Lentricchia [1982:143] reinforces Burke's point with the following example: "[U]nlike real estate, the language of privilege and authority is not the private property of any person or class. The linguistic symbols of authority, like 'rights' and 'freedom,' are appropriable—they can be seized by a collective and turned against those who appropriated them in order to dispossess yet earlier appropriators."

In his writing, Burke is especially insistent that *formal discourse* be studied carefully, since it often escapes public scrutiny. He felt that the "drama of human relations" could even be found in the wording of political constitutions, bureaucratic injunctions, academic treatises, and scientific discourse. Especially scientific discourse. Burke was concerned that the technological establishment (which grew up around him in the 1940s and 1950s) was escaping critical examination because of its rhetoric of nonrhetoric. The scientific word, Burke argued, is often exploitative and combative; it typically dissociates thought and feeling and too often rejects its communal responsibilities [Frank, 1969]. "Scientism," Burke argued, "needs to be counter-balanced by a stress on 'intuition,' 'imagination,' 'vision,' and 'revelation'" [Rueckert, 1963:38].

In terms of the politics of the late 1980s, Burke might, therefore, be attracted to the rhetoric of Jesse Jackson, not because of Jackson's political viewpoints, but because Jackson's rhetoric stressed social possibilities rather than systemic constraints, negotiation rather than determinism. Burke might worry that the technocratic realism of a Michael Dukakis or a George Bush would reduce politics to "mere motion" rather than to "dramatic action" and thus hide the *choice-making* that all politics involves. Burke always appreciated persuasion that owned up to its nature as persuasion. But whenever rhetoric denied itself, Burke perked up his ears.

2. *All life is drama.* Burke believes that drama is present whenever people congregate but that the essential drama of a situation is not revealed until rhetoric exploits it. The new journalists, writers who describe real events but who do so as novelist/journalists, exemplify Burke's point. For example, Truman Capote's *In Cold Blood* tells of an innocent farm family being slaughtered by persons they did not know. Before Capote got to this story, it was just another uninspiring crime in a rural setting. Because of his writing skills, however, Capote could restore the dramatic action hidden by the disembodied statistics of the local police blotter. Capote's rhetoric returned life to the victims who had died and humanized the story of the inhuman beasts who had perpetrated the crime.

The beat journalists in western Kansas had also written about this crime, but their reports did not help readers hear the dull thud of the death instruments or feel the rush of the murderers' adrenalin as they committed their crimes. Capote made his readers feel these things and more when he dramatized the murders. Thus, in Burke's terms, the new journalists might be better dubbed old journalists, since they *reestablish* the dramatic action of prior events, events whose drama would have seeped away if the writer's rhetoric had not taken hold.

Rhetoric is, therefore, a compass for dramatic action: It points out what is at stake, for whom, by affixing labels to activities. Without such labels, Burke says, people cannot describe what they feel, even to themselves. Burke was especially interested in definitional labels [Heath, 1986:96]. When Truman Capote titled his book *In Cold Blood*, for example, he revealed his view of the crime's motivational dynamics. Similarly, when the FBI referred to campus disturbances as "riots" in the 1960s, it hoped to expose the students as "barbarians" and pave the way for the "heroic" procedures it would use to halt the agitation. More recently, just after the Democrats left the Omni convention hall in 1988, right-to-life groups vowed to continue their convention-inspired protests, arguing that Atlanta had become "the Selma of 1988," thereby co-opting the dramatic action of the civil rights protests of several decades earlier.

To appreciate rhetoric, then, one must understand a culture's library of dramas. As Rueckert [1963:20] observes, the "quest" drama alone has inspired countless works of literature, including *The Odyssey*, *The Aeneid*, *The Adventures of Huckleberry Finn*, and *The Heart of Darkness*. Quests are also found in the rhetoric of the U.S. space program, the war against cancer, and détente with the Soviet Union. Becoming aware of these formulae, says Brummett [1984d:4], especially when they are used in nonnarrative discourse (for example, in Congressional testimony), can help the critic disestablish dangerous forms of dramatic action. So, for example, although Joe McCarthy used the quest motif to depict himself as a stalwart searcher after Communists in the 1950s, his fanaticism eventually resulted in the seeker becoming the sought. One of his opponents caught on to his histrionics and tore apart his theatre of the absurd with a single, memorable statement: "Let us not assassinate this lad further, Senator. You have done enough. Have you no decency, sir, at long last? Have you left no sense of decency" [Cohn, 1968:197]?

3. *Dramas feature human motives.* This is a key Burkean assumption. It says that the central purpose of drama is to spotlight why people do what they do. It also says that our natural curiosity about human motives can seduce us. As an illustration, let us consider the headlines from a randomly chosen front page of *The New York Times* (Sunday, March 27, 1988):

"SCHULTZ WILL MAKE NEW MIDEAST TRIP IN QUEST FOR PEACE"

"REGIME IN PANAMA SEIZES FLOUR MILLS AND CANAL DOCKS"

"NUCLEAR ARMS AND NEW JOBS CLASH IN IDAHO"

"ARMED TRUCE DIVIDES CHAD AND LIBYANS"

"DROUGHT IN WEST BRINGING RATIONING AND THREAT TO CROPS"

"ALONG U.S. BORDER, A THIRD WORLD IS REBORN"

Dramatism is not difficult to find here: a dangerous and uncertain peace trip, more exploitation of the weak by the strong, a potential class war in Idaho, yet another imbroglio among old enemies, a threat of drought, the rebirth of a nation. But these are not just random happenings; they are also motivated. In each case, the *Times*'s headline writers have taken us behind the scenes to show that someone is acting for/with/against someone else for some set of reasons. Droughts, of course, have no reasons, but, even there, some (as yet unspecified) person is being said to take action for some (as yet unspecified) purpose. The job of the newspaper headline, then, is not just to describe action but to reveal motive. *This* is what makes us read newspapers.

Even a staid journal like *The New York Times* cannot resist the motival mandate. With regard to the Schultz visit, for example, a Mr. Redman of the State Department is quoted as saying "the trip does not reflect increased expectations of a breakthrough in the negotiations, but is a continuation of the diplomatic approach that the United States has pursued without substantial results in recent months." One quickly recognizes the rhetoric of governance here: Trips for peace are symbolic, as are explanations of trips for peace, as are newspaper reports of explanations of trips for peace. In other words, the details of the story *contradict* the bold headline, thereby providing the careful reader with crucial information about the forthcoming trip: There has been no real change in Middle East attitudes; the upcoming trip is a routine one; even if it were special, the actions of the U.S. would still be constrained by the other players in the international game. In short, without these additional (motival) details, there is really no story at all.

With regard to motive, the critic's job is (1) to inspect discourse for its model of motivation and (2) to explain the rhetor's dramatic actions parsimoniously. That is a tall order. Motives, after all, are complex, overlapping, and sometimes contradictory. So Burke begins simply by examining a rhetoric's **vocabulary of motives**—the language it uses to explain human behavior—in order to outline that rhetoric's theory of volition. It is this motivational apparatus, says Burke, that makes one piece of rhetoric different from another.

For example, a scientist may describe drinking-while-driving as "conditioned behavior," a phrase that downplays motive, while the libertarian and the religious cleric may highlight motives but do so oppositely (for example, "drinking as personal freedom" vs. "drinking as sin"). For the scientist, decisions are made by the brain; for the libertarian they are made by the mind; for the preacher they are made by the conscience. Each sketches a different theory of life: a matter of random reinforcement, a question of political conversion, part of a divine plan. Each differs as to human possibility (there is much, some, none) and each proposes a unique solution to problems (scientific analysis, political propaganda, moral submission). Different still is the rhetoric of Mothers Against Drunk Driving. For them, drinking is a social act, often a public act, and only the *public's motives*—not the driver's motives—are relevant to the discussion. MADD's vocabulary of motives is, therefore, neither long nor textured: "Killing while drinking and driving is murder, plain and simple."

4. *Hierarchy is fundamental to human symbolism.* Every page of the daily newspaper shows the centrality of hierarchy. *Page 1:* "Henderson Elected Mayor in Landslide." *Editorial Page:* "Trash Collectors Should Strike." *Obituary Page:* "Prominent Physician, Church Deacon, Dies." *Sports Page:* "Tway Loses British Open by One Stroke." *Society Page:* "Harvard Grad Marries Social Worker." *Entertainment Page: "Son of Rocky* Debuts Locally." In these ways and more, the newspaper tells who has gotten how far in life, which is why young brides and old mayors alike prepare their press releases carefully. Even after death, hierarchy remains, and so the good doctor's survivors labor over his obituary notice. Yet it is also true that people read newspapers not just to find out about the rich and powerful but to regain hope that the trash collectors among them will receive justice as well.

Hierarchy is, by definition, incremental, so dramatic tension is highest when the increments are small (for example, when a championship slips away with one bad putt). Hierarchy is also bidirectional: it recounts failure as well as triumph. Should *Son of Rocky* ever be filmed, it would no doubt depict a young man brought up in luxury who somehow loses his fortune. Cast headlong into life's gutter, Rocky Jr. would retrace his father's pugilistic steps until he, like Dad, becomes older, wiser, and, given improved ticket distribution, considerably richer.

Burke says that people are "goaded by hierarchy" to do more and be more and have more. But Burke's hierarchies are not just monetary. Values, too, are hierarchical, which is why preachers preach. Knowledge is hierarchical, which is why teachers teach. Beauty is hierarchical, which is why there are cosmetics commercials. Even though none of us has yet found an ideal person, idea, or object, the *principle* of hierarchy goads us on. Despite a world filled with injustice, many feel that "Jesus is the answer." Despite the sorry track record of consumer products, others "Buy Panasonic, the last TV you'll ever own." In their heart of hearts, many people harbor religious doubts and even more distrust home appliances. And yet the principle of hierarchy will not let them rest. They become gluttons for the rhetoric of perfection.

Rhetoric is filled with overstatements, because it so often focuses on the end-points of the hierarchy, inspiring us with the highest highs, frightening us with the lowest lows. As Nichols [1969:279] observes, the rhetoric of Karl Marx had special power for many, because his political cosmos was structured so hierarchically: The worker worked for the state, the state worked for the worker, all worked for the motherland. As a result, the peasant could perform his menial chores happily, knowing that he or she was contributing *directly* to the great historical drama of Communism. Griffin [1969:460] argues that many other successful movements have used similar motivational tactics when positing an ideal order, a heaven, the good society, utopia, etc.

Burke [1966:18] says that rhetoric can also tilt in the opposite direction when it describes perfect evil: the Christian's devil, the Nazi's Jew, Israel's PLO, etc. The general principle seems to be that persuasion profits directly from the "hierarchical energy" contained in an audience's values. Brummett [1981a:260] reports that Ronald Reagan profited in precisely this way when telling voters that their economic habits (spending a great deal, owing a great deal) were consistent with the traditional American values of "free enterprise," "economic growth," and "renewed productivity." Reagan's opponents at the time said that his rhetoric made the American people comfortable with their prejudices, but perhaps a better charge was that Mr. Reagan made them comfortable with their hierarchies.

5. *Rhetoric promises transcendence.* If hierarchy gives rhetoric a quantitative dimension (how much, how often, how high), transcendence gives it a qualitative dimension (how good, how grand, how noble). Hierarchy argues that people can get more; transcendence argues that they can become better. Hierarchy suggests how people can improve; transcendence tells them why they should. Rhetoric has transcendent themes because people want to feel they are doing something important with their lives, that they are rising above the ordinary. According to Burke, meeting these needs turns rhetoric into a kind of **secular prayer.** Perhaps this is why black preachers have been such an important emotional resource in their communities throughout American history. They secularized Christian motifs for black slaves (and, later, for the black unemployed), assuring them that their hard physical labors would earn them rewards in tomorrow's tomorrow. Transcendence can also be found at the other end of life's hierarchy: An aging millionaire suddenly decides to become an aging philanthropist as well. Those who practice the art of philanthropic solicitation know full well that some people will trade millions for meaning. Like hierarchy, the need for transcendence goads us too.

Transcendence is also an incorporative device. When a U.S. president speaks of "all Americans," momentarily at least Texans cease to be Texans and New Yorkers New Yorkers. At that same time, American doctors become less medical and American farmers less agricultural. Similarly, each time we give the Elks' handshake or wear the company softball uniform, we transcend to another level of symbolic identity, acquiring new "motives" for what we do. Moving upward in this way gives people a sense of drama and also offers them new explanations for their actions: "I am standing in this long line to vote not because I am a masochist but because I am a patriot." Naturally, Burke was wary of transcendent rhetorics, since so much evil has been done at their behest. And yet his reading of history resigned him to their drumbeat. From the time of the pharaoh's pyramids to that of the modern organizational chart, people have been attracted to hierarchies and to the transcendent rhetorics that help them scale these hierarchies.

6. *Rhetoric is fueled by the negative.* Burke is fascinated by the negative. He accounts for the omnipresence of rhetoric by looking to the inevitable divisions among people and between people and their personal goals. This makes people "relentlessly rhetorical" [Rueckert, 1982:22] as they try to bridge the gap between themselves and their dreams. Burke also regards people as guilt-ridden by nature, who, when sharing rhetoric with one another, use "collectivist effort" [Rueckert, 1963:47] to slay the "guilty part" of themselves and become "purified." In doing so, rhetoric serves important, realistic purposes by becoming an intellectual defense against ignorance, an emotional

defense against estrangement, a spiritual defense against impurity. In these ways, rhetoric becomes, like literature, what Burke would call **equipment for living.**

"C-SPAN junkies" who fear nuclear holocaust and who, as a result, gorge themselves on Congressional rhetoric seem to use rhetoric as equipment for living. They do so because such speechmaking is highly controlled and, importantly, boring ("Why should I be afraid when the Representatives in the chamber are falling asleep"). Similarly, people watch soap operas to steel themselves against cancer, infidelity, drug use, aging, and loneliness. Each day, soap-opera characters confront these evils and persevere (there *will* be a show again tomorrow!), thereby providing viewers with steady doses of emotional medicine. In other words, "passive" television viewing may not be passive at all, but a safe, active way of coping with real and potential psychological loss.

Burke says that nature itself is completely "positive," that it is people who invented the negative, which is why, wherever he looked, Burke found formulas of guilt and redemption. As Rueckert [1963:130] says, "a 'No Trespassing' sign on a piece of property is the infusion of a linguistic negative into nature" (the fenced-in pasture has no "preference" as to who walks where) and "the proposition that adultery and fornication are sinful is the infusion of a linguistic negative into pure sensory experience" (the sex drive does not require a spouse). Rhetoric, in short, puts people in charge of people by saying "thou shalt not." Why celebrate the Fourth of July? To stave off tyranny. Why attend a funeral? To conquer death, at least temporarily. Why buy aluminum siding? Because weather can be brutal. Christian soldiers march onward because there is sin; Madonna sings of love because there is hate; Jane Fonda shouts encouragement in her workout tapes because there is blubber. In each case, a rhetor steps forward to shout "no!" to nature.

In nature, time passes. In nature, memory fades. But Carlson and Hocking [1988:211] discovered that slips of paper continue to be collected each day at the Vietnam War Memorial in Washington, D.C., deposited there by ordinary citizens so that *they*, not nature, will have the last word: "Finally, America has awakened and taken home those of us who live and remember you and all the others . . . I kept your spirit alive 'til America woke up, sir. I'm done. Rest well my friend, my Lieutenant." Similarly, as Bostdorff [1987:45] observes, political cartoonist Tony Auth could not personally fire James Watt (a pro-business Secretary of the Interior in the Reagan administration), but he could symbolically rearrange nature by creating a Ronald Reagan National Forest and populating its hillsides with oil derricks.

In both examples, rhetoric has reduced evil to a **scapegoat,** a person, group, or idea treated as the incarnation of evil. Hitler, of course, used this technique, but Burke argued that this same principle is employed whenever people build a sense of unity by identifying a common enemy. Sometimes, the scapegoat is made obvious (like James Watt) and sometimes it is not (a "sleeping America" in the War Memorial example). At still other times, the scapegoat is not a person at all but an object (demon rum), an idea (reckless liberalism), or even a bodily process (the AA's notion that alcoholism is a disease). Burke notes that while rhetoric often scapegoats others (an operation he calls **victimage**), it can also scapegoat the self (what he calls **mortification**). In either case, rhetoric cleanses the soul of sin and provides new "attitudes" for use in daily decision making.

Burke was ambivalent about his discovery of the negative. He understood that any group must develop a shared conception of evil if it is to develop a social order. He realized that morals must be taught somewhere, either through formal institutions (church or school) or through everyday experience (popular entertainment, family interaction). If commercial advertisements, for example, inadvertently teach people how to deal with romantic or work problems, they serve an educational function. But Burke would also note that these same ads purge something or someone to get their messages across. For example, when Crest urges that we brush three times a day "to avoid that trip to the dentist's office," the image of the dental profession suffers once again. Similarly, Burke would be bothered, as was Brummett [1985], to learn that young, sexually active, women were overwhelmingly chosen for victimage in contemporary horror films. What lessons about life are being taught here? That youth is bad? That sex is bad? That women are bad? Rhetoric may indeed be equipment for living, but, we must ask, what sort of life is that equipment endorsing?

THE METHODS OF DRAMATISM

Burke's interpreters often describe his critical approach as a system of conceptual principles, but it is more a loose confederation of ideas that Burke uses erratically but often brilliantly. Not being Kenneth Burkes, we must proceed more carefully. The key to Burke's brand of criticism is asking how and why a text is dramatized, and the principles examined in the first section of this chapter became Burke's basic critical vantage point. They can become our vantage point as well. Phrased as critical probes, they are:

1. Can principles of **hierarchy** be found in the discourse? Who or what has great value, little value? Is movement up the hierarchy

---

RHETORIC AND MASS ENTERTAINMENT

Critical Profile 11.1   Soap Standards

The business of soap operas is selling sin. Or so goes the common criticism. But research on the effects of soaps on moral standards remains inconclusive. Traditionally, research has focused "on the moral content of the programs and the number of instances in which moral dilemmas arise." For John C. Sutherland and Shelly J. Siniawsky, however, this quantitative approach to soap opera research is insufficient. "Merely tabulating the instances in which moral questions arise does not reveal how these questions were resolved. It may be that moral dilemmas are treated and resolved in a manner that is consistent with a moral code." In other words, if soaps *punish* rather than condone the sins they portray, they may not be liberalizing standards at all but rather *guarding* traditional moral values.

In an effort to determine how soaps actually deal with sin, Sutherland and Siniawsky followed reports of "All My Children" and "General Hospital" in *Soap Opera Digest*. They tracked the occurrence of dilemmas involving fourteen moral standards critics claim are most frequently violated on soaps, among which were: premarital/extramarital sex, abortion, incest, divorce, alcohol abuse, blackmail, deception, and so forth.

What were the researchers' conclusions? First, deceit, murder, and sex were the most frequently occurring moral issues. Second, although not all of the moral issues raised were resolved within the period studied, most moral violations were ultimately resolved *consistently with traditional moral standards.* Moreover, these two soaps actually tended to *punish* those who violated moral standards "either socially or economically." In other words, soaps were found to support the status quo and to reinforce traditional morals (in a backhanded sort of way).

In short, "the issue of soap operas' presentation of moral issues is not as clear-cut as many would have the public believe." Given Sutherland and Siniawsky's revelation that at least two soaps *do* have "standards," that they punish more often than they condone sin, could it be that further research will reveal soap operas to have become the modern bulwark against societal disintegration? Are soaps becoming a kind of secular televangelism that sustains Judeo-Christian morality each weekday afternoon? For some, that would be a chilling thought indeed.

Profiled by: Kerry Riley
Citation: Sutherland & Siniawsky (1982)

---

possible or are things "set"? Are there many gradations or only a few? Are the hierarchial stages clear or hazy?

2. What is the rhetor's **vocabulary of motives?** Why do things turn out as they do in life? Why do people think and act as they

Critical Profile 11.2   Winning Means Having to Say You're Sorry

Sports championships are more important to many people than governmental elections. Like politics, sports in the United States is an institution. Also like politics, sports operates largely through unwritten rules. To discover such rules is to understand the values and workings of the institution at hand. For this reason, Noreen Kruse of the University of Iowa examined when and how public outcries required sports figures to defend their personal characters.

For what must athletes apologize? According to Kruse, it is any action or statement that appears to threaten the team's chance of winning. "Sins" in the world of team sports include: fighting with teammates, leaving one's team for a higher salary, displaying a frivolous attitude on the field, not playing up to one's abilities, and expressing racist sentiments. Kruse concludes that "even when sport personalities' questionable actions appear to be related only indirectly to team success, those individuals may attempt to convince others that their conduct should not be used as evidence of bad character."

Are behavioral norms different in sports than in society generally? Perhaps, says Kruse. Former Green Bay Packer coach Bart Starr, for example, did not have to offer a public apology for violating National Football League rules in conducting a tryout for running back Duane Thomas. Starr noted that other teams were cheating and asserted, "We don't cheat. But we're going to go to the limit within the rules. And we're going to bend them within the framework." Despite his outspokenness on this occasion, Starr told reporters that if his remarks were publicly repeated, "your asses are not going to come through this door again." When the stories were, in fact, printed, Starr closed practices, canceled press conferences, and barred the reporters from the post-game locker rooms. The only response from Packer fans was to accuse the reporters of being "villains and traitors."

Sports figures apologize with the same tactics used by other public figures. They may assert that their improper actions were involuntary, accidental, justified, or provoked. By expressing regret, the athletic lore holds, athletes can help restore their team's chances of winning. By winning, and by giving fans the psychological boost they expect from athletic competition, the sports figure can be certain that all is forgiven. Studying what must be said to "get back on the team," whether in sports or politics, allows a critic to see through rhetorical trappings to the core values of an institution. For the sensitive critic, a public apology serves as a kind of cultural X-ray, revealing what is good, what is bad, what is possible, what is not. Athletes are a notoriously conservative group. When admitting their transgressions, they use rhetoric in its most conservative form—to make what has been true truer still. In other words, when the Fall tryouts are held, only mainstreamers need apply.

Profiled by: John Llewellyn
Citation: Kruse (1981)

Critical Profile 11.3   The Wonderful, Imperialist World of Disney

The name of Walt Disney is synonymous with wholesome children's entertainment. Indeed, the magic of Disney has enthralled generations of children around the world. But do the effects of Mickey Mouse and Donald
Duck comics end with the amusement of the reader? Or does the reader's
laughter mask the sounds of ideological wailing on the part of Walt Disney
Productions? And are children the only audience being addressed by
Mickey, Donald, and friends?

These questions were the focus of Ariel Dorfman and Armand Mattelart's
classic study of the Disney empire. They set out to uncover the capitalist
ideology and assumptions that lay beneath the surface of Disney's comics.
They discovered that the "wonderful world" represented by Disney is a persuasive tool used not only to socialize American children but also to reinforce the status quo that subjects Disney's readers in Third World countries
to the dominance of American imperialism. They argue that a strict analogy
can be found in Disney's cartoons: The Thirld World is to the United States
as children are to adults.

The adventure-to-foreign-lands motif is a standard story line in the Disney comics, note Dorfman and Mattelart, due in part to the sense of a natural order imparted from the theme of a return to foreign (primitive) lands.
Furthermore, the depiction of the native and his relationship to the Disney
characters serves to reinforce, and thus legitimize, the imperialist system.
Under such a system, the person who possesses advanced technology profits both monetarily and through socio-political control and thus is thought
to be superior to people without such knowledge.

One of the strips Dorfman and Mattelart discuss illustrates these points.
Moby Duck and Donald, having been captured by the Aridians, attempt to
extricate themselves by blowing soap bubbles. Enchanted by the bubbles,
the natives become distracted, the bubbles being magical to members of a
society lacking advanced technological capacity (the Aridian leader even
compares his people to children). Moby reinforces this connection: "It's only
a secret passed on from generation to generation," he says, effectively maintaining the distinction between the mystical and the technological, between
the child and the adult. Moby indicates that he will reveal this "secret" in
exchange for his freedom, proving Dorfman and Mattelart's contention that
"civilization is . . . to be administered by foreigners." The Aridian leader
responds by offering gold and jewels if only he, too, can learn the secret.

Thus, the noble savage consents to his own despoliation, "stand[ing] as
an exact replica of the relations between metropolis and satellite, between
empire and colony, between master and slave." Also as a consequence, Disney's readers are reinforced in thinking of their world as the "First World,"
of technology as having a kind of moral sanctity, and of primitive peoples
as deserving of second-class status. In short, it seems that persuasion lurks
everywhere, even in the funny papers.

Profiled by: Amy M. Korzick
Citation: Dorfman and Mattelart (1975)

do? Are their motives described clearly or mysteriously? Does the rhetor give personal reasons for speaking? Why or why not?

3. Who or what is being **scapegoated?** Is the scapegoating obvious or subtle? If the scapegoat is within ourselves, what sort of mortification is needed to purge it? If the scapegoat is another person or group, why have they been selected for victimage?
4. Are strategies of **transcendence** in evidence? What will help the audience get beyond the problems described? Are the transcendent forces human (a group, a nation) or extrahuman (God, fate)? Are they concrete (new legislation) or abstract (renewed spirit)?

Burke feels that we cannot speak without dramatizing, so questions of this sort are not really alien intrusions into a text. The average suburban cocktail party proves this. Informal chatter about the Neighborhood Watch Program (a transcendent solution), who is sleeping with whom (mortification and victimage), why good elementary teachers are hard to find (motive), and who might get promoted at the plant (hierarchy) are the very stuff of day-to-day drama. As the party drinks and dramatizing are ingested, the increasingly loud buzz of conversation proves the increasing influence of both. Burke, of course, was interested in weightier matters than those discussed at 7:00 P.M. in the suburbs. He was interested in texts like this:

> When I speak to you today and thus to millions of other Americans, I have more right to do this than anyone else. I have grown out of you yourselves. Once I myself stood among you, I was among you in the war for four and one-half years and now I speak to you to whom I feel myself to be bound still today, and for whom in the final analysis I carry on the struggle. As far as I was concerned the struggle was not necessary. Nor would I wage it for a class or any certain stratum of society. I lead the struggle for the masses of millions of our honest, industriously working, and creative people. . . .
>
> In my youth I was a worker like you, and then I worked my way up by industry, by study, and I can say, by starving. In my innermost being, however, I have always remained what I was before. When, after the war, I entered political life, I did so with the conviction that our people was poorly advised by its political leadership, that a horrible future awaited the American people as a result of this bad leadership. I acted then with the most sincere self-justification because I did not belong to those who were in any way responsible for the war. I was just as little responsible for the war as anyone among you, for at that time I was, just like you, an unknown person, whom fate passed over in the order of the day. In any case I have not counted myself among those who set themselves against their own nation at the time.

I was convinced that one had to enter the struggle for the destiny of the nation, if sooner or later the entire people was not to suffer a terrible ordeal. That is what separated me from the others who turned against America. When the war was over I, as a front soldier, assumed the right to represent that which I had recognized to be right. Before this I had not made any speeches, nor had I engaged in any activity. I was simply a man who earned his daily bread. Not until I saw after the conclusion of the war that the political leadership did not live up to what it had promised the nation, but that the contrary was true, did I go among the people and work with six other quite insignificant workers and found a movement.

I began with six or seven men. Today it is the greatest American Movement; this is so not by chance and not because the way was made easy for me, but because the ideas upon which I built are right. It was only for this reason that they could be carried through. For you can imagine, my friends, that when a man in my station in life begins a movement, success does not just fly to him. That is self-understood. One needs great tenacity and a tremendous will to begin such an enterprise at all. And I should like to say this to you: If I had this faith, I had it only because I knew the people and because I had no doubts as to the quality of the American people. The intellectual groups did not give me the courage to begin this gigantic work; I took courage because I knew the American worker and the American farmer. I knew that these two classes would one day become the bearers of the new spirit and that the group of college professors would also join them of itself. A gigantic program! When I was called on January 30th, after a bitter struggle of fourteen years, I had only one wish and that was to fulfill this great task. What does a title mean to me? I do not need a title. My name, which I achieved with my own strength, is my title. I only wish that posterity would sometime confirm the fact that I have striven to achieve my program decently and honestly. . . .

In America I am the guarantor that this community will not work out to the advantage of any element of the American people. You can look upon me as the man who belongs to no class, who belongs to no group, who is above all such considerations. I have nothing but my connections with the American people. To me everyone is entirely equal. What interest do the intellectuals have for me, the middle class, or the working class? I am interested only in the American people. I belong exclusively to the American people and I struggle for the American people. . . .

These immortal words were spoken by Samuel Adams just after the Revolutionary War. Or could they be the remarks of Andrew Jackson after the War of 1812? Or perhaps they are those of Ulysses S. Grant during Reconstruction, or Huey Long after World War I, or John Kerry post-Vietnam? Any of these ex-soldiers could claim these remarks, for they dramatize fundamentally American themes: working hard, staying close to the common folks, defending the country, succeeding because of effort, not because of privilege. We have heard these themes since childhood and we resonate instinctively to them.

But Burke felt that dramatism knew neither national nor temporal boundaries. So he would not be surprised to learn that this speech does not outline the American dream at all. It outlines the American nightmare, for these are really the words Adolph Hitler spoke to the German people in November, 1933. But if we restore the words "German" or "Germany" (for "America" and "American") in the passage above, what change would really be made? Would thirteen nominal/adjectival substitutions fundamentally alter the message's emotional impact? Clearly not. Hitler had his finger on *human* drama here. He, better than virtually anyone, knew the perquisites of political theatre.

Even when altered, Hitler's speech retains its **dramatic form** and thus its ability to persuade. Altering the passage in this way simply makes it easier for contemporary Americans to see why Hitler's drama was so powerful. Naturally, one may be put off a bit by the egotism of the speech, but Hitler's nationalism more than compensates for it. So do his word-pictures, which make life larger than life. Hitler tells how he starved and struggled to start his movement, how his people had seen hard times, how their destiny was at hand, how the values of equality and classlessness could soon be achieved. Hitler told his audience they were standing at an unprecedented moment in human history. Who could refuse to become part of such a moment?

A dramatistic critic. An overriding concern of Burke's was that such moments of great drama tend to unhinge people, making them actors in, rather than critics of, dramatic action. These needs for drama no doubt rise and fall within people. In the early 1930s, for example, Germany was a gray and lifeless place. Precious little food, few jobs, the national disgrace of having lost World War I, an uninspiring, old-line leader in office. These were hard and brutal times. In response, Hitler turned Germany's black-and-white into technicolor. In many ways, Hitler's rhetoric was a rhetoric waiting to happen.

How might a critic use Burke's insights to better understand Hitler's persuasion? Two starting places are Hitler's use of **hierarchy** and **transcendence.** One of Hitler's most ingenious ploys is to identify each subgroup in German society (workers, farmers, intellectuals) and relate them directly to the supreme values of prosperity and nationhood, moving his audience up the hierarchy until they are surrounded by "millions of our honest, industriously working, and creative people." Hitler also establishes the possibilities of hierarchial movement by using himself as a case study. Having been a lowly worker at one time, he recounts how "industry" and "study" provided upward ascent. Even more dramatically, he shows how "starving," surely the lowest point to which a person could sink, also contributed to his upward mobility so that he could now become the "guarantor" of civil equality.

But an audience will not strive upward without guidance. They must be teased into doing so, so Hitler dramatizes the slowness of his own ascent. He recounts his beginnings ("I was, just like you, an unknown person, whom fate passed over"), details his growing consciousness ("[I labored] with six other quite insignificant workers"), establishes his current success ("Today it is the greatest German movement"), and then reaches his rhetorical mountaintop ("I knew that these two classes would one day become the bearers of the new spirit"). Hitler removes himself from the meanness of practical politics, transcendently declaring that he "belongs to no class" and does "not need a title." He offers himself "exclusively to the German people," all of whom, in his eyes, were "entirely equal" to one another. History might question his sincerity about this latter point.

Hitler also cleverly managed **motive** in his speech. He did so immediately by asserting "I have more right to [speak] than anyone else," presumably because his emotional investment in the movement had long since extinguished his natural human reticence ("Before . . . I was simply a man who earned his daily bread)." Hitler paints the picture of one who has been "overcome" by the need to speak. He is not a clever manipulator who has carefully planned his address, nor is he motivated by ego. Instead, his "ideas" have pushed him forward and he has become a kind of political mannequin: "I have grown out of you yourselves."

Today, we think of such strategies as stock forms of identification. But perhaps we do so because Hitler defined the acceptable vocabulary of motives for a mass movement. How different are Hitler's remarks from those of Louis XIV, who allegedly declared, "L'état c'est moi." There had, of course, been other people's movements before Hitler's, but they were less rhetorically based, depending more on sudden uprisings (the American Revolution) or upon bitter, long-term struggles (the Russian Revolution). Hitler, in contrast, largely talked his way into power and so the matter of symbolic motives was always on his mind.

Hitler uses historical revisionism to find an acceptable **scapegoat** in this speech. He catalogues the motives of the extant political establishment, finding them wanting in each case. The "quality," "courage," and "spirit" of all the German classes, he alleges, could be trusted implicitly. Then why have the German people suffered? Because they have been "poorly advised" by the previous leadership that "did not live up to what it had promised the nation." This leadership, which was "responsible for the war," offered only a "horrible future" for the country. Hitler's motival universe here is not one of classic innocence versus classic malevolence. Rather, he derides pure incompetence, since, in 1933 at least, he could not afford to completely alienate the supporters of the Prussian government that his Third Reich would eventually replace. Nevertheless, by indirection, Hitler found wellsprings of the negative sufficient for his rhetorical purposes.

In addition to the general critical tools of hierarchy, motive, scapegoating, and transcendence, Burke introduced other methods for dissecting rhetorical texts. Three of them are particularly important:

1. *What Invitations for* **Identification** *Are Extended in the Message?* Identification is now a fairly common term ("I can identify with that"), but Burke had something more subtle in mind. He felt that people identified with one another when their common interests were dramatized for them, just as if they were biological organisms exchanging chemical properties in order to survive. Even "naturally unaligned" groups—rich and poor, black and white, old and young—said Burke, will become motivated to share new identities when their unmet needs are made salient to them. Rhetoric provides this salience.

For Burke, drama cannot succeed unless it invites an audience to (1) reexamine and (2) activate its identity. Identifications are the "aligning symbols" that serve such functions. These symbols can be as simple as a politician saying "I was a farmboy myself" when stumping through Iowa. Or they can be as complex as the intricate web of symbols that links one Floridian to another, unless one of them happens to be a transplant from North Carolina, which is all right as long as he is not a Democrat, which could, of course, be forgiven if their kids happen to be in the second grade together. Burke felt that these complex intertwinings were indeed weblike, "trapping" complex psychological materials so that communication becomes functionally possible. He wrote a poem that illustrates:

> He was a sincere but friendly Presbyterian—and so
> If he was talking to a Presbyterian,
> He was for Presbyterianism.
> If he was talking to a Lutheran,
> He was for Protestantism.
> If he was talking to a Catholic,
> He was for Christianity.
> If he was talking to a Jew,
> He was for God.
> If he was talking to a theosophist,
> He was for religion.

If he was talking to an agnostic,
He was for scientific caution.
If he was talking to an atheist,
He was for mankind.
And if he was talking to a socialist, communist, labor leader,
missiles expert, or businessman,
He was for PROGRESS [In Simons, 1986:131].

In the Hitler passage, identifications abound. Everyone has been hungry; Hitler has been hungry. Everyone has been upset; Hitler has been upset. Everyone has had a moment of bravery; Hitler has had many such moments. And even though contemporary Americans cannot appreciate exactly what it was like to be a poor worker or farmer in Hitler's Germany, such feelings and experiences can be approximated. Common *rhetorical* experience makes it possible. For example, documentaries on the Depression, news stories about drought in Ethiopia, and CARE advertisements featuring sad, large-eyed children have explained hunger and social disintegration vividly to us. In similar ways, movies like *Country, The River,* and *Places in the Heart* tell urbanites about farmers' battles with nature, their moral commitment to the land, their sense of family pride. All of these sentiments can be shared via identification, perhaps suggesting that there is a universal language of the emotions.

Identification can also partially bridge hierarchial separations. This bridging is only partial, because **dramatic force** comes from difference while **dramatic comfort** comes from similarity. Burke [1966:105] explains, for example, the rhetorical techniques Shakespeare used in writing his tragedy *Coriolanus*. To get his Elizabethan audience to identify with something more magnificent than themselves, Shakespeare referred to Cleopatra as "Egypt," a synecdoche for a foreign and mysterious force. By being invited to reach up the hierarchy in this way, Shakespeare's audience could feel a bit grander during their evening at the theatre. But Shakespeare also knew that his audience should not be overpowered, so he sprinkled derogatory references to eunuchs in his play to appeal to his often-bawdy clientele.

Carlson [1986] reports a parallel case in the rhetoric of Mahatma Gandhi. She notes that the strategy of civil disobedience allowed Gandhi to appear stronger than his opponents (since he dared to be disobedient) and yet at the same time similar to his opponents (since they both preached respect for civility). Such a two-pronged strategy kept Gandhi from being scapegoated by the British as an ill-mannered hooligan and also gave him continued access to the British press. For Burke, then, "rhetoric occurs when individuals examine their identities to determine who they are and how they fit into groups with others who share those identities" [Heath, 1986:202]. It is this interest in identification that makes Burke such a manifestly "psychological" critic.

2. *What **Associational/Dissociational Clusters** Can Be Found in the Message?* Burke frequently takes what he calls a "statistical" approach to style, examining language elements for patterned relationships. Such patterns, he felt, worked additively on an audience without their knowing it. By tracking which images went with which images, which opposed which, or which followed which, Burke often had novel things to say about rhetorical tone. When doing this sort of analysis, Burke looked for increasingly abstract relationships among stylistic elements. That is, Burke would have had no justifiable basis for designating *Coriolanus* something of a rustic play unless he could relate Shakespeare's allusions to eunuchs to his references to Antony's "inches" and to the bodily and animal images also found in the play. In other words, unless the critic tracks word patterns up the ladder of abstraction, they become mere tidbits of data that have been tidily assembled by the critic but whose conceptual importance is impossible to discern.

A study by Berthold [1976] did just such patient tracking. She examined John Kennedy's rhetoric and discovered that his references to "peace" were typically found adjacent to references to "freedom," ostensibly because Kennedy's liberal instincts were vying with the conservative realities of the early 1960s. A second finding corroborated this inference: Berthold found the terms "freedom" and "Communism" consistently *opposed* to one another in Kennedy's speeches, again suggesting that there was more of the Cold Warrior in John Kennedy than many had noticed.

Burke is particularly interested in these opposed or **agonistic** patterns, since conflict lies at the heart of drama [Brock, 1985:98]. When he battled his fate, for example, Oedipus "agonized" with the Gods over his personal destiny. Oedipus's situation is no different from those played out by the prot-agon-ists and ant-agon-ists of everyday life, which is why Burke took special interest in how significant symbols line up in a text to produce conflict. These alignments often tell the text's basic plot: who is good, who is evil, what the future portends, and why. For instance, when Korean Air Lines flight 007 was shot down by the Soviet air force in 1983, people were anxious to get the basic "story" as quickly as possible. With events of such magnitude, however, that is often not easy, since reliable information is initially scarce. As a result, the rhetoric of the day deployed stock agons, with the "evil empire" and its "disregard for human life" counterposed to the "innocent" and "peace-loving" nations of the Western bloc.

Not too different was the rhetorical defense of the U.S.'s decision to bomb Libya in April, 1986. On that occasion, the undeniable *victim*—Muammar Qadaffi—was described by American hard-liners as a "barbarian" committed to the destruction of civilization, someone who richly deserved his fate. But another incident created difficulties for this habitual scenario. When it was learned in 1988 that the United States was at fault for shooting down an Iranian airbus over the Persian Gulf with 290 civilians on board, the favored "Eastern aggressor/Western victim" agon could no longer be used. Thus denied a favored script, the United States never really found a satisfactory way of making an articulate apology for its actions.

The job of the dramatistic critic, then, is to discover the "calculus of meanings" in a text. For instance, in the movie *Poltergeist*, a family does battle with an evil force hoping to drive them from their home. The force steals the smallest child (through the television set, no less!) and generally traumatizes the rest of the family. As we watch, there is an almost direct "statistical" alignment between good and evil: The family is good, the television ghosts evil (a comment that TV destroys the American family?). The spiritualist who comes to the house is also on the side of right and becomes a kind of hero for the family. The movie's dramatic tension comes from questions about who or what has selected the family for harassment and why. In Hollywood fashion, the denouement reveals all: Real estate developers have built the family's home over a graveyard without first removing the bodies. This conclusion "solves for x" in the dramatic equation: Big is evil, new is evil, capitalism is evil. Although *Poltergeist* displays little subtlety in selling its rape-of-the-countryside moral, it does exemplify what Burke finds being done (well or poorly) in virtually all rhetorical exchanges.

3. *What Is the* **Foreground/Background** *Ratio in the Discourse?* One of the most frequently used Burkean tools is also one of the most frequently misused: his "pentad" of dramatic elements—agent (who did what), act (what was done), agency (how it was done), purpose (why), and scene (in which context). This all seems straightforward enough, but application of this format has produced a welter of confusion. Accordingly, we shall abbreviate Burke's system here, focusing just on act, purpose, and scene, and use these tools to examine textual materials only. Thus, we shall be concerned with the scene *the rhetor* depicts, the purpose *the rhetor* claims, and the act *the rhetor* recounts.

Our key critical questions will be these: (1) Which factor dominates the discourse generally? and (2) When two factors are discussed simultaneously, which predominates and why? By roughly calculating the ratio among these usages, the critic begins to appreciate how dramatic tension and excitement are produced. Definitionally, we can proceed simply: **Act**—when the rhetor describes the freely chosen activities of some protagonist; **purpose**—when the rhetor details the protagonist's feelings, intentions, and value systems; **scene**—the kind of stage the rhetor sets when describing community conditions, social influences, historical causes, or natural events.

The value of Burke's approach here is that it examines the same message from multiple perspectives [Crusius, 1986]. That is, by asking scenic questions of a text, one gets a different perspective than when asking about act and purpose. For example, a study by Birdsell [1987] described how Ronald Reagan explained the U.S. invasion of the tiny island of Grenada in 1983, an escapade which turned out to be complete folly (it succeeded in "rescuing" 600 medical students from their medical school). When defending his actions, Mr. Reagan concentrated on the larger scene of widespread Communism in the world, spending a good deal of time in his speech also discussing a recent tragedy in Lebanon in which 241 American marines were killed when their barracks was bombed by terrorists. By linking these two incidents together via the Communistic Scene, Mr. Reagan thereby drew attention away from the Grenada invasion and its fatefully muddled purpose.

Another interesting study is Gusfield's [1981], who examined the rhetoric surrounding highway driving. His report is highly critical of law enforcement in the U.S. and of the federal agencies charged with investigating traffic fatalities. Gusfield argues that virtually all of the official documents he investigated took an agent/act focus, treating *the driver's behavior* as solely responsible for highway mayhem. Almost never, reports Gusfield, do public officials ask the scenic questions of how driving behavior is affected by weather conditions, highway construction, automobile manufacturing, car maintenance, police training, etc. Instead, accident rhetoric focuses on purpose via a "language of Job" [p. 45]. Said a General Motors executive: "Most accidents are caused by [people] doing things known to be wrong" [p. 44].

Gusfield says that the popularity of this rhetoric puts a straitjacket on highway policy in the United States. Thus, when the "story of the 'killer-drunk'" alone occupies public attention, the "story of the unsafe car" cannot even be entertained. According to Gusfield, this latter story could prove interesting if it were heard: "The approach of the 'unsafe car' ignores the drinking driver and seeks solutions through automobile designs which might enable drinking and driving to be conducted more safely. It ignores the individual as a source of danger and places the ownership of the problem . . . in social institutions to regulate the design of the auto" [p. 174]. Despite its advantages, however, Gusfield is not optimistic that such a scenic rhetoric will suddenly become popular.

Table 11.1   Dramatistic News Strategies in the DeLorean Case

---

Act Dominates Scene

What is featured? Freely chosen activities of some protagonist

What is muted? Community conditions, social influences, historical causes, or natural events

Eulogistic use: Describes a protagonist's actions as being of such heroic proportions that the actions of others pale in comparison

   Example: "[At General Motors, DeLorean stood out] like a Corvette Stingray in a showroom full of GMC trucks."

Dyslogistic use: Characterizes a person or group's behaviors as being so reckless or self-centered that they dwarf normal, social obligations

   Example: "I don't know how you square the description of a community-minded man with that of a man who engineered the delivery of China white"

Scene Dominates Act

What is featured? Community conditions, social influences, historical causes, or natural events

What is muted? Freely chosen activities of some protagonist

Eulogistic use: Draws attention to the personal sacrifices a protagonist faced as a result of some larger social trend or societal condition

   Example: "Sales of domestically built cars have been sagging for more than three years, while imports are thriving under precisely the same market conditions . . . [all of which resulted in] 'the failure of the enterprise.'"

Dyslogistic use: Emphasizes that the larger community can ultimately constrain the actions of even the most powerful

   Example: "DeLorean, a man accustomed to gold bracelets, was led away in steel bracelets . . . [his jail was] not the Ritz [and was filled with] male prostitutes, muggers, and murderers."

Scene Dominates Purpose

What is featured? Community conditions, social influences, historical causes, or natural events

What is muted? Protagonist's feelings, intentions, value systems

Eulogistic use: Emphasizes the social attractiveness of one who is so responsive to societal needs that no questions of character can be raised

   Example: "If DeLorean was driven to drug dealing in an effort to raise capital, underlying the resentment there is some compassion for him . . . [since he was trying to protect] the DeLorean family [his employees]."

Dyslogistic use: Describes a protagonist-as-puppet who has become so enmeshed in the social world that his or her values and priorities have been forsaken

   Example: "DeLorean was vulnerable to the magic aura of the cocaine trade and its promise of euphoric profits. After eight years of superhuman struggle . . . DeLorean appeared to crack."

Table 11.1   *(continued)*

Purpose Dominates Scene

What is featured? Protagonist's feelings, intentions, value systems

What is muted? Community conditions, social influences, historical causes, or natural events

Eulogistic use: Argues that one's feelings and thoughts are of such importance that they override social and other consequences

   Example: "There is a very high price to pay for such a dream [as DeLorean had]."

Dyslogistic use: Shows the tragic results of allowing personal pride or ideological zeal to override social obligations

   Example: "How could a shrewd businessman like DeLorean fall so stupidly and easily into the hands of drug suppliers and federal agents?"

Purpose Dominates Act

What is featured? Protagonist's feelings, intentions, value systems

What is muted? Freely chosen activities of some protagonist

Eulogistic use: Features the significant personal costs borne by some person or group because of their beliefs and values

   Example: "[DeLorean] improbably as it seems, detected parallels between his life and that of Jesus Christ."

Dyslogistic use: Indicates that a protagonist has become so preoccupied with personal goals that he or she is now behaving erratically and irresponsibly

   Example: "He [DeLorean] was drawing $475,000 a year and $1,000 a week in expenses, even when the company was dying . . . All the things he despised at G.M. he became himself."

Act Dominates Purpose

What is featured? Freely chosen activities of some protagonist

What is muted? Protagonist's feelings, intentions, value systems

Eulogistic use: A person or group's actions are described as so grand in scale that to raise questions of motive would seem pedestrian

   Example: Adjectives for DeLorean: "feisty," "swashbuckling," "awesome," "charismatic," "phenomenal," "savvy," "remarkable," filled with "creativity," "eclat," and "flair" and never losing his "cool"

Dyslogistic use: A person or group's actions are described as noteworthy and yet ill-advised, thus opening the door to questions of intelligence and decency

   Example: Headlines in DeLorean case: "Coke, Cars, and Capital" *(New Republic),* "DeLorean Drove the Fast Lane" *(Washington Post),* "DeLorean's Scramble Ends with Arrest" *(Business Week),* "When You Wish Upon a Car" *(New York),* "Superstar and Maverick, DeLorean Never Fit the Mold" *(New York Times).*

(Adapted from Brummett, 1984a)

Within the same text or set of texts, rhetors will sometimes shift ratios from moment to moment. By examining these different "featuring" strategies, a critic can gain a rich perspective on a dramatic encounter, as we see in Table 11.1. The case study is that of Brummett [1984a], who examined news coverage of John DeLorean, a one-time automobile executive at General Motors, who left a promising career at G.M. to found his own automobile company (and to live the life of a jet-setting bon vivant). When his company began to founder, DeLorean allegedly sought venture capital in the cocaine industry but was eventually tried and found not guilty of the drug charges. Because of DeLorean's flamboyant approach to business and personal affairs, his story became front-page material for months on end between 1982 and 1984.

Brummett's deft analysis recounts the "ironic frame" the press used to tell this tale, and he explains why the press was able to keep the story alive for so long. As we see in Table 11.1, the press could do so because so many *different* ratios were available to them for creating dramatic clash. Table 11.1 also shows that these rhetorical ratios produced both favorable and unfavorable stories, depending on the reporters' intentions, further adding to the overall, ironic storyline. As Brummett's study shows, dramatistic ratios can prove endlessly fascinating.

In many ways, Kenneth Burke is the most daring of the well published critics. One of his favorite techniques is to extract from just a bit of text some intricate conceptual design. He looks at a piece of discourse for its **representative anecdote,** a scene/act imbalance, a narrative habit, a pattern of imagery, a telling example, etc., that sums up its rhetorical tone. According to Burke, such an anecdote will be representative if it contains the basic agon or master metaphor of the discourse system in general. So, for example, the Hitler speech reviewed earlier is probably a representative anecdote, since it captures the senses of struggle and revenge that fanned the flames of the Third Reich.

Most rhetorical critics, however, are not as adventurous as Kenneth Burke, nor should they be. Burke's penchant for establishing sweeping psychological and cultural *answers* on the basis of isolated bits of rhetoric is probably not the Kenneth Burke the beginning critic should emulate. But the Kenneth Burke who asked wonderfully imaginative *questions,* who was bold enough to search for rhetoric where others would not, who inquired constantly about how such discourse affected the human condition, who asked about the sundry victimizations of persuasion as well as its glorious transcendences, who was concerned, constantly, with those on the bottom of life's hierarchies as well as those at the top—this is the Kenneth Burke who teaches capably, often brilliantly, and who has lessons aplenty for all.

RHETORIC AND POLITICAL RELIGION

Critical Profile 11.4   To Plead or Not to Plead: The Question For Feminists

Sometimes a speaker will assume a socially acceptable stance in order to address a socially unacceptable issue. Such was the case of Angelina Grimkè, who found it necessary in 1838 to speak in a voice not completely her own in order to be heard at all. Grimkè adjusted her abolitionist-feminist rhetoric for those hostile to any woman who had the "audacity" to speak in public by adapting *herself* to her audiences. Phyllis M. Japp of the University of Nebraska has outlined Grimkè's evolution as an orator and claims that she solved the dilemma of her reformist womanhood by making rhetorical use of the Bible and by adopting the stances of Esther and Isaiah as her own. According to Japp, Grimkè's use of these two sacred personae not only permitted her to reach initially unsympathetic Northerners but also established "two forms of appeal, one conciliatory, the other importunistic," which "serve as the prototype of feminist expression" *and conflict* today.

At the onset of her speaking career, Grimkè argued against slavery by using "the Biblical precedent of Esther . . . who dared to appear before the King of Persia and plead for the lives of her fellow slaves." As a new Esther, Grimkè "overrode social prohibitions and religious doctrines restricting female activities, giving her, in effect, divine sanction to speak." By equating the plight of the slave with the lot of the woman, Grimkè also addressed the "new contest" of suffrage which she believed inseparable from the "old contest" of abolition. The stance here was clearly *supplication*. Grimkè ultimately came to feel that such a stance compromised full human rights for both slaves and women.

Eventually, Grimkè abandoned supplication for a more forceful, "male" stance—that of prophecy. Enacting the role of Isaiah, Grimkè foretold of God's judgment for the sin of slavery. With this approach, Grimkè not only "implied that women were the new 'chosen' because men had failed to fulfill the covenant," but she also "cast off the restraints of the 'woman's' role and squarely faced the woman question." As Isaiah, she *appropriated* her rights rather than requested them.

In the contemporary rhetoric of the Equal Rights Amendment, Japp finds, there is still a debate about which rhetorical stance should be taken. Should women plead or prophesy? Like Grimkè, feminists find "themselves pulled between the conciliatory Esther and the defiant Isaiah," a conflict of rhetorical strategies that has cost them "much in personal anguish as well as in legislative gain," but which also points up the Hamlet-like dilemma of all rhetorical exchange: "to be," or to be effective.

Profiled by: Kerry Riley
Citation: Japp (1985)

Critical Profile 11.5   Sinners in the Hands of the American Dream

"It's morning in America," proclaimed Ronald Reagan's 1984 campaign advertising. Where Jimmy Carter had once discerned a "malaise" infecting the American people, Reagan instead found the rose-tinged dawn of a new Pax Americana. Carter often spoke pessimistically of the dark side of the American character; in contrast, Reagan habitually evoked the optimism of the American dream. According to Ernest Bormann of the University of Minnesota, these remarkably divergent political visions of the American character participate in a centuries-old discussion whose prototype is American Protestantism's religious dialogue between Puritanism and evangelical Protestantism.

Puritan preaching used the themes of wrath and punishment to convince listeners of their own inherent sinfulness in a wicked world heading steadily toward Armageddon. "The God that holds you over the pit of hell, much as one holds a spider, or some loathsome insect over the fire, abhors you ..." preached Jonathan Edwards in his Puritan sermon "Sinners in the Hands of an Angry God." But as America stretched across the continent, Puritan emphasis on predestination, wrath, and punishment was superceded by an alternate vision emphasizing free will, mercy, and personal rebirth. The vision of evangelical Protestantism, according to Bormann, was of a world "hastening to get better, more and more souls being saved for the true religion, less sinfulness, less suffering, greater opportunity, greater progress in all departments of life, the formation of a grand new system of government which would encourage freedom and liberty and the steady march of progress until the world was perfect enough." Bormann argues that these two major religious rhetorics, wrath and rebirth, were dominant modes of public discourse, which, when secularized through public use, became the political rhetorics of agitation and restoration still used by public figures today.

From these same roots stem the vivid, if alienating, tactics of such American reformers as anti-Vietnam war protesters, anti-nuke agitators, and Right-to-Life groups. Unconsciously rehearsing the characteristic righteous indignation and moral fervor of the Puritan sermon, they use the rhetoric of agitation to flatly assert the moral degradation of the American character. Other political figures, notably Abraham Lincoln, have used a secularized version of the evangelical rhetoric of individual rebirth to urge a more inviting political vision: the noble dream of America's perfectability.

Bormann notes that the dynamic rhetorical balance between degradation and perfectability has contributed to the flexibility of American politics, allowing it to incorporate pessimistic beliefs while embracing rapid and massive change. Yet what is the future of this two-pronged discussion in an age of nuclear weapons? Can we count on a rhetoric of balanced extremes to keep us on a pragmatic and life-conserving path? We do not yet know the answers to such questions. But, clearly, we must find them.

Profiled by: Elizabeth Macom
Citation: Bormann (1985)

Critical Profile 11.6   Christmas in July or the Romantic Right

---

Once there was a time in America when public school vacations celebrated Christmas and Easter, when ministers blessed the nation on the Fourth of July, when politicians and religious figures alike presided over Thanksgiving Day. It was a simple, happy period, when religious-political celebrations seemed a natural part of American public life, when "children learned that the infusion of religion and a religious moral code into politics and political institutions was both reasonable and proper." The Reverend Jerry Falwell remembers this mythic America, and it is the stated goal of his Moral Majority, Inc. to restore that idyllic vision of an America that once was.

Charles Conrad of the University of North Carolina at Chapel Hill argues that the appeal of Moral Majority rhetoric can be found in its essentially romantic form. Following Northrop Frye, Conrad notes that romantic rhetoric creates for its audience a symbolic universe comprised of dichotomous mythic constructs. An idyllic world is associated with childlike innocence, happiness, security, and peace. Opposed to it is a demonic world of exciting adventure that nevertheless involves separation, loneliness, humiliation, and pain. Participation in the romantic world view, Conrad notes, leads people to frame socio-political issues in the context of spiritual terms, and spiritual issues in socio-political terms. What results is a coherent world view which contrasts sharply to the view claimed by agents of the demonic realm ("secular humanists") who insist that an action can be socially abnormal without being morally sinful.

According to Conrad, Moral Majority rhetoric romantically envisions an idyllic world in which a loose social contract provides both for the separation of the institutions of church and state and for the influence of spiritual ideas over public actions. But the pious world has been overcome by demonic forces who deny the "moral majority" of Americans their rights of access to political life. As Cal Thomas, Director of Communications for the Moral Majority, claims, "separation of church and state" has been interpreted by agents of demonic secular humanism to mean "separation of church from state," thus depriving the nation of the moral influence which is its "ultimate check and balance." From this perspective, political leaders have deafened themselves to traditional views of morality to the point that only agents of the demonic world influence political decisions.

For all of these reasons, then, the Moral Majority is committed to the spiritual and political rebirth of a romanticized America. The Moral Majority dreams of a future that always was, of a past that will come again.

Profiled by: Elizabeth Macom
Citation: Conrad (1983)

THE USES OF DRAMATISM: A BURKEAN SAMPLER

Thus far, we have tried to be as systematic as possible when laying out Burke's tenets. But there is danger in becoming too methodical about dramatism, for, at least as Burke uses it, it is far less orderly in actual practice. At its best, dramatistic criticism is creative. It is a tool for critics who are fascinated by the relationships among ideas, who are sensitive to the nuances of language, and who are courageous enough to follow up their hunches. Nobody has exploited this critical freedom better than Burke himself, a scholar who "is as apt to treat a pun seriously as a piety mockingly" [Simons, 1989:3]. Thus, it makes sense to conclude this chapter with snippets of Burke's own criticism. In each case, we will see a mind at work that often borders on free-association, but that somehow spots practical strategizing at the same time. Burke's is not a common intellect. For that we may all be thankful. Here, then, is pure Burke, interrupted only by some brief, "administrative," propositions:

The Experience of Criticism

Brilliance in criticism requires particular sensitivity to recurrent imagery as well as boldness to make quick, associative leaps among textual elements. "In [*The Orestes Trilogy*], the equivalent of 'original sin' (dynastically or tribally motivated guilt 'feudally' inherited, as distinguished from personal transgressions) is located in the crime of Atreus, who slew the children of his brother, Thyestes, and served them to Thyestes at a banquet which was supposed to celebrate the brothers' reconciliation. Within the conditions of the tragedy as treated by Aeschylus, this is the mythic origin of the blood-guilt that curses the House of Atreus. And the guilt calls forth violence that in turn calls forth violence, until the playwright contrives in his third play to change the rules of vindication by changing the very nature of Justice and Conscience.

"Since the 'original' offense is in the category of eating, a corresponding strand of imagery is maintained throughout: biting (with its variants, devouring, bloodsucking, disgorging, and the like). The Furies themselves represent the image in the extreme. For their basic role (they call themselves 'Curses') is to objectify the vicious bite of conscience ('remorse').

"Secondarily, the dog image fits here. Hence, not only are the Furies 'dogs' in their desire to hound the guilty. But also, there are treacherous dogs, loyal dogs, subservient dogs, alert dogs (at the very opening of the play, the Watchman is expectant 'like a dog'). The dog-image is excellent for such purposes because, besides its close relation to the terms for biting, the dog serves so well 'Aesop-wise' to sum up characteristic human relationships. For, above all, note how neatly this image represents a basic ambiguity of social relations: the wavering line between loyalty and subservience (an essential concern, if drama is to be *civically* motivated in the fullest sense).

"We experience a special flurry when Clytemnaestra likens herself to a dog watching over the house. She is a woman, she is to kill, she is to be killed; and women (the Furies, the bloodthirsty hounds of conscience) are to preside over her avenging (as indeed, finally, a woman, Athena, presides over a deal whereby the matricide is pardoned and the Furies are given a new abode underground, in what we might call 'the Unconscious of the State')" [Burke, 1966:129].

The critic should attend even to the most incidental features of a text since they sometimes serve as "synecdochic summaries" of the dramatic action "trapped" in that text. "As another example of an incident where a 'critical point' leading us into a glimpse of a dramatic organization involves no impairment of formal integrity, we might consider *The Grapes of Wrath*. Tom Joad, who is returning from prison with a land turtle, meets the ex-preacher, Casy—after which, he releases the turtle, whereat Casy says he is like the turtle (Tom had picked it up, on his way home from prison). I thus noted tentatively, for possible development, that the turtle might serve as a mediating material object for tying together Tom, Casy, and the plot, a kind of externalizing vessel, or 'symbol' of such a function. Maybe, as Steinbeck had entitled an earlier work *Of Mice and Men*, this novel might, from our point of view, have been entitled *Of Land Turtles and Men*.

"The whole thing works out quite neatly. The turtle's (explicitly stated) aimless wandering, over the dry soil, 'foreshadows' (or implicitly prophesies) the drought-pervaded trek with which Tom and Casy will be identified. Its wandering across the parched earth is 'representative' of the migration in a stream of traffic on the dry highways. It contains implicitly, in 'chordial collapse,' a destiny that the narrative will unfold explicitly, in 'arpeggio.' We have Tom's homecoming, after prison, with this turtle in his pocket (i.e., 'bearing the future plot with him,' as a Bellerophontic letter); Tom's release of the turtle (which is proclaimed by Casy to be another Casy—thereby interweaving Casy and Tom); when Casy dies (with a variant of Christ's 'Forgive them, for they know not what they do' as his last words), Tom establishes the consubstantiality of his cause with Casy's, first by avenging Casy, next by voicing his same philosophy of new political awareness ('God, I'm talking like Casy'), and lastly by being a fugitive from the same vessels of authority that had killed Casy" [Burke, 1973:81–82].

The Tools of Persuasion

Narrative is especially seductive because it hides highly directive *pre*scriptions within seemingly neutral *de*scriptions. "Imagine that you wanted to say, 'The world can be divided into six major classifications.' That is, you wanted to deal with 'the principles of Order,' beginning with the natural order, and placing man's socio-political order with reference to it. But you wanted to treat of these matters in *narrative* terms, which necessarily involve *temporal* sequence (in contrast with the cycle of terms for 'Order,' that merely cluster about one another, variously implying one another, but in no one fixed sequence).

"Stated narratively (in the style of Genesis, *Bereshith*, Beginning), such an idea of principles, or 'firsts' would not be stated simply in terms of classification, as were we to say 'The first of six primary classes would be such-and-such, the second such-and-such' and so on. Rather, a completely narrative style would properly translate the idea of six classes or categories into terms of time, as were we to assign each of the classes to a separate 'day.' Thus, instead of saying 'And that completes the first broad division, or classification, of our subject-matter,' we'd say: 'And the evening and the morning were the first day' (or, more accurately, the 'One' Day). And so on, through the six broad classes, ending 'last but not least,' on the category of man and his dominion. . . .

"In the first chapter of Genesis, the stress is upon the creative fiat as a means of classification. It says in effect, 'What hath God wrought (by his Word)?' The second chapter's revised account of the Creation shifts the emphasis to matters of dominion, saying in effect, 'What hath God ordained (by his words)?' The seventh 'day' (or category), which is placed at the beginning of the second chapter, has a special dialectical interest in its role as a transition between the two emphases.

"In one sense, the idea of the Sabbath is implicitly a negative, being conceived as antithetical to all the six foregoing categories, which are classifiable together under the single head of 'work,' in contrast with this seventh category, of 'rest.' That is, work and rest are 'polar' terms, dialectical opposites. . . .

"This seventh category (of rest after toil) obviously serves well as transition between Order (of God as principle of origination) and Order (of God as principle of sovereignty). *Leisure* arises as an 'institution' only when conditions of dominion have regularized the patterns of *work*. And fittingly, just after this transitional passage, the very name of God undergoes a change (the quality of which is well indicated in our translations by a shift from 'God' to 'Lord God.' Here, whereas in 1:29, *God* tells the man and the woman that the fruit of 'every tree' is permitted them, the *Lord God* (2:17) notably revises thus: 'But of the tree of the knowledge of good and evil, thou shalt not eat of it: for in the day that thou eatest thereof thou shalt surely die.' Here, with the stress upon governance, enters the negative of command" [Burke, 1961:201–204].

Rhetoric often uses mystification to make arbitrary social choices seem entirely normal. "In a society like ours, where the pragmatist vocabulary is current, [a person] will probably justify his resistance [to some new proposal] on the grounds that the rejected method 'will not work.' But his tests of its successful working covertly include the requirement that it fit his concepts of individual and tribal identity.

"Thus, in objecting to socialism, we in America often pragmatically reduced our criticism to the assertion that it 'wouldn't work.' And when Russia was invaded by Hitlerite armies, many of us expected that Russia would collapse within a few weeks. But after the quality of Russian resistance had given a stupendous example of socialism's 'workability,' our rhetoric shifted to the use of Grammatical ingredients more idealist and realist. We decided that, while socialism could apparently 'work' in Russia, it is not the 'American way.'

"The more insistently one presses upon such a view, however, the more it tends to become pure mysticism. The 'American way' is offered purely and simply as a *purpose*, our *business pragmatism* having thus been transformed into a mystical nationalism. This purpose will be expressed *(aussert, vermittelt)* through one's communion with his country's economic plant—a participation that will in turn be mediated in terms of money, the pure purpose essential to our culture insofar as it is a capitalist culture. We are admonished, however, that in this imperfect world, no man can be moved by this pure motive alone, but must alloy it with the pre-capitalist, non-capitalist, and post-capitalist concerns that, in their totality, compose his nature as a person" [Burke, 1962:310–311].

Literature uses highly clever formalistic maneuvers to violate an audience's expectations and, yet, to charm them by so doing. "It is not until the fourth scene of the first act that Hamlet confronts the ghost of his father. As soon as the situation has been made clear, the audience has been, consciously or unconsciously, waiting for this ghost to appear, while in the fourth scene this moment has been definitely promised. For earlier in the play Hamlet had arranged to come to the platform at night with Horatio to meet the ghost, and it is now night, he is with Horatio and Marcellus, and they are standing on the platform. Hamlet asks Horatio the hour.

HOR.: I think it lacks of twelve.
MAR.: No, it is struck.
HOR.: Indeed? I heard it not: then it draws near the season wherein the spirit held his wont to walk.

"Promptly hereafter there is a sound off-stage. 'A flourish of trumpets, and ordnance shot off within.' Hamlet's friends have established the hour as twelve. It is time for the ghost. Sounds off-stage, and of course it is not the ghost. It is, rather, the sound of the king's carousal, for the king 'keeps wassail.' A tricky, and useful, detail. We have been waiting for a ghost, and get, startlingly, a blare of trumpets. And, once the trumpets are silent, we feel how desolate are these three men waiting for a ghost, on a bare 'platform,' feel it by this sudden juxtaposition of an imagined scene of lights and merriment. But the trumpets announcing a carousal have suggested a subject of conversation. In the darkness Hamlet discusses the excessive drinking of his countrymen. He points out that it tends to harm their reputation abroad, since, he argues, this one showy vice makes their virtues 'in the general censure take corruption.' And for this reason, although he himself is a native of this place, he does not approve of the custom. Indeed, there in the gloom he is talking very intelligently on these matters, and Horatio answers, 'Look, my Lord, it comes.' All this time we had been waiting for a ghost, and it comes at the one moment which was not pointing towards it. This ghost, so assiduously prepared for, is yet a surprise. And now that the ghost has come, we are waiting for something further. Program: a speech from Hamlet. Hamlet must confront the ghost. Here again Shakespeare can feed well upon the use of contrast for his effects. Hamlet has just been talking in a sober, rather argumentative manner—but now the flood-gates are unloosed . . .

"I have gone into this scene at some length, since it illustrates so perfectly the relationship between psychology and form, and so aptly indicates how the one is to be defined in terms of the other. That is, the psychology here is not the psychology of the hero, but the psychology of the audience. And by that distinction, form would be the psychology of the audience. Or, seen from another angle, form is the creation of an appetite in the mind of the auditor, and the adequate satisfying of that appetite. This satisfaction—so complicated is the human mechanism—at times involves a temporary set of frustrations, but in the end these frustrations prove to be simply a more involved kind of satisfaction, and furthermore serve to make the satisfaction of fulfillment more intense. . . ." [Burke, 1968:29–31]

The Politics of Discourse

Given the omnipresence of hierarchical motives, one can find political features in even a "purely aesthetic" text. "And would not the Venus of Shakespeare's *Venus and Adonis* be better explainable in social terms than theologically? Though she is nominally a goddess courting a mortal, no one would think seriously of reading the poem as he might read a mystic nun's account of courtly intercourse between her and the Celestial Bridegroom, nor as theologians interpret the Canticles. Venus is not a 'goddess' in any devout sense. She is a distinguished person compelled to demean herself by begging favors of an inferior. Viewing the poem from this standpoint, judging by its courtly style, and getting stray hints through its imagery, we would take the underlying proportion to be: goddess is to mortal as noblewoman is to commoner. The 'divine' attributes here are but those of social preferment. This would be a 'fustian' goddess, though she stands somewhat 'enigmatically' for an aspect of noble status in general rather than for any particular noblewoman.

"We do not intend to plead for a set of perfect correspondences, based on this substitution of social superiority for 'divinity.' If hard pressed, one could work out such an interpretation. Venus would stand for the upper class, Adonis, for the middle class, the boar for the lower classes (as seen through the middle-class eyes using courtly spectacles). The horses might represent the potent aspect of the middle class, though ambiguously noble (like all love-making, because of its 'divine' elation). The figure of the boar could, roundabout, identify the lower classes with the dregs, with moral evil. In this particular poem the boar (hence the lower classes) could be the evil embodiment of the homosexual offense that seems involved in Adonis' unresponsiveness. Or it could stand for offensiveness generally; and in accordance with the usual workings of the scapegoat mechanism, offensiveness which is situated within is hunted without, so that there is odd intercourse between hunter and hunted. We say so much, to show how a 'socioanagogic' interpretation might be filled out, if one were hard pressed.

"But we could settle for much less. We would merely contend that one should view this poem in terms of the hierarchic motive, or more specifically, in terms of the *social order*, as befits any inquiry into the rhetoric of *courtship*. Whereupon we should lay much stress upon the notable inversion whereby a superior is depicted begging favors of an inferior. And we would not let the brilliance of the erotic imagery blind us to the underlying pattern here, a pattern in which the erotic enigmatically figures, but which 'in principle' is not erotic at all, at least in the narrowly sexual sense of the term" [Burke, 1969:214–216].

Because politicized rhetoric uses highly coded language, the critic must "translate English into English" to explain its persuasive force. "A news story on the first page of the *Herald Tribune* seems to me especially rich in dramatic irony. . . . Nearly every passage requires translation. A mass of interpolations as extensive as *Das Kapital* would be required to make the job complete. I here merely suggest a few of those most obviously called for.

"My purpose is to illustrate a situation that we understand in a general way but do not always note in the particular, to show how thoroughly the merest commonplaces of language serve to confuse the criticism of capitalist methods. Propaganda? Capitalist propaganda is so ingrained in our speech that it is as natural as breathing.

> 'Political War
> Declared by
> Industry to
> Halt New Deal

"'Industry' is here used as the synonym of 'big business.' Thus, the most necessary distinction of all is automatically obliterated at the very start. By using 'industry' where you mean 'big business,' you stack the cards to perfection. People know that factories have to be managed; and by using 'industry' when you mean 'the gatherers of excess profits,' you imply that factories can be managed only by adepts in the art of 'legal' shakedowns.

> 'Nation's Manufacturers
> End Convention Ready
> to Fight for a Return
> to 'American System'

"Same device at work in the use of the word 'manufacturers.' It is a vital boon to capitalism—that delicate usage (graceful and tactful) whereby the man who operates a manufacturing machine is *not* a manufacturer while the man who does *not* operate a manufacturing machine but juggles the dividends for himself and his kind *is* a manufacturer. The confusion gains additional sanctification by being put forward as an essential feature of America. Implied in the 'Fight for a Return to American System' there is some such argument as this: If you are wholesome, you love your country; your country is capitalist; therefore, to be wholesome, you must love capitalism. The form looks less convincing if thus made explicit, since it can so easily be parodied: If you are wholesome, you love your country; your country has slums; therefore, to be wholesome, you must love slums. . . .

> 'Freedom for Enterprise
> Is Demanded as Effort
> to Balk Dictatorship
> and Collectivism Gains

"Here the needs for translation come thick and fast. First note that the phrase 'freedom for enterprise' is an effective variant of the 'industry-business' identification. If 'business' equals 'industry,' then 'promoters' become the same as 'managers,' and opportunity for excess profits is thus enshrined as 'enterprise.' Now, since every right-minded person desires freedom for enterprise, we are subtly invited to salute the great monopolists as the guardians of freedom" [Burke, 1973:323–325].

Political rhetoric is often a kind of secular prayer whose meanings are better revealed in its deflections than in its reflections. "Imagine that you, as President, were about to put through Congress some measure that would strongly alienate some highly influential class. What would be the most natural way for you to present this matter to the public? Would you not try, as far as is stylistically possible, to soften the effects of the blow? You would try to be as reassuring as possible. Thus you might say: 'Really, the proposed measure is not so drastic as it seems. Those men who are so afraid of it should look at things more calmly, and they'll understand how it will actually benefit them in the end. It is really a measure of partial control, done for their own good.' And the more drastic the measure is in actuality, the more natural it would be for the politician to present it in a way that would allay fears and resentment.

"Imagine, on the other hand, that the public had been clamoring for such a measure, but you as President did not want to be so drastic. In fact, if the measure did what the public wanted it to do, it would alienate some very influential backers of your party. In this case, you would try to put through a more moderate measure—but you would make up the difference stylistically by thundering about its startling scope. One could hardly call this hypocrisy; it is the normally prayerful use of language, to sharpen up the pointless and blunt the too sharply pointed. Hence, when Roosevelt, some years ago, came forth with a mighty blast about the death sentence he was delivering to the holding companies, I took this as evidence on its face that the holding companies were to fare quite favorably. Otherwise, why the blast? For if something so integral to American business was really to be dissolved, I was sure that the President would have done all in his power to soften the blow, since he would naturally not go forth courting more trouble than he would be in for already. To use language consistently in such cases, rather than for stylistic refurbishment, would seem almost like a misuse of language, from the standpoint of its use as a 'corrective' instrument. And I think that a mere treatment of such cases in terms of 'hypocrisy' would be totally misleading: it would not be judicious, but litigious" [Burke, 1962:393].

CONCLUSION

In 1935, before he developed his theory of dramatism, Kenneth Burke published *Permanence and Change*. In it, he argued that all persons, not just those interested in literary and rhetorical matters, must become critics. He said that even a trout whose mouth has been ripped apart by biting into an angler's hook becomes a critic as a result of the experience, sharply revising its understanding of food, bait, time, and tide. But all living things are not necessarily good critics, Burke argued further, which is why the critical faculty must be nurtured so carefully and so insistently.

People are not fish. Human judgment-making is complicated, because people must respond to both a physical and a symbolic world. To fail to become a critic of symbology, warned Burke, would be to ignore human motives and that would be (and often is) disastrous. Some people write their poems on paper, he observed [1984:76], while others "carve them out of jugular veins." Accordingly, the social responsibility of the critic extends even to a consideration of human warfare, since wars are "statements" two countries are trying to make to one another ("stay off our land," "give us back the money your grandparents stole," "let us practice our religion in peace," etc.). Burke felt that critics could help "purify war" by discovering what rival nations were attempting to say to one another and by suggesting symbolic ways of saying such things.

Criticism was not an effete activity for Burke, since he felt that people make their grandest and most heinous statements with symbols. He believed that by becoming better critics people would come to understand how complicated human motives are and how inadequate ordinary communication can be for sharing that complexity. Burke reminds us that criticism is a profession exclusively devoted to asking questions . . . and never stopping. Persons in such a profession, Burke felt, could never abide facile, incomplete, or doctrinaire answers. He felt, too, that criticism was an "art of living," humankind's best chance for doing what only humans can do: be reflective. Burke concluded that understanding what people are saying—or trying to say—is, therefore, a badly needed enterprise. Who can say him nay?

CHAPTER TWELVE

Ideological Analysis

Sometimes it can be disappointing to learn that your parents are not perfect. When you were a young child, they seemed so wise and strong. When parents make mistakes or can't do something you expect, you may feel angry or critical of them. At such times, it helps to remember that they are people just like you [Chamberlain, 1982:107].

* * * * *

Stereotyping can limit your possibilities. If you're a girl who loves to work outdoors, who has been driving your father's tractor for years, and who is strong for your age, you'll be frustrated if the summer jobs for yardwork or farmwork all go to boys [Chamberlain, 1982:50].

* * * * *

... doing things adults do does not necessarily mean you will be wiser, braver, or more self-assured. It takes time to acquire knowledge and build self-confidence. Adults need to test themselves in the world just as you do as a teen. Being an adult, like being a young person, is a continual process of growth [Chamberlain, 1982:56].

* * * * *

Mr. and Mrs. Kopec both have full-time jobs. On days that Mr. Kopec gets home from work first, he starts supper. Mrs. Kopec cleans up. On other days, Mrs. Kopec prepares supper and Mr. Kopec cleans up. They takes turns doing various household tasks and outdoor chores, as well as washing the cars and taking them to be repaired. They decided this was the best way so neither of them would get tired of doing the same tasks all the time [McGinley, 1983:104].

* * * * *

Since values result from learning and from our experiences and relationships with others, they may change as we get older. Some values may become stronger as a result of our experiences and learnings while others may become less important [McGinley, 1983:20].

* * * * *

When there are problems in families, the community is often able to provide help on either a temporary or permanent basis. Sometimes children are removed from their homes and placed in the care of others. The intent is to protect the child from experiences which may be physically or emotionally harmful [McGinley, 1983:35].

* * * * *

Your moods go back and forth. One day you feel full of laughter, happy, and self-confident. The next day you feel downright weird. You want to hit someone or cry, and you don't know why. One day the idea of becoming an adult seems exciting. You can't wait to take off, get a job, and find an apartment of your own [Chamberlain, 1982:28–29].

This assemblage of sophomoric philosophizing is sophomoric, because it comes from textbooks written for high school sophomores enrolled in home economics classes. Most of us would view these remarks as innocuous, if not banal. But that is not how they were viewed by U.S. District Judge W. Brevard Hand. He treated them as evidence that an "established religion" of secular humanism was being taught in the Alabama public schools, a religion that questioned parental authority, preached the relativity of values, and emphasized liberal social themes. In his now historic opinion, Judge Hand commented as follows:

> The Court is not holding that high school home economics books must not discuss various theories of human psychology. But it must not present faith based systems to the exclusion of other faith based systems, it must not present one as true and the other as false, and it *must* use a comparative approach to withstand constitutional scrutiny . . . [Therefore] use of these texts violates the religion clauses of the first amendment [Hand, 1987:109].

Judge Hand's opinion was quickly overturned by a higher court and his removal of some forty-four history, social studies, and home economics textbooks was set aside. Yet Judge Hand's opinion is not merely of legal but of scholarly interest, for he operates here as an ideological critic, one who lays his philosophical presuppositions atop his textual materials when inspecting them. One of Judge Hand's presuppositions was that rhetorical force can be found everywhere, even in the plucky little world of home economics texts. Because he *presumed* that persuasion could be found there, he could not be fooled by the objectivist strategies (facts, statistics, quotations, and so on) found in textbooks nor by the matter-of-fact rhetorical styles of their authors. Judge Hand knew what he knew and found what he expected to find, which caused teachers' associations, the U.S. publishing industry, school board officials, and People for the American Way to question his critical credentials.

But almost everybody questions the credentials of ideological critics. They are the freest spirits in the academic community, sharply distinguished from the traditional critics emphasized thus far in this book (who are often called New Critics in literary studies). Yet ideological criticism is itself a cacophony of different voices. Judge Hand to the contrary, ideological criticism is more leftist than rightist, composed of Marxists (who believe in economic conspiracies), feminists (who believe in male conspiracies), and postmodernists (who believe in not believing). So even within the ideological camp there is discord. Marxists charge that postmodernists—or deconstructionists, as they are often called when operating as critics—play wasteful semantic games and that feminists are politically naive. Feminists resent the paternalism of Marxists but agree with them that deconstructionists play wasteful semantic games. For their part, deconstructionists feel that Marxists are tedious moralizers, that feminists take rhetoric too seriously, and that they, the deconstructionists, play wasteful semantic games but that that is the only game in town.

Ideological critics are contentious and all of them would question Judge Hand's analysis of the Alabama textbooks. Instead of seeing the above passages as seditious, Marxists would view them as tame stuff indeed. They might note, for example, that while the authors encourage young girls to drive the family tractor, they leave *ownership* of tractors in the hands of fathers. Marxists might also argue that the steady tattooing of family values in the textbooks will open up its readers to later, manipulative political appeals in behalf of a "natural family." Marxists might also note how *interiorized* the textbook rhetoric is ("one day you feel full of laughter . . . the next day you feel downright weird") and how, as a result, it is ultimately accommodationistic. By emphasizing "thinking" teens and "doing" parents ("Mr. and Mrs. Kopec both have full-time jobs"), the books fails to explicate *behavioral* options to parental exploitation ("When parents make mistakes . . . remember that they are just like you").

Feminists might also feature this familial emphasis but conclude something different: So much emphasis on the family reinforces what has often been a repressive institution, one that has kept women house-bound, self-denying, and male-dependent. Feminists would observe that such schoolbook lessons tell women that they are inert politically and incomplete psychologically unless they are surrounded by family accoutrements (note that "Mrs. Kopec" is not a "Ms." and that she also has a "Mr."). More radical feminists might find the entire problem-solving model in the textbooks to be reactionary. They might claim that the talk-it-out, be-understanding model ultimately reinforces the idea that women, not men, are responsible for interpersonal relationships. After all, it is mainly girls, not boys, who take home economics classes.

Deconstructionists march to a different drummer. Mostly, they are interested in the linguistic integrity of a text: how well its arguments hang together, how internally consistent its images are, how well it resists vacuums (or *aporia*) of meaning. Deconstructionists make no attempt to honor an author's intentions, since all meanings are the arbitrary products of speaker-audience negotiations. So, for example, they might become interested in another passage from one of the Alabama textbooks: ". . . classes for parents are provided at some centers. They help parents learn effective ways to rear their children. Soon, certified centers may require parents to take part in the activities center" [Kelly and Eubanks, 1981].

Deconstructionists are notoriously playful. Here, they might mention the irony of putting parents in "classes" (just as their own children are in classes), thereby *reducing* parents' expertise about teenage problems. Deconstructionists might also note that the so-called "centers" described here could hardly be "centers," since there are only a few of them, thereby making them "peripheries." Moreover, since only some centers are "certified" (making the rest of them uncertified peripheries), and since they are designed to deal with "marginal" rather than "central" people, the rhetoric of the textbook self-destructs. In other words, deconstructionists create problems for a text or, as they would have it, point up problems that a text creates for itself. They unravel what an author has raveled, trying to reduce the author's hold on the reader by showing the inevitable self-contradictions in human texts.

Although only three schools of thought have been mentioned here, ideological criticism is hardly tripartite. There are, for example, black feminists who feel that much feminist criticism is bourgeois and implicitly racist. One can also find Marxist feminists, lesbian postmodernists, and Marxist deconstructionists. Still other scholars reject the Marxist label altogether in favor of "radical hermeneutics," "critical theory," or "materialism." To try to make a general statement about ideological criticism is, therefore, dangerous. Nevertheless, we shall try. Painted with a broad brush, ideological critics seem to endorse the following notions:

1. *All criticism is political.* As Jameson [1981:58] argues, virtually any statement one makes has latent historical or theoretical assumptions. Whenever we look at something, we do so with all of our habitual ways of looking, including our biases, hunches, and uncertainties. Thus, to enjoy a Dr. Pepper commercial featuring dancing teenagers and their dancing grandparents may expose our belief that physical energy is central to a meaningful life. This assumption may betray yet other assumptions we have about aging (that it is best when it looks

like nonaging) as well as about politics (that state funding for the care of sedentary geriatric patients should not be increased). Thus, a phrase like "ideological criticism" is redundant, since, its proponents feel, nobody can become a critic without betraying self-interest. Ideological critics feel that they are simply more honest about their political premises than traditional critics.

2. *Criticism should be criticism.* Ideological critics are opposed to the traditionalists, who analyze a text's rhetorical devices without getting personally involved. While traditionalists like Hill [1983:122] try to focus on "the data in the text" without becoming "rhetorical partisans," ideological critics want to become part of the public dialogue. Josephine Donovan [1979:79], a feminist critic, pronounces her critical manifesto with gusto: "No longer will we accept the totalitarian dogma of the formalists that there is but one way to read a text . . . Instead, we will recognize that critics and readers are whole persons who come to literature with tunnels of experience through which they view the happenings in the text." While all critics study what is present and absent in a text, ideological critics also study what is right and wrong about it.

3. *Criticism should be expansionistic.* Ideological critics often study previously ignored texts. In contrast, says Wander [1983:3], traditional critics typically study texts produced by "the monopoly of officialdom"—white, Anglo-Saxon, centrist males—and thereby produce rhetorical theories of doubtful generalizability. To correct for such limitations, says Lentricchia [1983:15], the ideological critic tries "to re-read culture so as to amplify and strategically position the marginalized voices of the ruled, exploited, oppressed, and excluded." So, for example, deconstructionists study the works of modernists who have stood literary conventions on their heads. Feminists examine the secret writings of nineteenth-century women who had no public outlet for their talents. Marxists study youthful "punk" cultures to "open a space within which . . . resistance may be heard" [Grossberg, 1984:416]. In short, ideological critics listen to voices that have been systematically muted.

4. *Criticism should be oppositional.* Ideological critics feel that traditionalists have been too willing to honor the text the author had in mind. The very title of E. D. Hirsch's traditionalist classic, *Validity in Interpretation* [1967], suggests that the only way to know a text is the author's way, resulting in a gospel of "intentionalism" that reproduces the author's "attitudes, his cultural givens, in short, his world" [Divver, 1987:67]. Ideological critics show no such obeisance to the author. They become "resistant readers" [Fetterly, 1987] who accept no utterance at face value and instead examine a text for what they find interesting, whether or not it coincides with the author's implied prescrip-

tions-for-interpretation. The ideological critic practices what Ricoeur has called a "hermeneutics of suspicion" [Ruthven, 1984:35], an ominous sounding phrase but one that keeps the critic from being caught up in an author's rhetorical web.

Thus far in this book, we have discussed a variety of traditional approaches to criticism. But it is now time to welcome a new family to the critical neighborhood, a family that is, admittedly, fractious. They often say outrageous things, become tedious in their preachment, and ask intriguing questions that they cannot always answer. It is for this last reason that we must welcome them, however, for despite their impertinences ideological critics are producing some of the most interesting contemporary studies. As a kind of gentle godfather to this movement, Kenneth Burke counseled that criticism should be more than just an intellectual exercise. It was Burke who urged us to "take our work home" with us, to become "responsible to the larger social project" [Lentricchia, 1983:151]. If criticism is to be insightful, as it must be, probing, as it can be, and pluralistic, as it should be, how can we not listen to these new, disturbing voices?

THE POSTMODERN CRITIQUE

Deconstructionists win few popularity contests. Born out of the social turmoil that swept through Europe in the 1960s, deconstruction is "intensely skeptical of all claims to truth" [Norris, 1982:57]. To deconstruct is to take apart a rhetorical message, to examine how well a text "holds" its author's ideas without revealing unintended meanings. Given such obstreperous goals, it is not surprising that deconstruction was spawned by frustration. The founders of deconstruction were French thinkers—Jacques Derrida, Michel Foucault, and Roland Barthes—who disdained the Western establishment that fostered the Vietnam war, student repression, and racial segregation. They are often termed *post*modernists because they rejected the excessive capitalism underpinning "modern" conveniences and "modern" self-assuredness. Moreover, they charged establishment academics with spawning positivism (a love of things scientific), formalism (a reverence for traditional texts), and structuralism (a commitment to study such texts scientifically). Deconstructionists are also, then, *post*structuralists. They do not view language "as a complex but stable system whose constituents can be securely established" but as "an unreliable structure that violates its own rules" [Barney, 1987:179].

Deconstructionists are often accused of being anarchists, who treat communication as an impossibility and who are, as a result, nothing more than radical debunkers. According to their detractors, deconstructionists flee from the hard, patient work of disciplined criticism. But hard, patient, disciplined criticism is often unenlightening, they respond, and too often becomes "mere paraphrasing" of a message rather than "genuinely analytical reading" [Young, 1981:26]. The alternative, say the deconstructionists, is criticism that challenges rather than confirms critics' assumptions, that explores rather than retraces textual features, that subverts rather than accepts literary or rhetorical artistry. Deconstructionists resist the charge that they are political saboteurs costumed as critics, arguing that the nature of textuality demands their approach once three crucial premises are granted:

1. *Meaning is problematic.* The mystery of language is the central issue for deconstructionists. They feel that language is polysemous, that the "same" word means different things to different people and different things to the same person on different occasions. Accordingly, deconstruction turns into linguistic skepticism [Norris, 1982:174] because of what Derrida calls the constant "deferral" of meaning in a text. One factor demanding such deferral, says Moi [1985:106], is **language structure.** She notes, for example, that the letter "b" has no inherent meaning but only "gets" meaning when grouped with other letters (for example, to make "bat" or "bit"). "B" must, therefore, "defer" its meaning to these other elements to establish understandability. Similarly, "bat" and "bit" must defer their meaning once again to form "batch" or "bitter." If instablility is true at such elementary levels, the deconstructionists argue, how can a critic expect to settle, once and for all, the complete meaning of a verbal text?

Verbal context further complicates the picture, says Ryan [1982:12], who notes that the "God" in "God damn" and in "God of our Fathers" are very different Gods indeed. As a result, says Sumner [1979:149], every text will have a "surplus of meaning," which changes the critic's job considerably. Rather than looking for a message's "best" meaning, deconstructionists seek out its widest range of meanings by asking the question: In how many *different* ways might people come to undertand this text?

Social context makes meaning even harder to establish. Take a statement like the following, says Belsey [1980:52], and then ask if its interpretaion is unproblematic: "Democracy will ensure that we extend the boundaries of civilization." Would this statement sound different, Belsey asks, to residents of Western democracies (who would think of free speech, consumer choice, and open elections) than to residents of the Third World (who might think of colonial exploitation, guerrilla warfare, and cultural decadence)? Belsey says that such a statement would sound different still if mouthed by a conservative Member of

Parliament in Great Britain, by a committed socialist, or by the International Vice President of Pepsi Cola. This sentence will not stand still, Belsey argues, and we cannot pretend in criticism that it will.

Given these roadblocks to easy meaning, someone must become equipped to deal with what Culler [1982:220] calls "the uncanny irrationality of texts." Someone must realize that chaos is not something the radical critic adds to a text but something that constitutes the text initially [Barney, 1987:186]. Someone must ask the questions about "real meaning" the traditionalists have been afraid to ask. The deconstructionist is that someone.

2. *All messages are intertwined.* No text can be understood unless viewed in the light of what we saw described in Chapter Three as its persuasive field, the messages to which that text responds and which respond to it. The ideal critic, says Barthes [1981:39], views the text as an "intertext," as something woven by the threads of other texts. The critic looks for the traces of these other messages within the text so that its "pluralistic" effects can be guaged. This means that deconstructionists "often show scant respect for the wholeness or integrity of individual works" [Culler, 1982:220], but are more interested in the general themes that echo throughout society. While deconstructionists sometimes visit with an individual text, they rarely stay for long.

To take a pedestrian example of intertextuality, we might ask why radio call-in shows are so popular. A deconstructionist might observe that they contain (and are contained by) back-yard gossip, doctrinaire preaching, psychological counseling, classroom instruction, obscene phone-calling, stage drama, and commerical salesmanship. Each of these discourse systems carries its own "charge" for listeners, which can "detonate" from time to time, thereby increasing the show's overall rhetorical "explosion." And because these subdiscourses are mutually implicative, their power is increased all the more. Hence the job of the deconstructionist: to reveal the seams in the fabric of talk-radio by asking whether listeners really wish to become addicted to discourse emerging from the rather squalid worlds of doctrinaire preaching and obscene phone-calling. Thus, by examining intertextuality, deconstructionists trace "a path among textual strata in order to stir up and expose forgotten and dormant sediments of meaning which have accumulated and settled into the text's fabric" [Harari, 1979:37].

Deconstructionists say that we cannot escape from intertextuality, that subtexts affect not only how we listen and read but also how we are *prepared* to listen and read. So, for example, even with an empirical event like the Civil War, people will view it differently depending upon the texts (Northern myths versus Southern myths) heard previously, texts "which can be deciphered endlessly without ever rendering an ultimate meaning-determination or a full truth" [Ryan, 1982:24].

Because of this complexity, deconstructionists feel that criticism must challenge the univocal interpretation of any text. As Foucault [1981:70] points out, for example, madness and hypersexuality have been the objects of scorn *and reverence* at different points in human history. Thus, unless a text's meanings are pluralized, an old rhetoric may gain new, unwarranted popularity because its "textual history" has been forgotten or not plainly established in the first place.

3. *Rhetoric is problematic.* Heretofore, most deconstructionists have analyzed literature, unmasking an author by demonstrating the clever tricks used to fabricate rationality in a fictional world. While traditional critics have assumed that the author knew "what he was doing" [Harvey, 1987:143], deconstructionists have made no such assumption. They have proclaimed "the Death of the Author" [Belsey, 1980:139], approaching texts in ways that might well horrify their creators. Foucault [1981:67] and his colleagues think of discourse as a "violence which we do to things," a deliberate intrusion into ongoing reality. So deconstructionists often call authors to task for the "texts" they wittingly or unwittingly reproduce anew. Not wishing to become leeches on someone else's writings, these critics often use texts merely to *illustrate* arguments that they, the critics, want to forward.

Because deconstruction has been used primarily in literary studies, its full power has not yet been tapped, since literature is, after all, self-consciously fictive. Literature does not expect readers to grant it factual status, only "truth" status. "Poetry is the foreknowledge of criticism," say DeMan [1983:31]; it does not present itself as a final authority but only as an initial, teasing voice. Rhetoric is different. It expects to be taken seriously. Because it does so, the critic must work especially hard to reveal its necessary contradictions and gaps of meaning. This is why Eagleton [1983:145] has emphasized that *all* language is metaphorical—including the languages of philosophy, politics, law, and commerce—and that, because it acknowledges this fact, literature is "less deluded than other forms of discourse."

In a sense, then, deconstructionists approach rhetoric as if it were literature. They emphasize rhetoric's fabricated status so that people will learn to question the Declaration of Independence just as sharply as they do *The Canterbury Tales.* Equally, the deconstructionist approaches literature as if it were rhetoric, warning readers not to become so relaxed in the presence of literature that they forget that it can also affect their social attitudes and expectations. Tracking rhetorical devices in a text—whether rhetorical or literary—sheds light on how an author privileges one meaning over its many alternatives. By "pluralizing" a text in this way, the critic regains control over that text. Or, at least, so say the deconstructionists.

Given these three, rather frustrating, premises, what is a critic to do? How does one deconstruct a text? And why would one want to do so? The deconstructionist's answers to these questions of purpose and method often prove frustrating. For one thing, they rarely worry about producing answers. Their business is producing (or reproducing) questions. Deconstruction is, therefore, never a completed process. Its goals are (1) to "exhaust" a text so that its multiple meanings become clearer and (2) to contrast what an author intends for a text with the other intentions a critic might find in it [Harvey, 1985:209].

As for critical method, there is none. Not really. Rather, the critic operates creatively, teasing out themes, inconsistencies, and pontifications in a text, starting down one path and then another, looking for semantic uncertainty until it is time to stop. (A deconstructionist never *concludes*.) When doing criticism, a deconstructionist will frequently "seize on some apparently peripheral fragment in the work—a footnote, a recurrent minor term or image, a casual allusion—and work it tenaciously through to the point where it threatens to dismantle the oppositions that govern the text as a whole. The tactic of the deconstructive critic . . . is to show how texts come to embarrass their own ruling systems of logic" [Eagleton, 1983:133].

But while deconstructionists dismiss questions of purpose (a delusion, they feel) and method (the refuge of pendants, they feel), they do ask some questions persistently. To avoid complete bewilderment, we will use these questions during a sample deconstruction. But what should be deconstructed? What sort of text deserves the rather rough treatment deconstruction hands out? Aune [1983:260] provides a clue when he recalls that Derrida & Co. were especially suspicious of the "transcendental significations" of formalized rhetoric. Derrida had in mind such things as legal statutes, religious coda, scientific reports, and political oratory. He might also have had Jerry Ford in mind. We will assume that he did, and here consider the simple set of remarks President Ford gave on July 1, 1976, just prior to the opening of a Centennial safe that had been sealed at the U.S. Capitol a century before. Mr. Ford spoke thusly:

[1] Thank you very much, Senator Mansfield, Mr. Speaker, Senator Scott, Senator Brooke, Congressman Boggs, distinguished Members of the House and Senate, ladies and gentlemen:

[2] Obviously, I am deeply honored to have the opportunity this afternoon to open this historic Centennial safe. It contains many items of interest to us today as we celebrate the completion of our second century. But it symbolizes much more than a valuable collection of mementos; it symbolizes something about the United States of America that is so mighty and so inspiring that it cannot be locked up in a safe—I mean the American spirit.

[3] When this safe was sealed, Americans looked forward to the future, to this year of 1976. There was no doubt in their minds that a President of a free government would participate in a ceremony here in the United States Capitol Building.

[4] Just as American men and women 200 years ago looked to the future, those who sealed this safe 100 years ago also looked to the future. So it is today with Americans. But there is no safe big enough to contain the hopes, the energies, the abilities of our people. Our real national treasure does not have to be kept under lock and key in a safe or in a vault. America's wealth is not in material objects, but in our great heritage, our freedom, and our belief in ourselves.

[5] A century ago the population of the United States numbered over 40 million; today we have more than five times as many. But the growth of our population has not lessened our devotion to the principles that inspired Americans in 1776 or 1876.

[6] In 1876 our immense wealth, both natural and inventive, commanded world-wide attention. We grew from coast to coast in greater industrial and agricultural development than humanity had ever known. In 1876 America was still emerging from a terrible fraternal war. A lesser people might have been unequal to the challenge, but 1976 finds the confidence of 1876 confirmed.

[7] Today there is far greater equality of opportunity, liberty, and justice for all of our citizens in every corner of America. There is rising prosperity for our Nation and peace and progress for our people.

[8] We look back to the evening of July 4, 1776. It was then, after the adoption of the Declaration of Independence, that the Continental Congress resolved that Franklin, Adams, and Jefferson begin work on a seal as a national symbol. We are all familiar with the front part of that great seal. But the reverse side, which also appears on every dollar bill, is especially instructive. It depicts a pyramid which is not completed and a single eye gazing out radiantly. The unfinished pyramid represents the work that remains for Americans to do. The Latin motto below is freely translated: "God has favored our undertaking." Two hundred years later, we know God has.

[9] Though we may differ, as Americans have throughout the past, we share a common purpose: It is the achievement of a future in keeping with our glorious past. The American Republic provides for continued growth through a convergence of views and interests, but that growth must be spiritual as well as material.

[10] As we look inside this safe, let us look inside ourselves. Let us look into our hearts and into our hopes.

[11] On Sunday we start a new century, a century of the individual. We have given meaning to our life as a nation. Let us now welcome a century in which we give new meaning to our lives as individuals. Let us look inside ourselves to unleash the God-given treasures stored within. And let us look outside ourselves to the needs of our families, our friends, our communities, our Nation, and our moral and spiritual consciousness.

[12] Thank you very much. [Ford 1976a:1941–1943]

Most Americans would judge this a fine speech. It says nothing terribly new, but is says old things in a pleasing way. Mr. Ford develops a trite metaphorical theme (spiritual values as riches), touches on the expected bits of Americana (the Revolutionary War, Adams and Jefferson), and ends his speech by looking toward a glorious future. There is nothing startling here but nothing distasteful either. Even the most cynical observer would judge the speech harmless. Not so, says the deconstructionist: This speech subverts the dignity of the average citizen and promotes a new American oligarchy. Preposterous, most Americans would exclaim. Where is the proof?

Since deconstruction is "the undoing of finality in all its philosophic forms" [Ryan, 1982:34], the deconstructionist might first examine any **absolute language** implicitly promising listeners that they can rise above partiality. President Ford's brave phrases—"so mighty and so inspiring," "our great heritage," "devotion to the principles"— merely float in rhetorical space, the deconstructionist would argue. Similarly, when Ford speaks of "we," "us," or "Americans," he conceives of a dormant citizenry. Of the twenty-one such references in the speech, over half refer to *looking*, not acting. Americans look forward and backward; they look inside their hearts and inside their national safe. But what sort of citizen is a "looking" citizen, the deconstructionist would ask? Why does Ford use only three behavioral verbs to describe what Americans are like? How can such an inert speech comfort an audience? And if the American people are not "acting," who is?

The speech's **figurative language** answers this latter question. According to deconstructionists, people depend heavily on metaphors for meaning but too often forget they are dealing with imagery. The deconstructionist would note, for example, that during Mr. Ford's speech-act he not only opens a safe inside the Capitol but also uses that safe figuratively. Why choose the metaphor of a safe, the deconstructionist would ask, when most Americans have no immediate connection with a convenience the upper class uses to hide its money? Is Mr. Ford really describing a *national* safe or is he just taunting blue-collar Americans by alluding to valuables they do not possess residing in a safe they do not own? Besides, how "safe" can a safe be for ordinary people when it is opened but once every hundred years and then only by the ruling-class individuals who have its keys?

Deconstructionists might observe that there is even a certain cruelty to Mr. Ford's teasing here, since the safe we are locked out of *contains our hopes:* "As we look inside this safe, let us look inside ourselves. Let us look into our hearts and into our hopes." So, it appears, we are (1) inside a safe that (2) we do not own and (3) for which we do not have a key. We are thus a people trapped and isolated, separated from our fellow citizens by steel walls, a people who cannot even hope for community since the President has urged us to "give new meaning to our lives *as individuals.*"

But why do the American people deserve this fate? Too many of them were born on the wrong side of the tracks says Mr. Ford via his **abstract language.** "[T]hrough abstractions," says Ryan [1982:50,56], people can be manipulated by making things "seem outside the movement of time and the productive processes of society." Such is the case with Mr. Ford's concept of "wealth," which he says lies "not in material objects" but is "spiritual as well." Is Ford arguing here that monetary and spirtual wealth are necessarily separate, with some people deserving one and some another? Apparently so, since he claims that *our* "real national treasure does not have to be kept in a vault." But why can't *we* have secured riches, Mr. Ford? Because there is "no safe big enough to contain the hopes . . . of our people," he replies. Thus, we must resign ourselves to the lot of all nonelites (only *"work* remains for Americans to do") and to inequality as well ("We may differ, as Americans have throughout the past"). The American Dream, it appears, is ultimately just a dream.

Deconstructionists also key on **hierarchical language** because of their theory of meaning: A thing can only be known by its opposite; if one thing is good, other things must be less good and still others more good. This sense of relativitity is rarely explicated in a text, which is not to say that it is not there (by implication). Mr. Ford's unfinished pyramid on the back of the dollar bill is a case in point. By the time he makes this allusion, Mr. Ford has already affirmed (in paragraph 6) that there are greater and "lesser" people in the world. Presumably, this means that some people are on the pyramid's bottom and some at its top. When finishing the construction of such a pyramid, one would presumably work at (for?) its apex and not at (for?) its base. This implies that the real beneficiaries in the future will be those who are already at the top of the pyramid, powerful persons looking with "a single eye gazing out radiantly" on the day-laborers in society.

Might Mr. Ford's hierarchy be leveled in the future? Apparently not, since we can only look toward "a future *in keeping with* our glorious past," a past that Mr. Ford admits included a civil war, insufficient opportunity for the nation's citizens, denial of liberty, and an inadequate judicial system. While there apparently will be some increases for "our citizens in every corner of America," one wonders whether cornered citizens will even notice such improvements, sitting as they do at the base of the Ford pyramid.

Deconstructionists are particularly devilish when it comes to **inconsistent language.** For example, despite his lionizing of "spiritual treasures," Ford declares that the "valuable collection of mementos" in the national vault symbolizes "something" (some-*thing*) important, thereby endorsing materialist values. He repeats this theme when recollecting that "our immense weath . . . commanded world-wide attention" in 1876, attention he clearly appreciates. If Mr. Ford were not a materialist, why did he choose the dollar bill as his central rhetorical image? Moreover, why did he tell us to look "outside ourselves" to the "needs of our families, our friends, our communities"? If these needs are truly *outside* ourselves, how can we possibly deal with them? And how can we trust in the future when it took until 1976 to "find the confidence" needed to persevere: "Two hundred years later, we know God has [favored our undertaking]." With a heavenly time lag of this magnitude, can this really be called a speech of hope?

Much more sophisticated deconstructions than this one have been performed in the past and many of them have inspected the same five "trouble spots" isolated in the Ford text. Ryan [1982:136], for example, examined a report from the Carnegie Commission on Higher Education. He argues that while the report lauded "academic freedom," it really camouflaged "the link between education and business behind a benign vocabulary," thereby endorsing "academic constriction" rather than its opposite. In a similar vein, Perlman [1976] notes that Brazilian peasants were described as "marginalized" in official documents but were actually quite *central* to Brazilian society as a source of cheap labor. On a very different front, Belsey [1980:114—117] observes how Sherlock Holmes detective stories praise the scientific method and yet how women of "shadowy sexuality" often steal the show, thereby casting doubt on scientific rationality. A similar theme was traced by Ryan [1982:146], who examined how "philosophic reason" became utilitarian when articulated by business leaders accused of air and water pollution. As one business leader remarked: "I don't think it's realistic to ask a corporation to do [too much] . . . The cost-benefit [ratio] can get out of line."

Given deconstruction's often bizarre flights of fancy, what are we to make of it? Deconstructions can be cute, but are they valid? Useful? Important? Any message, after all, could be "destroyed" in the way we have destroyed Mr. Ford's speech. That is a crucial fact, the deconstructionists would reply. After all, if a carefully crafted, simple, speech like Ford's can be shown to be pessimistic, reactionary, materialistic, isolationistic, and hierarchial rather than their opposites, should we not be especially on guard when presented with vastly more subtle rhetorical materials?

Perhaps, but was our deconstruction really fair? Did it not put words into Mr. Ford's mouth? Not really, for Ford's vacuums of meaning came from *his own remarks*. Admittedly, we did not interpret the President's words as he would have preferred. But why should we? Why should critics help Ford fashion his message? Aren't critics free agents? Must they slavishly conform to the author's rhetorical directions? Besides, is Gerald Ford not a grown adult? If he could not make his words stand still, why should the critic compensate for him? It is rather important, after all, that Ford's language could not obviate problems that have plagued American democracy throughout its history: poverty in a land of opportunity, militarism in a land of peace, godlessness in a land of churches. If these inconsistencies have not been resolved in two hundred years, how could Jerry Ford resolve them in one five-minute speech? Ultimately, then, there is nothing magical about deconstruction except this: It forces a text to be honest with itself.

Perhaps the sharpest challenge to deconstruction is that, in the example above, President Ford's *actual listeners* probably never noticed what Johnson [1981:166] calls the "warring forces of signification" in a text. Indeed, Mr. Ford's listeners were probably charmed by his oration. Do not such real-life responses give the lie to deconstruction? Only if the critic wishes to become an audience member and not a critic. In deconstruction, it is the critic who must highlight the conflicts in texts, thereby making those texts problematic for the wider community. The deconstructionist is essentially a consciousness-raiser, spotting trouble in a text where there seems to be none. Ultimately, the question becomes one of who will have the last word—Jerry Ford or the critic. It is not to Mr. Ford's advantage to have his speeches deconstructed.

The most devastating critique of deconstruction is that of the Marxists, who find it to be too gamelike. It produces an "infinite regression" in texts, warns Barney [1987:199], "a kind of 'textual fiddling while Rome burns,'" says Norris [1982:131], an "elitist cult and reactionary force," says Felperin [1985:111]. While "millions have been killed because they were Marxists," observes Ryan [1982:1], "no one will be obliged to die because s/he is a deconstructionist." As we will see, Marxists are fond of making such grand statements. But the deconstructionists and the Marxist have much in common, because they both expose "the complicity between rhetoric, power, and authority" [Cain, 1984:241] and can, therefore, be liberating. But liberation for what end, asks the Marxist? What social policies does deconstruction put in place? How will people's lives be improved because contrariety is found in a text? About such matters, the deconstructionist is typically silent.

RHETORIC AND PERSONAL CHANGE
Critical Profile 12.1   There's Money in Advice

Why are self-help books so popular these days and what are the implications of such popularity? George Dillon, then of the University of Maryland, examined such questions when he studied contemporary advice books on topics ranging from child care and sexual relations to financial investing and English composition. Advice books, he says, "pretend" to be oral conversations by scripting a role for the reader and then engaging in dialogue with this imagined audience.

Dillon's analysis includes an interesting discussion of investment books that predict "an imminent hyperinflationary crisis." Such books as Howard Ruff's *How to Prosper during the Coming Bad Years* and Douglas Casey's *Crisis Investing*, argues Dillon, are "violently hyperbolic" and use a "figurative mode of expression running to images of destruction, disease, and parasitism." They are based on the premise that "traditional wisdom and institutions cannot deal with the present reality," which is "out of control." But Dillon points to the disparity between such hyperbolic statements of the problem and the fairly tame solutions offered, solutions that are often merely vacuous restatements of traditional advice. Ruff, for example, justifies both "paying off the property" and taking out a second mortgage, "Either approach is OK," says consultant Ruff.

The key to understanding this disparity, Dillon feels, is that many of the "metaphors of uncontrollable, malign forces" also convey *control* as well. For example, while talking about the approaching economic crash, Ruff creates the image of a car headed "for the precipice" and states, "it doesn't matter whether we go soaring over the cliff with our foot on the accelerator (inflation), or skidding with our foot on the brake (deflation)." In either case, Dillon observes, the "implication [is] that we are in the driver's seat, potentially powerful even in our powerlessness." Crisis investment books, therefore, offer a world in which "free-swinging writing can enact feelings of mastery and control," and they offer this verbal play as a substitute for meaningful human action: If I can't be powerful, I want to at least feel powerful and talk powerfully. Indeed, as Dillon points out, the ultimate purpose of many crisis investment books is to get the reader to subscribe to the author's "rather expensive investment newsletters." In other words, self-help books empower their readers by getting them to feel that *the act of reading* about a problem is in many senses superior to the act of actually solving it.

Profiled by: David R. Harvey
Citation: Dillon (1986)

Critical Profile 12.2   The Rhetoric of Urgency

The consent form for federally-funded sterilization operations reads: I UNDERSTAND THAT THE STERILIZATION MUST BE CONSIDERED PERMANENT AND NOT REVERSIBLE. I HAVE DECIDED THAT I DO NOT WANT TO BECOME PREGNANT, BEAR CHILDREN OR FATHER CHILDREN. In a similar vein, an environmental group warns that without immediate action a treasured species of duck-billed platypus will disappear forever. Throughout the byways of commercial America, store signs read: FINAL CLOSEOUT! PRICES MAY NEVER BE THIS LOW AGAIN! Claims like these, claims that argue that a certain decision must be made *now* because its consequences cannot be reversed, have become routine. These arguments play on people's fears of permanent loss, on their need to have some say about the future. And although this rhetoric-of-urgency is prevalent, says J. Robert Cox of the University of North Carolina, its prevalence has not sapped its rhetorical appeal.

In a sense, any choice a person makes has a touch of the irreparable to it. Most people understand that they cannot experience a particular moment twice, that life is full of one-shot opportunities. But the potency of a rhetorical claim based on irreparability, Cox argues, rests in its insistence that we choose among competing—*and equally irreparable*—alternatives. As a result, persuasion of this sort forces its audience to make value judgments at the most fundamental level. "Which is worth more," the political campaigner asks, "a lovely, fragile wilderness or a lumber industry that provides wood, jobs, and important by-products? You can't have it both ways." Rhetoric that paints this either-or scenario organizes people's choices for them (often artificially) and closes them off to short-term, more expedient modes of decision making. After all, Cox notes, "The object or act which qualifies as irreparable is necessarily unique; . . . its existence is precarious . . . [its value is dependent upon] a transitory state of affairs."

When confronted with the rhetoric of the irreparable, people often suspend their normal reasoning processes. Because this is so, Cox sees important ethical questions beckoning: Who, for example, should be "permitted" to base arguments on the never-again? It is one thing for a physician to point out the irreparability of sterilization procedures to a teenager and quite another for a salesperson to announce a "final" close-out sale on sit-down lawnmowers. Also, if arguments about irreparability are used indiscreetly, will listeners begin to turn a deaf ear to all such rhetoric, even to that of properly "licensed" spokespersons (for example, nuclear armaments experts). Moreover, since the rhetoric of irreparability is often such a radical rhetoric ("There is no time to waste!" "Life itself hangs in the balance"), Cox warns that it can provoke equally radical—and equally irreparable—responses (for example, the firebombing of an abortion clinic). In other words, this rhetoric must be met by the coolest heads available, since it so dramatically encourages the response: "What else have I to lose if 'all' is already lost?"

Profiled by: Susan Whalen
Citation: Cox (1982)

Critical Profile 12.3   Separate Keys to the Executive Washroom?

According to Dr. Jolene Koester of the University of Missouri, the contemporary women's movement has led more women to seek managerial success. One response to help the wave of aspiring female managers has come in the form of numerous self-help books. With so many books on the market, Koester wondered what sorts of advice about success were being offered to contemporary women. After reviewing twenty-eight popular advice books, among them *The Women's Guide to Management Success* and *Games Mother Never Taught You: Corporate Gamesmanship for Women,* Koester found that the message women were getting was that they themselves were the "source of their own success or failure" and that gender was the "ultimate factor" in every situation.

Koester's analysis reveals that authors use various instructional strategies for building models of success. Predominant among them is the use of behavioral scripts to teach women how their gender and individual actions operate in the organizational world. All such scenarios revolve around the issue of gender. For example, one author tells women, "If you have to tell your boss not to send you for coffee, you must have already told him nonverbally that you were ready to go." Scenarios such as these give women the idea that they alone are responsible for every action they take and every reaction they generate. Koester argues that this is a deceptive notion. She explains that while women may initially feel optimistic by believing that the only obstacle to success is their own desire to achieve it, eventually women will learn that they cannot change everyone's attitudes and behaviors toward them. The woman who accepts the "tenet that she is in control of her own fate will repeatedly come face-to-face with failure," says Koester.

Popular advice books, therefore, give women "incomplete, contradictory and debilitating advice," claims Koester. They imply that factors like job performance, technical skills, and professional competence are of secondary importance to, or completely irrelevant to, success. To suggest to women that gender is the greatest liability to success is to personalize an issue that is highly political and economic and to individualize a woman's feelings, thus isolating her from the collective actions (that is, women's groups, professional groups, etc.) available for changing her life. Consequently, when it comes to making decisions or handling conflict, Koester believes there is great danger in store for women who follow the advice that "a woman manager is a woman first and a manager second."

Profiled by: Yvonne Becerra
Citation: Koester (1982)

THE MARXIST CRITIQUE

The Marxist critic takes a very old story—a story of exploitation—and tells it again and again. What is the plot of this story? That the ruling classes use rhetoric to justify their exalted positions, rationalize the meager existences of the downtrodden, and inhibit insurrection. How do they do so? Through education, religion, political patronage, banking systems, nationalism, bureaucracies, and manufacturing processes. Why does rhetoric enter the picture? Because each of these systems of exploitation needs an attractive public face. And what does the critic do? Expose the constantly changing disguises of repression.

Even in this simplistic rendering, it is clear why Marxist thought captivates many. In the world of criticism, it especially captivates those who have tired of traditional criticism and, more recently, of deconstruction. According to the Marxist, traditionalists "appreciate" rather than critique discourse, thereby making criticism a decadent activity, like collecting bottle caps or frequenting Woody Allen film festivals. Such criticism stands too far away from its object of analysis and ultimately becomes boring, predictable, and socially irresponsible: "Becoming certificated [in criticism] is a matter of being able to talk and write in certain ways ... Those employed to teach [it to] you will remember whether or not you were able to speak it proficiently long after they have forgotten what you said" [Eagleton, 1983:201].

In short, Marxists aim to make a difference in the world of politics by making a row in the world of criticism. Unlike their cousins on the left, the deconstructionists, Marxists will risk being both repetitious and tendentious if it will open people's eyes to the political manipulations surrounding (and suppressing) them. For Marxists, a text is worth studying not for its inherent worth but because it signals such manipulation. They base their criticism on the following premises:

1. *Economic factors determine rhetoric.* There is no plainer way of stating the most fundamental presupposition of Marxist criticism. And the word "determine" is central to this proposition, for it holds that the possibilities for communication are set by society's structural and economic mechanisms. These mechanisms make only certain thoughts thinkable and, hence, only certain messages sayable and hearable. Although this "vulgar" form of Marxism has become less popular as Marxist theory has matured, Marx's fundamental dictum still informs most such criticism: "Consciousness does not determine life; life determines consciousness" [Eagleton, 1976:4].

Why is this true? Because society needs to reproduce itself from age to age and, therefore, needs a rhetoric capable of making its favored institutions compelling and dynamic. If a politico-economic "base" is to remain viable, it must produce "superstructures" (religious, social, cultural, and educational systems) capable of sustaining that base. Thus, it is not enough for a capitalistic system to produce goods (its economic base); it must also find a rhetoric to make such production continuingly necessary. So, says King [1987:73], "Americans have been told to feel that their bodies are filthy, rotting masses of chemicals and that their odors and body faults must be constantly disguised, or they will be found out and ridiculed. [Marxist] theorists point to the enormous sales of soaps and deodorants as proof that the engineered insecurity of the masses is a fact of life."

2. *Messages are produced, not created.* This proposition proceeds logically from the first: If the base dominates the superstructure, then human texts are fashioned automatically. The implications of this proposition are stark and unsettling: People's most unique thoughts are little more than the thoughts "granted" them by the larger social system. So, for example, a high school sophomore who feels she is dressed distinctively when wearing her Calvin Kleins is not just deluded but trebly deluded: (1) She is wearing jeans because that is what the powerful cotton industry in the United States has made available for her to wear; (2) she has chosen the Calvin Klein brand because it can be purchased locally, meaning that in comparison to its competitors Calvin Klein, Inc. has best managed to keep wages low and profits high; and (3) she feels distinctive because the Calvin Klein ads have depicted independent women doing independent things while wearing their Calvins.

Our high school sophomore would naturally be outraged by this analysis, feeling that her choice of clothing was, in fact, *her choice.* She must embrace this delusion, the Marxist says, for without "false consciousness" the social and economic system would fail. Delusions like these result from what Williams [1977] and others call **hegemony,** an all-encompassing master text so broadly based in society that it can no longer be seen by either speaker or audience. "The author does not make the materials with which he works," claims Eagleton [1976:29], just as "the worker in a car-assembly plant fashions his product from already-processed materials." So, says Eagleton [1975:52], the three-volume novel became popular in Victorian England not because writers wished to write them or readers read them but because publishers found them profitable to produce and formed a cartel with the newly emerging circulating libraries for their distribution. In short, while we may wish to believe that ideas spring from nothingness, the Marxist finds this a silly notion.

3. *Ideologies leave textual evidence.* Generally speaking, Marxist critics treat an individual message as a fragment of "the textual coherence of contemporary cultural experience" [McGee, 1987:8]. Marxist critics differ with one another about how easy it is to find such coher-

ence, but few doubt it can be found. The basic critical operation for the Marxist is thus one of "rewriting" a text so that its ideological imprintings can be observed. For the Marxist, true critical consciousness is being able to know even "yourself as the product of a historical process that has deposited its traces in you" [Lentricchia, 1983:11]. This is similar to the cultural critic's challenge (as seen in Chapter Ten), but Marxism adds a new dimension—the State—by looking for the political and economic truths a text honors.

But it is often hard to find ideology trapped inside texts, because it hides "within the naturalized, altogether acceptable and normal operations of authority which define social order" [Merod, 1987:161]. For example, the Marxist might note that American companies often vie with one another to support U.S. Olympic teams. These corporate/nationalistic linkages do not just make for good public relations, but have two other benefits in addition: (1) The televised athletic competition reinforces free market competitiveness and (2) the private sector's capitalistic message is linked directly to the public sector's patriotic message. This is why Marxist critics so often study popular culture, where such contrivances and collusions have become so naturalized that they can no longer be seen (What could be more natural than running and jumping?).

4. *Established institutions need rhetoric.* Rhetoric is often thought of as the tool of the downtrodden, a way of changing the status quo. But Marxist critics have shown that the establishment also depends on public discourse, even if it does so less colorfully. Religious leaders attend political gatherings, business executives appear on the nightly news, and Hollywood personalities, well-paid athletes, and military leaders move about constantly in each other's company, forming a kind of U.S. cultural establishment. Their rhetorical skills make for what Thompson [1984:68] calls "cultural capital," which, when combined with having an education, gaining access to the media, and learning bureaucratic routines, makes some people very powerful.

This shower of establishment rhetoric often makes us forget what we know. We know, for example, that individuals have different amounts of money. But in capitalistic societies, rhetorics develop to make these differences seem both natural and necessary. Still other rhetorics develop to prove they need not be permanent: the rags-to-riches tale, the lottery millionaire myth, the Bill Cosby story, and so forth. Cultural rituals, political oratory, and television dramas cooperate to make what we see with our eyes (disparity) different from what we come to accept (justifiable disparity). At times, these differential allocations are even made to seem *attractive* (for example, the rather forgettable Goldie Hawn movie *Overboard*, in which a bored heiress falls off her yacht, loses her memory, moves in with a laborer, and eventually find her essential self in his poor-but-honest embrace). These messages bombard us so constantly and so unobtrusively, says Corcoran [1984:142], that we are not just awakened to establishment values but deadened to all other values as well.

Given these assumptions about rhetoric, what do Marxist critics do? At the risk of generalizing about a diverse group, it seems that they do two main things. *The first goal of Marxist criticism is to historicize messages.* Marxists remind us constantly that rhetoric is crafted by particular people for particular people. They steer clear of what Bennett [1979:147] calls the "metaphysic of the text" (a text in pure form) by repopulating it. So, for example, a Marxist critic would never treat a documentary on Central America as a mere example of its genre. Rather, the critic would want to know *who* financed the film, under *whom* the director studied and why, why *this* political figure and not *that* political figure was profiled in the film, *who* was made to seem a devil and *who* an angel, *to whom* the documentary was distributed and through *whose* agency.

Naturally, one need not be a Marxist to be interested in such questions. But Marxists take special pains to remember (1) that each piece of rhetoric contains the marks of its unique historical situation and (2) that rhetoric has a powerful (and dangerous) capacity to make the world abstract. This is why Marxists are interested in a rhetorical image's **material conditions** (who lives and who dies in the documentary, what sorts of food people eat in the restaurant scenes, what type of work they perform in the fields). According to the Marxist, traditional criticism all too often overlooks such facts by "aestheticizing" a text. The Marxist critic would discover whether the documentarist placed a First World or a Third World lens on the camera, whether peasant rituals were treated paternalistically, whether the film accurately depicted the reality of prostitution in Central America, and whether a rock beat or a Latin beat was featured in the nightclub scenes. In other words, a Marxist critic would never forget that the Central American documentary ultimately dealt with Central Americans.

The second goal of Marxist criticism is to comfort the afflicted and afflict the comfortable, often by amplifying voices that have been previously muted. So, for example, Jameson [1981] urged examination of the oral epics of tribal society, the fairy tales developed by the European underclasses, and the melodramas written for pennies by paupers. Similarly, Genovese [1976] studied how black slaves transformed their oppressors' Christianity into a religious style better suited to their own cultural patterns. Yet another brand of Marxist criticism studies the "symbolic violence" done to oppressed groups by mainstream messages (how ghetto residents watching *Dallas* decode its obscene consumerism). By examining such matters, Marxists radicalize scholarship and become, in a sense, critically insubordinate [Merod, 1987:158].

But, we must now ask, how do Marxists actually do their criticism? As with all critics, they ask questions. Specifically, they look for rhetorical features that have been "over-determined" by socio-economic conditions. We shall consider five common ways of isolating these features by examining a humble guide to student parking regulations at the University of Texas. Like so many bureaucratic tomes, this document is almost comically dense. Among its highlights are the following:

(1) PERMITS REQUIRED FOR ACCESS & PARKING: Only vehicles conspicuously displaying proper University permits (as specified in Section VI, infra) may enter or park on the main campus Monday through Friday from 7:30 A.M. to 5:00 P.M. Purchase of a permit does not guarantee a parking place on campus (Section II, infra).

(2) DISPLAY OF PERMITS: Parking permits must be properly affixed to or displayed on the vehicle(s) as described in Section VI infra. Decals which are taped or affixed by unauthorized materials will subject the holder to a University citation. Additionally, the permit will be revoked and the holder may lose all parking privileges (Section VIII, infra). . . .

(4) REMOVAL OF PERMITS: Permits shall be removed when there is a change of vehicle ownership; when association with the University is terminated; when a replacement permit (decal) has been issued to take the place of a previously issued permit (decal); or upon expiration or revocation (Section VI, infra).

(5) OWNERSHIP OF PERMIT: Ownership of the parking permit remains with the University. Purchase of a parking permit signifies that an individual has been granted the privilege of parking a motor vehicle on University property (Section IV, infra). . . .

(14) BICYCLES AND SKATES: Bicycles must be operated in accordance with the ordinances of the City of Austin, the specific applicable provisions of these regulations, all provisions of these regulations concerning parking restrictions and traffic and applicable state laws. Rollerskating (including skate boards) is not permitted on any part of the campus (Section IV, infra). . . .

(17) POSTED SIGNS: Posted signs, whether permanent or temporary, must be obeyed at all times and take precedence over painted curbs, pavement markings and designations shown on any University map. . . .

(20) REGISTRATION OF TWO VEHICLES: Holders of Class D, F or O permits may register an alternate vehicle at no extra cost. Holders of Class A, C or G permits may register one additional motorcylce, or moped (Section VI, infra). . . .

(21) ENFORCEMENT AND IMPOUNDMENTS: Failure to abide by these regulations may be the basis for disciplinary action against students, and

faculty/staff (Section V, infra). Upon notice, violators may subject their vehicle(s) to impoundment pending payment of overdue charges (Section VIII, infra). Students may also be barred from readmission and have grades, degree, refunds or official transcripts withheld pending payment of overdue charges (Section VIII, infra). Vehicles may also be impounded for specific violations (Section VII, infra).

(22) APPEAL OF CITATION: University parking and traffic citations may be appealed, **within five (5) working days** from date of citation by filing a Citation Appeal Form with the Parking and Traffic Office. (See Section VIII for detailed procedures.) Court Appearance citations are handled by the appropriate state or municipal court.

(23) VISITORS: All visitors need permits to park on campus UNLESS parked at a paid parking meter or at the University Visitor Center or in the parking garage. OFFICIAL VISITORS are those who conduct important business with the University or who are not otherwise eligible for annual parking permits. Official Visitors may obtain temporary visitor parking permits from the guards at the traffic control stations. These permits entitle the holder to park *only* in a space designated "Official Visitor." Permits must be clearly visible and hanging from the rear view mirror support (Section VI, infra).

(24) PEDESTRIANS—RIGHTS AND DUTIES: Pedestrians are subject to all official traffic control devices. They have the right-of-way at marked crosswalks, in intersections and on sidewalks extending across a service drive, building entrance or driveway. Pedestrians crossing a street at any point other than within a marked crosswalk or within an unmarked crosswalk at an intersection shall yield the right-of-way to all vehicles on said street. Pedestrians shall not leave curb or other place of safety and walk or run into the path of a vehicle which is so close that it is impossible for the driver to yield. They may cross an intersection diagonally only where permitted by special pavement marking.

(25) INOPERABLE VEHICLES: If a vehicle becomes inoperable, a telephone call shall be placed to the University Police Department (471-4441). The police will either render assistance or authorize temporary parking. Temporary parking shall not exceed 24 hours and must not create an obstruction or hazard. Vehicles shall not be left without written permission from UTPD. Hand written notes are NOT acceptable [Quick Reference, 1986].

Documents like this abound in any bureaucracy, where they are defended as necessary for carrying out mundane affairs. If people were allowed to park a dune buggy backward in the reflection pool at high noon, bureaucrats would argue, all order would disappear from a parking infrastructure that is fragile at best with some 48,000 students descending on the campus daily. To make interdependence possible on such a campus, bureaucrats continue, rules-of-the-road must be formulated and then shared widely in a society prizing informed consent.

But why do such documents sound the way they do? Do they keep the "extant modes of production" in force, as the Marxists argue? Are students' consciousnesses "colonized" when they passively accept such reading materials?

To answer such questions, Marxist critics might first consider **structural strategies,** given their interest in the ideology of form. Eagleton [1975:56] notes, for example, that John Milton's decision to write *Paradise Lost* in his native tongue, to use the vernacular *form*, was a thunderous rejection of the aristocratic values of his day. In contrast, our list of parking regulations is mainstream. It is highly ordered (note the numbered paragraphs), thereby warning students that any response they might make to it must also be orthodox in form (and hence in content). The document's voice is muted, so no personal interchange with its author is encouraged. Moreover, it is a document-within-a-document (note the cross-references), thus threatening students with an endless welter of paperwork should they become obstreperous. It is steamlined in appearance (note the simple, declarative sentences), suggesting that it exhausts all knowledge on the subject. In short, the document's overall form suggests that *the University* knows all and that it knows best. In thereby "reproducing authority," the document maintains the traditional administrator/student power imbalance found on any college campus.

Marxists are also interested in **homogenizing strategies** that (1) downplay individual desires, (2) simulate a collective consciousness not based on fact, and (3) posit totalistic models for appropriate behavior. Clearly, our parking document works hard at homogenization. It issues common permits to all University personnel (paragraph 1); it creates a kind of Grand Overseer out of University, city, and state authorities (paragraphs 14 and 22); and it affixes its *own* labels to everyone, even to miscellaneous persons (paragraph 23). Moreover, the document specifies public norms and excoriates countercultural behavior. Paragraph 14 eliminates the free-spirited skateboarders. Paragraph 25 forbids handwritten notes of apology. And paragraph 24 even specifies proper walking behavior! All of this would be too much for Marxist critics, who feel that rhetoric should expose diversity rather than suppress it. They feel that an homogenizing rhetoric, in contrast, serves a privileged few by providing "the constant assurance of the social bond" and thereby effacing "the intolerable fact of social division" [Thompson, 1984:30].

While Marxists are interested in **utopian strategies,** our prosaic parking document has few of them. Still, there is a constant invocation of what McGee [1980] calls ideographs, ultimate terms that point toward the operating social consensus. Terms like "ownership," "privileges," "regulations," "eligibility," and "the University" reflect an ideal world where matters of authority have been long since settled, where orderliness reigns supreme, where one knows one's place. But there is no real delineation of this ideal state here, perhaps because bureaucrats must guard against preachment. Marxists would be of two minds about this document: They would appreciate its austerity, but they would worry that by not arguing explicitly for its utopian ideals, it removes them from public scrutiny, thereby instantiating them in the audience's minds.

Marxists feel that utopianism typically serves the interests of the exploiters rather than the exploited. As Eagleton [1976:45] reports, Marx's own tastes in literature tended to the "realist, satirical, radical writers" who were hostile to Romanticism, a movement that Marx felt "concealed the sordid prose of bourgeois life." In other words, because utopian visions are so rich and yet so malleable, they can be used to sanctify the unsanctifiable, something evidenced in the 1990s by Afrikaners who use the Christian vision to defend apartheid.

Marxists are particularly sensitive to the **dialectical strategies** of rhetoric. They feel that each text contains evidence of the oppositions facing its creator (and its creator's culture) and that good criticism "reads the code" of these oppositions. Although our parking document tries to put its best foot forward, even it betrays stresses and strains: University versus city jurisdiction (paragraph 14), permanent versus temporary students (paragraph 4), drivers versus pedestrians (paragraph 24), visitors with "important business" versus informal visitors (paragraph 23). And there are other tensions, tensions produced by creative students (who try to display decals "taped or affixed by unauthorized materials"), tardy students (whose citations are not appealed "within five (5) working days"), and litigious students (who try to play one rule against another: "posted signs ... take precedence over painted curbs").

Often, these dialectical themes unwittingly "reproduce the hierarchy" of the University community, with faculty members, but not students, able to "register an alternate vehicle at no extra cost" (paragraph 20) and with penalties specified for students but not for faculty (paragraph 21). The job of rhetoric, then, is to explain, justify, and ultimately resolve such dialectical tensions. According to the Marxists, these resolutions typically favor established sources of power. It is clear, after all, that even though the parking document deals exclusively with student life on campus, it was *not* written by students.

Rhetorically speaking, one of the most remarkable things about the parking document is that it is so unremarkable. Its words tumble from on high—sensible, rational, drained of emotion. And yet look what happens: It establishes a park-for-pay system with differential allocations of resources, with career-threatening sanctions for untoward behavior, with governance vested in a small number of unnamed persons, and with all signs of student individuality punished severely. The

Marxist would quickly draw a parallel between this mini-society (this textual fragment) and the larger society of which it is a part (the master text).

And their case would be strongest when focusing on the **strategies of omission** it employs. Like the deconstructionist, the Marxist examines the not-said because it often speaks the unspeakable: that which cannot be argued clearly because it cannot be argued at all. Imagine the rhetoric required, for example, to justify the following propositions: a parking permit is a privilege, not a right (paragraph 5); "parking cooperatives" are illegal and immoral (paragraph 4); a student-purchased decal belongs to the University (paragraph 5); economic penalties for parking misbehavior are legitimate (paragraph 21); one's right to redress wrongs lasts less than a week (paragraph 22); even pedestrians have duties specifiable by a *public* University (paragraph 24). Defending even one of these premises would be time-consuming, but most time-consuming of all would be defending how a University's prerogatives supercede those of the Almighty and the suicide-prone: "Pedestrians shall not leave curb or other place of safety and . . . run into the path of a vehicle which is so close that it is impossible for the driver to yield" (paragraph 24).

Naturally, an experienced bureaucrat could eventually generate enough words to justify these nonarguments. But ideology obviates the need to do so, functioning like a "linguistic legislature which defines what is available for public discussion and what is not" [Thompson, 1984:85]. Reacting against such trends, Marxist critics try to make rhetoric work harder by exploring what it wishes to conceal: its unargued premises. Unless required to do so, rhetoric will follow the path of least resistance, tapping values rooted in the political and economic priorities a society has already established. Thus, even though rhetoric is an art (and therefore a contrivance), it rarely admits to that status. That is why Roland Barthes has described the "healthy" sign as "one which draws attention to its own arbitrariness—which does not try to palm itself off as 'natural'" [Eagleton, 1983:135]. The Marxist would find few signs of such health in the average set of parking regulations.

Marxist critics study such things as parking regulations because their ordinariness allows them to deliver ideology to our doorsteps daily. A study by Mumby and Spitzack [1983] also examined the impact of everyday messages. They found that television news commentators emphasize politicians' *roles* rather than their moral obligations, thereby giving these leaders an "ideology of impersonality" that helped to explain away their ethical lapses. A related study by Corcoran [1986] traced U.S. news magazine coverage of a Soviet attack on a Korean airliner and found that such reports amounted to little more than nationalistic cheerleading, even though subsequent events cast doubt on the Soviets' responsibility for the incident. Studies like these show how dependent on the mass media political leaders are for keeping ideological beliefs available, relevant, and powerful for their citizens. Another study by Thomas [1985] also traced ideology in the media, finding that religious programs designed for the working class (Rex Humbard) differed considerably from programs pitched to the upwardly mobile (The 700 Club). The former minimized worldly achievements (concentrating instead on piety and spiritual devotion), while the latter found God's hand at work in their viewers' economic successes. Capitalistic ideology and the economic benefits of a good education are even reinforced on TV quiz shows, which "demonstrate symbolically that the rewards a society offers really *are* available for all, that the free-enterprise, equal-opportunity system *works*. All you need is a bit more luck than the next bloke and the bedroom suite falls into your lap" [Fiske, 1983:143].

A central theme in Marxist criticism is that ideology operates most powerfully when audiences are relaxed. Schwartzman's [1987] study of the industrial propaganda in Walt Disney's EPCOT illustrates. He found that the various pavilions in Orlando depicted an unusual amount of harmony on the world scene, which he read as a powerful endorsement of current U.S. foreign policy by the highly self-involved (and internationally minded) corporate sponsors. Television dramas also nurture established world views, says Selnow [1986], who found that the problem-solving model dramatized in prime-time shows (for example, *Miami Vice*) reinforced the same work ethic emphasized in U.S. politics, schools, and churches.

Not all popular rhetoric parrots establishment values. Countercultural texts also invade the private space of the average citizen. Jameson's [1981] analysis of *Lord Jim*, for example, shows how graphically Joseph Conrad depicted the brutal working conditions of nineteenth-century seamen, which Jameson interprets as Conrad's critique of the political ethos of his age. In a similar vein, Eagleton's [1975:161] survey of writers from George Eliot to D. H. Lawrence found them questioning the favored, but misguided, "organic" model of society in which all citizens work cooperatively for the common good. As Balibar and Macherey [1981:96] observe, such aesthetic rhetoric is well suited to ideological tasks (of both the Left and the Right) because its touch is such a gentle one:

> The literary text . . . does not seem a mechanical imposition, forced, revealed like a religious dogma, on individuals who must repeat it faithfully. Instead it appears as if offered for interpretations, a free choice, for the subjective private use of individuals. It is the privileged agent of ideological subjection, in the democratic and "critical" form of "freedom of thought."

Marxist criticism is not for everyone. Its detractors are many. Some object to its circularity: Exploitation is posited; its marks are sought in a text; the text is then used to prove the exploitation. The Marxist approach "assumes what it cannot demonstrate," argue some [Real, 1984:76]. It turns "the text's force against itself," argue others [Felperin, 1985:32–33], by "roughing it up, so to speak, until it says what is ideologically required by the interpreter's community." Because many Marxist critics approach texts more probatively than playfully, they often become heavy-handed, seizing on a minor rhetorical feature cordial to their case and missing a more important one. Their "sneering self-confidence," says Felperin [1985:61], often makes them too short-sighted. In can also make them too broad-sighted: When historicizing texts, Marxist critics sometimes become quite bad historians.

While some accuse Marxists of applying their model too forcefully, others question the model itself. Deconstructionists, for example, reject the notion of base/superstructure relationships. Economic forces, historical events, and political entanglements come to people *through texts*, they say, so "the firm and privileged ground of Marxist history as the basis for a scientific study of literature turns out to be not only firm or privileged, but not even a ground at all; it is more like an abyss" [Felperin, 1985:68]. Others question the Marxist vision of the audience. At times, that is, Marxists see the public as dull-witted oafs who must be awakened to the exploitations they cannot see. At other times, they seize upon the subtlest rhetorical themes and imply that these same oafs would also notice, and be affected by, such manipulations. Fiske [1986] tries to resolve such ambiguities by noting that people can learn to "read against the ideology." So, for example, some black viewers root for the black villain in a television drama even though the actors do their best to direct viewers' sympathies elsewhere. Still, until we know more about what audiences actually "do" with the messages directed at them, we should probably not all rush out to become Marxist critics.

But perhaps some of us should walk in that direction. After all, one need not adopt Marxist politics to profit from Marxist scholarship. Criticism has always been at its best when alternative models could be counted upon to produce controversy. And with Marxists about, there will be no shortage of controversy. Their critique of traditional criticism is not mild: They say that it is too orthodox in its critical assumptions, too establishmentarian in its choice of texts, too naive in its understanding of rhetorical effects, and too scientistic in its methodologies. They argue that traditional criticism is too intellectually smug, too politically bourgeois, and too Western in outlook as well. These rebukes are probably overstated. But the Marxist critique cannot be ignored, since it calls into question the *assumptions* critics make about rhetoric, about criticism, and about life itself. No self-respecting critic could resist such an important call for introspection.

RHETORIC AND CULTURAL IDENTITY

Critical Profile 12.4   Separate Dishes or a Melting Pot?

America has often been characterized as a melting pot where persons of any background can become "Americans" by losing the distinctive flavor of their ethnic origins. With the rise of national and ethnic minority consciousness in the 1960's, some leaders began questioning the appropriateness of the melting pot metaphor. Rather than losing cultural distinctiveness, such leaders argued, each group should celebrate the unique and tasty additions it makes to the national stew.

This debate has continued into the 1980s and the 1990s as gay and lesbian activists have sought passage of laws prohibiting discrimination on the basis of sexual orientation in housing and employment, reports James Chesebro, now of Queens College in New York. Some gay activists have argued that a straightforward, *separatist* approach to persuasion will serve the movement best. They believe that there is a "relatively precise subculture that exists apart from heterosexuals" and that "members of this 'subculture' . . . [are] distinct from the norms of American culture." They point with pride to the strides same-sex couples have made in eliminating sex role stereotypes in their relationships.

Other activists argue that if gay people "are to be mainstreamed, [they] can no longer be viewed as a unified and isolated subculture." These activists urge an *accommodationist* stance and point to the negative stereotypes that plague gay people—promiscuity, mental illness, and moral depravity—ultimately suggesting that until gays are seen as "distributed randomly across all socioeconomic, cultural, intellectual, political, geographic, and professional groupings," they will continue to face social and legal discrimination.

Which rhetorical approach best serves the gay community? Is it possible for gay men and women to be seen as different yet equal? Must they believe like everyone else in order to be special? Should activists compromise their personal beliefs for the good of the movement? Should the twenty-two million gay people in the United States suffer political setbacks simply because an activist is unwilling to compromise a favorite persuasive approach?

As with so many important human questions, no final answers are possible. Gay activists, like blacks, women, and environmentalists before them, will continue to search for a rhetorical style that best balances their needs. Rhetorical exchange often thrusts such hard choices upon us and the diversity of the United States often makes these hard choices even harder. So, then, will the peppers of the new American melting pot mask their true flavors while reflecting those of the morsels surrounding them, or will they sharply awaken the national palate?

Profiled by: Nancy Roth
Citation: Chesebro (1980)

Critical Profile 12.5   The Case of the Peuple Quebecois

In the fall of 1979, the government of Quebec issued a formal statement of policy—commonly referred to as "The White Paper"—that proposed a new political order. According to this policy, Quebec would become a sovereign state, linked economically to Canada but culturally and politically separated from it. If the citizens of Quebec voted favorably on a referendum calling for a separate state, Quebec would gain a new constitutional status and freedom from what the White Paper termed an "oppressor government." A new people would be formed, its proponents argued, a group called the "peuple quebecois."

As a rhetorical document, the job of the White Paper was to get Quebecers to see themselves as non-Canadians. The Paper recounted the history and struggles of Quebec citizens, emphasizing the commitments and concerns that set them apart from run-of-the-mill Canadians. Although the referendum ultimately failed, over 45 percent of the French-speaking voters of Quebec favored it. So, while Quebec was not ready for independence, the White Paper did serve as a stark example of what Maurice Charland of Concordia University has called a "constitutive" rhetoric.

The real trick of such rhetoric is to turn an aggregate sharing physical space into a group sharing psychological space. Naturally, people are usually unwilling to renounce their old attitudes as self-centered, short-sighted, and undistinguished unless they can do so gracefully. Rhetoric provides the grace. It urges people to climb outside of themselves and to examine themselves anew. So, for example, on the assumption that *labels precede realities*, one activist urged residents of Quebec to "assert themselves not as French-speaking Canadians, but as Quebecois, citizens who, for the moment, suffer the want of a country that is their own." Refashioning written histories is also a popular device found in constitutive rhetorics, as past facts are reconsidered in light of modern political preferences. Thus, new histories were written for Quebec as they had been written for Russia after Stalinization, for China after Mao, and for the American South after the Civil War. Out of such doctrinaire and revisionistic histories, a "people" is often born.

According to Charland, the case of the peuple quebecois illustrates that political groups "become real only through rhetoric." That is, a nation becomes a nation psychologically not just because of its vernacular or geography or economy or tribal customs but also because of how it talks about those realities. Normally, the cultural definitions that emerge from such talk are enormously subtle and evolve over many generations. The Quebec case was an interesting one because certain social activists *tried to hasten* these slow, evolutionary processes. Charland says that without rhetoric people could not describe themselves. Equally, he argues, without rhetoric they could not *be* themselves.

Profiled by: Susan Whalen
Citation: Charland (1987)

Critical Profile 12.6   The Neo-Liberal's Identity Crisis

What was the essential difference between Jimmy Carter and Gary Hart? According to Michael Weiler of the University of Pittsburgh, Carter was a (thinly disguised) traditional liberal politician, while Hart represented a new political species, the "neo-liberal." Like traditional, postwar liberals, neo-Liberals advocate utilitarian policies based on "the greatest good for the greatest number" and see general economic prosperity as a means to this utilitarian end. Unlike traditional liberals, however, neo-Liberals rhetorically disassociate themselves from the effects of traditional liberalism: big government and exclusive attention to minority problems. They do this, Weiler holds, not so much by advocating substantially different solutions but by making distinctive rhetorical appeals.

One appeal Weiler found in neo-Liberal rhetoric he calls "entrepreneurial." He notes that recent liberals have "responded to the economic hardships of the 1970s with two suggestions: reindustrialization or reorientation." Traditional liberals support the former suggestion and advocate massive capital investment in failing heavy industries. Neo-Liberals, however, favor reorientation and advocate capital investment in "high-tech" industries "where the U.S. might be expected to enjoy a comparative advantage." Weiler claims that this choice gives neo-Liberals a rhetorical advantage over the traditional liberal, since "computer chips are more exciting than concrete slabs." This "high-tech" entrepreneurial appeal works well for neo-Liberals since it associates them with the nineteenth-century liberal ideology yet separates them from the "rugged individualist" image popular in conservative rhetoric. The neo-Liberal entrepreneur has not "brought himself up by the boot straps" but rather is "well-schooled, well-financed and born into comfort, if not affluence." Further, the neo-Liberal entrepreneur does not work for a large company, but rather "heads a company of recent origin and diminutive size." This works to the neo-Liberal's advantage, since small organizations do not seem as impersonal and oppressive as large corporations.

But, as Weiler notes, this entrepreneurial appeal also causes problems for neo-Liberals, since "it is a borrowed concept from the neo-Liberal's ideological counterpart, the neo-Conservative" and therefore makes it hard for some voters to tell the difference between, say, Michael Dukakis and Jack Kemp. The basic difference, says Weiler, is that neo-Liberals value a "new breed of entrepreneur," one independent of huge corporations and removed from the "inefficiency of big business." Thus, neo-Liberals "are free to criticize particular businesses and business leaders without adopting an anti-business bias," the rhetorical equivalent of having one's cake and eating it too.

Profiled by: David R. Harvey
Citation: Weiler (1984)

THE FEMINIST CRITIQUE

Feminist criticism is often angry criticism. One of its practitioners, Kate Millett, has been described as "neither submissive nor ladylike: her style is that of a hard-nosed street kid out to challenge the author's authority at every turn" [Moi, 1985:25]. Like Marxist critics, feminists use a political template when examining textual materials. But "Whereas Marxism argues that women are defined by the work they do or do not do," says Humm [1986:72], "feminism argues that women are defined by the sexuality which they express or are repressed by." No longer can a text be judged innocent until proven guilty, says the feminist. Because patriarchy runs so deep in modern society, virtually any message will bear its traces. This realization makes the feminist critic naturally suspicious of docile criticism that slavishly endorses established, repressive rhetorical practices.

Because feminists have much in common with the ideological critics already discussed, we can narrow our focus here to the assumptions and approaches unique to feminism. Like the deconstructionists and Marxists, feminists see society's distribution of power as fundamentally unfair. But while deconstructionists are bothered by intellectual hegemony and Marxists by economic hegemony, feminists seek to overturn gender-based repressions that cut across theoretical and political boundaries. Their criticism is informed by the following assumptions:

1. *Rhetorical acts are androcentric* (male-dominated). Feminists insist that they do not introduce politics into a text but expose the politics already there. For example, it may seem natural for a male U.S. president to sing the praises of the "father of our country" on Washington's birthday and then relinquish the podium to a male prelate intoning the benediction, "Our Father, who art in heaven." Feminists would quickly point out that this "natural" androcentrism is nothing but a grand contrivance: Ceremonies are conducted by those who already have power (presidents and ministers) and who are also heir to a rich tradition of masculine motifs (as in the Washington myth and the King James bible). As a result, the very act of participating in these ceremonies reinforces the power of those who speak (men) and saps the power of those who listen (women). And feminists would note that even when *minority* speakers speak, they do so as male lawyers (Ralph Nader), male fundamentalists (Jerry Falwell), male ecologists (Robert Redford), and male integrationists (Jesse Jackson).

The male bias in symbolic activity is not new. Donovan [1980:216] reports, for example, that prior to the nineteenth century women could not study Latin (the language of education, religion, and the law) and thus were denied the key to the door of power: "Only when the Latin influence had weakened . . . and only after the rhetoric of the home and the forum had once again merged, could women hope to have equal access to the means of literary creation." This is not to say that women had no expressive outlets, for they often wrote in private though not permitted to speak in public. But even here they tended to write escapist novels. As Gilbert and Gubar [1986:109,111] say, "the woman novelist, safely shut in prose, may fantasize about freedom with a certain impunity," but she cannot turn her hand to lyric poetry, since it requires "the utterance of a strong and assertive 'I.'"

Literary creation is one thing, public discourse quite another. Because rhetoric is so often found at the crossroads of power, women who have tried to enter the public forum have often been treated badly. An interesting study by Berg and Berry [1986], for example, looked at female religious prophets in the seventeenth century who were labeled "spiritual whores" by the theologians of the day, not because their message was subversive, but because they presumed to fill a tradition-ally male role. Because the act of speaking is an act of assertion, women have had to go to great lengths to claim the rhetorical practices avail-able to them. So, for example, Humm [1986:6–8] notes that women writers have shown a special preference for animal and plant imagery and for supernatural references, perhaps because these were the only textual practices allowed them by those who had excluded them from public decision making.

2. *Rhetorical texts are androcentric.* Feminist criticism employs two different modes. In the **universalizing mode,** a critic examines a text for its general descriptions of the human condition and then asks how "general" those descriptions really are. This sort of criticism is demanded, says Showalter [1985:143], because texts have heretofore asked women to "identify against themselves" by presuming that *male* standards for beauty, truth, and justice are equivalent to all *human* standards. That these masculine premises have been accepted so implicitly, without self-reflectiveness, especially bothers feminists. As Ruthven [1984:64–65] points out, "men are able to conceive of their own subjectivity as being non-gendered, and therefore wonder why feminists make such a fuss about gender. But because women are not aligned with the universal, they are much more inclined to see them-selves as women than men are to see themselves as men."

Accordingly, says Rich [1972:20], critics must practice what she calls re-vision, the act of "entering an old text from a new critical direc-tion," so that these male-centered premises can be rethought anew. Take, for example, a standard piece of American eloquence: John Ken-nedy's inaugural address. Feminists would urge us to reexamine this *master*piece to see if what Kennedy endorsed for all Americans was, specifically, endorsable by women. Early in his address, Kennedy [1961a:267] made the following declaration:

> We dare not forget today that we are the heirs of that first revolution. Let the word go forth from this time and this place, to friend and foe alike, that the torch has passed to a new generation of Americans— born in this century, tempered by war, disciplined by a hard and bitter peace, proud of our ancient heritage—and unwilling to witness or permit the slow undoing of those human rights to which this Nation has always been committed, and to which we are committed today at home and around the world.

What is alleged to be universally true here? That forgetting is unconscionable; that pride is a human virtue; that the U.S. must tend the international community. The feminist would find the invisible hand of patriarchy here and be moved to ask: Must we make the (male) asumption that wars are good and that old wars are especially good? Must we honor the (male) need to pass on the "torches" of war, bequeathing to our heirs yesterday's victories as well as a taste for tomorrow's battles? Must oratory always appeal to the (male) taste for a "hard and bitter" peace? Are these the only *human* options available? Must all Americans become men on inauguration day?

And what of these much-despised processes of "witnessing," "permitting," and "undoing" that Kennedy decries? Must they be subjugated in each case to the more masculine "daring," "disciplining," and "tempering" he evisions for his audience? When we speak as a nation, must we always shout in the masculine style ("let the word go forth") rather than converse in the feminine style? Might we not at least once try what women have so often urged: to treat old grievances as *old* grievances ("we dare not forget") and to end, not continue, militaristic expansionism ("at home and around the world")? Must the children of fathers *and of mothers* accept Mr. Kennedy's torch of war? In short, feminists would be suspicious of all high-blown oratory like Kennedy's and want to examine anew (and through feminist eyes) virtually all of the great historical texts in rhetoric and literature.

3. *Traditional criticism is androcentric.* The **particularizing mode** of feminist scholarship tries to find the authentic female voice by calling into question the established universal norms for literary and rhetorical excellence. For example, novels that present an "overview of the human experience" are esteemed, says Baym [1985:67], while texts offering detailed portrayals "of wealthy New Yorkers, Yugoslavian immigrants [and] Southern rustics" are ignored. More than sixty years ago, Virginia Woolf [1929:77] understood the bias against such small-scale works: "This is an important book . . . because it deals with war.

This is an insignificant book because it deals with the feelings of women in a drawing room." In reaction to such biases, feminists are beginning to use the phrase "women's writing" rather than "women's literature" to define their interests, since the former, more generous phrase, includes the schoolbooks, diaries, and letters that were the only outlets available to generations of literarily inclined women.

Feminists fear that unless the female voice is found, the androcentric imperative will flourish. Why learn half a story about discourse, they ask, when the full story is also available? Kolodny [1985:158], for example, argues that an analysis of *Paradise Lost* should analyze "its complex hierarchial structures," but also not "fail to note the implications of gender within that hierarchy." Such an analysis should discuss "the poem's thematic reworking of classical notions of marital and epic prowess," but also realize "that Eve is stylistically edited out of that process." In other words, unless we strain harder to hear what women are saying (or what men are saying for women in their behalf), we will not be able to answer Eagleton's [1986:5] intriguing question: "Is Margaret Thatcher speaking as a woman or is she merely the ventriloquist's dummy for the male voice?"

Positing a female voice is one thing. Discovering its exact features is quite another. The female voice represents "process, plurality, diversity," says Ruthven [1984:100]. "Women think in circles rather than lines," says Humm [1986:14], employing "associational rather than sequential logic." Still other characteristics are offered: The female voice is subjective rather than objective; fluent, not forced; personal, not impersonal; open, not closed. But not all feminists are pleased with the notion of a female voice. They worry that such discussions will further stigmatize women and isolate them from power bases. They worry that since male language features—strength, precision, categorization—are so often posited as the rhetorical ideal, women who buck this language style will be shortchanged once again.

Other feminist critics persist in their search for the female voice. For example, Tompkins [1985:88] decided to take *Uncle Tom's Cabin* more seriously than it had been taken by the traditional (male) critics who decried its gross sentimentality: "'O, Topsy, poor child, I love you!' said Eva with a sudden burst of feeling and laying her little thin, white hand on Topsy's shoulder." We must understand this book as *rhetorical* literature, says Tompkins, and realize that women, too, can change public perceptions. Harriet Beecher Stowe "relocate[d] the center of power in American life," she says [1985:100], "placing it not in the government, nor in the courts of law, nor in the marketplace, but in the kitchen." Recognizing that Stowe spoke a special language—of the heart, not the head, of rhetoric, not literature—helped Tompkins account for one of the most influential social forces in American history.

Operating on these three major premises, feminist criticism has been especially productive during the last two decades. While traditionalists in the U.S. have often dismissed deconstruction as "too French" and Marxism as "too Soviet," feminist criticism is more "local" and hence has been harder for them to put off. But they have resisted the feminist attempt to blur literature and rhetoric. Yet this is exactly what Register [1975:19,21,23] does when arguing that while "literature must allow forthright and honest self-expression," it must also account for feminist sensitivities. Register wants to see more female role-models in literature but, seemingly conflicted, also recommends that literary characters "not be idealized beyond plausibility." Similarly, she recommends that "factual information about discrimination" be integrated into stories, but quickly urges that care be taken "so that its presence seem natural." The difficulties Register has here are the fate of any critic trying to do description and prescription simultaneously, which is to say, it is the fate of any ideological critic.

There are three common foci in feminist criticism. One deals with the **intellectual conventions** found in public discourse, since, as feminists argue, patriarchy endorses only certain (male) modes of thinking. Abstractions, for example, are problematic for feminists, who argue that while men may be driven to battle by such ultimate terms as duty, honor, and country, women's appreciation for physicality and immediacy makes them more naturally resistant to such siren calls. Similarly, feminists criticize the male preference for dichotomizing, because it keeps people from seeing life's gradations. But this problem is even more serious, they argue, since the most basic dichotomy—male/good, female/bad—subverts women in particular. Ruthven [1984:72] notes, for instance, that while male characters have been given full definition in literature, female characters have been given binary options: "sensuous roses or virginal lilies, pedestalled goddesses or downtrodden slaves, Eves or Marys, Madonnas or Magdalenes, damned whores or God's police."

Feminists have special antipathy for political discourse, since it is so shot through with these dichotomies and abstractions, leading men to conflict rather than negotiation, to martyrdom rather than flexibility, to independence rather than interdependence. The historical reality of women—as bearers of children, as nurses to the sick, as preparers of food—have made them essentialists. Feminists offer these concretizing experiences as ideal antitdotes to even the most eloquent political rhetoric: **"Let every nation know, whether it wishes us well or ill** [The only two possibilities?], **that we** [Who? Are Peorians included?] **shall pay any price** [Are you speaking of money here?], **bear any burden, meet any hardship** [Could you be more specific? Will this hardship make me bleed?], **support any friend, oppose any foe** [Who's a friend, Who's a foe? Are there no other options?], **in order to assure the survival** [Have things gotten that bad already?] **and the success** [Measured how?] **of liberty** [What does liberty look like, feel like?]" [Kennedy, 1961:268].

Feminist critics are also interested in the **mythic conventions** used in rhetoric. Not surprisingly, they have found that many standard mythic patterns have marginalized women, if not victimized them. Ruthven [1984:80], for example, argues that the typical story line in a fairy tale is of a passive princess "who waits patiently on top of the Glass Hill for the first man to climb it" and who, as a result, is "symbolically dead" and can only be brought to life by a man. Radway's [1984:212–213] study of why modern women read paperback romance novels stirs up parallel concerns. She finds similar kinds of passivity there and, although she notes that reading such fiction is a somewhat "rebellious" act, it is also mythically entrapping: "They do nothing to challenge [women's] separation from one another brought about by the patriarchal culture's insistence that they never work in the public world to maintain themselves but rather live symbiotically as the property and responsibility of men."

Because they are reinforced so often and so artfully, myths die hard, if they die at all. Phillips [1978], for example, did an interesting study of the profiles of women presented in *Ms.* and *Family Circle.* Naturally, she found major differences in the profiles, but, surprisingly, found more important similarities. The women praised in *Ms.* were depicted as being rewarded not by upward mobility or prestige (so often the rewards of men) but for their social instincts: producing beautiful music, helping the poor, and organizing workers. Rarely, says Phillips, does one find stories of women "who have climbed the ladder of success and status"; even in *Ms.* the women are, at best, "liberal, but not liberated" [p. 27].

True liberation, it appears, is a male property. Baym [1985] found, for example, that perhaps the hardiest mythic plot line in American literature is of a man tearing himself away from "society's" female domination and setting out for a "wilderness" where he could afford, at last, to be fully a man. American rhetoric has tapped this mythic reservoir as well. From Westward expansion to space exploration to fifth-generation computing, *de*socializing myths—man as his own inventor—have motivated the nation to do much and spend much.

These grand treks have inspired boys to become men and men to become immortal. Meanwhile, at home, women wait.

Feminists also focus on the **role conventions** of discourse. Perhaps the most cherished role, the role of authority, has been an especially male preserve. Male doctors have issued the public warnings about breast cancer; male psychologists have offered counsel about child care; male governors have announced the membership of the State Commission on Women. The comparatively few female authorities available have spoken about women's rights, not human rights, about family budgets, not the national budget, about the war between the sexes, not the wars between the continents. This has resulted in a kind of rhetorical ghettoing of women and set up a perfect dilemma: People who cannot be heard cannot be taken seriously; people who cannot be taken seriously should not be heard.

The *projected* roles of women—how they are portrayed in rhetoric and literature—are also frequently demeaning. These roles, too, have consequences. Not only do they affect how men see women but also how women see themselves. As Simone de Beauvoir has said, "One is not born, but rather becomes a woman" [Ruthven, 1984:45]. An example of such portrayals is found in the work of Barbatsis, et al. [1983], who did a comprehensive analysis of television programming. They found that men talked most of the time on television shows (even in cartoons), that females received significantly more orders than did males, and that women asked more questions than they gave answers. Even in romantic fiction, says Snitow [1986:138], women's roles are circumscribed. Despite the comforting familiarity of such characterizations from a literary viewpoint, one can only wonder about their *rhetorical* impact on women's attitudes:

> When women try to picture excitement, the society offers them one vision, romance. When women try to imagine companionship, the society offers them one vision, male, sexual companionship. When women try to fantasize about success, mastery, the society offers them one vision, the power to attract a man. When women try to fantasize about sex, the society offers them taboos on most of its imaginable expressions except those that deal directly with arousing and satisfying men. When women try to project a unique self, the society offers them very few attractive images. True completion for women is nearly always presented as social, domestic, sexual.

Feminist cricitism is not a monolithic activity. Nor is it universally glum. Byars [1987] notes, for example, that a number of "feminine discourses" are emerging on television and that shows like *Kate and Allie* and *Cagney and Lacey*, both of which projected successful "women's communities, " have done a great deal for women. Another study by Brown [1987] of a Pepsi advertisement featuring Geraldine Ferraro (see Figure 12.1) shows the subtlety that feminist criticism often musters. In her study, Brown holds that the Ferraro ad is open to both patriarchal and feminist readings. She notes, for example, that the man's voice-

Figure 12.1
Text of the Ferraro Advertisement

Video	Audio
1. Sunlit, Victorian sun porch. One woman at a table in lounge chair (extreme back lighting), reading a newspaper. Another walks in in pants, younger, apparently serving something.	D1:/"Looking for a job, Mom?"/ (Seagull noises in background.)
2. Newspaper picture of man (too fast to see who, but looks political).	
3. GF	GF: /"Very funny."/
4. Legs coming in a screen door (in a long skirt).	
5. Laura coming in door (face).	D2 (Laura):/"Well, I am."/
6. Daughter 1. Parts of face (locked down camera so face moves within the frame—side view—last shot, eyes).	D1: /"What's it this week, Laura, marine biology?"/
7. GF. Newspaper in front of her mouth, we see her eyes.	GF: /"Aren't we still hoping to be a star of stage and screen?"/
8. Pepsi being poured into glass. Woman's hand picks up glass from the top and pulls it upward.	D2 (Laura): /"Come on Mom,/ (Sounds of ice cubes clinking.)
9. Laura drinking it (cut on the movement).	/"It's a tough choice."/
10. GF. Face, eyes and mouth.	GF: /"Sure its tough when you can be anything you want to be."/
11. Skirted woman taking seat at the table. (Shot from under the table).	
12. Sunlit porch (same as shot 1). The three women are now sitting around the table.	Male VO: /"When you make a choice, what's right is what feels right./
13. Diet Pepsi can—glass goes through the bottom of frame right to left (shot from above and side).	/"Diet Pepsi."/
14. GF. Face (side view, one eye screen right; edge of newspaper screen left).	GF: /"You know, there's one choice I'll never regret."/
15. Laura. Face (mouth to eyes) sways back and forth slightly.	D2 (Laura): /"Politics?"/
16. GF and daughter. (GF screen right, daughter screen left; two eyes at first).	GF /"Unh-unh. Being a mother."/
17. Pepsi cans. Side view.	Male VO: /"Diet Pepsi—the one calorie choice of a new generation."/
Super in: The one calorie Choice of A New Generation	

over in the ad reflects the usual "male omniscience" and, at the same time, reflects female economic subservience. She also mentions that the ad is shot at home (women's primary place?) and in a family setting (women's primary duty?). And she notes that the newspaper depicted in the ad has a male face on its front page (woman-as-reader, not actor?) and that the ad itself features food preparation (the only source of female authority?).

But Brown also points out that the ad features Geraldine Ferraro and not Miss America, the same Ferraro who supported abortion rights in her 1984 vice presidential campaign. Moreover, says Brown, the ad depicts Ferraro's real daughters and not paper cut-outs. "These are not fictive characters," says Brown [p. 349], "they are people—endowed with moral freedom and motives." Also, unlike traditional messages about women, the advertisement shows motherhood as an active rather than expected choice. In addition, virtually all of the verbal content features women-as-deciders ("Sure it's tough when you can be anything you want to be") rather than women as dancing marionettes. Nonverbally, Brown observes, the lines in Ferraro's face are clearly shown, revealing her to be neither young nor beautiful, no idealized female object crafted for the male stare. Also, Ferraro's gaze is active and powerful, not a "licensed withdrawal." For all of these reasons, Brown concludes, feminists "can find moments of purchase within this ad" [p. 351].

Numerous objections have been made to feminist criticism: Its ideological commitments blind it to rhetorical subtleties; it describes texts poorly in its rush to prescription; its accusatory tone makes it predictable, boring; its often derogatory analyses of popular discourse make it elitist and condescending. But feminist criticism's greatest advantage is the encouragement it gives the critic to re-see traditional texts. As Ruthven [1984:13] says, it is not so important that we all "write feminist criticism" as that we "incorporate the lessons of feminism into everything [we] write." And those lessons are twofold: to question what we think we know about rhetoric in case it is only what men know and to assess the consequences of rhetoric that historically have treated half of us as inconsequential. Surely these are lessons useful for all critics—men as well as women. And if women prosper, especially, because these lessons are learned, would that not be an acceptable gratuity indeed?

CONCLUSION

It is hard to project the future of ideological criticism in the United States. In many ways, it runs against the grain of American pluralism.

Because it is so angry, so irreverent, and so cynical, it threatens the optimistic, liberal credo of the American establishment. For all of these reasons, ideological criticism may always be a minority practice. But even for ideological critics this may not be entirely unfortunate. After all, a minority discourse always has a special claim on our attention. It asks constantly if we know what we are doing and, if we know, how we know. It requires us to examine where we go for our premises and why we go there and not elsewhere. It asks if our critical practices are of benefit to anyone in particular and, if not, why not.

Ideological critics sense a certain systematic unfairness in the world. And they see rhetoric as a tool for turning such unfairness into social routines and thenceforth into public policy. Thus, they offer a critique. In doing so, they operate as critics always have, which should remind us that criticism itself is a minority business. There are powerful people in the world. There always have been. They use rhetoric to maintain their power. They always will. Somebody, therefore, must call attention to how they do what they do and ask if it is right that they do so. This challenge is challenge enough for legions of rhetorical critics, since the odds so heavily favor the producers of rhetoric and, hence, the producers of power. So for reasons both conceptual and practical, it makes little sense to purge a minority of a minority. Surely there is work enough for all.

Appendixes

APPENDIX A

Finding Texts for Criticism: A Sampler

by Deborah Smith-Howell

When starting any critical project, the critic faces a task that at first seems simple but that quickly becomes formidable—how to locate the desired materials for analysis. Because so much rhetoric is either ephemeral or situation-bound, the critic must search out information that is not automatically collected and distributed. In other cases, fortunately, speakers, organizations, or editors do think toward the future, capturing rhetoric and preserving it for later, "unintended" audiences. Thus, rather than being discouraged by the lack of materials available for analysis, the critic is sometimes overwhelmed by the wealth of messages accessible and worthy of rhetorical analysis. With this Appendix, we will show how the critic can find a variety of texts suitable for detailed critical study.

Clearly, no appendix can present all of the sources useful for finding rhetorical texts. But the suggestions offered here may stimulate the reader to think of new avenues for rhetorical investigation. The lists of citations in each category are not intended to be comprehensive or representative. Instead, they provide a starting place for the critic.

In this appendix, we present ten types of printed materials and one general category of audio-visual materials. Each of the general classifications is divided into subcategories containing increasingly specific items. The categories are not mutually exclusive—material from one might be equally useful in another context. In addition to the usual bibliographic information, the citations include the Library of Congress number used to house library materials. Users should realize, however, that Library of Congress numbers are not necessarily the same from one library to the next and so it may well become necessary to do a local check on the identifications provided here.

Searching for materials sometimes takes time. For a particularly ambitious project, a critic may have to send away for appropriate texts. But it is interesting to note how willing groups and individuals often are to share these materials with interested persons. Thus, patience, persistence, and the price of postage can sometimes be the critic's greatest allies.

1.0 SPEECHES

The speech is one of the most familiar items for rhetorical criticism. Speeches from varying eras, speakers, and occasions can be found easily in virtually any major library. Of course, searches become more complicated when the target is either very specific or unfamiliar, but quantity is almost never a problem.

1.1 Serial Collections of Speeches

One of the most useful sources **(1.1a)** provides access to contemporary as well as historical speeches. The *Congressional Record* includes transcripts of political speeches as well as texts that are not specifically related to the American political scene. For instance, the *Record* frequently includes commemoration speeches for individuals, groups, and localities as well as letters or speeches given by various constituents—materials that are entered into the *Record* by Senators and Representatives. *Representative American Speeches* **(1.1b)**, an annual collection published since 1938, presents speeches selected to illustrate the social and political issues of the time. As a periodical appearing twice a month since 1934, *Vital Speeches* **(1.1c)** is an excellent source of recent speeches from many disciplines and thus a virtual gold mine for the rhetorical critic.

1.1a *Congressional Record: Proceedings and Debates* (Washington, D.C.: U.S. Government Printing Office). [J 11 .R5]

1.1b *Representative American Speeches* (New York: H.W. Wilson Co.). [PS 668 .R146]

1.1c *Vital Speeches of the Day.* [PN 6121]

1.2 Collections of Great Speeches

Collections of the world's "great speeches" are useful for accessing rhetoric that has either stood the test of time or figures importantly in some major historical controversy. In these collections, critics will find speeches ranging from Pericles' Funeral Oration to William Jennings Byran's Cross of Gold Speech. In such collections, the critic has easy access to the speeches of antiquity and to other generally recognized masterpieces.

1.2a   Boutwell, W. D. *Great Speeches from Pericles to Kennedy* (New York: Scholastic Book Services, 1965). [PN 6122 .G7]

1.2b   Copeland, L. G. *World's Greatest Speeches* (Garden City, NY: Garden City Publishing Company, 1942). [PN 6121 .C65]

1.2c   Peterson, H. *A Treasury of the World's Greatest Speeches* (New York: Simon and Schuster, 1954). [PN 6121 .P4]

1.2d   Shurle, E. D. *Masterpieces of Modern Oratory* (Boston: Ginn and Company, 1906). [PS 662 .S53]

1.3 *Collections of American Speeches*

Collections of American public address help the cultural critic interested in examining the concept of Americanicity and allow access to both the popular and the enduring in American rhetoric. For instance, collections like those below include speeches such as Puritan preacher Jonathan Edwards' "Sinners in the Hands of an Angry God" as well as actor Alan Alda's "Commencement Address at Drew University."

1.3a   Andrews, J., and D. Zarefsky. *American Voices: Significant Texts in American History, 1640–1945* (White Plains, NY: Longman, 1989). [E 173.A7596]

1.3b   Andrews, J., and D. Zarefsky. *Contemporary American Voices: Significant Texts in American History, 1945 to Present* (White Plains, NY: Longman, forthcoming).

1.3c   Baird, A. C. *American Public Addresses: 1740–1952* (New York: McGraw-Hill Book Company, 1956). [PS 662 .B27]

1.3d   Birley, R. *Speeches and Documents in American History* (London: Oxford University Press, 1962). [E 183 .B53 1962]

1.3e   Linkugel, W. A., R. R. Allen, R. L. Johannesen. *Contemporary American Speeches*. 6th ed. (Dubuque, IA: Kendall/Hunt Publishing Company, 1988). [PS 668 .L5 1988]

1.3f   Oliver, R. T., & E. E. White. *Selected Speeches from American History* (Boston: Allyn and Bacon, 1966). [PS 661.04]

1.4 *Collections of Speeches by Period*

These collections concentrate on specific issues or specific people and are useful for comparing how different speakers at different times addressed similar issues. For example, the Issues collections are organized by idea rather than by speaker and incorporate modest, grass-roots orators as well as those of greater stature. With collections of this type, the critic is able to examine an historic controversy, such as slavery, in all of its conflictual and emotional dimensions.

1.4a   Brandt, C. G., & E. M. Shafter, Jr. *Selected American Speeches on Basic Issues (1850–1950)* (Boston: Houghton Mifflin Company, 1960). [E178.6 .B85]

1.4b   Hawthorne, J. *Orations of American Orators* (New York: Colonial Press, 1900). [PN 6121 .M2]

1.4c   Packard, F. C., Jr. *Great Americans Speak* (New York: Charles Scribner's Sons, 1951). [PS 662 .P3]

1.4d   Wrage, E. J., & B. Baskerville. *American Forum, Speeches on Historic Issues, 1788–1900* (Seattle: University of Washington Press, 1967). [PS 662 .W7]

1.5 Collections of Speeches by Topic

In these anthologies, the editors have chosen materials focusing on specific topics. Using these collections, the critic can access information not readily available in the broader sources above and will find them particularly useful in movement studies. Perusal of the Subject Index in a library's card catalog will provide hundreds of similar collections.

1.5a   Dunbar, A. M. *Masterpieces of Negro Eloquence.* Reprint (New York: Johnson Reprint Corp., 1970). [PS 663 .N4 N4]

1.5b   Kennedy, P. S., & G. H. O'Shields. *We Shall Be Heard: Women Speakers in America* (Dubuque, IA: Kendall/Hunt Publishing Company, 1983). [HQ 1410 .W4 1983]

1.5c   O'Neill, D. J. *Speeches by Black Americans* (Encino, CA: Dickenson Publishing Company, 1971). [PS 663 .N4 O5]

1.5d   Rawson, L. *Alvan Stewart's Writings and Speeches on Slavery* (New York: A. B. Burdick, 1860). [E 441 .S634]

1.5e   Snyder, W. L. *Great Speeches by Great Lawyers: A Collection of Arguments and Speeches before Courts and Juries.* Original 1881 (Littleton, CO: F.B. Rothman, 1981). [K 181 .G73 1981]

1.5f   Zacharias, D. W. *In Pursuit of Peace: Speeches of the Sixties* (New York: Random House, 1970). [JX 1963 .Z25]

1.6 Speech/Analysis Collections

In addition to providing texts and background material for the speeches they include, these authors/editors also provide analysis and evaluation of the texts and thus illustrate the critical art itself.

1.6a Campbell, K. K. *Critiques of Contemporary Rhetoric* (Belmont, CA: Wadsworth Publishing Company, 1972). [PE 1417 .C255 1972]

1.6b Jamieson, K. M. *Critical Anthology of Public Speeches* (Palo Alto, CA: Science Research Associates, 1978). [PS 662 .C7]

1.6c Makay, J. J., & W. R. Brown. *The Rhetorical Dialogue: Contemporary Concepts and Cases* (Dubuque, IA: W.C. Brown Company, 1972). [P 91 .M285]

1.6d Rohler, L., & R. Cook. *Great Speeches for Criticism and Analysis* (Greenwood, IN: Alistair Press, 1986). [PN 4121 .G7 1986]

1.6e Ryan, H. R. *American Rhetoric from Roosevelt to Reagan: A Collection of Speeches and Critical Essays* (Prospect Heights, IL: Waveland Press, 1983). [PS 668 .A43 1983]

1.7 Individual Speakers

Many well-known, as well as rather obscure, speakers have had collections of their speeches published. Once again, a library's Subject Index will provide immediate access to volume after volume of speeches produced by particular individuals. In searching for speech collections of particular speakers, critics should recognize that the publishing of speeches produced by ministers, politicians, and others was a fairly standard practice in the eighteenth, nineteenth, and early twentieth centuries. In more recent times, this has become less common.

1.7a *Black Elk Speaks: Being the Life Story of a Holy Man of the Oglala Sioux.* As told through J. G. Neihardt (Lincoln, NE: University of Nebraska Press, 1979). [E99.03 .B49 1079]

1.7b Bryan, W. J. *Speeches of William Jennings Bryan,* 2 vols. (New York: Funk and Wagnalls, 1913). [E 660 .B93]

1.7c King, M. L. *The Words of Martin Luther King, Jr.* Selected by Coretta Scott King (New York: Newmarket Press, 1983). [E 185.97 .K5 A25 1983]

1.7d   Malcolm X. *Malcolm X Speaks: Selected Speeches and State-ments.* Edited with prefatory note by George Breitman (New York: Merit Publishers, 1965). [E 185.61 .L58]

1.7e   McCarthy, J. R. *Major Speeches and Debates of Senator Joe McCarthy Delivered in the United States Senate, 1950–1951* (Washington, D.C.: Government Printing Office). [E 743.5 .M2]

1.7f   Sakharov, Andrei D. *Sakharov Speaks.* Edited and foreword by Harrison E. Salisbury (New York: Alfred A. Knopf, 1974). [DK 274 .S277 1974]

1.7g   Twain, M. *Mark Twain's Speeches* (New York: Harper, 1923). [PS 1322 .S5 1923]

2.0 INSTITUTIONAL POLITICS

Many rhetorical critics are interested primarily in political dis-course. While this emphasis is apparent even in the speech anthologies just presented, critics can also find other, more specific, sources useful for examining political rhetoric.

2.1 Presidential Papers

The critic's task is simplified when investigating the modern pres-idency by the general availability of *Public Papers of the President* **(2.1b)**. *Public Papers* are currently available for the Hoover administra-tion, the Truman presidency, and each president thereafter. These vol-umes include virtually every statement (oral or written) made by a sit-ting president. The records of earlier presidents are available through collections **(2.1c)** or other organized records **(2.1a, 2.1d, 2.1f)**. The *Weekly Compilation of Presidential Documents* **(2.1e)** was initiated in 1965 and contains essentially the same information as *Public Papers* but is available in most libraries almost immediately after a given pres-idential statement is made in public.

2.1a   Fitzpatrick, J. C. (Ed.) *The Writings of George Washington from the Original Manuscript Sources* (Washington, D.C.: U.S. Government Printing Office, 1931). [E 312.7 1931]

2.1b   *Public Papers of the President* (Washington, D.C.: U.S. Government Printing Office). [J 80 .A283]

2.1c   Richardson, J. D. (Ed.) *Messages and Papers of the Presidents, 1789–1897.* 10 vols. (New York: Bureau of National Litera-ture). [J 81 .B96]

2.1d Roosevelt, F. D. *The Public Papers and Addresses of Franklin D. Roosevelt* (New York: Russell & Russell, 1969). [J 82 .D6 1969]

2.1e *Weekly Compilation of Presidential Documents* (Washington, D.C.: U.S. Government Printing Office). [J 80 .A284]

2.1f Wilson, W. *Selected Literary and Political Papers and Addresses of Woodrow Wilson, III* (New York: Grosset & Dunlap, 1921). [E 660 .W725]

2.2 Presidential Research Guides

In addition to accessing presidential texts, critics may be interested in examining the background information available from presidential libraries and from other special collections. Goehlert and Martin **(2.2b)** provide a guide to general presidential materials while Burton, et al. **(2.2a)** and Viet **(2.2c)** focus on the presidential libraries. Burton, et al. **(2.2a)** briefly describe almost 5000 items or collections available in seven presidential libraries (the book does not include the Carter library). For example, there is an entry for "Acheson, Dean Gooderhan" that describes a "66ft" collection in the John F. Kennedy Library, and mentions a nonpublished "finding aid" available at the library. Viet **(2.2c)** gives an overview of the presidential library system, including how to use the various libraries and where to find papers or documents of presidents preceding Hoover, presidents who do not have libraries dedicated to their administrations.

2.2a Burton, D. A., J. B. Rhoads, & R. W. Smock. *Guide to Manuscripts in the Presidential Libraries, 1939–1985* (College Park, MD: Research Materials Corporation, 1985). [CD 3029.82 .B87 1985]

2.2b Goehlert, R. U., & F. S. Martin. *The Presidency: A Research Guide* (Santa Barbara, CA: ABC-CLIO Information Services, 1985). [Z 1249 .P7 G63 1985]

2.2c Viet, F. *Presidential Libraries and Collections* (New York: Greenwood Press, 1987). [CD 3029.82 .V45 1987]

2.3 Special Collections of Presidential Rhetoric

Collections are available of specific genres of presidential address.

2.3a *Inaugural Addresses of the Presidents of the United States, 1789–1985* (Washington, D.C.: U.S. Government Printing Office, 1985). [J81 .I528 1985]

2.3b   Israel, F. L. (Ed.) *State of the Union Messages of the Presidents* (New York: Chelsea House, 1966). [J 81 .C66]

2.4 Presidential Campaigns

While it is relatively easy to locate complete textual records of a presidency, the records of campaigns are not as complete. While the speeches of a sitting president seeking reelection are included in *Public Papers*, finding more general materials on the campaign itself or on the opposition candidate may be a problem. Occasionally, one can find collections of campaign speeches produced by all of the participants **(2.4a, 2.4d)** and, additionally, Schlesinger and Israel have provided a wealth of documents in their *History of American Presidential Elections* **(2.4c)**. Candidates who have not been elected have also had their statements published in special collections **(2.4b, 2.4e)** on occasion. In the 1976 campaign and in the campaigns following it, the Government Printing Office has published virtually complete records of the contests **(2.4f)**. Volume One **(2.4f)** of this collection presents documents from the Carter campaign, including speeches, statements, press conferences, and position papers. The equivalent material from the Ford campaign is included in Volume Two. Volume Three contains the presidential and vice-presidential debates.

2.4a   Bush, G. *Campaign Speeches of American Presidential Candidates: 1948–1984* (New York: Frederick Ungar Publishing, 1985). [E 743 .C236]

2.4b   McGovern, G. *An American Journey: The Presidential Campaign Speeches of George McGovern* (New York: Random House, 1974). [E 840.8 .M34 A52]

2.4c   Schlesinger, A. M. Jr., & F. L. Israel, (Eds.) *History of American Presidential Elections.* 4 vols. (New York: Chelsea House & McGraw Hill, 1971). [E 183 .S28]

2.4d   Singer, A. *Campaign Speeches of American Presidential Candidates: 1928–1972* (New York: Frederick Ungar Publishing, 1973). [E 743 .C235]

2.4e   Stevenson, A. *Major Campaign Speeches of Adlai E. Stevenson* (New York: Random House, 1953). [E 816 .S69]

2.4f   *The Presidential Campaign, 1976.* 3 Vols. (Washington, D.C.: U.S. Government Printing Office, 1978). [JK 526 1976 .U52 1978]

2.5 Political Parties

In addition to candidate-specific materials, party-based information is also available, including official documents, public statements,
platform material, and convention records.

2.5a Chester, E. W. (Ed.) *A Guide to Political Platforms* (Hamden,
CT: Archon Books, 1977). [JK 2261 .C48]

2.5b Congressional Quarterly, Inc. *National Party Conventions,
1831–1984.* (Washington, D.C.: Congressional Quarterly,
1987). [JK 2255 .N374 1987]

2.5c Johnson, D. B. *National Party Platforms, 1840–1976* (Urbana,
IL: University of Illinois Press, 1978). [JK 2255 .J64 1978]

2.5d Johnson, D. B. *National Party Platforms, 1980* (Urbana, IL:
University of Illinois Press, 1982). [JK 2255 .J643]

2.5e Schlesinger, A. M. Jr. *History of U.S. Political Parties, 1789–
1972* (New York: Chelsea House Publishers, 1973). [JK 2261
.S35]

2.6 Primary Indexes for Government Documents

No matter what sort of discourse a critic is interested in, government documents are a treasure trove of information. For example,
because Congress holds hearings on topics ranging from rock music
lyrics to immigration law, critics may find useful statements from a
wide (often wild) assortment of individuals and groups concerned with
a hearing's subject matter. Accessing such materials is relatively easy
when one uses the indexes to government documents. The Congressional Information Service **(2.6a, 2.6b)** provides guides to all materials
published by the U.S. Congress.

Many libraries, even if they are not government depositories, contain the CIS material on microforms. *The Monthly Catalog* **(2.6d)** is the
traditional index for such materials and it includes congressional materials as well as those issued by other governmental bodies. For
instance, *The Monthly Catalog* lists all films distributed by government
agencies, even those intended for foreign audiences that are not usually available to U.S. audiences. *The Index to U.S. Government Periodicals* **(2.6c)** indexes items issued by the various bureaucratic agencies
and by researchers focusing on topics such as economics, political science, sociology, business, and education.

2.6a   *CIS Index* (Washington, D.C.: Congressional Information Service, Inc.). [KF 49 .C62]

2.6b   *CIS U.S. Congressional Committee Prints Index* (Washington, D.C.: Congressional Information Service, Inc.). [Z 1223 .Z7 C66]

2.6c   *Index to U.S. Government Periodicals* (Chicago: Infordata International, Inc.). [AI 3 .I5334 DOCS]

2.6d   *Monthly Catalog* (Washington, D.C.: U.S. Government Printing Office). [Z 1223 .A18]

2.7 Indexes to Government Materials

More specific indexes are available to the researcher. For instance, by using the *Declassified Documents Catalog* **(2.7d)**, a critic could locate any document recently removed from a classified, unavailable status. The *Federal Index* **(2.7a)** indexes the *Congressional Record, Federal Register, Weekly Compilation of Presidential Documents* and *Law Week*. Additionally, other sources **(2.7b, 2.7c)** provide access to specific material issued by the GAO (reports, statements and speeches related to cost effectiveness of government programs) or related to the U.S. Code (all government rules and regulations).

2.7a   *Federal Index* (Bethesda, MD: National Standards Association). [J K1 .F3337 DOCS]

2.7b   *GAO Documents* (Washington, D.C.: U.S. Government Accounting Office). [HJ 9802 .U5474]

2.7c   *U.S. Code Congressional and Administrative News* (St. Paul, MN: West Publishing Company). [KF 48 .A1]

2.7d   *The Declassified Documents Catalog* (Woodbridge, CT: Research Publications, Inc.). [Z 1223 29 .D4]

2.8 Political Action Committees

While PACs are a fairly recent phenomenon, they have become an important part of American politics. Anyone interested in studying the materials produced by the PACs might contact the organizations through directories like those listed below.

2.8a   Weinberger, W., and D.U. Greevy. *The PAC Directory* (Cambridge, MA: Ballinger Publishing Company, 1982). [JK 1991 .P22]

2.8b Zuckerman, E. *Almanac of Federal PAC's*. (Washington, D.C.: Amward Publications, Inc., 1986). [JK 1991 .A455 1986]

2.9 Agency Directories

When examining political decision making, a researcher may wish to learn more about individuals involved or about a group's organizational structure. For instance, one source **(2.9a)** provides information on 2700 federal committees (such as presidential advisory committees and public advisory committees). Listings in this directory **(2.9a)** include names, addresses, history, programs, publications, and meetings. Another directory **(2.9d)** describes over 5000 items related to Congress, executive agencies, and private and special interest groups with offices in Washington, D.C. Each entry gives the name of the organization, the Director's address and telephone number, and a description of the organization's purposes and operations.

2.9a *Encyclopedia of Government Advisory Organizations* (Detroit: Gale Research Company, 1975, with semi-annual updates in *New Governmental Advisory Organizations*). [JK 468 .C7 .E52 1975 DOCS]

2.9b *Federal Regulatory Directory, 1979–80* (Washington, D.C.: Congressional Quarterly, Inc., 1979). [KF 5406 .A15 F4]

2.9c *Official Congressional Directory* (Washington, D.C.: Government Printing Office, available from 1809–present). [JK 1011 .A3278 DOCS]

2.9d *Washington Information Directory* (Washington, D.C.: Congressional Quarterly, Inc., available from 1974–present). [F 192.3 .C66 REF]

2.10 Government Propaganda

Since virtually all institutions engage in distributing "information" about themselves or others, their efforts are a natural source of intrigue for the rhetorical critic. Of course, these propagandizing institutions do not label their products thusly. Therefore, the rhetorical critic will find texts for analysis in diverse locations, many of which bear objective-sounding labels. For instance, *The Monthly Catalog* **(2.6d)** lists all films produced by the U.S. government for distribution in foreign countries as well as pamphlets concerning AIDS, education, consumer product safety, etc. The following section suggests avenues for locating and examining propaganda. For instance, one source **(2.10b)** is actually a collection of texts for Voice of America, which pledged in its first broadcast "The news may be good. The news may be bad. But we shall tell you the truth." Other sources (such as **2.10c** and **2.10e**) provide analysis of propaganda material as well as texts and additional references.

2.10a   Black, J. B. *Organising the Propaganda Instrument: The British Experience* (The Hague: Martines Nijhoff, 1975). [DA 588 .B54]

2.10b   *Catalogue of Selected Voice of America Documents* (Washington, D.C.: U.S. Information Agency). [DOCS I A1.2:U8715]

2.10c   Mackenzie, J. M. *Propaganda and Empire: The Manipulation of British Public Opinion, 1880–1960* (Dover, NH: Manchester University Press, 1984). [JU 1011 .M34 1984]

2.10d   *Subject Index, Radio Free Europe Research.* [DR 1 .R344]

2.10e   Ruff, L. J. *Mobilizing Women for War: German and American Propaganda, 1939–1945* (Princeton, NJ: Princeton University Press, 1978). [D 810 .W7 R8]

2.10f   Cline, M. W., C. E. Christiansen, and J. M. Fontaine, (Eds.). *Scholar's Guide to Intelligence Literature: Bibliography of the Russell J. Bowen Collection* (Frederick, MD: University Publications of America, Inc., 1983). [JF 1525 .I6 S364 1983]

3.0 LEGAL DISCOURSE

Recently, rhetorical scholars have turned their attention to examining communication in the legal environment. While traditional analyses of legal arguments are important and useful, critics have also become interested in the stories created in the trial setting, the language used by attorneys and judges, and the nonverbal climate of the courtroom. Additionally, analysis of court decisions provides insight into American culture, American values, and how these features change over time.

3.1 Court Decisions

To locate texts of court decisions, the critic will want to utilize some version of the West Reporter system **(3.1b, 3.1c, 3.1d)**. West Publishing Company distributes a *Reporter* for Supreme Court decisions **(3.1d)**, U.S. Courts of Appeals, and Temporary Courts of Appeals **(3.1b)**, U.S. District Courts and U.S. Courts of International Trade **(3.1c)** as well as a system of regional reporters for all other courts. The *General Digest* provides a brief description of court decisions with a descriptive word index and table of cases **(3.1e)**. Other indexes are available for Supreme Court decisions **(3.1f, 3.1a)**.

3.1a   Blandord, L.A., & P. R. Evans (Eds.) *Supreme Court of the United States: An Index to Opinions Arranged by Justice* (Millwood, NY.: Kraus International Publications, 1983). [KF 101.6 .B57 1983]

3.1b   *Federal Reporter* (St. Paul, MN: West Publishing Company). [KF 293]

3.1c   *Federal Supplement* (St Paul, MN: West Publishing Company). [KF 2933]

3.1d   *Supreme Court Reporter* (St. Paul, MN: West Publishing Company). [KF 101 .U52]

3.1e   *West's General Digest* (St. Paul, MN: West Publishing Company). [KF 141]

3.1f   U.S. *Supreme Court Bulletin* (Commerce Clearing House, Inc.) [KF 101.1 .C65]

3.2 State-based Information

While texts of court decisions are available in many general libraries and in all law libraries, the critic interested in trial deliberations must usually write to specific individuals or offices to obtain verbatim transcripts of a given trial **(3.2a, 3.2c)**. While some trials are now videotaped, critics must locate and negotiate for copies through the specific court in the same manner as obtaining a transcript. Researchers interested in court records, state legislative proceedings, state political party deliberations, lobbying publications, and other local discourse might use the following directories to locate the persons responsible for providing such information.

3.2a   *BNA's Directory of State Courts, Judges, and Clerks* (Washington, D.C.: Bureau of National Affairs, 1986). [KF 8700 .A19 K56]

3.2b   *Guide to State Legislative Materials* (Littleton, CO: Fred B. Rothman and Company, 1983). [KF 1 .G8 1983]

3.2c   *National Directory of State Agencies* (Bethesda, MD: National Standards Association, Inc., 1986). [JK 2443 .N37 1986]

3.2d   *State Legislative Sourcebook 1987: A Resource Guide to Legislative Information in the Fifty States* (Topeka, KS: Government Research Service, 1986). [JK 2495 .S689 1987]

3.3 Legal Publications

The *Index* (**3.3b**) provides the critic with access to printed materials emanating from law reviews and other general legal periodicals. The *Directory* (**3.3c**) enables a researcher to locate the names and addresses of individuals responsible for legal archiving. The critic interested in courtroom behavior will almost always have to rely on the helpfulness of such individuals rather than expect to find published material in a local library.

3.3a   Hicks, F.C. *Famous American Jury Speeches* (St. Paul, MN: West Publishing Company, 1925). [KF 211 .H53]

3.3b   *Index to Legal Periodicals* (Bronx, NY: H.W. Wilson Company). [K 1 .I5]

3.3c   Wasserman, P., and M. Kaszubski. *Law and Legal Information Directory* (Detroit, MI: Gale Research Company, 1980). [KF 190 .L35]

4.0 INTERNATIONAL POLITICS

While the critic may not immediately recognize it, most libraries provide access to a wide range of material on international affairs. This material includes such items as United Nations documents as well as proceedings of other foreign governmental bodies that have been translated into English.

4.1 United Nations

While *Sow the Wind* (**4.1a**) consists of speeches made by leaders of various countries (all available in English), other sources in this section are indexes useful for either locating material in a library or ordering the material from some other source. These indexes (**4.1b** through **4.1e**) allow access to many of the publications of the United Nations. One source (**4.1b**) focuses on the proceedings of the U.N. General Assembly in New York City while another (**4.1e**) catalogs materials available from a single U.N. agency. Other resource materials are available regarding the U.N. but these general and specific indexes should provide a starting point for the critic interested in the cross-cultural aspects of discourse.

4.1a   Prosser, M. H. (Ed.) *Sow the Wind, Reap the Whirlwind: Heads of State Address the United Nations* (New York: William Morrow and Company, 1970). [JX 1977 .P728]

4.1b *Index to Proceedings of the General Assembly* (New York: UN Publications). [JX 1977 .A44]

4.1c *UNDOC: Current Index* (New York: UN Publications). [JX 1977 .A2 A2545]

4.1d *United Nations Document Index* (New York: UN Publications). [JX 1977 .A2 A25 DOCS]

4.1e *UNESCO List of Documents and Publications* (Paris: UN Educational, Scientific, and Cultural Organization). [AS 4 .U8 A1334]

4.2 Legislative Records

As indicated earlier, many libraries house the proceedings of foreign legislative bodies. For example, some publications **(4.2b, 4.2c, 4.2d, 4.2e)** contain such records for Canada and South Africa (the latter is translated into English). Yet another source **(4.2a)** is an aid to searching United Kingdom records and thus might have special interest for U.S. researchers.

4.2a Bond, M. P. (Ed.) *Guide to the Records of Parliament* (London: Her Majesty's Stationery Office, 1971). [CD 1063 .B63]

4.2b *Debates: House of Commons Canada* (Quebec: Canadian Government Publishing Centre).

4.2c *Debates of the Senate Canada* (Quebec: Canadian Government Publishing Centre).

4.2d *South African Parliament Debates of the Senate* (Cape Town: The Government Printer). [J 705 .J212]

4.3 Written Documents

Other documents (constitutions, treaty agreements, etc.) might be of interest to the rhetorical analyst. In one source **(4.3a)**, for example, copies of the constitutions from many countries have been translated into English and these provide an interesting perspective on international values.

4.3a Blaustein, A. P., & H. F. Gisbert (Eds.) *Constitutions of the Countries of the World*. 18 binders. (Dobbs Ferry, NY: Oceana Publications Inc., 1987). [JF 11 .B5235]

4.3b Israel, F. I. (Ed.) *Major Peace Treaties of Modern History, 1648–1967* (New York: Chelsea House Publishers, 1967). [JX 121 .I8]

4.3c   *U.S. Treaties and Other International Agreements, 1776–.* [JX 231 .K4]

4.3d   *Treaty Series: Treaties and International Agreements Registered or Filed and Recorded with the Secretariat of the United Nations* (New York: United Nations, 1946/47–). [JX 170 .U35]

4.4 Statements and Documents

These sources illustrate materials that have been translated into English and that are generally available in U.S. libraries. Such documents and speeches may be potentially useful to the critic interested in the rhetoric of a particular person, place, or issue on the world scene.

4.4a   Castro, F. *Fidel Castro's Speeches.* 2 vols. (New York: Pathfinder Press, 1981). [F 1788.22 C3A5 1981]

4.4b   Churchill, W. *Churchill Speaks; The Major Speeches of Sir Winston S. Churchill, 1897–1963* (New York: Chelsea House Publishers, 1975). [DA 566.9 .C5 A3624]

4.4c   Compton, G. (Tr.) *Mao's China: Party Reform Documents 1942–1944* (Seattle: University of Washington Press, 1952).

4.4d   Curtis, E., & R. B. McDowell (Eds.) *Irish Historical Documents, 1172–1922* (London: Methuen and Company, Ltd., 1943). [DA 905 .C8]

4.4e   *Speeches of Adolf Hitler: April 1922–August 1939.* N. H. Bagnes (Ed.) (London: Oxford University Press, 1942). [DD 247 .H5 A73 1942a]

4.4f   Nehru, J. *India's Foreign Policy: Selected Speeches, September 1946–April 1961* (Delhi: Publications Division, Minister of Information and Broadcasting, Government of India, 1961). [DS 481 .N35 A3424]

4.4g   Stalin, J. *War Speeches, Orders of the Day, and Answers to Foreign Press Correspondents during the Great Patriotic War, July 3, 1941–June 22, 1945* (London: Hutchinson and Co., 1946). [D 764 .S844]

4.5 International Political Groups

While actual contact with terrorist organizations might not be possible or desirable for a critic, the directories in this section illustrate that the average college or university library is a good resource for both traditional and nontraditional rhetorical documents.

4.5a   Degenhardt, H. W. *Political Dissent: An International Guide to Dissident, Extra-Parliamentary, Guerrilla and Illegal Political Movements* (Detroit: Gale Research Company, 1983). [JC 328.3 .D43 1983]

4.5b   Janke, P. (Ed.) *Guerrilla and Terrorist Organisations: A World Directory and Bibliography* (New York: Macmillan Publishing Company, 1983). [JC 328.6 .J36 1983]

5.0 SOCIAL MOVEMENTS

In studying rhetorical movements, the critic will probably rely on both textual materials generally available (such as those found in the speech collections mentioned earlier) as well as on previously uncollected discourse distributed by the movement itself. Therefore, sources useful to the movement critic include directories, bibliographies, and document collections.

5.1 General Information

The sources in this section apply to a variety of movements. By using one source **(5.1a)**, the critic can learn the location and availability of materials gathered in libraries throughout the United States. From another **(5.1b)**, a researcher can find the names, addresses, size, and publications of virtually any organized grouping in the United States— whether political, social, religious, or educational. Yet another **(5.1c)** is an example of the bibliographies available for studying movement discourse.

5.1a   *Directory of Archives and Manuscript Repositories* (Washington, D.C.: National Historical Publications and Records Commission, 1978). [CD 3020 .U54 1978]

5.1b   *Encyclopedia of Associations* (Detroit: Gale Research Company, 1987). [H5 17 .G3]

5.1c   Muller, R. H., T. J. Spahn, & J. M. Spahn (Eds.) *From Radical Left to Extreme Right* Vol. 1 (Ann Arbor, MI: Campus Publishers, 1970); Spahn, T. J., & J. M. Spahn, (Eds.) Vols. 2 & 3 (Metuchen, NJ: The Scarerow Press, Inc., 1972, 1976). [JA 3 .M1970]

5.2 Student Protest

The student protest movement of the 1960s has received considerable attention both during and after its era. Several resources **(5.2a,**

5.2b, 5.2c, 5.2d) provide speeches and pamphlets that will be of considerable interest to the rhetorical analyst, and another **(5.2e)** is a bibiliography of additional materials on the movement.

5.2a   Albert, J. C., & S. E. Albert. *The Sixties Papers: Documents of a Rebellious Decade.* (New York: Praeger, 1984). [HN 65 .S563]

5.2b   Cohen, M., & D. Hale. (Eds.) *The New Student Left: An Anthology.* (Boston: Beacon Press, 1967). [LA 229 .C6 1967]

5.2c   Draper, H. *Berkeley: The New Student Revolt.* (New York: Grove Press, 1965). [LD 760 .D7]

5.2d   Lipset, S. M., & S. S. Wolin.*The Berkeley Student Revolt: Facts and Interpretation.* (New York: Doubleday, 1965). [LD 760 .L5]

5.2e   Phillips, D. E. *Student Protest, 1960–1970; An Analysis of the Issues and Speeches.* (Lanham, MD: UP of America, 1985). [LA 229 .E483]

5.3 Women's Movement—History

The sources in this section allow access to original texts, collections of documents, and a directory to other materials dealing with the women's movement. One source **(5.3b)** is a guide to the archives and manuscripts of women, while others **(5.3c** and **5.3d)** contain materials by and about women. Yet another **(5.3e)** provides materials from the late nineteenth century and early twentieth century women's movement.

5.3a   Campbell, K. K. *Man Cannot Speak for Her: Key Texts of the Early Feminists* (New York: Greenwood Press, 1989). [HQ 1154 .C28 1989].

5.3b   Hinding, A. (Ed.) *Women's History Sources: A Guide to Archives and Manuscript Collections in the United States* (New York: R.R. Bowker Company, 1979). [HQ 1410 .H56]

5.3c   Papachristou, J. *Women Together: A History in Documents of the Women's Movement in the United States* (New York: Knopf, 1976). [HQ 1426 .P34]

5.3d   Rossi, A. S. *The Feminist Papers: From Adams to Beauvoir* (New York: Columbia University Press, 1973). [HQ 1154 .R746]

5.3e   Stanton, E., S. Anthony, & M. J. Gage (Eds.) *History of Woman Suffrage,* 3 Vols. (Rochester, 1887). [JK 1896 .S8]

RHETORIC AND THE AMERICAN SOUTH

Critical Profile 13.1   Creating the "Nigger" Myth

"Nigger" is one of the most offensive words in American English. Why is that? The word "nigger" is simply a derivative of the Spanish word *negro,* which means "black." From such innocent origins, how did the word "nigger" gain its derogatory connotations? Cal Logue of the University of Georgia provides at least part of the answer. Logue studied the rhetoric of Southern whites during Reconstruction after the Civil War. Before the Civil War, whites in the South controlled blacks through the legalized institution of slavery. When slavery was abolished, the whites resorted to rhetorical means of control. According to Logue, the public rhetoric of this period in the South forced the "nigger" myth "as a means of confining Blacks to their formerly enslaved status." That is, white power was maintained rhetorically by degrading the image of blacks.

White Southern rhetoric served its purpose by defining blacks as something less than human, or at best as marginally human, and at the same time aroused fears of contamination of the "superior" white race. Southern editors referred to blacks as "starved monkeys" and "wild beasts." Sarcasm and satire became the favorite weapons of white editors:

> Naturalists now visting the city . . . have been engaged in classifying the animals and have found no difficulty in assigning the most of them to one or other of the three groups *Limladae, Cebidae Lemuridae* (monkey tribe) with a few specimens of the Pithecus Satyrus *(orang outang)* but they have grave suspicions of the presence of a genuine *troglodytesgorilla.*

Logue includes several satirical sketches of black legislators that were printed in *XIX Century* magazine and reprinted in the Atlanta *Constitution.* These sketches mocked blacks and at the same time stirred deep-seated fears in white readers. For example, one such sketch pretended to present the arguments of "Rev. & Hon. Plenty Small" for social equality. In the caricature, Rev. Small claims that "Adam an Ebe was cullud pussons in de riginashun" and that "de blush on de cheek ob de fair sec ob de op'sit race, am only de faint streke ob de rich cullur which de Lord 'llow to stay."

Such caricatures derided the language and logic of blacks while raising fears among white readers that the blacks would contaminate the fair sex of the white race. In creating the "nigger" myth, spokesmen for the white South bequeathed a linguistic legacy that nurtures home-grown American racism to this very day.

Profiled by: Jim Mackin
Citation: Logue (1976)

Critical Profile 13.2   One Constitution, Many Interpreters

Southern rhetoric, that richly costumed oratory of mythic fame, is, like most rhetoric, exploitative. Its orators retell often apocryphal tales of the past, invent embellished stories of glorified futures, and rail against pressures being applied from "the outside." Waldo Braden of Louisiana State University has demonstrated that Southern orators have also exploited the Constitution of the United States in order to support their belief in racial segregation. Braden quickly points out, however, that any rhetor in any region or nation can "add" meaning to or "subtract" meaning from any document, the Constitution included, as circumstances, and ideology, dictate.

In his study, Braden points out that the Constitution was used in some places in support of the Civil Rights movement, while in the South the same document was exploited to defend against interference from "the NAACP, the Supreme Court, the northern press, left-wing educators, left-wing pseudoscientists, professional agitators, Communists, communist front organizations, and foundations" that favored desegregation. Braden argues that skillful interpretation of the Constitution to serve the ends of segregation was accomplished by the "manipulation of the setting, control of the media, and exploitation of emotion." Among the orator's tools was graphic imagery of Constitution-hating scoundrels bent on forcing the South to abandon its tradition of racial segregation.

Those images were sharpened, Braden points out, by using the Constitution itself to defend segregation in two ways. First, Southern orators asserted that the Constitution guaranteed individual states the right to establish laws governing the relationships among their citizens. Second, Southern orators described those who opposed this interpretation as "devoid of mercy and gallantry," illegally forcing the Southern states to accept the Fourteenth Amendment. Judge Thomas P. Brady, for example, declared: "The South is the citadel of conservatism. It is a fortress for constitutional government." Similarly, Senator James O. Eastland argued that "our position [favoring segregation] is sound under the constitution and the laws of the United States . . ." and is aimed at "the preservation of the American system of government with its dual powers which provide for additional liberty and freedom." Other opponents of desegregation described how the Constitution was being subverted by Supreme Court Justices who had "exchanged their judicial robes for the caps and gowns of sociology professors and proceeded to tear the heart from the American Constitution. . . ."

Perhaps more than anything else, Braden's study shows how clearly "the law of the land" is really just a product of who is able to make the most persuasive case when, where, for whom, and by what means. Constitutions, treaties, and laws are merely formalized rhetorics having neither inherent meaning nor inherent worth—they amount only to what can be negotiated socially at a particular time and a particular place.

Profiled by: Donald Nobles
Citation: Braden (1983)

Critical Profile 13.3   Rehabilitating the Southern Myth

The South has always seemed distinct from the rest of the United States. Professor Stephen Smith of the University of Arkansas shows that, in the modern South, this distinctiveness may be rooted in mythological practices rather than in the actual facts of life in the region. New symbols and new myths, says Smith, have replaced the myths of the Old South, the Lost Cause, and the perennial notion of a "New South." Smith observes that social change in the South was impeded because "generations of orators in crisis after crisis have returned repeatedly to the old symbols and the old myth to explain reality for the region."

But things have been changing lately, even in the South. The stressful period from the Brown decision in 1954 to the passage of the Voting Rights Act of 1965 saw the emergence of a new myth that promised better answers and a brighter future for the contemporary South. The new myth promoted themes of equality, regional distinctiveness, and appreciation of place and community. Smith explains that the communications media have enhanced acceptance of the theme of equality: "The South now has an electronic folklore with much more egalitarian icons and symbols."

The modern theme of southern distinctiveness is advanced by media treatments of such things as Southern music, food, sports, and heroes. "Country" music, for example, remains primarily Southern country music. Smith reports that Southern locations accounted for 75 percent of the places named in a sample of country music. Also, such lyrics are much more favorable to the South than to other regions. Despite the franchised proliferation of formerly regional fried chicken delicacies, the media continue to treat Southern food in distinctive ways. Catfish, barbecue, grits, and cornbread remain objects of veneration. Broadcasts from Tuscaloosa and Athens reinforce the fact that football, a national pastime, is a Southern religion. The contemporary South has new and simple heroes, often advanced by the media. Jefferson Davis and Robert E. Lee yielded center stage in the 1960s and 1970s to Andy Griffith and the Waltons.

Smith notes that, for institutional reasons, the mass media often retain a myth long after its factual base has eroded. In contemporary times, the South is becoming more technological than agricultural, more urban than rural, more Republican than populist, more educated than uneducated. Also, racial tolerance is found more often in some parts of the South than in some parts of the North; Episcopal and Methodist churches are springing up alongside Baptist and Assembly of God churches; and Southern politicians increasingly sound more pluralistic than partisan, more internationalist than regionalist. In other words, on an empirical level, the South is becoming more like the rest of the United States each day. But the myth of Southern distinctiveness will not die as easily, largely because it is reinforced constantly by a backward-looking, and often lazy, mass media industry. The myth of Southern distinctiveness is hardy not just because it is important to Southerners, but because it is useful to all persons looking for a simple story to tell.

Profiled by: John Llewellyn
Citation: Smith (1985)

5.4 Women's Movement—Contemporary

The following sources are examples of resource guides (5.4a, 5.4b) and texts for the contemporary women's movement.

5.4a   Doss, M. M. *Women's Organizations: A National Directory* (Garrett Park, MD: Garrett Park Press, 1986). [HQ 1883 .W65 1986]

5.4b   Harrison, C. E. *Women's Movement Media: A Source Guide* (New York: R.R. Bowker Company, 1975). [HQ 1420 .H5775]

5.4c   Kante, H., S. Lefanu, S. Shah, & C. Spetting. *Sweeping Statements: Writings from the Women's Movement, 1981–1983* (London: The Women's Press, Ltd., 1984). [HQ 1154 .S933 1984]

5.5 Peace Movement

By utilizing the directories and guides in this section, a researcher can locate a wide variety of materials focusing on contemporary peace and human rights movements, both of which have had remarkable longevity in American life.

5.5a   Bernstein, E., R. Elias, & Associates. *Peace Resource Book* (Cambridge, MA: Ballinger Publishing Company, 1986). [JX 1905.5 .A64 1986]

5.5b   *Checklist of Human Rights Documents.* Monthly Index. (Stanfordville, NJ: Earl M. Coleman, 1976–1980). [JC 585 .C4355]

5.5c   Fine, M., & P. M. Steven (Eds.) *American Peace Directory* (Cambridge, MA: Ballinger Publishing Company, 1984). [JX 1905 .A64]

5.5d   Trzyna, T. C. (Ed.) *International Peace Directory* (Claremont, CA: California Institute of Public Affairs, 1984). [JX 1905.5 .I58]

5.6 Black Protest

Black protest has received a great deal of attention in recent times but as the sources below indicate, the black protest movement has had

a considerable history as well. The sources below contain texts span-
ning many centuries. One source **(5.6c)**, for example, ranges from narratives from the slave trade days to the speeches of the radical activist
Malcolm X.

5.6a   Burke, J. M. *Civil Rights: A Current Guide to the People,
Organizations, and Events* (New York: R.R. Bowker Company, 1974). [JC 599 .U5 B85 1974]

5.6b   Ducas, G. (Ed.) *Great Documents in Black American History*
(New York: Praeger Publishers, 1970). [E 184.6 .D83
1970]

5.6c   Frazier, T. R. *Afro-American History: Primary Sources* (New
York: Harcourt, Brace, and World, Inc., 1970). [E 184.6
F7]

5.6d   Grant, J. *Black Protest: History, Documents, and Analysis, 1619
to the Present* (New York: Fawcett World Library, 1968).
[E 185 .G75]

5.6e   Jacobs, D. M. *Antebellum Black Newspapers: Indices to New
York's Freedom's Journal 1827–29, The Rights of All 1829, The
Weekly Advocate 1837, and The Colored American 1837–1841*
(Westport, CT: Greenwood Press, 1976). [E 185.5 .J33]

5.6f   Johnson, R. B., & J. L. Johnson (Eds.) *The Black Resource
Guide* (Washington, D.C.: R.B. Johnson, publisher, 1986).
[E 185.5 .B565 1986]

5.7 Ethnic Groups

Researchers might be interested in the rhetoric of various ethnic
groups and movements. One method of finding such information is to
consult directories that provide names of organizations, leaders, and
publications and then write to them for primary materials. Additionally, some bibliographies (for example, **5.7b**) aid in locating materials
on specific groups or events.

5.7a   Caballero, C. (Compiler) *Chicano Organizations Directory*
(New York: Neal-Schuman Publishers, Inc., 1985). [E 184
.M5 C26 1985]

5.7b   Miller, W. C. *A Comprehensive Bibliography for the Study of
American Minorities* (New York: New York University Press,
1976). [Z 1361 .F4 M529]

5.7c   Wasserman, P. & A. E. Kinnington. *Ethnic Information Sources of the United States.* 2nd Ed. (Detroit: Gale Research Company, 1983). [E 184 .A1 W27 1983]

5.7d   Wynan, L. R. *Encyclopedic Directory of Ethnic Organizations in the United States* (Littleton, CO: Libraries Unlimited, Inc., 1975). [E 184 .A1 W94]

5.8 Environmental Issues

While environmental and conservationist groups would be listed in *The Encyclopedia of Associations* (as are virtually all other organized groups), a critic could also consult more specific guides to the special literature of the movement and to the organizations promoting it.

5.8a   *Environmental Periodicals Bibliography* (Santa Barbara, CA: Environmental Studies Institute). [TA 170 .E5953]

5.8b   *World Environmental Directory* (Silver Spring, MD: Business Publishers, Inc., 1980). [TD 12 .W65]

6.0 MEDIA STUDIES

Mass media such as newspapers, radio, television, and film provide interesting subject matter for rhetorical analysis. Regardless of the study's focus, the analyst can, with some diligence, locate materials from a variety of media outlets.

6.1 Television and Radio News

While television and radio news are now an increasingly common focus for rhetorical analysis, getting access to textual materials, particularly historical materials, sometimes takes effort. Of course, a critic may make arrangements to record certain programs or events off-air if he or she knows about a particular news feature sufficiently in advance. For instance, an analyst interested in news coverage of presidential candidates might video or audio record evening newscasts for a given time period. Additionally, researchers should check local libraries to determine what their ever-increasing audio-visual collections contain.

For many researchers, the Vanderbilt Archives **(6.1d)** will provide the best avenue for accessing television news programs, since it records the nightly network newscasts of all major networks and other news specials and then makes these materials available to scholars. By using the index to this collection **(6.1d)**, the critic can determine what material he or she desires and then follow the procedures listed in the index for ordering such materials. Other sources, such as written transcripts of news programs **(6.1b, 6.1e)**, can also be useful for analyzing television or radio news.

6.1a Adams, W., and F. Schreibman. *Television Network News: Issues in Content Analysis* (Washington, D.C.: George Washington University, 1978). [PN 4784 .B75 T4]

6.1b *Face the Nation: The Collected Transcripts from the CBS Radio and Television Broadcasts, 1954–1977* (CBS News). [E743 .C59]

6.1c *Subject Guide to the Radio and Television Collection of the Museum of Broadcasting* (New York: Museum of Broadcasting, 1979). [PN 1991.9 .M84 1979]

6.1d *Television News Index and Abstracts* (Nashville: Joint Universities Libraries, 1972–). [PN 4784 .T4 T4555]

6.1e *CBS News Index* (Ann Arbor, MI: University Microfilms International). [PN 4888 .T4 C17a 1985]

6.2 Editorials

Critics interested in topical coverage, argumentative strategies, commentary, and other press reactions might well examine newspaper editorials. Editorials can be retrieved through newspaper indexes (see **6.8**) as well as through collections. The sources in this section illustrate some of the collections of editorials available, including two organized around the original source **(6.2a, 6.2b)**, one based on excellence **(6.2d)**, and a third that is a general, ongoing collection **(6.2c)**.

6.2a *Casual Essays of the Sun* (New York: Robert Grier Cooke, 1905).

6.2b *Century of Tribune Editorials.* Original 1947. (Freeport, NY: Books for Libraries Press, 1970). [E 178.6 .C535 1970]

6.2c *Editorials On File* (New York: Facts on File, Inc., 1969–). [D839 .E3]

6.2d Sloan, W. D. (Ed.) *Pulitzer Prize Editorials: America's Best Editorial Writing, 1917–1979* (Ames, IA: Iowa State University Press, 1980). [PN 4726 .P8]

6.3 Editorialist Collections

Since many writers publish collections of their articles, the critic interested in an individual commentator or perspective might use a library's card catalog as a basis for analysis. Examples of these collections include:

6.3a   Buchwald, A. *While Reagan Slept* (New York: Putnam, 1983). [PS 3503 .U1828 G48 1983]

6.3b   Goodman, E. *At Large* (New York: Summit Books, 1981). [AC 8 .G7619]

6.3c   Will, G. *The Pursuit of Happiness and Other Sobering Thoughts* (New York: Harper and Row, 1978). [AC 8 .W613 1978]

6.4 Editorial Cartoon Collections

For many people, political cartoons offer a humorous and powerful commentary on current events. When examining political cartoons, an analyst might use collections organized according to the original source or according to their personal excellence.

6.4a   Brooks, C. (Ed.) *Best Editorial Cartoons* (Gretna, LA: Pelican Publishing Company, 1972–). [E 839.5 .B45]

6.4b   Freeman, R. B., & R. Samuelwest (Eds.) *Best Political Cartoons of 1978* (Lansdale, PA: Puck Press, 1978). [E 872 .B47]

6.4c   *Editorial Cartoons, 1913–1965* (St. Louis Post-Dispatch). [NC 1428 .S35]

6.4d   *Can Board Chairmen Get Measles: Thirty Years of Great Cartoons from the Wall Street Journal.* Selected by C. Preston (New York: Crown Publishers, 1982). [NC 1428 .W33 C3 1982]

6.5 Cartoonist Collections

Like columnists, cartoonists also publish collections of their materials in bound volumes. Additionally, there are some indexes available (for example, one source **[6.5e]** indexes Gary Trudeau's *Doonesbury* cartoons).

6.5a   Block, H. *Herblock on All Fronts: Texts and Cartoons* (New York: New American Library, 1980). [E 872 .B57]

6.5b   Oliphant, P. *The Year of Living Perilously* (Kansas City: Andrews, McMeel, and Parker, 1984). [E 876 .0453 1984]

6.5c   Peters, M. *Win One for the Geezer: The Cartoons of Mike Peters* (New York: Bantam Books, 1982). [NC 1429 .P45 A4 1982]

6.5d   Sargent, B. *Big Brother Blues: The Editorial Cartoons of Ben Sargent* (Austin, TX: Texas Monthly Press, 1984). [E 876. S27 1984]

6.5e   Satin, A.D. *A Doonesbury Index, 1970–1983* (Metuchen, NJ: The Scarecrow Press, 1985). [PN 6728 .D65 T937 1985]

6.5f   Shields, M. *On the Campaign Trail* (Chapel Hill, NC: Algonquin Books, 1985). [E 879 .S55 1985]

6.5g   Trudeau, G. *Doonesbury Dossier* (New York: Holt, Rinehart, Winston, 1984). [PN 6728 .D65 T7245]

6.6 Movies/Video

Of course, a critic interested in analyzing film might conveniently visit local theaters and video-rental outlets. Several sources **(6.6e, 6.6g, 6.6h, 6.6i)** provide information about the availability of films on videotape. *Videolog* **(6.6h)** is an index housed in some video stores that lists films available on tape and that provides information on relevant directors and actors. Other sources, **(6.6a, 6.6b, 6.6c)** provide resource materials useful in locating specific information. Additional sources **(6.6e, 6.6f)** provide title lists and other information that can help locate particular documents.

6.6a   American Film Institute. *The American Film Institute Catalog of Motion Pictures Produced in the United States: Feature Films, 1921–1930; Feature Films, 1961–1970* (New York; R.R. Bowker, Co., 1971). [PN 1998 .A57]

6.6b   Bukalski, P. *Film Research* (Boston: G.K. Hall & Co., 1972). [PN 1995 .B821]

6.6c   Bottesman, R., and H. M. Geduld *Guidebook to Film: An Eleven-in-One Reference* (New York: Holt, Rinehart, and Winston, 1972). [PN 1998 .A1 G6]

6.6d   Gifford, D. *The British Film Catalog, 1895–1970: A Guide to Entertainment Films* (Newton Abbot: David & Charles, 1973). [PN 1993.5 .G7 1973b]

6.6e   Matlin, L. *TV Movies and Video Guide* (New York: New American Library, 1987).

6.6f   McCarty, C. *Published Screenplays: A Checklist* (Kent, OH: Kent State University Press, 1971). [PN 1995 .M333]

6.6g *Rating the Movies* (Skokie, IL: Publications International, Inc., 1986).

6.6h *Videolog* (San Diego: Trade Service Publication, Inc., 1987).

6.6i *The Video Source Book* (Syosset, NY: The National Video Clearinghouse, Inc., 1979). [PN 1998 .N4935]

6.7 Radio and Television Programs

In addition to news, analysts may be interested in the entertainment programs offered by radio and television. With these studies, critics focus on the cultural values portrayed in dramas and comedies and also do ideological commentary. Some scripts are published and generally available **(6.7a)**, while others require correspondence and time to locate. Critics should check their own libraries and media facilities to determine what is available locally, and should also plan taping sessions for specific programs as needed.

6.7a Poteet, G. H. *Published Radio, Television, and Film Scripts: A Bibliography* (Troy, NY: Whitson Publishing Company, 1975). [PN 1991.77 .P684]

6.7b *Motion Pictures: A Catalog of Books, Periodicals, Screenplays, Television Scripts, and Production Stills.* Compiled by Theatre Arts Library, UCLA (Boston: G.K. Hall, 1972). [PN 1994 .A52 1976]

6.7c Terrace, V. *Encyclopedia of Television Programs, 1947–1979* (South Brunswick, NJ: A.S. Barnes, 1980). [PN 1992.3 .U5 T46 1980]

6.7d Terrace, V. *Radio's Golden Years: The Encyclopedia of Radio Programs, 1930–1960* (San Diego, CA: A.S. Barnes, 1981). [PN 1991.3 .U6 T47]

6.8 Indexes for National Newspapers and Magazines

Rhetorical analysts may want access to the texts of magazines and newspapers in order to examine specific types of discourse, to determine the significance of and reactions to particular speeches and issues, as well as to study the rhetorical aspects of media coverage. *Readers Guide* **(6.8a)** indexes many general and popular magazines and periodicals. Newspapers with national distribution usually have an index that allows easy searches for material. Most libraries have many newspapers available on microform.

6.8a *Reader's Guide to Periodicals* (Bronx, NY: H.W. Wilson, Co.). [AI 3 .R48]

6.8b *Index to the Christian Science Monitor* (Wooster, OH: Bell and Howell, Co.). [AI 21 .C46]

6.8c *Los Angeles Times Index* (Ann Arbor, MI: University Microfilms, a Bell and Howell Information Company). [AI 21 .L686]

6.8d *New York Times Index* (New York: New York Times Company). [AI 21 .N44]

6.8e *Wall Street Journal Index* (New York: Dow Jones and Company, Inc.). [HG 1 .W26]

6.8f *The Official Washington Post Index* (Woodbridge, CT: Research Publications, Inc.). [AI 21 .W33 054]

6.9 Regional Newspaper Indexes

In addition to the largest nationally oriented newspapers, some of the major regional papers have indexes that greatly aid in scholarly searches. Critics investigating topics linked to specific geographical areas (such as some of the Western environmental concerns) or to region-specific political concerns (such as the early civil rights movement) will find the regional indexes particularly valuable. Additionally, the regional newspapers provide a way of examining local reactions to national issues (for instance, by looking at letters to the editor).

6.9a *Atlanta Constitution Index* (Ann Arbor, MI: University Microfilms, a Bell and Howell Information Co.). [AI 21 .A94]

6.9b *Chicago Tribune Index* (Wooster, OH: Bell and Howell, Co.). [AI 21 .C4754]

6.9c *New Orleans Times Picayune and the States Item Index* (Wooster, OH: Bell and Howell, Co.). [AI 21 .N4255]

6.10 Alternative Press

In addition to the mainstream newspapers and periodicals, critics may be interested in the wealth of "alternative" or "underground" presses in the United States. This material will be especially valuable in movement studies as well as for critiquing the biases and critical perspectives of traditional media outlets.

6.10a   Daniel, W. C. *Black Journals of the United States* (Westport, CT: Greenwood Press, 1982). [PN 4882.5 .D36]

6.10b   Glesing, R. J. *The Underground Press in America* (Bloomington, IN: Indiana University Press, 1970). [PN 4888 .U5 G5]

6.10c   Littlefield, D. F., & J. W. Parins *American Indian and Alaska Native Newspapers and Periodicals Vol. 1 1826–1924, Vol. 2 1925–1970* (Westport, CT: Greenwood Press, 1984,1986). [PN 4883 .L57]

6.10d   Murphy, S. *Other Voices: Black, Chicano, and American Indian Press* (Dayton, OH: Pflaum, 1974). [PN 4882 .M8]

6.10e   *Undergrounds: A Union List of Alternative Periodicals in Libraries of the United States and Canada.* J. P. Danky (Compiler) (Madison, WI: State Historical Society of Wisconsin, 1974). [PN 4888 .U5 D328]

6.11 Documentaries

Perhaps one of the most interesting types of modern persuasion is the media documentary. Information regarding documentaries may be found in such indexes as the *Television News Index and Abstracts* **(6.1d)** or the *CBS News Index* **(6.1e)**. Additional indexes such as those listed in this section can also be useful, particularly those produced by the news division of television networks. For instance, *CBS News: Television Broadcasts in Microform* **(6.11b)** provides transcripts of all network news television broadcasts, including regular and special news coverage, the documentary series *CBS Reports*, and shows such as *60 Minutes*. In addition to indexed material, the critic should also investigate the resources available on his or her own campus and local libraries. Many libraries have tapes of television and film documentaries that would be of interest to the rhetorical scholar such as PBS's *Eyes on the Prize*, a historical documentary of the American civil rights movement.

6.11a   *CBS News Almanac* [AY 67 .N5 755 1978]

6.11b   *CBS News: Television Broadcasts in Microform* (Ann Arbor, MI: University Microfilms International).

6.11c   *PBS Video: Program Catalogue* (Alexandria, VA: Public Broadcasting Service). [LB 1044.9 .V5 P2]

6.12 Music

Songs and music reflect the culture, values, issues, and problems of a society. The rhetorical critic interested in any or all of these areas may productively analyze the music associated with groups, movements and time periods.

6.12a   Cooper, B.L. *Resource Guide to Themes in Contemporary American Song Lyrics, 1950–1985* (Westport, CT: Greenwood Press, 1986). [ML 156.4 .P6 C66 1986]

6.12b   Denisoff, R.S. *American Protest Songs of War and Peace: A Selected Bibliography and Discography* (Los Angeles: Center for the Study of Armament and Disarmament, 1970). [ML 128 .W2 D5]

6.12c   Duncan, E. *Lyrics from the Old Song Books* (Freeport, NY: Books for Libraries, 1971, reprint 1927 edition). [PR 1187 .D8 1971]

6.12d   Heffle, B. *Jazz Bibliography: International Literature on Jazz, Blues, Spirituals, Gospel, and Ragtime Music* (London: Munchen, 1981). [ML 128 .J3 H461]

6.12e   Lomax, A. *Hardhitting Songs for Hard-Hit People: American Folk Songs of the Depression and Labor Movement of the 1930's* (New York: Oak Publications, 1967). [M 1629 .L83 H4]

6.12f   Sandahl, L. J. *Rock Films: A Guide to Three Decades of Musicals, Concerts, Documentaries, and Soundtracks.* (New York: Facts on File Publications, 1987).

6.12g   Work, J. W. *American Negro Songs and Spirituals: A Comprehensive Collection of 230 Folk Songs, Religious and Secular.* (New York: Crown Publishers, 1940). [M 1670 .W93 A446]

7.0 ADVERTISING

Advertisements, particularly television ads, constitute one of the most common, yet elusive, forms of persuasion in contemporary society. In analyzing advertising, the critic can collect print ads from sources such as newspapers and periodicals and perhaps record televised ads off-air (observing, of course, all legal regulations pertaining to such taping). Additionally, researchers should also check collections available from local libraries.

7.1 Texts

Collections of advertising texts are difficult to find. Occasionally, a critic may find some "best ads" collections (7.1b) that provide examples of advertisements used in various industries. Additionally, background information and some examples will be found in the trade journal

Advertising Age. For critics interested in slogans, collections and indexes are available **(7.1c, 7.1d)**.

7.1a   *Advertising Age*

7.1b   Reeves, R. (Ed.) *The 400 Best Read Ads of 1968* (New York: Corinthian Editions, Inc., 1968). [HF 5813 .U6 F63]

7.1c   Sharp, H. S. *Advertising Slogans of America* (Metuchen, NJ: The Scarecrow Press, Inc., 1984). [HF 6135 .S53 1984]

7.1d   Urdany, L., & C. D. Tobbins. *Slogans* (Detroit: Gale Research Company, 1984). [HF 6135 .S57]

7.2 Advertising Resource Guides

When examining advertisements, researchers might also consult directories that lead to the people and organizations responsible for the ads.

7.2a   Lipstein, B., & W. J. McGuire. *Evaluating Advertising: A Bibliography of the Communication Process* (New York: Advertising Research Foundation, 1978). [HF 5823 .L567]

7.2b   Pollay, R. W. (Ed.) *Information Sources in Advertising History* (Westport, CT: Greenwood Press, 1979). [HF 5811 .P64]

7.2c   *Standard Directory of Advertising Agencies* (New York: National Register Publishing Company, annual). [HF 5805 .S72]

7.2d   *Standard Directory of Advertisers* (New York: National Register Publishing Company, annual). [HF 5805 .S7]

7.2e   *Trade Names Directory.* 3 Vols. (Detroit: Gale Research Company). [T 223 .V4 A22]

8.0 SCIENCE AND CORPORATE AFFAIRS

In recent years, scholars have increasingly focused on the rhetorical dimensions of science and business. When examining such matters, the critic can examine popularizations of science and corporate activities as well as the communication shared within such organizations by their members.

8.1 Science Texts

Since many popular periodicals are designed for lay audiences, critics may wish to utilize them as rhetorical texts **(8.1a, 8.1b, 8.1c)**.

Additionally, scripts from televised science programs are sometimes available **(8.1d)**. If an individual is interested in obtaining a copy or script of a televised program, he or she should contact the local network affiliate for information. For example, PBS program scripts are sometimes available, but one must contact the station responsible for producing the program (for example, *Nova* is produced by Boston station WGBH and *Austin City Limits* by Austin, Texas station KLRU).

8.1a *Popular Science.* [AP 2 .P8]

8.1b *Science.* [Q 1 .S35 NS]

8.1c *Science News.* [Q 1 .S76]

8.1d *Nova.* Box 322 Boston, MA 02124

8.2 Science Directories

In addition to popular literature, critics can examine discourse produced within scientific groups. One means of accessing this literature is through directories of science-related organizations, many of which are more than willing to send materials produced in-house.

8.2a *Directory of American Research and Technology.* 20th ed. (New York: R. R. Bowker Company, 1986). [T 176 165]

8.2b *Research Center Directory.* 11th ed. (Detroit: Gale Research Company, 1987). [AS 25 .D5]

8.2c *Scientific and Technical Organizations and Agencies Directory.* (Detroit: Gale Research Company, 1985). [Q 145 .S36 1985]

8.3 Corporate Sources

While numerous books focusing on corporate behavior and strategies are available, critics might also examine general business publications and in-house communications. The critic can begin to locate such materials via indexes and directories, although it often takes a good deal of correspondence with the companies in question to secure actual textual materials.

8.3a *Business Information Sources.* L. M. Daniells (Compiler) (Berkeley: University of California Press, 1985). [HF 5030 .D16 1985]

8.3b *Business Periodical Index* (New York: H.W. Wilson Company). [HF 5001 .B883]

8.3c *Directory of Corporate Affiliations* (Skokie, IL: National Register Publishing Company, annual). [HG 4057 .A2195]

8.3d   *Encyclopedia of Business Information Sources.* 6th ed. J. Woy (Ed.) (Detroit: Gale Research Company, 1986). [HF 5353 .E9 1986]

8.3e   *Training and Development Organizations Directory.* 3rd ed. (Detroit: Gale Research Company, 1983). [HD 30.42 .U5 T72]

9.0 RELIGION

When analyzing religious messages, critics examine sermons, rituals, liturgy, and social/political involvement. Regardless of the study's focus, critics can easily locate a wide variety of religious materials, since so many different religious groups proselytize so heavily in the United States. Normally, these groups are more than willing to share their rhetorical wares with others.

9.1 Collections of Sermons

There are many sermon collections available from ancient to contemporary preaching and covering all types of religions. One resource **(9.1f)**, for example, is a catalog listing the extensive audio and video collection of the Reinger seminary.

9.1a   *American Jewish Pulpit: A Collection of Sermons by the Most Eminent American Rabbis.* (Cincinnati: Block and Company, 1881). [BM 735 .A43]

9.1b   Holland, D. (Ed.) *Sermons in American History* (Nashville: Abingdon Press, 1971). [BV 4241 .S4186]

9.1c   Latimer, H. *Selected Sermons* (Charlottesville, VA: The University Press of Virginia, 1968). [BX 5133 .L3 S4]

9.1d   Morris, E. C. *Sermons, Addresses, and Reminiscences and Important Correspondence, Black Bapists.* Reprint, original 1901 (New York: Arno Press, 1980). [BX 6447 .M67 1980]

9.1e   Pope John Paul II. *Addresses and Homilies in Mexico.* [BX 1756 .J636 1979]

9.1f   *Reinger Recording Library Catalog* (Richmond, VA: Union Theological Seminary, 1981). [Z 717 .U5 1981]

9.2 Religious Texts

Religious documents, such as sacred texts or doctrinal statements, may be of interest to the rhetorical analyst and can be accessed through sources like the following:

9.2a   Adams, Charles J. *A Reader's Guide to the Great Religions.* 2nd ed. (New York: Free Press, 1977). [BL 80.2 .A35 1977]

9.2b   Carlen, C. (Ed.) *The Papal Encyclicals, 1740–1981* (Raleigh, NC: McGrath Publishing Company, 1981). [BX 860 .C37 1981]

9.2c   Dunn, C. W. (Ed.) *American Political Theology: Historical Perspectives and Theoretical Analysis* (New York: Praeger Publishers, 1984). [BL 2525 .D86]

9.2d   Jack, H. A. (Ed.) *Religion for Peace: Proceedings of the Kyoto Conferences on Religion and Peace* (New Delhi: Grace Peace Foundation, 1973). [BL 65 .P4 W67 1970]

9.3 Religious Periodicals

An additional, potentially rich, source of religious textual materials can be found in periodicals published by religious organizations and groups. For instance, *Sojourners* **(9.3d)** emphasizes religious activism from a liberal perspective, producing tracts on such issues as the sanctuary movement and nuclear freeze. Periodicals from many different religious positions may be accessed by using indexes such as those mentioned in this section.

9.3a   *Index to Jewish Periodicals* (Cleveland Heights, OH: College of Jewish Studies Press, 1963–). [BM 157 .I53]

9.3b   *Religion Index One: Periodicals* (Chicago: American Theological Library Association, 1977–). [BL 48 .A44]

9.3c   *Religion Index Two: Multi-Author Works* (Chicago: American Theological Library Association, 1976–). [BL 48 .A442]

9.3d   *Sojourners.* [BR 115 .W6 S55]

10.0 LITERATURE

When a critic chooses literature as an area for rhetorical analysis, he or she has a virtually infinite number of texts available for study. By using specific reference works and focused collections, the researcher can quickly search for the works most appropriate to his or her interest.

10.1 Indexes

Indexes provide a quick and easy means for examining specific types of literature.

10.1a   *Comprehensive Index to Little Magazines, 1890–1970.* M. Sader (Ed.) (Millwood, NY: Kraus-Thomson Org., 1976). [PN 4836 .S235]

10.1b   *Granger's Index to Poetry.* 8th ed. (New York: Columbia University Press, 1986.) [PN 1022 .G7 1986]

10.1c   *Play Index. 1949–.* (New York: H.W. Wilson Company). [PN 1625 .P553]

10.1d   *Short Story Index.* (New York: H.W. Wilson Company, 1986). [PS 374 .S5 C6652 1985]

10.1e   *The International Directory of Little Magazines and Small Presses.* 22nd ed. (Paradise, CA: Dustbooks). [Z 6944 .L5 D5]

10.2 Theatre

When thinking of theatre as material for rhetorical criticism, the critic will find plays published individually, in a variety of "best" collections, and in collections organized by issue, race, sex, time, and other distinctive characteristics.

10.2a   *Best American Plays: Seventh Series 1967–1973.* C. Barnes (Ed.) (New York: Crown Publishers, 1975). [PS 634 .B4 7th]

10.2b   *Coming to Terms: American Plays and the Vietnam War* (New York: Theatre Communications Group, Inc., 1985). [PS 627 V53 C6]

10.2c   Ostrow, E.J. (Ed.) *Center Stage: An Anthology of 21 Black American Plays* (Oakland, CA: Sea Urchin Press, 1981). [PS 628 .N4 C4]

10.2d   Pereira, E. *Contemporary South African Plays* (Johannesburg: Ravan Press, 1977). [PR 9366.6 .C65]

10.3 Poetry

Similar to dramatic literature, poetry is found in books of one poet's work and in anthologies focusing on thematic or generic commonalities.

10.3a   Matthews, J. D. *Black Voices Shout: An Anthology of Poetry* (Austin, TX: Troubadour Press, 1974). [PR 9365.35 .N4 M3]

10.3b   Pater, A. F. *Anthology of Magazine Verse and Yearbook of American Poetry* (Beverly Hills, CA: Monitor Book Company, 1985). [PS 614 .A678 1985]

10.3c   Ray, D. *From A to Z: 200 Contemporary American Poets* (Chicago: Swallow Press, 1981). [PS 15 .F69]

10.3d   Scott, D. *Bread and Roses: An Anthology of Nineteenth and Twentieth Century Poetry by Women Writers* (London: Virago Press, 1982). [PN 6109.9]

11.0 AUDIO AND VIDEO RECORDINGS

While the preceding sections focused on specific content areas for rhetorical analysis, this last section is broader. When searching for audio and video records of rhetorical events, the critic should check with library, departmental, and audio-visual archives in his or her local area. Many libraries and schools have a wealth of recorded materials not generally publicized. In some cases, the critic may use the audio-visual material as a supplement to analysis of a written text. For instance, viewing a video of a Hitler rally or a civil rights protest march will add the color and drama to the event that often cannot be detected in a printed text. In other situations, the audio-visual material itself may become the primary focus of analysis.

11.1 General Guides

A useful source **(11.1a)** provides specific information for obtaining a variety of audio-visual materials. Gold **(11.1b)** explains the importance of audio material in rhetorical analysis and also describes several significant collections. The University of Texas Film Library guide **(11.1d)** is but one example of a university's media collection. Most major universities will have similar guides to their special holdings. One recent publication **(11.1c)** catalogs a wide array of educational and instructional videocassettes (on such topics as health care, travel, nature, marriage and family relationships, etc.) and thus is a fine guide to popular culture materials.

11.1a   *Educators' Guide to Free Tapes, Scripts, and Transcriptions* (Randolph, WI: Educators' Progress Service).

11.1b   Gold, E. R. "Recorded Sound Collections: New Materials to Explore the Past." (*Central States Speech Journal.* 1980: 143–151.) [PN 4001 .C45]

11.1c   *The Knowledge Collection* (New York: McGraw Hill, 1988).

11.1d   *Learning Resource Guide: Film Library* (University of Texas at Austin, 1986).

11.2 Audio-Visual Indexes

By using the following indexes, the critic can find a wealth of material suitable for analysis. As always, it normally takes some amount of persistence and time to locate the precise sort of material suitable for polished rhetorical analysis.

11.2a   *American Folklore: Films and Videotapes* (Memphis, TN: Center for Southern Folklore, 1976). [GR 105 .C45]

11.2b   *Educational Film/Video Locator.* 3rd ed. (New York: R.R. Bowker Company, 1986). [LB 1044 .Z9 E4]

11.2c   *National Union Catalogue: Motion Pictures and Filmstrips* (Washington, D.C.: Library of Congress, 1953–). [Z 881 .U49]

11.2d   *Library of Congress Catalogue: Music and Phonorecords* (Washington, D.C.: Library of Congress, 1953–). [ML 136 .U5 L45]

11.2e   *Native North American Music and Oral Data: Catalogue of Sound Recordings, 1893–1976.* D.S. Lee (Ed.) [ML 156.2 .I55]

11.2f   *Preliminary Directory of Sound Recordings Collections in the United States and Canada.* Association for Recorded Sound Collections (New York: The New York Public Library, 1977). [ML 19 .A85]

11.2g   *Scholar's Guide to Washington, D.C. for Audio Resources: Sound Recordings in the Arts, Humanities, and Social, Physical, and Life Sciences.* J. P. Heintze (Ed.) [ML 15 .W2 H44 1985]

CONCLUSION

In this Appendix, we have presented many sources and ideas for rhetorical analysis and yet these represent only a small portion of the materials available to the practicing critic. Nevertheless, we hope to have assisted researchers in finding specific material for analysis, stimulated the reader to think about new directions for criticism, and demonstrated the breadth of materials available. In short, while sometimes a formidable task, finding texts for criticism is hardly an impossible dream.

APPENDIX B

Providing Context for Criticism: Some Suggestions

by David B. McLennan

Experienced as well as novice critics are often surprised by the many steps involved in doing a complete job of criticism. The essential critical act—discovering interesting and important patterns in rhetorical messages—is, of course, the *sine qua non* without which no impressive critical report can be written. But perceptiveness about textual matters alone is not enough. Even after intriguing rhetorical features are discovered, the critic still has important questions to answer: Is this an authentic text? What is the social, cultural, and political background of the audience in question? What are the speaker's philosophical orientation and life experiences? What have other speakers said on this topic? Has other research been done on this rhetorical controversy previously?

Sometimes just trying to determine how to *start* a major critical project can be disconcerting. But libraries are filled with resources to help us answer these basic research questions, so despair is hardly in order. In this Appendix, we will introduce the reader to several ways of gathering basic facts about rhetorical events, information that can be useful for interpreting what has been previously gleaned from careful textual inspection.

Let us suppose, for example, that a critic chooses Ronald Reagan's foreign policy rhetoric as the subject for study. Obtaining speeches outlining President Reagan's stance on this topic only begins the process of analysis. Essential background information on United States foreign policy must also be obtained to understand how Reagan's rhetoric fit or deviated from the presidential norm, what important terms such as "detente" and "Strategic Defense Initiative" meant to Americans in the 1980s, how the President's past discourse shaped the messages currently being analyzed, and what factors within Reagan's multiple audiences influenced his rhetorical choices. Background information of this sort lets the critic know why Mr. Reagan's rhetoric sounded like it did and also tells the critic how his or her analysis differs from that of other researchers in the area. Only after these basic questions have been answered can the critic be assured that the resulting criticism is both comprehensive and authoritative.

For the beginning critic, this Appendix can be viewed as a primer for doing a "background check" on the speech-act in question. The experienced critic will also find valuable materials that will save many frustrating hours of aimless searching. Unlike many reference guides, however, the arrangement used here is functional rather than topical: Each heading constitutes a common critical question needing a scholarly answer. While not attempting to survey all existing materials a critic might need, this guide suggests ways to research (1) the speaker's background, (2) the general topic of the discourse in question, (3) the specific topic, (4) significant information about the audience, (5) their social background, (6) the general rhetorical environment, (7) major critical studies on like subjects, (8) critical studies in scholarly journals, (9) critical studies in published anthologies, and (10) materials available through computer searches.

In addition to sources for accessing academic research, there are two kinds of works listed below: reference books, which contain summary or statistical information, and bibliographies (lists of works on particular periods or subjects). Reference books (dictionaries, encyclopedias, biography collections, etc.) are useful for obtaining specific facts or for organizing a general outline for a critical report. Bibliographies do not themselves contain historical information but serve as guides to finding previously published studies on a given topic. Both kinds of works reduce the time a critic must spend doing extratextual, background research.

As an additional aid to the critic, Library of Congress call numbers have been inserted after each citation provided. While L.C. numbers will vary somewhat from library to library, those provided here will shorten the time spent looking for library materials. Naturally, none of these reference helps can alone produce insightful criticism. But library materials can produce *informed* criticism and that is surely the first step on the road to real insight.

1.0 GATHERING INFORMATION ABOUT THE SPEAKER

An important consideration for any analyst is understanding the person who produced the rhetorical message. Biographical information may yield not only demographic answers important to understanding the speaker/audience relationship but can also hint at how a speaker's past may have influenced his or her current rhetoric. Research on Ronald Reagan, for example, reveals that because he grew up during the Depression, came to maturity during Franklin Roosevelt's presidency, acquired training as a sportscaster and actor, and had his ideological roots developed during the bountiful nineteen fifties and turbulent nineteen sixties, his rhetoric of the eighties had a truly distinctive, some say revolutionary, flavor. In countless ways, then, biographical research can enhance critical understanding.

Biographical collections contain synopses of well-known individuals' lives, outlining especially their milestones and accomplishments. Certain biographical collections are appropriate for use depending on the time period being studied, on a speaker's place of birth, or on his or her occupation. If the critic desires a complete listing of available biography collections, the *Biography Index* **(1.1a)** would be appropriate. But by knowing the approximate date and national origin of the speaker, the critic can use *Who Was Who in America* **(1.2c)** to learn more about a former leader (such as Patrick Henry) or *Who's Who in America* **(1.3d)** to research a current speaker (such as Geraldine Ferraro), or the *Biographical Dictionary of the American Congress* **(1.4a)** if the speaker is a member of a specialized group or of a certain profession (such as Chrysler Corporation head, Lee Iacocca).

1.1 Guide to Biography Collections

1.1a *Biography Index: A Cumulative Guide to Biographical Material in Books and Magazines* (New York: H. W. Wilson Company, 1949–present). [Z 5301 .B5]

1.2 Biography Collections—Historical

1.2a *Who Was Who.* (British) Vol. I, 1897–1915; Vol. II, 1916–1928; Vol. III, 1929–1940; Vol. IV, 1941–1950 (London: Allen and Unwin, 1953). [DA 28 .W65]

1.2b *Who Was Who in America.* Vol. I, 1897–1942; Vol. II, 1943–1950; Vol. III, 1951–1960 (Chicago: Marquis Who's Who, 1943, 1950, 1962). The years covered in each volume indicate the dates of death for those included. [E 176 .W64]

1.2c *Who Was Who in America: Historical Volume, 1607–1896* (Chicago: Marquis Who's Who, 1963). [E 176 .W64]

1.3 Biography Collections—Past to Present

1.3a   *Dictionary of National Biography* (Oxford: Oxford University Press, 1922). Leslie Stephan and Sidney Lee, eds. Supplement (Boston: G. K. Hall, 1966). [DA 28 .D4]

1.3b   *Dictionary of American Biography* (New York: Charles Scribner's Sons, 1928–1958), including supplements. If the subject died after 1928, check the supplements. Supplement I covers deaths through the end of 1935; supplement II, 1940; supplement III, 1945. [E 17]

1.3c   *National Cyclopedia of American Biography* (Ann Arbor: University Microfilms, 1967). [E 176 .N28]

1.3d   *Who's Who in America* (Chicago: Marquis Who's Who, 1897–present). [E 176 .W64]

1.3e   *New York Time Obituary Index.* [CT 213 .N47]

1.3f   *Current Biography* (New York: H. W. Wilson Co., 1940–present). To locate the volume, check *Current Biography: Cumulated Index, 1940–1970.* [CT 100 .I5]

1.3g   *International Who's Who* (London: Europa, 1935–present). [CT 213 .N47]

1.4 Biography Collections—Specialized (Occupation or Group)

1.4a   *Biographical Dictionary of the American Congress, 1774–1961* (Washington, D.C.: Government Printing Office, 1961). [JK 1010 .A54 1961]

1.4b   *Biographic Register of the United States State Department* (Washington, D.C.: Government Printing Office, 1869–present). This is an annual volume; subjects are catalogued according to the years in which they served in the State Department. [JK 1010 .W64]

1.4c   *Biographic Dictionary of the United States Executive, 1774–1971* (Westport, CT: Greenwood, 1971). [E 176 .B576]

1.4d   *Who's Who of American Women* (Chicago: Marquis Who's Who, 1973). [CT 3260 .W5]

1.4e   *Who Was Who in American Politics.* [E 176 .M873]

2.0 UNDERSTANDING THE GENERAL TOPIC

Since one cannot understand a message fully unless one understands the topic with which it deals, encyclopedias and yearbooks can provide answers to the basic questions surrounding a given subject matter: who, what, where, why, when, and how. Knowing the answer to these questions helps the critic better understand how a given message came to be.

Encyclopedias define important terms, present general information on a particular subject, relate geographical facts, array statistical data, and much more. They thus are a good beginning point for any comprehensive critical investigation. For example, a critic investigating President Franklin D. Roosevelt's first inaugural address could use encyclopedias to gather general information about the Depression, statistics on unemployment in 1932, and the meaning of such key terms as "Black Tuesday." However, encyclopedias do not contain serious development or interpretation of historical subjects and should not be depended upon for substantive analyses of an event or time period. In the Roosevelt case, for example, important political analyses concerning factors leading up to the Depression and Roosevelt's response to them would be difficult to discern from such general resources, forcing the critic to consider more detailed scholarly materials.

General questions can be answered by consulting such encyclopedias as the *Encyclopedia Britannica* (**2.1a**), while commentaries on specific time periods are better found in specialized encyclopedias dealing with world or American history (**2.2a** and **2.2b**, for example). Still other resources contain such detailed information as membership figures for the American Catholic Church, the theological foundations of the Muslim faith (**2.3b** and **2.3d**), or the activities of specific associations like the American Communist Party (**2.3a**).

Yearbooks, in turn, summarize factual information and offer the critic a way of understanding such things as trends in voting behavior (**2.4a** and **2.4b**) or worldwide expenditures on food and armaments (**2.4c**). Analysis of George Bush's foreign policy rhetoric, for example, might be better understood after researching the historical background of the arms race and levels of arms expenditures for the superpowers in the late 1980s. Through such inquiries, a critic can more fully understand the context in which a message was produced.

2.1 General Encyclopedias

2.1a *Encyclopedia Britannica* (Chicago: Encyclopedia Brittannica Corporation, 1970). (See Revised Editions.) [G 1019 .E5]

2.1b *Encyclopedia Americana* (New York: The Americana Corporation). [AE 5 .B333]

2.1c *Collier's Encyclopedia* (New York: Crowell Collier and Macmillan). [AE 5 .C682 1985]

2.1d   *Compton's Pictured Encyclopedia and Fact-Index* (Chicago: Encyclopedia Britannica, Inc.). [A 65 .C73]

2.2 Historical Encyclopedias

2.2a   *An Encyclopedia of World History, Ancient, Medieval and Modern, Chronologically Arranged* (Boston: Houghton Mifflin Company, 1972). William L. Langer, ed. [D 21 .L27 1972]

2.2b   *Harper Encyclopedia of the United States History from 458 A.D. to 1972* (New York: Harper & Row, 1973). [E174 .L92]

2.2c   *Encyclopedia of American History* (New York: Harper and Row, 1979). [E 174.5 M847 1979]

2.3 Specialized Encyclopedias

2.3a   *Encyclopedia of Associations* (Detroit: Gale Research Co., 1987) (annual). Karin E. Koeh and Susan B. Martin, eds. [HS 17 .G3]

2.3b   *The Encyclopedia of American Religions* (Wilmington, NC: McGrath Publishing Co., 1978). J. Gordon Melton. [BL 2530 .U6 M443]

2.3c   *International Encyclopedia of the Social Sciences* (New York: Macmillan, 1968). David L. Sills, ed. [H 40 .A2 I5 1979]

2.3d   *Sacrementum Mundi: An Encyclopedia of Theology* (New York: Herder and Herder, c1968–1970). [BR 95 .S23 1968]

2.4 Yearbooks and Statistical Resources

2.4a   *Statesman's Yearbook* (New York: Macmillan, 1864–present). [JA 51 .S7]

2.4b   *Political Handbook of the World* (New York: Harper & Row, 1927–present). Council on Foreign Relations. Walter H. Mallory, ed. [JF 37 .P6]

2.4c   *Historical Tables, 58 B.C.–A.D. 1955.* (New York: St. Martin's Press, 1956). Sigfrid H. Steinberg. [D 11 .S8 1973]

2.4d   *Historical Statistics of the United States, Colonial Times to 1957* (Washington, D.C.: Bureau of the Census, 1960). [HA 202 .A385]

2.4e   *Statistical Abstract of the United States* (Washington, D.C.: Government Printing Office, 1878–present). Annual. [HA 202 .U572]

3.0 RESEARCHING THE SPECIFIC TOPIC

Government documents are invaluable in researching the background of any rhetorical message, but especially for those produced in political or governmental circles. For example, if one were researching a Supreme Court opinion or a speech delivered on the floor of Congress, government documents would provide not only complete reprintings of these texts but also summaries of the discussions surrounding the messages being studied (that is, the persuasive field).

The works listed below are guides to books, pamphlets, speeches, treaties, hearings, reports, etc., issued by public agencies. Happily, the major publications of the U.S. government are available at many libraries. General questions concerning what is available through the Government Printing Office are answered by consulting subject guides to these voluminous sources (**3.2a, 3.2b,** or **3.2c**), while more specific questions concerning such items as Congressional speeches or debates are answered in others (**3.3d**).

3.1 International Agencies

3.1a   *Guide to League of Nations Publications: A Bibliographical Survey of the Work of the League, 1920–1947* (New York: Columbia University Press, 1951). Hans Aufricht, comp. [JX 1975 .A947]

3.1b   *United Nations Documents Index* (New York: United Nations Library, 1950–present). This volume is issued annually. [JX 1977 .A7]

3.2 United States Government Publications—General Guides

3.2a   *United States Government Publications* (New York: H. W. Wilson, 1949). Anne Boyd, comp. [Z 1223 .Z7B7]

3.2b   *Subject Guide to United States Government Publications* (Chicago: American Library Association, 1947). Herbert Hirshberg and Carl Melinat, comps. [Z 1223 .Z7H57]

3.2c   *A Popular Guide to Government Publications* (New York: Columbia University Press, 1968). William P. Leidy, comp. [Z 1223 .Z7L4 1976]

3.2d   *Subject Guide to Major United States Government Publications* (Chicago: American Library Association, 1968). Ellen P. Jackson, comp. [Z 1223 .Z7532 1968]

3.2e   *Government Publications and Their Use* (Washington, D.C.: Brookings Institute, 1961). Lawrence Schmeckebier and Roy Eastin, eds. [JA 37 .B72]

3.3 United States Government Publications—Specific

3.3a   *Monthly Catalogue of United States Government Publications* (Washington, D.C.: Government Printing Office, 1895–present). [Z 1223 .A18]

3.3b   *Checklist of United States Public Documents, 1789–1909* (Washington, D.C.: Government Printing Office, 1911 and J. W. Edwards, 1958). [Z1223 .A113]

3.3c   *Catalogue of Public Documents of the United States, 1893–1940* (Washington, D.C.: Government Printing Office, 1895–1945). [O 15 .73 .Un35]

3.3d   *Congressional Record: United States Congress* (Washington, D.C.: Government Printing Office, 1873–present). [J 11 .R5]

4.0 GATHERING INFORMATION ABOUT THE AUDIENCE

Newspapers are often an excellent resource for understanding a rhetorical event and may be used as primary source material. As such, newspapers become an important means of understanding what the people of a given time were reading about and what they were saying about the times in which they lived. For example, the editorial pages of important newspapers such as the *Washington Post* and *The New York Times* would be important resources for a critic seeking general commentary about, say, the Iran-Contra crisis of the late 1980s.

In most cases, the critic will have access to only a few newspapers held in his or her school or public library. To discover which newspapers exist and where they are held, newspaper directories can be most helpful **(4.1a and 4.1b)**. Newspaper indexes are also important time-savers for the critic because they are arranged topically. As a result, the critic need not know the date of the event's occurrence to find when particular newspapers contained articles or editorials on a particular subject. Using such indexes, a critic may search for information about a specific event (such as the assassination of President John Kennedy) by knowing the exact date. However, a critic could find articles dealing with events not confined to a particular day or week (such as the Civil

Rights Movement) by employing an index topic heading **(4.1a, 4.2b, 4.2c, and 4.2d)**.

Additionally, oral history collections transmit similar important information about the audiences responding to a particular rhetorical event, including what stories remained important for groups of people. A critic could, for example, employ Columbia University's *Oral History Collection* **(4.3a)** when studying certain subcultures (such as residents of Appalachia who possess information about a topic and who have passed that information down to their descendants in oral instead of written form).

4.1 Newspaper Directories

4.1a *American Newspapers, 1821–1936: A Union List of Files Available in the United States and Canada* (New York: H. W. Wilson, 1937). Winifred Gerould, ed. [Z 6945 .A53]

4.1b *Newspaper in Microfilm: A Union Check List* (Washington, D.C.: Library of Congress, 1963). George Schwegman, Jr., ed. [Z6945 .N64]

4.2 Newspaper Indexes

4.2a *New York Times Index* (New York: New York Times, 1913–present). [AI 21 .N45]

4.2b *New York Daily Tribune Index* (New York: Tribune Association, 1876–1907).

4.2c *Official Index to the Times* [of London] (London: 1907–present). [AI 21 .T46]

4.2d *Christian Science Monitor Index* (Corvallis, OR: 1960–present). [AI 21 .C462C40]

4.3 Oral History Collections

4.3a *The Oral History Collection of Columbia University* (New York: Columbia University Oral History Research Office, 1964). [O 16 .773 .C7230]

4.3b *Oral History in the United States: A Directory* (New York: Oral History Association, 1971). Gary L. Shumway, comp. Locates and describes oral history collections. [E 175.4 .S58]

5.0 RESEARCHING THE SOCIAL BACKGROUND OF THE MESSAGE

A subject bibliography lists printed works on a particular topic. The bibliographies listed here represent only a small sample of the available works on particular persons, time periods, or events, but they are the most well respected and accessible works. Topical in nature, these bibliographies list works useful for discovering the general historical background of a particular rhetorical event. These sources go into more detail than do the more general encyclopedias mentioned earlier. Therefore, their usefulness increases with the depth of analysis required of the critic. If, for example, one wanted to know about the social and cultural trends during the Jacksonian era as background for analyzing the debates over a national bank, one would consult *American Social History Before 1860* **(5.1e)**. Here, a detailed understanding of the factionalism dividing the country on this issue could be gained, as well as of the many audience constraints placed on Andrew Jackson's rhetoric. A specialized bibliography such as *The History of American Presidential Elections: 1798–1968* **(5.2b)** catalogues those articles dealing with specific events (such as the Kennedy-Nixon debates before the 1960 presidential election). A critic interested in the genesis of presidential debates and their effects upon elections would definitely consult these readings. Furthermore, a division is set aside here for women and blacks **(5.3)** because of researchers' increasing interest in the discourse these groups produce.

5.1 General History

5.1a   *American Historical Association Guide to Historical Literature.* (New York: Macmillan, 1961). George F. Howe et al., eds.

5.1b   *Historical Bibliographies* (New York: Russell, 1965). Edith M. Coulter and Melanie Gerstenfeld, eds. [O 16 .9 .C832H 1965]

5.1c   *Harvard Guide to American History* (Cambridge, MA: Harvard University Press, 1974). Oscar Handlin et al., eds. [Z 1236 .H27]

5.1d   *American Social History Since 1860.* (New York: Appleton Century Crofts, 1970). Robert H. Bremner, ed. [Z 1361 .C6B7]

5.1e   *American Social History Before 1860.* (New York: Appleton Century Crofts, 1970). Gerald G. Grob, ed. [O 16 30973 .G892]

5.2 Specialized Bibliographies—General Political

5.2a *Guide to the Diplomatic History of the United States, 1775–1921* (Washington, D.C.: Government Printing Office, 1935). Samuel F. Bemis and Grace G. Griffin, eds. [E 183.7 .B457]

5.2b *History of American Presidential Elections: 1789–1968* (New York: McGraw-Hill, 1971). Arthur M. Schlesinger, Jr., ed. [E 183.S28]

5.2c *Index to United States Documents Relating to Foreign Affairs, 1828–1861* (Washington, D.C.: Carnegie Institute, 1914–1921). Adelaide R. Hasse, ed. [Z 1223 .Z3 H2]

5.3 Specialized Bibliographies—Special Groups

5.3a *The Negro in America: A Bibliography* (Cambridge, MA: Harvard University Press, 1970). Elizabeth W. Miller, comp. [Z 1361 .N39 M5]

5.3b *The Negro in the United States: A Research Guide* (Bloomington, IN: University of Indiana Press, 1965. Edwin K. Welsch, comp. [Z 1361 .N39]

5.3c *The American Woman in Colonial and Revolutionary Times, 1565–1800: A Syllabus with Bibliography* (Philadelphia: University of Pennsylvania Press, 1962). Eurenie Leonard, et al., eds. [HQ 1423 .L4321]

5.3d *Notable American Women, 1607–1950: A Bibliographical Dictionary* (Cambridge, MA: Harvard University Press, 1971). Edwin T. James, ed. [CT 3260 .N57]

5.3e *American Ethnic Groups: A Sourcebook for the 1970's* (Mt. Pleasant, IA: Social Science and Sociological Resources, 1973). Jack Kinton, ed. [Z 1361 .E4 K55 1976]

5.3f *Religion in American Life* (Princeton, NJ: Princeton University Press, 1961). Nelson R. Burr, ed. [BR 515 .B875]

6.0 UNDERSTANDING THE VERBAL ENVIRONMENT

Important to any critic's rhetorical analysis is an understanding of the "climate of communication" surrounding a particular event. Such climates include how historical changes have affected a term's meaning, colloquial expressions used in popular rhetoric, or terminology used to discuss new ideas. This verbal environment also includes how terms operated within a specific historical context—for example, how "suffrage" became an important term for the women's movement of the mid-to-late 1800s.

Included in the following list are general and specialized dictionaries the critic may use to understand how language functioned in certain historical epochs. For example, if a critic wanted to understand the origin of a term such as "ideology," he or she might consult such different sources as the *Oxford English Dictionary* **(6.1a)** in search of the word's etymology or look at *White's Political Dictionary* **(6.2e)** for an understanding of how the term functioned in common political parlance. By understanding how terminology was used at a particular time, a critic can begin to understand how ideas were popularized and, hence, made useful in everyday persuasion.

6.1 Dictionaries—General

6.1a *Oxford English Dictionary* (Oxford: Clarendon Press, 1888–1928). James A. H. Murray et al., eds. "A New English Dictionary on Historical Principles." [PE 1625 .W3 1959]

6.1b *Grolier's International Dictionary* (Danbury, CT: Grolier Inc., 1981). [PE 1625 .67 1981]

6.2 Dictionaries—Specialized

6.2a *Webster's Guide to American History* (Springfield, MA: G. and C. Merriam, 1971). [E 174 .5 .W5]

6.2b *Concise Dictionary of American History* (New York: Charles Scribner's Sons, 1962). Thomas C. Cochran and Wayne Andrews, eds. [E 174 .D522 1983]

6.2c *Dictionary of American History* (New York: Charles Scribner's Sons, 1942–1961). James T. Adams, ed. (Revised edition, 1983) [E 174 .D522 1983]

6.2d *Dictionary of Social Science* (Washington, D.C.: Public Affairs Press, 1959). John T. Zadrozny, ed. [H 41 .73]

6.2e *White's Political Dictionary* (New York: World Publishing Company, 1947). Wilbur White, ed. ([D 419 .W5 1948]

RHETORIC AND RELIGIOUS EXPERIENCE

Critical Profile 13.4   The Quaker Rhetoric of Rudeness and Rejection

What is the typical image of a Quaker? Peaceful, gentle, and above all, polite? Not so, says Richard Bauman, now of Indiana University. Bauman studied the rhetoric of the early Quakers in seventeenth-century England and found that the first generation of Quakers was considered both rude and arrogant, even obscene. In fact, long before nude "streakers" shocked the American public in the late 1960s, English Quakers used nudity as a form of public protest. Offending the manners of their fellow citizens was one of the means the Quakers used to establish their separate identity as a religious movement.

The rhetorical style that separated the Quakers from other seventeenth-century Britons was what the Quakers called "plain speech." Plain speech was not just plain. It was also minimal speech. "Let thy words be few" was the Quaker maxim. "Carnal talk" and "idle words," such as giving or acknowledging a greeting, were to be shunned. Saying "Good morning" to a neighbor would be an invitation to idle chatter, which was also sinful. In addition, plain speech demanded literalness. If a Quaker said "Good morning" to a non-Quaker it would be a lie, because the unsaved non-Quaker could only be expected to have an evil morning.

Even the Quaker use of the pronoun "thou" was considered rude by most of their fellow citizens. Accepted usage in the 1650s for most of the British was to address equals and superiors as "you" and inferiors as "thou." Quaker insistence on using "thou" thus provoked hostility in others, who took it as a sign of contempt.

Although Quaker speech aimed at literalness, some Quakers tried to use nonverbal metaphors. These were usually shocking actions aimed at members of other churches. Quakers would appear naked in public to signify the danger of "not being clothed with the spirit of the Lord" and as an indication that these others must be stripped of their false faith. Unfortunately, these esoteric meanings were not clear to non-Quakers, who simply saw them as an insult to public morality.

By their words and actions, the Quakers managed to offend most of their fellow citizens. The result was ostracism and persecution. However, the separation that ensued increased the Quakers' cohesion. Persecution simply proved to the Quakers that they were "taking up the cross" and so gaining salvation. Thus, in a roundabout way, the strange rhetorical style of the Quakers succeeded in making them both a separate and a unified social movement.

Profiled by: Jim Mackin
Citation: Bauman (1983)

Critical Profile 13.5   The Rhythm of Public Discourse

In contrast to most rhetorical analysis that focuses on the *linguistic* features of messages, Bruce A. Rosenberg, now of Brown University, has studied a *paralinguistic* factor, namely, rhythm. Inspired by an earlier study of the now extinct oral tradition of the Yugoslavian *guslars* ("supposedly the last remaining singers of oral epics in the West"), Rosenberg wanted to learn more about oral composition. More specifically, he hoped to test the notion "that the epic singer composed his oral poems by the judicious manipulation of metrically consistent phrases, some memorized and some spontaneously composed, which enabled him to spin out stories at great length." Before he could study such rhythmic phrases or "oral formulas," however, Rosenberg had to find an existing oral tradition.

In the chanted sermons of American folk preachers, Rosenberg discovered a thriving tradition of oral composition. "Originally from the South, many preachers (most of whom are Negro) compose their sermons spontaneously by using techniques identical to those employed by [the] *guslars.*" These sermons differ from other epic narratives, however, in that they almost never rhyme. But Rosenberg claims that they are, nonetheless, poetic by virtue of their metrical lines and use of language. He calls this preaching style a "folk art."

Rosenberg qualifies his categorization of folk preaching as an oral tradition in yet another way. Although folk sermons are characterized by formulas, they mediate (often "ineptly") between oratory and oral narrative. That is, most sermons will be partly spoken and partly chanted. Moreover, much of the preacher's performance as an "epic singer" is dependent on the fervor of the congregation's synchronized input. Audience participation ("That's preaching!" or "Amen!") encourages the preacher's chanting. Each preacher has a personal repertoire of phrases (such as "Ain't God alright?") used to heighten the congregation's emotional response to the sermon.

In the rhythmic interplay between preacher and congregation the sermon becomes an oral narrative. In fact, the rhythm of the cooperative chant—regardless of the preacher's words themselves—becomes the essence of religious rhetoric. According to Rosenberg, moments such as these make folk preaching a rare species of traditional oral narrative, a folk art still in evidence throughout the United States today.

Profiled by: Kerry Riley
Citation: Rosenberg (1970)

7.0 ACCESSING POPULAR COMMENTARY

Examining what other careful observers have said about a given rhetorical event often proves useful to the critic. Such an examination insures that the critic's report does not merely replicate existing knowl-

---

Critical Profile 13.6 The Puritan: Relic or Close Relative?

Why is there so often a split in religious rhetoric between the heart and the head? For instance, why do some televangelists argue for immediate *emotional* conversion to Christianity while others use *logical-rational* exhortations, encouraging us to find salvation in a life based on Christian ideals? Is this disparity in rhetorical approaches a recent development? Is it simply a matter of opposing doctrines or biblical interpretations? Eugene E. White of Penn State University argues that the antagonism between emotionalism and rationalism in religion is neither new nor simply a matter of interpretation. This split is an inheritance from the Great Awakening, an attempt on the part of Puritan revivalists in the 1740s to regain social control that traditional, more rational, forms of preaching had failed to maintain for them.

According to White, the inflammatory rhetoric of the revivalists, replete with images of hell and eternal damnation, disrupted "the precarious balance which the founding Puritans maintained between reason and emotion." The fear appeals of the Great Awakening made emotion, for the first time, an *issue* in religion. By radically disturbing the equilibrium of religious discourse, the Great Awakening stands as "the most important social movement in the Colonies prior to the Revolution." As instigator of the heart-head conflict in religion, Puritan rhetoric is more than an uninteresting "ancestral relic." Indeed, there is perhaps no better model for understanding the contemporary religious scene with its smorgasbord of choices—communes, meditation, evangelism, tongue-speaking, and so forth.

The Great Awakening culminated in the horrific sermons of Jonathan Edwards. His speaking was characterized by a consummate use of proximity and concreteness. Consider part of his description of hell:

> [The unconverted] never will be able to find any cooling stream or fountain . . . no, nor so much as a drop of water to cool their tongues . . . and will have no rest day or night for ever and ever . . . There will be great struggles, lamentable groans and pantings, and it may be convulsions . . . imagine yourself to be cast into a fiery oven, or a great furnace . . . O then, how would your hearts sink, if you knew you must bear it for ever and ever!

Fear appeals such as Edwards's tipped the balance in Puritanism toward emotionalism, a legacy that continues to make salvation a matter of the heart rather than the head for many ministers in the twentieth century.

Profiled by: Kerry Riley
Citation: White (1972)

edge. In addition, by surveying what has been said, a critic may come to understand where his or her special insights fit into the existing corpus of knowledge. For example, much has been written in popular periodicals about President Ronald Reagan's avoidance of press conferences in the latter part of his presidency, but a critic might discover that very little has been writen about how Mr. Reagan altered the press conference's essential *form*, thus providing a possible inroad to research. A thorough review of the literature may produce an answer to such a question, saving the critic the embarrassment of merely duplicating someone else's effort.

Because rhetoric is a *popular* art, it is often helpful to examine commentaries written for the general public. Particularly useful in this regard are such weeklies as *Newsweek* or the *National Review*. While thousands of publications exist worldwide, periodical guides (for example, **7.1a** and **7.1b**) can help to narrow the search by providing the general content and location of the most important periodicals. Once those periodicals have been located, indexes may be employed to find articles related to the specific subject under consideration. Such indexes are usually organized by subject and contain all articles on a given topic that appeared in the periodicals indexed. When attempting to discover popular reactions to President Kennedy's visit to the Berlin Wall, for example (where Kennedy gave his famous "Ich Bin Ein Berliner" speech), one might employ indexes such as *The Reader's Guide to Periodical Literature* or *The Essay and General Literature Index* (**7.2a** and **7.2e**).

Specialized indexes are also available. A critic studying the same Kennedy speech, for example, might check *Heresies* and *Foreign Affairs* (**7.3d** or **7.3f**) for articles with a more scholarly bent. These latter periodicals will provide the critic with more in-depth accounts of such events as the Soviet Union's shift in policy during the Stalin regime, a phenomenon that George Kennan outlined in his famous 1947 article in *Foreign Affairs*.

7.1 Periodical Guides

7.1a   *Union Lists of Serials in Libraries of the United States and Canada* (New York: H. W. Wilson, 1943). [Z 6945 .U45]

7.1b   *New Serial Titles: A Union List of Serials Commencing Publication after December 31, 1949* (Washington, D.C.: Library of Congress, 1953–present). [Z 6945 .U5S43]

7.1c   *World List of Historical Periodicals* (New York: H. W. Wilson, 1939). Pierre Caron and Marc Jaryc, eds. [Z 6201 .A1C3]

7.1d *Historical Periodicals: An Annotated World List of Historical and Related Serial Periodicals* (Santa Barbara, CA: Clio Press, 1961). Eric H. Boehm and Lalit Adolphus, eds. [Z 6205 .B6]

7.2 Periodical Indexes—General

7.2a *Reader's Guide to Periodical Literature* (New York: H. W. Wilson, 1900–present). [AI 3 .R48]

7.2b *Nineteenth Century Reader's Guide to Periodical Literature* (New York: H. W. Wilson, 1944). [AI 3 .R496]

7.2c *Poole's Index to Periodical Literature, 1802–1881* (Boston: Houghton Mifflin Co., 1891). There is a supplement covering 1882–1906. [AI 3 .P7]

7.2d *International Index to Periodicals* (New York: H. W. Wilson). [AI 3 .R49]

7.2e *Essay and General Literature Index* (New York: H. W. Wilson, 1800–present). This work lists articles published in collections of readings rather than in periodicals. [AI 3 .E75]

7.3 Specialized Periodical Indexes

7.3a *Historical Abstracts, 1775–1945: Bibliography of the World's Periodical Literature* (Santa Barbara, CA: Clio Press, 1955–present). Eric H. Boehm, ed. [D 299 .H52]

7.3b *Social Science and Humanities Index* (New York: H. W. Wilson, 1907–present). Please note that after 1975 the one index split to become the *Social Science Index* and the *Humanities Index*. [AI 3 .S6]

7.3c *Women's Magazines 1693–1968* (London: Michael Joseph, 1970). Cynthia White, comp. [PN 5124 .W6005]

7.3d *From Radical Left to Extreme Right* (Ann Arbor: Campus Publishers, 1970–present). Robert H. Muller, et al. This index covers periodicals of dissent and protest. [Z 7165 .U5M8]

7.3e *American Historical Review: General Index for Volumes XLI–LX, 1935–1955* (New York: Macmillan, 1962). [E 171 .A53]

7.3f *Foreign Affairs 50-Year Index: Vols. 1–50, 1922–1972.* (New York: Council on Foreign Relations, 1973). Robert J. Palmer, comp. [P 410 .F6]

8.0 ACCESSING SCHOLARLY COMMENTARY (JOURNALS)

Studies of particular rhetorical events exist in English, history, political science, sociology, as well as in communication-related journals. Reviewing the current literature on a particular topic often suggests not only what academics have said about rhetorical events but also gives indispensable insights into the relevant background information about that topic. For example, historians and political scientists, as well as communication scholars, have often commented upon the rhetorical failings of President Jimmy Carter. By reading these analyses before analyzing his July, 1979, address on the energy crisis, a critic would understand how Carter's own rhetorical history affected what he said in that much-noted (and little-appreciated) speech.

Some journals have their own cumulative indexes (like that of *Foreign Affairs* listed above) and thus can be a useful place to begin one's research. Particularly helpful for rhetorical scholars, however, is the *Index to Journals in Communication Studies Through 1985*—Annandale, VA: Speech Communication Association, 1987. Ronald J. Matlon and Peter C. Facciola, compilers. [Z 5630 .N37 1987]. This publication indexes articles in communication journals by author, subject (for example, the rhetoric of film), and by periodical (for example, *Quarterly Journal of Speech*).

In addition to the major communication journals listed below are journals from English, political science, history, and sociology. While many articles in these journals deal with more general theoretical issues within those disciplines, rhetorical scholars can often find within them message-based studies that shed direct light on rhetorical exchanges. For example, English scholars such as Edward Corbett have written on civil rights protest rhetoric in *College Composition and Communication* (**8.3c**), while political scientist Jeffrey Tulis has published articles dealing with presidential rhetoric in *Presidential Studies Quarterly* (**8.5a**). Historian Norman Graebner has written on foreign policy rhetoric in various history journals (**8.4a** and **8.4f**) and Talcott Parsons's discussions of social movements in sociology journals (**8.6a, 8.6b,** and **8.6c**) should be read by any student of rhetorical movements.

Unpublished doctoral dissertations also contain extensive background research and innovative interpretations of a large number of rhetorical events. Over 417,000 dissertations awarded by North American institutions are indexed in the *Comprehensive Dissertation Index*, which covers all academic disciplines. Critics should consult these indexes for abstracts about particular subjects by first checking the appropriate volume of *Dissertation Abstracts* (**8.7a**). (See, for example, the Literature and Languages volume for communication-related dissertations.) Then, the critic can survey particular dissertations by title and author for those relevant to his or her study. If appropriate dissertations are found through the abstracts, microfilm copies of the entire work may be obtained through interlibrary loan or purchased directly through Dissertation Publishing, University Microfilms International, 300 North Zeeb Road, P. O. Box 1764, Ann Arbor, Michigan 48106.

8.1 Communication Journals—Critical Studies

8.1a *Quarterly Journal of Speech* [PN 4071 .P3]
8.1b *Southern Speech Communication Journal* [PN 4071 .S65]
8.1c *Communication Quarterly* [PN 4071 .T6]
8.1d *Western Speech Communication Journal* [PN 4071 .W5]
8.1e *Central States Speech Journal* [PN 4062 .C45]
8.1f *Philosophy and Rhetoric* [B 1 .P572]
8.1g *Rhetorica* [PN 183 .R485]
8.1h *Communication Monographs* [PN 4077 .S6]

8.2 Mass Communication Journals (Often containing critical studies)

8.2a *Critical Studies in Mass Communication* [P 87 .C94]
8.2b *Journal of Communication* [808.05 .J826]
8.2c *Journalism Quarterly* [PN 4700 .J7]
8.2d *Communication* [D 87 .C8648]

8.3 English Literature Journals (Often containing critical studies)

8.3a *American Quarterly* [AP 2 .A3985]
8.3b *American Studies* [E 169.1 A437]
8.3c *College Composition and Communication* [PE 1001 .C6]
8.3d *Pretext*
8.3e *Style* [PE 1 .S89]

8.4 History Journals (Occasional studies of historically significant texts)

8.4a   Current History [D 410 .C8]
8.4b   Journal of Economic History [HC 10 .J63]
8.4c   American Historical Review [E 171 .A53]
8.4d   Journal of American History [F 351 .M69]
8.4e   Journal of Southern History [F 266 .T68]
8.4f   Journal of Modern History [D 1 .J62]

8.4 Political Science Journals (Occasional communication studies)

8.4a   American Journal of Political Science [JA 1 .A49646]
8.4b   American Political Science Review [JA 1 A6]
8.4c   Journal of Politics [JA 1 J67]
8.4d   Political Quarterly [JA 8 P61]
8.4e   Politics and Society [H1 P83]
8.4f   Polity [JA1 .P65]

8.5 Specialized Political Science Journals (Frequent communication studies)

8.5a   Presidential Studies Quarterly [JK 501 C44]
8.5b   Public Opinion [HN 90 P8 P82]
8.5c   Public Opinion Quarterly [HM 1 P8]
8.5d   Political Communication and Persuasion [JF 1525 .D8 P64]

8.6 Sociology Journals (Occasional critical studies)

8.6a   American Journal of Sociology [HM 1 A7]
8.6b   American Sociological Review [HM 1 A75]
8.6c   Annual Review of Sociology [HM 1 A763]
8.6d   Journal for the Scientific Study of Religion [RL 1 .J6]
8.6e   Sociological Quarterly [HM 1 .S69]
8.6f   Sociological Review [305 .S013]

8.7 Indexes to Doctoral Dissertations

8.7a *Dissertation Abstracts: Abstracts of Dissertations and Monographs in Microfilm* (Ann Arbor: University Microfilms). [Z 5053 .D57]

8.7b *Dissertations in History.* William F. Kuehl, ed. [Z 6201 .K8]

9.0 ACCESSING SCHOLARLY COMMENTARY (ANTHOLOGIES)

Some particularly important research has been compiled in published collections. While some of these critical studies may have been reprinted from journal articles, much of the research is original and cannot be accessed otherwise. Novice scholars should especially note how editors categorize these articles for hints on directions for possible new research. Particularly important are the following collections:

9.1 Studies of Speakers and Speeches—Historical

9.1a *A History and Criticism of American Public Address.* Vols. I–II (New York: McGraw-Hill Book Co., 1943). William N. Brigance, ed. [PS 400 .B75]

9.1b *A History and Criticism of American Public Address,* Vol. III (New York: Longmans, Green & Co., 1955). Marie Hochmuth, ed. [PS 400 .S66 112]

9.1c *American Orators Before 1900: Critical Studies and Sources* (Westport, CT: Greenwood Press, 1987). Bernard K. Duffy and Halford R. Ryan, eds. [PN 4055 .U5 A4 1987]

9.1d *American Rhetoric: Context and Criticism* (Carbondale, IL: Southern Illinois University Press, 1989). T. Benson, ed. [PE 2827. A44]

9.1e *History of Public Speaking in America* (Boston: Allyn and Bacon, Inc., 1965). Robert T. Oliver. [815.09 .OL4H]

9.1f *Historical Studies of Rhetoric and Rhetoricians* (Ithaca, NY: Cornell University Press, 1962). Raymond Howes, ed. [PN 4021 .H6]

9.1g *Studies in Rhetoric and Public Speaking in Honor of J. A. Winans* (New York: Russell and Russell, 1926). A. M. Drummond, ed. [PN 4012 .S7]

9.2 Studies of Speakers and Speeches—Historical: Specialized

9.2a   *The Oratory of Southern Demagogues* (Baton Rouge: Louisiana State University Press, 1973). Cal Logue and Howard Dorgan, eds. [PS 407.07]

9.2b   *Oratory in the Old South: 1828–1860* (Baton Rouge: Louisiana State University Press, 1970). Waldo W. Braden, ed. [PS 407 .07]

9.2c   *Oratory in the New South* (Baton Rouge: Louisiana State University Press, 1978). Waldo W. Braden, ed. [PS 407 .069]

9.2d   *The Rhetoric of Protest and Reform, 1878–1898* (Athens, OH: Ohio University Press, 1980). P. H. Boase, ed. [HN 90 .R49]

9.3 Studies of Speakers and Speeches—Contemporary and Specialized Topics

9.3a   *Essays in Presidential Rhetoric* (Dubuque, IA: Kendall/ Hunt, 1983). Theodore Windt and Beth Ingold, eds. [E 840 .P732]

9.3b   *Rhetoric of the People* (Amsterdam: Rudopi NV, 1974). Howard Barrett, ed. [PN 4055 .U5 B3]

9.3c   *American Orators of the Twentieth Century* (Westport, CT: Greenwood Press, 1987). Bernard K. Duffy and Halford R. Ryan, eds. [PN 4193 .P6A44]

9.3d   *Rhetoric in Transition: Studies in the Nature and Uses of Rhetoric* (University Park, PA: The Pennsylvania State University Press, 1980). Eugene E. White, ed. [PN 4061 .R47]

9.3e   *American Rhetoric from Roosevelt to Reagan* (Prospect Heights, IL: Waveland Press, 1983). Halford R. Ryan, ed. [PS 668 .A43]

9.3f   *Texts in Context: Critical Dialogues on Significant Episodes in American Political Rhetoric* (Davis, CA.: Hermagoras Press, 1989). Michael Leff and Fred Kauffeld, eds.

9.3g   *Oratorical Encounters: Selected Studies and Sources of Twentieth-Century Political Accusations and Apologies* (New York: Greenwood Press, 1988). Halford R. Ryan, ed. [PN 4193 P6 O68]

9.3h   *The Rhetoric of Black Power* (New York: Harper and Row, 1969). R. L. Scott and W. Brockriede, eds. [323.1196 .073]

9.4 Communication Collections—Theoretical Iss

9.4a   *Explorations in Rhetorical Criticism* (University Park, PA: The Pennsylvania State University Press, 1973). G. P. Mohrmann, Charles J. Stewart, Donovan J. Ochs, eds. [PN 4061 .M6]

9.4b   *Form and Genre: Shaping Rhetorical Action* (Annandale, VA: Speech Communication Association, 1978). Kathleen H. Jamieson and Karlyn K. Campbell, eds. [PN 4012 .F675]

9.4c   *Form, Genre, and the Study of Political Discourse* (Columbia, SC: University of South Carolina Press, 1986). H. W. Simons and A. A. Aghazarian, eds. [PN 239 .P64 F67]

9.4d   *Methods of Rhetorical Criticism* (Detroit: Wayne State University Press, 1980). B. Brock and R. Scott, eds. [PN 4061 .S037]

9.5 Communication Collections—Mass Media Focus

9.5a   *Rhetorical Dimensions in Media: A Casebook* (Dubuque, IA: Kendall/Hunt Publishing, 1984). T. W. Benson and M. J. Medhurst, eds. [P 91 .R46 1984]

9.5b   *Television: The Critical View* (New York: Oxford University Press, 1982). H. Newcomb, ed. [PN 1992.3 .V5 .T37]

9.5c   *American History, American Television* (New York: Frederick Ungar Publishing Co., 1983). J. E. O'Conner, ed. [PN 1992.3 .U5 .A48]

9.5d   *Television in Society* (New Brunswick, NJ: Transaction Books, 1987). A. A. Berger, ed. [PN 1992.6 .T417]

9.5e   *The New Television: A Public/Private Act.* (Cambridge, MA: Harvard University Press, 1978). D. Davis and A. Simmons, eds. [PN 1992.4 R56]

9.6 Political Science Collections—Communication Focus

9.6a   *The History and Philosophy of Rhetoric and Political Discourse,* Vol. I & II (Lanham, MD: University Press of America, 1987). Kenneth W. Thompson, ed. [PN 175. H57 1987]

9.6b   *Race for the Presidency: The Media and the Nomination Process.* (Englewood Cliffs, NJ: Prentice-Hall, 1978). J. D. Barber, ed. [JK 521 .R32]

9.6c   *International Handbook of Political Science* (Westport, CT: Greenwood Press, 1982). W. G. Andrews, ed. [JA 71 .I57]

9.6d   *Political Communication Yearbook: 1984* (Beverly Hills, CA: Sage Publications, 1985). D. N. Nimmo and L. L. Kaid, eds. [JA 1 .P56]

9.6e   *Politically Speaking: Cross-Cultural Studies of Rhetoric and Philosophy* (Philadelphia: Institute for the Study of Human Issues, 1981). R. Paine, ed. [PN 4193 .P64]

9.7 Sociology/Anthropology—(With focus on communication)

9.7a   *Research in Social Movements, Conflicts, and Change, Vol. 1* (Greenwich, CT: JAI Press, 1978). [HN 1 .R47]

9.7b   *Political Language and Oratory in Traditional Society* (London: Academic Press, 1975). M. Block, ed. [PN 493 .P6]

9.8 Collections of Research on Popular Culture

9.8a   *The Rhetorics of Popular Culture: Advertising, Advocacy, and Entertainment* (Westport, CT: Greenwood Press, forthcoming). Robert L. Root, ed.

9.8b   *Oxford Companion to American Literature* (New York: Oxford University Press, 1983). James D. Hart, ed. [PS 21 .H3 1983]

9.8c   *The Oxford Companion to American Theatre* (New York: Oxford University Press, 1984). Gerald Bordman, ed. [PN 2220 .B6 1984]

9.8d   *The Oxford Companion to Film* (New York: Oxford, 1976). Liz-Anne Bawden, ed. Contains articles on genres, directors, producers, actors, and notable films. [PN 1993.45 .B3]

9.8e   *Harvard Encyclopedia of American Ethnic Groups* (Cambridge, MA: Belknap Press of Harvard University Press, 1980). Stephen Thernstrom, ed. [E 184 .A1 H35]

9.8f   *Handbook of American Popular Culture* (Westport, CT: Greenwood Press, 1978–). M. Thomas Inge, ed. [E 169.1 .N2643]

10.0 COMPUTERIZED SEARCHES

Many of the above indexes are available through computer-based information services that greatly facilitate the modern scholar's research efforts. While not all libraries have computer-search capabilities, those that do offer these services have a variety of data bases from which to search for articles, manuscripts, and books as well as a variety of ways in which to search for them. Listed below are those the critic might find potentially useful. Also included is a brief description of how to use them.

ERIC

The ERIC database is a major source for locating literature on all aspects of education. Available in most research libraries for no charge, the computer database is the equivalent of two printed indexes: *Current Index to Journals in Education* (CIJE), which indexes articles from over 775 journals, and *Resources in Education* (RIE), which indexes and abstracts non-journal literature. Here, convention papers not published in scholarly journals may be found on microfiche. While most academic libraries have a large portion of the material listed in RIE available in hard copy, the remaining essays are easily accessible through the ERIC microfiche collection. CAUTION: Databases often have only the most recent years of ERIC indexes. Other fee-based online searches or printed indexes may yield more literature.

To use the ERIC database, the critic must be able to choose key search concepts corresponding to those used in the *Thesaurus of ERIC Descriptors*, 10th Edition. These descriptors (index terms) are those actually used to search the indexes. Once these descriptors are entered into the database, output is produced consisting of citations to journal articles (EJ numbers) and to documents on microfiche (ED numbers). These citations may direct the critic to journals with published articles dealing with a specific subject or a microfiche number, which may be used by reference librarians to acquire the needed essay.

DIALOG

DIALOG is useful in retrieving social science and humanities information in general. For example, DIALOG can access over 120 American political science journals, as well as CIS's (Congressional Information Service's indexes to Congressional Publications) and others. Basically, DIALOG works similarly to the ERIC system with descriptors being used to search a great variety of indexes. Dialog is a fee-based user service.

LEXIS

LEXIS gives access to a variety of legal information, including court opinions, and permits searches by significant words in case law. The search is done in the law itself, not in abstracts or digests. Among the materials accessible through LEXIS: decisions of all federal courts, the case law of the fifty states, *Shepard's Citations, The Federal Register, The Code of Federal Regulations,* briefs submitted to the U.S. Supreme Court, specialized Federal law libraries in specialized areas such as patent, copyright, communications, energy, labor, contracts, bankruptcy, materials from French and British law libraries, etc. Much of the 15th edition of *Encyclopedia Britannica* is also now available through LEXIS. Rhetorical scholars interested in finding not only opinions of the Supreme Court but also opinions of lower courts on the same topic should use LEXIS as a time-saving device. LEXIS is a fee-based system in most libraries.

NEXIS

NEXIS provides access to texts from newspapers, magazines, wire services, and encyclopedias. NEXIS stores online the texts of more than fifty publications. Among the databases accessible through NEXIS: *Congressional Quarterly Weekly Report, Editorial Research Reports, Dun's Business Month,* The AP, UPI, and PR newswires, *Economic Week, The ABA Banking Journal, The Economist, Advertising Compliance Service, Latin American Political Report,* among others.

BIBL

The BIBL File contains reference periodicals, pamphlets, GPO (Government Printing Office) publications, United Nations documents, and special interest/lobbyist publications. The Congressional Research Service's Library Services Division determines the significance of the material to its congressional users and enters it into the file. Typically, a citation lists the author's name, article title, title of publication, volume, date, and pagination for periodicals or place of publication, publisher, and date of monographs, as well as annotations and descriptions.

LCCC (Library of Congress Computerized Catalog)

The LCCC File contains over a million records representing the books in the Library's MARC data base, English-language books printed from 1968 on or catalogued since 1969, French-language books from 1973, and German, Portuguese, and Spanish-language books since 1975; additional languages are being added to the file. A bibliographic reference from this file usually includes the author's name, monograph title, place of publication, publisher, and date, as well as descriptive annotations, subject headings, LC and Dewey Decimal classification numbers, LC card number, and the International Standard Book Number (ISBN). A scholar may request a list of all publications in his or her area of interest for easy reference by paying a fee and requesting a search provided by the Library of Congress, Cataloging Distribution Service, Customer Services Section, Washington, D.C. 20540.

CONCLUSION

In a successful critical project, certain fundamental questions must inevitably be addressed by the scholar: What is the speaker's background? What real-life events gave rise to the discourse in question? What audience factors constrained what could be said? What was the effect of language choice on how the message was received? What research already exists on this topic? Answering these broad questions not only assures thoroughness on the scholar's part but also adds manifestly to the precision and authority of the resulting analysis. And it is precision and authority, after all, that separates the genuinely insightful piece of criticism from the merely anecdotal one. In short, while library research is often demanding, it is almost never unproductive. Providing context for criticism can be done well and it can be done poorly. We hope that this appendix makes the former option the most likely option.

References

Popular References

Ackerman, G. "Remarks on the Anniversary of the First Condominium Conversion," Reprinted from the *Congressional Record* by *Harper's*, October, p. 16.

"Are They Harmless Observances?" *Awake*, February 8, **1974**, pp. 27–28.

Boone, P., et al. *The Solution to Crisis-America* (Van Nuys, CA.: Bible Voice, Inc., **1970**).

"Budgets," *Harper's*, March, **1984**, p. 33.

Carter, J. "Energy and National Goals," July 15, 1979, *Weekly Compilations of Presidential Documents*, 15:29 **(1979)**, 1235–1241.

Chamberlain, V. *Teen Guide*, Fifth Edition (New York: McGraw-Hill, **1982**).

Cohn, R. "I Have Just Resigned the Presidency . . . ," in *New York*, March, **1974**, p. 48.

————. *McCarthy* (New York: Lancer Books, **1968**).

Eisenhower, D. "Commencement Address at the University of Notre Dame," June 5, **1960**, *Public Papers of the Presidents, 1960–1*, 461–468.

————. "The Korean Armistice," July 26, **1953**, *Vital Speeches of the Day*, 19:21 **(1953)**, 642.

————."Remarks to the Easter Egg Rollers on the White House Lawn," April 7, **1958**, *Public Papers of the Presidents, 1958*, 65.

————."Text of General Eisenhower's Reply," August 14, **1952**, *Public Papers of the Presidents, 1952*, 517–518.

Erlich, P. "Eco-Catastrophe!," June 9, 1970, in K. Campbell (Ed.), *Critiques of Contemporary Rhetoric* (Belmont, CA: Wadsworth, **1972)**, pp. 111–123.

Ford, G. "Remarks to American Society of Newspaper Editors," April 16, 1975, *Weekly Compilations of Presidential Documents*, 11:16 **(1975)**, 388–393.

————."Remarks at the Centennial Safe Opening at the Capitol," July 1, 1976, *Public Papers of the Presidents,1976a*:2, 1941–1943.

————."Remarks at the Waco Suspension Bridge in Waco, Texas," April 29, 1976, *Public Papers of the Presidents,1976b*:2, 1335–1336.

"Fox and Jacobs Fetes Grand Opening in Ember Oaks," *Dallas Times Herald*, August 21, **1988**, J5.

Gallagher, W. N. "Throw this Away" (Publicly Circulated Letter, August, **1984**).

Goldwater, B. "Foreign Policy," October 21, **1964**, *Vital Speeches of the Day*, 31:2 **(1964)**, 36–38.

Gould, F. J. *Funeral Services Without Theology* (Girard, KS.: Haldeman-Julius Publ., **n.d.**).

Greenfield, J. "This is Your Chief Executive . . . ," in *New York*, March, **1974**, p. 51.

Hand, W. B. *Douglas T. Smith, et al. vs. Board of School Commissioners of Mobile County, et al. and George G. Wallace, Governor of Alabama, et. al., U.S. District Court, Southern District, Alabama* (Civil Action No. 82-0544-BH, 82-0792-BH, **1987**).

Hill, H. "Prelude to Seventy-Six Trombones," *The Music Man* by M. Willson (New York: G. P. Putnam's, **1958**).

Hitler, A. "Speech at Siemensstadt, Berlin," November 10, 1933. Fugitive translation. Partially translated in A. Hitler, *My New Order*, Ed. R. DeSales (New York: Reynal and Hitchcock, **1941**), as well as in N. Baynes (Ed.), *The Speeches of Adolf Hitler, April 1922–August, 1939* (London: Oxford University Press, **1942**), and F. Prange (Ed.), *Hitler's Words* (Washington: American Council on Public Affairs, **1944**).

Johnson, J. H. *Religion Is a Gigantic Fraud* (No publisher cited, **n.d.**).

Johnson, L. "Address at the 10th District Rally," August 24, **1960,** Special Files, Box # 4, Lyndon Baines Johnson Presidential Library, Austin, Texas.

————."Medicare Program," June 15, 1966, *Weekly Compilations of Presidential Documents*, 2:24 **(1966a),** 774–780.

————."Remarks at a Party Rally in Chicago," May 17, 1966, *Weekly Compilations of Presidental Documents*, 2:20 **(1966b),** 657–660.

Kelly, J., and E. Eubanks. *Today's Teen* (Peoria, IL: Charles Bennett Co., **1981**).

Kennedy, J. "Commencement Address at San Diego State College," June 6, 1963, *Public Papers of the Presidents*, **1963a**, 445–448.

————."Inaugural Address," *Inaugural Addresses of the Presidents of the United States, From George Washington to John F. Kennedy* (Washington, D.C.: U.S. Government Printing Office, **1961a**).

————. "A Moral Imperative," June 11, 1963, *Vital Speeches of the Day*, 29:18 **(1963b),** 546–547.

————. "Remarks to the Greater Houston Ministerial Association," September 12, 1960," in T. H. White, *The Making of the President, 1960* (New York: Atheneum, **1961c**), pp. 427–430.

————. "Remarks at a Meeting of the Democratic National Committee," January 21, 1961, *Public Papers of the Presidents*, *1961b*, 4–5.

King, M. L. "I Have a Dream," in R. Hill (Ed.), *The Rhetoric of Racial Revolt* (Denver: Golden Bell Press, **1964**), pp. 371–375.

"Kiss Someone You Love When You Get This Letter and Make Magic," (Publicly Circulated Letter, **1985**).

"Legend Oaks: Live a Legendary Lifestyle," *Austin American-Statesman*, August 21, **1988,** F12.

Macdonald, C. "Two Brothers in a Field of Absence," in *Alternate Means of Transport: Poems* (New York: Knopf, **1985**), pp. 75–76.

Manson, C. "Interview," *Harper's*, September, 1985, pp. 28–29. (Originally published as "Manson at 50" in *California*, May, **1985**.)

McDonald's Corporation. "More about What We're All About and McDonald's Good Food." (Nationally circulated advertisement, **1987**).

McGinley, H. *Caring, Deciding, and Growing* (Lexington, MA: Ginn and Co., **1983**).

Nixon, R. "Address to the Nation Announcing Decision to Resign the Office of the President of the United States," August 8, 1974, *Public Papers of the Presidents*, **1974a**, 626–630.

————. "Cambodia," April 30, 1970, in W. Linkugel, et al. (Eds.), *Contemporary American Speeches*, 4th Edition (Belmont, CA: Wadsworth **1978**), 281–287.

————. "The Expense Fund Speech," *U.S. News and World Report* (October 3, **1952**), pp. 66–70.

————. "Letter to Pat Boone," reprinted in P. Boone, et al., *The Solution to Crisis-America* (Van Nuys, CA: Bible Voice, Inc., **1970b**), p. 18.

————. "The President's News Conference of August 22, 1973," *Public Papers of the Presidents,* **1973a,** 710–725.

————. "Remarks on Departure from the White House," August 9, 1974, *Public Papers of the Presidents,* **1974b,** 630–633.

————. "Second Inaugural Address," January 20, 1973, *Public Papers of the Presidents,* **1973b,** 12–15.

O'Hair, M. "History of Atheists' Fight for Radio Time," *The Atheist Viewpoint* (New York: Arno Press, **1972**), pp. 1–5.

Orwell, G. *Animal Farm* (New York: Harcourt Brace Jovanovich, [1946], **1960**).

Patton, G. "Speech to the Troops in July, 1944," in W. B. Mellor, *Patton: Fighting Man* (New York: Putnam, **1946**).

Peale, N. V. *Help Yourself with God's Help* (Pawling, NY: Foundation for Christian Living, **1976**).

Pershing, J. "My Fellow Soldiers," February 28, **1919,** General Orders No. 38A, G.H.Q. American Expeditionary Forces.

"Prayer at the Funeral Service," *Book of Common Prayer: According to the Uses of the Episcopal Church* (New York: Church Hymnal Corp., [1789], **1979**), pp. 482–485.

Prinz, J. "Speech at the March on Washington," August 28, **1963,** Original recording.

"Quick Reference to Parking and Traffic Regulations," University of Texas at Austin, **1986.**

Reagan, R. "Address to the Nation on the Iran Arms Controversy," *New York Times,* March 5, **1987,** p. 12.

————. "First Inaugural Address," January 20, 1981, in W. Linkugel, et al., (Eds.), *Contemporary American Speeches* (Dubuque, IA: Kendall/Hunt Publishers, **1982**), pp. 375–380.

————. "Presidential Debate of October 21, 1984," *Weekly Compilations of Presidential Documents,* 20:43 **(1984),** 1591–1610.

————. "Salute to a Stronger America," November 13, 1981, *Weekly Compilations of Presidential Documents,* 17:47 **(1981),** 1257–1261.

Sandler, R. "Blowing Smoke," *Harper's,* August, 1987, pp. 15–16. Reprinted from *Philip Morris Magazine,* Spring, **1987.**

Schlesinger, A. "I Stand Before You Tonight . . . ," in *New York,* March, **1974,** p. 49.

Shakespeare, W. "King Lear," in H. Craig (Ed.), *The Complete Works of Shakespeare* (Chicago: Scott, Foresman [1603], **1961**), 979–1016.

Shelton, R. *Ideals of a Klansman* (Denham Springs, LA: Invisible Empire Knights of the Ku Klux Klan, **n.d.**).

Sinclair, G. *Americans,* Westbound Records, Detroit, Michigan, **1973.**

Truman, H. "Democratic Aims and Achievements," May 15, 1950, *Vital Speeches of the Day,* 16:16 **(1950),** 496–498.

————. "Message to Dwight Eisenhower Inviting Him to a Luncheon and Briefing at the White House," August 14, 1952, *Public Papers of the Presidents,* **1952,** 517.

————. "Peace Comes High," October 15, 1951, *Vital Speeches of the Day,* 18:2 **(1951)**, 34–36.

U.S. Army, "Eleven Point Checklist for Job Hunters," Flyer circulated nationally in April, **1972.**

Vail Resort Association. "Ski, Mix, Meet" (Nationally circulated advertisement, **n.d.**).

von Hoffman, N. "Andy Jackson's Boy," *Washington Post,* January 24, **1973,** B1.

Webelos Scout Book (Boy Scouts of America, **1979**).

Webster, D. "The Bunker Hill Monument," in W. Parrish and M. Hochmuth (Eds.), *American Speeches* (New York: Longmans, [1825] **1954**), pp. 101–121.

"Weston Lakes Has Superlative Golf, Swimming, Tennis, Croquet," *Houston Post (Homefinder),* August 21, **1988**, p. 5.

Wiesel, E. "Plea to Reagan," *New York Times,* April 20, **1985**, p. 22.

"Wimbledon Country," *Houston Post (Homefinder),* August 21, **1988**, p. 3.

WKBW, "War of the Worlds," Radio program broadcast annually since October, **1968.** Transcribed by author.

Scholarly References

Abrams, R. *Preachers Present Arms* (New York: Round Table Press, **1933**).

Adams, W. C. "Whose Lives Count?: TV Coverage of Natural Disasters," *Journal of Communication,* 36:2 **(1986)**, 113–122.

Andrews, J. "The Passionate Negation: The Chartist Movement in Rhetorical Perspective," *Quarterly Journal of Speech,* 59 **(1973)**, 196–208.

Antczak, F. *Thought and Character: The Rhetoric of Democratic Education* (Ames, IA: Iowa State University Press, **1985**).

Arendt, H. *Eichmann in Jerusalem: A Report on the Banality of Evil* (New York: Viking, **1963**).

Arnold, C. *Criticism of Oral Rhetoric* (Columbus, OH: Merrill, **1974**).

————. "*Inventio* and *Pronuntiatio* in a 'New Rhetoric,'" Paper presented at the annual convention of the Central States Speech Association, April, **1972.**

————. "Oral Rhetoric, Rhetoric, and Literature," *Philosophy and Rhetoric,* 1 **(1968)**, 191–210.

————. "Reflections on American Public Discourse," *Central States Speech Journal,* 28 **(1977)**, 73–85.

————. "What's Reasonable?", *Communication Quarterly,* 19 **(1971)**, 19–23.

Asante, M., and D. Atwater, "The Rhetorical Condition as Symbolic Structure in Discourse," *Communication Quarterly,* 34 **(1986)**, 170–177.

Aune, J. "Beyond Deconstruction: The Symbol and Social Reality," *Southern Speech Communication Journal,* 48 **(1983)**, 255–268.

Austin, J. L. *How to Do Things with Words* (New York: Oxford University Press, **1970**).

Bailey, R. "Authorship Attribution in a Forensic Setting," in D. Ager, et al. (Eds.), *Advances in Computer-Aided Literary and Linguistic Research* (Birmingham: University of Aston, **1979**), 1–20.

Balibar, E., and P. Macherey, "On Literature as an Ideological Form," in R. Young (Ed.), *Untying the Text: A Post-Structuralist Reader* (London: Routledge and Kegan Paul, **1981**), pp. 79–100.

Balthrop, W. "Culture, Myth and Ideology as Public Argument: An Interpretation of the Ascent and Demise of 'Southern Culture,'" *Communication Monographs*, 51 **(1984)**, 339–352.

Barbatsis, G., et al., "A Struggle for Dominance: Relational Communication Patterns in Television Drama," *Communication Quarterly*, 31 **(1983)**, 148–155.

Barney, R. "Uncanny Criticism in the United States," in J. Natoli (Ed.), *Tracing Literary Theory* (Urbana, IL: University of Illinois Press, **1987**), pp. 177–212.

Barthes, R. "Theory of the Text," in R. Young (Ed.), *Untying the Text: A Post-Structuralist Reader* (London: Routledge and Kegan Paul, **1981**), pp. 31–47.

Baskerville, B. *The People's Voice: The Orator in American Society* (Lexington, KY: University of Kentucky Press, **1979**).

Bass, J. "The Appeal to Efficiency as Narrative Closure: Lyndon Johnson and the Dominican Crisis, 1965," *Southern Speech Communication Journal*, 50 **(1985)**, 103–120.

Bate, B., and L. Self, "The Rhetoric of Career Success Books for Women," *Journal of Communication*, 33:2 **(1983)**, 149–165.

Bauman, R. *Let Your Words Be Few: Symbolism of Speaking and Silence among Seventeenth Century Quakers* (New York: Cambridge University Press, **1983**).

Baym, N. "Melodramas of Beset Manhood: How Theories of American Fiction Exclude Women Authors," in E. Showalter (Ed.), *The New Feminist Criticism: Essays on Women, Literature, and Theory* (New York: Pantheon, **1985**), pp. 63–80.

Beardsley, M. "Style and Good Style," in G. Love and M. Payne (Eds.), *Contemporary Essays on Style* (Glenview, IL: Scott, Foresman, **1969**), pp. 3–14.

Belsey, C. *Critical Practice* (London: Methuen, **1980**).

Benjamin, J. "Performatives as a Rhetorical Construct," *Philosophy and Rhetoric*, 9 **(1976)**, 84–95.

Bennett, T. *Formalism and Marxism* (London: Methuen, **1979**).

Bennett, W. L. "Rhetorical Transformation of Evidence in Criminal Trials: Creating Grounds for Legal Judgment," *Quarterly Journal of Speech*, 65 **(1979)**, 311–323.

―――, and M. Edelman, "Toward a New Political Narrative," *Journal of Communication*, 35:4 **(1985)**, 156–171.

―――, and M. Feldman, *Constructing Reality in the Courtroom: Justice and Judgment in American Culture* (New Brunswick: Rutgers University Press, **1981**).

Benson, T. "Poisoned Minds," *Southern Speech Communication Journal*, 34 **(1968)**, 54–60.

―――. "The Rhetorical Structure of Frederick Wiseman's *Primate*," *Quarterly Journal of Speech*, 71 **(1985)**, 204–217.

Berg, C., and P. Berry, "'Spiritual Whoredom': An Essay on Female Prophets in the Seventeenth Century," in M. Eagleton (Ed.), *Feminist Literary Theory: A Reader* (London: Blackwell, **1986**), pp. 124–126.

Berthold, C. "Kenneth Burke's Cluster-Agon Method: Its Development and Application," *Central States Speech Journal,* 27 **(1976),** 302–309.

Birdsell, D. "Ronald Reagan on Lebanon and Grenada: Flexibility and Interpretation in the Application of Kenneth Burke's Pentad," *Quarterly Journal of Speech,* 73 **(1987),** 267–279.

Bitzer, L. "The Rhetorical Situation," *Philosophy and Rhetoric,* 1 **(1968),** 1–14.

Black, E. *Rhetorical Criticism: A Study in Method* (Madison, WI: University of Wisconsin Press, [1965], **1978a).**

————. "The Second Persona," *Quarterly Journal of Speech,* 56 **(1970),** 109–119.

————. "The Sentimental Style as Escapism, or the Devil with Dan'l. Webster," in K. Campbell and K. Jamieson (Eds.), *Form and Genre: Shaping Rhetorical Action* (Falls Church, VA: Speech Communication Association, **1978b),** pp. 75–86.

Blankenship, J. *A Sense of Style: An Introduction to Style for the Public Speaker* (Belmont, CA: Wadsworth, **1968).**

————. "Toward a Developmental Model of Form: ABC's Treatment of the Reagan Inaugural and the Iranian Hostage Release as Oxymoron," in H. Simons and A. Aghazarian (Eds.), *Form, Genre, and the Study of Political Discourse* (Columbia: University of South Carolina Press, **1986),** pp. 246–277.

Bloch, M. (Ed.), *Political Language and Oratory in Traditional Society* (London: Academic Press, **1975).**

Booth, W. *Critical Understanding: The Power and Limits of Pluralism* (Chicago: University of Chicago Press, **1979.).**

Bormann, E. "A Fantasy Theme Analysis of the Television Coverage of the Hostage Release and the Reagan Inaugural," *Quarterly Journal of Speech,* 68 **(1982),** 133–145.

————. "Fantasy and Rhetorical Vision: The Rhetorical Criticism of Social Reality," *Quarterly Journal of Speech,* 58 **(1972),** 396–407.

————. *The Force of Fantasy: Restoring the American Dream* (Carbondale, IL: Southern Illinois University Press, **1985).**

Bosmajian, H. "The Sources and Nature of Adolph Hitler's Techniques of Persuasion," *Central States Speech Journal,* 25 **(1974),** 240–248.

Bostdorff, D. "Making Light of James Watt: A Burkean Approach to the Form and Attitude of Political Cartoons," *Quarterly Journal of Speech,* 73 **(1987),** 43–59.

Braden, W. *The Oral Tradition in the South* (Baton Rouge, LA: Louisiana State University Press, **1983).**

Branham, R., and W. B. Pearce. "Between Text and Context: Toward a Rhetoric of Textual Reconstruction," *Quarterly Journal of Speech,* 71 **(1985),** 19–36.

Brinton, C. *The Anatomy of Revolution* (New York: Vintage, **1938).**

Brock, B. "Epistemology and Ontology in Kenneth Burke's Dramatism," *Communication Quarterly,* 33 **(1985),** 94–104.

Brockriede, W. "Rhetorical Criticism as Argument," *Quarterly Journal of Speech,* 60 **(1974),** 165–174.

Brown, B. "Family Intimacy in Magazine Advertising, 1920–1977," *Journal of Communication,* 32:3 **(1982),** 173–183.

Brown, M. *Kenneth Burke* (Minneapolis: University of Minnesota Press, **1969).**

Brown, M. E. "The Dialectic of the Feminine: Melodrama and Commodity in the Ferraro Pepsi Commercial," *Communication*, 9 **(1987)**, 335–354.

Brummett, B. "Burkean Comedy and Tragedy, Illustrated in Reactions to the Arrest of John DeLorean," *Central States Speech Journal*, 35 **(1984a)**, 217–227.

————. "Burkean Scapegoating, Mortification, and Transcendence in Presidential Campaign Rhetoric," *Central States Speech Journal*, 32 **(1981a)**, 254–264.

————. "Consensus Criticism," *Southern Speech Communication Journal*, 49 **(1984b)**, 111–124.

————. "Electric Literature as Equipment for Living: Haunted House Films," *Critical Studies in Mass Communication*, 2 **(1985)**, 247–261.

————. "Gastronomic Reference, Synecdoche, and Political Images," *Quarterly Journal of Speech*, 67 **(1981b)**, 138–145.

————. "Premillennial Apocalyptic as a Rhetorical Genre," *Central States Speech Journal*, 35 **(1984c)**, 84–93.

————. "The Representative Anecdote as a Burkean Method, Applied to Evangelical Rhetoric," *Southern Speech Communication Journal*, 50 **(1984d)**, 1–23.

Bryant, D. "Rhetoric: Its Functions and Its Scope," in D. Ehninger (Ed.), *Contemporary Rhetoric: A Coursebook* (Glenview, IL: Scott, Foresman, [1953] **1972**), pp. 15–38.

Brydon, S. "The Two Faces of Jimmy Carter: The Transformation of a Presidential Debater, 1976 and 1980," *Central States Speech Journal*, 36 **(1985)**, 138–151.

Bugliosi, V. *Helter Skelter: The True Stories of the Manson Murders* (New York: Norton, **1974**).

Burke, K. "Antony in Behalf of the Play," in S. E. Hyman (Ed.), *Perspectives by Incongruity* (Bloomington: Indiana University Press, **1964**), pp. 64–75.

————. *Counter-Statement* (Berkeley: University of California Press, [1931] **1968**).

————. *A Grammar of Motives* (Cleveland: World Publishing Co., **1962**).

————. *Language as Symbolic Action: Essays on Life, Literature and Method* (Berkeley: University of California Press, **1966**).

————. *Permanence and Change* (Berkeley: University of California Press, [1935], **1984**).

————. *The Philosophy of Literary Form* (Berkeley: University of California Press, [1941], **1973**).

————. *A Rhetoric of Motives* (Berkeley: University of California Press, [1950], **1969**).

————. *The Rhetoric of Religion: Studies in Logology* (Boston: Beacon Press, **1961**).

Byars, J. "Reading Feminine Discourse: Prime-time Television in the U.S.," *Communication*, 9 **(1987)**, 289–304.

Bytwerk, R. *Julius Streicher: The Man who Persuaded a Nation to Hate Jews* (New York: Stein and Day, **1983**).

Cain, W. E. *The Crisis in Criticism: Theory, Literature and Reform* (Baltimore: Johns Hopkins University Press, **1984**).

Campbell, J. "The Polemical Mr. Darwin," *Quarterly Journal of Speech,* 41 **(1975),** 375–390.

Campbell, K. "Critique of Spiro T. Agnew: An Exercise in Manichean Rhetoric," in K. Campbell (Ed.), *Critiques of Contemporary Rhetoric* (Belmont, CA: Wadsworth, **1972),** 94–110.

————. "Femininity and Feminism: To Be or Not to Be a Woman," *Communication Quarterly,* 31 **(1983),** 101–109.

————. "The Rhetoric of Women's Liberation: An Oxymoron," *Quarterly Journal of Speech,* 59 **(1973),** 74–86.

————. "Stanton's 'The Solitude of Self': A Rationale for Feminism, "*Quarterly Journal of Speech,* 66 **(1980),** 304–312

Campbell, R. "Securing the Middle Ground: Reporter Formulas in *60 Minutes,*" *Critical Studies in Mass Communication,* 4 **(1987),** 325–350.

Carbone, T. "Stylistic Variables as Related to Source Credibility: A Content Analysis Approach," *Communication Monographs,* 42 **(1975),** 99–106.

Carleton, W. "Theory Transformation in Communication: The Case of Henry Johnstone," *Quarterly Journal of Speech,* 61 **(1975),** 76–88.

Carlson, A. C. "Gandhi and the Comic Frame: 'Ad Bellum Purificandum,'" *Quarterly Journal of Speech,* 72 **(1986),** 446–455.

————, and J. Hocking, "Strategies of Redemption at the Vietnam Veterans Memorial," *Western Journal of Speech Communication,* 52 **(1988),** 203–215.

Carpenter, R. *The Eloquence of Frederick Jackson Turner* (San Marino, CA: Huntington Library, **1983).**

Charland, M. "Constitutive Rhetoric: The Case of the *Peuple Quebecois,*" *Quarterly Journal of Speech,* 73 **(1987),** 133–150.

Cheney, G. "The Rhetoric of Identification and the Study of Organizational Communication," *Quarterly Journal of Speech,* 69 **(1983),** 143–158.

Cherwitz, R., and J. Hikins. *Communication and Knowledge: An Investigation in Rhetorical Epistemology* (Columbia, SC: University of South Carolina Press, **1986).**

————, and K. Zagacki, "Consummatory Versus Justificatory Crisis Rhetoric," *Western Journal of Speech Communication,* 50 **(1986),** 307–324.

Chesebro, J. "Paradoxical Views of Homosexuality in the Rhetoric of Social Scientists: A Fantasy Theme Analysis," *Quarterly Journal of Speech,* 66 **(1980),** 127–139.

————, and C. Hamsher, "Contemporary Rhetorical Theory and Criticism: Dimensions of the New Rhetoric," *Speech Monographs,* 42 **(1975),** 311–334.

Clark, T. "An Exploration of Generic Aspects of Contemporary American Christian Sermons," *Quarterly Journal of Speech,* 63 **(1977),** 384–394.

Cline, R. "The Cronkite-Ford Interview at the 1980 Republican National Convention: A Therapeutic Analogue," *Central States Speech Journal,* 36 **(1985),** 92–139.

Condit, C. "The Function of Epideictic: The Boston Massacre Orations as Exemplar," *Communication Quarterly,* 33 **(1985),** 284–299.

————, and J. Selzer, "The Rhetoric of Objectivity in the Newspaper Coverage of a Murder Trial," *Critical Studies in Mass Communication,* 2 **(1985),** 197–216.

Conrad, C. "The Rhetoric of the Moral Majority: An Analysis of Romantic Form," *Quarterly Journal of Speech,* 69 **(1983),** 159–170.

Corcoran, F. "The Bear in the Back Yard: Myth, Ideology and Victimage in Soviet Funerals," *Communication Monographs,* 50 **(1983),** 305–320.

————. "KAL 007 and the Evil Empire: Mediated Disaster and Forms of Rationalization," *Critical Studies in Mass Communication,* 3 **(1986),** 297–316.

————. "Television as Ideological Apparatus: The Power and the Pleasure," *Critical Studies in Mass Communication,* 1 **(1984),** 131–145.

Cox, R. "The Die Is Cast: Topical and Ontological Dimensions of the *Locus* of the Irreparable," *Quarterly Journal of Speech,* 68 **(1982),** 227–239.

Crable, R. "Ike: Identification, Argument, and Paradoxical Appeal," *Quarterly Journal of Speech,* 63 **(1977),** 188–195.

————, and S. Vibbert, "Mobil's Epideictic Advocacy: 'Observations' of Prometheus-Bound," *Communication Monographs,* 50 **(1983),** 380–394.

Cragan, J., and D. Shields, "Foreign Policy Communication Dramas: How Mediated Rhetoric Played in Peoria in Campaign '76," *Quarterly Journal of Speech,* 63 **(1977),** 274–289.

Crusius, T. "A Case for Kenneth Burke's Dialectic and Rhetoric," *Philosophy and Rhetoric,* 19 **(1986),** 23–37.

Culler, J. *On Deconstruction: Theory and Criticism after Structuralism* (Ithaca, NY: Cornell University Press, **1982**).

Daniel, J., and G. Smitherman, "How I Got Over: Communication Dynamics in the Black Community," *Quarterly Journal of Speech,* 62 **(1976),** 26–39.

Darsey, J. *Vessels of the Word: Studies of the Prophetic Voice in American Public Address,* Unpublished Ph.D. Dissertation, University of Wisconsin, **1985.**

Daughton, S. "Lyndon Baines Johnson's Use of Metaphor and Speech Styles: 1939–1969," Paper Presented at the Annual Convention of the Southern Speech Communication Association, April, **1988.**

Davis, L. "Controversy and the Network Documentary: Critical Analysis of Form," *Communication Quarterly,* 26 **(1978),** 45–52.

Delia, J. "The Logical Fallacy, Cognitive Theory, and the Enthymeme: A Search for the Foundations of Reasoned Discourse," *Quarterly Journal of Speech,* 56 **(1970),** 140–148.

DeMan, P. *Blindness and Insight: Essays in the Rhetoric of Contemporary Criticism* (New York: Oxford, **1983**).

Dicks, V. "Courtroom Rhetorical Strategies: Forensic and Deliberative Perspectives," *Quarterly Journal of Speech,* 67 **(1981),** 178–192.

Dillon, G. *Rhetoric as Social Imagination: Explorations in the Interpersonal Function of Language* (Bloomington, IN: Indiana University Press, **1986**).

Divver, A. "Tracing Hermeneutics," in J. Natoli (Ed.), *Tracing Literary Theory* (Urbana, IL: University of Illinois Press, **1987**), pp. 54–79.

Donovan, J. "Afterword: Critical Re-Vision," in J. Donovan (Ed.), *Feminist Literary Criticism: Explorations in Theory* (Lexington, KY: University of Kentucky Press, **1975**), pp. 74–82.

————. "The Silence is Broken," in S. McConnell-Ginet, et al. (Eds.), *Women and Language in Literature and Society* (New York: Praeger, **1980**).

Dorfman, A., and A. Mattelart, *How to Read Donald Duck: Imperialist Ideology in the Disney Comic* (New York: International General, **1971**).

Douglass, R., and C. Arnold, "On Analysis of *Logos*: A Methodological Inquiry," *Quarterly Journal of Speech*, 56 **(1970)**, 22–32.

Downey, S. "The Evolution of Rhetorical Genres," A paper presented at the Annual Convention of the Speech Communication Association, November, **1982**.

Doyle, M. "The Rhetoric of Romance: A Fantasy Theme Analysis of Barbara Cartland Novels," *Southern Speech Communication Journal*, 51 **(1985)**, 24–48.

Duffy, B. "The Anti-Humanist Rhetoric of the Radical Right," *Southern Speech Communication Journal*, 49 **(1984)**, 339–360.

Eagleton, M. "Introduction," in M. Eagleton (Ed.), *Feminist Literary Theory: A Reader* (London: Blackwell, **1986**), pp. 1–6.

Eagleton, T. *Criticism and Ideology: A Study in Marxist Literary Theory* (London: Verso, **1975**).

————. *Literary Theory: An Introduction* (Minneapolis: University of Minnesota Press, **1983**).

————. *Marxism and Literary Criticism* (Berkeley: University of California Press, **1976**).

Edelman, M. *Political Language: Words that Succeed and Policies that Fail* (New York: Academic Press, **1977**).

————. *Politics as Symbolic Action: Mass Arousal and Quiescence* (Chicago: Markham, **1971**).

————. *The Symbolic Uses of Politics* (Urbana: University of Illinois Press, **1964**).

Ehninger, D., and W. Brockriede, *Decision by Debate* (New York: Dodd, Mead, **1963**).

Einhorn, L. "Basic Assumptions in the Virginia Ratification Debate: Patrick Henry vs. James Madison on the Nature of Man and Reason," *Southern Speech Communication Journal*, 46 **(1981)**, 327–340.

Elpenor (A pseudonym). "A Drunkard's Progress: AA and The Sobering Strength of Myth," *Harpers*, October **1986**, 42–48.

Enkvist, N. "On the Place of Style in Some Linguistic Theories," in S. Chatman (Ed.), *Literary Style: A Symposium* (London: Oxford, **1971**), pp. 47–64.

Erickson, P. *Reagan Speaks: The Making of an American Myth* (New York: New York University Press, **1986**).

Espy, W. *The Garden of Eloquence: A Rhetorical Bestiary* (New York: Dutton, **1983**).

Farrell, T. "Critical Modes in the Analysis of Discourse," *Western Journal of Speech Communication*, 44 **(1980)**, 300–314.

————, and T. Goodnight, "Accidental Rhetoric: The Root Metaphors of Three Mile Island," *Communication Monographs*, 49 **(1981)**, 271–300.

Felperin, H. *Beyond Deconstruction: The Uses and Abuses of Literary Theory* (Oxford: Clarendon, **1985**).

Fetterley, J. *The Resisting Reader* (Bloomington, IN: Indiana University Press, **1978**).

Finkelstein, L. "The Calendrical Rite of the Ascension to Power," *Western Journal of Speech Communication*, 45 **(1981)**, 51–59.

Fisher, J. "A Burkean Analysis of the Rhetorical Dimensions of a Multiple Murder and Suicide," *Quarterly Journal of Speech*, 60 **(1974)**, 174–189.

Fisher, W. *Human Communication as Narration: Toward a Philosophy of Reason, Value and Action* (Columbia, SC: University of South Carolina Press, **1987**).

————. "Narration as a Human Communication Paradigm: The Case of Public Moral Argument," *Communication Monographs*, 51 **(1984)**, 1–22.

————. "Romantic Democracy, Ronald Reagan, and Presidential Heroes," *Western Journal of Speech Communication*, 46 **(1982)**, 299–310.

Fiske, J. "The Discourses of TV Quiz Shows or, School + Luck = Success + Sex," *Central States Speech Journal*, 34 **(1983)**, 139–150.

————. "Television: Polysemy and Popularity," *Central States Speech Journal*, 3 **(1986)**, 391–408.

Foss, K. "Singing the Rhythm Blues: An Argumentative Analysis of the Birth-Control Debate in the Catholic Church," *Western Journal of Speech Communication*, 47 **(1983)**, 29–44.

Foss, S. "Ambiguity as Persuasion: The Vietnam Veterans Memorial," *Communication Quarterly*, 34:3 **(1986)**, 326–340.

Foucault, M. "The Order of Discourse," in R. Young (Ed.), *Untying the Text: A Post-Structuralist Reader* (London: Routledge and Kegan Paul, **1981**), pp. 48–78.

Frank, J. "Symbols and Civilization," in W. Rueckert (Ed.), *Critical Responses to Kenneth Burke* (Minneapolis: University of Minnesota Press, **1969**), pp. 401–406.

Frentz, T., and T. Farrell, "Conversion of America's Consciousness: The Rhetoric of *The Exorcist*," *Quarterly Journal of Speech*, 61 **(1975)**, 40–47.

Gaines, R. "Doing by Saying: Toward a Theory of Perlocution," *Quarterly Journal of Speech*, 65 **(1979)**, 207–217.

Genovese, E. *Roll Jordan Roll* (New York: Vintage, **1976**).

Gerlach, L., and V. Hine, "Five Factors Crucial to the Growth and Speed of a Modern Religious Movement," *Journal for the Scientific Study of Religion*, 7 **(1968)**, 23–40.

Gibson, W. *Tough, Sweet and Stuffy: An Essay on Modern Prose Styles* (Bloomington, IN: Indiana University Press, **1966**).

Gilberg, S., et al., "The State of the Union Address and the Press Agenda," *Journalism Quarterly*, 57 **(1980)**, 584–588.

Gilbert, S. "What Do Feminist Critics Want? A Postcard from a Volcano," in E. Showalter (Ed.), *The New Feminist Criticism: Essays on Women, Literature, and Theory* (New York: Pantheon, **1985**), pp. 29–45.

————, and S. Gubar, "Shakespeare's Sisters," in M. Eagleton (Ed.), *Feminist Literary Theory: A Reader* (London: Blackwell, **1986**), pp. 106–111.

Goffman, E. "The Lecture," in *Forms of Talk* (Philadelphia: University of Pennsylvania Press, **1981**), pp. 160–196.

Gold, G. "Cousin and the *Gros Chiens*: The Limits of Cajun Political Rhetoric," in R. Paine (Ed.), *Politically Speaking: Cross-Cultural Studies of Rhetoric* (Philadelphia: Institute for the Study of Human Issues, **1981**), pp. 143–164.

Goodwin, P., and J. Wenzel, "Proverbs and Practical Reasoning: A Study in Socio-Logic," *Quarterly Journal of Speech*, 65 **(1979)**, 289–302.

Graber, D. *Verbal Behavior and Politics* (Urbana, IL: University of Illinois Press, **1976)**.

Greenberg, B., and C. Atkin, "The Portrayal of Driving on Television, 1975–1980," *Journal of Communication*, 33:2 **(1983)**, 44–55.

Gregg, R. "The Ego-Function of the Rhetoric of Protest," *Philosophy and Rhetoric*, 4 **(1971)**, 71–91.

————. "Kenneth Burke's Prolegomena to the Study of the Rhetoric of Form," *Communication Quarterly*, 26 (1978:4), 3–13.

————. "The Rhetoric of Political Broadcasting," *Central States Speech Journal*, 28 **(1977)**, 221–237.

Griffin, L. "A Dramatistic Theory of the Rhetoric of Movements," in W. Rueckert (Ed.), *Critical Responses to Kenneth Burke* (Minneapolis: University of Minnesota Press, **1969)**, pp. 456–478.

————. "When Dreams Collide: Rhetorical Trajectories in the Assassination of President Kennedy," *Quarterly Journal of Speech*, 70 **(1984)**, 111–131.

Gronbeck, B. "Celluloid Rhetoric: On Genres of Documentary," in K. Campbell and K. Jamieson (Eds.), *Form and Genre: Shaping Rhetorical Action* (Falls Church, VA: Speech Communication Association, **1978a)**, pp. 139–161.

————. "The Rhetoric of Political Corruption: Sociolinguistic, Dialectical, and Ceremonial Processes," *Quarterly Journal of Speech*, 64 **(1978b)**, 155–172.

————. "Rhetorical Timing in Public Communication," *Central States Speech Journal*, 25 **(1974)**, 84–94.

Grossberg, L. "Strategies of Marxist Cultural Interpretation," *Central States Speech Journal*, 1 **(1984)**, 392–421.

Gusfield, J. *The Culture of Public Problems: Drinking-Driving and the Symbolic Order* (Chicago: University of Chicago Press, **1981)**.

Hankins, S. "Archetypal Alloy: Reagan's Rhetorical Image," *Central States Speech Journal*, 34 **(1983)**, 33–43.

Harari, J. "Critical Factions/Critical Fictions" in J. Harari (Ed.), *Textual Strategies: Perspectives in Post-Structuralist Criticism* (Ithaca, NY: Cornell University Press, **1979)**, pp. 17–72.

Harrell, J., et al., "Failure of Apology in American Politics: Nixon on Watergate," *Communication Monographs*, 42 **(1975)**, 245–261.

Hart, R. "On Applying Toulmin: The Analysis of Practical Discourse," in G. P. Mohrmann, et al. (Eds.), *Explorations in Rhetorical Criticism* (University Park, PA: Pennsylvania State University Press, **1973)**, pp. 75–95.

————. "Contemporary Scholarship in Public Address: A Research Editorial," *Western Journal of Speech Communication*, 50 **(1986a)**, 283–295.

————. "The Functions of Human Communication in the Maintenance of Public Values," ın C. Arnold and J. Bowers (Eds.), *Handbook of Rhetorical and Communication Theory* (Boston: Allyn and Bacon, **1984a)**, pp. 749–791.

————. "Of Genre, Computers, and the Reagan Inaugural," in H. Simons and A. Aghazarian (Eds.), *Form, Genre, and the Study of Political Discourse* (Columbia, SC: University of South Carolina Press, **1986b)**, pp. 278–298.

————. "The Language of the Modern Presidency," *Presidential Studies Quarterly,* 14 **(1984b),** 249–264.

————. *Philosophical Commonality and Speech Types,* Unpublished Ph.D. Dissertation, Pennsylvania State University, **1970.**

————. *The Political Pulpit* (W. Lafayette, IN: Purdue University Press, **1977**).

————."The Rhetoric of the True Believer," *Speech Monographs,* 38 **(1971),** 249–261.

————. *The Sound of Leadership: Presidential Communication in the Modern Age* (Chicago: University of Chicago Press, **1987**).

————. "Systematic Analysis of Political Discourse: The Development of DICTION," in K. Sanders, et al. (Eds.), *Political Communication Yearbook, 1984* (Carbondale, IL: Southern Illinois University Press, **1985**).

————. "Theory-Building and Rhetorical Criticism: An Informal Statement of Opinion," *Central States Speech Journal,* 27 **(1976),** 70–77.

————. "An Unquiet Desperation: Rhetorical Aspects of Popular Atheism in the United States," *Quarterly Journal of Speech,* 64 **(1978),** 33–46.

————. *Verbal Style and the Presidency* (New York: Academic Press, **1984d**).

————, and D. Burks, "Rhetorical Sensitivity and Social Interaction," *Speech Monographs,* 39 **(1972),** 75–91.

————, et al. *Public Communication* (New York: Harper, **1983**).

————, et al., "Rhetorical Features of Newscasts about the President," *Critical Studies in Mass Communication,* 1 **(1984c),** 260–286.

Harvey, I. "Contemporary French Thought and the Art of Rhetoric," *Philosophy and Rhetoric,* 18 **(1985),** 199–215.

————. "The Wellsprings of Deconstruction," in J. Natoli (Ed.), *Tracing Literary Theory* (Urbana, IL: University of Illinois Press, **1987**), pp. 127–147.

Haskins, W. "Rhetorical Vision of Equality: Analysis of the Rhetoric of the Southern Black Press During Reconstruction," *Communication Quarterly,* 29 **(1981),** 116–122.

Hatzenbuehler, R., and R. Ivie, *Congress Declares War: Rhetorical Leadership and Partisanship in the Early Republic* (Kent, OH: Kent State University Press, **1983**).

Hayes, J. "Gayspeak," *Quarterly Journal of Speech,* 62 **(1976),** 255–266.

Heath, R. "Kenneth Burke on Form," *Quarterly Journal of Speech,* 65 **(1979),** 392–404.

————. *Realism and Relativism: A Perspective on Kenneth Burke* (Macon, GA: Mercer University Press, **1986**).

Heisey, D. R., and J. D. Trebing, "Authority and Legitimacy: A Rhetorical Case Study of the Iranian Revolution," *Communication Monographs,* 53 **(1986),** 295–310.

Hensley, C. W. "Rhetorical Vision and the Persuasion of a Historical Movement: The Disciples of Christ in Nineteenth Century American Culture," *Quarterly Journal of Speech,* 61 **(1975),** 250–264.

Hikins, J., "The Rhetoric of 'Unconditional Surrender' and the Decision to Drop the Atomic Bomb," *Quarterly Journal of Speech,* 69 **(1983),** 379–400.

Hill, F. "A Turn against Ideology: Reply to Professor Wander," *Central States Speech Journal,* 34 **(1983),** 121–126.

Hill, M. *A Sociology of Religion* (London: Heinemann, **1973**).

Hillbruner, A. "Archetype and Signature: Nixon and the 1973 Inaugural," *Central States Speech Journal*, 25 **(1974)**, 169–181.

————. "Inequality, the Great Chain of Being, and Ante-Bellum Southern Oratory," *Southern Speech Communication Journal*, 25 **(1960)**, 172–189.

Himelstein, J. "Rhetorical Continuities in the Politics of Race: The Closed Society Revisited," *Southern Speech Communication Journal*, 48 **(1983)**, 153–166.

Himmelein, M. "Toward Hypotheses on Organization: Micro-Analysis of Message Structure," Unpublished M.A. Thesis, Purdue University, **1974.**

Hirsch, E. D. *Validity in Interpretation* (New Haven: Yale University Press, **1967)**.

Hogan, J. M. *The Panama Canal in American Politics: Domestic Advocacy and the Evolution of Policy* (Carbondale, IL: Southern Illinois University Press, **1986)**.

Hollihan, T. "Propagandizing in the Interest of War: A Rhetorical Study of the Committee on Public Information," *Southern Speech Communication Journal*, 49 **(1984)**, 241–257.

Hopper, R., et al. "Conversation Analysis Methods," in D. Ellis and W. Donohue (Eds.), *Contemporary Issues and Discourse Processes* (Hillsdale, NJ: Erlbaum, **1986)**, pp. 169–186.

Hubbard, R. C. "Relationship Styles in Popular Romance Novels, 1950 to 1983," *Communication Quarterly*, 33:2 **(1985)**, 113–125.

Hughey, J., et al. "Insidious Metaphors and the Changing Meaning of AIDS," Paper Presented at the Annual Convention of the Speech Communication Association, November, **1987.**

Humm, M. *Feminist Criticism: Women as Contemporary Critics* (New York: St. Martins, **1986)**.

Ilkka, R. "Rhetorical Dramatization in the Development of American Communism," *Quarterly Journal of Speech*, 63 **(1977)**, 413–427.

Ivie, R. "Images of Savagery in American Justifications for War," *Communication Monographs*, 47 **(1980)**, 279–294.

————. "Presidential Motives for War," *Quarterly Journal of Speech*, 50 **(1974)**, 337–345.

Jablonski, C. *Institutional Rhetoric and Radical Change: The Case of the Contemporary Roman Catholic Church in America, 1947–1977*, Unpublished Ph.D. Dissertation, Purdue University, **1979a.**

————. "Promoting Radical Change in the Roman Catholic Church: Rhetorical Requirements, Problems, and Strategies of the American Bishops," *Central States Speech Journal*, 31 **(1980)**, 282–289.

————. "Richard Nixon's Irish Wake: A Case of Generic Transference," *Central States Speech Journal*, 30 **(1979b)**, 164–173.

Jameson, F. *The Political Unconscious: Narrative as a Socially Symbolic Act* (Ithaca, NY: Cornell University Press, **1981)**.

Jamieson, K. "Antecedent Genre as Rhetorical Constraint," *Quarterly Journal of Speech*, 61 **(1975a)**, 406–415.

————. *Eloquence in an Electronic Age* (New York: Oxford University Press, **1988a)**.

————. "Generic Constraints and the Rhetorical Situation," *Philosophy and Rhetoric*, 6 **(1973)**, 162–170.

————. "The Metaphoric Cluster in the Rhetoric of Pope Paul VI and Edmund G. Brown, Jr.," *Quarterly Journal of Speech,* 66 **(1980),** 51–72.

————. *Packaging the Presidency: A History and Criticism of Presidential Campaign Advertising* (New York: Oxford Univeristy Press, **1984**).

————. "The Standardization and Modification of Rhetorical Genres: A Perspective," *Genre* (September , **1975b**), 183–193.

————. "Television, Presidential Campaigns and Debates," in J. Swerdlow (Ed.), *Presidential Debates: 1988 and Beyond* (Washington, D.C.: Congressional Quarterly Press, **1988b**), pp. 27–33.

————, and K. Campbell, "Rhetorical Hybrids: Fusions of Generic Elements," *Quarterly Journal of Speech,* 68 **(1982),** 146–157.

Japp, P. "Esther or Isaiah? The Abolitionist-Feminist Rhetoric of Angelina Grimkè," *Quarterly Journal of Speech,* 71 **(1985),** 335–348.

Jewett, R. *The Captain America Complex: The Dilemma of Zealous Nationalism* (Philadelphia: Westminster Press, **1973**).

Johannesen, R. "The Jeremiad and Jenkin Lloyd Jones," *Communication Monographs,* 52 **(1985),** 156–172.

Johnson, B. "The Critical Difference: Balzac's *Sarrasine* and Barthes's *S/Z,*" in R. Young (Ed.), *Untying the Text: A Post-Structuralist Reader* (London: Routledge and Kegan Paul, **1981**), pp. 162–174.

Johnson, B.M. "Images of the Enemy in Intergroup Conflict," *Central States Speech Journal,* 26 **(1975),** 84–92.

Johnstone, H. "Truth, Communication, and Rhetoric in Philosophy," *Revue Internationale de Philosophie,* 90:4 **(1969).**

Karlins, M., and H. Abelson, *Persuasion: How Opinions and Attitudes are Changed* (New York: Springer, **1978**).

Kaufer, D. "Analyzing Philosophy in Rhetoric: Darrow's Mechanism in the Defense of Leopold and Loeb," *Southern Speech Communication Journal,* 45 **(1980),** 363–377.

————. "Ironic Evaluations," *Communication Monographs,* 48 **(1981),** 25–38.

Kerr, H. "The Election Sermon: Primer for Revolutionaries," *Communication Monographs,* 29 **(1962),** 13–22.

Kessler, M. "The Role of Surrogate Speakers in the 1980 Presidential Campaign," *Quarterly Journal of Speech,* 67 **(1981),** 146–156.

Kidd, V. "Happily Ever After and Other Relationship Styles: Advice on Interpersonal Relations in Popular Magazines, 1951–1973," *Quarterly Journal of Speech,* 61 **(1975),** 31–39.

King, A. *Power and Communication* (Prospect Heights, IL: Waveland, **1987**).

————. "The Rhetoric of Power Maintenance," *Quarterly Journal of Speech,* 62 **(1976),** 127–134.

King, R. "Transforming Scandal into Tragedy: A Rhetoric of Political Apology," *Quarterly Journal of Speech,* 71 **(1985),** 289–301.

Kirkwood, W. "Parables as Metaphors and Examples," *Quarterly Journal of Speech,* 71 **(1985),** 422–440.

————. "Storytelling and Self-Confrontation: Parables as Communication Strategies," *Quarterly Journal of Speech,* 69 **(1983),** 58–74.

Klaus, C. "Reflections on Prose Style," in G. Love and M. Payne (Eds.), *Contemporary Essays on Style* (Glenview, IL.: Scott, Foresman, **1969**), pp. 52–62.

Knapp, M., et al. "Deception as a Communication Construct," *Human Communication Research,* 1 **(1974)**, 15–29.

Koester, J. "The Machiavellian Princess: Rhetorical Dramas for Women Managers," *Communication Quarterly,* 30 **(1982)**, 165–172.

Kolata, G. "Communicating Mathematics: Is It Possible?", *Science,* 187 **(1975)**, 732.

Kolodny, A. "Dancing through the Minefield: Some Observations on the Theory, Practice, and Politics of a Feminist Literary Criticism," in E. Showalter (Ed.), *The New Feminist Criticism: Essays on Women, Literature, and Theory* (New York: Pantheon, **1985**), pp. 144–167.

Kristol, I. *On the Democratic Idea in America* (New York: Harper and Row, **1972**).

Kruse, N. "Apologia in Team Sport," *Quarterly Journal of Speech,* 67 **(1981)**, 270–283.

Lake, R. "Enacting Red Power: The Consummatory Function in Native American Protest Rhetoric," *Quarterly Journal of Speech,* 69 **(1983)**, 127–142.

————. "Order and Disorder in Anti-Abortion Rhetoric: A Logological View," *Quarterly Journal of Speech,* 70 **(1984)**, 425–433.

Lakoff, G., and M. Johnson. *Metaphors We Live By* (Chicago: University of Chicago Press, **1980**).

Lanham, R. *Analyzing Prose* (New York: Scribners, **1983**).

Leathers, D. "Belief-Disbelief Systems: The Communicative Vacuum of the Radical Right," in G. Mohrmann, C. Stewart, and D. Ochs (Eds.), *Explorations in Rhetorical Criticism* (University Park: Pennsylvania State University Press, **1973**), pp. 124–137.

Leff, M. "Textual Criticism: The Legacy of G. P. Mohrmann," *Quarterly Journal of Speech,* 72 **(1986)**, 377–389.

Lentricchia, F. *Criticism and Social Change* (Chicago: University of Chicago Press, **1983**).

————. "Reading History in Kenneth Burke," in H. White and M. Brose (Eds.), *Representing Kenneth Burke* (Baltimore: Johns Hopkins University Press, **1982**), 119–149.

Lessl, T. *The Public Scientist: Rhetoric and the American Space Movement, 1975–1985,* Unpublished Ph.D. Dissertation, University of Texas at Austin, **1985.**

————. "Science and the Sacred Cosmos: The Ideological Rhetoric of Carl Sagan," *Quarterly Journal of Speech,* 71 **(1985)**, 175–187.

Lévi-Strauss, C. "The Structural Study of Myth," *Journal of American Folklore,* 68 **(1955)**, 250–261.

Lewis, L. "On the Genesis of Gray-Flanneled Puritans," *A.A.U.P. Bulletin,* Spring, **1972**, 21–29.

Logue, C. "Rhetorical Ridicule of Reconstruction Blacks," *Quarterly Journal of Speech,* 62 **(1976)**, 400–409.

Lucas, S. "Genre Criticism and Historical Context: The Case of George Washington's First Inaugural Address," *Southern Speech Communication Journal,* 51 **(1986)**, 354–370.

————. *Portents of Rebellion: Rhetoric and Revolution in Philadelphia, 1765–1776* (Philadelphia: Temple University Press, **1976**).

Mader, T. "On Presence in Rhetoric," *College Composition and Communication,* 24 **(1973)**, 375–381.

McCloskey, D. *The Rhetoric of Economics* (Madison, WI: University of Wisconsin Press, **1985**).

McCombs, M., and D. Shaw, "The Agenda-Setting Function of the Mass Media," *Public Opinion Quarterly*, 36 **(1972)**, 176–187.

McCormack, T. "The 'Wets' and the 'Drys': Binary Images of Women and Alcohol in Popular Culture," *Communication*, 9 **(1986)**, 43–64.

McDonald, L. "Myth, Politics, and Political Science," *Western Political Quarterly*, 22 **(1969)**, 141–150.

McGee, M. "The 'Ideograph': A Link Between Rhetoric and Ideology," *Quarterly Journal of Speech*, 66 **(1980)**, 1–16.

———. "Public Address and Culture Studies," Paper Presented at the Annual Meeting of the Central States Speech Association, April, **1987**.

———. "In Search of 'The People': A Rhetorical Alternative," *Quarterly Journal of Speech*, 61 **(1975)**, 235–249.

McGuire, M. B. "Religious Speaking and Religious Hearing: Rules and Responsibilities," A paper presented at the annual convention of the Society of the Scientific Study of Religion, **1976**.

McGuire, M. D. "Mythic Rhetoric in *Mein Kampf*: A Structuralist Critique," *Quarterly Journal of Speech*, 63 **(1977)**, 1–13.

McMillan, J. *The Rhetoric of the Modern Organization*, Unpublished Ph.D. Dissertation, University of Texas at Austin, **1982**.

Medhurst, M. "Resistance, Conservatism, and Theory Building: A Cautionary Note," *Western Journal of Speech Communication*, 49 **(1985)**, 103–115.

———, and M. Desousa, "Political Cartoons as Rhetorical Form," *Communication Monographs*, 48 **(1981)**, 197–236.

Merelman, R. "Learning and Legitimacy," *American Political Science Review*, 60 **(1966)**, 548–561.

Merod, J. *The Political Responsibility of the Critic* (Ithaca, NY: Cornell University Press, **1987**).

Merritt, R. *Symbols of American Community, 1735–1775* (New Haven: Yale University Press, **1966**).

Milic, L. "Rhetorical Choice and Stylistic Option: The Conscious and Unconscious Poles," in S. Chatman (Ed.), *Literary Style: A Symposium* (London: Oxford University Press, **1971**), pp. 77–94.

Minnick, W. *The Art of Persuasion* (Boston: Houghton-Mifflin, [1957], **1968**).

Moers, E. "Literary Women," in M. Eagleton (Ed.), *Feminist Literary Theory: A Reader* (London: Blackwell, **1986**), pp. 8–11.

Mohrmann, G. *Composition and Style in the Writing of Speeches* (Dubuque, IA: W. C. Brown, **1970**).

———, and F. Scott, "Popular Music and World War II: The Rhetoric of Continuation," *Quarterly Journal of Speech*, 62 **(1976)**, 145–156.

Moi, T. *Sexual/Textual Politics: Feminist Literary Theory* (London: Methuen, **1985**).

Morris, B. "The Communal Constraints on Parody: The Symbolic Death of Joe Bob Briggs," *Quarterly Journal of Speech*, 73 **(1987)**, 460–473.

Mumby, D., and C. Spitzack, "Ideology and Television News: A Metaphoric Analysis of Political Stories," *Central States Speech Journal*, 34 **(1983)**, 162–171.

Nelson, W. "Topoi: Functional in Human Recall," *Speech Monographs*, 38 **(1970)**, 121–126.

Nichols, M. H. "Kenneth Burke and the 'New Rhetoric,'" in W. Rueckert (Ed.), *Critical Responses to Kenneth Burke* (Minneapolis: University of Minnesota Press, **1969**), pp. 270–287.

Norris, C. *Deconstruction: Theory and Practice* (London: Methuen, **1982**).

Ohmann, R. "Prolegomena to the Analysis of Prose Style," in H. Martin (Ed.), *Style in Prose Fiction* (New York: Columbia University Press, **1959**), pp. 1–24.

Oliver, R. *Communication and Culture in Ancient India and China* (Syracuse: Syracuse University Press, **1971**).

Olson, L. "Portraits in Praise of a People: A Rhetorical Analysis of Norman Rockwell's Icons in Franklin D. Roosevelt's 'Four Freedoms' Campaign," *Quarterly Journal of Speech*, 69 **(1983)**, 15–28.

Oravec, C. "John Muir, Yosemite and the Sublime Response: A Study in the Rhetoric of Preservationism," *Quarterly Journal of Speech*, 67 **(1981)**, 245–259.

Orr, C. J. "Reporters Confront the President: Sustaining a Counterpoised Situation," *Quarterly Journal of Speech*, 66 **(1980)**, 17–32.

Orwell, G. *The Orwell Reader* (New York: Harcourt, **1956**).

Osborn, M. "The Evolution of the Archetypal Sea in Rhetoric and Poetic," *Quarterly Journal of Speech*, 63 **(1977)**, 347–363.

————. *Orientations to Rhetorical Style* (Chicago: Science Research Associates, **1976**).

————. "Rhetorical Depiction," in H. Simons and A. Aghazarian (Eds.), *Form, Genre, and the Study of Political Discourse* (Columbia, SC: University of South Carolina Press, **1986**), pp. 79–107.

Osgood, C., and E. Walker, "Motivation and Language Behavior: A Content Analysis of Suicide Notes," *Journal of Abnormal and Social Psychology*, 59 **(1959)**, 58–67.

Paletz, D. et al. *Politics in Public Service Advertising on Television* (New York: Praeger, **1977**).

Payne, D. *Coping with Failure: The Therapeutic Uses of Rhetoric* (Columbia, SC: University of South Carolina Press, **1989**).

Perelman, C. "The Rational and the Reasonable," in his *The New Rhetoric and the Humanities: Essays on Rhetoric and Its Applications* (Dordrecht, Holland: D. Reidel, **1979**).

Perlman, J. *The Myth of Marginality: Urban Poverty and Politics in Rio de Janeiro* (Berkeley, CA: University of California Press, **1976**).

Perry, S. "Rhetorical Functions of the Infestation Metaphor in Hitler's Rhetoric," *Central States Speech Journal*, 34 **(1983)**, 229–235.

Philipsen, G. "Mayor Daley's Council Speech: A Cultural Analysis," *Quarterly Journal of Speech*, 72 **(1986)**, 247–260.

————. "Speaking 'Like a Man' in Teamsterville: Cultural Patterns of Role Enactment in an Urban Neighborhood," *Quarterly Journal of Speech*, 61 **(1975)**, 13–22.

Phillips, E. B. "Magazine's Heroines: Is *Ms.* Just another Member of the *Family Circle?*" in G. Tuchman, et al. (Eds.), *Hearth and Home: Images of Women in the Mass Media* (New York: Oxford, **1978**), 116–129.

Pocock, J. *Politics, Language and Time: Essays on Political Thought and History* (New York: Atheneum, **1971**).

Prothro, J. "Verbal Shifts in the American Presidency: A Content Analysis," *American Political Science Review*, 50 **(1956)**, 726–739.

Radway, J. *Reading the Romance: Women, Patriarchy and Popular Literature* (Chapel Hill, NC: University of North Carolina Press, **1984**).

Rainville, R. E., and E. McCormick. "Extent of Covert Racial Prejudice in Pro Football Announcers' Speech," *Journalism Quarterly*, 54 **(1977)**, 20–26.

Real, M. "The Debate on Critical Theory and the Study of Communications," *Journal of Communication*, 34:4 **(1984)**, 72–80.

Register, C. "American Feminist Literary Criticism: A Bibliographical Introduction," in J. Donovan (Ed.), *Feminist Literary Criticism: Explorations in Theory* (Lexington, KY: University of Kentucky Press, **1975**), pp. 1–28.

Reid, R. "Apocalypticism and Typology: Rhetorical Dimensions of Symbolic Reality," *Quarterly Journal of Speech*, 69 **(1983)**, 229–248.

Rich, A. "When We Dead Awaken: Writing as Re-Vision," *College English*, 33 **(1972)**, 18–30.

Ritter, K. "American Political Rhetoric and the Jeremiad Tradition: Presidential Nomination Acceptance Addresses, 1960–1976," *Central States Speech Journal*, 31 **(1980)**, 153–171.

————. "Confrontation as Moral Drama: The Boston Massacre in Rhetorical Perspective," *Southern Speech Communication Journal*, 42 **(1977)**, 114–136.

————. "Drama and Legal Rhetoric: The Perjury Trials of Alger Hiss," *Western Journal of Speech Communication*, 49 **(1985)**, 83–102.

Rosenberg, B. *The Art of the American Folk Preacher* (New York: Oxford University Press, **1970**).

Rosenfield, L. "The Anatomy of Critical Discourse," in R. Scott and B. Brock (Eds.), *Methods of Rhetorical Criticism: A Twentieth Century Perspective* (New York: Harper and Row, [1968] **1972**), pp. 131–157.

————. "A Case Study in Speech Criticism: The Nixon-Truman Analog," *Communication Monographs*, 35 **(1968)**, 435–450.

Rueckert, W. *Kenneth Burke and the Drama of Human Relations* (Minneapolis: University of Minnesota Press, **1963**).

————. "Some of the Many Kenneth Burkes," in H. White and M. Brose (Eds.), *Representing Kenneth Burke* (Baltimore: Johns Hopkins University Press, **1982**), pp. 1–30.

Rushing, J. "The Rhetoric of the American Western Myth," *Communication Monographs*, 50 **(1983)**, 14–32.

Rutherford, J. "Structuralism," *Sociological Review Monographs*, 25 **(1977)**, 43–55.

Ruthven, K. K. *Feminist Literary Studies: An Introduction* (Cambridge: Cambridge University Press, **1984**).

Ryan, M. *Marxism and Deconstruction: A Critical Articulation* (Baltimore: Johns Hopkins University Press, **1982**).

Said, E. "The Text, the World, the Critic," in J. Harari (Ed.), *Textual Strategies: Perspectives in Post-Structuralist Criticism* (Ithaca, NY: Cornell University Press, **1979**), pp. 161–188.

Schwartzman, R. "The Substance of Paradox: Communication of Ideology at EPCOT and the Museum of Science and Industry," Paper Presented at the Annual Meeting of the International Communication Association, May, **1987.**

Scott, R. "Argument as a Critical Art: Re-Forming Understanding," *Argumentation,* 1 **(1987),** 57–71.

Sedelow, S., and W. Sedelow, "A Preface to Computational Stylistics," in J. Leed (Ed.), *The Computer and Literary Style* (Kent, OH: Kent State University Press, **1966),** pp. 1–13.

Selnow, G. "Solving Problems in Prime-Time Television," *Journal of Communication,* 36:2 **(1986),** 63–72.

Showalter, E. "Toward a Feminist Politics," in E. Showalter (Ed.), *The New Feminist Criticism: Essays on Women, Literature, and Theory* (New York: Pantheon, **1985),** pp. 125–143.

Simons, H. "Kenneth Burke and the Rhetoric of the Human Sciences," in H. Simons and T. Melia (Eds.), *The Legacy of Kenneth Burke* (Madison, WI: University of Wisconsin Press, **1989),** pp. 3–27.

————. *Persuasion: Understanding, Practice, and Analysis,* 2nd Edition (New York: Random House, **1986).**

Sinclair, D. "Rhetoric and Success: The Case of the Southern Baptists," Unpublished Ph.D. Dissertation, University of Texas at Austin, **1985.**

Smith, C. A. "The Hofstadter Hypothesis Revisited: The Nature of Evidence in Politically 'Paranoid' Discourse," *Southern Speech Communication Journal,* 42 **(1977),** 247–289.

Smith, C. R. "Richard Nixon's 1968 Acceptance Speech as a Model of Dual Audience Adaptation," *Today's Speech,* 19:4 **(1972),** 15–22.

Smith, S. *Myth, Media and the Southern Mind* (Fayetteville, AR: University of Arkansas Press, **1985).**

————. "Sounds of the South: The Rhetorical Saga of Country Music Lyrics," *Southern Speech Communication Journal,* 45 **(1980),** 164–172.

Snitow, A. "Mass Market Romance: Pornography for Women is Different," in M. Eagleton (Ed.), *Feminist Literary Theory: A Reader* (London: Blackwell, **1986),** pp. 134–139.

Snow, M. "Martin Luther King's 'Letter from Birmingham Jail' as Pauline Epistle," *Quarterly Journal of Speech,* 71 **(1985),** 318–334.

Solomon, M. "The Rhetoric of STOP ERA: Fatalistic Reaffirmation," *Southern Speech Communication Journal,* 44 **(1978),** 44–59.

————. "Robert Schuller: The American Dream in a Crystal Cathedral," *Central States Speech Journal,* 34 **(1983),** 172–186.

————. "Stopping ERA: A Pyrrhic Victory," *Communication Quarterly,* 31 **(1983),** 109–117.

Starosta, W. "Roots for an Older Rhetoric: On Rhetorical Effectiveness in the Third World," *Western Journal of Speech Communication,* 43 **(1979),** 278–287.

Stelzner, H. "The Quest Story and Nixon's November 3, 1969 Address," *Quarterly Journal of Speech,* 57 **(1971),** 163–172.

————. "'War Message,' December 8, 1941: An Approach to Language," *Communication Monographs,* 33 **(1966),** 419–437.

Stewart, C. "Civil War Preaching," in D. Holland (Ed.), *Preaching in American History* (Nashville: Abingdon Press, **1969**), pp. 352–374.

————. "The Pulpit in Time of Crisis: 1865 and 1963," *Communication Monographs*, 32 **(1965)**, 427–434.

Strine, M., and M. Pacanowsky, "How To Read Interpretive Accounts of Organizational Life: Narrative Bases of Textual Authority," *Southern Speech Communication Journal*, 50 **(1985)**, 283–297.

Sumner, C. *Reading Ideologies: An Investigation into the Marxist Theory of Ideology and Law* (London: Academic Press, **1979**).

Sutherland, J., and S. Siniawsky, "The Treatment and Resolution of Moral Violations on Soap Operas," *Journal of Communication*, 33:2 **(1982)**, 67–74.

Thomas, S. "The Route to Redemption: Religion and Social Class," *Journal of Communication*, 35:1 **(1985)**, 111–122.

Thompson, J. B. *Studies in the Theory of Ideology* (London: Polity, **1984**).

Tompkins, J. "Sentimental Power: *Uncle Tom's Cabin* and the Politics of Literary History," in E. Showalter (Ed.), *The New Feminist Criticism: Essays on Women, Literature, and Theory* (New York: Pantheon, **1985**), pp. 81–104.

Toulmin, S. *The Uses of Argument* (Cambridge: Cambridge University Press, **1958**).

Turner, G. *Stylistics* (Baltimore: Penguin, **1973**).

Vartabedian, R. "Nixon's Vietnam Rhetoric: A Case Study of Apologia as Generic Paradox," *Southern Speech Communication Journal*, 50 **(1985)**, 366–381.

Vermeer, J. *"For Immediate Release": Candidate Press Releases in American Political Campaigns* (Westport, CT: Greenwood Press, **1982**).

Vickery, M. "The Rhetoric of Commercial Nuclear Power: A Study of Technique," Unpublished Ph.D. Dissertation, University of Texas at Austin, **1988.**

Wallman, S. "Refractions of Rhetoric: Evidence for the Meaning of 'Race' in England," in R. Paine (Ed.), *Politically Speaking: Cross-Cultural Studies of Rhetoric* (Philadelphia: Institute for the Study of Human Issues, **1981**), pp. 143–164.

Wander, P. "The Ideological Turn in Criticism," *Central States Speech Journal*, 34 **(1983)**, 1–18.

————. "The Rhetoric of American Foreign Policy," *Quarterly Journal of Speech*, 70 **(1984)**, 339–361.

Ware, B., and W. Linkugel, "They Spoke in Defense of Themselves: On the Generic Criticism of Apologia," *Quarterly Journal of Speech*, 54 **(1973)**, 273–283.

Warner, W. L. "The Ritualization of the Past," in J. Combs and M. Mansfield (Eds.), *Drama in Life: The Uses of Communication in Society* (New York: Hastings House, **1976**), 371–388.

Warnick, B. "The Narrative Paradigm: Another Story," *Quarterly Journal of Speech*, 73 **(1987)**, 172–182.

————. "The Rhetoric of Conservative Resistance," *Southern Speech Communication Journal*, 42 **(1977)**, 256–273.

————. "Structuralism vs. Phenomenology: Implications for Rhetorical Criticism," *Quarterly Journal of Speech*, 65 **(1979)**, 260–261.

Weaver, R. *The Ethics of Rhetoric* (Chicago: Henry Regnery, **1953**).

Weiler, M. "The Rhetoric of Neo-Liberalism," *Quarterly Journal of Speech*, 70 **(1984)**, 362–378.

Weisman, E. "The Rhetoric of Holocaust Survivors: A Dramatistic Perspective," Unpublished Ph.D. Dissertation, Temple University, **1980.**

White, E. *Puritan Rhetoric: The Issue of Emotion in Religion* (Carbondale, IL: Southern Illinois University Press, **1972**).

White, R. "Hitler, Roosevelt, and the Nature of War Propaganda," *Journal of Abnormal and Social Psychology*, 44 **(1949)**, 157–174.

Whittenberger-Keith, K. *Paradox and Communication: The Case of Etiquette Manuals*, Unpublished Ph.D. Dissertation, University of Texas at Austin, **1989.**

Wichelns, H. "The Literary Criticism of Oratory," In R. Scott and B. Brock (Eds.), *Methods of Rhetorical Criticism: A Twentieth Century Perspective* (New York: Harper and Row, [1925] **1972**), pp. 27–60.

Wiethoff, W. "Rhetorical Enterprise in the Ministry of 'Reverend Ike,'" *Communication Monographs*, 44 **(1977)**, 52–59.

—————. "*Topoi* of Religious Controversy in the American Catholic Debate over Vernacular Reform," *Western Journal of Speech Communication*, 45 **(1981)**, 172–181.

Williams, M. *Community in a Black Pentacostalist Church: An Anthropological Study* (Pittsburgh: University of Pittsburgh Press, **1974**).

Williams, R. *Marxism and Literature* (London: Oxford, **1977**).

Wilson, J., and C. Arnold, *Public Speaking as a Liberal Art*, 3rd Edition (Boston: Allyn and Bacon, **1974**).

Windt, T. "The Diatribe: Last Resort for Protest," *Quarterly Journal of Speech*, 58 **(1972)**, 1–14.

Woodward, G. "Prime Ministers and Presidents: A Survey of the Differing Rhetorical Possibilities of High Office," *Communication Quarterly*, 27 **(1979)**, 41–49.

—————. "Reagan as Roosevelt: The Elasticity of Pseudo-Populist Appeals," *Central States Speech Journal*, 34 **(1983)**, 44–58.

Woolf, V. *A Room of One's Own* (New York: Harcourt, **1929**).

Young, R. "Post-Structuralism: An Introduction," in R. Young (Ed.), *Untying the Text: A Post-Structuralist Reader* (London: Routledge and Kegan Paul, **1981**), pp. 1–28.

Youngquist, M. "Three Blind Mice," quoted in W. Espy, *The Garden of Eloquence: A Rhetorical Bestiary* (New York: Dutton, **1983**), p. 153.

Zarefsky, D. *President Johnson's War on Poverty: Rhetoric and History* (University, AL: University of Alabama Press, **1986**).

—————, et al., "Reagan's Safety Net for the Truly Needy: The Rhetorical Uses of Definition," *Central States Speech Journal*, 35 **(1984)**, 113–119.

Zyskind, H. "A Case Study in Philosophic Rhetoric: Theodore Roosevelt," *Philosophy and Rhetoric*, 1 **(1968)**, 228–254.

Acknowledgments

3-4 "Two Brothers in a Field of Absence" from *Alternate Means of Transport*, by Cynthia Macdonald. Copyright © 1985 by Cynthia Macdonald. Reprinted by permission of Alfred A. Knopf, Inc.

5 From "Remarks on the Anniversary of the First Condominium Conversion." Reprinted from the *Congressional Record* by *Harper's*, October 1986, p. 16.

6-7 From "Plea to Reagan" by Elie Wiesel, *The New York Times*, April 20, 1985, p. 22.

21 From "Manson at 50," an interview by Keven Kennedy, *California* Magazine, May 1985. Reprinted by permission.

30 From "Message to Dwight Eisenhower Inviting Him to a Luncheon and Briefing at the White House," by President Harry S Truman, August 14, 1952, *Public Papers of the Presidents*, p. 517.

30-31 From "Text of General Eisenhower's Reply," August 14, 1952, *Public Papers of the Presidents*, pp. 517–518.

33-34 From *Religion Is a Gigantic Fraud* by J. H. Johnson.

49-52 From Edwin Black, *Rhetorical Criticism: A Study in Method.* The University of Wisconsin Press, 1978.

57-58 Excerpts from Addresses at Lincoln Memorial during Capital Civil Rights March by Rabbi Joachim Prinz, *The New York Times*, August 29, 1963. Copyright © by The New York Times Company. Reprinted by permission.

84-85 From "Speech to the Troops in July, 1944," in W. B. Mellor, *Patton: Fighting Man*, New York, Putnam, 1946.

87 One line from *The Music Man*, Book, Music and Lyrics by Meredith Willson (New York: G.P. Putnam's Sons). Copyright © 1958 by Meredith Willson; renewed © 1986 by Rosemary Willson. Reprinted by permission of the William Morris Agency.

87 Lyrics from "Ya Got Trouble" from *The Music Man* by Meredith Willson. Copyright © 1957, 1958 Frank Music Corp. and Meredith Willson Music; © renewed 1985, 1986 Frank Music Corp. and Meredith Willson Music. International Copyright Secured. All Rights Reserved. Used by permission.

96 "Universal Topics" from *Public Speaking as a Liberal Art*, Third Edition by John F. Wilson and Carroll C. Arnold. Copyright © 1974 by Allyn and Bacon, Inc. Reprinted by permission.

96-97 and 127 From *Public Communication*, Second Edition by Roderick P. Hart, Gustav W. Friedrich, and Barry Brummett. Copyright © 1983 by Roderick P. Hart, Gustav W. Friedrich, and Barry Brummett. Reprinted by permission of Harper & Row, Publishers, Inc.

111 From "Ski, Mix, Meet," Vail Resort Association.

112 From the advertisement "More about what we're all about and McDonald's good food." Copyright © 1987 McDonald's Corporation. Reprinted with permission.

114–116 From "The Expense Fund Speech," *U.S. News and World Report*, October 3, 1952, pp. 66–70.

119 From "What's Reasonable?" By Carroll Arnold, in *Communication Quarterly*, Vol. 19, 1971, pp. 19–23.

130, 134–135 From "The Expense Fund Speech."

152–153 From *King Lear* by William Shakespeare.

165–166 From "Presidential Debate of October 21, 1984," *Weekly Compilation of Presidential Documents*, 20:43, 1984, pp. 1591–1610.

168 From "The President's News Conference of August 22, 1973," *Public Papers of the Presidents*, pp. 710–725.

175ff. Transcript of WKBW radio's version of "War of the Worlds" is reprinted by permission of WKBW Radio, Buffalo, NY.

189 From "A Big, Big Man: A Commentary" by Nicholas von Hoffman as appeared in *The Washington Post*, January 24, 1973. Reprinted by permission of the author.

191–192 From "Richard Nixon's Irish Wake: A Case of Generic Transference" by Carol J. Jablonski, *Central States Speech Journal*. Kent, OH: Central States Speech Association, 1978.

196–197 From "Throw This Away" by Neil Gallagher, August, 1984.

210 From *Tough, Sweet & Stuffy* by Walker Gibson. Copyright © 1966 by Indiana University Press. Reprinted by permission.

210–211 Reprinted with permission of Charles Scribner's Sons, an imprint of Macmillan Publishing Company, from *A Farewell to Arms* by Ernest Hemingway. Copyright 1929 Charles Scribner's Sons; copyright renewed 1957 Ernest Hemingway.

211 From *Tough, Sweet & Stuffy* by Walker Gibson. Copyright © 1966 by Indiana University Press. Reprinted by permission.

212 *Smoking and Health*, Public Health Service Publication No. 1103, U.S. Government Printing Office, p. 5.

213 From *The Solution to Crisis America* by Pat Boone et al., Van Nuys, CA, Bible Voice, Inc., 1970.

217 From "Letter to Pat Boone" By Richard M. Nixon, reprinted in *The Solution to Crisis America*.

220–221 "Orientations to Rhetorical Style" by Michael Osborn, *Modcom* (Modules in Speech Communication). Chicago: Science Research Associates, Inc., 1976.

221–222 From "I Have a Dream" by Martin Luther King, Jr. Copyright © 1963 by Martin Luther King, Jr. Reprinted by permission of Joan Daves.

233 From *The Book of Common Prayer*, 1979, pp. 484–485.

235 From *Funeral Services without Theology* by F. J. Gould, Girard, KS, Haldeman-Julius, pp. 26–28.

241 From *The Orwell Reader* by George Orwell, New York, Harcourt, Brace & World, 1956, p. 363.

250–251 From *Stylistics* by G. Turner, Baltimore, Penguin, 1973, p. 25.

269-270 Excerpts from "Farewell to The Chief" as viewed by Roy Cohn, Arthur M. Schlesinger, and Jeff Greenfield, from *New York* Magazine, March 4, 1974. Copyright © 1974 by the NYM Corporation. Reprinted by permission of *New York* Magazine, Arthur M. Schlesinger, and Sterling Lord Literistic., Inc.

283-284 From "I'm Too Understanding to Mind" by Roberta Sandler, *Philip Morris Magazine*, Spring 1987. Reprinted by permission.

303-304 From "Americans" by Gordon Sinclair. Reprinted by permission of James D. Sinclair.

306-307 "What Is a Good Citizen?" from *Webelos Scout Book*, 1977 Printing. Copyright © 1967 Boy Scouts of America. Reprinted by permission.

308, 309, 311 From "On the Genesis of Gray-Flanneled Puritans" By Lionel Lewis, *A.A.U.P. Bulletin*, Vol. 58, No. 1, March 1972. Copyright © 1972 by the American Association of University Professors. Reprinted by permission.

310-311 From Minnick, Wayne, C., *The Art of Persuasion*, Second Edition. Copyright © 1968 by Houghton Mifflin Company. Used with permission.

312 Excerpt from #10, "How to Solve a Problem" in *Help Yourself . . . With God's Help* by Norman Vincent Peale. Copyright © 1976 by the Foundation for Christian Living. Reprinted by permission.

313 From "Energy and National Goals," by Jimmy Carter, July 15, 1979, *Weekly Compilations of Presidential Documents*, 15:29, 1979, pp. 1235–1241.

314 From "Robert Schuller: The American Dream in a Crystal Cathedral," by M. Solomon, *Central States Speech Journal*, Vol. 34, 1983, pp. 172–186.

322-325 From *Animal Farm* by George Orwell. Copyright 1946 by Harcourt Brace Jovanovich, Inc., renewed 1974 by Sonia Orwell. Reprinted by permission of the publisher, the Estate of the late Sonia Brownell Orwell and Martin Secker & Warburg Ltd.

334 From "Cousin and the *Gros Chiens:* the Limits of Cajun Political Rhetoric" by G. Gold from *Politically Speaking: Cross-Cultural Studies of Rhetoric*, edited by Robert Paine. Philadelphia: Institute for the Study of Human Issues, 1981, pp. 154–155.

335-337 From "Ideals of a Klansman" by Robert Shelton (Denham Springs, LA: Invisible Empire Knights of the Ku Klux Klan, n.d.).

340 From "Wimbledon Country," *Houston Post (Homefinder)*, August 21, 1988, p. 3; from "Legend Oaks: Live a Legendary Lifestyle," *Austin American-Statesman*, August 21, 1988, F12; from "Weston Lakes Has Superlative Golf, Swimming, Tennis, Croquet," *Houston Post (Homefinder)*, August 21, 1988, p. 5; from "Fox and Jacobs Fetes Grand Opening in Ember Oaks," *Dallas Times Herald*, August 21, 1988, J5.

345 From "Antony in Behalf of the Play" in *The Philosophy of Literary Form: Studies in Symbolic Action* by Kenneth Burke. Copyright © 1973 by The Regents of the University of California. Reprinted by permission of The University of California Press.

361-362 "He Was a Sincere, Etc." from *Collected Poems* by Kenneth Burke. Copyright © 1968 by Kenneth Burke. Reprinted by permission of The University of California Press.

372-373 From "Form and Persecution in the Oresteia" by Kenneth Burke, first published in the *Sewanee Review* 60, #3 (Summer 1952). Copyright 1952 by the University of the South. Excerpt reprinted with the permission of the editor.

374–375 From "Principles of Governance Stated Narratively" in *Rhetoric of Religion: Studies in Logology* by Kenneth Burke. Copyright © 1970 The Regents of the University of California. Reprinted by permission of The University of California Press.

375 From *A Grammar of Motives* by Kenneth Burke. Copyright © 1969 The Regents of the University of California. Reprinted by permission of The University of California Press.

375–376 From *Counter-Statement* by Kenneth Burke. Copyright 1931, 1953, 1968 by Kenneth Burke. Reprinted by permission of The University of California Press.

376–377 From *A Rhetoric of Motives* by Kenneth Burke. Copyright © 1969 The Regents of the University of California. Reprinted by permission of The University of California Press.

377–379 From *The Philosophy of Literary Form: Studies in Symbolic Action* by Kenneth Burke. Copyright © 1973 The Regents of the University of California. Reprinted by permission of The University of California Press.

379 From *A Grammar of Motives* by Kenneth Burke. Copyright © 1969 The Regents of the University of California. Reprinted by permission of The University of California Press.

382 From W. B. Hand, *Douglas T. Smith, et al. vs. Board of School Commissioners of Mobile Counter, et al., and George G. Wallace, Governor of Alabama, et al., U.S. District Court, Southern District, Alabama* (Civil Action No. 82-0544-BH, 82-0792-BH, 1987).

390–392 From "Remarks at the Centennial Safe Opening at the Capitol," by President Gerald Ford, July 1, 1976, *Public Papers of the Presidents,* pp. 1941–1943.

399 From *Literary Theory: An Introduction* by Terry Eagleton. Copyright © 1983 by Terry Eagleton. Reprinted by permission of the University of Minnesota Press and Basil Blackwell Ltd.

403–404 From "Quick Reference to Parking and Traffic Regulations," University of Texas at Austin, 1986.

415 From "Inaugural Address," by President John F. Kennedy, *Inaugural Addresses of the Presidents of the United States, From George Washington to John F. Kennedy,* Washington, D.C., U.S. Government Printing Office, 1961.

419 From *Feminist Literary Theory: A Reader* edited by Mary Eagleton. Copyright © 1986 by Mary Eagleton. Reprinted by permission of Basil Blackwell Ltd.

420 "The Geraldine Ferraro Pepsi Ad" as reprinted in "The Dialectic of the Feminine: Melodrama and Commodity in the Ferraro Pepsi Commercial" by M. E. Brown, *Communication,* Vol. 9, Nos. 3–4, 1987. Reprinted with permission of the trademark and copyright owner, © PepsiCo, Inc., 1987.

Index